Alexander Roberts, James Donaldson

Ante-Nicene Christian library

The writings of Irenæus

Alexander Roberts, James Donaldson

Ante-Nicene Christian library
The writings of Irenæus

ISBN/EAN: 9783742857002

Manufactured in Europe, USA, Canada, Australia, Japa

Cover: Foto ©Lupo / pixelio.de

Manufactured and distributed by brebook publishing software (www.brebook.com)

Alexander Roberts, James Donaldson

Ante-Nicene Christian library

ANTE-NICENE

CHRISTIAN LIBRARY:

TRANSLATIONS OF
THE WRITINGS OF THE FATHERS
DOWN TO A.D. 325.

EDITED BY THE
REV. ALEXANDER ROBERTS, D.D.,
AND
JAMES DONALDSON, LL.D.

VOL. IX.

IRENÆUS, VOL. II.—HIPPOLYTUS, VOL. II.
—FRAGMENTS OF THIRD CENTURY.

EDINBURGH:
T. & T. CLARK, 38, GEORGE STREET.
MDCCCLXIX.

THE WRITINGS

OF

IRENÆUS.

TRANSLATED BY

REV. ALEXANDER ROBERTS, D.D.,

AND

REV. W. H. RAMBAUT, A.B.

VOL. II.

EDINBURGH:
T. & T. CLARK, 38, GEORGE STREET.
LONDON: HAMILTON & CO.   DUBLIN: JOHN ROBERTSON & CO.
MDCCCLXIX.

CONTENTS.

BOOK IV. (*continued.*)

CHAP.		PAGE
31.	We should not hastily impute as crimes to the men of old time those actions which the Scripture has not condemned, but should rather seek in them types of things to come: an example of this in the incest committed by Lot, ...	1
32.	That one God was the author of both testaments, is confirmed by the authority of a presbyter who had been taught by the apostles, ...	4
33.	Whosoever confesses that one God is the author of both testaments, and diligently reads the Scriptures in company with the presbyters of the church, is a true spiritual disciple; and he will rightly understand and interpret all that the prophets have declared respecting Christ and the liberty of the new testament, . .	6
34.	Proof against the Marcionites, that the prophets referred in all their predictions to our Christ, . . .	18
35.	A refutation of those who allege that the prophets uttered some predictions under the inspiration of the Highest, others from the Demiurge. Disagreements of the Valentinians among themselves with regard to these same predictions, ...	22
36.	The prophets were sent from one and the same Father from whom the Son was sent, ...	26
37.	Men are possessed of free-will, and endowed with the faculty of making a choice. It is not true, therefore, that some are by nature good, and others bad, . . .	36
38.	Why man was not made perfect from the beginning, .	42

CHAP. | PAGE
39. Man is endowed with the faculty of distinguishing good and evil; so that, without compulsion, he has the power, by his own will and choice, to perform God's commandments, by doing which he avoids the evils prepared for the rebellious, ... 45
40. One and the same God the Father inflicts punishment on the reprobate, and bestows rewards on the elect, . 48
41. Those persons who do not believe in God, but who are disobedient, are angels and sons of the devil, not indeed by nature, but by imitation. Close of this book, and scope of the succeeding one, ... 50

BOOK V.

PREFACE, ... 54

1. Christ alone is able to teach divine things, and to redeem us: He, the same, took flesh of the Virgin Mary, not merely in appearance, but actually, by the operation of the Holy Spirit, in order to renovate us. Strictures on the conceits of Valentinus and Ebion, . . 55
2. When Christ visited us in His grace, He did not come to what did not belong to Him: also, by shedding His true blood for us, and exhibiting to us His true flesh in the Eucharist, He conferred upon our flesh the capacity of salvation, ... 58
3. The power and glory of God shine forth in the weakness of human flesh, as He will render our body a participator of the resurrection and of immortality, although He has formed it from the dust of the earth; He will also bestow upon it the enjoyment of immortality, just as He grants it this short life in common with the soul, . 61
4. Those persons are deceived who feign another God the Father besides the Creator of the world; for he must have been feeble and useless, or else malignant and full of envy, if he be either unable or unwilling to extend eternal life to our bodies, ... 64
5. The prolonged life of the ancients, the translation of Elijah and of Enoch in their own bodies, as well as the preservation of Jonah, of Shadrach, Meshach, and Abednego, in the midst of extreme peril, are clear demonstrations that God can raise up our bodies to life eternal, 65

CHAP.		PAGE
6.	God will bestow salvation upon the whole nature of man, consisting of body and soul in close union, since the Word took it upon Him, and adorned it with the gifts of the Holy Spirit, of whom our bodies are, and are termed, the temples, ...	67
7.	Inasmuch as Christ did rise in our flesh, it follows that we shall be also raised in the same; since the resurrection promised to us should not be referred to spirits naturally immortal, but to bodies in themselves mortal, ...	70
8.	The gifts of the Holy Spirit which we receive prepare us for incorruption, render us spiritual, and separate us from carnal men. These two classes are signified by the clean and unclean animals in the legal dispensation, .	72
9.	Showing how that passage of the apostle which the heretics pervert, should be understood: viz., "Flesh and blood shall not possess the kingdom of God," . .	75
10.	By a comparison drawn from the wild olive-tree, whose quality but not whose nature is changed by grafting, he proves more important things; he points out also that man without the Spirit is not capable of bringing forth fruit, or of inheriting the kingdom of God, .	78
11.	Treats upon the actions of carnal and of spiritual persons; also, that the spiritual cleansing is not to be referred to the substance of our bodies, but to the manner of our former life, ...	80
12.	Of the difference between life and death; of the breath of life and the vivifying Spirit: also how it is that the substance of flesh revives which once was dead, .	82
13.	In the dead who were raised by Christ we possess the highest proof of the resurrection; and our hearts are shown to be capable of life eternal, because they can now receive the Spirit of God, ...	87
14.	Unless the flesh were to be saved, the Word would not have taken upon Him flesh of the same substance as ours: from this it would follow that neither should we have been reconciled by Him, ...	91
15.	Proofs of the resurrection from Isaiah and Ezekiel; the same God who created us will also raise us up, . .	94
16.	Since our bodies return to the earth, it follows that they have their substance from it; also, by the advent of the Word, the image of God in us appeared in a clearer light, ...	98

CONTENTS.

CHAP.		PAGE
17.	There is but one Lord and one God, the Father and Creator of all things, who has loved us in Christ, given us commandments, and remitted our sins; whose Son and Word Christ proved Himself to be, when He forgave our sins,	100
18.	God the Father and His Word have formed all created things (which they use) by their own power and wisdom, not out of defect or ignorance. The Son of God, who received all power from the Father, would otherwise never have taken flesh upon Him,	103
19.	A comparison is instituted between the disobedient and sinning Eve and the Virgin Mary, her patroness. Various and discordant heresies are mentioned,	106
20.	Those pastors are to be heard to whom the apostles committed the churches, possessing one and the same doctrine of salvation; the heretics, on the other hand, are to be avoided. We must think soberly with regard to the mysteries of the faith,	108
21.	Christ is the Head of all things already mentioned. It was fitting that He should be sent by the Father, the Creator of all things, to assume human nature, and should be tempted by Satan, that He might fulfil the promises, and carry off a glorious and perfect victory,	110
22	The true Lord and the one God is declared by the law, and manifested by Christ His Son in the gospel; whom alone we should adore, and from Him we must look for all good things, not from Satan,	114
23.	The devil is well practised in falsehood, by which Adam having been led astray, sinned on the sixth day of the creation, in which day also he has been renewed by Christ,	116
24.	Of the constant falsehood of the devil, and of the powers and governments of the world, which we ought to obey, inasmuch as they are appointed of God, not of the devil,	119
25.	The fraud, pride, and tyrannical kingdom of Antichrist, as described by Daniel and Paul,	121
26.	John and Daniel have predicted the dissolution and desolation of the Roman Empire, which shall precede the end of the world and the eternal kingdom of Christ. The Gnostics are refuted, those tools of Satan, who invent another Father different from the Creator,	125
27.	The future judgment by Christ. Communion with and	

CONTENTS.

CHAP.		PAGE
	separation from the Divine Being. The eternal punishment of unbelievers, ...	128
28.	The distinction to be made between the righteous and the wicked. The future apostasy in the time of Antichrist, and the end of the world, ...	130
29.	All things have been created for the service of man. The deceits, wickedness, and apostate power of Antichrist. This was prefigured at the deluge, as afterwards by the persecution of Shadrach, Meshach, and Abednego, .	133
30.	Although certain as to the number of the name of Antichrist, yet we should come to no rash conclusions as to the name itself, because this number is capable of being fitted to many names. Reasons for this point being reserved by the Holy Spirit. Antichrist's reign and death, ...	135
31.	The preservation of our bodies is confirmed by the resurrection and ascension of Christ: the souls of the saints during the intermediate period are in a state of expectation of that time when they shall receive their perfect and consummated glory, ...	139
32.	In that flesh in which the saints have suffered so many afflictions, they shall receive the fruits of their labours; especially since all creation waits for this, and God promises it to Abraham and his seed, . . .	141
33.	Further proofs of the same proposition, drawn from the promises made by Christ, when He declared that He would drink of the fruit of the vine with His disciples in His Father's kingdom, while at the same time He promised to reward them an hundred-fold, and to make them partake of banquets. The blessing pronounced by Jacob had pointed out this already, as Papias and the elders have interpreted it, ...	143
34.	He fortifies his opinions with regard to the temporal and earthly kingdom of the saints after their resurrection, by the various testimonies of Isaiah, Ezekiel, Jeremiah, and Daniel; also by the parable of the servants watching, to whom the Lord promised that He would minister, ...	147
35.	He contends that these testimonies already alleged cannot be understood allegorically of celestial blessings, but that they shall have their fulfilment after the coming of Antichrist, and the resurrection, in the terrestrial Jerusalem. To the former prophecies he subjoins others	

CHAP.		PAGE
	drawn from Isaiah, Jeremiah, and the Apocalypse of John, ...	151
36.	Men shall be actually raised : the world shall not be annihilated; but there shall be various mansions for the saints, according to the rank allotted to each individual. All things shall be subject to God the Father, and so shall He be all in all, ...	155

FRAGMENTS FROM THE LOST WRITINGS OF IRENÆUS, 158

INDEX OF TEXTS, ... 189

INDEX OF PRINCIPAL SUBJECTS, ... 200

IRENÆUS AGAINST HERESIES.

BOOK IV.

CHAP. XXXI.—*We should not hastily impute as crimes to the men of old time those actions which the Scripture has not condemned, but should rather seek in them types of things to come: an example of this in the incest committed by Lot.*

1. 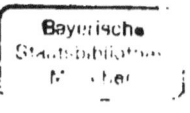WHEN recounting certain matters of this kind respecting them of old time, the presbyter [before mentioned] was in the habit of instructing us, and saying: "With respect to those misdeeds for which the Scriptures themselves blame the patriarchs and prophets, we ought not to inveigh against them, nor become like Ham, who ridiculed the shame of his father, and so fell under a curse; but we should [rather] give thanks to God in their behalf, inasmuch as their sins have been forgiven them through the advent of our Lord; for He said that they gave thanks [for us], and gloried in our salvation. With respect to those actions, again, on which the Scriptures pass no censure, but which are simply set down [as having occurred], we ought not to become the accusers [of those who committed them], for we are not more exact than God, nor can we be superior to our Master; but we should search for a type [in them]. For not one of those things which have been set down in Scripture without being condemned is without significance." An example is found in the case of Lot, who led forth his daughters from Sodom,

and these then conceived by their own father; and who left behind him within the confines [of the land] his wife, [who remains] a pillar of salt unto this day. For Lot, not acting under the impulse of his own will, nor at the prompting of carnal concupiscence, nor having any knowledge or thought of anything of the kind, did [in fact] work out a type [of future events]. As says the Scripture: "And that night the elder went in and lay with her father; and Lot knew not when she lay down, nor when she arose."[1] And the same thing took place in the case of the younger: "And he knew not," it is said, "when she slept with him, nor when she arose."[2] Since, therefore, Lot knew not [what he did], nor was a slave to lust [in his actions], the arrangement [designed by God] was carried out, by which the two daughters (that is, the two churches[3]), who gave birth to children begotten of one and the same father, were pointed out, apart from [the influence of] the lust of the flesh. For there was no other person, [as they supposed], who could impart to them quickening seed, and the means of their giving birth to children, as it is written: "And the elder said unto the younger, And there is not a man on the earth to enter in unto us after the manner of all the earth: come, let us make our father drunk with wine, and let us lie with him, and raise up seed from our father."[4]

2. Thus, after their simplicity and innocence, did these daughters [of Lot] so speak, imagining that all mankind had perished, even as the Sodomites had done, and that the anger of God had come down upon the whole earth. Wherefore also they are to be held excusable, since they supposed that they only, along with their father, were left for the preservation of the human race; and for this reason it was that they deceived their father. Moreover, by the words they used this fact was pointed out—that there is no other one who can confer upon the elder and younger church the

[1] Gen. xix. 33.   [2] Gen. xix. 35.
[3] "Id est duæ synagogæ," referring to the Jews and Gentiles. Some regard the words as a marginal gloss which has crept into the text.
[4] Gen. xix. 31, 32.

[power of] giving birth to children, besides our Father. Now the father of the human race is the Word of God, as Moses points out when he says, "Is not He thy father who hath obtained thee [by generation], and formed thee, and created thee?"[1] At what time, then, did He pour out upon the human race the life-giving seed—that is, the Spirit of the remission of sins, through means of whom we are quickened? Was it not then, when He was eating with men, and drinking wine upon the earth? For it is said, "The Son of man came eating and drinking;"[2] and when He had lain down, He fell asleep, and took repose. As He does Himself say in David, "I slept, and took repose."[3] And because He used thus to act while He dwelt and lived among us, He says again, "And my sleep became sweet unto me."[4] Now this whole matter was indicated through Lot, that the seed of the Father of all—that is, of the Spirit of God, by whom all things were made—was commingled and united with flesh—that is, with His own workmanship; by which commixture and unity the two synagogues—that is, the two churches—produced from their own father living sons to the living God.

3. And while these things were taking place, his wife remained in [the territory of] Sodom, no longer corruptible flesh, but a pillar of salt which endures for ever;[5] and by those natural processes[6] which appertain to the human race, indicating that the church also, which is the salt of the earth,[7] has been left behind within the confines of the earth, and subject to human sufferings; and while entire members are

---

[1] Deut. xxxii. 6, LXX.   [2] Matt. xi. 19.
[3] Ps. iii. 6.   [4] Jer. xxxi. 26.
[5] Comp. Clem. Rom. chap. xi. Josephus (*Antiq.* i. 11, 4) testifies that he had himself seen this pillar.
[6] The Latin is "per naturalia," which words, according to Harvey, correspond to δι' ἐμμηνορροίας. There is a poem entitled *Sodoma* preserved among the works of Tertullian and Cyprian which contains the following lines:
     "Dicitur et vivens, alio jam corpore, sexus
     Munificos solito dispungere sanguine menses."
[7] Matt. v. 13.

often taken away from it, the pillar of salt still endures,[1] thus typifying the foundation of the faith which maketh strong, and sends forward, children to their Father.

CHAP. XXXII.—*That one God was the author of both testaments, is confirmed by the authority of a presbyter who had been taught by the apostles.*

1. After this fashion also did a presbyter,[2] a disciple of the apostles, reason with respect to the two testaments, proving that both were truly from one and the same God. For [he maintained] that there was no other God besides Him who made and fashioned us, and that the discourse of those men has no foundation who affirm that this world of ours was made either by angels, or by any other power whatsoever, or by another God. For if a man be once moved away from the Creator of all things, and if he grant that this creation to which we belong was formed by any other or through any other [than the one God], he must of necessity fall into much inconsistency, and many contradictions of this sort; to which he will [be able to] furnish no explanations which can be regarded as either probable or true. And, for this reason, those who introduce other doctrines conceal from us the opinion which they themselves hold respecting God, because they are aware of the untenable[3] and absurd nature of their doctrine, and are afraid lest, should they be vanquished, they should have some difficulty in making good

---

[1] The poem just referred to also says in reference to this pillar:

"Ipsaque imago sibi formam sine corpore servans
Durat adhuc, et enim nuda statione sub æthram
Nec pluviis dilapsa situ, nec diruta ventis.
Quin etiam si quis mutilaverit advena formam,
Protinus ex sese suggestu vulnera complet."

[2] Harvey remarks here, that this can hardly be the same presbyter mentioned before, "who was only a hearer of those who had heard the apostles. Irenæus may here mean the venerable martyr Polycarp, bishop of Smyrna."

[3] "Quassum et futile." The text varies much in the MSS.

their escape. But if any one believes in [only] one God, who also made all things by the Word, as Moses likewise says, "God said, Let there be light: and there was light;"[1] and as we read in the Gospel, "All things were made by Him; and without Him was nothing made;"[2] and the Apostle Paul [says] in like manner, "There is one Lord, one faith, one baptism, one God and Father, who is above all, and through all, and in us all"[3]—this man will first of all "hold the head, from which the whole body is compacted and bound together, and, through means of every joint according to the measure of the ministration of each several part, maketh increase of the body to the edification of itself in love."[4] And then shall every word also seem consistent to him,[5] if he for his part diligently read the Scriptures in company with those who are presbyters in the church, among whom is the apostolic doctrine, as I have pointed out.

2. For all the apostles taught that there were indeed two testaments among the two peoples; but that it was one and the same God who appointed both for the advantage of those men (for whose[6] sakes the testaments were given) who were to believe in God, I have proved in the third book from the very teaching of the apostles; and that the first testament was not given without reason, or to no purpose, or in an accidental sort of manner; but that it subdued[7] those to whom it was given to the service of God, for their benefit (for God needs no service from men), and exhibited a type of heavenly things, inasmuch as man was not yet able to see the things of God through means of immediate vision;[8] and foreshadowed the images of those things which [now actually] exist in the church, in order that our faith might be firmly established; and contained a prophecy of things to come, in

---

[1] Gen. i. 3.   [2] John i. 3.   [3] Eph. iv. 5, 6.
[4] Eph. iv. 16; Col. ii. 19.   [5] "Constabit ci."
[6] We here read "secundum quos" with Massuet, instead of the usual "secundum quod."
[7] "Concurvans," corresponding to συγκάμπτων, which, says Harvey, "would be expressive of those who were brought under the law, as the neck of the steer is bent to the yoke."
[8] The Latin is, "per proprium visum."

order that man might learn that God has foreknowledge of all things.

CHAP. XXXIII.—*Whosoever confesses that one God is the author of both testaments, and diligently reads the Scriptures in company with the presbyters of the church, is a true spiritual disciple; and he will rightly understand and interpret all that the prophets have declared respecting Christ and the liberty of the new testament.*

1. A spiritual disciple of this sort truly receiving the Spirit of God, who was from the beginning, in all the dispensations of God, present with mankind, and announced things future, revealed things present, and narrated things past—[such a man] does indeed judge all men, but is himself judged by no man.[1] For he judges the Gentiles, "who serve the creature more than the Creator,"[2] and with a reprobate mind spend all their labour on vanity. And he also judges the Jews, who do not accept of the word of liberty, nor are willing to go forth free, although they have a Deliverer present [with them]; but they pretend, at a time unsuitable [for such conduct], to serve, [with observances] beyond [those required by] the law, God who stands in need of nothing, and do not recognise the advent of Christ, which He accomplished for the salvation of men, nor are willing to understand that all the prophets announced His two advents: the one, indeed, in which He became a man subject to stripes, and knowing what it is to bear infirmity,[3] and sat upon the foal of an ass,[4] and was a stone rejected by the builders,[5] and was led as a sheep to the slaughter,[6] and by the stretching forth of His hands destroyed Amalek;[7] while He gathered from the ends of the earth into His Father's fold the children who were scattered abroad,[8] and remembered His own dead ones who had formerly fallen asleep,[9] and came down to them that He might deliver them: but the second in which

[1] 1 Cor. ii. 15.
[2] Rom. i. 21.
[3] Isa. liii. 3.
[4] Zech. ix. 9.
[5] Ps. cxviii. 22.
[6] Isa. liii. 7.
[7] Ex. xvii. 11.
[8] Isa. xi. 12.
[9] Comp. book iii. 20, 4.

He will come on the clouds,¹ bringing on the day which burns as a furnace,² and smiting the earth with the word of His mouth,³ and slaying the impious with the breath of His lips, and having a fan in His hands, and cleansing His floor, and gathering the wheat indeed into His barn, but burning the chaff with unquenchable fire.⁴

2. Moreover, he shall also examine the doctrine of Marcion, [inquiring] how he holds that there are two gods, separated from each other by an infinite distance.⁵ Or how can *he* be good who draws away men that do not belong to him from him who made them, and calls them into his own kingdom? And why is his goodness, which does not save all [thus], defective? Also, why does he, indeed, seem to be good as respects men, but most unjust with regard to him who made men, inasmuch as he deprives him of his possessions? Moreover, how could the Lord, with any justice, if He belonged to another father, have acknowledged the bread to be His body, while He took it from that creation to which we belong, and affirmed the mixed cup to be His blood?⁶ And why did He acknowledge Himself to be the Son of man, if He had not gone through that birth which belongs to a human being? How, too, could He forgive us those sins for which we are answerable to our Maker and God? And how, again, supposing that He was not flesh, but was a man merely in appearance, could He have been crucified, and could blood and water have issued from His pierced side?⁷ What body, moreover, was it that those who buried Him consigned to the tomb? And what was that which rose again from the dead?

3. [This spiritual man] shall also judge all the followers of Valentinus, because they do indeed confess with the tongue one God the Father, and that all things derive their existence

---

¹ Dan. vii. 13.
² Mal. iv. 1.
³ Isa. xi. 4.
⁴ Matt. iii. 12; Luke iii. 17.
⁵ Harvey points this sentence interrogatively.
⁶ "Temperamentum calicis:" on which Harvey remarks that "the mixture of water with the wine in the holy Eucharist was the universal practice of antiquity ... the wine signifying the mystical Head of the church, the water the body."
⁷ John xix. 34.

from Him, but do at the same time maintain that He who formed all things is the fruit of an apostasy or defect. [He shall judge them, too, because] they do in like manner confess with the tongue one Lord Jesus Christ, the Son of God, but assign in their [system of] doctrine a production of his own to the Only-begotten, one of his own also to the Word, another to Christ, and yet another to the Saviour; so that, according to them, all these beings are indeed said [in Scripture to be], as it were, one; [while they maintain], notwithstanding, that each one of them should be understood [to exist] separately [from the rest], and to have [had] his own special origin, according to his peculiar conjunction. [It appears], then,[1] that their tongues alone, forsooth, have conceded the unity [of God], while their [real] opinion and their understanding (by their habit of investigating profundities) have fallen away from [this doctrine of] unity, and taken up the notion of manifold deities,—[this, I say, must appear] when they shall be examined by Christ as to the points [of doctrine] which they have invented. Him, too, they affirm to have been born at a later period than the Pleroma of the Æons, and that His production took place after [the occurrence of] a degeneracy or apostasy; and they maintain that, on account of the passion which was experienced by Sophia, they themselves were brought to the birth. But their own special prophet Homer, listening to whom they have invented such doctrines, shall himself reprove them, when he expresses himself as follows:

"Hateful to me that man as Hades' gates,
Who one thing thinks, while he another states."[2]

[This spiritual man] shall also judge the vain speeches of the perverse Gnostics, by showing that they are the disciples of Simon Magus.

4. He will judge also the Ebionites; [for] how can they be saved unless it was God who wrought out their salvation upon earth? Or how shall man pass into God, unless God has [first] passed into man? And how shall he (man) escape

---

[1] This sentence is very obscure in the Latin text.
[2] *Iliad,* ix. 312, 313.

from the generation subject to death, if not by means[1] of a new generation, given in a wonderful and unexpected manner (but as a sign of salvation) by God—[I mean] that regeneration which flows from the virgin through faith?[2] Or how shall they receive adoption from God if they remain in this [kind of] generation, which is naturally possessed by man in this world? And how could He (Christ) have been greater than Solomon,[3] or greater than Jonah, or have been the Lord of David,[4] who was of the same substance as they were? How, too, could He have subdued[5] him who was stronger than men,[6] who had not only overcome man, but also retained him under his power, and conquered him who had conquered, while he set free mankind who had been conquered, unless He had been greater than man who had thus been vanquished? But who else is superior to, and more eminent than, that man who was formed after the likeness of God, except the Son of God, after whose image man was created? And for this reason He did in these last days[7] exhibit the similitude; [for] the Son of God was made man, assuming the ancient production [of His hands] into His own nature,[8] as I have shown in the immediately preceding book.

5. He shall also judge those who describe Christ as [having become man] only in [human] opinion. For how can they imagine that they do themselves carry on a real discussion, when their Master was a mere imaginary being? Or how can they receive anything stedfast from Him, if He was a merely imagined being, and not a verity? And how can these men really be partakers of salvation, if He in whom they profess to believe, manifested Himself as a merely imaginary being? Everything, therefore, connected with these men is unreal, and

---

[1] The text is obscure, and the construction doubtful.
[2] The Latin here is, "quæ est ex virgine per fidem regenerationem." According to Massuet, "virgine" here refers not to Mary, but to the church. Grabe suspects that some words have been lost.
[3] Matt. xii. 41, 42.   [4] Matt. xxii. 43.
[5] Matt. xxii. 29; Luke xi. 21, 22.
[6] Literally, "who was strong against men."
[7] In fine: lit. "in the end."
[8] In semetipsum: lit. "unto Himself."

nothing [possessed of the character of] truth; and, in these circumstances, it may be made a question whether (since, perchance, they themselves in like manner are not men, but mere dumb animals) they do not present,[1] in most cases, simply a shadow of humanity.

6. He shall also judge false prophets, who, without having received the gift of prophecy from God, and not possessed of the fear of God, but either for the sake of vainglory, or with a view to some personal advantage, or acting in some other way under the influence of a wicked spirit, pretend to utter prophecies, while all the time they lie against God.

7. He shall also judge those who give rise to schisms, who are destitute of the love of God, and who look to their own special advantage rather than to the unity of the church; and who for trifling reasons, or any kind of reason which occurs to them, cut in pieces and divide the great and glorious body of Christ, and so far as in them lies, [positively] destroy it,— men who prate of peace while they give rise to war, and do in truth strain out a gnat, but swallow a camel.[2] For no reformation of so great importance can be effected by them, as will compensate for the mischief arising from their schism. He shall also judge all those who are beyond the pale of the truth, that is, who are outside the church; but he himself shall be judged by no one. For to him all things are consistent: he has a full faith in one God Almighty, of whom are all things; and in the Son of God, Jesus Christ our Lord, by whom are all things, and in the dispensations connected with Him, by means of which the Son of God became man; and a firm belief in the Spirit of God, who furnishes us with a knowledge of the truth, and has set forth the dispensations of the Father and the Son, in virtue of which He dwells with every generation of men,[3] according to the will of the Father.

---

[1] We here follow the reading "proferant:" the passage is difficult and obscure, but the meaning is as above.

[2] Matt. xxiii. 24.

[3] The Greek text here is σκηνοβατοῦν (lit. "to tabernacle:" comp. ἐσκήνωσεν, John i. 14) καθ ἑκάστην γενεὰν ἐν τοῖς ἀνθρώποις; the Latin is,

8. True knowledge[1] is [that which consists in] the doctrine of the apostles, and the ancient constitution[2] of the church throughout all the world, and the distinctive manifestation of the body[3] of Christ according to the successions of the bishops, by which they have handed down that church which exists in every place, and has come even unto us, being guarded and preserved,[4] without any forging of Scriptures, by a very complete system[5] of doctrine, and neither receiving addition nor [suffering] curtailment [in the truths which she believes]; and [it consists in] reading [the word of God] without falsification, and a lawful and diligent exposition in harmony with the Scriptures, both without danger and without blasphemy; and [above all, it consists in] the pre-eminent gift of love,[6] which is more precious than knowledge, more glorious than prophecy, and which excels all the other gifts [of God].

9. Wherefore the church does in every place, because of that love which she cherishes towards God, send forward, throughout all time, a multitude of martyrs to the Father; while all others[7] not only have nothing of this kind to point to among themselves, but even maintain that such witness-bearing is not at all necessary, for that their system of doctrines is the true witness [for Christ], with the exception, perhaps, that one or two among them, during the whole time

" Secundum quas (dispositiones) aderat generi humano." We have endeavoured to express the meaning of both.

[1] The following section is an important one, but very difficult to translate with undoubted accuracy. The editors differ considerably both as to the construction and the interpretation. We have done our best to represent the meaning in English, but may not have been altogether successful.

[2] The Greek is σύστημα; the Latin text has "status."

[3] The Latin is, "character corporis."

[4] The text here is, "custodita sine fictione scripturarum;" some prefer joining "scripturarum" to the following words.

[5] We follow Harvey's text, "tractatione;" others read "tractatio." According to Harvey, the creed of the church is denoted by "tractatione;" but Massuet renders the clause thus: ["True knowledge consists in] a very complete *tractatio* of the Scriptures, which has come down to us by being preserved ('custoditione' being read instead of 'custodita') without falsification."

[6] Comp. 2 Cor. viii. 1; 1 Cor. xiii.   [7] *i.e.* the heretics.

which has elapsed since the Lord appeared on earth, have occasionally, along with our martyrs, borne the reproach of the name (as if he too [the heretic] had obtained mercy), and have been led forth with them [to death], being, as it were, a sort of retinue granted unto them. For the church alone sustains with purity the reproach of those who suffer persecution for righteousness' sake, and endure all sorts of punishments, and are put to death because of the love which they bear to God, and their confession of His Son; often weakened indeed, yet immediately increasing her members, and becoming whole again, after the same manner as her type,[1] Lot's wife, who became a pillar of salt. Thus, too, [she passes through an experience] similar to that of the ancient prophets, as the Lord declares, "For so persecuted they the prophets who were before you;"[2] inasmuch as she does indeed, in a new fashion, suffer persecution from those who do not receive the word of God, while the self-same spirit rests upon her[3] [as upon these ancient prophets].

10. And indeed the prophets, along with other things which they predicted, also foretold this, that all those on whom the Spirit of God should rest, and who would obey the word of the Father, and serve Him according to their ability, should suffer persecution, and be stoned and slain. For the prophets prefigured in themselves all these things, because of their love to God, and on account of His word. For since they themselves were members of Christ, each one of them in his place as a member did, in accordance with this, set forth the prophecy [assigned him]; all of them, although many, prefiguring only one, and proclaiming the things which pertain to one. For just as the working of the whole body is exhibited through means of our members, while the figure of a complete man is not displayed by one member, but through means of all taken together, so also did all the prophets prefigure the one [Christ]; while every one of them, in his special place as a member, did, in accordance with this, fill up the [established] dispensation, and shadowed forth beforehand that particular working of Christ which was connected with that member.

[1] Comp. above, xxxi. 2.   [2] Matt. v. 12.   [3] Comp. 1 Pet. iv. 14.

11. For some of them, beholding Him in glory, saw His glorious life (*conversationem*) at the Father's right hand;[1] others beheld Him coming on the clouds as the Son of man;[2] and those who declared regarding Him, "They shall look on Him whom they have pierced,"[3] indicated His [second] advent, concerning which He Himself says, "Thinkest thou that when the Son of man cometh, He shall find faith on the earth?"[4] Paul also refers to this event when he says, "If, however, it is a righteous thing with God to recompense tribulation to them that trouble you, and to you that are troubled rest with us, at the revelation of the Lord Jesus from heaven, with His mighty angels, and in a flame of fire."[5] Others again, speaking of Him as a judge, and [referring], as if it were a burning furnace, [to] the day of the Lord, who "gathers the wheat into His barn, but will burn up the chaff with unquenchable fire,"[6] were accustomed to threaten those who were unbelieving, concerning whom also the Lord Himself declares, "Depart from me, ye cursed, into everlasting fire, which my Father has prepared for the devil and his angels."[7] And the apostle in like manner says [of them], "Who shall be punished with everlasting death from the face of the Lord, and from the glory of His power, when He shall come to be glorified in His saints, and to be admired in those who believe in Him."[8] There are also some [of them] who declare, "Thou art fairer than the children of men;"[9] and, "God, Thy God, hath anointed Thee with the oil of gladness above Thy fellows;"[10] and, "Gird Thy sword upon Thy thigh, O most Mighty, with Thy beauty and Thy fairness, and go forward and proceed prosperously; and rule Thou because of truth, and meekness, and righteousness."[11] And whatever other things of a like nature are spoken regarding Him, these indicated that beauty and splendour which exist in His

---

[1] Isa. vi. 1; Ps. cx. 1.   [2] Dan. vii. 13.   [3] Zech. xii. 10.
[4] Luke xviii. 8. There is nothing to correspond with "*putas*" in the received text.
[5] 2 Thess. i. 6–8.   [6] Matt. iii. 12.   [7] Matt. xxv. 41.
[8] 2 Thess. i. 9, 10.   [9] Ps. xlv. 2.   [10] Ps. xlv. 7.
[11] Ps. xlv. 3, 4.

kingdom, along with the transcendent and pre-eminent exaltation [belonging] to all who are under His sway, that those who hear might desire to be found there, doing such things as are pleasing to God. Again, there are those who say, "He is a man, and who shall know him?"[1] and, "I came unto the prophetess, and she bare a son, and His name is called Wonderful, Counsellor, the Mighty God;"[2] and those [of them] who proclaimed Him as Immanuel, [born] of the Virgin, exhibited the union of the Word of God with His own workmanship, [declaring] that the Word should become flesh, and the Son of God the Son of man (the pure One opening purely that pure womb which regenerates men unto God, and which He Himself made pure); and having become this which we also are, He [nevertheless] is the Mighty God, and possesses a generation which cannot be declared. And there are also some of them who say, "The Lord hath spoken in Zion, and uttered His voice from Jerusalem;"[3] and, "In Judah is God known;"[4]—these indicated His advent which took place in Judea. Those, again, who declare that "God comes from the south, and from a mountain thick with foliage,"[5] announced His advent at Bethlehem, as I have pointed out in the preceding book.[6] From that place, also, He who rules, and who feeds the people of His Father, has come. Those, again, who declare that at His coming "the lame man shall leap as an hart, and the tongue of the dumb shall [speak] plainly, and the eyes of the blind shall be opened, and the ears of the deaf shall hear,"[7] and that "the hands which hang down, and the feeble knees, shall be strengthened,"[8] and that "the dead which are in the grave shall arise,"[9] and that He Himself "shall take [upon Him] our weaknesses, and bear our sorrows,"[10]—[all these] pro-

---

[1] Jer. xvii. 9 (Sept.). Harvey here remarks: "The LXX read אָנֻשׁ instead of אֱנוֹשׁ. Thus, from a text that teaches us that *the heart is deceitful above all things*, the fathers extract a proof of the manhood of Christ."

[2] Isa. viii. 3, ix. 6, vii. 14.   [3] Joel iii. 16.   [4] Ps. lxxvi. 1.
[5] Hab. iii. 3.   [6] See III. xx. 4.   [7] Isa. xxxv. 5, 6.
[8] Isa. xxxv. 3.   [9] Isa. xxvi. 19.   [10] Isa. liii. 4.

claimed those works of healing which were accomplished by Him.

12. Some of them, moreover—[when they predicted that] as a weak and inglorious man, and as one who knew what it was to bear infirmity,[1] and sitting upon the foal of an ass,[2] He should come to Jerusalem; and that He should give His back to stripes,[3] and His cheeks to palms [which struck Him]; and that He should be led as a sheep to the slaughter;[4] and that He should have vinegar and gall given Him to drink;[5] and that He should be forsaken by His friends and those nearest to Him;[6] and that He should stretch forth His hands the whole day long;[7] and that He should be mocked and maligned by those who looked upon Him;[8] and that His garments should be parted, and lots cast upon His raiment;[9] and that He should be brought down to the dust of death,[10] with all [the other] things of a like nature—prophesied His coming in the character of a man as He entered Jerusalem, in which by His passion and crucifixion He endured all the things which have been mentioned. Others, again, when they said, "The holy Lord remembered His own dead ones who slept in the dust, and came down to them to raise them up, that He might save them,"[11] furnished us with the reason on account of which He suffered all these things. Those, moreover, who said, "In that day, saith the Lord, the sun shall go down at noon, and there shall be darkness over the earth in the clear day; and I will turn your feast days into mourning, and all your songs into lamentation,"[12] plainly announced that obscuration of the sun which at the time of His crucifixion took place from the sixth hour onwards, and that after this event, those days which were their festivals according to the law, and their songs, should be changed into grief and lamentation when they were handed over to the Gentiles.

[1] Isa. liii. 3.
[2] Zech. ix. 9.
[3] Isa. l. 6.
[4] Isa. liii. 7.
[5] Ps. lxix. 21.
[6] Ps. xxxviii. 11.
[7] Isa. lxv. 2.
[8] Ps. xxii. 7.
[9] Ps. xxii. 18.
[10] Ps. xxii. 15.
[11] Compare vol. i. of our translation, pp. 350, 454.
[12] Amos viii. 9, 10.

Jeremiah, too, makes this point still clearer, when he thus speaks concerning Jerusalem: "She that hath born [seven] languisheth; her soul hath become weary; her sun hath gone down while it was yet noon; she hath been confounded, and suffered reproach: the remainder of them will I give to the sword in the sight of their enemies."[1]

13. Those of them, again, who spoke of His having slumbered and taken sleep, and of His having risen again because the Lord sustained Him,[2] and who enjoined the principalities of heaven to set open the everlasting doors, that the King of glory might go in,[3] proclaimed beforehand His resurrection from the dead through the Father's power, and His reception into heaven. And when they expressed themselves thus, "His going forth is from the height of heaven, and His returning even to the highest heaven; and there is no one who can hide himself from His heat,"[4] they announced that very truth of His being taken up again to the place from which He came down, and that there is no one who can escape His righteous judgment. And those who said, "The Lord hath reigned; let the people be enraged: [even] He who sitteth upon the cherubim; let the earth be moved,"[5] were thus predicting partly that wrath from all nations which after His ascension came upon those who believed in Him, with the movement of the whole earth against the church; and partly the fact that, when He comes from heaven with His mighty angels, the whole earth shall be shaken, as He Himself declares, "There shall be a great earthquake, such as has not been from the beginning."[6] And again, when one says, "Whosoever is judged, let him stand opposite; and whosoever is justified, let him draw near to the servant[7] of God;"[8] and, "Woe unto you, for ye shall all wax old as doth a garment, and the moth shall eat you up;" and, "All flesh shall be humbled, and the Lord alone shall be exalted in the highest,"[9]—it is thus indicated that, after His passion and ascension, God shall cast down under His feet all who were

[1] Jer. xv. 9. [2] Ps. iii. 5. [3] Ps. xxiv. 7.
[4] Ps. xix. 6. [5] Ps. xcix. 1. [6] Matt. xxiv. 21.
[7] Or "son." [8] Isa. l. 8, 9 (loosely quoted). [9] Isa. ii. 17.

opposed to Him, and He shall be exalted above all, and there shall be no one who can be justified or compared to Him.

14. And those of them who declare that God would make a new covenant[1] with men, not such as that which He made with the fathers at Mount Horeb, and would give to men a new heart and a new spirit;[2] and again, "And remember ye not the things of old: behold, I make new things which shall now arise, and ye shall know it; and I will make a way in the desert, and rivers in a dry land, to give drink to my chosen people, my people whom I have acquired, that they may show forth my praise,"[3]—plainly announced that liberty which distinguishes the new covenant, and the new wine which is put into new bottles,[4] [that is], the faith which is in Christ, by which He has proclaimed the way of righteousness sprung up in the desert, and the streams of the Holy Spirit in a dry land, to give water to the elect people of God, whom He has acquired, that they might show forth His praise, but not that they might blaspheme Him who made these things, that is, God.

15. And all those other points which I have shown the prophets to have uttered by means of so long a series of Scriptures, he who is truly spiritual will interpret by pointing out, in regard to every one of the things which have been spoken, to what special point in the dispensation of the Lord it referred, and [by thus exhibiting] the entire system of the work of the Son of God, knowing always the same God, and always acknowledging the same Word of God, although He has [but] now been manifested to us; acknowledging also at all times the same Spirit of God, although He has been poured out upon us after a new fashion in these last times, [knowing that He descends] even from the creation of the world to its end upon the human race simply as such, from whom those who believe God and follow His word receive that salvation which flows from Him. Those, on the other hand, who depart from Him, and despise His precepts, and by their deeds bring dishonour on Him who made them, and

[1] Jer. xxxi. 31, 32.
[2] Ezek. xxxvi. 26.
[3] Isa. xliii. 19-21.
[4] Matt. ix. 17.

by their opinions blaspheme Him who nourishes them, heap up against themselves most righteous judgment.[1] He therefore (*i.e.* the spiritual man) sifts and tries them all, but he himself is tried by no man:[2] he neither blasphemes his Father, nor sets aside His dispensations, nor inveighs against the fathers, nor dishonours the prophets, by maintaining that they were [sent] from another God [than he worships], or again, that their prophecies were derived from different sources.[3]

CHAP. XXXIV.—*Proof against the Marcionites, that the prophets referred in all their predictions to our Christ.*

1. Now I shall simply say, in opposition to all the heretics, and principally against the followers of Marcion, and against those who are like to these, in maintaining that the prophets were from another God [than He who is announced in the gospel], read with earnest care that gospel which has been conveyed to us by the apostles, and read with earnest care the prophets, and you will find that the whole conduct, and all the doctrine, and all the sufferings of our Lord, were predicted through them. But if a thought of this kind should then suggest itself to you, to say, What then did the Lord bring to us by His advent?—know ye that He brought all [possible] novelty, by bringing Himself who had been announced. For this very thing was proclaimed beforehand, that a novelty should come to renew and quicken mankind. For the advent of the King is previously announced by those servants who are sent [before Him], in order to the preparation and equipment of those men who are to entertain their Lord. But when the King has actually come, and those who are His subjects have been filled with that joy which was proclaimed beforehand, and have attained to that liberty which He bestows, and share in the sight of Him, and have listened to His words, and have enjoyed the gifts which He confers, the question will not then be asked by any that are

[1] Rom. ii. 5.   [2] 1 Cor. ii. 15.
[3] "Ex alia et alia substantia fuisse prophetias."

possessed of sense what new thing the King has brought beyond [that proclaimed by] those who announced His coming. For He has brought Himself, and has bestowed on men those good things which were announced beforehand, which things the angels desired to look into.[1]

2. But the servants would then have been proved false, and not sent by the Lord, if Christ on His advent, by being found exactly such as He was previously announced, had not fulfilled their words. Wherefore He said, "Think not that I have come to destroy the law or the prophets; I came not to destroy, but to fulfil. For verily I say unto you, Until heaven and earth pass away, one jot or one tittle shall not pass from the law and the prophets till all come to pass."[2] For by His advent He Himself fulfilled all things, and does still fulfil in the church the new covenant foretold by the law, onwards to the consummation [of all things]. To this effect also Paul, His apostle, says in the Epistle to the Romans, "But now,[3] without the law, has the righteousness of God been manifested, being witnessed by the law and the prophets; for the just shall live by faith."[4] But this fact, that the just shall live by faith, had been previously announced[5] by the prophets.

3. But whence could the prophets have had power to predict the advent of the King, and to preach beforehand that liberty which was bestowed by Him, and previously to announce all things which were done by Christ, His words, His works, and His sufferings, and to predict the new covenant, if they had received prophetical inspiration from another God [than He who is revealed in the gospel], they being ignorant, as ye allege, of the ineffable Father, of His kingdom, and His dispensations, which the Son of God fulfilled when He came upon earth in these last times? Neither are ye in a position to say that these things came to pass by a certain kind of chance, as if they were spoken by the prophets in regard to some other person, while like events happened to

[1] 1 Pet. i. 12.
[3] Rom. iii. 21.
[5] Hab. ii. 4.
[2] Matt. v. 17, 18.
[4] Rom. i. 17.

the Lord. For all the prophets prophesied these same things, but they never came to pass in the case of any one of the ancients. For if these things had happened to any man among them of old time, those [prophets] who lived subsequently would certainly not have prophesied that these events should come to pass in the last times. Moreover, there is in fact none among the fathers, nor the prophets, nor the ancient kings, in whose case any one of these things properly and specifically took place. For all indeed prophesied as to the sufferings of Christ, but they themselves were far from enduring sufferings similar to what was predicted. And the points connected with the passion of the Lord, which were foretold, were realized in no other case. For neither did it happen at the death of any man among the ancients that the sun set at mid-day, nor was the veil of the temple rent, nor did the earth quake, nor were the rocks rent, nor did the dead rise up, nor was any one of these men [of old] raised up on the third day, nor received into heaven, nor at his assumption were the heavens opened, nor did the nations believe in the name of any other; nor did any from among them, having been dead and rising again, lay open the new covenant of liberty. Therefore the prophets spake not of any one else but of the Lord, in whom all these aforesaid tokens concurred.

4. If any one, however, advocating the cause of the Jews, do maintain that this new covenant consisted in the rearing of that temple which was built under Zerubbabel after the emigration to Babylon, and in the departure of the people from thence after the lapse of seventy years, let him know that the temple constructed of stones was indeed then rebuilt (for as yet that law was observed which had been made upon tables of stone), yet no new covenant was given, but they used the Mosaic law until the coming of the Lord; but from the Lord's advent, the new covenant which brings back peace, and the law which gives life, has gone forth over the whole earth, as the prophets said: "For out of Zion shall go forth the law, and the word of the Lord from Jerusalem; and He shall rebuke many people; and they shall break down their swords into ploughshares, and their spears into pruning-

hooks, and they shall no longer learn to fight."[1] If therefore another law and word, going forth from Jerusalem, brought in such a [reign of] peace among the Gentiles which received it (the word), and convinced, through them, many a nation of its folly, then [only] it appears that the prophets spake of some other person. But if the law of liberty, that is, the word of God, preached by the apostles (who went forth from Jerusalem) throughout all the earth, caused such a change in the state of things, that these [nations] did form the swords and war-lances into ploughshares, and changed them into pruning-hooks for reaping the corn, [that is], into instruments used for peaceful purposes, and that they are now unaccustomed to fighting, but when smitten, offer also the other cheek,[2] then the prophets have not spoken these things of any other person, but of Him who effected them. This person is our Lord, and in Him is that declaration borne out; since it is He Himself who has made the plough, and introduced the pruning-hook, that is, the first semination of man, which was the creation exhibited in Adam,[3] and the gathering in of the produce in the last times by the Word; and, for this reason, since He joined the beginning to the end, and is the Lord of both, He has finally displayed the plough, in that the wood has been joined on to the iron, and has thus cleansed His land; because the Word, having been firmly united to flesh, and in its mechanism fixed with pins,[4] has reclaimed the savage earth. In the beginning, He figured forth the pruning-hook by means of Abel, pointing out that there should be a gathering in of a righteous race of men. He says, "For behold how the just man perishes, and no man considers it; and righteous men are taken away, and no man layeth it to heart."[5] These things were acted beforehand in Abel, were also previously declared by the prophets,

---

[1] Isa. ii. 3, 4; Mic. iv. 2, 3.   [2] Matt. v. 39.   [3] Vol. i. p. 40.
[4] This is following Harvey's conjectural emendation of the text, viz. "talcis" for "talia." He considers the *pins* here as symbolical of the *nails* by which our Lord was fastened to the cross. The whole passage is almost hopelessly obscure, though the general meaning may be guessed.
[5] Isa. lvii. 1.

but were accomplished in the Lord's person; and the same [is still true] with regard to us, the body following the example of the Head.

5. Such are the arguments proper [to be used] in opposition to those who maintain that the prophets [were inspired] by a different God, and that our Lord [came] from another Father, if perchance [these heretics] may at length desist from such extreme folly. This is my earnest object in adducing these scriptural proofs, that confuting them, as far as in me lies, by these very passages, I may restrain them from such great blasphemy, and from insanely fabricating a multitude of gods.

CHAP. XXXV.—*A refutation of those who allege that the prophets uttered some predictions under the inspiration of the Highest, others from the Demiurge. Disagreements of the Valentinians among themselves with regard to these same predictions.*

1. Then again, in opposition to the Valentinians, and the other Gnostics, falsely so called, who maintain that some parts of Scripture were spoken at one time from the Pleroma (*a summitate*) through means of the seed [derived] from that place, but at another time from the intermediate abode through means of the audacious mother Prunica, but that many are due to the Creator of the world, from whom also the prophets had their mission, we say that it is altogether irrational to bring down the Father of the universe to such straits, as that He should not be possessed of His own proper instruments, by which the things in the Pleroma might be perfectly proclaimed. For of whom was He afraid, so that He should not reveal His will after His own way and independently, freely, and without being involved with that spirit which came into being in a state of degeneracy and ignorance? Was it that He feared that very many would be saved, when more should have listened to the unadulterated truth? Or, on the other hand, was He incapable of preparing for Himself those who should announce the Saviour's advent?

2. But if, when the Saviour came to this earth, He sent

His apostles into the world to proclaim with accuracy His advent, and to teach the Father's will, having nothing in common with the doctrine of the Gentiles or of the Jews, much more, while yet existing in the Pleroma, would He have appointed His own heralds to proclaim His future advent into this world, and having nothing in common with those prophecies originating from the Demiurge. But if, when within the Pleroma, He availed Himself of those prophets who were under the law, and declared His own matters through their instrumentality; much more would He, upon His arrival hither, have made use of these same teachers, and have preached the gospel to us by their means. Therefore let them not any longer assert that Peter and Paul and the other apostles proclaimed the truth, but that it was the scribes and Pharisees, and the others, through whom the law was propounded. But if, at His advent, He sent forth His own apostles in the spirit of truth, and not in that of error, He did the very same also in the case of the prophets; for the Word of God was always the selfsame: and if the Spirit from the Pleroma was, according to these men's system, the Spirit of light, the Spirit of truth, the Spirit of perfection, and the Spirit of knowledge, while that from the Demiurge was the spirit of ignorance, degeneracy, and error, and the offspring of obscurity; how can it be, that in one and the same being there exist perfection and defect, knowledge and ignorance, error and truth, light and darkness? But if it was impossible that such should happen in the case of the prophets, for they preached the word of the Lord from one God, and proclaimed the advent of His Son, much more would the Lord Himself never have uttered words, on one occasion from above, but on another from degeneracy below, thus becoming the teacher at once of knowledge and of ignorance; nor would He have ever glorified as Father at one time the Founder of the world, and at another Him who is above this one, as He does Himself declare : "No man putteth a piece of a new garment upon an old one, nor do they put new wine into old bottles."[1] Let these men, there-

[1] Luke v. 36, 37.

fore, either have nothing whatever to do with the prophets, as with those that are ancients, and allege no longer that these men, being sent beforehand by the Demiurge, spake certain things under that new influence which pertains to the Pleroma; or, on the other hand, let them be convinced by our Lord, when He declares that new wine cannot be put into old bottles.

3. But from what source could the offspring of their mother derive his knowledge of the mysteries within the Pleroma, and power to discourse regarding them? Suppose that the mother, while beyond the Pleroma, did bring forth this very offspring; but what is beyond the Pleroma they represent as being beyond the pale of knowledge, that is, ignorance. How, then, could that seed, which was conceived in ignorance, possess the power of declaring knowledge? Or how did the mother herself, a shapeless and undefined being, one cast out of doors as an abortion, obtain knowledge of the mysteries within the Pleroma, she who was organized outside it and given a form there, and prohibited by Horos from entering within, and who remains outside the Pleroma till the consummation [of all things], that is, beyond the pale of knowledge? Then, again, when they say that the Lord's passion is a type of the extension of the Christ above, which he effected through Horos, and so imparted a form to their mother, they are refuted in the other particulars [of the Lord's passion], for they have no semblance of a type to show with regard to them. For when did the Christ above have vinegar and gall given him to drink? Or when was his raiment parted? Or when was he pierced, and blood and water came forth? Or when did he sweat great drops of blood? And [the same may be demanded] as to the other particulars which happened to the Lord, of which the prophets have spoken. From whence, then, did the mother or her offspring divine the things which had not yet taken place, but which should occur afterwards?

4. They affirm that certain things still, besides these, were spoken from the Pleroma, but are confuted by those which are referred to in the Scriptures as bearing on the advent of Christ.

But what these are [that are spoken from the Pleroma] they are not agreed, but give different answers regarding them. For if any one, wishing to test them, do question one by one with regard to any passage those who are their leading men, he shall find one of them referring the passage in question to the Propator—that is, to Bythus; another attributing it to Arche—that is, to the Only-begotten; another to the Father of all—that is, to the Word; while another, again, will say that it was spoken of that one Æon who was [formed from the joint contributions] of the Æons in the Pleroma;[1] others [will regard the passage] as referring to Christ, while another [will refer it] to the Saviour. One, again, more skilled than these,[2] after a long protracted silence, declares that it was spoken of Horos; another that it signifies the Sophia which is within the Pleroma; another that it announces the mother outside the Pleroma; while another will mention the God who made the world (the Demiurge). Such are the variations existing among them with regard to one [passage], holding discordant opinions as to the same Scriptures; and when the same identical passage is read out, they all begin to purse up their eyebrows, and to shake their heads, and they say that they might indeed utter a discourse transcendently lofty, but that all cannot comprehend the greatness of that thought which is implied in it; and that, therefore, among the wise the chief thing is silence. For that Sige (*silence*) which is above must be typified by that silence which they preserve. Thus do they, as many as they are, all depart [from each other], holding so many opinions as to one thing, and bearing about their clever notions in secret within themselves. When, therefore, they shall have agreed among themselves as to the things predicted in the Scriptures, then also shall they be confuted by us. For, though holding wrong opinions, they do in the meanwhile, however, convict themselves, since they are not of one mind with regard to the same words. But as we follow for our teacher the one and only true God, and possess His words as the rule of truth, we do all speak alike with

---

[1] Vol. i. p. 11.
[2] Illorum; following the Greek form of the comparative degree.

regard to the same things, knowing but one God, the Creator of this universe, who sent the prophets, who led forth the people from the land of Egypt, who in these last times manifested His own Son, that He might put the unbelievers to confusion, and search out the fruit of righteousness.

CHAP. XXXVI.—*The prophets were sent from one and the same Father from whom the Son was sent.*

1. Which [God] the Lord does not reject, nor does He say that the prophets [spake] from another god than His Father; nor from any other essence, but from one and the same Father; nor that any other being made the things in the world, except His own Father, when He speaks as follows in His teaching: "There was a certain householder, and he planted a vineyard, and hedged it round about, and digged in it a winepress, and built a tower, and let it out to husbandmen, and went into a far country: And when the time of the fruit drew near, he sent his servants unto the husbandmen, that they might receive the fruits of it. And the husbandmen took his servants: they cut one to pieces, stoned another, and killed another. Again he sent other servants more than the first: and they did unto them likewise. But last of all he sent unto them his only son, saying, Perchance they will reverence my son. But when the husbandmen saw the son, they said among themselves, This is the heir; come, let us kill him, and we shall possess his inheritance. And they caught him, and cast him out of the vineyard, and slew him. When, therefore, the lord of the vineyard shall come, what will he do unto these husbandmen? They say unto him, He will miserably destroy these wicked men, and will let out his vineyard to other husbandmen, who shall render him the fruits in their seasons."[1] Again does the Lord say: "Have ye never read, The stone which the builders rejected, the same is become the head of the corner: this is the Lord's doing, and it is marvellous in our eyes? Therefore I say unto you, that the kingdom of God shall be

[1] Matt. xxi. 33–41.

taken from you, and given to a nation bringing forth the fruits thereof."[1] By these words He clearly points out to His disciples one and the same Householder—that is, one God the Father, who made all things by Himself; while [He shows] that there are various husbandmen, some obstinate, and proud, and worthless, and slayers of the Lord, but others who render Him, with all obedience, the fruits in their seasons; and that it is the same Householder who sends at one time His servants, at another His Son. From that Father, therefore, from whom the Son was sent to those husbandmen who slew Him, from Him also were the servants [sent]. But the Son, as coming from the Father with supreme authority (*principali auctoritate*), used to express Himself thus: "But I say unto you."[2] The servants, again, [who came] as from their Lord, spake after the manner of servants, [delivering a message]; and they therefore used to say, "Thus saith the Lord."

2. Whom these men did therefore preach to the unbelievers as Lord, Him did Christ teach to those who obey Him; and the God who had called those of the former dispensation, is the same as He who has received those of the latter. In other words, He who at first used that law which entails bondage, is also He who did in after times [call His people] by means of adoption. For God planted the vineyard of the human race when at the first He formed Adam and chose the fathers; then He let it out to husbandmen when He established the Mosaic dispensation: He hedged it round about, that is, He gave particular instructions with regard to their worship: He built a tower, [that is], He chose Jerusalem: He digged a winepress, that is, He prepared a receptacle of the prophetic Spirit. And thus did He send prophets prior to the transmigration to Babylon, and after that event others again in greater number than the former, to seek the fruits, saying thus to them (the Jews): "Thus saith the Lord, Cleanse your ways and your doings, execute just judgment, and look each one with pity and compassion on his brother: oppress not the widow nor the orphan, the proselyte nor the

[1] Matt. xxi. 42–44. [2] Matt. v. 22.

poor, and let none of you treasure up evil against his brother in your hearts, and love not false swearing. Wash you, make ye clean, put away evil from your hearts, learn to do well, seek judgment, protect the oppressed, judge the fatherless (*pupillo*), plead for the widow; and come, let us reason together, saith the Lord."[1] And again: "Keep thy tongue from evil, and thy lips that they speak no guile; depart from evil, and do good; seek peace, and pursue it."[2] In preaching these things, the prophets sought the fruits of righteousness. But last of all He sent to those unbelievers His own Son, our Lord Jesus Christ, whom the wicked husbandmen cast out of the vineyard when they had slain Him. Wherefore the Lord God did even give it up (no longer hedged around, but thrown open throughout all the world) to other husbandmen, who render the fruits in their seasons,—the beautiful elect tower being also raised everywhere. For the illustrious church is [now] everywhere, and everywhere is the winepress digged: because those who do receive the Spirit are everywhere. For inasmuch as the former have rejected the Son of God, and cast Him out of the vineyard when they slew Him, God has justly rejected them, and given to the Gentiles outside the vineyard the fruits of its cultivation. This is in accordance with what Jeremiah says, "The Lord hath rejected and cast off the nation which does these things; for the children of Judah have done evil in my sight, saith the Lord."[3] And again in like manner does Jeremiah speak: "I set watchmen over you; hearken to the sound of the trumpet; and they said, We will not hearken. Therefore have the Gentiles heard, and they who feed the flocks in them."[4] It is therefore one and the same Father who planted the vineyard, who led forth the people, who sent the prophets, who sent His own Son, and who gave the vineyard to those other husbandmen that render the fruits in their season.

3. And therefore did the Lord say to His disciples, to make us become good workmen: "Take heed to yourselves, and watch continually upon every occasion, lest at any time your

---

[1] Jer. vii. 3; Zech. vii. 9, 10, viii. 17; Isa. i. 17-19.
[2] Ps. xxxiv. 13, 14. [3] Jer. vii. 29, 30. [4] Jer. vi. 17, 18.

hearts be overcharged with surfeiting and drunkenness, and cares of this life, and that day shall come upon you unawares; for as a snare shall it come upon all dwelling upon the face of the earth."[1] "Let your loins, therefore, be girded about, and your lights burning, and ye like to men who wait for their lord, when he shall return from the wedding."[2] "For as it was in the days of Noe, they did eat and drink, they bought and sold, they married and were given in marriage, and they knew not, until Noe entered into the ark, and the flood came and destroyed them all; as also it was in the days of Lot, they did eat and drink, they bought and sold, they planted and builded, until the time that Lot went out of Sodom; it rained fire from heaven, and destroyed them all: so shall it also be at the coming of the Son of man."[3] "Watch ye therefore, for ye know not in what day your Lord shall come."[4] [In these passages] He declares one and the same Lord, who in the times of Noah brought the deluge because of men's disobedience, and who also in the days of Lot rained fire from heaven because of the multitude of sinners among the Sodomites, and who, on account of this same disobedience and similar sins, will bring on the day of judgment at the end of time (*in novissimo*); on which day He declares that it shall be more tolerable for Sodom and Gomorrah than for that city and house which shall not receive the word of His apostles. "And thou, Capernaum," He said, "is it that thou shalt be exalted to heaven?[5] Thou shalt go down to hell. For if the mighty works which have been done in thee had been done in Sodom, it would have remained unto this day. Verily I say unto you, that it shall be more tolerable for Sodom in the day of judgment than for you."[6]

4. Since the Son of God is always one and the same, He gives to those who believe on Him a well of water[7] [springing

---

[1] Luke xxi. 34, 35.
[2] Luke xii. 35, 36.
[3] Luke xvii. 26, etc.
[4] Matt. xxiv. 42.
[5] No other of the Greek fathers quotes this text as above; from which fact Grabe infers that the old Latin translator, or his transcribers, altered the words of Irenæus to suit the Latin versions.
[6] Matt. xi. 23, 24.
[7] John iv. 14.

up] to eternal life, but He causes the unfruitful fig-tree immediately to dry up; and in the days of Noah He justly brought on the deluge for the purpose of extinguishing that most infamous race of men then existent, who could not bring forth fruit to God, since the angels that sinned had commingled with them, and [acted as He did] in order that He might put a check upon the sins of these men, but [that at the same time] He might preserve the archetype,[1] the formation of Adam. And it was He who rained fire and brimstone from heaven, in the days of Lot, upon Sodom and Gomorrah, "an example of the righteous judgment of God,"[2] that all may know, "that every tree that bringeth not forth good fruit shall be cut down, and cast into the fire."[3] And it is He who uses [the words], that it will be more tolerable for Sodom in the general judgment than for those who beheld His wonders, and did not believe on Him, nor receive His doctrine.[4] For as He gave by His advent a greater privilege to those who believed on Him, and who do His will, so also did He point out that those who did not believe on Him should have a more severe punishment in the judgment; thus extending equal justice to all, and being to exact more from those to whom He gives the more; the more, however, not because He reveals the knowledge of another Father, as I have shown so fully and so repeatedly, but because He has, by means of His advent, poured upon the human race the greater gift of paternal grace.

5. If, however, what I have stated be insufficient to convince any one that the prophets were sent from one and the same Father, from whom also our Lord was sent, let such a one, opening the mouth of his heart, and calling upon the Master, Christ Jesus the Lord, listen to Him when He says,

---

[1] This is Massuet's conjectural emendation of the text, viz. *archetypum* for *arcætypum*. Grabe would insert *per* before *arcæ*, and he thinks the passage to have a reference to 1 Pet. iii. 20. Irenæus, in common with the other ancient fathers, believed that the fallen angels were the "sons of God" who commingled with "the daughters of men," and thus produced a race of spurious men.

[2] Jude 7.   [3] Matt. iii. 10.   [4] Matt. xi. 24; Luke x. 12.

"The kingdom of heaven is like unto a king who made a marriage for his son, and he sent forth his servants to call them who were bidden to the marriage." And when they would not obey, He goes on to say, "Again he sent other servants, saying, Tell them that are bidden, Come ye, I have prepared my dinner; my oxen and all the fatlings are killed, and everything is ready; come unto the wedding. But they made light of it, and went their way, some to their farm, and others to their merchandize; but the remnant took his servants, and some they treated despitefully, while others they slew. But when the king heard this, he was wroth, and sent his armies and destroyed these murderers, and burned up their city, and said to his servants, The wedding is indeed ready, but they which were bidden were not worthy. Go out therefore into the highways, and as many as ye shall find, gather in to the marriage. So the servants went out, and collected together as many as they found, bad and good, and the wedding was furnished with guests. But when the king came in to see the guests, he saw there a man not having on a wedding garment; and he said unto him, Friend, how camest thou hither, not having on a wedding garment? But he was speechless. Then said the king to his servants, Take him away, hand and foot, and cast him into outer darkness: there shall be weeping and gnashing of teeth. For many are called, but few are chosen."[1] Now, by these words of His, does the Lord clearly show all [these points, viz.] that there is one King and Lord, the Father of all, of whom He had previously said, "Neither shalt thou swear by Jerusalem, for it is the city of the great King;"[2] and that He had from the beginning prepared the marriage for His Son, and used, with the utmost kindness, to call, by the instrumentality of His servants, the men of the former dispensation to the wedding feast; and when they would not obey, He still invited them by sending out other servants, yet that even then they did not obey Him, but even stoned and slew

---

[1] Matt. xxii. 1, etc.
[2] Matt. v. 35. Instead of placing a period here, as the editors do, it seems to us preferable to carry on the construction.

those who brought them the message of invitation. He accordingly sent forth His armies and destroyed them, and burned down their city; but He called together from all the highways, that is, from all nations, [guests] to the marriage feast of His Son, as also He says by Jeremiah: "I have sent also unto you my servants the prophets to say, Return ye now, every man, from his very evil way, and amend your doings."[1] And again He says by the same prophet: "I have also sent unto you my servants the prophets throughout the day and before the light; yet they did not obey me, nor incline their ears unto me. And thou shalt speak this word to them: This is a people that obeyeth not the voice of the Lord, nor receiveth correction; faith has perished from their mouth."[2] The Lord, therefore, who has called us everywhere by the apostles, is He who called those of old by the prophets, as appears by the words of the Lord; and although they preached to various nations, the prophets were not from one God, and the apostles from another; but, [proceeding] from one and the same, some of them announced the Lord, others preached the Father, and others again foretold the advent of the Son of God, while yet others declared Him as already present to those who then were afar off.

6. Still further did He also make it manifest, that we ought, after our calling, to be also adorned with works of righteousness, so that the Spirit of God may rest upon us; for this is the wedding garment, of which also the apostle speaks, "Not for that we would be unclothed, but clothed upon, that mortality might be swallowed up by immortality."[3] But those who have indeed been called to God's supper, yet have not received the Holy Spirit, because of their wicked conduct "shall be," He declares, "cast into outer darkness."[4] He thus clearly shows that the very same King who gathered from all quarters the faithful to the marriage of His Son, and who grants them the incorruptible banquet, [also] orders that man to be cast into outer darkness who has not on a wedding garment, that is, one who despises it. For as in

---

[1] Jer. xxxv. 15.   [2] Jer. vii. 25, etc.
[3] 2 Cor. v. 4.   [4] Matt. xxii. 13.

the former covenant, "with many of them was He not well pleased;"[1] so also is it the case here, that "many are called, but few chosen."[2] It is not, then, one God who judges, and another Father who calls us together to salvation; nor one, forsooth, who confers eternal light, but another who orders those who have not on the wedding garment to be sent into outer darkness. But it is one and the same God, the Father of our Lord, from whom also the prophets had their mission, who does indeed, through His infinite kindness, call the unworthy; but He examines those who are called, [to ascertain] if they have on the garment fit and proper for the marriage of His Son, because nothing unbecoming or evil pleases Him. This is in accordance with what the Lord said to the man who had been healed: "Behold, thou art made whole; sin no more, lest a worse thing come unto thee." For He who is good, and righteous, and pure, and spotless, will endure nothing evil, nor unjust, nor detestable in His wedding chamber. This is the Father of our Lord, by whose providence all things consist, and all are administered by His command; and He confers His free gifts upon those who should [receive them]; but the most righteous Retributor metes out [punishment] according to their deserts, most deservedly, to the ungrateful and to those that are insensible of His kindness; and therefore does He say, "He sent His armies, and destroyed those murderers, and burned up their city."[4] He says here, "His armies," because all men are the property of God. For "the earth is the Lord's, and the fulness thereof; the world, and all that dwell therein."[5] Wherefore also the Apostle Paul says in the Epistle to the Romans, "For there is no power but of God; the powers that be are ordained of God. Whosoever resisteth the power, resisteth the ordinance of God; and they that resist shall receive unto themselves condemnation. For rulers are not for a terror to a good work, but to an evil. Wilt thou then not be afraid of the power? Do that which is good, and thou shalt have praise of the same; for he is the minister of God to thee for good. But if thou do that

[1] 1 Cor. x. 5.   [2] Matt. xxii. 14.   [3] John v. 14.
[4] Matt. xxii. 7.   [5] Ps. xxiv. 1.

which is evil, be afraid; for he beareth not the sword in vain: for he is the minister of God, the avenger for wrath upon him that doeth evil. Wherefore ye must needs be subject, not only for wrath, but also for conscience sake. For this cause pay ye tribute also; for they are God's ministers, attending continually upon this very thing."[1] Both the Lord, then, and the apostles announce as the one only God the Father, Him who gave the law, who sent the prophets, who made all things; and therefore does He say "He sent His armies," because every man, inasmuch as he is a man, is His workmanship, although he may be ignorant of his God. For He gives existence to all; He, "who maketh His sun to rise upon the evil and the good, and sendeth rain upon the just and unjust."[2]

7. And not alone by what has been stated, but also by the parable of the two sons, the younger of whom consumed his substance by living luxuriously with harlots, did the Lord teach one and the same Father, who did not even allow a kid to his elder son; but for him who had been lost, [namely] his younger son, he ordered the fatted calf to be killed, and he gave him the best robe.[3] Also by the parable of the workmen who were sent into the vineyard at different periods of the day, one and the same God is declared[4] as having called some in the beginning, when the world was first created; but others afterwards, and others during the intermediate period, others after a long lapse of time, and others again in the end of time; so that there are many workmen in their generations, but only one householder who calls them together. For there is but one vineyard, since there is also but one righteousness, and one dispensator, for there is one Spirit of God who arranges all things; and in like manner is there one hire, for they all received a penny each man, having [stamped upon it] the royal image and superscription, the knowledge of the Son of God, which is immortality. And therefore He began by giving the hire to those [who were engaged] last, because in the last times, when the Lord was revealed, He presented Himself to all [as their reward].

8. Then, in the case of the publican, who excelled the

[1] Rom. xiii. 1-7. [2] Matt. v. 45. [3] Luke xv. 11. [4] Matt. xx. 1, etc.

Pharisee in prayer, [we find] that it was not because he worshipped another Father that he received testimony from the Lord that he was justified rather [than the other]; but because with great humility, apart from all boasting and pride, he made confession to the same God.[1] The parable of the two sons also: those who are sent into the vineyard, of whom one indeed opposed his father, but afterwards repented, when repentance profited him nothing; the other, however, promised to go, at once assuring his father, but he did not go (for "every man is a liar;"[2] "to will is present with him, but he finds not means to perform"[3]),—[this parable, I say], points out one and the same Father. Then, again, this truth was clearly shown forth by the parable of the fig-tree, of which the Lord says, "Behold, now these three years I come seeking fruit on this fig-tree, but I find none"[4] (pointing onwards, by the prophets, to His advent, by whom He came from time to time, seeking the fruit of righteousness from them, which he did not find), and also by the circumstance that, for the reason already mentioned, the fig-tree should be hewn down. And, without using a parable, the Lord said to Jerusalem, "O Jerusalem, Jerusalem, thou that killest the prophets, and stonest those that are sent unto thee; how often would I have gathered thy children together, as a hen gathereth her chickens under her wings, and ye would not! Behold, your house shall be left unto you desolate."[5] For that which had been said in the parable, "Behold, for three years I come seeking fruit," and in clear terms, again, [where He says], "How often would I have gathered thy children together," shall be [found] a falsehood, if we do not understand His advent, which is [announced] by the prophets—if, in fact, He came to them but once, and then for the first time. But since He who chose the patriarchs and those [who lived under the first covenant], is the same Word of God who did both visit them through the prophetic Spirit, and us also who have been called together from all quarters by His advent; in addition to what has been already said, He truly declared,

[1] Luke xviii. 10. [2] Ps. cxvi. 2. [3] Rom. vii. 18.
[4] Luke xiii. 6. [5] Luke xiii. 34; Matt. xxiii. 37.

"Many shall come from the east and from the west, and shall recline with Abraham, and Isaac, and Jacob, in the kingdom of heaven. But the children of the kingdom shall go into outer darkness; there shall be weeping and gnashing of teeth."[1] If, then, those who do believe in Him through the preaching of His apostles throughout the east and west shall recline with Abraham, Isaac, and Jacob, in the kingdom of heaven, partaking with them of the [heavenly] banquet, one and the same God is set forth as He who did indeed choose the patriarchs, visited also the people, and called the Gentiles.

CHAP. XXXVII.—*Men are possessed of free will, and endowed with the faculty of making a choice. It is not true, therefore, that some are by nature good, and others bad.*

1. This expression [of our Lord], "How often would I have gathered thy children together, and thou wouldest not,"[2] set forth the ancient law of human liberty, because God made man a free [agent] from the beginning, possessing his own power, even as he does his own soul, to obey the behests (*ad utendum sententia*) of God voluntarily, and not by compulsion of God. For there is no coercion with God, but a good will [towards us] is present with Him continually. And therefore does He give good counsel to all. And in man, as well as in angels, He has placed the power of choice (for angels are rational beings), so that those who had yielded obedience might justly possess what is good, given indeed by God, but preserved by themselves. On the other hand, they who have not obeyed shall, with justice, be not found in possession of the good, and shall receive condign punishment: for God did kindly bestow on them what was good; but they themselves did not diligently keep it, nor deem it something precious, but poured contempt upon His supereminent goodness. Rejecting therefore the good, and as it were spuing it out, they shall all deservedly incur the just judgment of God, which also the Apostle Paul testifies in his Epistle to the Romans, where he says, "But dost thou despise the riches of His goodness, and patience, and long-

[1] Matt. viii. 11, 12.   [2] Matt. xxiii. 37.

suffering, being ignorant that the goodness of God leadeth thee to repentance? But according to thy hardness and impenitent heart, thou treasurest to thyself wrath against the day of wrath, and the revelation of the righteous judgment of God." "But glory and honour," he says, "to every one that doeth good."[1] God therefore has given that which is good, as the apostle tells us in this epistle, and they who work it shall receive glory and honour, because they have done that which is good when they had it in their power not to do it; but those who do it not shall receive the just judgment of God, because they did not work good when they had it in their power so to do.

2. But if some had been made by nature bad, and others good, these latter would not be deserving of praise for being good, for such were they created; nor would the former be reprehensible, for thus they were made [originally]. But since all men are of the same nature, able both to hold fast and to do what is good; and, on the other hand, having also the power to cast it from them and not to do it,—some do justly receive praise even among men who are under the control of good laws (and much more from God), and obtain deserved testimony of their choice of good in general, and of persevering therein; but the others are blamed, and receive a just condemnation, because of their rejection of what is fair and good. And therefore the prophets used to exhort men to what was good, to act justly and to work righteousness, as I have so largely demonstrated, because it is in our power so to do, and because by excessive negligence we might become forgetful, and thus stand in need of that good counsel which the good God has given us to know by means of the prophets.

3. For this reason the Lord also said, "Let your light so shine before men, that they may see your good deeds, and glorify your Father who is in heaven."[2] And, "Take heed to yourselves, lest perchance your hearts be overcharged with surfeiting, and drunkenness, and worldly cares."[3] And, "Let your loins be girded about, and your lamps burning, and ye like unto men that wait for their Lord, when He

[1] Rom. ii. 4, 5, 7. [2] Matt. v. 16. [3] Luke xxi. 34.

returns from the wedding, that when He cometh and knocketh, they may open to Him. Blessed is that servant whom his Lord, when He cometh, shall find so doing."[1] And again, "The servant who knows his Lord's will, and does it not, shall be beaten with many stripes."[2] And, "Why call ye me, Lord, Lord, and do not the things which I say?"[3] And again, "But if the servant say in his heart, The Lord delayeth, and begin to beat his fellow-servants, and to eat, and drink, and to be drunken, his Lord will come in a day on which he does not expect Him, and shall cut him in sunder, and appoint his portion with the hypocrites."[4] All such passages demonstrate the independent will[5] of man, and at the same time the counsel which God conveys to him, by which He exhorts us to submit ourselves to Him, and seeks to turn us away from [the sin of] unbelief against Him, without, however, in any way coercing us.

4. No doubt, if any one is unwilling to follow the gospel itself, it is in his power [to reject it], but it is not expedient. For it is in man's power to disobey God, and to forfeit what is good; but [such conduct] brings no small amount of injury and mischief. And on this account Paul says, "All things are lawful to me, but all things are not expedient;"[6] referring both to the liberty of man, in which respect "all things are lawful,". God exercising no compulsion in regard to him; and [by the expression] "not expedient" pointing out that we "should not use our liberty as a cloak of maliciousness,"[7] for this is not expedient. And again he says, "Speak ye every man truth with his neighbour."[8] And, "Let no corrupt communication proceed out of your mouth, neither filthiness, nor foolish talking, nor scurrility, which are not convenient, but rather giving of thanks."[9] And, "For ye were sometimes darkness, but now are ye light in the Lord; walk honestly as children of the light, not in rioting and drunkenness, not in chambering and wantonness, not in anger and

---

[1] Luke xii. 35, 36. [2] Luke xii. 47. [3] Luke vi. 46.
[4] Luke xii. 45, 46; Matt. xxiv. 48-51. [5] τὸ αὐτεξούσιον.
[6] 1 Cor. vi. 12. [7] 1 Pet. ii. 16. [8] Eph. iv. 25.
[9] Eph. iv. 29.

jealousy. And such were some of you; but ye have been washed, but ye have been sanctified in the name of our Lord."[1] If then it were not in our power to do or not to do these things, what reason had the apostle, and much more the Lord Himself, to give us counsel to do some things, and to abstain from others? But because man is possessed of free will from the beginning, and God is possessed of free will, in whose likeness man was created, advice is always given to him to keep fast the good, which thing is done by means of obedience to God.

5. And not merely in works, but also in faith, has God preserved the will of man free and under his own control, saying, "According to thy faith be it unto thee;"[2] thus showing that there is a faith specially belonging to man, since he has an opinion specially his own. And again, " All things are possible to him that believeth;"[3] and, " Go thy way; and as thou hast believed, so be it done unto thee."[4] Now all such expressions demonstrate that man is in his own power with respect to faith. And for this reason, "he that believeth in Him has eternal life; while he who believeth not the Son hath not eternal life, but the wrath of God shall remain upon him."[5] In the same manner therefore the Lord, both showing His own goodness, and indicating that man is in his own free will and his own power, said to Jerusalem, " How often have I wished to gather thy children together, as a hen [gathereth] her chickens under her wings, and ye would not! Wherefore your house shall be left unto you desolate."[6]

6. Those, again, who maintain the opposite to these [conclusions], do themselves present the Lord as destitute of power, as if, forsooth, He were unable to accomplish what He willed; or, on the other hand, as being ignorant that they were by nature "material," as these men express it, and such as cannot receive His immortality. "But He should not," say they, " have created angels of such a nature that they were capable of transgression, nor men who immediately proved ungrateful towards Him; for they were made

[1] 1 Cor. vi. 11. [2] Matt. ix. 29. [3] Mark ix. 23.
[4] Matt. viii. 13. [5] John iii. 36. [6] Matt. xxiii. 37, 38.

rational beings, endowed with the power of examining and judging, and were not [formed] as things irrational or of a [merely] animal nature, which can do nothing of their own will, but are drawn by necessity and compulsion to what is good, in which things there is one mind and one usage, working mechanically in one groove (*inflexibiles et sine judicio*), who are incapable of being anything else except just what they had been created." But upon this supposition, neither would what is good be grateful to them, nor communion with God be precious, nor would the good be very much to be sought after, which would present itself without their own proper endeavour, care, or study, but would be implanted of its own accord and without their concern. Thus it would come to pass, that their being good would be of no consequence, because they were so by nature rather than by will, and are possessors of good spontaneously, not by choice; and for this reason they would not understand this fact, that good is a comely thing, nor would they take pleasure in it. For how can those who are ignorant of good enjoy it? Or what credit is it to those who have not aimed at it? And what crown is it to those who have not followed in pursuit of it, like those victorious in the contest?

7. On this account, too, did the Lord assert that the kingdom of heaven was the portion of "the violent;" and He says, "The violent take it by force;"[1] that is, those who by strength and earnest striving are on the watch to snatch it away on the moment. On this account also Paul the Apostle says to the Corinthians, "Know ye not, that they who run in a racecourse, do all indeed run, but one receiveth the prize? So run, that ye may obtain. Every one also who engages in the contest is temperate in all things: now these men [do it] that they may obtain a corruptible crown, but we an incorruptible. But I so run, not as uncertainly; I fight, not as one beating the air; but I make my body livid, and bring it into subjection, lest by any means, when preaching to others, I may myself be rendered a castaway."[2] This able wrestler, therefore, exhorts us to the struggle for im-

[1] Matt. xi. 12.   [2] 1 Cor. ix. 24-27.

mortality, that we may be crowned, and may deem the crown precious, namely, that which is acquired by our struggle, but which does not encircle us of its own accord (*sed non ultro coalitam*). And the harder we strive, so much is it the more valuable; while so much the more valuable it is, so much the more should we esteem it. And indeed those things are not esteemed so highly which come spontaneously, as those which are reached by much anxious care. Since, then, this power has been conferred upon us, both the Lord has taught and the apostle has enjoined us the more to love God, that we may reach this [prize] for ourselves by striving after it. For otherwise, no doubt, this our good would be [virtually] irrational, because not the result of trial. Moreover, the faculty of seeing would not appear to be so desirable, unless we had known what a loss it were to be devoid of sight; and health, too, is rendered all the more estimable by an acquaintance with disease; light, also, by contrasting it with darkness; and life with death. Just in the same way is the heavenly kingdom honourable to those who have known the earthly one. But in proportion as it is more honourable, so much the more do we prize it; and if we have prized it more, we shall be the more glorious in the presence of God. The Lord has therefore endured all these things on our behalf, in order that we, having been instructed by means of them all, may be in all respects circumspect for the time to come, and that, having been rationally taught to love God, we may continue in His perfect love: for God has displayed long-suffering in the case of man's apostasy; while man has been instructed by means of it, as also the prophet says, "Thine own apostasy shall heal thee;"[1] God thus determining all things beforehand for the bringing of man to perfection, for his edification, and for the revelation of His dispensations, that goodness may both be made apparent, and righteousness perfected, and that the church may be fashioned after the image of His Son, and that man may finally be brought to maturity at some future time, becoming ripe through such privileges to see and comprehend God.

[1] Jer. ii. 19.

CHAP. XXXVIII.—*Why man was not made perfect from the beginning.*

1. If, however, any one say, "What then? Could not God have exhibited man as perfect from the beginning?" let him know that, inasmuch as God is indeed always the same and unbegotten as respects Himself, all things are possible to Him. But created things must be inferior to Him who created them, from the very fact of their later origin; for it was not possible for things recently created to have been uncreated. But inasmuch as they are not uncreated, for this very reason do they come short of the perfect. Because, as these things are of later date, so are they infantile; so are they unaccustomed to, and unexercised in, perfect discipline. For as it certainly is in the power of a mother to give strong food to her infant, [but she does not do so], as the child is not yet able to receive more substantial nourishment; so also it was possible for God Himself to have made man perfect from the first, but man could not receive this [perfection], being as yet an infant. And for this cause our Lord, in these last times, when He had summed up all things into Himself, came to us, not as He might have come, but as we were capable of beholding Him. He might easily have come to us in His immortal glory, but in that case we could never have endured the greatness of the glory; and therefore it was that He, who was the perfect bread of the Father, offered Himself to us as milk, [because we were] as infants. He did this when He appeared as a man, that we, being nourished, as it were, from the breast of His flesh, and having, by such a course of milk-nourishment, become accustomed to eat and drink the Word of God, may be able also to contain in ourselves the Bread of immortality, which is the Spirit of the Father.

2. And on this account does Paul declare to the Corinthians, "I have fed you with milk, not with meat, for hitherto ye were not able to bear it."[1] That is, ye have indeed learned the advent of our Lord as a man; nevertheless, because of your infirmity, the Spirit of the Father has not as yet rested

[1] 1 Cor. iii. 2.

upon you. "For when envying and strife," he says, "and dissensions are among you, are ye not carnal, and walk as men?"[1] That is, that the Spirit of the Father was not yet with them, on account of their imperfection and the shortcomings of their walk in life. As, therefore, the apostle had the power to give them strong meat—for those upon whom the apostles laid hands received the Holy Spirit, who is the food of life [eternal]—but they were not capable of receiving it, because they had the sentient faculties of the soul still feeble and undisciplined in the practice of things pertaining to God; so, in like manner, God had power at the beginning to grant perfection to man; but as the latter was only recently created, he could not possibly have received it, or even if he had received it, could he have contained it, or containing it, could he have retained it. It was for this reason that the Son of God, although He was perfect, passed through the state of infancy in common with the rest of mankind, partaking of it thus not for His own benefit, but for that of the infantile stage of man's existence, in order that man might be able to receive Him. There was nothing, therefore, impossible to and deficient in God, [implied in the fact] that man was not an uncreated being; but this merely applied to him who was lately created, [namely] man.

3. With God there are simultaneously exhibited power, wisdom, and goodness. His power and goodness [appear] in this, that of His own will He called into being and fashioned things having no previous existence; His wisdom [is shown] in His having made created things parts of one harmonious and consistent whole; and those things which, through His super-eminent kindness, receive growth and a long period of existence, do reflect the glory of the uncreated One, of that God who bestows what is good ungrudgingly. For from the very fact of these things having been created, [it follows] that they are not uncreated; but by their continuing in being throughout a long course of ages, they shall receive a faculty of the Uncreated, through the gratuitous bestowal of eternal existence upon them by God. And thus in all things God has

[1] 1 Cor. iii. 3.

the pre-eminence, who alone is uncreated, the first of all things, and the primary cause of the existence of all, while all other things remain under God's subjection. But being in subjection to God is continuance in immortality, and immortality is the glory of the uncreated One. By this arrangement, therefore, and these harmonies, and a sequence of this nature, man, a created and organized being, is rendered after the image and likeness of the uncreated God,—the Father planning everything well and giving His commands, the Son carrying these into execution and performing the work of creating, and the Spirit nourishing and increasing [what is made], but man making progress day by day, and ascending towards the perfect, that is, approximating to the uncreated One. For the Uncreated is perfect, that is, God. Now it was necessary that man should in the first instance be created; and having been created, should receive growth; and having received growth, should be strengthened; and having been strengthened, should abound; and having abounded, should recover [from the disease of sin]; and having recovered, should be glorified; and being glorified, should see his Lord. For God is He who is yet to be seen, and the beholding of God is productive of immortality, but immortality renders one nigh unto God.

4. Irrational, therefore, in every respect, are they who await not the time of increase, but ascribe to God the infirmity of their nature. Such persons know neither God nor themselves, being insatiable and ungrateful, unwilling to be at the outset what they have also been created—men subject to passions; but go beyond the law of the human race, and before that they become men, they wish to be even now like God their Creator, and they who are more destitute of reason than dumb animals [insist] that there is no distinction between the uncreated God and man, a creature of to-day. For these, [the dumb animals], bring no charge against God for not having made them men; but each one, just as he has been created, gives thanks that he has been created. For we cast blame upon Him, because we have not been made gods from the beginning, but at first merely men,

then at length gods; although God has adopted this course out of His pure benevolence, that no one may impute to Him invidiousness or grudgingness. He declares, "I have said, Ye are gods; and ye are all sons of the Highest."[1] But since we could not sustain the power of divinity, He adds, "But ye shall die like men," setting forth both truths—the kindness of His free gift, and our weakness, and also that we were possessed of power over ourselves. For after His great kindness He graciously conferred good [upon us], and made men like to Himself, [that is] in their own power; while at the same time by His prescience He knew the infirmity of human beings, and the consequences which would flow from it; but through [His] love and [His] power, He shall overcome the substance of created nature.[2] For it was necessary, at first, that nature should be exhibited; then, after that, that what was mortal should be conquered and swallowed up by immortality, and the corruptible by incorruptibility, and that man should be made after the image and likeness of God, having received the knowledge of good and evil.

CHAP. XXXIX.—*Man is endowed with the faculty of distinguishing good and evil; so that, without compulsion, he has the power, by his own will and choice, to perform God's commandments, by doing which he avoids the evils prepared for the rebellious.*

1. Man has received the knowledge of good and evil. It is good to obey God, and to believe in Him, and to keep His commandment, and this is the life of man; as not to obey God is evil, and this is his death. Since God, therefore, gave [to man] such mental power (*magnanimitatem*), man knew both the good of obedience and the evil of disobedience, that the eye of the mind, receiving experience of both, may with judgment make choice of the better things; and that he may never become indolent or neglectful of God's com-

---

[1] Ps. lxxxii. 6, 7.
[2] That is, that man's human nature should not prevent him from becoming a partaker of the divine.

mand; and learning by experience that it is an evil thing which deprives him of life, that is, disobedience to God, may never attempt it at all, but that, knowing that what preserves his life, namely, obedience to God, is good, he may diligently keep it with all earnestness. Wherefore he has also had a twofold experience, possessing knowledge of both kinds, that with discipline he may make choice of the better things. But how, if he had no knowledge of the contrary, could he have had instruction in that which is good? For there is thus a surer and an undoubted comprehension of matters submitted to us than the mere surmise arising from an opinion regarding them. For just as the tongue receives experience of sweet and bitter by means of tasting, and the eye discriminates between black and white by means of vision, and the ear recognises the distinctions of sounds by hearing; so also does the mind, receiving through the experience of both the knowledge of what is good, become more tenacious of its preservation, by acting in obedience to God: in the first place, casting away, by means of repentance, disobedience, as being something disagreeable and nauseous; and afterwards coming to understand what it really is, that it is contrary to goodness and sweetness, so that the mind may never even attempt to taste disobedience to God. But if any one do shun the knowledge of both these kinds of things, and the twofold perception of knowledge, he unawares divests himself of the character of a human being.

2. How, then, shall he be a God, who has not as yet been made a man? Or how can he be perfect who was but lately created? How, again, can he be immortal, who in his mortal nature did not obey his Maker? For it must be that thou, at the outset, shouldest hold the rank of a man, and then afterwards partake of the glory of God. For thou dost not make God, but God thee. If, then, thou art God's workmanship, await the hand of thy Maker which creates everything in due time; in due time as far as thou art concerned, whose creation is being carried out.[1] Offer to Him thy heart in a soft and tractable state, and preserve the form in

---

[1] Efficeris.

which the Creator has fashioned thee, having moisture in thyself, lest, by becoming hardened, thou lose the impressions of His fingers. But by preserving the framework thou shalt ascend to that which is perfect, for the moist clay which is in thee is hidden [there] by the workmanship of God. His hand fashioned thy substance; He will cover thee over [too] within and without with pure gold and silver, and He will adorn thee to such a degree, that even "the King Himself shall have pleasure in thy beauty."[1] But if thou, being obstinately hardened, dost reject the operation of His skill, and show thyself ungrateful towards Him, because thou wert created a [mere] man, by becoming thus ungrateful to God, thou hast at once lost both His workmanship and life. For creation is an attribute of the goodness of God; but to be created is that of human nature. If, then, thou shalt deliver up to Him what is thine, that is, faith towards Him and subjection, thou shalt receive His handiwork, and shalt be a perfect work of God.

3. If, however, thou wilt not believe in Him, and wilt flee from His hands, the cause of imperfection shall be in thee who didst not obey, but not in Him who called [thee]. For He commissioned [messengers] to call people to the marriage, but they who did not obey Him deprived themselves of the royal supper.[2] The skill of God, therefore, is not defective, for He has power of the stones to raise up children to Abraham;[3] but the man who does not obtain it, is the cause to himself of his own imperfection. Nor, [in like manner], does the light fail because of those who have blinded themselves; but while it remains the same as ever, those who are [thus] blinded are involved in darkness through their own fault. The light does never enslave any one by necessity; nor, again, does God exercise compulsion upon any one unwilling to accept the exercise of His skill. Those persons, therefore, who have apostatized from the light given by the Father, and transgressed the law of liberty, have done so through their own fault, since they have been created free agents, and possessed of power over themselves.

[1] Ps. xlv. 11.   [2] Matt. xxii. 3, etc.   [3] Matt. iii. 9.

4. But God, foreknowing all things, prepared fit habitations for both, kindly conferring that light which they desire on those who seek after the light of incorruption, and resort to it; but for the despisers and mockers who avoid and turn themselves away from this light, and who do, as it were, blind themselves, He has prepared darkness suitable to persons who oppose the light, and He has inflicted an appropriate punishment upon those who try to avoid being subject to Him. Submission to God is eternal rest, so that they who shun the light have a place worthy of their flight; and those who fly from eternal rest, have a habitation in accordance with their fleeing. Now, since all good things are with God, they who by their own determination fly from God, do defraud themselves of all good things; and having been [thus] defrauded of all good things with respect to God, they shall consequently fall under the just judgment of God. For those persons who shun rest shall justly incur punishment, and those who avoid the light shall justly dwell in darkness. For as in the case of this temporal light, those who shun it do deliver themselves over to darkness, so that they do themselves become the cause to themselves that they are destitute of light, and do inhabit darkness; and, as I have already observed, the light is not the cause of such an [unhappy] condition of existence to them; so those who fly from the eternal light of God, which contains in itself all good things, are themselves the cause to themselves of their inhabiting eternal darkness, destitute of all good things, having become to themselves the cause of [their consignment to] an abode of that nature.

CHAP. XL.—*One and the same God the Father inflicts punishment on the reprobate, and bestows rewards on the elect.*

1. It is therefore one and the same God the Father who has prepared good things with Himself for those who desire His fellowship, and who remain in subjection to Him; and who has prepared the eternal fire for the ringleader of the apostasy, the devil, and those who revolted with him, into which [fire] the Lord[1] has declared those men shall be sent

[1] Matt. xxv. 41.

who have been set apart by themselves on His left hand.
And this is what has been spoken by the prophet, "I am a
jealous God, making peace, and creating evil things;"[1] thus
making peace and friendship with those who repent and turn
to Him, and bringing [them to] unity, but preparing for the
impenitent, those who shun the light, eternal fire and outer
darkness, which are evils indeed to those persons who fall
into them.

2. If, however, it were truly one Father who confers rest,
and another God who has prepared the fire, their sons would
have been equally different [one from the other]; one, indeed, sending [men] into the Father's kingdom, but the other
into eternal fire. But inasmuch as one and the same Lord
has pointed out that the whole human race shall be divided
at the judgment, "as a shepherd divideth the sheep from the
goats,"[2] and that to some He will say, "Come, ye blessed
of my Father, receive the kingdom which has been prepared
for you,"[3] but to others, "Depart from me, ye cursed, into
everlasting fire, which my Father has prepared for the devil
and his angels,"[4] one and the same Father is manifestly
declared [in this passage], "making peace and creating evil
things," preparing fit things for both; as also there is one
Judge sending both into a fit place, as the Lord sets forth in
the parable of the tares and the wheat, where He says, "As
therefore the tares are gathered together, and burned in the
fire, so shall it be at the end of the world. The Son of man
shall send His angels, and they shall gather from His kingdom everything that offendeth, and those who work iniquity,
and shall send them into a furnace of fire: there shall be
weeping and gnashing of teeth. Then shall the just shine
forth as the sun in the kingdom of their Father."[5] The
Father, therefore, who has prepared the kingdom for the
righteous, into which the Son has received those worthy of it,
is He who has also prepared the furnace of fire, into which
these angels commissioned by the Son of man shall send
those persons who deserve it, according to God's command.

[1] Isa. xlv. 7.   [2] Matt. xxv. 32.   [3] Matt. xxv. 34.
[4] Matt. xxv. 41.   [5] Matt. xiii. 40–43.

3. The Lord, indeed, sowed good seed in His own field;[1] and He says, "The field is the world." But while men slept, the enemy came, and "sowed tares in the midst of the wheat, and went his way."[2] Hence we learn that this was the apostate angel and the enemy, because he was envious of God's workmanship, and took in hand to render this [workmanship] at enmity with God. For this cause also God has banished from His presence him who did of his own accord stealthily sow the tares, that is, him who brought about the transgression;[3] but He took compassion upon man, who, through want of care no doubt, but still wickedly [on the part of another], became involved in disobedience; and He turned the enmity by which [the devil] had designed to make [man] the enemy of God, against the author of it, by removing His own anger from man, turning it in another direction, and sending it instead upon the serpent. As also the Scripture tells us that God said to the serpent, "And I will place enmity between thee and the woman, and between thy seed and her seed. He[4] shall bruise thy head, and thou shalt bruise his heel."[5] And the Lord summed up in Himself this enmity, when He was made man from a woman, and trod upon his [the serpent's] head, as I have pointed out in the preceding book.

CHAP. XLI.—*Those persons who do not believe in God, but who are disobedient, are angels and sons of the devil, not indeed by nature, but by imitation. Close of this book, and scope of the succeeding one.*

1. Inasmuch as the Lord has said that there are certain angels, [viz. those] of the devil, for whom eternal fire is prepared; and as, again, He declares with regard to the tares,

---

[1] Matt. xiii. 34.   [2] Matt. xiii. 28.

[3] The old Latin translator varies from this (the Greek of which was recovered by Grabe from two ancient *Catenæ Patrum*), making the clause run thus, *that is, the transgression which he had himself introduced*, making the explanatory words to refer to the *tares*, and not, as in the Greek, to the *sower of the tares*.

[4] Following the reading of the LXX., αὐτός σου τηρήσει κεφαλήν.
[5] Gen. iii. 15.

"The tares are the children of the wicked one,"[1] it must be affirmed that He has ascribed all who are of the apostasy to him who is the ringleader of this transgression. But He made neither angels nor men so by nature. For we do not find that the devil created anything whatsoever, since indeed he is himself a creature of God, like the other angels. For God made all things, as also David says with regard to all things of the kind: "For He spake the word, and they were made; He commanded, and they were created."[2]

2. Since, therefore, all things were made by God, and since the devil has become the cause of apostasy to himself and others, justly does the Scripture always term those who remain in a state of apostasy "sons of the devil" and "angels of the wicked one" (*maligni*). For [the word] "son," as one before me has observed, has a twofold meaning: one [is a son] in the order of nature, because he was born a son; the other, in that he was made so, is reputed a son, although there be a difference between being born so and being made so. For the first is indeed born from the person referred to; but the second is made so by him, whether as respects his creation or by the teaching of his doctrine. For when any person has been taught from the mouth of another, he is termed the son of him who instructs him, and the latter [is called] his father. According to nature, then—that is, according to creation, so to speak—we are all sons of God, because we have all been created by God. But with respect to obedience and doctrine we are not all the sons of God: those only are so who believe in Him and do His will. And those who do not believe, and do not obey His will, are sons and angels of the devil, because they do the works of the devil. And that such is the case He has declared in Isaiah: "I have begotten and brought up children, but they have rebelled against me."[3] And again, where He says that these children are aliens: "Strange children have lied unto me."[4] According to nature, then, they are [His] children, because they have been so created; but with regard to their works, they are not His children.

[1] Matt. xiii. 38.
[2] Ps. cxlix. 5.
[3] Isa. i. 2.
[4] Ps. xviii. 45.

3. For as, among men, those sons who disobey their fathers, being disinherited, are still their sons in the course of nature, but by law are disinherited, for they do not become the heirs of their natural parents; so in the same way is it with God,—those who do not obey Him being disinherited by Him, have ceased to be His sons. Wherefore they cannot receive His inheritance: as David says, " Sinners are alienated from the womb; their anger is after the likeness of a serpent."[1] And therefore did the Lord term those whom He knew to be the offspring of men " a generation of vipers;"[2] because after the manner of these animals they go about in subtilty, and injure others. For He said, " Beware of the leaven of the Pharisees and of the Sadducees."[3] Speaking of Herod, too, He says, " Go ye and tell that fox,"[4] aiming at his wicked cunning and deceit. Wherefore the prophet David says, "Man, being placed in honour, is made like unto cattle."[5] And again Jeremiah says, " They are become like horses, furious about females; each one neighed after his neighbour's wife."[6] And Isaiah, when preaching in Judea, and reasoning with Israel, termed them " rulers of Sodom " and " people of Gomorrah;"[7] intimating that they were like the Sodomites in wickedness, and that the same description of sins was rife among them, calling them by the same name, because of the similarity of their conduct. And inasmuch as they were not by nature so created by God, but had power also to act rightly, the same person said to them, giving them good counsel, "Wash ye, make you clean; take away iniquity from your souls before mine eyes; cease from your iniquities."[8] Thus, no doubt, since they had transgressed and sinned in the same manner, so did they receive the same reproof as did the Sodomites. But when they should be converted and come to repentance, and cease from evil, they should have power to become the sons of God, and to receive the inheritance of immortality which is given by Him. For this reason, therefore, He has termed those " angels of the

---

[1] Ps. lviii. 3, 4.
[2] Matt. xxiii. 33.
[3] Matt. xvi. 6.
[4] Luke xiii. 32.
[5] Ps. xlix. 21.
[6] Jer. v. 8.
[7] Isa. i. 10.
[8] Isa. i. 16.

devil," and "children of the wicked one,"[1] who give heed to the devil, and do his works. But these are, at the same time, all created by the one and the same God. When, however, they believe and are subject to God, and go on and keep His doctrine, they are the sons of God; but when they have apostatized and fallen into transgression, they are ascribed to their chief, the devil—to him who first became the cause of apostasy to himself, and afterwards to others.

4. Inasmuch as the words of the Lord are numerous, while they all proclaim one and the same Father, the Creator of this world, it was incumbent also upon me, for their own sake, to refute by many [arguments] those who are involved in many errors, if by any means, when they are confuted by many [proofs], they may be converted to the truth and saved. But it is necessary to subjoin to this composition, in what follows, also the doctrine of Paul after the words of the Lord, to examine the opinion of this man, and expound the apostle, and to explain whatsoever [passages] have received other interpretations from the heretics, who have altogether misunderstood what Paul has spoken, and to point out the folly of their mad opinions; and to demonstrate from that same Paul, from whose [writings] they press questions upon us, that they are indeed utterers of falsehood, but that the apostle was a preacher of the truth, and that he taught all things agreeable to the preaching of the truth; [to the effect that] it was one God the Father who spake with Abraham, who gave the law, who sent the prophets beforehand, who in the last times sent His Son, and conferred salvation upon His own handiwork—that is, the substance of flesh. Arranging, then, in another book, the rest of the words of the Lord, which He taught concerning the Father not by parables, but by expressions taken in their obvious meaning (*sed simpliciter ipsis dictionibus*), and the exposition of the epistles of the blessed apostle, I shall, with God's aid, furnish thee with the complete work of the exposure and refutation of knowledge, falsely so called; thus practising myself and thee in [these] five books for presenting opposition to all heretics.

[1] Matt. xxv. 41, xiii. 38.

BOOK V.

PREFACE.

N the four preceding books, my very dear friend, which I put forth to thee, all the heretics have been exposed, and their doctrines brought to light, and these men refuted who have devised irreligious opinions. [I have accomplished this by adducing] something from the doctrine peculiar to each of these men, which they have left in their writings, as well as by using arguments of a more general nature, and applicable to them all.¹ Then I have pointed out the truth, and shown the preaching of the church, which the prophets proclaimed (as I have already demonstrated), but which Christ brought to perfection, and the apostles have handed down, from whom the church, receiving [these truths], and throughout all the world alone preserving them in their integrity (*bene*), has transmitted them to her sons. Then also—having disposed of all questions which the heretics propose to us, and having explained the doctrine of the apostles, and clearly set forth many of those things which were said and done by the Lord in parables—I shall endeavour, in this the fifth book of the entire work which treats of the exposure and refutation of knowledge falsely so called, to exhibit proofs from the rest of the Lord's doctrine and the apostolical epistles: [thus] complying with thy demand, as thou didst request of me (since indeed I have been assigned a place in the ministry of the word); and, labouring by every means in my power to

¹ Ex ratione universis ostensionibus procedente. The words are very obscure.

furnish thee with large assistance against the contradictions of the heretics, as also to reclaim the wanderers and convert them to the church of God, to confirm at the same time the minds of the neophytes, that they may preserve stedfast the faith which they have received, guarded by the church in its integrity, in order that they be in no way perverted by those who endeavour to teach them false doctrines, and lead them away from the truth. It will be incumbent upon thee, however, and all who may happen to read this writing, to peruse with great attention what I have already said, that thou mayest obtain a knowledge of the subjects against which I am contending. For it is thus that thou wilt both controvert them in a legitimate manner, and wilt be prepared to receive the proofs brought forward against them, casting away their doctrines as filth by means of the celestial faith; but following the only true and stedfast teacher, the Word of God, our Lord Jesus Christ, who did, through His transcendent love, become what we are, that He might bring us to be even what He is Himself.

CHAP. I.—*Christ alone is able to teach divine things, and to redeem us: He, the same, took flesh of the Virgin Mary, not merely in appearance, but actually, by the operation of the Holy Spirit, in order to renovate us. Strictures on the conceits of Valentinus and Ebion.*

1. For in no other way could we have learned the things of God, unless our Master, existing as the Word, had become man. For no other being had the power of revealing to us the things of the Father, except His own proper Word. For what other person "knew the mind of the Lord," or who else "has become His counsellor?"[1] Again, we could have learned in no other way than by seeing our Teacher, and hearing His voice with our own ears, that, having become imitators of His works as well as doers of His words, we may have communion with Him, receiving increase from the perfect One, and from Him who is prior to all creation. We—who were but lately

[1] Rom. xi. 34.

created by the only best and good Being, by Him also who has the gift of immortality, having been formed after His likeness (predestinated, according to the prescience of the Father, that we, who had as yet no existence, might come into being), and made the first-fruits of creation [1]—have received, in the times known beforehand, [the blessings of salvation] according to the ministration of the Word, who is perfect in all things, as the mighty Word, and very man, who, redeeming us by His own blood in a manner consonant to reason, gave Himself as a redemption for those who had been led into captivity. And since the apostasy tyrannized over us unjustly, and, though we were by nature the property of the omnipotent God, alienated us contrary to nature, rendering us its own disciples, the Word of God, powerful in all things, and not defective with regard to His own justice, did righteously turn against that apostasy, and redeem from it His own property, not by violent means, as the [apostasy] had obtained dominion over us at the beginning, when it insatiably snatched away what was not its own, but by means of persuasion, as became a God of counsel, who does not use violent means to obtain what He desires; so that neither should justice be infringed upon, nor the ancient handiwork of God go to destruction. Since the Lord thus has redeemed us through His own blood, giving His soul for our souls, and His flesh for our flesh, and has also poured out the Spirit of the Father for the union and communion of God and man, imparting indeed God to men by means of the Spirit, and, on the other hand, attaching man to God by His own incarnation, and bestowing upon us at His coming immortality durably and truly, by means of communion with God,—all the doctrines of the heretics fall to ruin.

2. Vain indeed are those who allege that He appeared in mere seeming. For these things were not done in appearance only, but in actual reality. But if He did appear as a man, when He was not a man, neither could the Holy Spirit have rested upon Him,—an occurrence which did actually take

[1] "Initium facturæ," which Grabe thinks should be thus translated with reference to Jas. i. 18.

place—as the Spirit is invisible; nor, [in that case], was there any degree of truth in Him, for He was not that which He seemed to be. But I have already remarked that Abraham and the other prophets beheld Him after a prophetical manner, foretelling in vision what should come to pass. If, then, such a being has now appeared in outward semblance different from what he was in reality, there has been a certain prophetical vision made to men; and another advent of His must be looked forward to, in which He shall be such as He has now been seen in a prophetic manner. And I have proved already, that it is the same thing to say that He appeared merely to outward seeming, and [to affirm] that He received nothing from Mary. For He would not have been one truly possessing flesh and blood, by which He redeemed us, unless He had summed up in Himself the ancient formation of Adam. Vain therefore are the disciples of Valentinus who put forth this opinion, in order that they may exclude the flesh from salvation, and cast aside what God has fashioned.

3. Vain also are the Ebionites, who do not receive by faith into their soul the union of God and man, but who remain in the old leaven of [the natural] birth, and who do not choose to understand that the Holy Ghost came upon Mary, and the power of the Most High did overshadow her:[1] wherefore also what was generated is a holy thing, and the Son of the Most High God the Father of all, who effected the incarnation of this being, and showed forth a new [kind of] generation; that as by the former generation we inherited death, so by this new generation we might inherit life. Therefore do these men reject the commixture of the heavenly wine,[2] and wish it to be water of the world only, not receiving God so as to have union with Him, but they remain in that Adam who had been conquered and was expelled from Paradise: not considering that as, at the beginning

---

[1] Luke i. 35.
[2] In allusion to the mixture of water in the eucharistic cup, as practised in these primitive times. The Ebionites and others used to consecrate the element of water alone.

of our formation in Adam, that breath of life which proceeded from God, having been united to what had been fashioned, animated the man, and manifested him as a being endowed with reason ; so also, in [the times of] the end, the Word of the Father and the Spirit of God, having become united with the ancient substance of Adam's formation, rendered man living and perfect, receptive of the perfect Father, in order that as in the natural [Adam] we all were dead, so in the spiritual we may all be made alive.[1] For never at any time did Adam escape the *hands*[2] of God, to whom the Father speaking, said, "Let us make man in our image, after our likeness." And for this reason in the last times (*fine*), not by the will of the flesh, nor by the will of man, but by the good pleasure of the Father,[3] His hands formed a living man, in order that Adam might be created [again] after the image and likeness of God.

CHAP. II.—*When Christ visited us in His grace, He did not come to what did not belong to Him : also, by shedding His true blood for us, and exhibiting to us His true flesh in the Eucharist, He conferred upon our flesh the capacity of salvation.*

1. And vain likewise are those who say that God came to those things which did not belong to Him, as if covetous of another's property ; in order that He might deliver up that man who had been created by another, to that God who had neither made nor formed anything, but who also was deprived from the beginning of His own proper formation of men. The advent, therefore, of Him whom these men represent as coming to the things of others, was not righteous ; nor did He truly redeem us by His own blood, if He did not really become man, restoring to His own handiwork what was said [of it] in the beginning, that man was made after the image and likeness of God ; not snatching away by stratagem the property of another, but taking possession of His own in a righteous and gracious manner. As far as concerned the

[1] 1 Cor. xv. 22.   [2] Viz. the Son and the Spirit.   [3] John i. 13.

apostasy, indeed, He redeems us righteously from it by His own blood; but as regards us who have been redeemed, [He does this] graciously. For we have given nothing to Him previously, nor does He desire anything from us, as if He stood in need of it; but we do stand in need of fellowship with Him. And for this reason it was that He graciously poured Himself out, that He might gather us into the bosom of the Father.

2. But vain in every respect are they who despise the entire dispensation of God, and disallow the salvation of the flesh, and treat with contempt its regeneration, maintaining that it is not capable of incorruption. But if this indeed do not attain salvation, then neither did the Lord redeem us with His blood, nor is the cup of the Eucharist the communion of His blood, nor the bread which we break the communion of His body.[1] For blood can only come from veins and flesh, and whatsoever else makes up the substance of man, such as the Word of God was actually made. By His own blood He redeemed us, as also His apostle declares, "In whom we have redemption through His blood, even the remission of sins."[2] And as we are His members, we are also nourished by means of the creation (and He Himself grants the creation to us, for He causes His sun to rise, and sends rain when He wills[3]). He has acknowledged the cup (which is a part of the creation) as His own blood, from which He bedews our blood; and the bread (also a part of the creation) He has established as His own body, from which He gives increase to our bodies.

3. When, therefore, the mingled cup and the manufactured bread receives the Word of God, and the Eucharist of the blood and the body of Christ is made,[4] from which things the substance of our flesh is increased and supported, how can they affirm that the flesh is incapable of receiving the gift of God, which is life eternal, which [flesh] is nourished from the body and blood of the Lord, and is a member of Him?—

---

[1] 1 Cor. x. 16.   [2] Col. i. 14.   [3] Matt. v. 45.

[4] The Greek text, of which a considerable portion remains here, would give, "and the Eucharist becomes the body of Christ."

even as the blessed Paul declares in his Epistle to the Ephesians, that " we are members of His body, of His flesh, and of His bones."[1] He does not speak these words of some spiritual and invisible man, for a spirit has not bones nor flesh;[2] but [he refers to] that dispensation [by which the Lord became] an actual man, consisting of flesh, and nerves, and bones,—that [flesh] which is nourished by the cup which is His blood, and receives increase from the bread which is His body. And just as a cutting from the vine planted in the ground fructifies in its season, or as a corn of wheat falling into the earth and becoming decomposed, rises with manifold increase by the Spirit of God, who contains all things, and then, through the wisdom of God, serves for the use of men, and having received the Word of God, becomes the Eucharist, which is the body and blood of Christ; so also our bodies, being nourished by it, and deposited in the earth, and suffering decomposition there, shall rise at their appointed time, the Word of God granting them resurrection to the glory of God, even the Father, who freely gives to this mortal immortality, and to this corruptible incorruption,[3] because the strength of God is made perfect in weakness,[4] in order that we may never become puffed up, as if we had life from ourselves, and exalted against God, our minds becoming ungrateful; but learning by experience that we possess eternal duration from the excelling power of this Being, not from our own nature, we may neither undervalue that glory which surrounds God as He is, nor be ignorant of our own nature, but that we may know what God can effect, and what benefits man receives, and thus never wander from the true comprehension of things as they are, that is, both with regard to God and with regard to man. And might it not be the case, perhaps, as I have already observed, that for this purpose God permitted our resolution into the common dust of mortality,[5] that we, being instructed by every mode, may be

---

[1] Eph. v. 30. [2] Luke xxiv. 39. [3] 1 Cor. xv. 53. [4] 2 Cor. xii. 3.

[5] This is Harvey's free rendering of the passage, which is in the Greek (as preserved in the Catena of John of Damascus): καὶ διὰ τοῦτο ἠνέσχετο ὁ Θεὸς τὴν εἰς τὴν γῆν ἡμῶν ἀνάλυσιν. In the Latin: Propter

accurate in all things for the future, being ignorant neither of God nor of ourselves?

CHAP. III.—*The power and glory of God shine forth in the weakness of human flesh, as He will render our body a participator of the resurrection and of immortality, although He has formed it from the dust of the earth; He will also bestow upon it the enjoyment of immortality, just as He grants it this short life in common with the soul.*

1. The Apostle Paul has, moreover, in the most lucid manner, pointed out that man has been delivered over to his own infirmity, lest, being uplifted, he might fall away from the truth. Thus he says in the second [Epistle] to the Corinthians: "And lest I should be lifted up by the sublimity of the revelations, there was given unto me a thorn in the flesh, the messenger of Satan to buffet me. And upon this I besought the Lord three times, that it might depart from me. But He said unto me, My grace is sufficient for thee; for strength is made perfect in weakness. Gladly therefore shall I rather glory in infirmities, that the power of Christ may dwell in me."[1] What, therefore? (as some may exclaim:) did the Lord wish, in that case, that His apostle should thus undergo buffeting, and that he should endure such infirmity? Even so it was; the word says it. For strength is made perfect in weakness, rendering him a better man who by means of his infirmity becomes acquainted with the power of God. For how could a man have learned that he is himself an infirm being, and mortal by nature, but that God is immortal and powerful, unless he had learned by experience what is in both? For there is nothing evil in learning one's infirmities by endurance; yea, rather, it has even the beneficial effect of preventing him from forming an undue opinion of his own nature (*non aberrare in natura sua*). But the

hoc passus est Deus fieri in nobis resolutionem. See the former volume, p. 348.

[1] 2 Cor. xii. 7-9.

being lifted up against God, and taking His glory to one's self, rendering man ungrateful, has brought much evil upon him. [And thus, I say, man must learn both things by experience], that he may not be destitute of truth and love either towards himself or his Creator.[1] But the experience of both confers upon him the true knowledge as to God and man, and increases his love towards God. Now, where there exists an increase of love, there a greater glory is wrought out by the power of God for those who love Him.

2. Those men, therefore, set aside the power of God, and do not consider what the word declares, when they dwell upon the infirmity of the flesh, but do not take into consideration the power of Him who raises it up from the dead. For if He does not vivify what is mortal, and does not bring back the corruptible to incorruption, He is not a God of power. But that He is powerful in all these respects, we ought to perceive from our origin, inasmuch as God, taking dust from the earth, formed man. And surely it is much more difficult and incredible, from non-existent bones, and nerves, and veins, and the rest of man's organization, to bring it about that all this should be, and to make man an animated and rational creature, than to reintegrate again that which had been created and then afterwards decomposed into earth (for the reasons already mentioned), having thus passed into those [elements] from which man, who had no previous existence, was formed. For He who in the beginning caused him to have being who as yet was not, just when He pleased, shall much more reinstate again those who had a former existence, when it is His will [that they should inherit] the life granted by Him. And that flesh shall also be found fit for and capable of receiving the power of God, which at the beginning received the skilful touches of God; so that one part became the eye for seeing; another, the ear for hearing; another, the hand for feeling and working; another, the

---

[1] We have adopted here the explanation of Massuet, who considers the preceding period as merely parenthetical. Both Grabe and Harvey, however, would make conjectural emendations in the text, which seem to us to be inadmissible.

sinews stretched out everywhere, and holding the limbs together; another, arteries and veins, passages for the blood and the air;[1] another, the various internal organs; another, the blood, which is the bond of union between soul and body. But why go [on in this strain]? Numbers would fail to express the multiplicity of parts in the human frame, which was made in no other way than by the great wisdom of God. But those things which partake of the skill and wisdom of God, do also partake of His power.

3. The flesh, therefore, is not destitute [of participation] in the constructive wisdom and power of God. But if the power of Him who is the bestower of life is made perfect in weakness—that is, in the flesh—let them inform us, when they maintain the incapacity of flesh to receive the life granted by God, whether they do say these things as being living men at present, and partakers of life, or acknowledge that, having no part in life whatever, they are at the present moment dead men. And if they really are dead men, how is it that they move about, and speak, and perform those other functions which are not the actions of the dead, but of the living? But if they are now alive, and if their whole body partakes of life, how can they venture the assertion that the flesh is not qualified to be a partaker of life, when they do confess that they have life at the present moment? It is just as if anybody were to take up a sponge full of water, or a torch on fire, and to declare that the sponge could not possibly partake of the water, or the torch of the fire. In this very manner do those men, by alleging that they are alive and bear life about in their members, contradict themselves afterwards, when they represent these members as not being capable of [receiving] life. But if the present temporal life, which is of such an inferior nature to eternal life, can nevertheless effect so much as to quicken our mortal members, why should not eternal life, being much more powerful than this, vivify the flesh, which has already held converse with, and

---

[1] The ancients erroneously supposed that the arteries were *air-vessels*, from the fact that these organs, after death, appear quite empty, from all the blood stagnating in the veins when death supervenes.

been accustomed to sustain, life? For that the flesh can really partake of life, is shown from the fact of its being alive; for it lives on, as long as it is God's purpose that it should do so. It is manifest, too, that God has the power to confer life upon it, inasmuch as He grants life to us who are in existence. And, therefore, since the Lord has power to infuse life into what He has fashioned, and since the flesh is capable of being quickened, what remains to prevent its participating in incorruption, which is a blissful and never-ending life granted by God?

CHAP. IV.—*Those persons are deceived who feign another God the Father besides the Creator of the world; for he must have been feeble and useless, or else malignant and full of envy, if he be either unable or unwilling to extend eternal life to our bodies.*

1. Those persons who feign the existence of another Father beyond the Creator, and who term him the good God, do deceive themselves; for they introduce him as a feeble, worthless, and negligent being, not to say malign and full of envy, inasmuch as they affirm that our bodies are not quickened by him. For when they say of things which it is manifest to all do remain immortal, such as the spirit and the soul, and such other things, that they are quickened by the Father, but that another thing [viz. the body] which is quickened in no different manner than by God granting [life] to it, is abandoned by life,—[they must either confess] that this proves their Father to be weak and powerless, or else envious and malignant. For since the Creator does even here quicken our mortal bodies, and promises them resurrection by the prophets, as I have pointed out; who [in that case] is shown to be more powerful, stronger, or truly good? Whether is it the Creator who vivifies the whole man, or is it their Father, falsely so called? He feigns to be the quickener of those things which are immortal by nature, to which things life is always present by their very nature; but he does not benevolently quicken those things which required his

assistance, that they might live, but leaves them carelessly to fall under the power of death. Whether is it the case, then, that their Father does not bestow life upon them when he has the power of so doing, or is it that he does not possess the power? If, on the one hand, it is because he cannot, he is, upon that supposition, not a powerful being, nor is he more perfect than the Creator; for the Creator grants, as we must perceive, what *He* is unable to afford. But if, on the other hand, [it be that he does not grant this] when he has the power of so doing, then he is proved to be not a good, but an envious and malignant Father.

2. If, again, they refer to any cause on account of which their Father does not impart life to bodies, then that cause must necessarily appear superior to the Father, since it restrains Him from the exercise of His benevolence; and His benevolence will thus be proved weak, on account of that cause which they bring forward. Now every one must perceive that bodies are capable of receiving life. For they live to the extent that God pleases that they should live; and that being so, the [heretics] cannot maintain that [these bodies] are utterly incapable of receiving life. If, therefore, on account of necessity and any other cause, those [bodies] which are capable of participating in life are not vivified, their Father shall be the slave of necessity and that cause, and not therefore a free agent, having His will under His own control.

CHAP. V.—*The prolonged life of the ancients, the translation of Elijah and of Enoch in their own bodies, as well as the preservation of Jonah, of Shadrach, Meshach, and Abednego, in the midst of extreme peril, are clear demonstrations that God can raise up our bodies to life eternal.*

1. [In order to learn] that bodies did continue in existence for a lengthened period, as long as it was God's good pleasure that they should flourish, let [these heretics] read the Scriptures, and they will find that our predecessors advanced beyond seven hundred, eight hundred, and nine hundred

years of age; and that their bodies kept pace with the protracted length of their days, and participated in life as long as God willed that they should live. But why do I refer to these men? For Enoch, when he pleased God, was translated in the same body in which he did please Him, thus pointing out by anticipation the translation of the just. Elijah, too, was caught up [when he was yet] in the substance of the [natural] form; thus exhibiting in prophecy the assumption of those who are spiritual, and that nothing stood in the way of their body being translated and caught up. For by means of the very same hands through which they were moulded at the beginning, did they receive this translation and assumption. For in Adam the hands of God had become accustomed to set in order, to rule, and to sustain His own workmanship, and to bring it and place it where they pleased. Where, then, was the first man placed? In paradise certainly, as the Scripture declares: "And God planted a garden [*paradisum*] eastward in Eden, and there He placed the man whom He had formed."[1] And then afterwards, when [man] proved disobedient, he was cast out thence into this world. Wherefore also the elders who were disciples of the apostles tell us that those who were translated were transferred to that place (for paradise has been prepared for righteous men, such as have the Spirit; in which place also Paul the apostle, when he was caught up, heard words which are unspeakable as regards us in our present condition[2]), and that there shall they who have been translated remain until the consummation [of all things], as a prelude to immortality.

2. If, however, any one imagine it impossible that men should survive for such a length of time, and that Elias was not caught up in the flesh, but that his flesh was consumed in the fiery chariot, let him consider that Jonah, when he had been cast into the deep, and swallowed down into the whale's belly, was by the command of God again thrown out safe upon the land.[3] And then, again, when Ananias, Azarias, and Misaël were cast into the furnace of fire sevenfold heated, they sustained no harm whatever, neither was the smell of

[1] Gen. ii. 8.   [2] 2 Cor. xii. 4.   [3] Jonah ii. 11.

fire perceived upon them. As, therefore, the hand of God was present with them, working out marvellous things in their case —[things] impossible [to be accomplished] by man's nature— what wonder was it, if also in the case of those who were translated it performed something wonderful, working in obedience to the will of God, even the Father? Now this is the Son of God, as the Scripture represents Nebuchadnezzar the king as having said, " Did not we cast three men bound into the furnace? and, lo, I do see four walking in the midst of the fire, and the fourth is like the Son of God."[1] Neither the nature of any created thing, therefore, nor the weakness of the flesh, can prevail against the will of God. For God is not subject to created things, but created things to God; and all things yield obedience to His will. Wherefore also the Lord declares, " The things which are impossible with men, are possible with God."[2] As, therefore, it might seem to the men of the present day, who are ignorant of God's appointment, to be a thing incredible and impossible that any man could live for such a number of years, yet those who were before us did live [to such an age], and those who were translated do live as an earnest of the future length of days; and [as it might also appear impossible] that from the whale's belly and from the fiery furnace men issued forth unhurt, yet they nevertheless did so, led forth as it were by the hand of God, for the purpose of declaring His power: so also now, although some, not knowing the power and promise of God, may oppose their own salvation, deeming it impossible for God, who raises up the dead, to have power to confer upon them eternal duration, yet the scepticism of men of this stamp shall not render the faithfulness of God of none effect.

CHAP. VI.—*God will bestow salvation upon the whole nature of man, consisting of body and soul in close union, since the Word took it upon Him, and adorned it with the gifts of the Holy Spirit, of whom our bodies are, and are termed, the temples.*

1. Now God shall be glorified in His handiwork, fitting it

[1] Dan. iii. 19–25. [2] Luke xviii. 27.

so as to be conformable to, and modelled after, His own Son. For by the hands of the Father, that is, by the Son and the Holy Spirit, man, and not [merely] a part of man, was made in the likeness of God. Now the soul and the spirit are certainly a *part* of the man, but certainly not *the* man; for the perfect man consists in the commingling and the union of the soul receiving the spirit of the Father, and the admixture of that fleshly nature which was moulded after the image of God. For this reason does the apostle declare, "We speak wisdom among them that are perfect,"[1] terming those persons "perfect" who have received the Spirit of God, and who through the Spirit of God do speak in all languages, as he used himself also to speak. In like manner we do also hear[2] many brethren in the church, who possess prophetic gifts, and who through the Spirit speak all kinds of languages, and bring to light for the general benefit the hidden things of men, and declare the mysteries of God, whom also the apostle terms "spiritual," they being spiritual because they partake of the Spirit, and not because their flesh has been stripped off and taken away, and because they have become purely spiritual. For if any one take away the substance of flesh, that is, of the handiwork [of God], and understand that which is purely spiritual, such then would not be a spiritual man, but would be the spirit of a man, or the Spirit of God. But when the spirit here blended with the soul is united to [God's] handiwork, the man is rendered spiritual and perfect because of the outpouring of the Spirit, and this is he who was made in the image and likeness of God. But if the Spirit be wanting to the soul, he who is such is indeed of an animal nature, and being left carnal, shall be an imperfect being, possessing indeed the image [of God] in his formation (*in plasmate*), but not receiving the similitude through the Spirit; and thus is this being imperfect. Thus also, if any one take away the image and set aside the handiwork, he cannot then understand this as being a man, but as either some part of a man, as I have already said, or as something else than a man. For that flesh which has been moulded is not a perfect man in itself,

---

[1] 1 Cor. ii. 6 [2] The old Latin has "audivimus," *have heard*.

but the body of a man, and part of a man. Neither is the soul itself, considered apart by itself, the man; but it is the soul of a man, and part of a man. Neither is the spirit a man, for it is called the spirit, and not a man; but the commingling and union of all these constitutes the perfect man. And for this cause does the apostle, explaining himself, make it clear that the saved man is a complete man as well as a spiritual man; saying thus in the first Epistle to the Thessalonians, "Now the God of peace sanctify you perfect (*perfectos*); and may your spirit, and soul, and body be preserved whole without complaint to the coming of the Lord Jesus Christ."[1] Now what was his object in praying that these three—that is, soul, body, and spirit—might be preserved to the coming of the Lord, unless he was aware of the [future] reintegration and union of the three, and [that they should be heirs of] one and the same salvation? For this cause also he declares that those are "the perfect" who present unto the Lord the three [component parts] without offence. Those, then, are the perfect who have had the Spirit of God remaining in them, and have preserved their souls and bodies blameless, holding fast the faith of God, that is, that faith which is [directed] towards God, and maintaining righteous dealings with respect to their neighbours.

2. Whence also he says, that this handiwork is "the temple of God," thus declaring: "Know ye not that ye are the temple of God, and that the Spirit of God dwelleth in you? If any man, therefore, will defile the temple of God, him will God destroy: for the temple of God is holy, which [temple] ye are."[2] Here he manifestly declares the body to be the temple in which the Spirit dwells. As also the Lord speaks in reference to Himself, "Destroy this temple, and in three days I will raise it up. He spake this, however," it is said, "of the temple of His body."[3] And not only does he (the apostle) acknowledge our bodies to be a temple, but even the temple of Christ, saying thus to the Corinthians, "Know ye not that your bodies are members of Christ? Shall I then take the members of Christ, and make them the

[1] 1 Thess. v. 23.   [2] 1 Cor. iii. 16.   [3] John ii. 19–21.

members of an harlot?"[1] He speaks these things, not in reference to some other spiritual man; for a being of such a nature could have nothing to do with an harlot: but he declares "our body," that is, the flesh which continues in sanctity and purity, to be "the members of Christ;" but that when it becomes one with an harlot, it becomes the members of an harlot. And for this reason he said, "If any man defile the temple of God, him will God destroy." How then is it not the utmost blasphemy to allege, that the temple of God, in which the Spirit of the Father dwells, and the members of Christ, do not partake of salvation, but are reduced to perdition? Also, that our bodies are raised not from their own substance, but by the power of God, he says to the Corinthians, "Now the body is not for fornication, but for the Lord, and the Lord for the body. But God hath both raised up the Lord, and shall raise us up by His own power."[2]

CHAP. VII.—*Inasmuch as Christ did rise in our flesh, it follows that we shall be also raised in the same; since the resurrection promised to us should not be referred to spirits naturally immortal, but to bodies in themselves mortal.*

1. In the same manner, therefore, as Christ did rise in the substance of flesh, and pointed out to His disciples the mark of the nails and the opening in His side[3] (now these are the tokens of that flesh which rose from the dead), so "shall He also," it is said, "raise us up by His own power."[4] And again to the Romans he says, "But if the Spirit of Him that raised up Jesus from the dead dwell in you, He that raised up Christ from the dead shall also quicken your mortal bodies."[5] What, then, are mortal bodies? Can they be souls? Nay, for souls are incorporeal when put in comparison with mortal bodies; for God "breathed into the face of man the breath of life, and man became a living soul." Now the breath

[1] 1 Cor. iii. 17. [2] 1 Cor. vi. 13, 14. [3] John xx. 20, 25, 27.
[4] 1 Cor. vi. 14. [5] Rom. viii. 11.

of life is an incorporeal thing. And certainly they cannot maintain that the very breath of life is mortal. Therefore David says, "My soul also shall live to Him,"[1] just as if its substance were immortal. Neither, on the other hand, can they say that the spirit is the mortal body. What therefore is there left to which we may apply the term "mortal body," unless it be the thing that was moulded, that is, the flesh, of which it is also said that God will vivify it? For this it is which dies and is decomposed, but not the soul or the spirit. For to die is to lose vital power, and to become henceforth breathless, inanimate, and devoid of motion, and to melt away into those [component parts] from which also it derived the commencement of [its] substance. But this event happens neither to the soul, for it is the breath of life; nor to the spirit, for the spirit is simple and not composite, so that it cannot be decomposed, and is itself the life of those who receive it. We must therefore conclude that it is in reference to the flesh that death is mentioned; which [flesh], after the soul's departure, becomes breathless and inanimate, and is decomposed gradually into the earth from which it was taken. This, then, is what is mortal. And it is this of which he also says, "He shall also quicken your mortal bodies." And therefore in reference to it he says, in the first [Epistle] to the Corinthians: "So also is the resurrection of the dead: it is sown in corruption, it rises in incorruption."[2] For he declares, "That which thou sowest cannot be quickened, unless first it die."[3]

2. But what is that which, like a grain of wheat, is sown in the earth and decays, unless it be the bodies which are laid in the earth, into which seeds are also cast? And for this reason he said, "It is sown in dishonour, it rises in glory."[4] For what is more ignoble than dead flesh? Or, on the other hand, what is more glorious than the same when it arises and partakes of incorruption? "It is sown in weakness, it is raised in power:"[5] in its own weakness certainly, because since it is earth it goes to earth; but [it is quickened]

[1] Ps. xxii. 31, LXX. [2] 1 Cor. xv. 42. [3] 1 Cor. xv. 36.
[4] 1 Cor. xv. 43. [5] 1 Cor. xv. 43.

by the power of God, who raises it from the dead. "It is sown an animal body, it rises a spiritual body."[1] He has taught, beyond all doubt, that such language was not used by him, either with reference to the soul or to the spirit, but to bodies that have become corpses. For these are animal bodies, that is, [bodies] which partake of life, which when they have lost, they succumb to death; then, rising through the Spirit's instrumentality, they become spiritual bodies, so that by the Spirit they possess a perpetual life. "For now," he says, "we know in part, and we prophesy in part, but then face to face."[2] And this it is which has been said also by Peter: "Whom having not seen, ye love; in whom now also, not seeing, ye believe; and believing, ye shall rejoice with joy unspeakable."[3] For our face shall see the face of the Lord,[4] and shall rejoice with joy unspeakable,—that is to say, when it shall behold its own Delight.

CHAP. VIII.—*The gifts of the Holy Spirit which we receive prepare us for incorruption, render us spiritual, and separate us from carnal men. These two classes are signified by the clean and unclean animals in the legal dispensation.*

1. But we do now receive a certain portion of His Spirit, tending towards perfection, and preparing us for incorruption, being little by little accustomed to receive and bear God; which also the apostle terms "an earnest," that is, a part of the honour which has been promised us by God, where he says in the Epistle to the Ephesians, "In which ye also, having heard the word of truth, the gospel of your salvation, believing in which ye have been sealed with the Holy Spirit of promise, which is the earnest of our inheritance."[5] This earnest, therefore, thus dwelling in us, renders

---

[1] 1 Cor. xv. 44.   [2] 1 Cor. xiii. 9, 12.   [3] 1 Pet. i. 8.
[4] Grabe, Massuet, and Stieren prefer to read, "the face of the living God;" while Harvey adopts the above, reading merely "Domini," and not "Dei vivi."
[5] Eph. i. 13, etc.

us spiritual even now, and the mortal is swallowed up by immortality.[1] "For ye," he declares, "are not in the flesh, but in the Spirit, if so be that the Spirit of God dwell in you."[2] This, however, does not take place by a casting away of the flesh, but by the impartation of the Spirit. For those to whom he was writing were not without flesh, but they were those who had received the Spirit of God, "by which we cry, Abba, Father."[3] If therefore, at the present time, having the earnest, we do cry, "Abba, Father," what shall it be when, on rising again, we behold Him face to face; when all the members shall burst out into a continuous hymn of triumph, glorifying Him who raised them from the dead, and gave the gift of eternal life? For if the earnest, gathering man into itself, does even now cause him to cry, "Abba, Father," what shall the complete grace of the Spirit effect, which shall be given to men by God? It will render us like unto Him, and accomplish the will[4] of the Father; for it shall make man after the image and likeness of God.

2. Those persons, then, who possess the earnest of the Spirit, and who are not enslaved by the lusts of the flesh, but are subject to the Spirit, and who in all things walk according to the light of reason, does the apostle properly term "spiritual," because the Spirit of God dwells in them. Now, spiritual men shall not be incorporeal spirits; but our substance, that is, the union of flesh and spirit, receiving the Spirit of God, makes up the spiritual man. But those who do indeed reject the Spirit's counsel, and are the slaves of fleshly lusts, and lead lives contrary to reason, and who, without restraint, plunge headlong into their own desires, having no longing after the Divine Spirit, do live after the manner of swine and of dogs; these men, [I say], does the apostle very properly term "carnal," because they have no thought of anything else except carnal things.

3. For the same reason, too, do the prophets compare them to irrational animals, on account of the irrationality of

---

[1] 2 Cor. v. 4.   [2] Rom. viii. 9.   [3] Rom. viii. 15.
[4] This is adopting Harvey's emendation of "voluntatem" for "voluntate."

their conduct, saying, "They have become as horses raging for the females; each one of them neighing after his neighbour's wife."[1] And again, "Man, when he was in honour, was made like unto cattle."[2] This denotes that, for his own fault, he is likened to cattle, by rivalling their irrational life. And we also, as the custom is, do designate men of this stamp as cattle and irrational beasts.

3. Now the law has figuratively predicted all these, delineating man by the [various] animals:[3] whatsoever of these, says [the Scripture], have a double hoof and ruminate, it proclaims as clean; but whatsoever of them do not possess one or other of these [properties], it sets aside by themselves as unclean. Who then are the clean? Those who make their way by faith steadily towards the Father and the Son; for this is denoted by the steadiness of those which divide the hoof; and they meditate day and night upon the words of God,[4] that they may be adorned with good works: for this is the meaning of the ruminants. The unclean, however, are those which do neither divide the hoof nor ruminate; that is, those persons who have neither faith in God, nor do meditate on His words: and such is the abomination of the Gentiles. But as to those animals which do indeed chew the cud, but have not the double hoof, and are themselves unclean, we have in them a figurative description of the Jews, who certainly have the words of God in their mouth, but who do not fix their rooted stedfastness in the Father and in the Son; wherefore they are an unstable generation. For those animals which have the hoof all in one piece easily slip; but those which have it divided are more sure-footed, their cleft hoofs succeeding each other as they advance, and the one hoof supporting the other. In like manner, too, those are unclean which have the double hoof but do not ruminate: this is plainly an indication of all heretics, and of those who do not meditate on the words of God, neither are adorned with works of righteousness; to whom also the Lord says, "Why call ye me Lord, Lord, and do not the things which

[1] Jer. v. 8.
[2] Ps. xlix. 20.
[3] Lev. xi. 2; Deut. xiv. 3, etc.
[4] Ps. i. 2.

I say to you?"[1] For men of this stamp do indeed say that they believe in the Father and the Son, but they never meditate as they should upon the things of God, neither are they adorned with works of righteousness; but, as I have already observed, they have adopted the lives of swine and of dogs, giving themselves over to filthiness, to gluttony, and recklessness of all sorts. Justly, therefore, did the apostle call all such " carnal " and " animal,"[2]—[all those, namely], who through their own unbelief and luxury do not receive the Divine Spirit, and in their various phases cast out from themselves the life-giving Word, and walk stupidly after their own lusts: the prophets, too, spake of them as beasts of burden and wild beasts; custom likewise has viewed them in the light of cattle and irrational creatures; and the law has pronounced them unclean.

CHAP. IX.—*Showing how that passage of the apostle which the heretics pervert, should be understood; viz.,* " *Flesh and blood shall not possess the kingdom of God.*"

1. Among the other [truths] proclaimed by the apostle, there is also this one, "That flesh and blood cannot inherit the kingdom of God."[3] This is [the passage] which is adduced by all the heretics in support of their folly, with an attempt to annoy us, and to point out that the handiwork of God is not saved. They do not take this fact into consideration, that there are three things out of which, as I have shown, the complete man is composed—flesh, soul, and spirit. One of these does indeed preserve and fashion [the man]— this is the spirit; while as to another it is united and formed —that is the flesh; then [comes] that which is between these two—that is the soul, which sometimes indeed, when it follows the spirit, is raised up by it, but sometimes it sympathizes with the flesh, and falls into carnal lusts. Those then, as many as they be, who have not that which saves and forms [us] into life [eternal], shall be, and shall be called, [mere] flesh and blood; for these are they who have not the Spirit

[1] Luke vi. 46. [2] 1 Cor. ii. 14, iii. 1, etc. [3] 1 Cor. xv. 50.

of God in themselves. Wherefore men of this stamp are spoken of by the Lord as "dead;" for, says He, "Let the dead bury their dead,"[1] because they have not the Spirit which quickens man.

2. On the other hand, as many as fear God and trust in His Son's advent, and who through faith do establish the Spirit of God in their hearts,—such men as these shall be properly called both "pure," and "spiritual," and "those living to God," because they possess the Spirit of the Father, who purifies man, and raises him up to the life of God. For as the Lord has testified that "the flesh is weak," so [does He also say] that "the spirit is willing."[2] For this latter is capable of working out its own suggestions. If, therefore, any one admix the ready inclination of the Spirit to be, as it were, a stimulus to the infirmity of the flesh, it inevitably follows that what is strong will prevail over the weak, so that the weakness of the flesh will be absorbed by the strength of the Spirit; and that the man in whom this takes place cannot in that case be carnal, but spiritual, because of the fellowship of the Spirit. Thus it is, therefore, that the martyrs bear their witness, and despise death, not after the infirmity of the flesh, but because of the readiness of the Spirit. For when the infirmity of the flesh is absorbed, it exhibits the Spirit as powerful; and again, when the Spirit absorbs the weakness [of the flesh], it possesses the flesh as an inheritance in itself, and from both of these is formed a living man,—living, indeed, because he partakes of the Spirit, but man, because of the substance of flesh.

3. The flesh, therefore, when destitute of the Spirit of God, is dead, not having life, and cannot possess the kingdom of God: [it is as] irrational blood, like water poured out upon the ground. And therefore he says, "As is the earthy, such are they that are earthy."[3] But where the Spirit of the Father is, there is a living man; [there is] the rational blood preserved by God for the avenging [of those that shed it]; [there is] the flesh possessed by the Spirit, forgetful indeed of what belongs to it, and adopting the quality of the Spirit,

[1] Luke x. 60. [2] Matt. xxvi. 41. [3] 1 Cor. xv. 48.

being made conformable to the Word of God. And on this account he (the apostle) declares, "As we have borne the image of him who is of the earth, we shall also bear the image of Him who is from heaven."[1] What, therefore, is the earthly? That which was fashioned. And what is the heavenly? The Spirit. As therefore he says, when we were destitute of the celestial Spirit, we walked in former times in the oldness of the flesh, not obeying God; so now let us, receiving the Spirit, walk in newness of life, obeying God. Inasmuch, therefore, as without the Spirit of God we cannot be saved, the apostle exhorts us through faith and chaste conversation to preserve the Spirit of God, lest, having become non-participators of the Divine Spirit, we lose the kingdom of heaven; and he exclaims, that flesh in itself, and blood, cannot possess the kingdom of God.

4. If, however, we must speak strictly, [we would say that] the flesh *does not* inherit, but *is* inherited; as also the Lord declares, "Blessed are the meek, for they shall possess the earth by inheritance;"[2] as if in the [future] kingdom, the earth, from whence exists the substance of our flesh, is to be possessed by inheritance. This is the reason for His wishing the temple (*i.e.* the flesh) to be clean, that the Spirit of God may take delight therein, as a bridegroom with a bride. As, therefore, the bride cannot [be said] to wed, but to be wedded, when the bridegroom comes and takes her, so also the flesh cannot by itself possess the kingdom of God by inheritance; but it can be taken *for* an inheritance into the kingdom of God. For a living person inherits the goods of the deceased; and it is one thing to inherit, another to be inherited. The former rules, and exercises power over, and orders the things inherited at his will; but the latter things are in a state of subjection, are under orders, and are ruled over by him who has obtained the inheritance. What, therefore, is it that lives? The Spirit of God, doubtless. What, again, are the possessions of the deceased? The various parts of the man, surely, which rot in the earth. But these are inherited by the Spirit when they are translated into the kingdom of heaven. For

[1] 1 Cor. xv. 49. [2] Matt. v. 5.

this cause, too, did Christ die, that the gospel covenant being manifested and known to the whole world, might in the first place set free His slaves; and then afterwards, as I have already shown, might constitute them heirs of His property, when the Spirit possesses them by inheritance. For he who lives inherits, but the flesh is inherited. In order that we may not lose life by losing that Spirit which possesses us, the apostle, exhorting us to the communion of the Spirit, has said, according to reason, in those words already quoted, "That flesh and blood cannot inherit the kingdom of God." Just as if he were to say, "Do not err; for unless the Word of God dwell with, and the Spirit of the Father be in you, and if ye shall live frivolously and carelessly as if ye were this only, viz. mere flesh and blood, ye cannot inherit the kingdom of God."

CHAP. X.—*By a comparison drawn from the wild olive-tree, whose quality but not whose nature is changed by grafting, he proves more important things; he points out also that man without the Spirit is not capable of bringing forth fruit, or of inheriting the kingdom of God.*

1. This truth, therefore, [he declares], in order that we may not reject the engrafting of the Spirit while pampering the flesh. "But thou, being a wild olive-tree," he says, "hast been grafted into the good olive-tree, and been made a partaker of the fatness of the olive-tree."[1] As, therefore, when the wild olive has been engrafted, if it remain in its former condition, viz. a wild olive, it is "cut off, and cast into the fire;"[2] but if it takes kindly to the graft, and is changed into the good olive-tree, it becomes a fruit-bearing olive, planted, as it were, in a king's park (*paradiso*): so likewise men, if they do truly progress by faith towards better things, and receive the Spirit of God, and bring forth the fruit thereof, shall be spiritual, as being planted in the paradise of God. But if they cast out the Spirit, and remain in their former condition, desirous of being of the flesh rather

[1] Rom. xi. 17. [2] Matt. vii. 19.

than of the Spirit, then it is very justly said with regard to men of this stamp, "That flesh and blood shall not inherit the kingdom of God;"[1] just as if any one were to say that the wild olive is not received into the paradise of God. Admirably therefore does the apostle exhibit our nature, and God's universal appointment, in his discourse about flesh and blood and the wild olive. For as the good olive, if neglected for a certain time, if left to grow wild and to run to wood, does itself become a wild olive; or again, if the wild olive be carefully tended and grafted, it naturally reverts to its former fruit-bearing condition: so men also, when they become careless, and bring forth for fruit the lusts of the flesh like woody produce, are rendered, by their own fault, unfruitful in righteousness. For when men sleep, the enemy sows the material of tares;[2] and for this cause did the Lord command His disciples to be on the watch.[3] And again, those persons who are not bringing forth the fruits of righteousness, and are, as it were, covered over and lost among brambles, if they use diligence, and receive the word of God as a graft,[4] arrive at the pristine nature of man—that which was created after the image and likeness of God.

2. But as the engrafted wild olive does not certainly lose the substance of its wood, but changes the quality of its fruit, and receives another name, being now not a wild olive, but a fruit-bearing olive, and is called so; so also, when man is grafted in by faith and receives the Spirit of God, he certainly does not lose the substance of flesh, but changes the quality of the fruit [brought forth, *i.e.*] of his works, and receives another name,[5] showing that he has become changed for the better, being now not [mere] flesh and blood, but a spiritual man, and is called such. Then, again, as the wild olive, if it be not grafted in, remains useless to its lord because of its woody quality, and is cut down as a tree bearing no fruit, and cast into the fire; so also man, if he does not receive through faith the engrafting of the Spirit, remains in his old condi-

---

[1] 1 Cor. xv. 50.   [2] Matt. xiii. 25.
[3] Matt. xxiv. 42, xxv. 13; Mark xiii. 33.
[4] Jas. i. 21.   [5] Rev. ii. 17.

tion, and being [mere] flesh and blood, he cannot inherit the kingdom of God. Rightly therefore does the apostle declare, "Flesh and blood cannot inherit the kingdom of God;"[1] and, "Those who are in the flesh cannot please God:"[2] not repudiating [by these words] the substance of flesh, but showing that into it the Spirit must be infused.[3] And for this reason he says, "This mortal must put on immortality, and this corruptible must put on incorruption."[4] And again he declares, "But ye are not in the flesh, but in the Spirit, if so be that the Spirit of God dwell in you."[5] He sets this forth still more plainly, where he says, "The body indeed is dead, because of sin; but the Spirit is life, because of righteousness. But if the Spirit of Him who raised up Jesus from the dead dwell in you, He that raised up Christ from the dead shall also quicken your mortal bodies, because of His Spirit dwelling in you."[6] And again he says, in the Epistle to the Romans, "For if ye live after the flesh, ye shall die."[7] [Now by these words] he does not prohibit them from living their lives in the flesh, for he was himself in the flesh when he wrote to them; but he cuts away the lusts of the flesh, those which bring death upon a man. And for this reason he says in continuation, "But if ye through the Spirit do mortify the works of the flesh, ye shall live. For whosoever are led by the Spirit of God, these are the sons of God."

CHAP. XI.—*Treats upon the actions of carnal and of spiritual persons; also, that the spiritual cleansing is not to be referred to the substance of our bodies, but to the manner of our former life.*

1. [The apostle], foreseeing the wicked speeches of unbelievers, has particularized the works which he terms carnal; and he explains himself, lest any room for doubt be left to

---

[1] 1 Cor. xv. 50.   [2] Rom. viii. 8.
[3] The Latin has, "sed infusionem Spiritus attrahens."
[4] 1 Cor. xv. 53.   [5] Rom. viii. 9.
[6] Rom. viii. 10, etc.   [7] Rom. viii. 13.

those who do dishonestly pervert his meaning, thus saying in the Epistle to the Galatians: "Now the works of the flesh are manifest, which are: adulteries, fornications, uncleanness, luxuriousness, idolatries, witchcrafts,[1] hatreds, contentions, jealousies, wraths, emulations, animosities, irritable speeches, dissensions, heresies, envyings, drunkenness, carousings, and such like; of which I warn you, as also I have warned you, that they who do such things shall not inherit the kingdom of God."[2] Thus does he point out to his hearers in a more explicit manner what it is [he means when he declares], "Flesh and blood shall not inherit the kingdom of God." For they who do these things, since they do indeed walk after the flesh, have not the power of living unto God. And then, again, he proceeds to tell us the spiritual actions which vivify a man, that is, the engrafting of the Spirit; thus saying, "But the fruit of the Spirit is love, joy, peace, long-suffering, goodness, benignity, faith, meekness, continence, chastity: against these there is no law."[3] As, therefore, he who has gone forward to the better things, and has brought forth the fruit of the Spirit, is saved altogether because of the communion of the Spirit; so also he who has continued in the aforesaid works of the flesh, being truly reckoned as carnal, because he did not receive the Spirit of God, shall not have power to inherit the kingdom of heaven. As, again, the same apostle testifies, saying to the Corinthians, "Know ye not that the unrighteous shall not inherit the kingdom of God? Do not err," he says: "neither fornicators, nor idolaters, nor adulterers, nor effeminate, nor abusers of themselves with mankind, nor thieves, nor covetous, nor revilers, nor rapacious persons, shall inherit the kingdom of God. And these ye indeed have been; but ye have been washed, but ye have been sanctified, but ye have been justified in the name of the Lord Jesus Christ, and in the Spirit of our God."[4] He shows in the clearest manner through what things it is that man goes to destruction, if he has continued to live after the flesh; and then, on the other hand, [he points out]

---

[1] Or, "poisonings."
[2] Gal. v. 19, etc.
[3] Gal. v. 22.
[4] 1 Cor. vi. 9–11.

through what things he is saved. Now he says that the things which save are the name of our Lord Jesus Christ, and the Spirit of our God.

2. Since, therefore, in that passage he recounts those works of the flesh which are without the Spirit, which bring death [upon their doers], he exclaimed at the end of his epistle, in accordance with what he had already declared, "And as we have borne the image of him who is of the earth, we shall also bear the image of Him who is from heaven. For this I say, brethren, that flesh and blood cannot inherit the kingdom of God."[1] Now this which he says, "as we have borne the image of him who is of the earth," is analogous to what has been declared, "And such indeed ye were; but ye have been washed, but ye have been sanctified, but ye have been justified in the name of our Lord Jesus Christ, and in the Spirit of our God." When, therefore, did we bear the image of him who is of the earth? Doubtless it was when those actions spoken of as "works of the flesh" used to be wrought in us. And then, again, when [do we bear] the image of the heavenly? Doubtless when he says, "Ye have been washed," believing in the name of the Lord, and receiving His Spirit. Now we have washed away, not the substance of our body, nor the image of our [primary] formation, but the former vain conversation. In these members, therefore, in which we were going to destruction by working the works of corruption, in these very members are we made alive by working the works of the Spirit.

CHAP. XII.—*Of the difference between life and death; of the breath of life and the vivifying Spirit: also how it is that the substance of flesh revives which once was dead.*

1. For as the flesh is capable of corruption, so is it also of incorruption; and as it is of death, so is it also of life. These two do mutually give way to each other; and both cannot remain in the same place, but one is driven out by the other, and the presence of the one destroys that of the other. If,

[1] 1 Cor. xv. 49, etc.

then, when death takes possession of a man, it drives life away from him, and proves him to be dead, much more does life, when it has obtained power over the man, drive out death, and restore him as living unto God. For if death brings mortality, why should not life, when it comes, vivify man? Just as Esaias the prophet says, "Death devoured when it had prevailed."[1] And again, "God has wiped away every tear from every face." Thus that former life is expelled, because it was not given by the Spirit, but by the breath.

2. For the breath of life, which also rendered man an animated being, is one thing, and the vivifying Spirit another, which also caused him to become spiritual. And for this reason Isaiah said, "Thus saith the Lord, who made heaven and established it, who founded the earth and the things therein, and gave breath to the people upon it, and Spirit to those walking upon it;"[2] thus telling us that breath is indeed given in common to all people upon earth, but that the Spirit is theirs alone who tread down earthly desires. And therefore Isaiah himself, distinguishing the things already mentioned, again exclaims, "For the Spirit shall go forth from me, and I have made every breath."[3] Thus does he attribute the Spirit as peculiar to God, which in the last times He pours forth upon the human race by the adoption of sons; but [he shows] that breath was common throughout the creation, and points it out as something created. Now what has been made is a different thing from him who makes it. The breath, then, is temporal, but the Spirit eternal. The breath, too, increases [in strength] for a short period, and continues for a certain time; after that it takes its departure, leaving its former abode destitute of breath. But when the Spirit pervades the man within and without, inasmuch as it continues there, it never leaves him. "But that is not first which is spiritual," says the apostle, speaking this as if with reference to us human beings; "but that is first which is animal, afterwards that which is spiritual,"[4] in accordance with reason. For there had been a necessity that, in the

[1] Isa. xxv. 8, LXX.   [2] Isa. xlii. 5.
[3] Isa. lvii. 16.   [4] 1 Cor. xv. 46.

first place, a human being should be fashioned, and that what was fashioned should receive the soul; afterwards that it should thus receive the communion of the Spirit. Wherefore also "the first Adam was made" by the Lord "a living soul, the second Adam a quickening spirit."[1] As, then, he who was made a living soul forfeited life when he turned aside to what was evil, so, on the other hand, the same individual, when he reverts to what is good, and receives the quickening Spirit, shall find life.

3. For it is not one thing which dies and another which is quickened, as neither is it one thing which is lost and another which is found, but the Lord came seeking for that same sheep which had been lost. What was it, then, which was dead? Undoubtedly it was the substance of the flesh; the same, too, which had lost the breath of life, and had become breathless and dead. This same, therefore, was what the Lord came to quicken, that as in Adam we do all die, as being of an animal nature, in Christ we may all live, as being spiritual, not laying aside God's handiwork, but the lusts of the flesh, and receiving the Holy Spirit; as the apostle says in the Epistle to the Colossians: "Mortify, therefore, your members which are upon the earth." And what these are he himself explains: "Fornication, uncleanness, inordinate affection, evil concupiscence, and covetousness, which is idolatry."[2] The laying aside of these is what the apostle preaches; and he declares that those who do such things, as being merely flesh and blood, cannot inherit the kingdom of heaven. For their soul, tending towards what is worse, and descending to earthly lusts, has become a partaker in the same designation which belongs to these [lusts, viz. "earthly"], which, when the apostle commands us to lay aside, he says in the same epistle, "Cast ye off the old man with his deeds."[3] But when he said this, he does not remove away the ancient formation [of man]; for in that case it would be incumbent on us to rid ourselves of its company by committing suicide.

4. But the apostle himself also, being one who had been formed in a womb, and had issued thence, wrote to us, and

[1] 1 Cor. xv. 45. [2] Col. iii. 5. [3] Col. iii. 9.

confessed in his Epistle to the Philippians that "to live in the flesh was the fruit of [his] work;"[1] thus expressing himself. Now the final result of the work of the Spirit is the salvation of the flesh.[2] For what other visible fruit is there of the invisible Spirit, than the rendering of the flesh mature and capable of incorruption? If then [he says], "To live in the flesh, this is the result of labour to me," he did not surely contemn the substance of flesh in that passage where he said, "Put ye off the old man with his works;"[3] but he points out that we should lay aside our former conversation, that which waxes old and becomes corrupt; and for this reason he goes on to say, "And put ye on the new man, that which is renewed in knowledge, after the image of Him who created him." In this, therefore, that he says, "which is renewed in knowledge," he demonstrates that he, the selfsame man who was in ignorance in times past, that is, in ignorance of God, is renewed by that knowledge which has respect to Him. For the knowledge of God renews man. And when he says, "after the image of the Creator," he sets forth the recapitulation of the same man, who was at the beginning made after the likeness of God.

5. And that he, the apostle, was the very same person who had been born from the womb, that is, of the ancient substance of flesh, he does himself declare in the Epistle to the Galatians: "But when it pleased God, who separated me from my mother's womb, and called me by His grace, to reveal His Son in me, that I might preach Him among the Gentiles,"[4] it was not, as I have already observed, one person who had been born from the womb, and another who preached the gospel of the Son of God; but that same individual who formerly was ignorant, and used to persecute the church, when the revelation was made to him from heaven, and the Lord conferred with him, as I have pointed out in the third book,[5] preached the gospel of Jesus Christ the Son of God, who was crucified under Pontius Pilate, his former ignorance

[1] Phil. i. 22.
[2] Following Harvey's explanation of a somewhat obscure passage.
[3] Col. iii. 10.   [4] Gal. i. 15, 16.   [5] Vol. i. pp. 306, 321.

being driven out by his subsequent knowledge: just as the blind men whom the Lord healed did certainly lose their blindness, but received the substance of their eyes perfect, and obtained the power of vision in the very same eyes with which they formerly did not see; the darkness being merely driven away by the power of vision, while the substance of the eyes was retained, in order that, by means of those eyes through which they had not seen, exercising again the visual power, they might give thanks to Him who had restored them again to sight. And thus, also, he whose withered hand was healed, and all who were healed generally, did not change those parts of their bodies which had at their birth come forth from the womb, but simply obtained these anew in a healthy condition.

6. For the Maker of all things, the Word of God, who did also from the beginning form man, when He found His handiwork impaired by wickedness, performed upon it all kinds of healing. At one time [He did so], as regards each separate member, as it is found in His own handiwork; and at another time He did once for all restore man sound and whole in all points, preparing him perfect for Himself unto the resurrection. For what was His object in healing [different] portions of the flesh, and restoring them to their original condition, if those parts which had been healed by Him were not in a position to obtain salvation? For if it was [merely] a temporary benefit which He conferred, He granted nothing of importance to those who were the subjects of His healing. Or how can they maintain that the flesh is incapable of receiving the life which flows from Him, when it received healing from Him? For life is brought about through healing, and incorruption through life. He, therefore, who confers healing, the same does also confer life; and He [who gives] life, also surrounds His own handiwork with incorruption.

CHAP. XIII.—*In the dead who were raised by Christ we possess the highest proof of the resurrection; and our hearts are shown to be capable of life eternal, because they can now receive the Spirit of God.*

1. Let our opponents—that is, they who speak against their own salvation—inform us [as to this point]: The deceased daughter of the high priest;[1] the widow's dead son, who was being carried out [to burial] near the gate [of the city];[2] and Lazarus, who had lain four days in the tomb,[3]—in what bodies did they rise again? In those same, no doubt, in which they had also died. For if it were not in the very same, then certainly those same individuals who had died did not rise again. For [the Scripture] says, "The Lord took the hand of the dead man, and said to him, Young man, I say unto thee, Arise. And the dead man sat up, and He commanded that something should be given him to eat; and He delivered him to his mother."[4] Again, He called Lazarus "with a loud voice, saying, Lazarus, come forth; and he that was dead came forth bound with bandages, feet and hands." This was symbolical of that man who had been bound in sins. And therefore the Lord said, "Loose him, and let him depart." As, therefore, those who were healed were made whole in those members which had in times past been afflicted; and the dead rose in the identical bodies, their limbs and bodies receiving health, and that life which was granted by the Lord, who prefigures eternal things by temporal, and shows that it is He who is Himself able to extend both healing and life to His handiwork, that His words concerning its [future] resurrection may also be believed; so also at the end, when the Lord utters His voice "by the last trumpet,"[5] the dead shall be raised, as He Him-

---

[1] Mark v. 22. Irenæus confounds the ruler of the synagogue with the high priest.
[2] Luke vii. 12.   [3] John ix. 30.
[4] The two miracles of raising the widow's son and the rabbi's daughter are here amalgamated.
[5] 1 Cor. xv. 52.

self declares: "The hour shall come, in which all the dead which are in the tombs shall hear the voice of the Son of man, and shall come forth; those that have done good to the resurrection of life, and those that have done evil to the resurrection of judgment."[1]

2. Vain, therefore, and truly miserable, are those who do not choose to see what is so manifest and clear, but shun the light of truth, blinding themselves like the tragic Œdipus. And as those who are not practised in wrestling, when they contend with others, laying hold with a determined grasp of some part of [their opponent's] body, really fall by means of that which they grasp, yet when they fall, imagine that they are gaining the victory, because they have obstinately kept their hold upon that part which they seized at the outset, and besides falling, become subjects of ridicule; so is it with respect to that [favourite] expression of the heretics: "Flesh and blood cannot inherit the kingdom of God;" while taking two expressions of Paul's, without having perceived the apostle's meaning, or examined critically the force of the terms, but keeping fast hold of the mere expressions by themselves, they die in consequence of their influence (περὶ αὐτὰς), overturning as far as in them lies the entire dispensation of God.

3. For thus they will allege that this passage refers to the flesh strictly so called, and not to fleshly works, as I have pointed out, so representing the apostle as contradicting himself. For immediately following, in the same epistle, he says conclusively, speaking thus in reference to the flesh: "For this corruptible must put on incorruption, and this mortal must put on immortality. So, when this mortal shall have put on immortality, then shall be brought to pass the saying which is written, Death is swallowed up in victory. O death, where is thy sting? O death, where is thy victory?"[2] Now these words shall be appropriately said at the time when this mortal and corruptible flesh, which is subject to death, which also is pressed down by a certain dominion of death, rising up into life, shall put on incorruption and immortality.

[1] John v. 28. [2] 1 Cor. xv. 53.

For then, indeed, shall death be truly vanquished, when that flesh which is held down by it shall go forth from under its dominion. And again, to the Philippians he says: "But our conversation is in heaven, from whence also we look for the Saviour, the Lord Jesus, who shall transfigure the body of our humiliation conformable to the body of His glory, even as He is able (*ita ut possit*) according to the working of His own power."[1] What, then, is this "body of humiliation" which the Lord shall transfigure, [so as to be] conformed to "the body of His glory?" Plainly it is this body composed of flesh, which is indeed humbled when it falls into the earth. Now its transformation [takes place thus], that while it is mortal and corruptible, it becomes immortal and incorruptible, not after its own proper substance, but after the mighty working of the Lord, who is able to invest the mortal with immortality, and the corruptible with incorruption. And therefore he says,[2] "that mortality may be swallowed up of life. He who has perfected us for this very thing is God, who also has given unto us the earnest of the Spirit."[3] He uses these words most manifestly in reference to the flesh; for the soul is not mortal, neither is the spirit. Now, what is mortal shall be swallowed up of life, when the flesh is dead no longer, but remains living and incorruptible, hymning the praises of God, who has perfected us for this very thing. In order, therefore, that we may be perfected for this, aptly does he say to the Corinthians, "Glorify God in your body."[4] Now God is He who gives rise to immortality.

4. That he uses these words with respect to the body of flesh, and to none other, he declares to the Corinthians manifestly, indubitably, and free from all ambiguity: "Always bearing about in our body the dying of Jesus,[5] that also the

---

[1] Phil. iii. 29, etc.

[2] The original Greek text is preserved here, as above; the Latin translator inserts, "in secunda ad Corinthios." Harvey observes: "The interpolation of the scriptural reference by the translator suggests the suspicion that the greater number of such references have come in from the margin."

[3] 2 Cor. v. 4. [4] 1 Cor. vi. 20.

[5] Agreeing with the Syriac version in omitting "the Lord" before the

life of Jesus Christ might be manifested in our body. For if we who live are delivered unto death for Jesus' sake, it is that the life of Jesus may also be manifested in our mortal flesh."[1] And that the Spirit lays hold on the flesh, he says in the same epistle, "That ye are the epistle of Christ, ministered by us, inscribed not with ink, but with the Spirit of the living God, not in tables of stone, but in the fleshly tables of the heart."[2] If, therefore, in the present time, fleshly hearts are made partakers of the Spirit, what is there astonishing if, in the resurrection, they receive that life which is granted by the Spirit? Of which resurrection the apostle speaks in the Epistle to the Philippians: "Having been made conformable to His death, if by any means I might attain to the resurrection which is from the dead."[3] In what other mortal flesh, therefore, can life be understood as being manifested, unless in that substance which is also put to death on account of that confession which is made of God?—as he has himself declared, "If, as a man, I have fought with beasts[4] at Ephesus, what advantageth it me if the dead rise not? For if the dead rise not, neither has Christ risen. Now, if Christ has not risen, our preaching is vain, and your faith is vain. In that case, too, we are found false witnesses for God, since we have testified that He raised up Christ, whom [upon that supposition] He did not raise up.[5] For if the dead rise not, neither has Christ risen. But if Christ be not risen, your faith is vain, since ye are yet in your sins. Therefore those who have fallen asleep in Christ have perished. If in this life only we have hope in Christ, we are more miserable than all men. But now Christ has risen from the dead, the first-fruits of those that sleep; for

---

word "Jesus," and in reading ἀεί as εἰ, which Harvey considers the true text.

[1] 2 Cor. iv. 10, etc.   [2] 2 Cor. iii. 3.   [3] Phil. iii. 11.

[4] The Syriac translation seems to take a literal meaning out of this passage: "If, as one of the sons of men, I have been cast forth to the wild beasts at Ephesus."

[5] This is in accordance with the Syriac, which omits the clause, εἴπερ ἄρα νεκροὶ οὐκ ἐγείρονται.

as by man [came] death, by man also [came] the resurrection of the dead."[1]

5. In all these passages, therefore, as I have already said, these men must either allege that the apostle expresses opinions contradicting himself, with respect to that statement, "Flesh and blood cannot inherit the kingdom of God;" or, on the other hand, they will be forced to make perverse and crooked interpretations of all the passages, so as to overturn and alter the sense of the words. For what sensible thing can they say, if they endeavour to interpret otherwise this which he writes: "For this corruptible must put on incorruption, and this mortal put on immortality;"[2] and, "That the life of Jesus may be made manifest in our mortal flesh;"[3] and all the other passages in which the apostle does manifestly and clearly declare the resurrection and incorruption of the flesh? And thus shall they be compelled to put a false interpretation upon passages such as these, they who do not choose to understand one correctly.

CHAP. XIV.—*Unless the flesh were to be saved, the Word would not have taken upon Him flesh of the same substance as ours: from this it would follow that neither should we have been reconciled by Him.*

1. And inasmuch as the apostle has not pronounced against the very substance of flesh and blood, that it cannot inherit the kingdom of God, the same apostle has everywhere adopted the term "flesh and blood" with regard to the Lord Jesus Christ, partly indeed to establish His human nature (for He did Himself speak of Himself as the Son of man), and partly that He might confirm the salvation of our flesh. For if the flesh were not in a position to be saved, the Word of God would in no wise have become flesh. And if the blood of the righteous were not to be inquired after, the Lord would certainly not have had blood [in His composition]. But inasmuch as blood cries out (*vocalis est*) from the beginning [of the world], God said to Cain, when he had slain his

[1] 1 Cor. xv. 13, etc.   [2] 1 Cor. xv. 53.   [3] 2 Cor. iv. 11.

brother, "The voice of thy brother's blood crieth to me."[1] And as their blood will be inquired after, he said to those with Noah, "For your blood of your souls will I require, [even] from the hand of all beasts;"[2] and again, "Whosoever will shed man's blood,[3] it shall be shed for his blood." In like manner, too, did the Lord say to those who should afterwards shed His blood, "All righteous blood shall be required which is shed upon the earth, from the blood of righteous Abel to the blood of Zacharias the son of Barachias, whom ye slew between the temple and the altar. Verily I say unto you, All these things shall come upon this generation."[4] He thus points out the recapitulation that should take place in His own person of the effusion of blood from the beginning, of all the righteous men and of the prophets, and that by means of Himself there should be a requisition of their blood. Now this [blood] could not be required unless it also had the capability of being saved; nor would the Lord have summed up these things in Himself, unless He had Himself been made flesh and blood after the way of the original formation [of man], saving in His own person at the end that which had in the beginning perished in Adam.

2. But if the Lord became incarnate for any other order of things, and took flesh of any other substance, He has not then summed up human nature in His own person, nor in that case can He be termed flesh. For flesh has been truly made [to consist in] a transmission of that thing moulded originally from the dust. But if it had been necessary for Him to draw the material [of his body] from another substance, the Father would at the beginning have moulded the material [of flesh] from a different substance [than from what He actually did]. But now the case stands thus, that the Word has saved that which really was [created, viz.] humanity which had perished, effecting by means of Himself that communion which should be held with it, and seeking

---

[1] Gen. iv. 10.   [2] Gen. ix. 5, 6, LXX.
[3] One of the MSS. reads here: Sanguis pro sanguine ejus effundetur.
[4] Matt. xxiii. 35, etc.; Luke xi. 50.

out its salvation. But the thing which had perished possessed flesh and blood. For the Lord, taking dust from the earth, moulded man; and it was upon his behalf that all the dispensation of the Lord's advent took place. He had Himself, therefore, flesh and blood, recapitulating in Himself not a certain other, but that original handiwork of the Father, seeking out that thing which had perished. And for this cause the apostle, in the Epistle to the Colossians, says, "And though ye were formerly alienated, and enemies to His knowledge by evil works, yet now ye have been reconciled in the body of His flesh, through His death, to present yourselves holy and chaste, and without fault in His sight."[1] He says, "Ye have been reconciled in the body of His flesh," because the righteous flesh has reconciled that flesh which was being kept under bondage in sin, and brought it into friendship with God.

3. If, then, any one allege that in this respect the flesh of the Lord was different from ours, because it indeed did not commit sin, neither was deceit found in His soul, while we, on the other hand, are sinners, he says what is the fact. But if he pretends that the Lord possessed another substance of flesh, the sayings respecting reconciliation will not agree with that man. For that thing is reconciled which had formerly been in enmity. Now, if the Lord had taken flesh from another substance, He would not, by so doing, have reconciled that one to God which had become inimical through transgression. But now, by means of communion with Himself, the Lord has reconciled man to God the Father, in reconciling us to Himself by the body of His own flesh, and redeeming us by His own blood, as the apostle says to the Ephesians, "In whom we have redemption through His blood, the remission of sins;"[2] and again to the same he says, "Ye who formerly were far off have been brought near in the blood of Christ;"[3] and again, "Abolishing in His flesh the enmities, [even] the law of commandments [contained] in ordinances."[4] And in every epistle the apostle plainly testifies, that through the flesh of our Lord, and through His blood, we have been saved.

[1] Col. i. 21, etc.   [2] Eph. i. 7.   [3] Eph. ii. 13.   [4] Eph. ii. 15.

4. If, therefore, flesh and blood are the things which procure for us life, it has not been declared of flesh and blood, in the literal meaning (*proprie*) of the terms, that they cannot inherit the kingdom of God; but [these words apply] to those carnal deeds already mentioned, which, perverting man to sin, deprive him of life. And for this reason he says, in the Epistle to the Romans: "Let not sin, therefore, reign in your mortal body, to be under its control: neither yield ye your members instruments of unrighteousness unto sin; but yield yourselves to God, as being alive from the dead, and your members as instruments of righteousness unto God."[1] In these same members, therefore, in which we used to serve sin, and bring forth fruit unto death, does He wish us to [be obedient] unto righteousness, that we may bring forth fruit unto life. Remember, therefore, my beloved friend, that thou hast been redeemed by the flesh of our Lord, re-established[2] by His blood; and "holding the Head, from which the whole body of the church, having been fitted together, takes increase"[3]—that is, acknowledging the advent in the flesh of the Son of God, and [His] divinity (*deum*), and looking forward with constancy to His human nature[4] (*hominem*), availing thyself also of these proofs drawn from Scripture—thou dost easily overthrow, as I have pointed out, all those notions of the heretics which were concocted afterwards.

CHAP. XV.—*Proofs of the resurrection from Isaiah and Ezekiel; the same God who created us will also raise us up.*

1. Now, that He who at the beginning created man, did promise him a second birth after his dissolution into earth,

[1] Rom. vi. 12, etc.
[2] "Et sanguine ejus redhibitus," corresponding to the Greek term ἀποκαταστάθεις. "Redhibere" is properly a *forensic* term, meaning to cause any article to be restored to the vendor.
[3] Col. ii. 19.
[4] Harvey restores the Greek thus, καὶ τὸν αὐτοῦ ἄνθρωπον βεβαίως ἐκδεχόμενος, which he thinks has a reference to the patient waiting for "Christ's second advent to judge the world." The phrase might also be translated, "and receiving stedfastly His human nature."

Esaias thus declares: "The dead shall rise again, and they who are in the tombs shall arise, and they who are in the earth shall rejoice. For the dew which is from Thee is health to them."[1] And again: "I will comfort you, and ye shall be comforted in Jerusalem: and ye shall see, and your heart shall rejoice, and your bones shall flourish as the grass; and the hand of the Lord shall be known to those who worship Him."[2] And Ezekiel speaks as follows: "And the hand of the Lord came upon me, and the Lord led me forth in the Spirit, and set me down in the midst of the plain, and this place was full of bones. And He caused me to pass by them round about: and, behold, there were many upon the surface of the plain very dry. And He said unto me, Son of man, can these bones live? And I said, Lord, Thou who hast made them dost know. And He said unto me, Prophesy upon these bones, and thou shalt say to them, Ye dry bones, hear the word of the Lord. Thus saith the Lord to these bones, Behold, I will cause the spirit of life to come upon you, and I will lay sinews upon you, and bring up flesh again upon you, and I will stretch skin upon you, and will put my Spirit into you, and ye shall live; and ye shall know that I am the Lord. And I prophesied as the Lord had commanded me. And it came to pass, when I was prophesying, that, behold, an earthquake, and the bones were drawn together, each one to its own articulation: and I beheld, and, lo, the sinews and flesh were produced upon them, and the skins rose upon them round about, but there was no breath in them. And He said unto me, Prophesy to the breath, Son of man, and say to the breath, These things saith the Lord, Come from the four winds (*spiritibus*), and breathe upon these dead, that they may live. So I prophesied as the Lord had commanded me, and the breath entered into them; and they did live, and stood upon their feet, an exceeding great gathering."[3] And again he says, "Thus saith the Lord, Behold, I will set your graves open, and cause you to come out of your graves, and bring you into the land of Israel; and ye shall know that I am the Lord, when I shall open your sepulchres, that I may

[1] Isa. xxvi. 19.   [2] Isa. lxvi. 13.   [3] Ezek. xxvii. 1, etc.

bring my people again out of the sepulchres: and I will put my Spirit into you, and ye shall live; and I will place you in your land, and ye shall know that I am the Lord. I have said, and I will do, saith the Lord."[1] As we at once perceive that the Creator (*Demiurgo*) is in this passage represented as vivifying our dead bodies, and promising resurrection to them, and resuscitation from their sepulchres and tombs, conferring upon them immortality also (He says, "For as the tree of life, so shall their days be"[2]), He is shown to be the only God who accomplishes these things, and as Himself the good Father, benevolently conferring life upon those who have not life from themselves.

2. And for this reason did the Lord most plainly manifest Himself and the Father to His disciples, lest, forsooth, they might seek after another God besides Him who formed man, and who gave him the breath of life; and that men might not rise to such a pitch of madness as to feign another Father above the Creator. And thus also He healed by a word all the others who were in a weakly condition because of sin; to whom also He said, "Behold, thou art made whole, sin no more, lest a worse thing come upon thee:"[3] pointing out by this, that, because of the sin of disobedience, infirmities have come upon men. To that man, however, who had been blind from his birth, He gave sight, not by means of a word, but by an outward action; doing this not without a purpose, or because it so happened, but that He might show forth the hand of God, that which at the beginning had moulded man. And therefore, when His disciples asked Him for what cause the man had been born blind, whether for his own or his parents' fault, He replied, "Neither hath this man sinned, nor his parents, but that the works of God should be made manifest in him."[4] Now the work of God is the fashioning of man. For, as the Scripture says, He made [man] by a kind of process: "And the Lord took clay from the earth, and formed man."[5] Wherefore also the Lord spat on the ground and made clay, and

---

[1] Ezek. xxxvii. 12, etc.   [2] Isa. lxv. 22.   [3] John v. 14.
[4] John ix. 3.   [5] Gen. ii. 7.

smeared it upon the eyes, pointing out the original fashioning [of man], how it was effected, and manifesting the hand of God to those who can understand by what [hand] man was formed out of the dust. For that which the artificer, the Word, had omitted to form in the womb, [viz. the blind man's eyes], He then supplied in public, that the works of God might be manifested in him, in order that we might not be seeking out another hand by which man was fashioned, nor another Father; knowing that this hand of God which formed us at the beginning, and which does form us in the womb, has in the last times sought us out who were lost, winning back His own, and taking up the lost sheep upon His shoulders, and with joy restoring it to the fold of life.

3. Now, that the Word of God forms us in the womb, He says to Jeremiah, "Before I formed thee in the womb, I knew thee; and before thou wentest forth from the belly, I sanctified thee, and appointed thee a prophet among the nations."[1] And Paul, too, says in like manner, "But when it pleased God, who separated me from my mother's womb, that I might declare Him among the nations."[2] As, therefore, we are by the Word formed in the womb, this very same Word formed the visual power in him who had been blind from his birth; showing openly who it is that fashions us in secret, since the Word Himself had been made manifest to men: and declaring the original formation of Adam, and the manner in which he was created, and by what hand he was fashioned, indicating the whole from a part. For the Lord who formed the visual powers is He who made the whole man, carrying out the will of the Father. And inasmuch as man, with respect to that formation which was after Adam, having fallen into transgression, needed the laver of regeneration, [the Lord] said to him [upon whom He had conferred sight], after He had smeared his eyes with the clay, "Go to Siloam, and wash;"[3] thus restoring to him both [his perfect] conformation, and that regeneration which takes place by means of the laver. And for this reason when he was washed he came seeing, that he might both

[1] Jer. i. 5.   [2] Gal. i. 15.   [3] John ix. 7.

know Him who had fashioned him, and that man might learn [to know] Him who has conferred upon him life.

4. All the followers of Valentinus, therefore, lose their case, when they say that man was not fashioned out of this earth, but from a fluid and diffused substance. For, from the earth out of which the Lord formed eyes for that man, from the same earth it is evident that man was also fashioned at the beginning. For it were incompatible that the eyes should indeed be formed from one source and the rest of the body from another; as neither would it be compatible that one [being] fashioned the body, and another the eyes. But He, the very same who formed Adam at the beginning, with whom also the Father spake, [saying], "Let us make man after our image and likeness,"[1] revealing Himself in these last times to men, formed visual organs (*visionem*) for him who had been blind [in that body which he had derived] from Adam. Wherefore also the Scripture, pointing out what should come to pass, says, that when Adam had hid himself because of his disobedience, the Lord came to him at eventide, called him forth, and said, "Where art thou?"[2] That means that in the last times the very same Word of God came to call man, reminding him of his doings, living in which he had been hidden from the Lord. For just as at that time God spake to Adam at eventide, searching him out; so in the last times, by means of the same voice, searching out his posterity, He has visited them.

CHAP. XVI.—*Since our bodies return to the earth, it follows that they have their substance from it; also, by the advent of the Word, the image of God in us appeared in a clearer light.*

1. And since Adam was moulded from this earth to which we belong, the Scripture tells us that God said to him, "In the sweat of thy face shalt thou eat thy bread, until thou turnest again to the dust from whence thou wert taken."[3] If then, after death, our bodies return to any other substance,

[1] Gen. i. 25.   [2] Gen. iii. 9.   [3] Gen. iii. 19.

it follows that from it also they have their substance. But if it be into this very [earth], it is manifest that it was also from it that man's frame was created; as also the Lord clearly showed, when from this very substance He formed eyes for the man [to whom He gave sight]. And thus was the hand of God plainly shown forth, by which Adam was fashioned, and we too have been formed; and since there is one and the same Father, whose voice from the beginning even to the end is present with His handiwork, and the substance from which we were formed is plainly declared through the Gospel, we should therefore not seek after another Father besides Him, nor [look for] another substance from which we have been formed, besides what was mentioned beforehand, and shown forth by the Lord; nor another hand of God besides that which, from the beginning even to the end, forms us and prepares us for life, and is present with His handiwork, and perfects it after the image and likeness of God.

2. And then, again, this Word was manifested when the Word of God was made man, assimilating Himself to man, and man to Himself, so that by means of his resemblance to the Son, man might become precious to the Father. For in times long past, it was *said* that man was created after the image of God, but it was not [actually] *shown;* for the Word was as yet invisible, after whose image man was created. Wherefore also he did easily lose the similitude. When, however, the Word of God became flesh, He confirmed both these: for He both showed forth the image truly, since He became Himself what was His image; and He re-established the similitude after a sure manner, by assimilating man to the invisible Father through means of the visible Word.

3. And not by the aforesaid things alone has the Lord manifested Himself, but [He has done this] also by means of His passion. For doing away with [the effects of] that disobedience of man which had taken place at the beginning by the occasion of a tree, "He became obedient unto death, even the death of the cross;"[1] rectifying that disobedience

[1] Phil. ii. 8.

which had occurred by reason of a tree, through that obedience which was [wrought out] upon the tree [of the cross]. Now He would not have come to do away, by means of that same [image], the disobedience which had been incurred towards our Maker if He proclaimed another Father. But inasmuch as it was by these things that we disobeyed God, and did not give credit to His word, so was it also by these same that He brought in obedience and consent as respects His Word; by which things He clearly shows forth God Himself, whom indeed we had offended in the first Adam, when he did not perform His commandment. In the second Adam, however, we are reconciled, being made obedient even unto death. For we were debtors to none other but to Him whose commandment we had transgressed at the beginning.

CHAP. XVII.—*There is but one Lord and one God, the Father and Creator of all things, who has loved us in Christ, given us commandments, and remitted our sins; whose Son and Word Christ proved Himself to be, when He forgave our sins.*

1. Now this being is the Creator (*Demiurgus*), who is, in respect of His love, the Father; but in respect of His power, He is Lord; and in respect of His wisdom, our Maker and Fashioner; by transgressing whose commandment we became His enemies. And therefore in the last times the Lord has restored us into friendship through His incarnation, having become "the Mediator between God and men;"[1] propitiating indeed for us the Father against whom we had sinned, and cancelling (*consolatus*) our disobedience by His own obedience; conferring also upon us the gift of communion with, and subjection to, our Maker. For this reason also He has taught us to say in prayer, "And forgive us our debts;"[2] since indeed He is our Father, whose debtors we were, having transgressed His commandments. But who is this Being? Is He some unknown one, and a Father who gives no com-

[1] 1 Tim. ii. 5.   [2] Matt. vi. 12.

mandment to any one? Or is He the God who is proclaimed in the Scriptures, to whom we were debtors, having transgressed His commandment? Now the commandment was given to man by the Word. For Adam, it is said, "heard the voice of the Lord God."[1] Rightly then does His Word say to man, "Thy sins are forgiven thee;"[2] He, the same against whom we had sinned in the beginning, grants forgiveness of sins in the end. But if indeed we had disobeyed the command of any other, while it was a different being who said, "Thy sins are forgiven thee;"[2] such an one is neither good, nor true, nor just. For how can he be good, who does not give from what belongs to himself? Or how can he be just, who snatches away the goods of another? And in what way can sins be truly remitted, unless that He against whom we have sinned has Himself granted remission "through the bowels of mercy of our God," in which "He has visited us"[3] through His Son?

2. And therefore, when He had healed the man sick of the palsy, [the evangelist] says: "The people upon seeing it glorified God, who gave such power unto men."[4] What God, then, did the bystanders glorify? Was it indeed that unknown Father invented by the heretics? And how could they glorify him who was altogether unknown to them? It is evident, therefore, that the Israelites glorified Him who has been proclaimed as God by the law and the prophets, who is also the Father of our Lord; and therefore He taught men, by the evidence of their senses through those signs which He accomplished, to give glory to God. If, however, He Himself had come from another Father, and men glorified a different Father when they beheld His miracles, He [in that case] rendered them ungrateful to that Father who had sent the gift of healing. But as the only-begotten Son had come for man's salvation from Him who is God, He did both stir up the incredulous by the miracles which He was in the habit of working, to give glory to the Father; and to the Pharisees, who did not admit the advent of His Son, and who

---

[1] Gen. iii. 8. [2] Matt. ix. 2; Luke v. 20.
[3] Luke i. 78. [4] Matt. ix. 8.

consequently did not believe in the remission [of sins] which was conferred by Him, He said, "That ye may know that the Son of man hath power to forgive sins."[1] And when He had said this, He commanded the paralytic man to take up the pallet upon which he was lying, and go into his house. By this work of His He confounded the unbelievers, and showed that He is Himself the voice of God, by which man received commandments, which he broke, and became a sinner; for the paralysis followed as a consequence of sins.

3. Therefore, by remitting sins, He did indeed heal man, while He also manifested Himself who He was. For if no one can forgive sins but God alone, while the Lord remitted them and healed men, it is plain that He was Himself the Word of God made the Son of man, receiving from the Father the power of remission of sins; since He was man, and since He was God, in order that since as man He suffered for us, so as God He might have compassion on us, and forgive us our debts, in which we were made debtors to God our Creator. And therefore David said beforehand, "Blessed are they whose iniquities are forgiven, and whose sins are covered. Blessed is the man to whom the Lord has not imputed sin;"[2] pointing out thus that remission of sins which follows upon His advent, by which "He has destroyed the handwriting" of our debt, and "fastened it to the cross;"[3] so that as by means of a tree we were made debtors to God, [so also] by means of a tree we may obtain the remission of our debt.

4. This fact has been strikingly set forth by many others, and especially through means of Elisha the prophet. For when his fellow-prophets were hewing wood for the construction of a tabernacle, and when the iron [head], shaken loose from the axe, had fallen into the Jordan and could not be found by them, upon Elisha's coming to the place, and learning what had happened, he threw some wood into the water. Then, when he had done this, the iron part of the axe floated up, and they took up from the surface of the water what they had previously lost.[4] By this action the prophet pointed out

---

[1] Matt. ix. 6.   [2] Ps. xxxii. 1, 2.
[3] Col. ii. 14.   [4] 2 Kings vi. 6.

that the sure word of God, which we had negligently lost by means of a tree, and were not in the way of finding again, we should receive anew by the dispensation of a tree, [viz. the cross of Christ]. For that the word of God is likened to an axe, John the Baptist declares [when he says] in reference to it, "But now also is the axe laid to the root of the trees."[1] Jeremiah also says to the same purport: "The word of God cleaveth the rock as an axe."[2] This word, then, what was hidden from us, did the dispensation of the tree make manifest, as I have already remarked. For as we lost it by means of a tree, by means of a tree again was it made manifest to all, showing the height, the length, the breadth, the depth in itself; and, as a certain man among our predecessors observed, "Through the extension of the hands of a divine person,[3] gathering together the two peoples to one God." For these were two hands, because there were two peoples scattered to the ends of the earth; but there was one head in the middle, as there is but one God, who is above all, and through all, and in us all.

CHAP. XVIII.—*God the Father and His Word have formed all created things (which they use) by their own power and wisdom, not out of defect or ignorance. The Son of God, who received all power from the Father, would otherwise never have taken flesh upon Him.*

1. And such or so important a dispensation He did not bring about by means of the creations of others, but by His own; neither by those things which were created out of ignorance and defect, but by those which had their substance from the wisdom and power of His Father. For He was neither unrighteous, so that He should covet the property of another; nor needy, that He could not by His own means impart life to His own, and make use of His own creation for

---

[1] Matt. iii. 10.   [2] Jer. xxxiii. 29.
[3] The Greek is preserved here, and reads, διὰ τῆς θείας ἐκτάσεως τῶν χειρῶν—literally, "through the divine extension of hands." The old Latin merely reads, "per extensionem manuum."

the salvation of man. For indeed the creation could not have sustained Him [on the cross], if He had sent forth [simply by commission] what was the fruit of ignorance and defect. Now we have repeatedly shown that the incarnate Word of God was suspended upon a tree, and even the very heretics do acknowledge that He was crucified. How, then, could the fruit of ignorance and defect sustain Him who contains the knowledge of all things, and is true and perfect? Or how could that creation which was concealed from the Father, and far removed from Him, have sustained His Word? And if this world were made by the angels (it matters not whether we suppose their ignorance or their cognizance of the Supreme God), when the Lord declared, "For I am in the Father, and the Father in me,"[1] how could this workmanship of the angels have borne to be burdened at once with the Father and the Son? How, again, could that creation which is beyond the Pleroma have contained Him who contains the entire Pleroma? Inasmuch, then, as all these things are impossible and incapable of proof, that preaching of the church is alone true [which proclaims] that His own creation bare Him, which subsists by the power, the skill, and the wisdom of God; which is sustained, indeed, after an invisible manner by the Father, but, on the contrary, after a visible manner it bore His Word: and this is the true [Word].

2. For the Father bears the creation and His own Word simultaneously, and the Word borne by the Father grants the Spirit to all as the Father wills.[2] To some He gives after the manner of creation what is made;[3] but to others [He gives] after the manner of adoption, that is, what is from God, namely generation. And thus one God the Father is declared, who is above all, and through all, and in all. The Father is indeed above all, and He is the Head of

---

[1] John xiv. 11.

[2] From this passage Harvey infers that Irenæus held the procession of the Holy Spirit from the Father and the Son,—a doctrine denied by the Oriental Church in after times.

[3] Grabe and Harvey insert the words, "quod est conditionis," but on slender authority.

Christ; but the Word is through all things, and is Himself the Head of the Church; while the Spirit is in us all, and He is the living water,[1] which the Lord grants to those who rightly believe in Him, and love Him, and who know that "there is one Father, who is above all, and through all, and in us all."[2] And to these things does John also, the disciple of the Lord, bear witness, when he speaks thus in the Gospel: "In the beginning was the Word, and the Word was with God, and the Word was God. This was in the beginning with God. All things were made by Him, and without Him was nothing made."[3] And then he said of the Word Himself: "He was in the world, and the world was made by Him, and the world knew Him not. To His own things He came, and His own people received Him not. However, as many as did receive Him, to these gave He power to become the sons of God, to those that believe in His name."[4] And again, showing the dispensation with regard to His human nature, John said: "And the Word was made flesh, and dwelt among us."[5] And in continuation he says, "And we beheld His glory, the glory as of the Only-begotten by the Father, full of grace and truth." He thus plainly points out to those willing to hear, that is, to those having ears, that there is one God, the Father over all, and one Word of God, who is through all, by whom all things have been made; and that this world belongs to Him, and was made by Him, according to the Father's will, and not by angels; nor by apostasy, defect, and ignorance; nor by any power of Prunicus, whom certain of them also call "the Mother;" nor by any other maker of the world ignorant of the Father.

3. For the Creator of the world is truly the Word of God: and this is our Lord, who in the last times was made man, existing in this world, and who in an invisible manner contains all things created, and is inherent in the entire creation, since the Word of God governs and arranges all things; and

---

[1] John vii. 39.
[2] Eph. iv. 6.
[3] John i. 1, etc.
[4] John i. 10, etc.
[5] John i. 14.

therefore He came to His own in a visible[1] manner, and was made flesh, and hung upon the tree, that He might sum up all things in Himself. "And His own peculiar people did not receive Him," as Moses declared this very thing among the people: "And thy life shall be hanging before thine eyes, and thou wilt not believe thy life."[2] Those therefore who did not receive Him did not receive life. "But to as many as received Him, to them gave He power to become the sons of God."[3] For it is He who has power from the Father over all things, since He is the Word of God, and very man, communicating with invisible beings after the manner of the intellect, and appointing a law observable to the outward senses, that all things should continue each in its own order; and He reigns manifestly over things visible and pertaining to men; and brings in just judgment and worthy upon all; as David also, clearly pointing to this, says, "Our God shall openly come, and will not keep silence."[4] Then he shows also the judgment which is brought in by Him, saying, "A fire shall burn in His sight, and a strong tempest shall rage round about Him. He shall call upon the heaven from above, and the earth, to judge His people."

CHAP. XIX.—*A comparison is instituted between the disobedient and sinning Eve and the Virgin Mary, her patroness. Various and discordant heresies are mentioned.*

1. That the Lord then was manifestly coming to His own things, and was sustaining them by means of that creation which is supported by Himself, and was making a recapitulation of that disobedience which had occurred in connection with a tree, through the obedience which was [exhibited by Himself when He hung] upon a tree, [the effects] also of that deception being done away with, by which that virgin Eve, who was already espoused to a man, was unhappily misled,— was happily announced, through means of the truth [spoken] by the angel to the Virgin Mary, who was [also espoused] to

---

[1] The text reads "invisibiliter," which seems clearly an error.
[2] Deut. xxviii. 66. [3] John i. 13. [4] Ps. l. 3, 4.

a man.[1] For just as the former was led astray by the word of an angel, so that she fled from God when she had transgressed His word; so did the latter, by an angelic communication, receive the glad tidings that she should sustain (*portaret*) God, being obedient to His word. And if the former did disobey God, yet the latter was persuaded to be obedient to God, in order that the Virgin Mary might become the patroness (*advocata*) of the virgin Eve. And thus, as the human race fell into bondage to death by means of a virgin, so is it rescued by a virgin; virginal disobedience having been balanced in the opposite scale by virginal obedience. For in the same way the sin of the first created man (*protoplasti*) receives amendment by the correction of the First-begotten, and the cunning of the serpent is conquered by the harmlessness of the dove, those bonds being unloosed by which we had been fast bound to death.

2. The heretics being all unlearned and ignorant of God's arrangements, and not acquainted with that dispensation by which He took upon Him human nature (*inscii ejus quæ est secundum hominem dispensationis*), inasmuch as they blind themselves with regard to the truth, do in fact speak against their own salvation. Some of them introduce another Father besides the Creator; some, again, say that the world and its substance was made by certain angels; certain others [maintain] that it was widely separated by Horos[2] from him whom they represent as being the Father—that it sprang forth (*floruisse*) of itself, and from itself was born. Then, again, others [of them assert] that it obtained substance in those things which are contained by the Father, from defect and ignorance; others still, despise the advent of the Lord manifest [to the senses], for they do not admit His incarnation; while others, ignoring the arrangement [that He should be born] of a virgin, maintain that He was begotten by Joseph. And still further, some affirm that neither their soul nor their body can receive eternal life, but merely the inner man.

---

[1] The text is here most uncertain and obscure.

[2] The text reads "porro," which makes no sense; so that Harvey looks upon it as a corruption of the reading "per Horum."

Moreover, they will have it that this [inner man] is that which is the understanding (*sensum*) in them, and which they decree as being the only thing to ascend to "the perfect." Others [maintain], as I have said in the first book, that while the soul is saved, their body does not participate in the salvation which comes from God; in which [book] I have also set forward the hypotheses of all these men, and in the second have pointed out their weakness and inconsistency.

CHAP. XX.—*Those pastors are to be heard to whom the apostles committed the churches, possessing one and the same doctrine of salvation; the heretics, on the other hand, are to be avoided. We must think soberly with regard to the mysteries of the faith.*

1. Now all these [heretics] are of much later date than the bishops to whom the apostles committed the churches; which fact I have in the third book taken all pains to demonstrate. It follows, then, as a matter of course, that these heretics aforementioned, since they are blind to the truth, and deviate from the [right] way, will walk in various roads; and therefore the footsteps of their doctrine are scattered here and there without agreement or connection. But the path of those belonging to the church circumscribes the whole world, as possessing the sure tradition from the apostles, and gives unto us to see that the faith of all is one and the same, since all receive one and the same God the Father, and believe in the same dispensation regarding the incarnation of the Son of God, and are cognizant of the same gift of the Spirit, and are conversant with the same commandments, and preserve the same form of ecclesiastical constitution,[1] and expect the same advent of the Lord, and await the same salvation of the complete man, that is, of the soul and body. And undoubtedly the preaching of the church is true and

---

[1] "Et eandem figuram ejus quæ est erga ecclesiam ordinationis custodientibus." Grabe supposes this refers to the ordained ministry of the church, but Harvey thinks it refers more probably to its general constitution.

stedfast, in which one and the same way of salvation is shown throughout the whole world. For to her is entrusted the light of God; and therefore the "wisdom" of God, by means of which she saves all men, "is declared in [its] going forth; it uttereth [its voice] faithfully in the streets, is preached on the tops of the walls, and speaks continually in the gates of the city."[1] For the church preaches the truth everywhere, and she is the seven-branched candlestick which bears the light of Christ.

2. Those, therefore, who desert the preaching of the church, call in question the knowledge of the holy presbyters, not taking into consideration of how much greater consequence is a religious man, even in a private station, than a blasphemous and impudent sophist.[2] Now, such are all the heretics, and those who imagine that they have hit upon something more beyond the truth, so that by following those things already mentioned, proceeding on their way variously, inharmoniously, and foolishly, not keeping always to the same opinions with regard to the same things, as blind men are led by the blind, they shall deservedly fall into the ditch of ignorance lying in their path, ever seeking and never finding out the truth.[3] It behoves us, therefore, to avoid their doctrines, and to take careful heed lest we suffer any injury from them; but to flee to the church, and be brought up in her bosom, and be nourished with the Lord's Scriptures. For the church has been planted as a garden (*paradisus*) in this world; therefore says the Spirit of God, "Thou mayest freely eat from every tree of the garden,"[4] that is, Eat ye from every Scripture of the Lord; but ye shall not eat with an uplifted mind, nor touch any heretical discord. For these men do profess that they have themselves the knowledge of good and evil; and they set their own impious minds above the God who made them. They therefore form opinions on what is beyond the limits of the understanding. For this cause also

---

[1] Prov. i. 20, 21.

[2] That is, the private Christian as contrasted with the sophist of the schools.

[3] 2 Tim. iii. 7.   [4] Gen. ii. 16.

the apostle says, "Be not wise beyond what it is fitting to be wise, but be wise prudently,"[1] that we be not cast forth by eating of the "knowledge" of these men (that knowledge which knows more than it should do) from the paradise of life. Into this paradise the Lord has introduced those who obey His call, "summing up in Himself all things which are in heaven, and which are on earth;"[2] but the things in heaven are spiritual, while those on earth constitute the dispensation in human nature (*secundum hominem est dispositio*). These things, therefore, He recapitulated in Himself: by uniting man to the Spirit, and causing the Spirit to dwell in man, He is Himself made the head of the Spirit, and gives the Spirit to be the head of man: for through Him (the Spirit) we see, and hear, and speak.

CHAP. XXI.—*Christ is the Head of all things already mentioned. It was fitting that He should be sent by the Father, the Creator of all things, to assume human nature, and should be tempted by Satan, that He might fulfil the promises, and carry off a glorious and perfect victory.*

1. He has therefore, in His work of recapitulation, summed up all things, both waging war against our enemy, and crushing him who had at the beginning led us away captives in Adam, and trampling upon his head, as thou canst perceive in Genesis that God said to the serpent, "And I will put enmity between thee and the woman, and between thy seed and her seed; He shall be on the watch for (*observabit*[3]) thy head, and thou on the watch for His heel."[4] For from that time, He who should be born of a woman, [namely] from the Virgin, after the likeness of Adam, was preached as keeping watch for the head of the serpent. This is the seed of which the apostle says in the Epistle to the Galatians, "that the law of works was established until the seed should come to whom the promise was made."[5] This fact is exhibited in

---

[1] Rom. xii. 3.   [2] Eph. i. 10.
[3] τηρήσει and τερίσει have probably been confounded.
[4] Gen. iii. 15.   [5] Gal. iii. 19.

a still clearer light in the same epistle, where he thus speaks: "But when the fulness of time was come, God sent forth His Son, made of a woman."[1] For indeed the enemy would not have been fairly vanquished, unless it had been a man [born] of woman who conquered him. For it was by means of a woman that he got the advantage over man at first, setting himself up as man's opponent. And therefore does the Lord profess Himself to be the Son of man, comprising in Himself that original man out of whom the woman was fashioned (*ex quo ea quæ secundum mulierem est plasmatio facta est*), in order that, as our species went down to death through a vanquished man, so we may ascend to life again through a victorious one; and as through a man death received the palm [of victory] against us, so again by a man we may receive the palm against death.

2. Now the Lord would not have recapitulated in Himself that ancient and primary enmity against the serpent, fulfilling the promise of the Creator (*Demiurgi*), and performing His command, if He had come from another Father. But as He is one and the same, who formed us at the beginning, and sent His Son at the end, the Lord did perform His command, being made of a woman, by both destroying our adversary, and perfecting man after the image and likeness of God. And for this reason He did not draw the means of confounding him from any other source than from the words of the law, and made use of the Father's commandment as a help towards the destruction and confusion of the apostate angel. Fasting forty days, like Moses and Elias, He afterwards hungered, first, in order that we may perceive that He was a real and substantial man—for it belongs to a man to suffer hunger when fasting; and secondly, that His opponent might have an opportunity of attacking Him. For as at the beginning it was by means of food that [the enemy] persuaded man, although not suffering hunger, to transgress God's commandments, so in the end he did not succeed in persuading Him that was an hungered to take that food which proceeded from God. For, when tempting

[1] Gal. iv. 4.

Him, he said, "If thou be the Son of God, command that these stones be made bread."[1] But the Lord repulsed him by the commandment of the law, saying, "It is written, Man doth not live by bread alone."[2] As to those words [of His enemy,] "If thou be the Son of God," [the Lord] made no remark; but by thus acknowledging His human nature He baffled His adversary, and exhausted the force of his first attack by means of His Father's word. The corruption of man, therefore, which occurred in paradise by both [of our first parents] eating, was done away with by [the Lord's] want of food in this world.[3] But he, being thus vanquished by the law, endeavoured again to make an assault by himself quoting a commandment of the law. For, bringing Him to the highest pinnacle of the temple, he said to Him, "If thou art the Son of God, cast thyself down. For it is written, That God shall give His angels charge concerning thee, and in their hands they shall bear thee up, lest perchance thou dash thy foot against a stone;"[4] thus concealing a falsehood under the guise of Scripture, as is done by all the heretics. For that was indeed written, [namely], "That He hath given His angels charge concerning Him;" but "cast thyself down from hence" no Scripture said in reference to Him: this kind of persuasion the devil produced from himself. The Lord therefore confuted him out of the law, when He said, "It is written again, Thou shalt not tempt the Lord thy God;"[5] pointing out by the word contained in the law that which is the duty of man, that he should not tempt God; and in regard to Himself, since He appeared in human form, [declaring] that He would not tempt the Lord his God.[6] The pride of reason, therefore, which was in the serpent, was put to nought by the humility

---

[1] Matt. iv. 3.   [2] Deut. viii. 3.

[3] The Latin of this obscure sentence is: Quæ ergo fuit in Paradiso repletio hominis per duplicem gustationem, dissoluta est per eam, quæ fuit in hoc mundo, indigentiam. Harvey thinks that *repletio* is an error of the translation reading ἀναπλήρωσις for ἀνατήρωσις. This conjecture is adopted above.

[4] Ps. lxxxix. 11.   [5] Deut. vi. 16.

[6] This sentence is one of great obscurity.

found in the man [Christ]; and now twice was the devil conquered from Scripture, when he was detected as advising things contrary to God's commandment, and was shown to be the enemy of God by [the expression of] his thoughts. He then, having been thus signally defeated, and then, as it were, concentrating his forces, drawing up in order all his available power for falsehood, in the third place "showed Him all the kingdoms of the world, and the glory of them,"[1] saying, as Luke relates, "All these will I give thee,—for they are delivered to me; and to whom I will, I give them,—if thou wilt fall down and worship me." The Lord then, exposing him in his true character, says, "Depart, Satan; for it is written, Thou shalt worship the Lord thy God, and Him only shalt thou serve."[2] He both revealed him by this name, and showed [at the same time] who He Himself was. For the Hebrew word "Satan" signifies an apostate. And thus, vanquishing him for the third time, He spurned him from Him finally as being conquered out of the law; and there was done away with that infringement of God's commandment which had occurred in Adam, by means of the precept of the law, which the Son of man observed, who did not transgress the commandment of God.

3. Who, then, is this Lord God to whom Christ bears witness, whom no man shall tempt, whom all should worship, and serve Him alone? It is, beyond all manner of doubt, that God who also gave the law. For these things had been predicted in the law, and by the words (*sententiam*) of the law the Lord showed that the law does indeed declare the Word of God from the Father; and the apostate angel of God is destroyed by its voice, being exposed in his true colours, and vanquished by the Son of man keeping the commandment of God. For as in the beginning he enticed man to transgress his Maker's law, and thereby got him into his power; yet his power consists in transgression and apostasy, and with these he bound man [to himself]; so again, on the other hand, it was necessary that through man himself he should, when conquered, be bound with the same chains with which

[1] Luke iv. 6, 7.   [2] Matt. iv. 10.

he had bound man, in order that man, being set free, might return to his Lord, leaving to him (Satan) those bonds by which he himself had been fettered, that is, sin. For when Satan is bound, man is set free; since "none can enter a strong man's house and spoil his goods, unless he first bind the strong man himself."[1] The Lord therefore exposes him as speaking contrary to the word of that God who made all things, and subdues him by means of the commandment. Now the law is the commandment of God. The Man proves him to be a fugitive from and a transgressor of the law, an apostate also from God. After [the Man had done this], the Word bound him securely as a fugitive from Himself, and made spoil of his goods,—namely, those men whom he held in bondage, and whom he unjustly used for his own purposes. And justly indeed is he led captive, who had led men unjustly into bondage; while man, who had been led captive in times past, was rescued from the grasp of his possessor, according to the tender mercy of God the Father, who had compassion on His own handiwork, and gave to it salvation, restoring it by means of the Word—that is, by Christ—in order that men might learn by actual proof that he receives incorruptibility not of himself, but by the free gift of God.

CHAP. XXII.—*The true Lord and the one God is declared by the law, and manifested by Christ his Son in the Gospel; whom alone we should adore, and from Him we must look for all good things, not from Satan.*

1. Thus then does the Lord plainly show that it was the true Lord and the one God who had been set forth by the law; for Him whom the law proclaimed as God, the same did Christ point out as the Father, whom also it behoves the disciples of Christ alone to serve. By means of the statements of the law, He put our adversary to utter confusion; and the law directs us to praise God the Creator (*Demiurgum*), and to serve Him alone. Since this is the case, we must not seek for another Father besides Him, or above Him, since

[1] Matt. xii. 29 and Mark iii. 27.

there is one God who justifies the circumcision by faith, and the uncircumcision through faith.[1] For if there were any other perfect Father above Him, He (Christ) would by no means have overthrown Satan by means of His words and commandments. For one ignorance cannot be done away with by means of another ignorance, any more than one defect by another defect. If, therefore, the law is due to ignorance and defect, how could the statements contained therein bring to nought the ignorance of the devil, and conquer the strong man? For a strong man can be conquered neither by an inferior nor by an equal, but by one possessed of greater power. But the Word of God is the superior above all, He who is loudly proclaimed in the law: "Hear, O Israel, the Lord thy God is one God;" and, "Thou shalt love the Lord thy God with all thy heart;" and, "Him shalt thou adore, and Him alone shalt thou serve."[2] Then in the Gospel, casting down the apostasy by means of these expressions, He did both overcome the strong man by His Father's voice, and He acknowledges the commandment of the law to express His own sentiments, when He says, "Thou shalt not tempt the Lord thy God."[3] For He did not confound the adversary by the saying of any other, but by that belonging to His own Father, and thus overcame the strong man.

2. He taught by His commandment that we who have been set free should, when hungry, take that food which is given by God; and that, when placed in the exalted position of every grace [that can be received], we should not, either by trusting to works of righteousness, or when adorned with supereminent [gifts of] ministration, by any means be lifted up with pride, nor should we tempt God, but should feel humility in all things, and have ready to hand [this saying], "Thou shalt not tempt the Lord thy God."[4] As also the apostle taught, saying, "Minding not high things, but consenting to things of low estate;"[5] that we should neither be ensnared with riches, nor mundane glory, nor present fancy,

[1] Rom. iii. 30.   [2] Deut. vi. 4, 5, 13.   [3] Matt. iv. 7.
[4] Deut. vi. 16.   [5] Rom. xii. 16.

but should know that we must "worship the Lord thy God, and serve Him alone," and give no heed to him who falsely promised things not his own, when he said, "All these will I give thee, if, falling down, thou wilt worship me." For he himself confesses that to adore him, and to do his will, is to fall from the glory of God. And in what thing either pleasant or good can that man who has fallen participate? Or what else can such a person hope for or expect, except death? For death is next neighbour to him who has fallen. Hence also it follows that he will not give what he has promised. For how can he make grants to him who has fallen? Moreover, since God rules over men and him too, and without the will of our Father in heaven not even a sparrow falls to the ground,[1] it follows that his declaration, "All these things are delivered unto me, and to whomsoever I will I give them," proceeds from him when puffed up with pride. For the creation is not subjected to his power, since indeed he is himself but one among created things. Nor shall he give away the rule over men to men; but both all other things, and all human affairs, are arranged according to God the Father's disposal. Besides, the Lord declares that "the devil is a liar from the beginning, and the truth is not in him."[2] If then he be a liar, and the truth be not in him, he certainly did not speak truth, but a lie, when he said, "For all these things are delivered to me, and to whomsoever I will I give them."[3]

CHAP. XXIII.—*The devil is well practised in falsehood, by which Adam having been led astray, sinned on the sixth day of the creation, in which day also he has been renewed by Christ.*

1. He had indeed been already accustomed to lie against God, for the purpose of leading men astray. For at the beginning, when God had given to man a variety of things for food, while He commanded him not to eat of one tree only, as the Scripture tells us that God said to Adam:

---
[1] Matt. x. 29. [2] John viii. 44. [3] Luke iv. 6.

"From every tree which is in the garden thou shalt eat food; but from the tree of knowledge of good and evil, from this ye shall not eat: for in the day that ye shall eat of it, ye shall die by death;"[1] he then, lying against the Lord, tempted man, as the Scripture says that the serpent said to the woman: "Has God indeed said this, Ye shall not eat from every tree of the garden?"[2] And when she had exposed the falsehood, and simply related the command, as He had said, "From every tree of the garden we shall eat; but of the fruit of the tree which is in the midst of the garden, God hath said, Ye shall not eat of it, neither shall ye touch it, lest ye die:"[3] when he had [thus] learned from the woman the command of God, having brought his cunning into play, he finally deceived her by a falsehood, saying, "Ye shall not die by death; for God knew that in the day ye shall eat of it your eyes shall be opened, and ye shall be as gods, knowing good and evil."[4] In the first place, then, in the garden of God he disputed about God, as if God was not there, for he was ignorant of the greatness of God; and then, in the next place, after he had learned from the woman that God had said that they should die if they tasted the aforesaid tree, opening his mouth, he uttered the third falsehood, "Ye shall not die by death." But that God was true, and the serpent a liar, was proved by the result, death having passed upon them who had eaten. For along with the fruit they did also fall under the power of death, because they did eat in disobedience; and disobedience to God entails death. Wherefore, as they became forfeit to death, from that [moment] they were handed over to it.

2. Thus, then, in the day that they did eat, in the same did they die, and became death's debtors, since it was one day of the creation. For it is said, "There was made in the evening, and there was made in the morning, one day." Now in this same day that they did eat, in that also did they die. But according to the cycle and progress of the days, after which one is termed first, another second, and another third, if anybody seeks diligently to learn upon what day out of the

[1] Gen. ii. 16, 17.   [2] Gen. iii. 1.   [3] Gen. iii. 2, 3.   [4] Gen. iii. 4.

seven it was that Adam died, he will find it by examining the dispensation of the Lord. For by summing up in Himself the whole human race from the beginning to the end, He has also summed up its death. From this it is clear that the Lord suffered death, in obedience to His Father, upon that day on which Adam died while he disobeyed God. Now he died on the same day in which he did eat. For God said, "In that day on which ye shall eat of it, ye shall die by death." The Lord, therefore, recapitulating in Himself this day, underwent His sufferings upon the day preceding the Sabbath, that is, the sixth day of the creation, on which day man was created; thus granting him a second creation by means of His passion, which is that [creation] out of death. And there are some, again, who relegate the death of Adam to the thousandth year; for since "a day of the Lord is as a thousand years,"[1] he did not overstep the thousand years, but died within them, thus bearing out the sentence of his sin. Whether, therefore, with respect to disobedience, which is death; whether [we consider] that, on account of that, they were delivered over to death, and made debtors to it; whether with respect to [the fact that on] one and the same day on which they ate they also died (for it is one day of the creation); whether [we regard this point], that, with respect to this cycle of days, they died on the day in which they did also eat, that is, the day of the preparation, which is termed "the pure supper," that is, the sixth day of the feast, which the Lord also exhibited when He suffered on that day; or whether [we reflect] that he (Adam) did not overstep the thousand years, but died within their limit,—it follows that, in regard to all these significations, God is indeed true. For they died who tasted of the tree; and the serpent is proved a liar and a murderer, as the Lord said of him: "For he is a murderer from the beginning, and the truth is not in him."[2]

[1] 2 Pet. iii. 8.   [2] John viii. 44.

CHAP. XXIV.—*Of the constant falsehood of the devil, and of the powers and governments of the world, which we ought to obey, inasmuch as they are appointed of God, not of the devil.*

1. As therefore the devil lied at the beginning, so did he also in the end, when he said, "All these are delivered unto me, and to whomsoever I will I give them."[1] For it is not he who has appointed the kingdoms of this world, but God; for "the heart of the king is in the hand of God."[2] And the Word also says by Solomon, "By me kings do reign, and princes administer justice. By me chiefs are raised up, and by me kings rule the earth."[3] Paul the apostle also says upon this same subject: "Be ye subject to all the higher powers; for there is no power but of God: now those which are have been ordained of God."[4] And again, in reference to them he says, "For he beareth not the sword in vain; for he is the minister of God, the avenger for wrath to him who does evil."[5] Now, that he spake these words, not in regard to angelical powers, nor of invisible rulers—as some venture to expound the passage—but of those of actual human authorities, [he shows when] he says, "For this cause pay ye tribute also: for they are God's ministers, doing service for this very thing."[6] This also the Lord confirmed, when He did not do what He was tempted to by the devil; but He gave directions that tribute should be paid to the tax-gatherers for Himself and Peter;[7] because "they are the ministers of God, serving for this very thing."

2. For since man, by departing from God, reached such a pitch of fury as even to look upon his brother as his enemy, and engaged without fear in every kind of restless conduct, and murder, and avarice; God imposed upon mankind the fear of man, as they did not acknowledge the fear of God, in order that, being subjected to the authority of men, and kept under restraint by their laws, they might attain

---

[1] Matt. iv. 9; Luke iv. 6.   [2] Prov. xxi. 1.   [3] Prov. viii. 15.
[4] Rom. xiii. 1.   [5] Rom. xiii. 4.   [6] Rom. xiii. 6.   [7] Matt. xvii. 27.

to some degree of justice, and exercise mutual forbearance through dread of the sword suspended full in their view, as the apostle says: "For he beareth not the sword in vain; for he is the minister of God, the avenger for wrath upon him who does evil." And for this reason too, magistrates themselves, having laws as a clothing of righteousness whenever they act in a just and legitimate manner, shall not be called in question for their conduct, nor be liable to punishment. But whatsoever they do to the subversion of justice, iniquitously, and impiously, and illegally, and tyrannically, in these things shall they also perish; for the just judgment of God comes equally upon all, and in no case is defective. Earthly rule, therefore, has been appointed by God for the benefit of nations, and not by the devil, who is never at rest at all, nay, who does not love to see even nations conducting themselves after a quiet manner, so that under the fear of human rule, men may not eat each other up like fishes; but that, by means of the establishment of laws, they may keep down an excess of wickedness among the nations. And considered from this point of view, those who exact tribute from us are "God's ministers, serving for this very purpose."

3. As, then, "the powers that be are ordained of God," it is clear that the devil lied when he said, "These are delivered unto me; and to whomsoever I will, I give them." For by the law of the same Being as calls men into existence are kings also appointed, adapted for those men who are at the time placed under their government. Some of these [rulers] are given for the correction and the benefit of their subjects, and for the preservation of justice; but others, for the purposes of fear and punishment and rebuke: others, as [the subjects] deserve it, are for deception, disgrace, and pride; while the just judgment of God, as I have observed already, passes equally upon all. The devil, however, as he is the apostate angel, can only go to this length, as he did at the beginning, [namely] to deceive and lead astray the mind of man into disobeying the commandments of God, and gradually to darken the hearts of those who would endeavour to

serve him, to the forgetting of the true God, but to the adoration of himself as God.

4. Just as if any one, being an apostate, and seizing in a hostile manner another man's territory, should harass the inhabitants of it, in order that he might claim for himself the glory of a king among those ignorant of his apostasy and robbery; so likewise also the devil, being one among those angels who are placed over the spirit of the air, as the Apostle Paul has declared in his Epistle to the Ephesians,[1] becoming envious of man, was rendered an apostate from the divine law: for envy is a thing foreign to God. And as his apostasy was exposed by man, and man became the [means of] searching out his thoughts (*et examinatio sententiæ ejus, homo factus est*), he has set himself to this with greater and greater determination, in opposition to man, envying his life, and wishing to involve him in his own apostate power. The Word of God, however, the Maker of all things, conquering him by means of human nature, and showing him to be an apostate, has, on the contrary, put him under the power of man. For He says, "Behold, I confer upon you the power of treading upon serpents and scorpions, and upon all the power of the enemy,"[2] in order that, as he obtained dominion over man by apostasy, so again his apostasy might be deprived of power by means of man turning back again to God.

CHAP. XXV.—*The fraud, pride, and tyrannical kingdom of Antichrist, as described by Daniel and Paul.*

1. And not only by the particulars already mentioned, but also by means of the events which shall occur in the time of Antichrist is it shown that he, being an apostate and a robber, is anxious to be adored as God; and that, although a mere slave, he wishes himself to be proclaimed as a king. For he (Antichrist) being endued with all the power of the devil, shall come, not as a righteous king, nor as a legitimate king, [*i.e.* one] in subjection to God, but an impious, unjust, and lawless one; as an apostate, iniquitous and

[1] Eph. ii. 2.   [2] Luke x. 19.

murderous; as a robber, concentrating in himself [all] satanic apostasy, and setting aside idols to persuade [men] that he himself is God, raising up himself as the only idol, having in himself the multifarious errors of the other idols. This he does, in order that they who do [now] worship the devil by means of many abominations, may serve himself by this one idol, of whom the apostle thus speaks in the second Epistle to the Thessalonians: "Unless there shall come a falling away first, and the man of sin shall be revealed, the son of perdition, who opposeth and exalteth himself above all that is called God, or that is worshipped; so that he sitteth in the temple of God, showing himself as if he were God." The apostle therefore clearly points out his apostasy, and that he is lifted up above all that is called God, or that is worshipped—that is, above every idol—for these are indeed so called by men, but are not [really] gods; and that he will endeavour in a tyrannical manner to set himself forth as God.

2. Moreover, he (the apostle) has also pointed out this which I have shown in many ways, that the temple in Jerusalem was made by the direction of the true God. For the apostle himself, speaking in his own person, distinctly called it the temple of God. Now I have shown in the third book, that no one is termed God by the apostles when speaking for themselves, except Him who truly is God, the Father of our Lord, by whose directions the temple which is at Jerusalem was constructed for those purposes which I have already mentioned; in which [temple] the enemy shall sit, endeavouring to show himself as Christ, as the Lord also declares: "But when ye shall see the abomination of desolation, which has been spoken of by Daniel the prophet, standing in the holy place (let him that readeth understand), then let those who are in Judea flee into the mountains; and he who is upon the house-top, let him not come down to take anything out of his house: for there shall then be great hardship, such as has not been from the beginning of the world until now, nor ever shall be."[1]

3. Daniel too, looking forward to the end of the last king-

[1] Matt. xxiv. 15, 21.

dom, *i.e.* the ten last kings, amongst whom the kingdom of those men shall be partitioned, and upon whom the son of perdition shall come, declares that ten horns shall spring from the beast, and that another little horn shall arise in the midst of them, and that three of the former shall be rooted up before his face. He says: "And, behold, eyes were in this horn as the eyes of a man, and a mouth speaking great things, and his look was more stout than his fellows. I was looking, and this horn made war against the saints, and prevailed against them, until the Ancient of days came and gave judgment to the saints of the most high God, and the time came, and the saints obtained the kingdom."[1] Then, further on, in the interpretation of the vision, there was said to him: "The fourth beast shall be the fourth kingdom upon earth, which shall excel all other kingdoms, and devour the whole earth, and tread it down, and cut it in pieces. And its ten horns are ten kings which shall arise; and after them shall arise another, who shall surpass in evil deeds all that were before him, and shall overthrow three kings; and he shall speak words against the most high God, and wear out the saints of the most high God, and shall purpose to change times and laws; and [everything] shall be given into his hand until a time of times and a half time,"[2] that is, for three years and six months, during which time, when he comes, he shall reign over the earth. Of whom also the Apostle Paul again, speaking in the second [Epistle] to the Thessalonians, and at the same time proclaiming the cause of his advent, thus says: "And then shall the wicked one be revealed, whom the Lord Jesus shall slay with the spirit of His mouth, and destroy by the presence of His coming; whose coming [*i.e.* the wicked one's] is after the working of Satan, in all power, and signs, and portents of lies, and with all deceivableness of wickedness for those who perish; because they did not receive the love of the truth, that they might be saved. And therefore God will send them the working of error, that they may believe a lie; that they all may be judged who did not believe the truth, but gave consent to iniquity."[3]

[1] Dan. vii. 8, etc. [2] Dan. vii. 23, etc. [3] 2 Thess. ii. 8.

4. The Lord also spoke as follows to those who did not believe in Him: "I have come in my Father's name, and ye have not received me: when another shall come in his own name, him ye will receive,"[1] calling Antichrist "the other," because he is alienated from the Lord. This is also the unjust judge, whom the Lord mentioned as one "who feared not God, neither regarded man,"[2] to whom the widow fled in her forgetfulness of God,—that is, the earthly Jerusalem,—to be avenged of her adversary. Which also he shall do in the time of his kingdom: he shall remove his kingdom into that [city], and shall sit in the temple of God, leading astray those who worship him, as if he were Christ. To this purpose Daniel says again: "And he shall desolate the holy place; and sin has been given for a sacrifice,[3] and righteousness been cast away in the earth, and he has been active (*fecit*), and gone on prosperously."[4] And the angel Gabriel, when explaining his vision, states with regard to this person: "And towards the end of their kingdom a king of a most fierce countenance shall arise, one understanding [dark] questions, and exceedingly powerful, full of wonders; and he shall corrupt, direct, influence (*faciet*), and put strong men down, the holy people likewise; and his yoke shall be directed as a wreath [round their neck]; deceit shall be in his hand, and he shall be lifted up in his heart: he shall also ruin many by deceit, and lead many to perdition, bruising them in his hand like eggs."[5] And then he points out the time that his tyranny shall last, during which the saints shall be put to flight, they who offer a pure sacrifice unto God: "And in the midst of the week," he says, "the sacrifice and the libation shall be taken away, and the abomination of desolation [shall be brought] into the temple: even unto the consummation of

---

[1] John v. 43.   [2] Luke xviii. 2, etc.

[3] This may refer to Antiochus Epiphanes, Antichrist's prototype, who offered swine upon the altar in the temple at Jerusalem. The LXX. version has, ἰδόθη ἐπὶ τὴν θυσίαν ἁμαρτία, i.e. sin has been given against (or, *upon*) the sacrifice.

[4] Dan. viii. 12.

[5] Dan. viii. 23, etc.

the time shall the desolation be complete."[1] Now three years and six months constitute the half-week.

5. From all these passages are revealed to us, not merely the particulars of the apostasy, and [the doings] of him who concentrates in himself every satanic error, but also that there is one and the same God the Father, who was declared by the prophets, but made manifest by Christ. For if what Daniel prophesied concerning the end has been confirmed by the Lord, when He said, "When ye shall see the abomination of desolation, which has been spoken of by Daniel the prophet"[2] (and the angel Gabriel gave the interpretation of the visions to Daniel, and he is the archangel of the Creator (*Demiurgi*), who also proclaimed to Mary the visible coming and the incarnation of Christ), then one and the same God is most manifestly pointed out, who sent the prophets, and made promise[3] of the Son, and called us into His knowledge.

CHAP. XXVI.—*John and Daniel have predicted the dissolution and desolation of the Roman Empire, which shall precede the end of the world and the eternal kingdom of Christ. The Gnostics are refuted, those tools of Satan, who invent another Father different from the Creator.*

1. In a still clearer light has John, in the Apocalypse, indicated to the Lord's disciples what shall happen in the last times, and concerning the ten kings who shall then arise, among whom the empire which now rules [the earth] shall be partitioned. He teaches us what the ten horns shall be which were seen by Daniel, telling us that thus it had been said to him: "And the ten horns which thou sawest are ten kings, who have received no kingdom as yet, but shall receive power as if kings one hour with the beast. These have one mind, and give their strength and power to the beast. These shall make war with the Lamb, and the Lamb shall overcome them, because He is the Lord of lords and the King of kings."[4]

---

[1] Dan. ix. 27.   [2] Matt. xxiv. 15.
[3] The MSS. have "præmisit," but Harvey suggests "promisit," which we have adopted.
[4] Rev. xvii. 12, etc.

It is manifest, therefore, that of these [potentates], he who is to come shall slay three, and subject the remainder to his power, and that he shall be himself the eighth among them. And they shall lay Babylon waste, and burn her with fire, and shall give their kingdom to the beast, and put the church to flight. After that they shall be destroyed by the coming of our Lord. For that the kingdom must be divided, and thus come to ruin, the Lord [declares when He] says: "Every kingdom divided against itself is brought to desolation, and every city or house divided against itself shall not stand."[1] It must be, therefore, that the kingdom, the city, and the house be divided into ten; and for this reason He has already foreshadowed the partition and division [which shall take place]. Daniel also says particularly, that the end of the fourth kingdom consists in the toes of the image seen by Nebuchadnezzar, upon which came the stone cut out without hands; and as he does himself say: "The feet were indeed the one part iron, the other part clay, until the stone was cut out without hands, and struck the image upon the iron and clay feet, and dashed them into pieces, even to the end."[2] Then afterwards, when interpreting this, he says: "And as thou sawest the feet and the toes, partly indeed of clay, and partly of iron, the kingdom shall be divided, and there shall be in it a root of iron, as thou sawest iron mixed with baked clay. And the toes were indeed the one part iron, but the other part clay."[3] The ten toes, therefore, are these ten kings, among whom the kingdom shall be partitioned, of whom some indeed shall be strong and active, or energetic; others, again, shall be sluggish and useless, and shall not agree; as also Daniel says: "Some part of the kingdom shall be strong, and part shall be broken from it. As thou sawest the iron mixed with the baked clay, there shall be minglings among the human race, but no cohesion one with the other, just as iron cannot be welded on to pottery ware."[4] And since an end shall take place, he says: "And in the days of these kings shall the God of heaven raise up a kingdom which shall never decay, and His king-

[1] Matt. xii. 25.   [2] Dan. ii. 33, 34.
[3] Dan. ii. 41, 42.   [4] Dan. ii. 42, 43.

dom shall not be left to another people. It shall break in pieces and shatter all kingdoms, and shall itself be exalted for ever. As thou sawest that the stone was cut without hands from the mountain, and brake in pieces the baked clay, the iron, the brass, the silver, and the gold, God has pointed out to the king what shall come to pass after these things; and the dream is true, and the interpretation trustworthy."[1]

2. If therefore the great God showed future things by Daniel, and confirmed them by His Son; and if Christ is the stone which is cut out without hands, who shall destroy temporal kingdoms, and introduce an eternal one, which is the resurrection of the just; as he declares, "The God of heaven shall raise up a kingdom which shall never be destroyed,"—let those thus confuted come to their senses, who reject the Creator (*Demiurgum*), and do not agree that the prophets were sent beforehand from the same Father from whom also the Lord came, but who assert that prophecies originated from diverse powers. For those things which have been predicted by the Creator alike through all the prophets has Christ fulfilled in the end, ministering to His Father's will, and completing His dispensations with regard to the human race. Let those persons, therefore, who blaspheme the Creator, either by openly expressed words, such as the disciples of Marcion, or by a perversion of the sense [of Scripture], as those of Valentinus and all the Gnostics falsely so called, be recognised as agents of Satan by all those who worship God; through whose agency Satan now, and not before, has been seen to speak against God, even Him who has prepared eternal fire for every kind of apostasy. For he did not venture to blaspheme his Lord openly of himself; as also in the beginning he led man astray through the instrumentality of the serpent, concealing himself as it were from God. Truly has Justin remarked:[2]

---

[1] Dan. ii. 44, 45.
[2] The Greek text is here preserved by Eusebius, *Hist. Eccl.* iv. 18; but we are not told from what work of Justin Martyr it is extracted. The work is now lost. An ancient catena continues the Greek for several lines further.

That before the Lord's appearance Satan never dared to blaspheme God, inasmuch as he did not yet know his own sentence, because it was contained in parables and allegories; but that after the Lord's appearance, when he had clearly ascertained from the words of Christ and His apostles that eternal fire has been prepared for him as he apostatized from God of his own free-will, and likewise for all who unrepentant continue in the apostasy, he now blasphemes, by means of such men, the Lord who brings judgment [upon him] as being already condemned, and imputes the guilt of his apostasy to his Maker, not to his own voluntary disposition. Just as it is with those who break the laws, when punishment overtakes them: they throw the blame upon those who frame the laws, but not upon themselves. In like manner do those men, filled with a satanic spirit, bring innumerable accusations against our Creator, who has both given to us the spirit of life, and established a law adapted for all; and they will not admit that the judgment of God is just. Wherefore also they set about imagining some other Father who neither cares about nor exercises a providence over our affairs, nay, one who even approves of all sins.

CHAP. XXVII.—*The future judgment by Christ. Communion with and separation from the Divine Being. The eternal punishment of unbelievers.*

1. If the Father, then, does not exercise judgment, [it follows] that judgment does not belong to Him, or that He consents to all those actions which take place; and if He does not judge, all persons will be equal, and accounted in the same condition. The advent of Christ will therefore be without an object, yea, absurd, inasmuch as [in that case] He exercises no judicial power. For "He came to divide a man against his father, and the daughter against the mother, and the daughter-in-law against the mother-in-law;"[1] and when two are in one bed, to take the one, and to leave the other; and of two women grinding at the mill, to take one

[1] Matt. x. 25.

and leave the other:[1] [also] at the time of the end, to order the reapers to collect first the tares together, and bind them in bundles, and burn them with unquenchable fire, but to gather up the wheat into the barn;[2] and to call the lambs into the kingdom prepared for them, but to send the goats into everlasting fire, which has been prepared by His Father for the devil and his angels.[3] And why is this? Has the Word come for the ruin and for the resurrection of many? For the ruin, certainly, of those who do not believe Him, to whom also He has threatened a greater damnation in the judgment-day than that of Sodom and Gomorrah;[4] but for the resurrection of believers, and those who do the will of His Father in heaven. If then the advent of the Son comes indeed alike to all, but is for the purpose of judging, and separating the believing from the unbelieving, since, as those who believe do His will agreeably to their own choice, and as, [also] agreeably to their own choice, the disobedient do not consent to His doctrine; it is manifest that His Father has made all in a like condition, each person having a choice of his own, and a free understanding; and that He has regard to all things, and exercises a providence over all, " making His sun to rise upon the evil and on the good, and sending rain upon the just and unjust."[5]

2. And to as many as continue in their love towards God, does He grant communion with Him. But communion with God is life and light, and the enjoyment of all the benefits which He has in store. But on as many as, according to their own choice, depart from God, He inflicts that separation from Himself which they have chosen of their own accord. But separation from God is death, and separation from light is darkness; and separation from God consists in the loss of all the benefits which He has in store. Those, therefore, who cast away by apostasy these forementioned things, being in fact destitute of all good, do experience every kind of punishment. God, however, does not punish them immediately of Himself, but that punishment falls upon them because they

[1] Luke xvii. 34. [2] Matt. xiii. 30. [3] Matt. xxv. 33, etc.
[4] Luke x. 12. [5] Matt. v. 45.

are destitute of all that is good. Now, good things are eternal and without end with God, and therefore the loss of these is also eternal and never-ending. It is in this matter just as occurs in the case of a flood of light: those who have blinded themselves, or have been blinded by others, are for ever deprived of the enjoyment of light. It is not, [however], that the light has inflicted upon them the penalty of blindness, but it is that the blindness itself has brought calamity upon them: and therefore the Lord declared, "He that believeth in me is not condemned,"[1] that is, is not separated from God, for he is united to God through faith. On the other hand, He says, "He that believeth not is condemned already, because he has not believed in the name of the only-begotten Son of God;" that is, he separated himself from God of his own accord. "For this is the condemnation, that light is come into this world, and men have loved darkness rather than light. For every one who doeth evil hateth the light, and cometh not to the light, lest his deeds should be reproved. But he that doeth truth cometh to the light, that his deeds may be made manifest, that he has wrought them in God."

CHAP. XXVIII.—*The distinction to be made between the righteous and the wicked. The future apostasy in the time of Antichrist, and the end of the world.*

1. Inasmuch, then, as in this world (αἰῶνι) some persons betake themselves to the light, and by faith unite themselves with God, but others shun the light, and separate themselves from God, the Word of God comes preparing a fit habitation for both. For those indeed who are in the light, that they may derive enjoyment from it, and from the good things contained in it; but for those in darkness, that they may partake in its calamities. And on this account He says, that those upon the right hand are called into the kingdom of heaven, but that those on the left He will send into eternal fire; for they have deprived themselves of all good.

2. And for this reason the apostle says: "Because they

[1] John iii. 18, 21.

received not the love of God, that they might be saved, therefore God shall also send them the operation of error, that they may believe a lie, that they all may be judged who have not believed the truth, but consented to unrighteousness."[1] For when he (Antichrist) is come, and of his own accord concentrates in his own person the apostasy, and accomplishes whatever he shall do according to his own will and choice, sitting also in the temple of God, so that his dupes may adore him as the Christ; wherefore also shall he deservedly "be cast into the lake of fire:"[2] [this will happen according to divine appointment], God by His prescience foreseeing all this, and at the proper time sending such a man, "that they may believe a lie, that they all may be judged who did not believe the truth, but consented to unrighteousness;" whose coming John has thus described in the Apocalypse: "And the beast which I had seen was like unto a leopard, and his feet as of a bear, and his mouth as the mouth of a lion; and the dragon conferred his own power upon him, and his throne, and great might. And one of his heads was as it were slain unto death; and his deadly wound was healed, and all the world wondered after the beast. And they worshipped the dragon because he gave power to the beast; and they worshipped the beast, saying, Who is like unto this beast, and who is able to make war with him? And there was given unto him a mouth speaking great things, and blasphemy and power was given to him during forty and two months. And he opened his mouth for blasphemy against God, to blaspheme His name and His tabernacle, and those who dwell in heaven. And power was given him over every tribe, and people, and tongue, and nation. And all who dwell upon the earth worshipped him, [every one] whose name was not written in the book of the Lamb slain from the foundation of the world. If any one have ears, let him hear. If any one shall lead into captivity, he shall go into captivity. If any shall slay with the sword, he must be slain with the sword. Here is the endurance and the faith of the saints."[3] After this he likewise describes his armour-bearer, whom he

[1] 2 Thess. ii. 10-12. [2] Rev. xix. 20. [3] Rev. xiii. 2, etc.

also terms a false prophet: "He spake as a dragon, and exercised all the power of the first beast in his sight, and caused the earth, and those that dwell therein, to adore the first beast, whose deadly wound was healed. And he shall perform great wonders, so that he can even cause fire to descend from heaven upon the earth in the sight of men, and he shall lead the inhabitants of the earth astray."[1] Let no one imagine that he performs these wonders by divine power, but by the working of magic. And we must not be surprised if, since the demons and apostate spirits are at his service, he through their means performs wonders, by which he leads the inhabitants of the earth astray. John says further: "And he shall order an image of the beast to be made, and he shall give breath to the image, so that the image shall speak; and he shall cause those to be slain who will not adore it." He says also: "And he will cause a mark [to be put] in the forehead and in the right hand, that no one may be able to buy or sell, unless he who has the mark of the name of the beast or the number of his name; and the number is six hundred and sixty-six,"[2] that is, six times a hundred, six times ten, and six units. [He gives this] as a summing up of the whole of that apostasy which has taken place during six thousand years.

3. For in as many days as this world was made, in so many thousand years shall it be concluded. And for this reason the Scripture says: "Thus the heaven and the earth were finished, and all their adornment. And God brought to a conclusion upon the sixth day the works that He had made; and God rested upon the seventh day from all His works."[3] This is an account of the things formerly created, as also it is a prophecy of what is to come. For the day of the Lord is as a thousand years;[4] and in six days created things were completed: it is evident, therefore, that they will come to an end at the sixth thousand year.

4. And therefore throughout all time, man, having been moulded at the beginning by the hands of God, that is, of

[1] Rev. xiii. 11, etc.
[2] Rev. xiii. 14, etc.
[3] Gen. ii. 2.
[4] 2 Pet. iii. 8.

the Son and of the Spirit, is made after the image and likeness of God: the chaff, indeed, which is the apostasy, being cast away; but the wheat, that is, those who bring forth fruit to God in faith, being gathered into the barn. And for this cause tribulation is necessary for those who are saved, that having been after a manner broken up, and rendered fine, and sprinkled over by the patience of the Word of God, and set on fire [for purification], they may be fitted for the royal banquet. As a certain man of ours said, when he was condemned to the wild beasts because of his testimony with respect to God: "I am the wheat of Christ, and am ground by the teeth of the wild beasts, that I may be found the pure bread of God."[1]

CHAP. XXIX.—*All things have been created for the service of man. The deceits, wickedness, and apostate power of Antichrist. This was prefigured at the deluge, as afterwards by the persecution of Shadrach, Meshach, and Abednego.*

1. In the previous books I have set forth the causes for which God permitted these things to be made, and have pointed out that all such have been created for the benefit of that human nature which is saved, ripening for immortality that which is [possessed] of its own free will and its own power, and preparing and rendering it more adapted for eternal subjection to God. And therefore the creation is suited to [the wants of] man; for man was not made for its sake, but creation for the sake of man. Those nations, however, who did not of themselves raise up their eyes unto heaven, nor returned thanks to their Maker, nor wished to behold the light of truth, but who were like blind mice concealed in the depths of ignorance, the word justly reckons

[1] This is quoted from the Epistle of Ignatius to the Romans, ch. iv. It is found in the two Greek recensions of his works, and also in the Syriac. See vol. i. pp. 212 and 282 of this series. The Latin translation is here followed: the Greek of Ignatius would give "the wheat of God," and omits "of God" towards the end, as quoted by Eusebius.

"as waste water from a sink, and as the turning-weight of a balance—in fact, as nothing;"[1] so far useful and serviceable to the just, as stubble conduces towards the growth of the wheat, and its straw, by means of combustion, serves for working gold. And therefore, when in the end the church shall be suddenly caught up from this, it is said, "There shall be tribulation such as has not been since the beginning, neither shall be."[2] For this is the last contest of the righteous, in which, when they overcome, they are crowned with incorruption.

2. And there is therefore in this beast, when he comes, a recapitulation made of all sorts of iniquity and of every deceit, in order that all apostate power, flowing into and being shut up in him, may be sent into the furnace of fire. Fittingly, therefore, shall his name possess the number six hundred and sixty-six, since he sums up in his own person all the commixture of wickedness which took place previous to the deluge, due to the apostasy of the angels. For Noah was six hundred years old when the deluge came upon the earth, sweeping away the rebellious world, for the sake of that most infamous generation which lived in the times of Noah. And [Antichrist] also sums up every error of devised idols since the flood, together with the slaying of the prophets and the cutting off of the just. For that image which was set up by Nebuchadnezzar had indeed a height of sixty cubits, while the breadth was six cubits; on account of which Ananias, Azarias, and Misaël, when they did not worship it, were cast into a furnace of fire, pointing out prophetically, by what happened to them, the wrath against the righteous which shall arise towards the [time of the] end. For that image, taken as a whole, was a prefiguring of this man's coming, decreeing that he should undoubtedly himself alone be worshipped by all men. Thus, then, the six hundred years of Noah, in whose time the deluge occurred because of the apostasy, and the number of the cubits of the image for which these just men were sent into the fiery furnace, do indicate the number of the name of that man in whom is concen-

[1] Isa. xl. 15.   [2] Matt. xxiv. 21.

Book v.]   IRENÆUS AGAINST HERESIES.   135

trated the whole apostasy of six thousand years, and unrighteousness, and wickedness, and false prophecy, and deception; for which things' sake a cataclysm of fire shall also come [upon the earth].

CHAP. XXX.—*Although certain as to the number of the name of Antichrist, yet we should come to no rash conclusions as to the name itself, because this number is capable of being fitted to many names. Reasons for this point being reserved by the Holy Spirit. Antichrist's reign and death.*

1. Such, then, being the state of the case, and this number being found in all the most approved and ancient copies[1] [of the Apocalypse], and those men who saw John face to face bearing their testimony [to it]; while reason also leads us to conclude that the number of the name of the beast, [if reckoned] according to the Greek mode of calculation by the [value of] the letters contained in it, will amount to six hundred and sixty and six; that is, the number of tens shall be equal to that of the hundreds, and the number of hundreds equal to that of the units (for that number which [expresses] the digit six being adhered to throughout, indicates the recapitulations of that apostasy, taken in its full extent, which occurred at the beginning, during the intermediate periods, and which shall take place at the end),—I do not know how it is that some have erred following the ordinary mode of speech, and have vitiated the middle number in the name, deducting the amount of fifty from it, so that instead of six decads they will have it that there is but one. [I am inclined to think that this occurred through the fault of the copyists, as is wont to happen, since numbers also are expressed by letters; so that the Greek letter which expresses the number sixty was easily expanded into the letter Iota of the

[1] ἐν πᾶσι τοῖς σπουδαίοις καὶ ἀρχαίοις ἀντιγράφοις. This passage is interesting, as showing how very soon the autographs of the New Testament must have perished, and various readings crept into the MSS. of the canonical books.

Greeks.]¹ Others then received this reading without examination; some in their simplicity, and upon their own responsibility, making use of this number expressing one decad; while some, in their inexperience, have ventured to seek out a name which should contain the erroneous and spurious number. Now, as regards those who have done this in simplicity, and without evil intent, we are at liberty to assume that pardon will be granted them by God. But as for those who, for the sake of vainglory, lay it down for certain that names containing the spurious number are to be accepted, and affirm that this name, hit upon by themselves, is that of him who is to come; such persons shall not come forth without loss, because they have led into error both themselves and those who confided in them. Now, in the first place, it is loss to wander from the truth, and to imagine that as being the case which is not; then again, as there shall be no light punishment [inflicted] upon him who either adds or subtracts anything from the Scripture,² under that such a person must necessarily fall. Moreover, another danger, by no means trifling, shall overtake those who falsely presume that they know the name of Antichrist. For if these men assume one [number], when this [Antichrist] shall come having another, they will be easily led away by him, as supposing him not to be the expected one, who must be guarded against.

2. These men, therefore, ought to learn [what really is the state of the case], and go back to the true number of the name, that they be not reckoned among false prophets. But, knowing the sure number declared by Scripture, that is, six hundred sixty and six, let them await, in the first place, the division of the kingdom into ten; then, in the next place, when these kings are reigning, and beginning to set their affairs in order, and advance their kingdom, [let them learn] to acknowledge that he who shall come claiming the kingdom for himself, and shall terrify those men of whom we

---

¹ That is, Ζ into ΕΙ, according to Harvey, who considers the whole of this clause as an evident interpolation. It does not occur in the Greek here preserved by Eusebius (*Hist. Eccl.* v. 8).

² Rev. xxii. 19.

have been speaking, having a name containing the aforesaid number, is truly the abomination of desolation. This, too, the apostle affirms: "When they shall say, Peace and safety, then sudden destruction shall come upon them."[1] And Jeremiah does not merely point out his sudden coming, but he even indicates the tribe from which he shall come, where he says, "We shall hear the voice of his swift horses from Dan; the whole earth shall be moved by the voice of the neighing of his galloping horses: he shall also come and devour the earth, and the fulness thereof, the city also, and they that dwell therein."[2] This, too, is the reason that this tribe is not reckoned in the Apocalypse along with those which are saved.[3]

3. It is therefore more certain, and less hazardous, to await the fulfilment of the prophecy, than to be making surmises, and casting about for any names that may present themselves, inasmuch as many names can be found possessing the number mentioned; and the same question will, after all, remain unsolved. For if there are many names found possessing this number, it will be asked which among them shall the coming man bear. It is not through a want of names containing the number of that name that I say this, but on account of the fear of God, and zeal for the truth: for the name *Evanthas* (*ΕΥΑΝΘΑΣ*) contains the required number, but I make no allegation regarding it. Then also *Lateinos* (*ΛΑΤΕΙΝΟΣ*) has the number six hundred and sixty-six; and it is a very probable [solution], this being the name of the last kingdom [of the four seen by Daniel]. For the Latins are they who at present bear rule: I will not, however, make any boast over this [coincidence]. *Teitan* too, (*ΤΕΙΤΑΝ*, the first syllable being written with the two Greek vowels ε and ι), among all the names which are found among us, is rather worthy of credit. For it has in itself the predicted number, and is composed of six letters, each syllable containing three letters; and [the word itself] is ancient, and removed from ordinary use; for among our kings we find none bearing this name Titan, nor have any of the idols which are worshipped in public among the Greeks and bar-

---

[1] 1 Thess. v. 3.   [2] Jer. viii. 16.   [3] Rev. vii. 5–7.

barians this appellation. Among many persons, too, this name is accounted divine, so that even the sun is termed "Titan" by those who do now possess [the rule]. This word, too, contains a certain outward appearance of vengeance, and of one inflicting merited punishment because he (Antichrist) pretends that he vindicates the oppressed.[1] And besides this, it is an ancient name, one worthy of credit, of royal dignity, and still further, a name belonging to a tyrant. Inasmuch, then, as this name "Titan" has so much to recommend it, there is a strong degree of probability, that from among the many [names suggested], we infer, that perchance he who is to come shall be called "Titan." We will not, however, incur the risk of pronouncing positively as to the name of Antichrist; for if it were necessary that his name should be distinctly revealed in this present time, it would have been announced by him who beheld the apocalyptic vision. For that was seen no very long time since, but almost in our day, towards the end of Domitian's reign.

4. But he indicates the number of the name now, that when this man comes we may avoid him, being aware who he is: the name, however, is suppressed, because it is not worthy of being proclaimed by the Holy Spirit. For if it had been declared by Him, he (Antichrist) might perhaps continue for a long period. But now as "he was, and is not, and shall ascend out of the abyss, and goes into perdition,"[2] as one who has no existence; so neither has his name been declared, for the name of that which does not exist is not proclaimed. But when this Antichrist shall have devastated all things in this world, he will reign for three years and six months, and sit in the temple at Jerusalem; and then the Lord will come from heaven in the clouds, in the glory of the Father, sending this man and those who follow him into the lake of fire; but bringing in for the righteous the times of the kingdom, that is, the rest, the hallowed seventh day;

---

[1] Massuet here quotes Cicero and Ovid in proof of the sun being termed *Titan*. The Titans waged war against the gods, to avenge themselves upon Saturn.

[2] Rev. xvii. 8.

and restoring to Abraham the promised inheritance, in which kingdom the Lord declared, that "many coming from the east and from the west should sit down with Abraham, Isaac, and Jacob."[1]

CHAP. XXXI.—*The preservation of our bodies is confirmed by the resurrection and ascension of Christ: the souls of the saints during the intermediate period are in a state of expectation of that time when they shall receive their perfect and consummated glory.*

1. Since, again, some who are reckoned among the orthodox go beyond the pre-arranged plan for the exaltation of the just, and are ignorant of the methods by which they are disciplined beforehand for incorruption, they thus entertain heretical opinions. For the heretics, despising the handiwork of God, and not admitting the salvation of their flesh, while they also treat the promise of God contemptuously, and pass beyond God altogether in the sentiments they form, affirm that immediately upon their death they shall pass above the heavens and the Demiurge, and go to the Mother (Achamoth) or to that Father whom they have feigned. Those persons, therefore, who disallow a resurrection affecting the whole man (*universam reprobant resurrectionem*), and as far as in them lies remove it from the midst [of the Christian scheme], how can they be wondered at, if again they know nothing as to the plan of the resurrection? For they do not choose to understand, that if these things are as they say, the Lord Himself, in whom they profess to believe, did not rise again upon the third day; but immediately upon His expiring on the cross, undoubtedly departed on high, leaving His body to the earth. But the case was, that for three days He dwelt in the place where the dead were, as the prophet says concerning Him: "And the Lord remembered His dead saints who slept formerly in the land of sepulture; and He descended to them, to rescue and save them."[2] And the Lord Himself says, "As Jonas re-

[1] Matt. viii. 11.   [2] See Book iii. 20, 4.

mained three days and three nights in the whale's belly, so shall the Son of man be in the heart of the earth."[1] Then also the apostle says, "But when He ascended, what is it but that He also descended into the lower parts of the earth?"[2] This, too, David says when prophesying of Him, "And Thou hast delivered my soul from the nethermost hell;"[3] and on His rising again the third day, He said to Mary, who was the first to see and to worship Him, "Touch me not, for I have not yet ascended to the Father; but go to the disciples, and say unto them, I ascend unto my Father, and unto your Father."[4]

2. If, then, the Lord observed the law of the dead, that He might become the first-begotten from the dead, and tarried until the third day "in the lower parts of the earth;"[5] then afterwards rising in the flesh, so that He even showed the print of the nails to His disciples,[6] He thus ascended to the Father;—[if all these things occurred, I say], how must these men not be put to confusion, who allege that "the lower parts" refer to this world of ours, but that their inner man, leaving the body here, ascends into the super-celestial place? For as the Lord "went away in the midst of the shadow of death,"[7] where the souls of the dead were, yet afterwards arose in the body, and after the resurrection was taken up [into heaven], it is manifest that the souls of His disciples also, upon whose account the Lord underwent these things, shall go away into the invisible place allotted to them by God, and there remain until the resurrection, awaiting that event; then receiving their bodies, and rising in their entirety, that is bodily, just as the Lord arose, they shall come thus into the presence of God. "For no disciple is above the Master, but every one that is perfect shall be as his Master."[8] As our Master, therefore, did not at once depart, taking flight [to heaven], but awaited the time of His resurrection prescribed by the Father, which had been also shown forth through Jonas, and rising again after three days

[1] Matt. xi. 40. [2] Eph. iv. 9. [3] Ps. lxxxvi. 23.
[4] John xx. 17. [5] Eph. iv. 9. [6] John xx. 20, 27.
[7] Ps. xxiii. 4. [8] Luke vi. 40.

was taken up [to heaven]; so ought we also to await the time of our resurrection prescribed by God and foretold by the prophets, and so, rising, be taken up, as many as the Lord shall account worthy of this [privilege].[1]

CHAP. XXXII.—*In that flesh in which the saints have suffered so many afflictions, they shall receive the fruits of their labours; especially since all creation waits for this, and God promises it to Abraham and his seed.*

Inasmuch, therefore, as the opinions of certain [orthodox persons] are derived from heretical discourses, they are both ignorant of God's dispensations, and of the mystery of the resurrection of the just, and of the [earthly] kingdom which is the commencement of incorruption, by means of which kingdom those who shall be worthy are accustomed gradually to partake of the divine nature (*capere Deum*[2]); and it is necessary to tell them respecting those things, that it behoves the righteous first to receive the promise of the inheritance which God promised to the fathers, and to reign in it, when they rise again to behold God in this creation which is renovated, and that the judgment should take place afterwards. For it is just that in that very creation in which they toiled or were afflicted, being proved in every way by suffering, they should receive the reward of their suffering; and that in the creation in which they were slain because of their love to God, in that they should be revived again; and that in the creation in which they endured servitude, in that they should reign. For God is rich in all things, and all things are His. It is fitting, therefore, that the creation itself, being restored to its primeval condition, should without restraint be

---

[1] The five following chapters were omitted in the earlier editions, but added by Feuardentius. Most MSS., too, did not contain them. It is probable that the scribes of the middle ages rejected them on account of their inculcating millenarian notions, which had been long extinct in the church. Quotations from these five chapters have been collected by Harvey from Syriac and Armenian MSS. lately come to light.

[2] Or, "gradually to comprehend God."

under the dominion of the righteous; and the apostle has made this plain in the Epistle to the Romans, when he thus speaks: "For the expectation of the creature waiteth for the manifestation of the sons of God. For the creature has been subjected to vanity, not willingly, but by reason of him who hath subjected the same in hope; since the creature itself shall also be delivered from the bondage of corruption into the glorious liberty of the sons of God."[1]

2. Thus, then, the promise of God, which He gave to Abraham, remains stedfast. For thus He said: "Lift up thine eyes, and look from this place where now thou art, towards the north and south, and east and west. For all the earth which thou seest, I will give to thee and to thy seed, even for ever."[2] And again He says, "Arise, and go through the length and breadth of the land, since I will give it unto thee;"[3] and [yet] he did not receive an inheritance in it, not even a footstep, but was always a stranger and a pilgrim therein.[4] And upon the death of Sarah his wife, when the Hittites were willing to bestow upon him a place where he might bury her, he declined it as a gift, but bought the burying-place (giving for it four hundred talents of silver) from Ephron the son of Zohar the Hittite.[5] Thus did he await patiently the promise of God, and was unwilling to appear to receive from men, what God had promised to give him, when He said again to him as follows: "I will give this land to thy seed, from the river of Egypt even unto the great river Euphrates."[6] If, then, God promised him the inheritance of the land, yet he did not receive it during all the time of his sojourn there, it must be, that together with his seed, that is, those who fear God and believe in Him, he shall receive it at the resurrection of the just. For his seed is the church, which receives the adoption to God through the Lord, as John the Baptist said: "For God is able from the stones to raise up children to Abraham."[7] Thus also the apostle says in the Epistle to the Galatians: "But ye,

---

[1] Rom. viii. 19, etc.   [2] Gen. xiii. 13, 14.   [3] Gen. xiii. 17.
[4] Acts vii. 5; Heb. xi. 13.   [5] Gen. xxiii. 11.   [6] Gen. xv. 13.
[7] Luke iii. 8.

brethren, as Isaac was, are the children of the promise."[1] And again, in the same epistle, he plainly declares that they who have believed in Christ do receive Christ, the promise to Abraham thus saying, "The promises were spoken to Abraham, and to his seed. Now He does not say, And of seeds, as if [He spake] of many, but as of one, And to thy seed, which is Christ."[2] And again, confirming his former words, he says, "Even as Abraham believed God, and it was accounted to him for righteousness. Know ye therefore, that they which are of faith are the children of Abraham. But the Scripture, foreseeing that God would justify the heathen through faith, declared to Abraham beforehand, That in thee shall all nations be blessed. So then they which are of faith shall be blessed with faithful Abraham."[3] Thus, then, they who are of faith shall be blessed with faithful Abraham, and these are the children of Abraham. Now God made promise of the earth to Abraham and his seed; yet neither Abraham nor his seed, that is, those who are justified by faith, do now receive any inheritance in it; but they shall receive it at the resurrection of the just. For God is true and faithful; and on this account He said, "Blessed are the meek, for they shall inherit the earth."[4]

CHAP. XXXIII.—*Further proofs of the same proposition, drawn from the promises made by Christ, when He declared that He would drink of the fruit of the vine with His disciples in His Father's kingdom, while at the same time He promised to reward them an hundred-fold, and to make them partake of banquets. The blessing pronounced by Jacob had pointed out this already, as Papias and the elders have interpreted it.*

1. For this reason, when about to undergo His sufferings, that He might declare to Abraham and those with him the glad tidings of the inheritance being thrown open, [Christ], after He had given thanks while holding the cup, and had

[1] Gal. iv. 28. [2] Gal. iii. 16.
[3] Gal. iii. 6, etc. [4] Matt. v. 5.

drunk of it, and given it to the disciples, said to them: "Drink ye all of it: this is my blood of the new covenant, which shall be shed for many for the remission of sins. But I say unto you, I will not drink henceforth of the fruit of this vine, until that day when I will drink it new with you in my Father's kingdom."[1] Thus, then, He will Himself renew the inheritance of the earth, and will re-organize the mystery of the glory of [His] sons; as David says, "He who hath renewed the face of the earth."[2] He promised to drink of the fruit of the vine with His disciples, thus indicating both these points: the inheritance of the earth in which the new fruit of the vine is drunk, and the resurrection of His disciples in the flesh. For the new flesh which rises again is the same which also received the new cup. And He cannot by any means be understood as drinking of the fruit of the vine when settled down with His [disciples] above in a super-celestial place; nor, again, are they who drink it devoid of flesh, for to drink of that which flows from the vine pertains to flesh, and not spirit.

2. And for this reason the Lord declared, " When thou makest a dinner or a supper, do not call thy friends, nor thy neighbours, nor thy kinsfolk, lest they ask thee in return, and so repay thee. But call the lame, the blind, and the poor, and thou shalt be blessed, since they cannot recompense thee, but a recompense shall be made thee at the resurrection of the just."[3] And again He says, "Whosoever shall have left lands, or houses, or parents, or brethren, or children because of me, he shall receive in this world an hundred-fold, and in that to come he shall inherit eternal life."[4] For what are the hundred-fold [rewards] in this world, the entertainments given to the poor, and the suppers for which a return is made? These are [to take place] in the times of the kingdom, that is, upon the seventh day, which has been sanctified, in which God rested from all the works which He created, which is the true Sabbath of the righteous, in which they shall not be engaged in any earthly occupation; but

[1] Matt. xxvi. 27.
[2] Ps. civ. 30.
[3] Luke xiv. 12, 13.
[4] Matt. xix. 29 ; Luke xviii. 29, 30.

shall have a table at hand prepared for them by God, supplying them with all sorts of dishes.

3. The blessing of Isaac with which he blessed his younger son Jacob has the same meaning, when he says, "Behold, the smell of my son is as the smell of a full field which the Lord has blessed."[1] But "the field is the world."[2] And therefore he added, "God give to thee of the dew of heaven, and of the fatness of the earth, plenty of corn and wine. And let the nations serve thee, and kings bow down to thee; and be thou lord over thy brother, and thy father's sons shall bow down to thee: cursed shall be he who shall curse thee, and blessed shall be he who shall bless thee."[3] If any one, then, does not accept these things as referring to the appointed kingdom, he must fall into much contradiction and contrariety, as is the case with the Jews, who are involved in absolute perplexity. For not only did not the nations in this life serve this Jacob; but even after he had received the blessing, he himself going forth [from his home], served his uncle Laban the Syrian for twenty years;[4] and not only was he not made lord of his brother, but he did himself bow down before his brother Esau, upon his return from Mesopotamia to his father, and offered many gifts to him.[5] Moreover, in what way did he inherit much corn and wine here, he who emigrated to Egypt because of the famine which possessed the land in which he was dwelling, and became subject to Pharaoh, who was then ruling over Egypt? The predicted blessing, therefore, belongs unquestionably to the times of the kingdom, when the righteous shall bear rule upon their rising from the dead;[6] when also the creation, having been renovated and set free, shall fructify with an abundance of all kinds of food, from the dew of heaven, and from the fertility of the earth: as the elders who saw John,

---

[1] Gen. xxvii. 27, etc. [2] Matt. xiii. 38. [3] Gen. xxvii. 28, 29.
[4] Gen. xxxi. 41. [5] Gen. xxxiii. 3.
[6] From this to the end of the section there is an Armenian version extant, to be found in the *Spicil. Solesm.* i. p. 1, edited by M. Pitra, Paris 1852, and which was taken by him from an Armenian MS. in the Mechitarist Library at Venice, described as being of the twelfth century.

the disciple of the Lord, related that they had heard from him how the Lord used to teach in regard to these times, and say: The days will come, in which vines shall grow, each having ten thousand branches, and in each branch ten thousand twigs, and in each true[1] twig ten thousand shoots, and in each one of the shoots ten thousand clusters, and on every one of the clusters ten thousand grapes, and every grape when pressed will give five and twenty metretes of wine. And when any one of the saints shall lay hold of a cluster,[2] another shall cry out, "I am a better cluster, take me; bless the Lord through me." In like manner [the Lord declared] that a grain of wheat would produce ten thousand ears, and that every ear should have ten thousand grains, and every grain would yield ten pounds (*quinque bilibres*) of clear, pure, fine flour; and that all other fruit-bearing trees,[3] and seeds and grass, would produce in similar proportions (*secundum congruentiam iis consequentem*); and that all animals feeding [only] on the productions of the earth, should [in those days] become peaceful and harmonious among each other, and be in perfect subjection to man.

4. And these things are borne witness to in writing by Papias, the hearer of John, and a companion of Polycarp, in his fourth book; for there were five books compiled (συντεταγμένα) by him. And he says in addition, "Now these things are credible to believers." And he says that, "when the traitor Judas did not give credit to them, and put the question, 'How then can things about to bring forth so abundantly be wrought by the Lord?' the Lord declared, 'They who shall come to these [times] shall see.'" When prophesying of these times, therefore, Esaias says: "The wolf also shall feed with the lamb, and the leopard shall take his rest with the kid; the calf also, and the bull, and the lion shall eat together; and a little boy shall lead them. The ox

---

[1] This word "true" is not found in the Armenian.

[2] Or, following Arm. vers., "But if any one shall lay hold of an holy cluster."

[3] The Arm. vers. is here followed; the old Latin reads, "Et reliqua autem poma."

and the bear shall feed together, and their young ones shall agree together; and the lion shall eat straw as well as the ox. And the infant boy shall thrust his hand into the asp's den, into the nest also of the adder's brood; and they shall do no harm, nor have power to hurt anything in my holy mountain." And again he says, in recapitulation, "Wolves and lambs shall then browse together, and the lion shall eat straw like the ox, and the serpent earth as if it were bread; and they shall neither hurt nor annoy anything in my holy mountain, saith the Lord."[1] I am quite aware that some persons endeavour to refer these words to the case of savage men, both of different nations and various habits, who come to believe, and when they have believed, act in harmony with the righteous. But although this is [true] now with regard to some men coming from various nations to the harmony of the faith, nevertheless in the resurrection of the just [the words shall also apply] to those animals mentioned. For God is rich in all things. And it is right that when the creation is restored, all the animals should obey and be in subjection to man, and revert to the food originally given by God (for they had been originally subjected in obedience to Adam), that is, the productions of the earth. But some other occasion, and not the present, is [to be sought] for showing that the lion shall [then] feed on straw. And this indicates the large size and rich quality of the fruits. For if that animal, the lion, feeds upon straw [at that period], of what a quality must the wheat itself be whose straw shall serve as suitable food for lions?

CHAP. XXXIV.—*He fortifies his opinions with regard to the temporal and earthly kingdom of the saints after their resurrection, by the various testimonies of Isaiah, Ezekiel, Jeremiah, and Daniel; also by the parable of the servants watching, to whom the Lord promised that He would minister.*

1. Then, too, Isaiah himself has plainly declared that there

[1] Isa. xl. 6, etc.

shall be joy of this nature at the resurrection of the just, when he says: "The dead shall rise again; those, too, who are in the tombs shall arise, and those who are in the earth shall rejoice. For the dew from Thee is health to them."[1] And this again Ezekiel also says: "Behold, I will open your tombs, and will bring you forth out of your graves; when I will draw my people from the sepulchres, and I will put breath in you, and ye shall live; and I will place you on your own land, and ye shall know that I am the Lord."[2] And again the same speaks thus: "These things, saith the Lord, I will gather Israel from all nations whither they have been driven, and I shall be sanctified in them in the sight of the sons of the nations: and they shall dwell in their own land, which I gave to my servant Jacob. And they shall dwell in it in peace; and they shall build houses, and plant vineyards, and dwell in hope, when I shall cause judgment to fall among all who have dishonoured them, among those who encircle them round about; and they shall know that I am the Lord their God, and the God of their fathers."[3] Now I have shown a short time ago that the church is the seed of Abraham; and for this reason, that we may know that He who in the New Testament "raises up from the stones children unto Abraham,"[4] is He who will gather, according to the Old Testament, those that shall be saved from all the nations, Jeremiah says: "Behold, the days come, saith the Lord, that they shall no more say, The Lord liveth, who led the children of Israel from the north, and from every region whither they had been driven; He will restore them to their own land which He gave to their fathers."[5]

2. That the whole creation shall, according to God's will, obtain a vast increase, that it may bring forth and sustain fruits such [as we have mentioned], Isaiah declares: "And there shall be upon every high mountain, and upon every prominent hill, water running everywhere in that day, when many shall perish, when walls shall fall. And the light of

[1] Isa. xxvi. 19.   [2] Ezek. xxxvii. 12, etc.   [3] Ezek. xxviii. 25, 26.
[4] Matt. iii. 9.   [5] Jer. xxiii. 7, 6.

the moon shall be as the light of the sun, seven times that of the day, when He shall heal the anguish of His people, and do away with the pain of His stroke."[1] Now "the pain of the stroke" means that inflicted at the beginning upon disobedient man in Adam, that is, death; which [stroke] the Lord will heal when He raises us from the dead, and restores the inheritance of the fathers, as Isaiah again says: "And thou shalt be confident in the Lord, and He will cause thee to pass over the whole earth, and feed thee with the inheritance of Jacob thy father."[2] This is what the Lord declared: "Happy are those servants whom the Lord when He cometh shall find watching. Verily I say unto you, that He shall gird Himself, and make them to sit down [to meat], and will come forth and serve them. And if He shall come in the evening watch, and find them so, blessed are they, because He shall make them sit down, and minister to them; or if this be in the second, or it be in the third, blessed are they."[3] Again John also says the very same in the Apocalypse: "Blessed and holy is he who has part in the first resurrection."[4] Then, too, Isaiah has declared the time when these events shall occur; he says: "And I said, Lord, how long? Until the cities be wasted without inhabitant, and the houses be without men, and the earth be left a desert. And after these things the Lord shall remove us men far away (*longe nos faciet Deus homines*), and those who shall remain shall multiply upon the earth."[5] Then Daniel also says this very thing: "And the kingdom and dominion, and the greatness of those under the heaven, is given to the saints of the Most High God, whose kingdom is everlasting, and all dominions shall serve and obey Him."[6] And lest the promise named should be understood as referring to this time, it was declared to the prophet: "And come thou, and stand in thy lot at the consummation of the days."[7]

3. Now, that the promises were not announced to the prophets and the fathers alone, but to the churches united

---

[1] Isa. xxx. 25, 26. [2] Isa. lviii. 14. [3] Luke xii. 37, 38.
[4] Rev. xx. 6. [5] Isa. vi. 11. [6] Dan. vii. 27.
[7] Dan. xii. 13.

to these from the nations, whom also the Spirit terms "the islands" (both because they are established in the midst of turbulence, suffer the storm of blasphemies, exist as a harbour of safety to those in peril, and are the refuge of those who love the height [of heaven], and strive to avoid Bythus, that is, the depth of error), Jeremiah thus declares: "Hear the word of the Lord, ye nations, and declare it to the isles afar off; say ye, that the Lord will scatter Israel, He will gather him, and keep him, as one feeding his flock of sheep. For the Lord hath redeemed Jacob, and rescued him from the hand of one stronger than he. And they shall come and rejoice in Mount Zion, and shall come to what is good, and into a land of wheat, and wine, and fruits, of animals and of sheep; and their soul shall be as a tree bearing fruit, and they shall hunger no more. At that time also shall the virgins rejoice in the company of the young men: the old men, too, shall be glad, and I will turn their sorrow into joy; and I will make them exult, and will magnify them, and satiate the souls of the priests the sons of Levi; and my people shall be satiated with my goodness."[1] Now, in the preceding book[2] I have shown that all the disciples of the Lord are Levites and priests, they who used in the temple to profane the Sabbath, but are blameless.[3] Promises of such a nature, therefore, do indicate in the clearest manner the feasting of that creation in the kingdom of the righteous, which God promises that He will Himself serve.

4. Then again, speaking of Jerusalem, and of Him reigning there, Isaiah declares, "Thus saith the Lord, Happy is he who hath seed in Zion, and servants in Jerusalem. Behold, a righteous king shall reign, and princes shall rule with judgment."[4] And with regard to the foundation on which it shall be rebuilt, he says: "Behold, I will lay in order for thee a carbuncle stone, and sapphire for thy foundations; and I will lay thy ramparts with jasper, and thy gates with crystal, and thy wall with choice stones: and all thy children shall be taught of God, and great shall be the peace of thy

[1] Jer. xxxi. 10, etc.
[2] See iv. 8, 3.
[3] Matt. xii. 5.
[4] Isa. xxxi. 9, xxxii. 1.

children; and in righteousness shalt thou be built up."¹ And yet again does he say the same thing: "Behold, I make Jerusalem a rejoicing, and my people [a joy]; for the voice of weeping shall be no more heard in her, nor the voice of crying. Also there shall not be there any immature [one], nor an old man who does not fulfil his time: for the youth shall be of a hundred years; and the sinner shall die a hundred years old, yet shall be accursed. And they shall build houses, and inhabit them themselves; and shall plant vineyards, and eat the fruit of them themselves, and shall drink wine. And they shall not build, and others inhabit; neither shall they prepare the vineyard, and others eat. For as the days of the tree of life shall be the days of the people in thee; for the works of their hands shall endure."²

CHAP. XXXV.—*He contends that these testimonies already alleged cannot be understood allegorically of celestial blessings, but that they shall have their fulfilment after the coming of Antichrist, and the resurrection, in the terrestrial Jerusalem. To the former prophecies he subjoins others drawn from Isaiah, Jeremiah, and the Apocalypse of John.*

1. If, however, any shall endeavour to allegorize [prophecies] of this kind, they shall not be found consistent with themselves in all points, and shall be confuted by the teaching of the very expressions [in question]. For example: "When the cities" of the Gentiles "shall be desolate, so that they be not inhabited, and the houses so that there shall be no men in them, and the land shall be left desolate."³ "For, behold," says Isaiah, "the day of the Lord cometh past remedy, full of fury and wrath, to lay waste the city of the earth, and to root sinners out of it."⁴ And again he says, "Let him be taken away, that he behold not the glory of God."⁵ And when these things are done, he says, "God will remove men far away, and those that are left shall multiply

¹ Isa. liv. 11–14.   ² Isa. lxv. 18.   ³ Isa. vi. 11.
⁴ Isa. xiii. 9.   ⁵ Isa. xxvi. 10.

in the earth."[1] "And they shall build houses, and shall inhabit them themselves: and plant vineyards, and eat of them themselves."[2] For all these and other words were unquestionably spoken in reference to the resurrection of the just, which takes place after the coming of Antichrist, and the destruction of all nations under his rule; in [the times of] which [resurrection] the righteous shall reign in the earth, waxing stronger by the sight of the Lord: and through Him they shall become accustomed to partake in the glory of God the Father, and shall enjoy in the kingdom intercourse and communion with the holy angels, and union with spiritual beings; and [with respect to] those whom the Lord shall find in the flesh, awaiting Him from heaven, and who have suffered tribulation, as well as escaped the hands of the Wicked one. For it is in reference to them that the prophet says: "And those that are left shall multiply upon the earth." And Jeremiah[3] the prophet has pointed out, that as many believers as God has prepared for this purpose, to multiply those left upon earth, should both be under the rule of the saints to minister to this Jerusalem, and that [His] kingdom shall be in it, saying, "Look around Jerusalem towards the east, and behold the joy which comes to thee from God Himself. Behold, thy sons shall come whom thou hast sent forth: they shall come in a band from the east even unto the west, by the word of that Holy One, rejoicing in that splendour which is from thy God. O Jerusalem, put off thy robe of mourning and of affliction, and put on that beauty of eternal splendour from thy God. Gird thyself with the double garment of that righteousness proceeding from thy God; place the mitre of eternal glory upon thine head. For God will show thy glory to the whole earth under heaven. For thy name shall for ever be called by God Himself, the peace of righteousness and glory to him that worships God. Arise, Jerusalem, stand on high, and look towards the east, and behold thy sons from the

---

[1] Isa. vi. 12.   [2] Isa. lxv. 21

[3] The long quotation following is not found in Jeremiah, but in the apocryphal book of Baruch, chap. iv. 36, etc., and the whole of chap. v.

rising of the sun, even to the west, by the word of that Holy One, rejoicing in the very remembrance of God. For the footmen have gone forth from thee, while they were drawn away by the enemy. God shall bring them in to thee, being borne with glory as the throne of a kingdom. For God has decreed that every high mountain shall be brought low, and the eternal hills, and that the valleys be filled, so that the surface of the earth be rendered smooth, that Israel, the glory of God, may walk in safety. The woods, too, shall make shady places, and every sweet-smelling tree shall be for Israel itself by the command of God. For God shall go before with joy in the light of His splendour, with the pity and righteousness which proceeds from Him."

2. Now all these things being such as they are, cannot be understood in reference to super-celestial matters; " for God," it is said, " will show to the whole earth that is under heaven thy glory." But in the times of the kingdom, the earth has been called again by Christ [to its pristine condition], and Jerusalem rebuilt after the pattern of the Jerusalem above, of which the prophet Isaiah says, " Behold, I have depicted thy walls upon my hands, and thou art always in my sight."[1] And the apostle, too, writing to the Galatians, says in like manner, " But the Jerusalem which is above is free, which is the mother of us all."[2] He does not say this with any thought of an erratic Æon, or of any other power which departed from the Pleroma, or of Prunicus, but of the Jerusalem which has been delineated on [God's] hands. And in the Apocalypse John saw this new [Jerusalem] descending upon the new earth.[3] For after the times of the kingdom, he says, "I saw a great white throne, and Him who sat upon it, from whose face the earth fled away, and the heaven; and there was no more place for them."[4] And he sets forth, too, the things connected with the general resurrection and the judgment, mentioning " the dead, great and small." " The sea," he says, " gave up the dead which it had in it, and death and hell delivered up the dead that they contained; and the books were opened. Moreover," he

[1] Isa. xlix. 16. [2] Gal. iv. 26. [3] Rev. xxi. 2. [4] Rev. xx. 11.

says, "the book of life was opened, and the dead were judged out of those things that were written in the books, according to their works; and death and hell were sent into the lake of fire, the second death."[1] Now this is what is called Gehenna, which the Lord styled eternal fire.[2] "And if any one," it is said, "was not found written in the book of life, he was sent into the lake of fire."[3] And after this, he says, "I saw a new heaven and a new earth, for the first heaven and earth have passed away; also there was no more sea. And I saw the holy city, new Jerusalem, coming down from heaven, as a bride adorned for her husband." "And I heard," it is said, "a great voice from the throne, saying, Behold, the tabernacle of God is with men, and He will dwell with them; and they shall be His people, and God Himself shall be with them as their God. And He will wipe away every tear from their eyes; and death shall be no more, neither sorrow, nor crying, neither shall there be any more pain, because the former things have passed away."[4] Isaiah also declares the very same: "For there shall be a new heaven and a new earth; and there shall be no remembrance of the former, neither shall the heart think about them, but they shall find in it joy and exultation."[5] Now this is what has been said by the apostle: "For the fashion of this world passeth away."[6] To the same purpose did the Lord also declare, "Heaven and earth shall pass away."[7] When these things, therefore, pass away above the earth, John, the Lord's disciple, says that the new Jerusalem above shall [then] descend, as a bride adorned for her husband; and that this is the tabernacle of God, in which God will dwell with men. Of this Jerusalem the former one is an image—that Jerusalem of the former earth in which the righteous are disciplined beforehand for incorruption and prepared for salvation. And of this tabernacle Moses received the pattern in the mount;[8] and nothing is capable of being allegorized, but all things are stedfast, and true, and substantial, having

[1] Rev. xx. 12-14. [2] Matt. xxv. 41. [3] Rev. xx. 15.
[4] Rev. xxi. 1-4. [5] Isa. lxv. 17, 18. [6] 1 Cor. vii. 31.
[7] Matt. xxvi. 35. [8] Ex. xxv. 40.

been made by God for righteous men's enjoyment. For as it is God truly who raises up man, so also does man truly rise from the dead, and not allegorically, as I have shown repeatedly. And as he rises actually, so also shall he be actually disciplined beforehand for incorruption, and shall go forwards and flourish in the times of the kingdom, in order that he may be capable of receiving the glory of the Father. Then, when all things are made new, he shall truly dwell in the city of God. For it is said, "He that sitteth on the throne said, Behold, I make all things new. And the Lord says, Write all this; for these words are faithful and true. And He said to me, They are done."[1] And this is the truth of the matter.

CHAP. XXXVI.—*Men shall be actually raised: the world shall not be annihilated; but there shall be various mansions for the saints, according to the rank allotted to each individual. All things shall be subject to God the Father, and so shall He be all in all.*

1. For since there are real men, so must there also be a real establishment (*plantationem*), that they vanish not away among non-existent things, but progress among those which have an actual existence. For neither is the substance nor the essence of the creation annihilated (for faithful and true is He who has established it), but "the *fashion* of the world passeth away;"[2] that is, those things among which transgression has occurred, since man has grown old in them. And therefore this [present] fashion has been formed temporary, God foreknowing all things; as I have pointed out in the preceding book,[3] and have also shown, as far as was possible, the cause of the creation of this world of temporal things. But when this [present] fashion [of things] passes away, and man has been renewed, and flourishes in an incorruptible state, so as to preclude the possibility of becoming old, [then] there shall be the new heaven and the new earth, in which the new man shall remain [continually],

[1] Rev. xxi. 5, 6.   [2] 1 Cor. vii. 31.   [3] Lib. iv. 5, 6.

FRAGMENTS FROM THE LOST WRITINGS OF IRENÆUS.

I.

ADJURE thee, who shält transcribe this book,[1] by our Lord Jesus Christ, and by His glorious appearing, when He comes to judge the living and the dead, that thou compare what thou hast transcribed, and be careful to set it right according to this copy from which thou hast transcribed; also, that thou in like manner copy down this adjuration, and insert it in the transcript.

II.

These[2] opinions, Florinus, that I may speak in mild terms, are not of sound doctrine; these opinions are not consonant to the church, and involve their votaries in the utmost impiety; these opinions, even the heretics beyond the church's pale have never ventured to broach; these opinions, those presbyters who preceded us, and who were conversant with the apostles, did not hand down to thee. For, while I was yet a boy, I saw thee in Lower Asia with Polycarp, distinguishing thyself in the royal court,[3] and endeavouring to gain his approbation. For I have a more vivid recollection of what occurred at that time than of recent events (inas-

[1] This fragment is quoted by Eusebius, *Hist. Eccl.* v. 20. It occurred at the close of the lost treatise of Irenæus entitled *De Ogdoade*.

[2] This interesting extract we also owe to Eusebius, who (*ut sup.*) took it from the work *De Ogdoade*, written after this former friend of Irenæus had lapsed to Valentinianism. Florinus had previously held that God was the author of evil, which sentiment Irenæus opposed in a treatise, now lost, called περὶ μοναρχίας.

[3] Comp. vol. i. p. 476, and Phil. iv. 22.

much as the experiences of childhood, keeping pace with the growth of the soul, become incorporated with it); so that I can even describe the place where the blessed Polycarp used to sit and discourse—his going out, too, and his coming in—his general mode of life and personal appearance, together with the discourses which he delivered to the people; also how he would speak of his familiar intercourse with John, and with the rest of those who had seen the Lord; and how he would call their words to remembrance. Whatsoever things he had heard from them respecting the Lord, both with regard to His miracles and His teaching, Polycarp having thus received [information] from the eye-witnesses of the Word of life, would recount them all in harmony with the Scriptures. These things, through God's mercy which was upon me, I then listened to attentively, and treasured them up not on paper, but in my heart; and I am continually, by God's grace, revolving these things accurately in my mind. And I can bear witness before God, that if that blessed and apostolical presbyter had heard any such thing, he would have cried out, and stopped his ears, exclaiming as he was wont to do: "O good God, for what times hast Thou reserved me, that I should endure these things?" And he would have fled from the very spot where, sitting or standing, he had heard such words. This fact, too, can be made clear, from his epistles which he despatched, whether to the neighbouring churches to confirm them, or to certain of the brethren, admonishing and exhorting them.

III.

For[1] the controversy is not merely as regards the day, but

[1] See preface to vol. i. p. xviii. We are indebted again to Eusebius for this valuable fragment from the Epistle of Irenæus to Victor Bishop of Rome (*Hist. Eccl.* v. 24; copied also by Nicephorus, iv. 39). It appears to have been a synodical epistle to the head of the Roman church, the historian saying that it was written by Irenæus, "in the name of (ἐκ προσώπου) those brethren over whom he ruled throughout Gaul." Neither are these expressions to be limited to the church at Lyons, for the same authority records (v. 23) that it was the testimony "of the dioceses throughout Gaul, which Irenæus superintended" (Harvey).

also as regards the form itself of the fast.[1] For some consider themselves bound to fast one day, others two days, others still more, while others [do so during] forty: the diurnal and the nocturnal hours they measure out together as their [fasting] day.[2] And this variety among the observers [of the fasts] had not its origin in our time, but long before in that of our predecessors, some of whom probably, being not very accurate in their observance of it, handed down to posterity the custom as it had, through simplicity or private fancy, been [introduced among them]. And yet nevertheless all these lived in peace one with another, and we also keep peace together. Thus, in fact, the difference [in observing] the fast establishes the harmony of [our common] faith.[3] And the presbyters preceding Soter in the government of the church which thou dost now rule—I mean, Anicetus and Pius, Hyginus and Telesphorus, and Sixtus— did neither themselves observe it [after that fashion], nor permit those with them[4] to do so. Notwithstanding this, those who did not keep [the feast in this way] were peacefully disposed towards those who came to them from other dioceses in which it was [so] observed, although such observance was [felt] in more decided contrariety [as presented] to those who did not fall in with it; and none were ever cast out [of the church] for this matter. On the contrary, those presbyters who preceded thee, and who did not observe [this custom], sent the Eucharist to those of other dioceses who did observe it.[5] And when the blessed Polycarp was sojourning

---

[1] According to Harvey, the early paschal controversy resolved itself into two particulars: (*a*) as regards the precise day on which our Lord's resurrection should be celebrated; (*b*) as regards the custom of the fast preceding it.

[2] Both reading and punctuation are here subjects of controversy. We have followed Massuet and Harvey.

[3] "The observance of *a* day, though not everywhere the same, showed unity, so far as faith in the Lord's resurrection was concerned."—HARVEY.

[4] Following the reading of Rufinus, the ordinary text has μετ' αὐτούς, *i.e.* after them.

[5] This practice was afterwards forbidden by the Council of Laodicea, A.D. 320.

in Rome in the time of Anicetus, although a slight controversy had arisen among them as to certain other points, they were at once well inclined towards each other [with regard to the matter in hand], not willing that any quarrel should arise between them upon this head. For neither could Anicetus persuade Polycarp to forego the observance [in his own way], inasmuch as these things had been always [so] observed by John the disciple of our Lord, and by other apostles with whom he had been conversant; nor, on the other hand, could Polycarp succeed in persuading Anicetus to keep [the observance in his way], for he maintained that he was bound to adhere to the usage of the presbyters who preceded him. And in this state of affairs they held fellowship with each other; and Anicetus conceded to Polycarp in the church the celebration of the Eucharist, by way of showing him respect; so that they parted in peace one from the other, maintaining peace with the whole church, both those who did observe [this custom] and those who did not.[1]

IV.

As[2] long as any one has the means of doing good to his neighbours, and does not do so, he shall be reckoned à stranger to the love of the Lord.[3]

V.

The[4] will and the energy of God is the effective and foreseeing cause of every time and place and age, and of every

---

[1] It was perhaps in reference to this pleasing episode in the annals of the church, that the Council of Arles, A.D. 314, decreed that the holy Eucharist should be consecrated by any foreign bishop present at its celebration.
[2] Quoted by Maximus Bishop of Turin, A.D. 422, *Serm.* vii. *de Eleemos.*, as from the Epistle to Pope Victor. It is also found in some other ancient writers.
[3] One of the MSS. reads here τοῦ Θεοῦ, of God.
[4] Also quoted by Maximus Turinensis, *Op.* ii. 152, who refers it to Irenæus' *Sermo de Fide*, which work, not being referred to by Eusebius or Jerome, causes Massuet to doubt the authenticity of the fragment. Harvey, however, accepts it.

nature. The will is the reason (λόγος) of the intellectual soul, which [reason] is within us, inasmuch as it is the faculty belonging to it which is endowed with freedom of action. The will is the mind desiring [some object], and an appetite possessed of intelligence, yearning after that thing which is desired.

VI.

Since[1] God is vast, and the Architect of the world, and omnipotent, He created things that reach to immensity both by the Architect of the world and by an omnipotent will, and with a new effect, potently and efficaciously, in order that the entire fulness of those things which have been produced might come into being, although they had no previous existence—that is, whatever does not fall under [our] observation, and also what lies before our eyes. And so does He contain all things in particular, and leads them on to their own proper result, on account of which they were called into being and produced, in no way changed into anything else than what it (the end) had originally been by nature. For this is the property of the working of God, not merely to proceed to the infinitude of the understanding, or even to overpass [our] powers of mind, reason and speech, time and place, and every age; but also to go beyond substance, and fulness or perfection.

VII.

This[2] [custom], of not bending the knee upon Sunday,

---

[1] We owe this fragment also to Maximus, who quoted it from the same work, *de Fide*, written by Irenæus to Demetrius, a deacon of Vienne. This and the last fragment were first printed by Feuardentius, who obtained them from Faber; no reference, however, being given as to the source from whence the Latin version was derived. The Greek of this Fragment vi. is not extant.

[2] Taken from a work (*Quæs. et Resp. ad. Othod.*) ascribed to Justin Martyr, but certainly written after the Nicene Council. It is evident that this is not an exact quotation from Irenæus, but a summary of his words. The "Sunday" here referred to must be Easter Sunday. Massuet's emendation of the text has been adopted, ἐπ' αὐτοῦ for ἐπ' αὐτῶν.

is a symbol of the resurrection, through which we have been set free, by the grace of Christ, from sins, and from death, which has been put to death under Him. Now this custom took its rise from apostolic times, as the blessed Irenæus, the martyr and bishop of Lyons, declares in his treatise *On Easter*, in which he makes mention of Pentecost also; upon which [feast] we do not bend the knee, because it is of equal significance with the Lord's day, for the reason already alleged concerning it.

VIII.

For [1] as the ark [of the covenant] was gilded within and without with pure gold, so was also the body of Christ pure and resplendent; for it was adorned within by the Word, and shielded without by the Spirit, in order that from both [materials] the splendour of the natures might be clearly shown forth.

IX.

Ever,[2] indeed, speaking well of the deserving, but never ill of the undeserving, we also shall attain to the glory and kingdom of God.

X.

It is indeed proper to God, and befitting His character, to show mercy and pity, and to bring salvation to His creatures, even though they be brought under danger of destruction. "For with Him," says the Scripture, "is propitiation."[3]

---

[1] Cited by Leontius of Byzantium, who flourished about the year A.D. 600; but he does not mention the writing of Irenæus from which it is extracted. Massuet conjectures that it is from the *De Ogdoade*, addressed to the apostate Florinus.

[2] This fragment and the next three are from the *Parallela* of John of Damascus. Frag. ix. x. xii. seem to be quotations from the treatise of Irenæus on the resurrection. No. xi. is extracted from his *Miscellaneous Dissertations*, a work mentioned by Eusebius, βιβλίον τι διαλέξεων διαφόρων.

[3] Ps. cxxx. 7.

XI.

The business of the Christian is nothing else than to be ever preparing for death (μελετᾶν ἀποθνήσκειν).

XII.

We therefore have formed the belief that [our] bodies also do rise again. For although they go to corruption, yet they do not perish; for the earth, receiving the remains, preserves them, even like fertile seed mixed with more fertile ground. Again, as a bare grain is sown, and, germinating by the command of God its Creator, rises again, clothed upon and glorious, but not before it has died and suffered decomposition, and become mingled with the earth; so [it is seen from this, that] we have not entertained a vain belief in the resurrection of the body. But although it is dissolved at the appointed time, because of the primeval disobedience, it is placed, as it were, in the crucible of the earth, to be re-cast again; not then as this corruptible [body], but pure, and no longer subject to decay: so that to each body its own soul shall be restored; and when it is clothed upon with this, it shall not experience sorrow, but shall rejoice, continuing permanently in a state of purity, having for its companion a just consort, not an insidious one, possessing in every respect the things pertaining to it, it shall receive these with perfect accuracy;[1] it shall not receive bodies diverse from what they had been, nor delivered from suffering or disease, nor as [rendered] glorious, but as they departed this life, in sins or in righteous actions: and such as they were, such shall they be clothed with upon resuming life; and such as they were in unbelief, such shall they be faithfully judged.

XIII.

For[2] when the Greeks, having arrested the slaves of

---

[1] This sentence in the original seems incomplete; we have followed the conjectural restoration of Harvey.

[2] " This extract is found in Œcumenius upon 1 Pet. c. iii. p. 198;

Christian catechumens, then used force against them, in order to learn from them some secret thing [practised] among Christians, these slaves, having nothing to say that would meet the wishes of their tormentors, except that they had heard from their masters that the divine communion was the body and blood of Christ, and imagining that it was actually flesh and blood, gave their inquisitors answer to that effect. Then these latter, assuming such to be the case with regard to the practices of Christians, gave information regarding it to other Greeks, and sought to compel the martyrs Sanctus and Blandina to confess, under the influence of torture, [that the allegation was correct]. To these men Blandina replied very admirably in these words: "How should those persons endure such [accusations], who, for the sake of the practice [of piety], did not avail themselves even of the flesh that was permitted [them to eat]?"

XIV.

How[1] is it possible to say that the serpent, created by God dumb and irrational, was endowed with reason and speech? For if it had the power of itself to speak, to discern, to understand, and to reply to what was spoken by the woman, there would have been nothing to prevent every serpent from doing this also. If, however, they say again that it was according to the divine will and dispensation that this [serpent] spake with a human voice to Eve, they render God the author of sin. Neither was it possible for the evil demon to impart speech to a speechless nature, and thus from that which is not to produce that which is; for if that were the case, he never would have ceased (with the view of leading men astray) from conferring with and deceiving them by means of serpents, and beasts, and birds. From what quarter, too, did it, being a beast, obtain infor-

and the words used by him indicate, as Grabe has justly observed, that he only condensed a longer passage."—HARVEY.

[1] From the *Contemplations* of Anastasius Sinaita, who flourished A.D. 685. Harvey doubts as to this fragment being a genuine production of Irenæus; and its whole style of reasoning confirms the suspicion.

mation regarding the injunction of God to the man given to him alone, and in secret, not even the woman herself being aware of it? Why also did it not prefer to make its attack upon the man instead of the woman? And if thou sayest that it attacked her as being the weaker of the two, [I reply that], on the contrary, she was the stronger, since she appears to have been the helper of the man in the transgression of the commandment. For she did by herself alone resist the serpent, and it was after holding out for a while and making opposition that she ate of the tree, being circumvented by craft; whereas Adam, making no fight whatever, nor refusal, partook of the fruit handed to him by the woman, which is an indication of the utmost imbecility and effeminacy of mind. And the woman indeed, having been vanquished in the contest by a demon, is deserving of pardon; but Adam shall deserve none, for he was worsted by a woman,—he who, in his own person, had received the command from God. But the woman, having heard of the command from Adam, treated it with contempt, either because she deemed it unworthy of God to speak by means of it, or because she had her doubts, perhaps even held the opinion that the command was given to her by Adam of his own accord. The serpent found her working alone, so that he was enabled to confer with her apart. Observing her then either eating or not eating from the trees, he put before her the fruit of the [forbidden] tree. And if he saw her eating, it is manifest that she was partaker of a body subject to corruption. "For everything going in at the mouth, is cast out into the draught."[1] If then corruptible, it is obvious that she was also mortal. But if mortal, then there was certainly no curse; nor was that a [condemnatory] sentence, when the voice of God spake to the man, "For earth thou art, and unto earth shalt thou return,"[2] as the true course of things proceeds [now and always]. Then again, if the serpent observed the woman not eating, how did he induce her to eat who never had eaten? And who pointed out to this accursed manslaying serpent that the sentence of death pronounced against

[1] Matt. xv. 17. [2] Gen. iii. 19.

them by God would not take [immediate] effect, when He said, "For in the day that ye eat thereof, ye shall surely die?" And not this merely, but that along with the impunity[1] [attending their sin] the eyes of those should be opened who had not seen until then? But with the opening [of their eyes] referred to, they made entrance upon the path of death.

XV.

When,[2] in times of old, Balaam spake these things in parables, he was not acknowledged; and now, when Christ has appeared and fulfilled them, He was not believed. Wherefore [Balaam], foreseeing this, and wondering at it, exclaimed, "Alas! alas! who shall live when God brings these things to pass?"[3]

XVI.

Expounding again the law to that generation which followed those who were slain in the wilderness, he published Deuteronomy; not as giving to them a different law from that which had been appointed for their fathers, but as recapitulating this latter, in order that they, by hearing what had happened to their fathers, might fear God with their whole heart.

XVII.

By these Christ was typified, and acknowledged, and brought into the world; for He was prefigured in Joseph: then from Levi and Judah He was descended according to the flesh, as King and Priest; and He was acknowledged by

---

[1] The Greek reads the barbarous word ἀόριξίᾳ, which Massuet thinks is a corruption of ἀθανασίᾳ, immortality. We have, however, followed the conjecture of Harvey, who would substitute ἀπληξίᾳ, which seems to agree better with the context.

[2] This and the eight following fragments may be referred to the *Miscellaneous Dissertations* of our author; see note on Frag. ix. They are found in three mss. in the Imperial Collection at Paris, on the Pentateuch, Joshua, Judges, and Ruth.

[3] Num. xxiv. 23.

Simeon in the temple: through Zebulon He was believed in among the Gentiles, as says the prophet, "the land of Zabulon;"[1] and through Benjamin [that is, Paul] He was glorified, by being preached throughout all the world.[2]

XVIII.

And this was not without meaning; but that by means of the number of the ten men,[3] he (Gideon) might appear as having Jesus for a helper, as [is indicated] by the compact entered into with them. And when he did not choose to partake with them in their idol-worship, they threw the blame upon him: for "Jerubbaal" signifies the judgment-seat of Baal.

XIX.

"Take unto thee Joshua ('Ιησοῦν) the son of Nun."[4] For it was proper that Moses should lead the people out of Egypt, but that Jesus (*Joshua*) should lead them into the inheritance. Also that Moses, as was the case with the law, should cease to be, but that Joshua ('Ιησοῦν), as the word, and no untrue type of the Word made flesh (ἐνυποστάτου), should be a preacher to the people. Then again, [it was fit] that Moses should give manna as food to the fathers, but Joshua wheat;[5] as the first-fruits of life, a type of the body of Christ, as also the Scripture declares that the manna of the Lord ceased when the people had eaten wheat from the land.[6]

[1] Isa. ix. 1.
[2] Compare the statement of Clemens Romanus, vol. i. p. 11 of this series, where, speaking of St. Paul, he says: "After preaching both in the east and west. . . . having taught righteousness to the whole world, and come to the extreme limit of the west."
[3] See Judg. vi. 27. It is not very clear how Irenæus makes out this allegory, but it is thought that he refers to the initial letter in the name 'Ιησοῦς, which stands for *ten* in the Greek enumeration. Compare the *Epistle of Barnabas*, vol. i. p. 117 of this series.
[4] Num. xxvii. 18.
[5] Harvey conceives the reading here (which is doubtful) to have been τὸν νέον σῖτον, the new wheat; and sees an allusion to the wave-sheaf of the new corn offered in the temple on the morning of our Lord's resurrection.
[6] Josh. v. 12.

XX.

"And[1] he laid his hands upon him."[2] The countenance of Joshua was also glorified by the imposition of the hands of Moses, but not to the same degree [as that of Moses]. Inasmuch, then, as he had obtained a certain degree of grace, [the Lord] said, "And thou shalt confer upon him of thy glory."[3] For [in this case] the thing given does not cease to belong to the giver.

XXI.

But he does not give, as Christ did, by means of breathing, because he is not the fount of the Spirit.

XXII.

"Thou shalt not go with them, neither shalt thou curse the people."[4] He does not hint at anything with regard to the people, for they all lay before his view, but [he refers] to the mystery of Christ pointed out beforehand. For as He was to be born of the fathers according to the flesh, the Spirit gives instructions to the man (Balaam) beforehand, lest, going forth in ignorance, he might pronounce a curse upon the people.[5] Not, indeed, that [his curse] could take any effect contrary to the will of God; but [this was done] as an exhibition of the providence of God which He exercised towards them on account of their forefathers.

XXIII.

"And he mounted upon his ass."[6] The ass was the type of the body of Christ, upon whom all men, resting from their labours, are borne as in a chariot. For the Saviour has taken

---

[1] Massuet seems to more than doubt the genuineness of this fragment and the next, and would ascribe them to the pen of Apollinaris, bishop of Hierapolis in Phrygia, a contemporary of Irenæus. Harvey passes over these two fragments.

[2] Num. xxvii. 23. [3] Num. xxvii. 20. [4] Num. xxii. 12.

[5] The conjectural emendation of Harvey has been adopted here, but the text is very corrupt and uncertain.

[6] Num. xxii. 22, 23.

up the burden of our sins.[1] Now the angel who appeared to Balaam was the Word Himself; and in His hand He held a sword, to indicate the power which He had from above.

XXIV.

"God is not as a man."[2] He thus shows that all men are indeed guilty of falsehood, inasmuch as they change from one thing to another ($\mu\epsilon\tau\alpha\phi\epsilon\rho\delta\mu\epsilon\nu o\iota$); but such is not the case with God, for He always continues true, perfecting whatever He wishes.

XXV.

"To inflict vengeance from the Lord on Midian."[3] For this man (Balaam), when he speaks no longer in the Spirit of God, but contrary to God's law, by setting up a different law with regard to fornication,[4] is certainly not then to be counted as a prophet, but as a soothsayer. For he who did not keep to the commandment of God, received the just recompense of his own evil devices.[5]

XXVI.

Know[6] thou that every man is either empty or full. For if he has not the Holy Spirit, he has no knowledge of the Creator; he has not received Jesus Christ the Life; he knows not the Father who is in heaven; if he does not live after the dictates of reason, after the heavenly law, he is not a sober-minded person, nor does he act uprightly: such an one is empty. If, on the other hand, he receives God, who says, "I will dwell with them, and walk in them, and I will be their God,"[7] such an one is not empty, but full.

---

[1] From one of the MSS. Stieren would insert $\epsilon\nu$ $\tau\tilde{\omega}$ $\iota\delta\iota\omega$ $\sigma\omega\mu\alpha\tau\iota$, in His own body; see 1 Pet. ii. 24.

[2] Num. xxiii. 19. [3] Num. xxxi. 3.
[4] Num. xxxi. 16. [5] Num. xxxi. 8.

[6] It is not certain from what work of Irenæus this extract is derived; Harvey thinks it to be from his work $\pi\epsilon\rho\iota$ $\epsilon\pi\iota\sigma\tau\eta\mu\eta\varsigma$, i.e. concerning Knowledge.

[7] Lev. xxvi. 12.

XXVII.

The little boy, therefore, who guided Samson by the hand,[1] pre-typified John the Baptist, who showed to the people the faith in Christ. And the house in which they were assembled signifies the world, in which dwell the various heathen and unbelieving nations, offering sacrifice to their idols. Moreover, the two pillars are the two covenants. The fact, then, of Samson leaning himself upon the pillars, [indicates] this, that the people, when instructed, recognised the mystery of Christ.

XXVIII.

"And the man of God said, Where did it fall? And he showed him the place. And he cut down a tree, and cast it in there, and the iron floated."[2] This was a sign that souls should be borne aloft (ἀναγωγῆς ψυχῶν) through the instrumentality of wood, upon which He suffered who can lead those souls aloft that follow His ascension. This event was also an indication of the fact, that when the holy soul of Christ descended [to Hades], many souls ascended and were seen in their bodies.[3] For just as the wood, which is the lighter body, was submerged in the water; but the iron, the heavier one, floated: so, when the Word of God became one with flesh, by a physical and hypostatic union, the heavy and terrestrial [part], having been rendered immortal, was borne up into heaven, by the divine nature, after the resurrection.

XXIX.

The[4] Gospel according to Matthew was written to the Jews. For they laid particular stress upon the fact that Christ [should be] of the seed of David. Matthew also, who had a still greater desire [to establish this point], took par-

---

[1] Judg. xvi. 26.   [2] 2 Kings vi. 6. Comp. book v. chap. xvii. 4.
[3] Matt. xxvii. 52.
[4] Edited by P. Possin, in a *Catena Patrum* on St. Matthew. See book iii. chap. xi. 8.

ticular pains to afford them convincing proof that Christ is of the seed of David; and therefore he commences with [an account of] His genealogy.

XXX.[1]

"The axe unto the root,"[2] he says, urging us to the knowledge of the truth, and purifying us by means of fear, as well as preparing [us] to bring forth fruit in due season.

XXXI.

Observe[3] that, by means of the grain of mustard seed in the parable, the heavenly doctrine is denoted which is sown like seed in the world, as in a field, [seed] which has an inherent force, fiery and powerful. For the Judge of the whole world is thus proclaimed, who, having been hidden in the heart of the earth in a tomb for three days, and having become a great tree, has stretched forth His branches to the ends of the earth. Sprouting out from Him, the twelve apostles, having become fair and fruitful boughs, were made a shelter for the nations as for the fowls of heaven, under which boughs, all having taken refuge, as birds flocking to a nest, have been made partakers of that wholesome and celestial food which is derived from them.

XXXII.[4]

Josephus says, that when Moses had been brought up in the royal palaces, he was chosen as general against the Ethiopians; and having proved victorious, obtained in marriage the daughter of that king, since indeed, out of her affection for him, she delivered the city up to him.[5]

---

[1] From the same *Catena*. Compare book v. chap. xvii. 4.

[2] Matt. iii. 10.

[3] First edited in Latin by Corderius, afterwards in Greek by Grabe, and also by Dr Cramer in his *Catena* on St. Luke.

[4] Massuet's Fragment xxxii. is here passed over; it is found in book iii. chap. xviii. 7.

[5] See Josephus' *Antiquities*, book ii. chap. x., where we read that this king's daughter was called Tharbis. Immediately upon the sur-

Why was it, that when these two (Aaron and Miriam) had both acted with despite towards him (Moses), the latter alone was adjudged punishment?[1] First, because the woman was the more culpable, since both nature and the law place the woman in a subordinate condition to the man. Or perhaps it was that Aaron was to a certain degree excusable, in consideration of his being the elder [brother], and adorned with the dignity of high priest. Then again, inasmuch as the leper was accounted by the law unclean, while at the same time the origin and foundation of the priesthood lay in Aaron, [the Lord] did not award a similar punishment to him, lest this stigma should attach itself to the entire [sacerdotal] race; but by means of his sister's [example] He awoke his fears, and taught him the same lesson. For Miriam's punishment affected him to such an extent, that no sooner did she experience it, than he entreated [Moses], who had been injured, that he would by his intercession do away with the affliction. And he did not neglect to do so, but at once poured forth his supplication. Upon this the Lord, who loves mankind, made him understand how He had not chastened her as a judge, but as a father; for He said, "If her father had spit in her face, should she not be ashamed? Let her be shut out from the camp seven days, and after that let her come in again."[2]

XXXIII.

Inasmuch[3] as certain men, impelled by what considerations I know not, remove from God the half of His creative power,

render of this city (Saba, afterwards called Meroë) Moses married her, and returned to Egypt. Whiston, in the notes to his translation of Josephus, says, "Nor, perhaps, did St. Stephen refer to anything else when he said of Moses, before he was sent by God to the Israelites, that he was not only learned in all the wisdom of the Egyptians, but was also mighty in words and in deeds" (Acts vii. 22).

[1] Num. xii. 1, etc.   [2] Num. xii. 14.

[3] Harvey considers this fragment to be a part of the work of Irenæus referred to by Photius under the title *De Universo*, or *de Substantiâ Mundi*. It is to be found in Codex 3011 of the Bodleian Library, Oxford.

by asserting that He is merely the cause of quality resident in matter, and by maintaining that matter itself is uncreated, come now let us put the question, What is at any time . . . is immutable. Matter, then, is immutable. But if matter be immutable, and the immutable suffers no change in regard to quality, it does not form the substance of the world. For which reason it seems to them superfluous, that God has annexed qualities to matter, since indeed matter admits of no possible alteration, it being in itself an uncreated thing. But further, if matter be uncreated, it has been made altogether according to a certain quality, and this immutable, so that it cannot be receptive of more qualities, nor can it be the thing of which the world is made. But if the world be not made from it, [this theory] entirely excludes God from exercising power on the creation [of the world].

XXXIV.

"And[1] dipped himself," says [the Scripture], "seven times in Jordan."[2] It was not for nothing that Naaman of old, when suffering from leprosy, was purified upon his being baptized, but [it served] as an indication to us. For as we are lepers in sin, we are made clean, by means of the sacred water and the invocation of the Lord, from our old transgressions; being spiritually regenerated as new-born babes, even as the Lord has declared: "Except a man be born again through water and the Spirit, he shall not enter into the kingdom of heaven."[4]

XXXV.

If the corpse of Elisha raised a dead man,[1] how much more shall God, when He has quickened men's dead bodies, bring them up for judgment?

---

[1] This and the next fragment first appeared in the Benedictine edition reprinted at Venice, 1734. They were taken from a MS. *Catena* on the books of Kings in the Coislin Collection.

[2] 2 Kings v. 14.   [3] John iii. 5.   [4] 2 Kings xiii. 21.

XXXVI.

True[1] knowledge, then, consists in the understanding of Christ, which Paul terms the wisdom of God hidden in a mystery, which "the natural man receiveth not,"[2] the doctrine of the cross; of which if any man "taste,"[3] he will not accede to the disputations and quibbles of proud and puffed-up men,[4] who go into matters of which they have no perception.[5] For the truth is unsophisticated (ἀσχημάτιστος); and "the word is nigh thee, in thy mouth and in thy heart,"[6] as the same apostle declares, being easy of comprehension to those who are obedient. For it renders us like to Christ, if we experience "the power of His resurrection and the fellowship of His sufferings."[7] For this is the affinity[8] of the apostolical teaching and the most holy "faith delivered unto us,"[9] which the unlearned receive, and those of slender knowledge have taught, not "giving heed to endless genealogies,"[10] but studying rather [to observe] a straightforward course of life; lest, having been deprived of the Divine Spirit, they fail to attain to the kingdom of heaven. For truly the first thing is to deny one's self and to follow Christ; and those who do this are borne onward to perfection, having fulfilled all their Teacher's will, becoming sons of God by spiritual regeneration, and heirs of the kingdom of heaven; those who seek which first shall not be forsaken.

---

[1] This extract and the next three were discovered in the year 1715 by Pfaff, a learned Lutheran, in the Royal Library at Turin. The MSS. from which they were taken were neither catalogued nor classified, and have now disappeared from the collection. It is impossible to say with any degree of probability from what treatises of our author these four fragments have been culled. For a full account of their history, see Stieren's edition of Irenæus, vol. ii. p. 381.

[2] 1 Cor. ii. 14.
[3] 1 Pet. ii. 3.
[4] 1 Tim. vi. 4, 5.
[5] Col. ii. 18.
[6] Rom. x. 8; Deut. xxx. 14.
[7] Phil. iii. 10.
[8] Harvey's conjectural emendation, ἐπιπλοκή for ἐπιλογή, has been adopted here.
[9] Jude 3.
[10] 1 Tim. i. 4.

XXXVII.

Those who have become acquainted with the secondary (*i.e.* under Christ) constitutions of the apostles,[1] are aware that the Lord instituted a new oblation in the new covenant, according to [the declaration of] Malachi the prophet. For, " from the rising of the sun even to the setting my name has been glorified among the Gentiles, and in every place incense is offered to my name, and a pure sacrifice;"[2] as John also declares in the Apocalypse: " The incense is the prayers of the saints."[3] Then again, Paul exhorts us " to present our bodies a living sacrifice, holy, acceptable unto God, which is your reasonable service."[4] And again, " Let us offer the sacrifice of praise, that is, the fruit of the lips."[5] Now those oblations are not according to the law, the handwriting of which the Lord took away from the midst by cancelling it;[6] but they are according to the Spirit, for we must worship God " in spirit and in truth."[7] And therefore the oblation of the Eucharist is not a carnal one, but a spiritual; and in this respect it is pure. For we make an oblation to God of the bread and the cup of blessing, giving Him thanks in that He has commanded the earth to bring forth these fruits for our nourishment. And then, when we have perfected the oblation, we invoke the Holy Spirit, that He may exhibit this sacrifice, both the bread the body of Christ, and the cup the blood of Christ, in order that the receivers of these antitypes[8] may obtain remission of sins and life eternal. Those

---

[1] ταῖς δευτέραις τῶν ἀποστόλων διατάξεσι. Harvey thinks that these words imply, " the formal constitution, which the apostles, acting under the impulse of the Spirit, though still in a secondary capacity, gave to the church."

[2] Mal. i. 11.

[3] Rev. v. 8. The same view of the eucharistic oblation, etc., is found in book iv. chap. xvii. : as also in Justin Martyr ; see p. 139 of his works in this series.

[4] Rom. xii. 1.   [5] Heb. xiii. 15.   [6] Col. ii. 14.   [7] John iv. 24.

[8] Harvey explains this word ἀντιτύπων as meaning an " exact counterpart." He refers to the word where it occurs in *Contra Hæreses*, lib. i. chap. xxiv., as confirmatory of his view. See vol. i. p. 24, line 20, where

persons, then, who perform these oblations in remembrance of the Lord, do not fall in with Jewish views, but, performing the service after a spiritual manner, they shall be called sons of wisdom.

XXXVIII.

The[1] apostles ordained, that "we should not judge any one in respect to meat or drink, or in regard to a feast day, or the new moons, or the sabbaths."[2] Whence then these contentions? whence these schisms? We keep the feast, but in the leaven of malice and wickedness, cutting in pieces the church of God; and we preserve what belongs to its exterior, that we may cast away these better things, faith and love. We have heard from the prophetic words that these feasts and fasts are displeasing to the Lord.[3]

XXXIX.

Christ,[4] who was called the Son of God before the ages, was manifested in the fulness of time, in order that He might cleanse us through His blood, who were under the power of sin, presenting us as pure sons to His Father, if we yield ourselves obediently to the chastisement of the Spirit. And in the end of time He shall come to do away with all evil, and to reconcile all things, in order that there may be an end of all impurities.

---

this word is translated "emblem" by him. Towards the end of his long note he says: "ἀντίτυπος here conveys the idea of identity between the body of Christ and the consecrated bread. The two are not co-existent as distinct substances, *consubstantially*; but the bread, through the energy of the word, is the Lord's body."

[1] Taken apparently from the *Epistle to Blastus, de Schismate*. Compare a similar passage, lib. iv. chap. xxxiii. 7.

[2] Col. ii. 16.   [3] Isa. i. 14.

[4] "From the same collection at Turin. The passage seems to be of cognate matter with the treatise *De Resurrec.* Pfaff referred it either to the διαλέξεις διάφοροι or to the ἐπιδείξις ἀποστολικοῦ κηρύγματος."— HARVEY.

XL.

"And[1] he found the jaw-bone of an ass."[2] It is to be observed that, after [Samson had committed] fornication, the holy Scripture no longer speaks of the things happily accomplished by him in connection with the formula, "The Spirit of the Lord came upon him."[3] For thus, according to the holy apostle, the sin of fornication is perpetrated against the body, as involving also sin against the temple of God.[4]

XLI.

This[5] indicates the persecution against the church set on foot by the nations who still continue in unbelief. But he (Samson) who suffered those things, trusted that there would be a retaliation against those waging this war. But retaliation through what means? First of all, by his betaking himself to the Rock[6] not cognizable to the senses;[7] secondly, by the finding of the jaw-bone of an ass. Now the type of the jaw-bone is the body of Christ.

XLII.

Speaking always well of the worthy, but never ill of the unworthy, we also shall attain to the glory and kingdom of God.

XLIII.

In[8] these things there was signified by prophecy that the

---

[1] This and the four following fragments are taken from MSS. in the Vatican Library at Rome. They are apparently quoted from the homiletical expositions of the historical books already referred to.

[2] Judg. xv. 15.   [3] Judg. xiv. 6–19.   [4] 1 Cor. iii. 16, 17.

[5] These words were evidently written during a season of persecution in Gaul; but what that persecution was, it is useless to conjecture.

[6] Judg. xv. 11.

[7] That is, when he fled to the rock Etam, he typified the true believer taking refuge in the spiritual Rock, Christ.

[8] Most probably from a homily upon the third and fourth chapters of Ezekiel. It is found repeated in Stieren's and Migne's edition as Fragment xlviii. extracted from a *Catena* on the Book of Judges.

people, having become transgressors, shall be bound by the chains of their own sins. But the breaking of the bonds of their own accord indicates that, upon repentance, they shall be again loosed from the shackles of sin.

XLIV.

It[1] is not an easy thing for a soul, under the influence of error, to be persuaded of the contrary opinion.

XLV.

" And[2] Balaam the son of Beor they slew with the sword."[3] For, speaking no longer by the Spirit of God, but setting up another law of fornication contrary to the law of God,[4] this man shall no longer be reckoned as a prophet, but as a soothsayer. For, as he did not continue in the commandment of God, he received the just reward of his evil devices.

XLVI.

"The[5] god of the world;"[6] that is, Satan, who was designated God to those who believe not.

XLVII.

The[7] birth of John [the Baptist] brought the dumbness of Zacharias to an end. For he did not burden his father, when

---

[1] We give this brief fragment as it appears in the editions of Stieren, Migne, and Harvey, who speculate as to its origin. They seem to have overlooked the fact that it is the Greek original of the old Latin, *non facile est ab errore apprehensam resipiscere animam,*—a sentence found towards the end of book iii. chap. ii.; see vol. i. p. 260, lines 23, 24, of our translation.

[2] With the exception of the initial text, this fragment is almost identical with No. xxv.

[3] Num. xxxi. 8.   [4] Rev. ii. 14.

[5] From the *Catena* on St. Paul's Epistles to the Corinthians, edited by Dr. Cramer, and reprinted by Stieren.

[6] 2 Cor. iv. 4.

[7] Extracted from a MS. of Greek theology in the Palatine Library at Vienna. The succeeding fragment in the editions of Harvey, Migne, and Stieren, is omitted, as it is merely a transcript of lib. iii. ch. x. 4; see vol. i. p. 285, lines 8-12.

the voice issued forth from silence; but as when not believed it rendered him tongue-tied, so did the voice sounding out clearly set his father free, to whom he had both been announced and born. Now the voice and the burning light[1] were a precursor of the Word and the Light.

XLVIII.

As[2] therefore seventy tongues are indicated by number, and from[3] dispersion the tongues are gathered into one by means of their interpretation; so is that ark declared a type of the body of Christ, which is both pure and immaculate. For[4] as that ark was gilded with pure gold both within and without, so also is the body of Christ pure and resplendent, being adorned within by the Word, and shielded on the outside by the Spirit, in order that from both [materials] the splendour of the natures might be exhibited together.

XLIX.

Now[5] therefore, by means of this which has been already brought forth a long time since, the Word has assigned an interpretation. We are convinced that there exist [so to speak] two men in each one of us. The one is confessedly a hidden thing, while the other stands apparent; one is corporeal, the other spiritual; although the generation of both may be compared to that of twins. For both are revealed to the world as but one, for the soul was not anterior to the body in its essence; nor, in regard to its formation, did the body precede the soul: but both these were produced at one time; and their nourishment consists in purity and sweetness.

[1] John v. 35.
[2] This fragment commences a series derived from the Nitrian Collection of Syriac MSS. in the British Museum.
[3] The Syriac text is here corrupt and obscure.
[4] See No. viii., which is the same as the remainder of this fragment.
[5] The Syriac MS. introduces this quotation as follows: "From the holy Irenæus Bp. of Lyons, from the first section of his interpretation of the Song of Songs."

L.

For[1] then there shall in truth be a common joy consummated to all those who believe unto life, and in each individual shall be confirmed the mystery of the Resurrection, and the hope of incorruption, and the commencement of the eternal kingdom, when God shall have destroyed death and the devil. For that human nature and flesh which has risen again from the dead shall die no more; but after it had been changed to incorruption, and made like to spirit, when the heaven was opened, [our Lord] full of glory offered it (the flesh) to the Father.

LI.

Now,[2] however, inasmuch as the books of these men may possibly have escaped your observation, but have come under our notice, I call your attention to them, that for the sake of your reputation you may expel these writings from among you, as bringing disgrace upon you, since their author boasts himself as being one of your company. For they constitute a stumbling-block to many, who simply and unreservedly receive, as coming from a presbyter, the blasphemy which they utter against God. Just [consider] the writer of these things, how by means of them he does not injure assistants [in divine service] only, who happen to be prepared in mind for blasphemies against God, but also damages those among us, since by his books he imbues their minds with false doctrines concerning God.

---

[1] This extract is introduced as follows: "For Irenæus Bishop of Lyons, who was a contemporary of the disciple of the apostle, Polycarp Bishop of Smyrna, and martyr, and for this reason is held in just estimation, wrote to an Alexandrian to the effect that it is right, with respect to the feast of the Resurrection, that we should celebrate it upon the first day of the week." This shows us that the extract must have been taken from the work *Against Schism* addressed to Blastus.

[2] From the same MS. as the preceding fragment. It is thus introduced: "And Irenæus Bp. of Lyons, to Victor Bp. of Rome, concerning Florinus, a presbyter, who was a partisan of the error of Valentinus, and published an abominable book, thus wrote."

LII.

The[1] sacred books acknowledge with regard to Christ, that as He is the Son of man, so is the same Being not a [mere] man; and as He is flesh, so is He also spirit, and the Word of God, and God. And as He was born of Mary in the last times, so did He also proceed from God as the First-begotten of every creature; and as He hungered, so did He satisfy [others]; and as He thirsted, so did He of old cause the Jews to drink, for the "Rock was Christ"[2] Himself: thus does Jesus now give to His believing people power to drink spiritual waters, which spring up to life eternal.[3] And as He was the son of David, so was He also the Lord of David. And as He was from Abraham, so did He also exist before Abraham.[4] And as He was the servant of God, so is He the Son of God, and Lord of the universe. And as He was spit upon ignominiously, so also did He breathe the Holy Spirit into His disciples.[5] And as He was saddened, so also did He give joy to His people. And as He was capable of being handled and touched, so again did He, in a non-apprehensible form, pass through the midst of those who sought to injure Him,[6] and entered without impediment through closed doors.[7] And as He slept, so did He also rule the sea, the winds, and the storms. And as He suffered, so also is He alive, and life-giving, and healing all our infirmity. And as He died, so is He also the Resurrection of the dead. He suffered shame on earth, while He is higher than all glory and praise in heaven; who, "though He was crucified through weakness, yet He liveth by divine power;"[8] who "descended into the lower parts of the earth," and who "ascended up above the heavens;"[9] for whom a manger sufficed, yet who filled all things; who was dead, yet who liveth for ever and ever. Amen.

---

[1] This extract had already been printed by M. Petra in his *Spicilegium Solesmense*, p. 6.
[2] 1 Cor. x. 4.
[3] John iv. 14.
[4] John viii. 58.
[5] John xx. 22.
[6] John viii. 59.
[7] John xx. 26.
[8] 2 Cor. xiii. 4.
[9] Eph. iv. 9, 10.

LIII.

With[1] regard to Christ, the law and the prophets and the evangelists have proclaimed that He was born of a virgin, that He suffered upon a beam of wood, and that He appeared from the dead; that He also ascended to the heavens, and was glorified by the Father, and is the Eternal King; that He is the perfect Intelligence, the Word of God, who was begotten before the light; that He was the Founder of the universe, along with it (light), and the Maker of man; that He is All in all: Patriarch among the patriarchs; Law in the laws; Chief Priest among priests; Ruler among kings; the Prophet among prophets; the Angel among angels; the Man among men; Son in the Father; God in God; King to all eternity. For it is He who sailed [in the ark] along with Noah, and who guided Abraham; who was bound along with Isaac, and was a Wanderer with Jacob; the Shepherd of those who are saved, and the Bridegroom of the church; the Chief also of the cherubim, the Prince of the angelic powers; God of God; Son of the Father; Jesus Christ; King for ever and ever. Amen.

LIV.

The[2] law and the prophets and evangelists have declared that Christ was born of a virgin, and suffered on the cross; was raised also from the dead, and taken up to heaven; that He was glorified, and reigns for ever. He is Himself termed the Perfect Intellect, the Word of God. He is the First-begotten,[3] after a transcendent manner, the Creator of man; All in all; Patriarch among the patriarchs; Law in the law; the Priest among priests; among kings Prime Leader;

---

[1] This extract from the Syriac is a shorter form of the next fragment, which seems to be interpolated in some places. The latter is from an Armenian MS. in the Mechitarist Library at Venice.

[2] This fragment is thus introduced in the Armenian copy: "From St. Irenæus, bishop, follower of the apostles, on the Lord's resurrection."

[3] The Armenian text is confused here; we have adopted the conjectural emendation of Quatremere.

the Prophet among the prophets; the Angel among angels; the Man among men; Son in the Father; God in God; King to all eternity. He was sold with Joseph, and He guided Abraham; was bound along with Isaac, and wandered with Jacob; with Moses He was Leader, and, respecting the people, Legislator. He preached in the prophets; was incarnate of a virgin; born in Bethlehem; received by John, and baptized in Jordan; was tempted in the desert, and proved to be the Lord. He gathered the apostles together, and preached the kingdom of heaven; gave light to the blind, and raised the dead; was seen in the temple, but was not held by the people as worthy of credit; was arrested by the priests, conducted before Herod, and condemned in the presence of Pilate; He manifested Himself in the body, was suspended upon a beam of wood, and raised from the dead; shown to the apostles, and, having been carried up to heaven, sitteth on the right hand of the Father, and has been glorified by Him as the Resurrection of the dead. Moreover, He is the Salvation of the lost, the Light to those dwelling in darkness, and Redemption to those who have been born; the Shepherd of the saved, and the Bridegroom of the church; the Charioteer of the cherubim, the Leader of the angelic host; God of God; Jesus Christ our Saviour.

LV.

"Then[1] drew near unto Him the mother of Zebedee's children, with her sons, worshipping, and seeking a certain thing from Him."[2] These people are certainly not void of understanding, nor are the words set forth in that passage of no signification: being stated beforehand like a preface, they have some agreement with those points formerly expounded.

"Then drew near." Sometimes virtue excites our ad-

---

[1] From an Armenian MS. in the Library of the Mechitarist Convent at Vienna, edited by M. Pitra, who considers this fragment as of very doubtful authority. It commences with this heading: "From the second series of Homilies of Saint Irenæus, follower of the Apostles; a Homily upon the Sons of Zebedee."

[2] Matt. xx. 20.

miration, not merely on account of the display which is given of it, but also of the occasion when it was manifested. I may refer, for example, to the premature fruit of the grape, or of the fig, or to any fruit whatsoever, from which, during its process [of growth], no man expects maturity or full development; yet, although any one may perceive that it is still somewhat imperfect, he does not for that reason despise as useless the immature grape when plucked, but he gathers it with pleasure as appearing early in the season; nor does he consider whether the grape is possessed of perfect sweetness; nay, he at once experiences satisfaction from the thought that this one has appeared before the rest. Just in the same way does God also, when He perceives the faithful possessing wisdom though still imperfect, and but a small degree of faith, overlook their defect in this respect, and therefore does not reject them; nay, but on the contrary, He kindly welcomes and accepts them as premature fruits, and honours the mind, whatsoever it may be, which is stamped with virtue, although not yet perfect. He makes allowance for it, as being among the harbingers of the vintage,[1] and esteems it highly, inasmuch as, being of a readier disposition than the rest, it has forestalled, as it were, the blessing to itself.

Abraham therefore, Isaac, and Jacob, our fathers, are to be esteemed before all, since they did indeed afford us such early examples of virtue. How many martyrs can be compared to Daniel? How many martyrs, I ask, can rival the three youths in Babylon, although the memory of the former has not been brought before us so conspicuously as that of the latter? These were truly first-fruits, and indications of the [succeeding] fructification. Hence God has directed their life to be recorded, as a model for those who should come after.

And that their virtue was thus accepted by God, as the first-fruits of the produce, hear what He has Himself declared: "As a grape," He says, "I have found Israel in the wilderness, and as first-ripe figs your fathers."[2] Call

---

[1] That is, the wine which flows from the grapes before they are trodden out.

[2] Hos. ix. 10.

not therefore the faith of Abraham merely blessed because he believed. Do you wish to look upon Abraham with admiration? Then behold how that one man alone professed piety when in the world six hundred had been contaminated with error. Dost thou wish Daniel to carry thee away to amazement? Behold that [city] Babylon, haughty in the flower and pride of impiousness, and its inhabitants completely given over to sin of every description. But he, emerging from the depth, spat out the brine of sins, and rejoiced to plunge into the sweet waters of piety. And now, in like manner, with regard to that mother of Zebedee's children, do not admire merely what she said, but also the time at which she uttered these words. For when was it that she drew near to the Redeemer? Not after the resurrection, nor after the preaching of His name, nor after the establishment of His kingdom; but it was when the Lord said, "Behold, we go up to Jerusalem, and the Son of man shall be delivered to the chief priests and the scribes; and they shall kill Him, and on the third day He shall rise again."[1]

These things the Saviour told in reference to His sufferings and cross; to these persons He predicted His passion. Nor did He conceal the fact that it should be of a most ignominious kind, at the hands of the chief priests. This woman, however, had attached another meaning to the dispensation of His sufferings. The Saviour was foretelling death; and she asked for the glory of immortality. The Lord was asserting that He must stand arraigned before impious judges; but she, taking no note of that judgment, requested as of the judge: "Grant," she said, "that these my two sons may sit, one on the right hand, and the other on the left, in Thy glory." In the one case the passion is referred to, in the other the kingdom is understood. The Saviour was speaking of the cross, while she had in view the glory which admits no suffering. This woman, therefore, as I have already said, is worthy of our admiration, not merely for what she sought, but also for the occasion of her making the request.

She did indeed suffer, not merely as a pious person, but

[1] Matt. xx. 18.

also as a woman. For, having been instructed by His words, she considered and believed that it would come to pass, that the kingdom of Christ should flourish in glory, and walk in its vastness throughout the world, and be increased by the preaching of piety. She understood, as was [in fact] the case, that He who appeared in a lowly guise had delivered and received every promise. I will inquire upon another occasion, when I come to treat upon this humility, whether the Lord rejected her petition concerning His kingdom. But she thought that the same confidence would not be possessed by her, when, at the appearance of the angels, He should be ministered to by the angels, and receive service from the entire heavenly host. Taking the Saviour, therefore, apart in a retired place, she earnestly desired of Him those things which transcend every human nature.

INDEXES.

I.—INDEX OF TEXTS.

	VOL. PAGE		VOL. PAGE
Gen. i. 1,	i. 123	Gen. xxiii. 11,	i. 142
i. 2,	i. 74	xxiv. 22, 25,	i. 76
i. 3,	ii. 5	xxv. 23,	i. 452
i. 25,	ii. 98	xxv. 26,	i. 452
i. 26,	i. 89, 107, 363, 377, 439	xxvii. 27, 28, 29,	ii. 145
i. 28,	i. 406	xxxi. 2,	i. 67
ii. 2,	ii. 132	xxxi. 11,	i. 404
ii. 5,	i. 358	xxxi. 41,	ii. 145
ii. 7,	i. 253, 439, ii. 96	xxxiii. 3,	ii. 145
ii. 8,	ii. 66	xxxv. 22,	i. 77
ii. 16,	ii. 109	xxxviii.	i. 459
ii. 16, 17,	ii. 117	xlii.	i. 77
ii. 25,	i. 361	xlix. 10-12,	i. 404
iii. 3, 4,	ii. 117	xlix. 18,	i. 284
iii. 9,	ii. 98	xlix. 28,	i. 77
iii. 13,	i. 366	Ex. i. 13, 14,	i. 477
iii. 14,	i. 364	iii. 4,	i. 404
iii. 15,	ii. 50, 110	iii. 6,	i. 387
iii. 16,	i. 364	iii. 7, 8,	i. 396, 411
iii. 19,	ii. 98, 166	iii. 8,	i. 270
iv. 7,	i. 365, 432, 433	iii. 14,	i. 270
iv. 10,	ii. 92	iii. 19,	i. 475
vi. 15,	i. 77	vii. 1,	i. 272
vi. 18,	i. 76	vii. 9,	i. 357
ix. 5, 6,	ii. 92	viii. 19,	i. 357
ix. 27,	i. 268	ix. 35,	i. 474
xii. 3,	i. 451	xi. 2,	i. 476
xiii. 13, 14, 15, 17,	ii. 142	xiii. 2,	i. 14
xv. 5,	i. 278, 395	xvii. 11,	ii. 11
xv. 13,	ii. 142	xvii. 16,	i. 328
xv. 19,	i. 76	xx. 5,	i. 103
xvii. 9-11,	i. 422	xx. 12,	i. 403
xvii. 12,	i. 76	xxi. 13,	i. 422
xvii. 17,	i. 394	xxiv. 4,	i. 77
xviii. 1,	i. 396	xxv. 10,	i. 207
xviii. 30,	i. 404	xxv. 17,	i. 207
xix. 22,	i. 388	xxv. 23,	i. 207
xix. 24,	i. 269	xxv. 31,	i. 207
xix. 31, 32,	ii. 2	xxv. 32,	i. 207
xix. 33,	ii. 2	xxv. 40,	i. 418, ii. 154
xix. 35,	ii. 2	xxvi. 1,	i. 75, 76, 208
xxii. 6,	i. 388	xxvi. 2,	i. 208

… INDEX OF TEXTS.

	VOL. PAGE		VOL. PAGE
Ex. xxvi. 7,	i. 208	Deut. xviii. 1,	i. 399
xxvi. 8,	i. 77	xxi. 23,	i. 339
xxvi. 16,	i. 208	xxviii. 66,	i. 405, ii. 106
xxvi. 26,	i. 208	xxx. 14,	ii. 175
xxvi. 37,	i. 210	xxx. 19, 20,	i. 424
xxvii. 1,	i. 210	xxxii. 1,	i. 379
xxviii. 1,	i. 210	xxxii. 4,	i. 344
xxviii. 2,	i. 77	xxxii. 6,	i. 405, ii. 2
xxviii. 5,	i. 210	xxxii. 8, LXX.,	i. 307
xxviii. 17,	i. 76	xxxii. 9,	i. 307
xxx. 23,	i. 208	xxxiii. 9,	i. 398
xxx. 34,	i. 208	Josh. iii. 12,	i. 77
xxxii. 6,	i. 469	iv. 3,	i. 77
xxxiii. 2, 3,	i. 420	v. 12,	ii. 168
xxxiii. 7,	i. 463	x. 17,	i. 210
xxxiii. 20,	i. 78, 442	Judg. vi. 27,	ii. 168
xxxiii. 20-22,	i. 446	vi. 37,	i. 335
xxxiv. 6, 7,	i. 445	xiv. 6-19,	ii. 178
xxxvi. 8,	i. 76	xv. 11,	ii. 178
xxxvi. 21,	i. 76	xv. 15,	ii. 178
Lev. x. 1, 2,	i. 462	xvi. 26,	ii. 171
xi. 2,	ii. 74	1 Sam. ix. 22,	i. 76
xxvi. 12,	ii. 170	xi. 27,	i. 465
Num. xii. 1,	ii. 173	xii. 1,	i. 466
xii. 7,	i. 272	xii. 3,	i. 464
xii. 8,	i. 406	xv. 22,	i. 426
xii. 14,	ii. 173	xvi. 10,	i. 76
xiv. 30,	i. 474	xviii.	i. 465
xv. 32,	i. 398	xx. 5,	i. 76
xvi. 15,	i. 464	2 Sam. v. 7,	i. 384
xvi. 33,	i. 463	1 Kings iv. 34,	i. 467
xviii. 20,	i. 399	viii. 27,	i. 467
xxi. 8,	i. 382	x. 1,	i. 467
xxii. 12, 22, 23,	ii. 169	xi. 1,	i. 467
xxiii. 19,	ii. 170	xi. 31,	i. 76
xxiv. 17,	i. 279	xiv. 10,	i. 463
xxiv. 23,	ii. 167	xviii. 21,	i. 271
xxvii. 18,	ii. 168	xviii. 36,	i. 271
xxvii. 20, 23,	ii. 169	xix. 11, 12,	i. 446
xxxi. 3,	ii. 170	2 Kings v. 14,	ii. 174
xxxi. 8,	ii. 170	vi. 6,	ii. 102, 174
xxxi. 16,	ii. 170	xiii. 21,	ii. 174
xxxviii. 8,	ii. 179	Ps. ii. 8,	i. 453
Deut. iv. 14,	i. 424	iii. 5,	ii. 16
iv. 19,	i. 272	iii. 6,	ii. 3
iv. 24,	i. 445	viii. 1,	i. 63
v. 2,	i. 423	viii. 3,	i. 407
v. 8,	i. 272	ix. 12,	i. 341
v. 22,	i. 419, 424	xiv. 3,	i. 78
v. 24,	i. 443	xviii. 45,	ii. 51
vi. 4, 6, 13,	i. 379	xix. 1,	i. 63
vi. 16,	ii. 112, 115	xix. 6,	ii. 16
viii. 3,	i. 424, ii. 112	xxi. 4,	i. 252
x. 12,	i. 424	xxii. 7,	ii. 15
x. 10,	i. 423	xxii. 15,	i. 445, ii. 15
xiv. 3, etc.,	ii. 74	xxii. 18,	ii. 15
xvi. 6,	i. 432	xxii. 31, LXX.,	ii. 71
xvi. 56,	i. 404	xxiii. 4,	ii. 140

INDEX OF TEXTS.

	VOL. PAGE		VOL. PAGE
Ps. xxiv. 7,	ii. 16	Ps. cxlviii. 5, 6,	i. 252
xxxii. 1, 2,	ii. 102	cxlix. 5,	ii. 51
xxxii. 11,	i. 324	Prov. i. 7,	i. 366
xxxiii. 6,	i. 85, 276	i. 20, 21,	ii. 109
xxxiii. 9,	i. 123	iii. 19, 20,	ii. 441
xxxiv. 1,	ii. 33	v. 22,	i. 280
xxxiv. 13, 14,	i. 429, ii. 28	viii. 15,	ii. 119
xxxv. 9,	i. 407	viii. 22-25,	i. 441
xxxviii. 11,	ii. 15	viii. 27-31,	i. 441
xl. 6,	i. 426	ix. 10,	i. 366
xlv. 2, 3, 4, 7,	ii. 13	xix. 17,	i. 436
xlv. 6,	i. 269	xxi. 1,	ii. 119
xlv. 11,	ii. 47	Isa. i. 2,	i. 379, ii. 51
xlv. 17,	i. 362, 387	i. 3,	i. 78
xlix. 12,	i. 385	i. 8,	i. 385
xlix. 20,	ii. 74	i. 8, 9,	ii. 16
xlix. 21,	ii. 52	i. 10, 16,	ii. 52
l. 1, 3,	i. 269	i. 11,	i. 427
l. 3, 4,	ii. 106	i. 14,	ii. 177
l. 9,	i. 427	i. 17-19,	ii. 28
l. 14, 15,	i. 427	i. 22,	i. 409
li. 12,	i. 334	i. 23,	i. 381
li. 17,	i. 426	ii. 17,	ii. 16
lviii. 3,	i. 282	ii. 34,	ii. 21
lviii. 3, 4,	ii. 52	iv. 4,	ii. 454
lxviii. 18,	i. 192	v. 6,	i. 335
lxix. 21,	i. 346, ii. 15	v. 12,	i. 197, 380
lxix. 26,	i. 297	vi. 1,	ii. 13
lxix. 27,	i. 360	vi. 5,	i. 445
lxxii. 1,	i. 269	vi. 10,	i. 474
lxxvi. 1,	i. 279, ii. 14	vi. 11,	ii. 149, 151
lxxviii. 5,	i. 326	vi. 12,	ii. 152
lxxx. 1,	i. 293	vii. 4,	i. 349
lxxxi. 9,	i. 270	vii. 10-17,	i. 355
lxxxii. 6,	i. 270	vii. 11,	i. 366
lxxxii. 6, 7,	i. 344, ii. 45	vii. 13,	i. 346, 355
lxxxiv. 16,	i. 471	vii. 14,	i. 346, 351, ii. 14
lxxxv. 11,	i. 266	viii. 3,	1. 327, ii. 14
lxxxvi. 23,	ii. 140	viii. 4,	i. 327
lxxxix. 11,	ii. 112	viii. 14,	i. 338
xci. 13,	i. 367	ix. 1,	ii. 168
xcv. 4,	i. 285	ix. 6,	i. 326, 346, ii. 14
xcv. 8,	i. 297	xi. 1,	i. 280
xcvi. 1,	i. 400	xi. 2,	i. 334, 336
xcvi. 2,	ii. 35	xi. 12,	ii. 6
xcvi. 5,	i. 270	xii. 2,	i. 284
xcviii. 2,	i. 284	xii. 4,	i. 386, ii. 7
xcix. 1,	ii. 16	xiii. 9,	ii. 151
cii. 25-27,	i. 383	xxv. 3,	i. 350
civ. 2, 4,	i. 231	xxv. 8,	ii. 83
cix. 8,	i. 191, 297	xxv. 9,	i. 401
cx. 1,	i. 226, 269, 287, 327	xxvi. 10,	ii. 151
cxviii. 22,	ii. 6	xxvi. 19,	ii. 14, 95, 148
cxxiv. 8,	i. 285	xxvii. 6,	i. 384
cxxx. 7,	ii. 163	xxviii. 16,	i. 357
cxxx. 11,	i. 279	xxix. 13,	i. 411
cxxxiv. 8,	i. 379	xxx. 1,	i. 433
cxlviii. 5,	i. 123	xxx. 25,	ii. 149

INDEX OF TEXTS.

Reference	Vol. Page	Reference	Vol. Page
Isa. xxxi. 9,	ii. 150	Jer. vi. 17, 18,	ii. 28
xxxii. 1,	ii. 150	vi. 20,	i. 428
xxxiii. 20,	i. 350	vii. 2, 3,	i. 428
xxxv. 3,	ii. 14	vii. 3,	ii. 28
xxxv. 5, 6,	ii. 14	vii. 21,	i. 428
xl. 6,	ii. 147	vii. 25,	ii. 32
xl. 12,	i. 437	vii. 29, 30,	ii. 28
xl. 12, 22,	i. 231	viii. 16,	ii. 137
xl. 15,	ii. 134	ix. 2,	i. 460
xlii. 3,	i. 446	ix. 24,	i. 428
xlii. 5,	i. 379, ii. 83	x. 11,	i. 271
xlii. 10,	i. 400	xi. 15,	i. 429
xliii. 5,	i. 417	xv. 9,	ii. 16
xliii. 10,	i. 270, 386	xvii. 9,	i. 239, 345, ii. 14
xliii. 19, 27,	ii. 17	xxii. 17,	i. 413
xliii. 23, 24,	i. 429	xxii. 24, 25,	i. 357
xliv. 9,	i. 270	xxii. 28, etc.,	i. 357
xlv. 5, 6,	i. 23, 103	xxiii. 7, 6,	ii. 148
xlv. 7,	ii. 49	xxiii. 20,	i. 461
xlvi. 2,	i. 429	xxiii. 23,	i. 438
xlvi. 9,	i. 23, 143	xxxi. 10,	ii. 150
xlviii. 32,	i. 71	xxxi. 11,	i. 276
xlix. 16,	ii. 153	xxxi. 26,	ii. 3
l. 6,	ii. 15	xxxi. 31,	i. 400
li. 6,	i. 383	xxxi. 31, 32,	ii. 17
liii. 2,	i. 346	xxxiii. 29,	ii. 103
liii. 3,	ii. 6, 15	xxxv. 15,	ii. 32
liii. 4,	ii. 14	xxxvi. 30, 31,	i. 358
liii. 7,	ii. 6, 15	Lam. iv. 20,	i. 284
liii. 7, 8,	i. 305	Ezek. i. 1,	i. 407
liii. 8,	i. 224, 345	ii. 1,	i. 407
liv. 1,	i. 45	xx. 12,	i. 422
liv. 11-14,	ii. 151	xx. 24,	i. 419
lvii. 1,	ii. 21	xxvii. 1,	ii. 95
lvii. 16,	ii. 83	xxviii. 25, 26,	ii. 148
lviii. 8,	i. 155	xxxvi. 26,	ii. 17
lviii. 6,	i. 429	xxxvii. 12,	ii. 96, 148
lviii. 14,	ii. 149	Dan. ii. 33, 34,	ii. 126
lx. 17,	i. 464	ii. 34,	i. 356
lxi. 1,	i. 280, 334, 336, 456	ii. 41, 42,	ii. 126
lxi. 2,	i. 196	ii. 42, 43,	ii. 126
lxiii. 9,	i. 350	ii. 44, 45,	ii. 127
lxiv. 4,	ii. 157	iii. 19,	ii. 25, 67
lxv. 1,	i. 269, 279	iii. 26,	i. 448
lxv. 2,	ii. 15	vii. 4,	i. 448
lxv. 17, 18,	ii. 154	vii. 8, 23,	ii. 123
lxv. 18,	ii. 151	vii. 10,	i. 138
lxv. 22,	ii. 96	vii. 13,	i. 346, ii. 7, 13
lxvi. 1,	i. 381	vii. 13, 14,	i. 448
lxvi. 3,	i. 434	viii. 12, 23,	ii. 124
lxvi. 13,	ii. 95	ix. 27,	ii. 125
lxvi. 22,	ii. 156	xii. 3,	i. 462
Jer. i. 5,	ii. 97	xii. 4, 7,	i. 461
ii. 13,	370	xii. 9, 10,	i. 79
ii. 19,	ii. 41	Hos. i. 2, 3,	i. 449
iv. 22,	i. 381	i. 6-9,	i. 450
v. 3,	ii. 74	ii. 23,	i. 45
v. 8,	ii. 52	iv. 1,	i. 78

INDEX OF TEXTS.

	VOL. PAGE		VOL. PAGE
Hos. vi. 6,	i. 430	Matt. v. 14,	i. 395
vii. 27,	ii. 149	v. 16,	i. 142, ii. 37
ix. 10,	ii. 185	v. 17, 18,	ii. 19
xii. 10,	i. 310, 443	v. 18,	i. 13
xii. 13,	ii. 149	v. 20,	i. 413
Joel ii. 28,	i. 297	v. 21,	i. 243, 413
iii. 16,	i. 351, ii. 14	v. 22,	i. 425, ii. 27
Amos i. 2,	i. 351	v. 23, 24,	i. 431
v. 25, 26,	i. 420	v. 26, 27,	i. 95
viii. 9, 11,	ii. 15	v. 27, 28,	i. 413
ix. 11, 12,	i. 312	v. 28,	i. 425
Jonah i. 9,	i. 348	v. 33,	i. 413
ii. 2,	i. 348	v. 34,	i. 381
ii. 11,	ii. 66	v. 35,	i. 383, ii. 35
iii. 8, 9,	i. 347	v. 39,	i. 342, ii. 21
Mic. iv. 23,	ii. 21	v. 41,	i. 414
vii. 9,	i. 350	v. 44,	i. 342
Hab. ii. 4,	ii. 19	v. 45,	i. 142, 197, 372, 414,
iii. 2,	i. 330		ii. 34, 59, 129
iii. 3,	ii. 14	vi. 3,	i. 479
iii. 5,	i. 351	vi. 9,	i. 142
Zech. vii. 9, 10,	i. 429, ii. 28	vi. 12,	ii. 100
vii. 16, 17,	i. 429	vi. 19,	i. 422
viii. 17,	ii. 28	vi. 24,	i. 275
ix. 9,	i. 346, ii. 6, 15	vii. 1, 2,	i. 478
xii. 10,	ii. 13	vii. 5,	i. 478
Mal. i. 2,	i. 452	vii. 7,	i. 160, 181, 232
i. 10, 11,	i. 430	vii. 15,	i. 2
i. 11,	ii. 176	vii. 19,	ii. 78
ii. 10,	i. 440	vii. 25,	i. 219
iii. 1,	i. 290	viii. 9,	i. 31
iv. 1,	i. 385, ii. 7	viii. 11,	i. 397
Matt. i. 1,	i. 324	viii. 11, 12,	ii. 36
i. 1, 18,	i. 294	viii. 13,	ii. 39
i. 12-16,	i. 357	ix. 2,	ii. 101
i. 18,	i. 324, 354	ix. 6,	ii. 102
i. 20,	i. 279	ix. 8,	ii. 101
i. 20, etc.,	i. 456	ix. 17,	ii. 17
i. 23,	i. 279, 354	ix. 29,	ii. 39
ii. 2,	i. 279	x. 6,	i. 315, 382
ii. 15,	i. 279	x. 8,	i. 18, 246
ii. 16,	i. 328	x. 10,	i. 399
iii. 3,	i. 278	x. 15,	i. 472
iii. 7,	i. 278	x. 17, 18,	i. 341
iii. 9,	i. 395, 459, ii. 148	x. 20,	i. 334
iii. 10,	i. 399, ii. 30, 103, 172	x. 21,	i. 14
iii. 11,	i. 385	x. 24,	i. 14, 224
iii. 12,	ii. 7, 13	x. 25,	ii. 128
iii. 16,	i. 279	x. 26,	i. 2
iv. 3,	i. 392, ii. 112	x. 28,	i. 341
iv. 7,	ii. 115	x. 29,	i. 216, ii. 116
iv. 9,	ii. 119	x. 30,	i. 215
iv. 10,	ii. 113	xi. 9,	i. 281, 290
v. 5,	i. 359, ii. 77, 143	xi. 11,	i. 281
v. 8,	i. 401, 442	xi. 12,	ii. 40
v. 12,	ii. 12	xi. 19,	ii. 3
v. 13,	ii. 3	xi. 23, 24,	ii. 29, 30
v. 13, 14,	i. 25	xi. 25,	i. 379

IREN.—VOL. II.   N

INDEX OF TEXTS.

Reference	Vol. Page
Matt. xi. 25-27,	i. 80
xi. 27,	i. 133
xi. 28,	i. 80
xi. 40,	ii. 140
xii. 5,	ii. 150
xii. 6,	i. 400
xii. 7,	i. 430
xii. 18,	i. 292
xii. 25,	ii. 126
xii. 29,	i. 276, 342, 363, ii. 114
xii. 31,	i. 296
xii. 36,	i. 184, 425
xii. 41,	ii. 9
xii. 41, 42,	i. 357
xii. 43,	i. 72
xiii. 11-16,	i. 474
xiii. 17,	i. 405, 454
xiii. 25,	ii. 79
xiii. 30,	ii. 129
xiii. 34,	ii. 50
xiii. 38,	i. 461, ii. 51, 53, 145
xiii. 40-43,	ii. 49
xiii. 43,	i. 243
xiii. 44,	i. 461
xiii. 52,	i. 399, 462
xiv. 19, 21,	i. 209
xv. 3,	i. 409
xv. 3, 4,	i. 403
xvi. 6,	ii. 52
xvi. 13,	ii. 340
xvi. 16,	i. 345
xvi. 17,	i. 315, 357, ii. 166
xvi. 21,	i. 340
xvi. 24, 25,	i. 349
xvii. 1, etc.,	i. 209
xvii. 3, etc.,	i. 446
xvii. 7,	i. 61
xvii. 27,	ii. 119
xviii. 8, 9,	i. 470
xviii. 10,	i. 58
xviii. 12,	i. 88
xix. 7, 8,	i. 420
xix. 17, 18,	i. 411
xix. 21,	i. 414
xix. 29,	ii. 144
xix. 30,	i. 362
xx.	ii. 34
xx. 1-16,	i. 6
xx. 16,	i. 362, 420, 470
xx. 18,	ii. 186
xxi. 8,	i. 381
xxi. 13,	i. 407
xxi. 16,	i. 407
xxi. 23,	i. 80
xxi. 31,	i. 451
xxii. 1, etc.,	ii. 31
xxii. 7,	ii. 33
xxii. 10, 11,	ii. 156

Reference	Vol. Page
Matt. xxii. 13,	ii. 32
xxii. 14,	ii. 33
xxii. 21,	i. 275
xxii. 29,	i. 386, 387, ii. 9
xxii. 33-41,	ii. 26
xxii. 42-44,	ii. 27
xxii. 43,	i. 357, ii. 9
xxiii. 2-4,	i. 410
xxiii. 9,	i. 378
xxiii. 13,	ii. 52
xxiii. 24,	i. 341, ii. 10
xxiii. 26,	i. 433
xxiii. 27,	i. 433
xxiii. 34,	i. 400
xxiii. 35,	ii. 92
xxiii. 37,	ii. 35, 36, 39
xxiv. 15, 21,	ii. 122, 125
xxiv. 21,	ii. 16, 134
xxiv. 28,	i. 417
xxiv. 42,	ii. 29, 79
xxiv. 45, 46,	i. 464
xxiv. 48,	i. 463, ii. 38
xxv. 2,	i. 209
xxv. 5,	i. 218
xxv. 13,	ii. 79
xxv. 14,	i. 336
xxv. 21,	i. 407
xxv. 32, 34,	ii. 49
xxv. 34,	i. 436, 472
xxv. 35, 36,	i. 479
xxv. 41,	i. 138, 243, 470, ii. 13, 48, 53
xxvi. 24,	i. 193, 472
xxvi. 26,	i. 430
xxvi. 27,	ii. 144
xxvi. 35,	ii. 154
xxvi. 38,	i. 33, 360
xxvi. 39,	i. 33
xxvi. 41,	ii. 76
xxvii. 46,	i. 33
xxvii. 52,	ii. 171
xxviii. 19,	i. 334
Mark i. 1,	i. 326
i. 24,	i. 392
iii. 27,	ii. 114
iv. 28,	i. 435
v. 22,	i. 87
v. 31,	i. 13
vi. 42, 44,	i. 209
viii. 31,	i. 328
ix. 2,	i. 67
x. 17,	i. 79
x. 38,	i. 81
xiii. 32,	i. 224
xiii. 33,	ii. 79
xiv. 21,	i. 193
xvi. 19,	i. 287
Luke i. 2,	i. 318, 376

INDEX OF TEXTS.

	VOL. PAGE		VOL. PAGE
Luke i. 6,	i. 281	Luke x. 12,	ii. 30, 129
i. 8,	i. 281	x. 13,	ii. 121
i. 15,	i. 281	x. 16,	i. 258
i. 17,	i. 287, 290	x. 18,	i. 336
i. 26,	i. 282	x. 19,	i. 192, 367, ii. 121
i. 32,	i. 282, 327	x. 21,	i. 379
i. 33,	i. 279	x. 22,	i. 389, 393, 396
i. 35,	i. 354, ii. 57	x. 35,	i. 336
i. 38,	i. 361	x. 60,	ii. 76
i. 42,	i. 357	xi.	i. 319
i. 46,	i. 282, 394	xi. 21, 22,	ii. 9
i. 68,	i. 283	xi. 40,	i. 225
i. 69,	i. 326	xi. 50,	ii. 92
i. 71, 75,	i. 442	xii. 20,	i. 319
i. 76,	i. 283	xii. 35, 36,	ii. 38
i. 78,	i. 283, ii. 101	xii. 37, 38,	i. 149
ii. 8,	i. 394	xii. 45, 46,	i. 403, ii. 38
ii. 11,	i. 284	xii. 47,	ii. 38
ii. 20,	i. 285	xii. 50,	i. 81
ii. 22,	i. 286	xii. 58,	i. 95
ii. 23,	i. 14	xiii.	i. 319, 320
ii. 28,	i. 35, 327	xiii. 6,	ii. 35
ii. 29,	i. 286, 327, 394	xiii. 15, 16,	i. 397
ii. 36,	i. 35	xiii. 16,	i. 204
ii. 38,	i. 286	xiii. 28,	i. 397
ii. 42,	i. 12	xiii. 32,	ii. 53
ii. 49,	i. 79	xiii. 34,	ii. 35
iii. 8,	ii. 142	xiv. 12,	ii. 144
iii. 11,	i. 479	xiv. 14,	ii. 157
iii. 17,	ii. 7	xiv. 27,	i. 14
iii. 23,	i. 6, 201	xv. 4,	i. 69
iv. 6,	ii. 116, 119	xv. 4-8,	i. 35
iv. 6, 7,	ii. 113	xv. 8,	i. 69
iv. 18,	i. 456	xv. 11,	ii. 34
v.	i. 319	xv. 22, 23,	i. 418
v. 20,	ii. 101	xvi.	i. 319
v. 31, 32,	i. 267	xvi. 9,	i. 479
v. 36, 37,	ii. 23	xvi. 11,	i. 253
vi. 3, 4,	i. 398	xvi. 16,	i. 385
vi. 13,	i. 12	xvi. 19,	i. 251, 380
vi. 24,	i. 319	xvi. 28,	i. 209
vi. 29,	i. 414	xvi. 31,	i. 380
vi. 40,	ii. 140	xvii.	i. 319
vi. 46,	ii. 38, 75	xvii. 5,	i. 319
vii.	i. 319	xvii. 24,	ii. 129
vii. 8,	i. 31	xvii. 26,	ii. 29
vii. 12,	ii. 67	xviii.	i. 319, 320
vii. 26,	i. 290	xviii. 2,	ii. 124
vii. 35,	i. 35	xviii. 8,	ii. 13
vii. 43,	i. 348	xviii. 10,	ii. 35
viii. 41,	i. 33	xviii. 18,	i. 79
viii. 51,	i. 209	xviii. 27,	i. 146, 442, ii. 67
ix. 13, 14,	i. 209	xviii. 29, 30,	ii. 144
ix. 22,	i. 328	xix.	i. 319
ix. 57, 58,	i. 33	xix. 5,	i. 34
ix. 60,	i. 34	xix. 8,	i. 412
ix. 61, 62,	i. 34	xix. 26,	i. 27
x. 1,	i. 194	xix. 42,	i. 80

INDEX OF TEXTS.

	VOL. PAGE		VOL. PAGE
Luke xxi. 4,	i. 432	John viii. 58,	i. 416, ii. 182
xxi. 34,	ii. 37	viii. 59,	ii. 182
xxi. 34, 35,	ii. 29	ix. 1,	i. 177
xxiii. 24,	i. 341	ix. 3,	ii. 96
xxiv.	i. 320	ix. 7,	ii. 97
xxiv. 25,	i. 328	ix. 30,	ii. 87
xxiv. 39,	ii. 60	xi. 25,	i. 387
xxiv. 44,	i. 328	xi. 54,	i. 199
John i. 1,	i. 288, 293, ii. 305	xii. 1,	i. 99
i. 1, 2, 3, 4,	i. 36	xii. 27,	i. 33
i. 3,	i. 85, 123, 276, 358, ii. 5	xii. 32,	i. 382
i. 5,	i. 37	xiii. 5,	i. 454
i. 6,	i. 290	xiv. 2,	i. 347, ii. 156
i. 10, 11,	i. 289, ii. 105	xiv. 6,	i. 266
i. 13,	i. 245, ii. 58, 106	xiv. 6, 7,	i. 395
i. 13, 14,	i. 325	xiv. 7, 9, 10,	i. 315
i. 14,	i. 284, 289, 290, ii. 10, 105	xiv. 11,	ii. 104
i. 15, 16,	i. 284	xiv. 16,	i. 295
i. 18,	i. 291, 444, 447	xiv. 28,	i. 227
i. 29,	i. 283	xv. 15,	i. 415
i. 47,	i. 292	xv. 16,	i. 417
i. 49,	i. 292	xvi. 7,	i. 335
i. 50,	i. 401	xvii. 5,	i. 416
ii. 3,	i. 291	xvii. 12,	i. 193
ii. 4,	i. 330	xvii. 16,	i. 27
ii. 19-21,	ii. 69	xvii. 24,	i. 417
ii. 23,	i. 198	xix. 11,	i. 434
ii. 25,	i. 280	xix. 15,	i. 452
iii. 5,	ii. 174	xix. 34,	ii. 7
iii. 14,	i. 382	xx. 17,	ii. 140
iii. 18-21,	ii. 130	xx. 20, 27,	ii. 140
iv. 6,	i. 360	xx. 22,	ii. 182
iv. 14,	ii. 29, 182	xx. 24,	i. 77
iv. 24,	ii. 176	xx. 25-27,	ii. 70
iv. 35,	i. 455	xx. 26,	ii. 182
iv. 37,	i. 460	xx. 31,	i. 328
iv. 41,	i. 382	Acts i. 7,	i. 362
iv. 50,	i. 198	i. 16,	i. 297
v. 1,	i. 198	i. 20,	i. 191
v. 5,	i. 204	ii. 22-27,	i. 297
v. 14,	ii. 33, 96	ii. 30-37,	i. 298
v. 28,	ii. 88	ii. 37, 38,	i. 298
v. 35,	ii. 180	ii. 41,	i. 457
v. 39, 40,	i. 403	iii. 6,	i. 299
v. 43,	ii. 124	iii. 12,	i. 300
v. 46,	i. 403	iii. 15,	i. 200
v. 46, 47,	i. 379	iv. 2,	i. 300
vi. 1,	i. 199	iv. 4,	i. 457
vi. 9,	i. 209	iv. 8, etc.,	i. 300
vi. 11,	i. 291	iv. 22,	i. 301
vi. 69,	i. 292	iv. 24,	i. 301
vii. 30,	i. 330	iv. 31,	i. 302
vii. 39,	ii. 105	iv. 33,	i. 302
viii. 34,	i. 275	v. 30,	i. 302
viii. 36,	i. 344	v. 42,	i. 302
viii. 44,	ii. 116, 118	vii. 2-8,	i. 308
viii. 56,	i. 388	vii. 5, 6,	ii. 142
viii. 56, 57,	i. 202	vii. 38,	i. 420

INDEX OF TEXTS.

	VOL. PAGE		VOL. PAGE
Acts vii. 56,	i. 310	Rom. viii. 10,	ii. 80, 175
viii. 9-11,	i. 86	viii. 11,	i. 333, ii. 70
viii. 9, 18,	i. 246	viii. 13,	ii. 80
viii. 20, 21, 23,	i. 86	viii. 15,	i. 270, 404, ii. 73
viii. 27,	i. 456	viii. 19,	ii. 142
viii. 32,	i. 405	viii. 21,	ii. 157
viii. 37,	i. 405	viii. 34,	i. 333
ix. 15, 16,	i. 321	viii. 36,	i. 198, 422
ix. 20,	i. 306	ix. 5,	i. 326
x. 1,	i. 303	ix. 10-13,	i. 452
x. 15,	i. 304	ix. 13,	i. 452
x. 28, 29,	i. 313	ix. 25,	i. 44, 278
x. 34, 35,	i. 304	ix. 25, 26,	i. 450
x. 37-44,	i. 304	x. 3, 4,	i. 411
x. 47,	i. 313	x. 6, 7,	i. 338
xiv. 15-17,	i. 307	x. 9,	i. 338
xv. 14,	i. 312, 349	x. 15,	i. 314
xv. 15,	i. 311	xi. 16,	i. 34
xvi. 8,	i. 316	xi. 17,	ii. 78
xvi. 13,	i. 316	xi. 21, 17,	i. 468
xvii. 24,	i. 307	xi. 26,	i. 382
xx. 5, 6,	i. 316	xi. 32,	i. 44, 349
xx. 25,	i. 318	xi. 33,	i. 45
xxi.	i. 317	xi. 34,	i. 55
xxii. 8,	i. 321	xi. 36,	i. 14
xxvi. 15,	i. 321	xii. 1,	ii. 176
xxvii.	i. 317	xii. 3,	ii. 110
xxviii. 11,	i. 317	xii. 16,	ii. 115
Rom. i. 1-4,	i. 326	xiii. 1,	ii. 119
i. 3, 4,	i. 360	xiii. 1-7,	ii. 34
i. 17,	ii. 19	xiii. 4,	ii. 119
i. 18,	i. 471	xiii. 6,	ii. 119
i. 21,	ii. 6	xiii. 10,	i. 410
i. 25,	i. 143	xiv. 9.	i. 338
i. 28,	i. 475	xiv. 15,	i. 339
ii. 5,	ii. 18	1 Cor. i. 18,	i. 15
ii. 27,	i. 412	i. 23,	i. 338
iii. 8,	ii. 94	i. 26-28,	i. 189
iii. 11,	i. 78	i. 29,	i. 348
iii. 21,	ii. 19	ii. 6,	i. 35, 259, ii. 68
iii. 23,	i. 468	ii. 9,	ii. 157
iii. 30,	i. 455, ii. 115	ii. 10,	i. 226
iv. 3,	i. 396	ii. 14,	i. 34, ii. 75, 175
iv. 12,	i. 395	ii. 15,	i. 34, ii. 6, 18
v. 14,	i. 243, 360	iii. 1,	ii. 75
v. 17,	i. 332	iii. 2,	ii. 42
v. 19,	i. 244, 358	iii. 3,	ii. 43
v. 20,	i. 368	iii. 7,	ii. 460
vi. 3, 4,	i. 332	iii. 16,	ii. 69
vi. 7,	i. 367	iii. 16, 17,	ii. 178
vi. 9,	i. 333	iii. 17,	i. 399, ii. 70
vi. 12, 13,	ii. 94	iv. 4,	i. 401
vii. 18,	i. 349, ii. 34	v. 6,	i. 470
vii. 24,	i. 351	v. 11,	i. 470
viii. 3,	i. 349	vi. 9, 10,	i. 470
viii. 5,	ii. 80	vi. 9-11,	ii. 81
viii. 8,	ii. 80	vi. 11,	ii. 39
viii. 9,	ii. 73, 80	vi. 12,	ii. 38

INDEX OF TEXTS.

	VOL. PAGE		VOL. PAGE
1 Cor. vi. 13,	ii. 70	2 Cor. iv. 11,	ii. 91
vi. 20,	ii. 89	v. 4,	i. 188, ii. 32, 72, 89
vii. 5,	i. 420	vii. 2,	i. 464
vii. 6,	i. 420	viii. 1,	ii. 11
vii. 12,	i. 420	x. 5,	ii. 33
vii. 14,	i. 450	xii. 2, 3, 4,	i. 235
vii. 25,	i. 421	xii. 3,	i. 236, ii. 60
vii. 31,	i. 383, ii. 154, 155	xii. 4,	ii. 66
viii. 1,	i. 215	xii. 7-9,	ii. 61
viii. 4, etc.,	i. 272	xii. 9,	i. 347
viii. 11,	i. 339	xiii.	ii. 11
ix. 24,	ii. 40	xiii. 4,	ii. 179
x. 1, etc.,	i. 469	Gal. i. 1,	i. 315
x. 4,	ii. 182	i. 15, 16,	ii. 85, 97
x. 11,	i. 418	ii. 1, 2,	i. 315
x. 16,	i. 336, ii. 59	ii. 5,	i. 315
xi. 4, 5,	i. 296	ii. 8,	i. 314
xi. 10,	i. 33	ii. 12, 13,	i. 313
xii. 4, 5, 6,	i. 226	iii. 5-9,	i. 451
xii. 4-7,	i. 443	iii. 6,	ii. 143
xii. 28,	i. 291, 370, 464	iii. 13,	i. 339
xiii. 2,	i. 410	iii. 16,	ii. 143
xiii. 9,	i. 226, 227	iii. 19,	i. 274, ii. 110
xiii. 9, 10,	i. 401	iii. 24,	i. 382
xiii. 9, 12,	ii. 172	iv. 4,	i. 330, 358, ii. 111
xiii. 13,	i. 222, 410	iv. 5,	i. 326
xiv. 20,	i. 474	iv. 8,	i. 143
xv. 3. 4,	i. 339	iv. 8, 9,	i. 272
xv. 8,	i. 33	iv. 24,	i. 45
xv. 10,	i. 457	iv. 26,	ii. 153
xv. 11,	i. 314	iv. 28,	i. 395
xv. 12,	i. 339	v. 19,	ii. 81
xv. 13,	ii. 91	v. 21,	i. 26
xv. 20-22,	i. 362	vi. 14,	i. 15
xv. 22,	i. 368, ii. 58	Eph. i. 7,	ii. 93
xv. 25, 26,	ii. 156	i. 10,	i. 14, 42, 110
xv. 26,	i. 367	i. 13,	ii. 72
xv. 27, 28,	ii. 157	i. 21,	i. 438, 458
xv. 30,	i. 111	ii. 2,	ii. 121
xv. 36,	ii. 71	ii. 7,	i. 387
xv. 41,	i. 175	ii. 13,	i. 339, ii. 93
xv. 42,	ii. 71	ii. 15,	ii. 93
xv. 43,	ii. 71	ii. 17,	i. 268
xv. 44,	i. 188, ii. 72	ii. 20,	i. 459
xv. 45,	ii. 85	iii. 21,	i. 12
xv. 46,	ii. 82	iv. 5, 6,	ii. 5, 105
xv. 48,	i. 34, ii. 76	iv. 6,	i. 123, 440
xv. 49,	ii. 77, 83	iv. 8,	i. 192
xv. 50,	ii. 75, 79, 80	iv. 9,	i. 454, ii. 140
xv. 52,	ii. 87	iv. 9, 10,	ii. 182
xv. 53,	ii. 60, 80, 88, 91	iv. 25, 29,	ii. 38
xv. 54,	i. 44	v. 6, 7,	i. 470
xv. 54, 55,	i. 367	v. 13,	i. 37
2 Cor. ii. 15, 16,	i. 473	v. 30,	ii. 60
ii. 17,	i. 464	v. 32,	i. 35
iii. 3,	ii. 90	vi. 12,	i. 42
iv. 4,	i. 272, 475, ii. 179	Col. i. 14,	ii. 59
iv. 10,	ii. 90	i. 14, 15,	i. 326

INDEX OF TEXTS.

	VOL. PAGE		VOL. PAGE
Col. i. 16,	i. 19	Jas. i. 18,	ii. 56
i. 18,	i. 200, 440	i. 21,	ii. 79
i. 21,	ii. 93	ii. 23,	i. 416, 423
ii. 9,	i. 14	1 Pet. i. 8,	i. 401, ii. 72
ii. 11,	i. 422	i. 12,	i. 177, ii. 19, 157
ii. 14,	ii. 102, 176	ii. 3,	ii. 175
ii. 16,	ii. 177	ii. 5-9,	i. 398
ii. 18,	ii. 175	ii. 16,	i. 425, ii. 38
ii. 19,	ii. 5, 94	ii. 23,	i. 333, 440
iii. 5,	ii. 85	ii. 24,	ii. 170
iii. 9,	ii. 84	iii. 20,	i. 76
iii. 10,	ii. 85	iv. 14,	ii. 12
iii. 11,	i. 14	2 Pet. iii. 8,	ii. 118, 132
iv. 14,	i. 317	1 John ii. 1,	i. 336
Phil. i. 22,	ii. 85	ii. 18,	i. 339
ii. 8,	i. 458, ii. 96	v. 1,	i. 332
ii. 9,	ii. 175	2 John 7, 8,	i. 331
ii. 10, 11,	i. 42	11,	i. 71
ii. 15,	i. 388	Jude 3,	ii. 175
iii. 2, 9,	ii. 89	7,	ii. 30
iii. 11,	ii. 90	Rev. i. 5,	i. 362
iv. 17,	i. 399	i. 12,	i. 448
iv. 18,	i. 434	i. 15,	i. 418
1 Thess. ii. 10-12,	ii. 69	i. 17,	i. 448
v. 3,	ii. 137	ii. 6,	i. 98
v. 23,	ii. 69	ii. 17,	ii. 79
2 Thess. i. 6-10,	i. 471	iii. 7,	i. 440
i. 9, 10,	ii. 13	iv. 7,	i. 293
ii. 4,	i. 272	v. 6,	i. 449
ii. 8,	i. 274, ii. 123	v. 8,	i. 431, ii. 176
ii. 11,	i. 475	vi. 2,	i. 452
1 Tim. i. 1,	ii. 175	vii. 5-7,	ii. 137
i. 9,	i. 423	xi. 19,	i. 436
ii. 5,	ii. 100	xii. 14,	i. 242
iii. 15,	i. 293	xiii. 2,	ii. 131
iv. 2,	i. 196	xiii. 11, 14,	ii. 132
vi. 4,	i. 308	xv. xvi.	i. 480
vi. 4, 5,	ii. 175	xvii. 8,	ii. 138
vi. 20,	i. 89, 116	xvii. 12,	ii. 125
2 Tim. ii. 17, 18,	i. 241	xix. 11-17,	i. 449
ii. 23,	i. 376	xix. 20,	ii. 131
iii. 6,	i. 56	xx. 6,	ii. 149
iii. 7,	i. 402, ii. 109	xx. 11,	ii. 153
iv. 3,	i. 195	xx. 12-14,	ii. 154
iv. 10, 11,	i. 317	xx. 15,	i. 154
Tit. iii. 10,	i. 71, 263	xxi. 1-4,	ii. 154
Heb. i. 3,	i. 238	xxi. 2,	ii. 153
iii. 5,	i. 272	xxi. 5, 6,	ii. 155
x. 9,	i. 426	xxii. 17,	i. 264
xi. 13,	ii. 142	xxii. 19,	ii. 136
xiii. 15,	ii. 142		

II.—INDEX OF PRINCIPAL SUBJECTS.

AARON and Miriam, their sin against Moses, and its punishment, ii. 173.
Abel and Cain, the offerings of, i. 432.
Abominations, the, practised by the Valentinians, i. 26, etc.
Abraham, saw the day of Christ, 388, 394, etc.; vain attempt of Marcion to exclude him from Christ's salvation, 396, etc.; had faith identical with ours, 451; both covenants prefigured in, 459, 460; waited for the promises of God, ii. 142, 143.
Abraxas, Basilides' doctrine of, i. 93.
Acceptable year of the Lord, the, i. 197.
Achamoth, an account of, i. 16; origin of the visible world from, 17, etc.; shall at last enter the Pleroma, 28; asserted to be referred to in Scripture, 33-35.
Adam and Eve, the story of, according to the Ophites, i. 107, 108.
Adam, the first, made a partaker of salvation, i. 362; his repentance signified by the girdle which he made, 366; why driven out of Paradise, 367; in Paradise, ii. 66; sinned on the sixth day of creation, 116-118; death of, 118.
Adam, analogy between the first and the second, i. 359.
Æon, the twelfth, the sufferings of, not to be deduced from Scripture, i. 190; nor typified by the woman with the issue of blood, 203.
Æons, the thirty, of Valentinus, i. 4, etc.; English equivalents of the Greek names of, 5, 6, note; how the thirty are said to be indicated in Scripture, 12; the production of, 152, etc., 168, etc.; further inquiry into and refutation of the speculations respecting, 172-179; the theory of, further exposed, 180, etc., 184, etc.; the twelve apostles not types of the twelve, 194; the thirty, not typified by the baptism of Jesus in His thirtieth year, 196.
Agape, i. 212.

Αἰών, meaning of the term, i. 444.
Aletheia, the Æon so called, i. 5, 7; how her passion is said to be indicated in Scripture, 13; of Ptolemy, 49; revealed by Tetrad, 59, etc.
Aletheia, the numerical value of, does not square with Valentinianism, i. 212.
Anaxagoras, i. 162.
Anaximander, i. 162.
Angels, the world not made by, i. 120, 121; could not be ignorant of the Supreme God, 132.
Angels of the devil, ii. 50, etc.
Animal men, the, of the Valentinians, i. 25, 33.
Animals, clean and unclean, ii. 74.
Anthropos and Ecclesia, the Æons so named, i. 5, 7, 50, 106.
Antichrist, the fraud, pride, and tyranny of the kingdom of, ii. 121-125; concentrates in himself the apostasy, 131; the number of the name of, 135.
Antiphanes, the theogony of, i. 160.
Apator, i. 21.
Apocryphal Scriptures, the, of the Marcosians, i. 79.
Apostles, the twelve, not types of the twelve Æons, i. 194.
Apostles, the, did not begin to preach till endued with the Holy Spirit, i. 258; preached one God, 259; the doctrine of, 296-314; the labours of, lessened by their predecessors, 455.
Aquila and Theodotian, their interpretation of Isa. vii. 14 referred to, i. 351, 352.
Ark of the covenant, i. 207, ii. 163.
Autogenes, i. 102.
Axe, the, made to float by means of wood, ii. 171.
Axe, the, laid at the root, ii. 172.

Balaam, ii. 167; forbidden to curse Israel, 169; his ass a type, 169, 170; slain, 170.
Baptism of Jesus in his thirtieth year not a type of the thirty Æons, i. 196.
Barbeliotes or Borborians, the, i. 101.

INDEX OF PRINCIPAL SUBJECTS. 201

Basilides, the doctrines of, i. 90, etc.; absurd notion of, as to the death of Jesus, 91; this notion of, refuted, 253.
Beast, the, ii. 131, etc., 134, etc.
Bishops, a succession of, in various churches, i. 261, etc.; first, of Rome, 261, 262.
Blandina, the martyr, ii. 165.
Blood, the, of Christ, redeems, ii. 58, 59.
Blood, the Christians accused of eating, how the calumny originated, ii. 165.
Bodies, the, of men, temples of the Holy Ghost, ii. 69; from the earth, 98.
Body and soul, the views of heretics respecting the future destiny of, refuted, i. 228.
Bread and wine in the Eucharist, ii. 59.
Breath of life, the, ii. 83.
Bythus, i. 4, 7, 49; absurdity of, 124.

Cain, i. 365; and Abel, the respective offerings of, 432.
Cainites, the doctrines of the, i. 113.
Carnal and spiritual, ii. 80, etc.
Carpocrates, the doctrines of, i. 93; the followers of, practised magic and incantations, 94; immorality of the system of, 94, 95; his views of the devil, 95; his followers branded with external marks, and have images of Jesus, etc., 96.
Centurion, the, of the Gospels, asserted by the Valentinians to be the Demiurge, i. 30.
Cerdo, the doctrines of, i. 98.
Cerinthus, the doctrines of, i. 97.
Christ, Valentinus' views of, i. 14, 25, 28, 29, 46, 51; the origin of, according to the Ophites, 104; the descent of, upon Jesus, according to the Ophites, 111, 112; the apostles of, their preaching, 266; and Jesus, the same, the only-begotten Son of God, 223-233; not, but the Holy Spirit, descended upon Jesus, 334; and Jesus of Nazareth proved from the writings of Paul to be one and the same, 337, etc.; did not flee away from Jesus at the cross, 340; did not suffer in appearance merely, 342; assumed actual flesh, conceived and born of the Virgin, 359, etc.; the advent of, foretold, 404; the advent of, foreknown and desired by righteous men, 405; did not abolish the law, 408; is the end of the law, 411; did not abrogate the natural precepts of the law, but removed the bondage, 412; came for the sake of men of all ages, 433, etc.; is the treasure hid in the field, 461; descended into regions beneath the earth, 467; foreseen and foretold by the prophets, ii. 13-17; the prophets referred all their predictions to, 18, etc.; alone able to redeem us, 55, etc.; took flesh, not seemingly, but really, 56; conferred on our flesh the capacity of salvation, 58-61; his resurrection a proof of ours, 70, etc.; the dead raised by, a proof of the resurrection, 87; fitting that He should take human nature and be tempted by the devil, 110, etc.; His victory over Satan, *ibid.*; temptation of, 111, etc.; His kingdom eternal, 127, 128; the resurrection of, 139, 140; how prefigured, 167, 168; testimony of the sacred books to, 182, 183, 184.
Christians, calumnies against the, ii. 165.
Church, the, her gifts, i. 246; performs nothing by incantations or curious arts, *ibid.*; of Rome, founded by Peter and Paul, 261; the catholic, the depository of truth, 264, etc.
Clean and unclean, ii. 74.
Colorbasus, the doctrines of, i. 49, etc.
Commandment, the first and greatest, i. 411.
Communion with God, ii. 129.
Cosmocrator, the, i. 23.
Covenant, the new, ii. 19, 20.
Covenants, one author and one end to both, i. 399, etc.; the oneness of both proved by Jesus' reproof of customs repugnant to the former, 408.
Created things, made after the image of invisible things, according to the Marcosians, i. 72, etc.
Created things, not images of Æons within the Pleroma, i. 134-140; not a shadow of the Pleroma, 140-142.
Creation, the, of all things out of nothing by God, i. 144-146.
Creator, but one, of the world, i. 142.

202 INDEX OF PRINCIPAL SUBJECTS.

Creator, the, made all things, spiritual and material, i. 237, 239; is the Word, ii. 105.
Creator, the, could not be ignorant of the Supreme God, i. 132, 133.

Day, the, does not square with the theory of Valentinus, i. 211.
Day of retribution, the, i. 197.
Dead, the, raised by Christ, a proof of the resurrection, ii. 87.
Death, the, and life, ii. 82.
Decalogue, the, at first inscribed on the hearts of men, i. 419; not cancelled by Christ, 424, 425.
Demiurge, the, the formation of, according to Valentinus, i. 20; the creator of all things outside the Pleroma, 21; ignorant of what he created, 22; ignorant of the offspring of his mother Achamoth, 24; passes into the intermediate habitation, 28; instructed by the Saviour, 20; is the centurion of the Gospels, *ibid.*; views of the heretics respecting, exposed and confuted, 184, etc.; declared by the heretics to be animal, 231; if animal, how could he make things spiritual? 237, 239.
Devil, views of the Carpocratians respecting, i. 95.
Devil, practised in falsehoods, he tempted man, ii. 116, 117; his lie in regard to the government of the world, 119, 120.
Devil, the sons of the, ii. 51.
Deuteronomy, ii. 167.
Diatheses, the, of Ptolemy, i. 49.
Disciples, the true spiritual, ii. 6, etc.
Discriminating faculty, the, in man, ii. 45.
Disobedient, the, are the angels of the devil, ii. 49.
Duodecad, the, of Valentinus, how said to be indicated in Scripture, i. 12.
Dyad, the, of Valentinus, i. 45.

Earthly things, types of heavenly, i. 436.
Ebionites, the, i. 97; refutation of, who disparaged the writings of Paul, 320, etc.; strictures on, ii. 57.
Ecclesia, the, of the Valentinians, i. 24; of Ptolemy, 50.
Egyptians, the Israelites commanded to spoil the goods of, an exposition and vindication, i. 475-480.

Elements, the twenty-four, of Marcus, i. 64, etc.
Elijah, ii. 66.
Elisha, ii. 102.
Emanations, the, of Valentinus and others, an account of, 4-35, 45, etc., 49, etc., 64, etc.; ridicule poured on, 47, 48.
Encratites, the, i. 100.
Enmity, the, put between Eve and the serpent, i. 367.
Ennœæ, i. 4, 5, 49, 101, etc., 104.
Enoch, the translation of, ii. 65, 66.
Enthymesis, the, of Sophia or Achamoth, i. 9, 21; the absurdity of, 180, etc.; the treachery of Judas not a type of, 191-193.
Error, how often set off, i. 2.
Eucharist, the, i. 435, ii. 59.
Evanthas, ii. 137.
Eve and the Virgin Mary compared, ii. 106, etc.
Eve, the story of, according to the Ophites, i. 107.

Faith, the unity of the, in the universal church, i. 42, etc.
Faith of Abraham, the, the same as ours, i. 45.
Father, the, the world made by, through the Word, i. 120-123.
Father, the, how no one knows, but the Son, i. 389; reveals the Son, 391.
Fear produces (according to Valentinus) animal substances, i. 22, 23.
Five, the number, the frequent use of, in Scripture, i. 208-210.
Flesh, the, as nourished by the body of the Lord, incorruptible, i. 435; made capable of salvation, ii. 59-64; quickened, 84, etc.; saved by the Word taking flesh, 91; the saints having suffered in, shall receive their rewards in, 141, etc., 143, etc.
Flesh and blood, ii. 75-78.
Flesh, the works of the, ii. 80, etc.
Florinus, ii. 158.
Free-will, man endowed with, ii. 37-41.
Fruit of the belly and of the loins, i. 355.

Gentiles, the conversion of, more difficult than that of the Jews, i. 457-459.
Gideon, a type, i. 335, ii. 68.
Gifts, the, of the Holy Spirit, ii. 72.

INDEX OF PRINCIPAL SUBJECTS. 203

Gnostics, the hypocrisy and pride of, i. 321.
God, but one, proved against Marcion and others, i. 117-120; the world made by, 120-123; created all things out of nothing, 144-146; not to be sought after by means of syllables and letters, 212, etc.; many things, the knowledge of which must be left in His hands, 221, 222; alone knows all things, 224; all things made by, 235; different names of, in the Hebrew Scriptures, 254, 255; one, proclaimed by Christ and the apostles, 266; the Holy Ghost throughout the Old Testament mentions but one, 268; objection to the doctrine of one, deduced from 2 Cor. iv. 5, answered, 273; objection from Matt. vi. 24 answered, 275; proved to be one and the same, the Creator, from the Gospel of Matthew, 277; from Mark and Luke, 281; from John, 287-292, 296, etc., showed Himself to be merciful and mighty to save, after the fall of man, 347, etc.; His providential rule over the world, 371; just to punish and good to save, 371, 372; but one, who is the Father, 377, 378; the unity of, proved from Moses, the prophets, and Christ, 378-382; immutable and eternal, 382; the destruction of Jerusalem derogates nothing from His majesty, 383; but one, announced by the law and the prophets, whom Christ confesses as His Father, 386, etc.; has placed man under law for man's own benefit, 416, etc.; needs nothing from man, 426, 427; formed all things by the Word and Spirit, 439-444; declared by the Son, 444; seen by men, 426, 427; yet invisible, 446; not the author of sin, 471; the author of both testaments, ii. 4, etc.; attributes of, 43; the misery of departure from, 47; one and the same, inflicts punishments and bestows rewards, 48, etc.; His power and glory will shine forth in the resurrection, 61, etc.; those deceived who feign another, 64, etc.; the image of, in which man was made, 99; unity of, reaffirmed, 100; pardons our sins, 100, etc.; and the Word, formed all things by their own power, 103, etc.; declared by the law and manifested in Christ, 114, etc.; communion with, 129, 130; His infinitude, 162; always true and faithful, 170.
God of this world, the, i. 273.
Gods, the so-called, in the Old Testament, i. 270.
Good works not necessary for Valentinian heretics, i. 26.
Gospels, the four, there can be neither more nor fewer, i. 293; symbolized by the four living creatures, 293, 294; respective characteristics of, 294; those who destroy the form of, vain and unlearned, 295.
Government, civil, of God, and to be obeyed, ii. 119, etc.
Grain of mustard seed, the, ii. 172.
Greater and less, application of the phrase, i. 400-403.
Grief, evil spirits said by Valentinus to derive their origin from, i. 23.

Heaven, the, of Valentinus, i. 21, 22.
Heavens, the new, different abodes in, ii. 155, 156.
Helena and Simon Magus, i. 87, 88.
Henotes, i. 47.
Heresies, of recent origin, i. 265, 266.
Heretics, the, resort to Scripture to support their opinions, i. 11, 74, 78, 79; modes of initiation practised by, 28-84; deviation of, from the truth, 84, etc.; their perverse interpretations of Scripture, 144; have fallen into an abyss of error, 146, etc.; the first order of productions maintained by (viz. Æons), indefensible, 152, etc.; borrow their systems from the heathen, 160-168; miracles claimed to be wrought by, 241, etc.; blasphemous doctrines of, further exposed, 242, etc.; follow neither Scripture nor tradition, 259; refutation of, from the orderly succession of bishops in the churches, 260; tossed about by every wind of doctrine, 269-271; unlearned, ignorant, and divided in opinion, ii. 107; to be avoided, 108, etc.
Holy Spirit, the, descended on Jesus at His baptism, not Christ nor the Saviour, i. 334.
Holy Spirit, gifts of the, ii. 172.

INDEX OF PRINCIPAL SUBJECTS.

Homer, laid under contribution by the Valentinians, curious instances of, i. 40, 41.
Hope, i. 211.
Horos and Stauros, i. 8, 9, 14.

Ialdabaoth, i. 106, 107.
I AM THAT I AM, i. 270.
Iao, i. 17.
Ignorance, human, of divine things, i. 219-228.
Image of God, the, in which man was created, ii. 99.
Immorality, the, of the Valentinian heretics, i. 26, 27.
Initiation, modes of, practised by the heretics, i. 82.
Intermediate state, the, ii. 140.
Isaac, the history of, symbolical, i. 451, 452; the blessing of, ii. 145.
Isaiah, his prophecy respecting the virgin conceiving, vindicated against Theodotian, Aquila, and the Ebionites, 351, etc.

Jacob, the actions of, typical, i. 452.
Jerusalem, the destruction of, derogates nothing from the majesty of God, i. 383, etc.
Jesus, the significance of the letters of the name, i. 215.
Jesus, how certain Æons are said to be indicated by the name of, i. 13; meaning of the letters of the name of, 60; the generation of, according to Marcus, 66; according to Basilides, was not crucified, but Simon of Cyrene in His stead, 91; descent of the Christ upon, according to the Ophites, 111, 112; His baptism when thirty years old, not a type of the thirty Æons, 197; passed through every stage of life, to sanctify all, 199; the ministry of, extended over ten years, 201, 202; lived at least till near fifty years old, 202; His teaching, 242, 243; the baptism of, 279, the same with Christ, the only-begotten Son of God, perfect God and perfect man, 323; with Him nothing incomplete — His time, 330, 331; neither Christ nor Saviour, but the Holy Spirit descended upon Him at His baptism, 334, etc.; and Christ, proved from the writings of Paul to be one and the same, 337, etc.; not a mere man, but very God, 344; became man so as to be capable of being tempted and crucified, 346; His birth foretold by Isaiah, 354; His reply to the Sadducees, 386, 387. [See Christ.]
John, and Cerinthus, a curious story relating to, i. 263.
Joshua, ii. 168.
Judas not an emblem of the twelfth Æon, i. 191-193.
Judgment, the future, by Jesus Christ, ii. 49, 128, etc.
Justin quoted against Marcion, i. 390.

Keltæ, the, i. 3.
Kingdom, the, of Christ, eternal, ii. 127, 128.
Kingdom, the earthly, of the saints after their resurrection, ii. 147-151; the prophecies respecting, not allegorical, 151, etc.
Knee, bending the, a symbol of the resurrection, ii. 163.
Knowledge, puffs up, i. 215; perfect, not attainable in this life, 219-228.
Knowledge, the true, ii. 11, 175.

Lateinos, ii. 137.
Law, the old and the new, has but one author, i. 399, etc.; Christ did not abrogate the natural precepts of, but removed the bondage of, 412, etc.; man was placed under, for his own benefit, 416; originally inscribed on the hearts of men, but afterwards, as the Mosaic, made by God to bridle the desires of the Jews, 419-421; perfect righteousness not obtained by, 421-425.
Letters and syllables, the absurd theories of Marcion respecting, i. 56-64, 65-71; absurdity of arguments derived from, 204; God not to be sought after by means of, 212, etc.
Levitical dispensation, the, not appointed by God for His own sake, i. 425, etc.
Life and death, ii. 82, etc.
Linus, bishop of Rome, i. 261.
Living creatures, the symbolic import of the four, i. 293.
Logos, the Æon so called, and Sige, i. 150; absurdity of the Valentinian account of the generation of, 175, etc., 224.

INDEX OF PRINCIPAL SUBJECTS. 205

Lord, the, is one God, the Father, i. 377; testimony of Moses to, 378, etc.
Lot and his daughters, the typical import of the story of, ii. 1-3; the wife of, turned into a pillar of salt, 3, 4.
Luke, and Paul, i. 316; refutation of the Ebionites who tried to disparage the authority of Paul from the writings of, 320.

Magic, our Lord's miracles not performed by, i. 245.
Magical practices, the, of Marcus, i. 51, etc.
Man, the first, according to the Ophites, i. 104, 105.
Man, God's mercy to, after the fall, i. 347; the object of God's longsuffering, 348; needs a greater than man to save, 349, 350; why not at first made perfect, ii. 42, etc.; endowed with the faculty of distinguishing good and evil, 45; the whole nature of, has salvation conferred on it, 67, etc.; unfruitful, without the Holy Spirit, 78, etc.; all things created for the service of, 133; every, either empty or full, 170.
Man, the threefold kind, feigned by the heretics, i. 24; the respective destinations of the threefold kind of, 28, 33, 34.
Mansions, the many, ii. 156.
Marcion, the doctrines of, i. 98; mutilates the Gospels, *ibid.*; vain attempt of, to exclude Abraham from Christ's salvation, 396, etc.
Marcionites, the, refuted, in relation to prophecy, ii. 18, etc.
Marcosians, the, absurd interpretations of, i. 69-72; absurd theories of, respecting things created, 72-74; appeal of, to Moses, 74-77; cite Scripture to prove that the Father was unknown before the coming of Christ, 78; the apocryphal Scriptures of, 79; pervert the Gospels, 79, 80; views of, respecting redemption, 81-84; departure of, from the truth, 84-86.
Marcus, the deceitful arts and nefarious practices of, i. 51; pretends to confer the gift of prophecy, 52, 53; corrupts women, 54; hypothesis of, respecting letters and syllables, 56-64; pretended revelations of Sige to, 64-69.
Mary, would hasten on Jesus, but is checked by Him, i. 330; and Eve, compared, ii. 106.
Matter, ii. 173, 174.
Men possessed of free-will, ii. 36; not true that some are by nature good, and some bad, 37.
Men, spiritual, ii. 6, etc., 73-80, etc.
Men, the three kinds of, feigned by the heretics, i. 24-27.
Menander, successor to Simon Magus, i. 89.
Mercy, not to be exaggerated at the expense of justice, i. 471.
Metropator, i. 21.
Miracles claimed to be performed by heretics, i. 241; performed by Christ and His disciples, 245.
Moral faculty, the, in man, ii. 45.
Monogenes, the, of Valentinus, i. 5, 7; of Ptolemy, 49.
Monotes, i. 47.
Months, the, do not fall in with the Valentinian theories of Æons, i. 211.
Moses, ii. 172; Aaron and Miriam sin against, 173.
Mother, the, of the Valentinian heresy, i. 185-190.

Naaman cleansed of his leprosy, ii. 174.
Names of God, different, in the Hebrew Scriptures, i. 254, 255.
Names of our Lord, i. 205, 206.
New covenant, the, ii. 19, 20.
Nicolaitanes, the, i. 97.
Nous, or Monogenes, i. 5, 7, 49, 106.
Number of the beast, the, ii. 135-139.
Numbers and letters, the folly of deriving arguments from, i. 204-212.

Oblation, the new, instituted by Christ, ii. 76.
Oblations and sacrifices, i. 431, etc.
Ogdoad, the first, of Valentinus, i. 5, 21; John asserted to have set forth, 34-38, 45, 46, 47.
Old Testament, the, everywhere mentions and predicts the advent of Christ, i. 403.
Olive, the wild, the symbolical significance of, ii. 78, etc.
Ophites, the, i. 104.

Papias, quoted, ii. 146.
Parables, ii. 34, 35.
Parables, the proper mode of interpreting, i. 217.
Paschal solemnities, differences in the observance of, ii. 159, 160.
Passion of the twelfth Æon, how said to be indicated in Scripture, i. 13; not to be proved from Scripture, 190-193.
Passions, animal, produce, according to Valentinus, material substances, i. 22.
Pastors, the, to whom the apostles committed the churches, to be heard, ii. 108, etc.
Patriarchs and prophets foretold the advent of Christ, i. 455.
Paul, caught up into the third heavens, i. 335, 336; and Peter, founders of the church of Rome, 261; sometimes uses words not in their grammatical sequence, 273; knew no mysteries unrevealed to the other apostles, 316; refutation of the Ebionites who disparaged the writings of, 320, etc.
Perfect, why man was not made, ii. 42.
Persecution foretold, ii. 12.
Pharaoh's heart hardened, how, ii. 471.
Plato, quoted, i. 373.
Pleroma, the, of Valentinus, i. 5, 14; shown to be absurd, 124, 168, 170.
Polycarp, conversed with the apostles, i. 262, 263; his reply to Marcion, 263; the epistle of, 263, 264; Irenæus' testimony respecting, 158, 159.
Predictions of the prophets, the, ii. 12, etc.; all uttered under the same inspiration, 22.
Presbyters, the, ought to be obeyed, i. 462; false, 463; faithful, 463, 464.
Proarche, the, of Valentinus, i. 47.
Production, the first order of, maintained by heretics proved to be indefensible, i. 152, etc.; and absurd, 168, 180.
Prophets, the, refutation of the notion that they uttered their predictions under the inspiration of different gods, i. 254, ii. 22; their predictions, 12, etc.; referred all their predictions to Christ, 18,
etc.; sent by the same Father who sent the Son, 26, etc.
Propator, the, of Valentinus, i. 4, 7; of Ptolemy, 50.
Protarchontes, i. 103.
Providence of God, the world ruled by, i. 371.
Prunicus, i. 104, 106, 107, 108.
Ptolemy the heresiarch, the doctrines of, i. 49, etc.
Ptolemy, the son of Lagus, procures a translation of the Jewish Scriptures to be made, i. 352, 353.
Pythagoras, the heretics borrow from, i. 164.

Redemption, the views of, entertained by heretics, i. 81, etc.
Resurrection, the, of the dead, asserted by Jesus against the Sadducees, i. 386, 387; of the flesh asserted, ii. 61, etc.; of the body, 64, etc.; various proofs of, from the Old Testament, 63, etc.; proved by the resurrection of Christ, 70, etc., 87, etc.; proofs of, from Isaiah and Ezekiel, 94; an actual, 155, etc.; illustrated, 164.
Retribution, the day of, i. 197.
Ridicule, poured upon the emanations and nomenclature of Valentinus, i. 47, etc.
Righteous, the, and the wicked, ii. 130.
Righteousness, perfect, not conferred by the law, i. 421-425.
Rod, the, of Moses, i. 357.
Roman empire, the dissolution of the, predicted, ii. 125.
Rome, the church of, founded and organized by Peter and Paul, i. 261; the first bishops of, 261, 262.

Sabaoth, i. 255 and note.
Sabbath-day, the law did not prohibit the hungry eating food ready to hand on the, i. 398.
Sacrifices, not required by God for their own sake, i. 426, 427-431; further remarks on, 431.
Sadducees, the reply of Jesus to the question asked by the, i. 387.
Samson, and the boy who guided him, types, ii. 171; further reference to, 178.
Satan, ii. 113; blasphemes God, 127, 128.

INDEX OF PRINCIPAL SUBJECTS. 207

Saturninus, the doctrines of, i. 89, 90.

Saviour, the, asserted by the Valentinians to be derived from all the Æons, i. 14, 25; various opinions of, among the heretics, 50.

Scriptures, the, appealed to by the heretics, i. 11, 15; how perverted by the heretics, 31, etc.; refutation of false interpretations of, 38, etc.; perverted by the Marcosians to support their absurdities, 74-80; perverse interpretations of the heretics, 144; proper method of interpreting the obscure passages of, 217-219; translation of the Hebrew, into Greek, 251; interpreted with fidelity by the LXX. translators, 253.

Seed, Valentinian absurdities respecting, exposed, i. 184-190.

Seeing God, i. 441, 442, 443, 444, 445, 446, 447.

Separatists, to be shunned, i. 463, 464.

Septuagint, the story of the origin of, i. 352, 353.

Serpent, the, cursed, i. 366; speculations respecting, ii. 165, 166.

Sethians, the doctrines of the, i. 104.

Shadrach, etc., in the fiery furnace, ii. 66.

Sige, i. 4 and note, 7; pretended revelation made by, to Marcus, 65; and Logos, mutually contradictory and repugnant, 150.

Simeon and Jesus, i. 327.

Simon of Cyrene, curious opinion of Basilides respecting, i. 91.

Simon Magus, i. 86; the pretensions of, 86, 87; honoured with a statue, 87; and Helena, 87, 88; the priests of, 88; succeeded by Menander, 89.

Sin, God not the author of, refutation of the Marcionites, 474, etc.

Sin, the pardon of, ii, 100, 101.

Sins of former times, recorded in Scripture for a warning to us, i. 465.

Son, meaning of the term, ii. 51.

Son of God, the, not made man in appearance only, i. 342-344; everywhere set forth in the Old Testament, 403, etc.

Son, the, reveals the Father, i. 390, 395; revealed by the Father, 391.

Sons of the devil, ii. 51.

Soul and body, views of the heretics relating to the future destruction of, refuted, i. 228, etc.

Souls, absurdity of the doctrine of the transmigration of, i. 247-250; existence of, after death, 250, 251; immortal, although they had a beginning, 251-253.

Soter, i. 205.

Sophia, the Æon so called, i. 6; her passion, 7, 8; another name of Achamoth, 16, 103; could have produced nothing apart from her consort, 149; exposure of the absurdity of the whole Valentinian theory respecting, 180, etc.

Spirit, the Holy, gifts of the, ii. 72.

Spiritual, the absurdity of heretics claiming to be, while they declare the Demiurge to be animal, i. 331.

Spiritual men, ii. 6, 73; and animal, 80, etc.

Spoiling the Egyptians, the act examined and vindicated, i. 475.

Stauros and Horos, i. 14, 15, 29.

Stesichorus, the story of, i. 87, 88.

Stone, the, cut out without hands, i. 356.

Tatian, the doctrines of, i. 100; refuted in his denial of the salvation of Adam, 368.

Teaching, the, of Jesus, opposed to the opinions of heretics, i. 242, 243.

Teitan, ii. 137.

Temptation, the, of Christ, ii. 111-113.

Testaments, the two, God the author of both, ii. 4.

Tetrad, the first, i. 5; of Marcus reveals Aletheia, 59.

Thamar, her labour typical, i. 459, 460.

Thelesis, i. 49.

Theodotian and Aquila, their interpretation of Isa. vii. 14 refuted, i. 351, 352.

Translation, the, of Enoch and Elijah, ii. 66.

Transmigration of souls, the, the absurdity of the doctrine of, i. 247-250.

Treasure hid in a field, the, i. 461.

Triacontad, the, of the heretics, i. 147.

Truth, the, to be found in the catholic church, i. 264.

Types, earthly, of heavenly things, i. 436, etc.
Unity, the, of the faith of the universal church, i. 42.
Unity, the, of God, i. 268, etc., ii. 100, 114.
Utter emptiness, the, of Valentinus, i. 48.

Vacuum, the absurdity of the, of the heretics, i. 125.
Valentinian views of Jesus refuted from the apostolic writings, i. 323.
Valentinians, the, their immoral opinions and practices, i. 26, 27; how they pervert Scripture to support their own opinions, 31, etc.; refutation of their false interpretations of Scripture, 38, etc.; quote Homer to support their views, 40, 41; the inconsistent and contradictory opinions of, 45, etc.
Valentinus, the absurd ideas held by, i. 4; his system derived from the heathen, with only a change of terms, 160-167; recapitulation of arguments against the views of, 239, etc.
Virgin, Jesus born of a, i. 348, 359-362; prophecy of Isaiah relating to, 351, etc.
Virgin Mary, the, and Eve, a comparison between, ii. 106.

Visions of God, i. 446, 447, 448, 449, 450.
Will, the freedom of the, in man, ii. 36, etc.
Wine, and water, the mixture of, ii. 57; and bread, in the Eucharist, 59.
Woman, the, with the issue of blood, not a type of the suffering Æon, i. 203.
Word, the, the world made through, i. 122; reveals the Father, 390, 391; always with the Father, 440; all things created by, 441; declares God, 444; takes flesh to save the flesh, ii. 91; the image of God, 99; the Creator, 105.
Works of the flesh, the, ii. 80.
World, the, not made by angels, but by God through the Word, i. 120-123, 124, 125; not formed by any other beings within the territory contained by the Father, 129, etc.; the Creator of, one, 142; ruled by the providence of God, 371; to be annihilated, ii. 80.

Year, the divisions of, do not really suit the Valentinian theory of Æons, i. 210, 212.
Year of the Lord, the acceptable, ii. 197.

Zoe, i. 5.

THE END.

THE WRITINGS

OF

HIPPOLYTUS, BISHOP OF PORTUS.
VOL. II.

FRAGMENTS OF WRITINGS

OF

THIRD CENTURY.

TRANSLATED BY

REV. S. D. F. SALMOND, M.A.

EDINBURGH:
T. & T. CLARK, 38, GEORGE STREET.
MDCCCLXIX.

MURRAY AND GIBB, EDINBURGH,
PRINTERS TO HER MAJESTY'S STATIONERY OFFICE.

CONTENTS.

THE EXTANT WORKS AND FRAGMENTS OF HIPPOLYTUS.

PART II.—DOGMATICAL AND HISTORICAL.

	PAGE
Treatise on Christ and Antichrist,	3
Expository Treatise against the Jews,	41
Fragment of the Discourse of St. Hippolytus against the Greeks,	46
Against the Heresy of one Noetus,	51
Against Beron and Helix,	71
The Discourse on the Holy Theophany,	80
FRAGMENTS OF DISCOURSES OR HOMILIES BY HIPPOLYTUS,	88
FRAGMENTS FROM OTHER WRITINGS OF HIPPOLYTUS,	94
The Story of a Maiden of Corinth, and a certain Person Magistrianus,	95

APPENDIX TO PART II. OF THE WORKS OF HIPPOLYTUS—

A Discourse by the most blessed Hippolytus, Bishop and Martyr, on the End of the World, and on Antichrist, and on the Second Coming of our Lord Jesus Christ,	98
Hippolytus on the Twelve Apostles,	130
The same Hippolytus on the Seventy Apostles,	132
Heads of the Canons of Abulides or Hippolytus,	135
Canons of the Church of Alexandria,	137

FRAGMENTS.

THE EPISTLES OF POPE ZEPHYRINUS—

Introductory Notice,	144
The First Epistle,	145
The Second Epistle,	148

CONTENTS.

	PAGE
FRAGMENTS OF CAIUS—	
Introductory Notice,	153
1. From a Dialogue or Disputation against Proclus, a Defender of the Sect of the Cataphrygians,	154
2. Fragments of an Anonymous Work against the Heresy of Artemon, ascribed by some to Caius,	155
3. Canon Muratorianus—an Acephalous Fragment on the Canon of the Sacred Scriptures, ascribed by some to Caius,	159
THE EXTANT WRITINGS OF JULIUS AFRICANUS—	
Introductory Notice,	163
1. The Epistle of Africanus to Aristides,	164
2. The Extant Fragments of the Five Books of the Chronography of Julius Africanus,	171
The Passion of St. Symphorosa and her Seven Sons,	191
Africanus' Narrative of Events happening in Persia on the Birth of Christ,	195
THE EPISTLES OF POPE CALLISTUS—	
The First Epistle,	203
The Second Epistle,	207
THE EPISTLE OF POPE URBAN FIRST,	217
THE EXTANT WRITINGS OF ASTERIUS URBANUS,	224
THE EPISTLES OF POPE PONTIANUS—	
The First Epistle,	232
The Second Epistle,	234
POPE ANTERUS—	
The Epistle,	240
THE EPISTLES OF POPE FABIAN—	
The First Epistle,	249
The Second Epistle,	255
The Third Epistle,	265
DECREES OF FABIAN,	272
FRAGMENTS OF THE EPISTLES OF ALEXANDER,	275
INDEX OF TEXTS,	279
INDEX OF SUBJECTS,	286

THE EXTANT WORKS AND FRAGMENTS

OF

HIPPOLYTUS,

BISHOP OF PORTUS, AND MARTYR.

PART II.—DOGMATICAL AND HISTORICAL.

TREATISE ON CHRIST AND ANTICHRIST.

[Gallandi, *Bibl. vet. Patr.* ii. p. 417, Venice 1765.]

1. AS it was your desire, my beloved brother Theophilus,[1] to be thoroughly informed on those topics which I put summarily before you, I have thought it right to set these matters of inquiry clearly forth to your view, drawing largely from the holy Scriptures themselves as from a holy fountain, in order that you may not only have the pleasure of hearing them on the testimony of men,[2] but may also be able, by surveying them in the light of (divine) authority, to glorify God in all. For this will be as a sure supply furnished you by us for your journey in this present life, so that by ready argument applying things ill understood and apprehended by most, you may sow them in the ground of your heart, as in a rich and clean soil.[3] By these, too, you will be able to silence those who

---

[1] Perhaps the same Theophilus whom Methodius, a contemporary of Hippolytus, addresses as Epiphanius, vol. i. pp. 640, 560, 590. From this introduction, too, it is clear that they are in error who take this book to be a homily. (Fabricius.)

[2] In the text the reading is τῶν ὄντων, for which τῶν ὤτων = *of the ears*, is proposed by some, and ἀνθρώπων = *of men*, by others. In the manuscripts the abbreviation ανων is often found for ἀνθρώπων.

[3] In the text we find ὡς πίων καθαρὰ γῆ, for which grammar requires ὡς πίονι καθαρᾷ γῇ. Combefisius proposes ὡσπεροῦν καθαρᾷ γῇ = *as in clean ground*. Others would read ὡς πυρόν, etc. = *like grain in clean ground*.

oppose and gainsay the word of salvation. Only see that you do not give these things over to unbelieving and blasphemous tongues, for that is no common danger. But impart them to pious and faithful men, who desire to live holily and righteously with fear. For it is not to no purpose that the blessed apostle exhorts Timothy, and says, " O Timothy, keep that which is committed to thy trust, avoiding profane and vain babblings, and oppositions of science falsely so called; which some professing have erred concerning the faith."[1] And again, "Thou therefore, my son, be strong in the grace that is in Christ Jesus. And the things that thou hast heard of me in many exhortations, the same commit thou to faithful men,[2] who shall be able to teach others also."[3] If, then, the blessed (apostle) delivered these things with a pious caution, which could be easily known by all, as he perceived in the spirit that " all men have not faith,"[4] how much greater will be our danger, if, rashly and without thought, we commit the revelations of God to profane and unworthy men?

2. For as the blessed prophets were made, so to speak, eyes for us, they foresaw through faith the mysteries of the word, and became ministers of these[5] things also to succeeding generations, not only reporting the past, but also announcing the present and the future, so that the prophet might not appear to be one only for the time being, but might also predict the future for all generations, and so be reckoned a (true) prophet. For these fathers were furnished with the Spirit, and largely honoured by the Word Himself; and just as it is with instruments of music, so had they the Word always, like the plectrum,[6] in union with them, and when moved by Him the prophets announced what God willed.

[1] 1 Tim. vi. 20, 21.
[2] This reading, παρακλήσεων for μαρτύρων (= witnesses), which is peculiar to Hippolytus alone, is all the more remarkable as so thoroughly suiting Paul's meaning in the passage.
[3] 2 Tim. ii. 1, 2. [4] 2 Thess. iii. 2.
[5] The text reads ἅτινα = which. Gudius proposes τινά = some.
[6] The plectrum was the instrument with which the lyre was struck. The text is in confusion here. Combefisius corrects it, as we render it, ὀργάνων δίκην ἡνωμένον ἔχοντες ἐν ἑαυτοῖς.

For they spake not of their own power¹ (let there be no mistake as to that²), neither did they declare what pleased themselves. But first of all they were endowed with wisdom by the Word, and then again were rightly instructed in the future by means of visions. And then, when thus themselves fully convinced, they spake those things which³ were revealed by God to them alone, and concealed from all others. For with what reason should the prophet be called a prophet, unless he in spirit foresaw the future? For if the prophet spake of any chance event, he would not be a prophet then in speaking of things which were under the eye of all. But one who sets forth in detail things yet to be, was rightly judged a prophet. Wherefore prophets were with good reason called from the very first "seers."⁴ And hence we, too, who are rightly instructed in what was declared aforetime by them, speak not of our own capacity. For we do not attempt to make any change one way or another among ourselves in the words that were spoken of old by them, but we make the Scriptures in which these are written public, and read them to those who can believe rightly; for that is a common benefit for both parties: for him who speaks, in holding in memory and setting forth correctly things uttered of old;⁵ and for him who hears, in giving attention to the things spoken. Since, then, in this there is a work assigned to both parties together, viz. to him who speaks, that he speak forth faithfully without regard to risk,⁶ and to him who hears, that he hear and receive in faith that which is spoken, I beseech you to strive together with me in prayer to God.

3. Do you wish then to know in what manner the Word of God, who was again the Son of God,⁷ as He was of old

---

¹ 2 Pet. i. 21.
² The text reads μὴ πλανῶ (= that I may not deceive). Some propose ὡς πλάνοι = as deceivers.
³ This is according to the emendation of Combefisius.
⁴ 1 Sam. ix. 9.
⁵ In the text it is προκείμενα (= things before us or proposed to us), for which Combefisius proposes, as in our rendering, προειρημένα.
⁶ The original is ἀκίνδυνον.
⁷ Isa. xlii. 1; Matt. xii. 18. The text is αὐτὸς πάλιν ὁ τοῦ Θεοῦ

the Word, communicated His revelations to the blessed prophets in former times? Well, as the Word shows His compassion and His denial of all respect of persons by all the saints, He enlightens them,[1] and adapts them to that which is advantageous for us, like a skilful physician, understanding the weakness of men. And the ignorant He loves to teach, and the erring He turns again to His own true way. And by those who live by faith He is easily found; and to those of pure eye and holy heart, who desire to knock at the door, He opens immediately. For He casts away none of His servants as unworthy of the divine mysteries. He does not esteem the rich man more highly than the poor, nor does He despise the poor man for his poverty. He does not disdain the barbarian, nor does He set the eunuch aside as no man. He does not hate the female on account of the woman's act of disobedience in the beginning, nor does He reject the male on account of the man's transgression. But He seeks all, and desires to save all, wishing to make all the children of God, and calling all the saints unto one perfect man. For there is also one Son (or Servant) of God, by whom we too, receiving the regeneration through the Holy Spirit, desire to come all unto one perfect and heavenly man.[2]

4. For whereas the Word of God was without flesh,[3] He took upon Himself the holy flesh by the holy Virgin, and prepared a robe which He wove for Himself, like a bridegroom, in the sufferings of the cross, in order that by uniting His own power with our mortal body, and by mixing[4] the incorruptible with the corruptible, and the strong with the weak, He might save perishing man. The web-beam, therefore, is the passion of the Lord upon the cross, and the warp on it

παῖς. See Macarius, *Divinitas D. N. S. C.* book iv. ch. xiii. p. 460, and Grabe on Bull's *Defens. Fid. Nic.* p. 101.

[1] Reading αὐτούς for αὐτόν.   [2] Eph. iv. 13.
[3] The text has ὦν = being, for which read ἦν = was.
[4] μίξας. Thomassin, *De Incarnatione Verbi*, iii. 5, cites the most distinguished of the Greek and Latin fathers, who taught that a mingling (*commistio*), without confusion indeed, but yet most thorough, of the two natures, is the bond and nexus of the personal unity.

is the power of the Holy Spirit, and the woof is the holy flesh wrought (woven) by the Spirit, and the thread is the grace which by the love of Christ binds and unites the two in one, and the combs (or rods) are the Word; and the workers are the patriarchs and prophets who weave the fair, long, perfect tunic for Christ; and the Word passing through these, like the combs (or rods), completes through them that which His Father willeth.

5. But as time now presses for the consideration of the question immediately in hand, and as what has been already said in the introduction with regard to the glory of God, may suffice, it is proper that we take the holy Scriptures themselves in hand, and find out from them what, and of what manner, the coming of Antichrist is; on what occasion and at what time that impious one shall be revealed; and whence and from what tribe (he shall come); and what his name is, which is indicated by the number in the Scripture; and how he shall work error among the people, gathering them from the ends of the earth; and (how) he shall stir up tribulation and persecution against the saints; and how he shall glorify himself as God; and what his end shall be; and how the sudden appearing of the Lord shall be revealed from heaven; and what the conflagration of the whole world shall be; and what the glorious and heavenly kingdom of the saints is to be, when they reign together with Christ; and what the punishment of the wicked by fire.

6. Now, as our Lord Jesus Christ, who is also God, was prophesied of under the figure of a lion,[1] on account of His royalty and glory, in the same way have the Scriptures also aforetime spoken of Antichrist as a lion, on account of his tyranny and violence. For the deceiver seeks to liken himself in all things to the Son of God Christ is a lion, so Antichrist is also a lion; Christ is a king,[2] so Antichrist is also a king. The Saviour was manifested as a lamb;[3] so he too, in like manner, will appear as a lamb, though within he is a wolf. The Saviour came into the world in the circumcision, and he will come in the same manner. The Lord sent

[1] Rev. v. 5. [2] John xviii. 37. [3] John i. 29.

apostles among all the nations, and he in like manner will send false apostles. The Saviour gathered together the sheep that were scattered abroad,[1] and he in like manner will bring together a people that is scattered abroad. The Lord gave a seal to those who believed on Him, and he will give one in like manner. The Saviour appeared in the form of man, and he too will come in the form of a man. The Saviour raised up and showed His holy flesh like a temple,[2] and he will raise a temple of stone in Jerusalem. And his seductive arts we shall exhibit in what follows. But for the present let us turn to the question in hand.

7. Now the blessed Jacob speaks to the following effect in his benedictions, testifying prophetically of our Lord and Saviour: "Judah, let thy brethren praise thee: thy hand shall be on the neck of thine enemies; thy father's children shall bow down before thee. Judah is a lion's whelp: from the shoot, my son, thou art gone up: he stooped down, he couched as a lion, and as a lion's whelp; who shall rouse him up? A ruler shall not depart from Judah, nor a leader from his thighs, until he come for whom it is reserved; and he shall be the expectation of the nations. Binding his ass to a vine, and his ass's colt to the vine tendril; he shall wash his garment in wine, and his clothes in the blood of the grapes. His eyes shall be gladsome as with wine, and his teeth shall be whiter than milk."[3]

8. Knowing, then, as I do, how to explain these things in detail, I deem it right at present to quote the words themselves. But since the expressions themselves urge us to speak of them, I shall not omit to do so. For these are truly divine and glorious things, and things well calculated to benefit the soul. The prophet, in using the expression, *a lion's whelp*, means him who sprang from Judah and David according to the flesh, who was not made indeed of the seed of David, but was conceived by the (power of the) Holy Ghost, and came forth[4] from the holy shoot of earth. For

---

[1] John xi. 52.   [2] John ii. 19.   [3] Gen. xlix. 8–12.
[4] The text has τούτου—προερχομένου, for which we read, with Combefisius, προερχόμενον.

Isaiah says, "There shall come forth a rod out of the root of Jesse, and a flower shall grow up out of it."[1] That which is called by Isaiah a *flower*, Jacob calls a shoot. For first he shot forth, and then he flourished in the world. And the expression, "he stooped down, he couched as a lion, and as a lion's whelp," refers to the three days' sleep (death, couching) of Christ; as also Isaiah says, "How is faithful Sion become an harlot! it was full of judgment; in which righteousness lodged (couched); but now murderers."[2] And David says to the same effect, "I laid me down (couched) and slept; I awaked: for the Lord will sustain me;"[3] in which words he points to the fact of his sleep and rising again. And Jacob says, "Who shall rouse him up?" And that is just what David and Paul both refer to, as when Paul says, "and God the Father, who raised Him from the dead."[4]

9. And in saying, "A ruler shall not depart from Judah, nor a leader from his thighs, until he come for whom it is reserved; and he shall be the expectation of the nations," he referred the fulfilment (of that prophecy) to Christ. For He is our expectation. For we expect Him, (and) by faith we behold Him as He comes from heaven with power.

10. "Binding his ass to a vine:" that means that He unites His people of the circumcision with His own calling (vocation). For He was the vine.[5] "And his ass's colt to the vine-tendril:" that denotes the people of the Gentiles, as He calls the circumcision and the uncircumcision unto one faith.

11. "He shall wash his garment in wine," that is, according to that voice of His Father which came down by the Holy Ghost at the Jordan.[6] "And his clothes in the blood

---

[1] Isa. xi. 1.   [2] Isa. i. 21.   [3] Ps. iii. 5.
[4] Gal. i. 1.   [5] John xv. 1.

[6] The text gives simply, τὴν τοῦ ἁγίου, etc. = the *paternal voice of the Holy Ghost*, etc. As this would seem to represent the Holy Ghost as the Father of Christ, Combefisius proposes, as in our rendering, κατὰ τὴν διὰ τοῦ ἁγίου, etc. The *wine*, therefore, is taken as a figure of His *deity*, and the garment as a figure of His *humanity*; and the sense would be, that He has the latter imbued with the former in a way peculiar to Himself — even as the voice at the Jordan declared Him to be the

of the grape." In the blood of what grape, then, but just
His own flesh, which hung upon the tree like a cluster of
grapes?—from whose side also flowed two streams, of blood
and water, in which the nations are washed and purified,
which (nations) He may be supposed to have as a robe about
Him.[1]

12. "His eyes gladsome with wine." And what are the
eyes of Christ but the blessed prophets, who foresaw in the
Spirit, and announced beforehand, the sufferings that were to
befall Him, and rejoiced in seeing Him in power with spiritual
eyes, being furnished (for their vocation) by the word Himself and His grace?

13. And in saying, "And his teeth (shall be) whiter than
milk," he referred to the commandments that proceed from the
holy mouth of Christ, and which are pure (purify) as milk.

14. Thus did the Scriptures preach beforetime of this
lion and lion's whelp. And in like manner also we find it
written regarding Antichrist. For Moses speaks thus: "Dan
is a lion's whelp, and he shall leap from Bashan."[2] But that
no one may err by supposing that this is said of the Saviour,
let him attend carefully to the matter. "Dan," he says, "is
a lion's whelp;" and in naming the tribe of Dan, he declared
clearly the tribe from which Antichrist is destined to spring.
For as Christ springs from the tribe of Judah, so Antichrist
is to spring from the tribe of Dan. And that the case stands
thus, we see also from the words of Jacob: "Let Dan be a
serpent, lying upon the ground, biting the horse's heel."[3]
What, then, is meant by the serpent but Antichrist, that
deceiver who is mentioned in Genesis,[4] who deceived Eve and
supplanted Adam ($\pi\tau\epsilon\rho\nu i\sigma a\varsigma$, bruised Adam's heel)? But
since it is necessary to prove this assertion by sufficient testi-
mony, we shall not shrink from the task.

15. That it is in reality out of the tribe of Dan, then, that

Father's Son, not His Son by adoption, but His *own* Son, anointed as
man with divinity itself.

[1] The nations are compared to a robe about Christ, as something
foreign to Himself, and deriving all their gifts from Him.

[2] Deut. xxxiii. 22.   [3] Gen. xlix. 17.   [4] Gen. iii. 1.

that tyrant and king, that dread judge, that son of the devil, is destined to spring and arise, the prophet testifies when he says, "Dan shall judge his people, as (he is) also one tribe in Israel."[1] But some one may say that this refers to Samson, who sprang from the tribe of Dan, and judged the people twenty years. Well, the prophecy had its partial fulfilment in Samson, but its complete fulfilment is reserved for Antichrist. For Jeremiah also speaks to this effect: "From Dan we are to hear the sound of the swiftness of his horses: the whole land trembled [at the sound of the neighing, of the driving of his horses"[2]]. And another prophet says: "He shall gather together all his strength, from the east even to the west. They whom he calls, and they whom he calls not, shall go with him. He shall make the sea white with the sails of his ships, and the plain black with the shields of his armaments. And whosoever shall oppose him in war shall fall by the sword."[3] That these things, then, are said of no one else but that tyrant, and shameless one, and adversary of God, we shall show in what follows.

16. But Isaiah also speaks thus: "And it shall come to pass, that when the Lord hath performed His whole work upon Mount Zion and on Jerusalem, He will punish (visit) the stout mind, the king of Assyria, and the greatness (height) of the glory of his eyes. For he said, By my strength will I do it, and by the wisdom of my understanding I will remove the bounds of the peoples, and will rob them of their strength: and I will make the inhabited cities tremble, and will gather the whole world in my hand like a nest, and I will lift it up like eggs that are left. And there is no one that shall escape or gainsay me, [and open the mouth and chatter. Shall the axe boast itself without him that heweth therewith? or shall the saw magnify itself without him that shaketh (draweth) it? As if one should raise a rod or a staff, and the staff should lift itself up]: and not thus. But the Lord shall send dishonour unto thy honour; and into thy glory a burning fire shall burn. And the light of Israel shall

[1] Gen. xlix. 16.   [2] Jer. viii. 16.
[3] Perhaps from an apocryphal book, as also below in ch. liv.

be a fire, and shall sanctify him in flame, and shall consume the forest like grass."[1]

17. And again he says in another place: " How hath the exactor ceased, and how hath the oppressor ceased!"[2] God hath broken the yoke of the rulers of sinners, He who smote the people in wrath, and with an incurable stroke: He that strikes the people with an incurable stroke, which He did not spare. He ceased (rested) confidently: the whole earth shouts with rejoicing. The trees of Lebanon rejoiced at thee, and the cedar of Lebanon, (saying), Since thou art laid down, no feller is come up against us. Hell from beneath is moved at meeting thee: all the mighty ones, the rulers of the earth, are gathered together—the lords from their thrones. All the kings of the nations, all they shall answer together, and shall say, And thou, too, art taken as we; and thou art reckoned among us. Thy pomp is brought down to earth, thy great rejoicing: they will spread decay under thee; and the worm shall be thy covering.[3] How art thou fallen from heaven, O Lucifer, son of the morning (*lit.* that risest early)! He is cast down to the ground who sends off to all the nations. And thou didst say in thy mind, I will ascend into heaven, I will set my throne above the stars of heaven: I will sit down upon the lofty mountains towards the north: I will ascend above the clouds: I will be like the Most High. Yet now thou shalt be brought down to hell, and to the foundations of the earth! They that see thee shall wonder at thee, and shall say, This is the man that excited the earth, that did shake kings, that made the whole world a wilderness, and destroyed the cities, that released not those in prison.[4] All the kings of the earth did lie in honour, every one in his own house; but thou shalt be cast out on the mountains like a loathsome carcase, with many who fall, pierced through with the sword, and going down to hell. As a garment stained with blood is not pure, so neither shalt thou be comely (or clean); because thou hast destroyed my land, and slain

---

[1] Isa. x. 12-17. [2] ἐπισπουδαστής.
[3] κατακάλυμμα; other reading, κατάλειμμα = remains.
[4] The text gives ἐπαγωγῇ. Combefisius prefers ἀπαγωγῇ = *trial*.

my people. Thou shalt not abide, enduring for ever, a wicked seed. Prepare thy children for slaughter, for the sins of thy father, that they rise not, neither possess my land."[1]

18. Ezekiel also speaks of him to the same effect, thus: "Thus saith the Lord God, Because thine heart is lifted up, and thou hast said, I am God, I sit in the seat of God, in the midst of the sea; yet art thou a man, and not God, (though) thou hast set thine heart as the heart of God. Art thou wiser than Daniel? Have the wise not instructed thee in their wisdom? With thy wisdom or with thine understanding hast thou gotten thee power, and gold and silver in thy treasures? By thy great wisdom and by thy traffic[2] hast thou increased thy power? Thy heart is lifted up in thy power. Therefore thus saith the Lord God: Because thou hast set thine heart as the heart of God: behold, therefore I will bring strangers[3] upon thee, plagues from the nations: and they shall draw their swords against thee, and against the beauty of thy wisdom; and they shall level thy beauty to destruction; and they shall bring thee down; and thou shalt die by the death of the wounded in the midst of the sea. Wilt thou yet say [before them that slay thee, I am God? But thou art a man, and no God, in the hand of them that wound thee. Thou shalt die the deaths of the uncircumcised by the hand of] strangers: for I have spoken it, saith the Lord."[4]

19. These words then being thus presented, let us observe somewhat in detail what Daniel says in his visions. For in distinguishing the kingdoms that are to rise after these things, he showed also the coming of Antichrist in the last times, and the consummation of the whole world. In expounding the vision of Nebuchadnezzar, then, he speaks thus: "Thou, O king, sawest, and behold a great image standing before thy face: the head of which was of fine gold, its arms and shoulders of silver, its belly and its thighs of brass, and its

---

[1] Isa. xiv. 4-21.
[2] *i.e.* according to the reading, $ἐμπορίᾳ$. The text is $ἐμπειρίᾳ =$ *experience*.
[3] There is another reading, $λιμοὺς$ (= *famines*) $τῶν ἐθνῶν$.
[4] Ezek. xxviii. 2-10.

legs of iron, (and) its feet part of iron and part of clay. Thou sawest, then, till that a stone was cut out without hands, and smote the image upon the feet that were of iron and clay, and brake them to an end. Then were the clay, the iron, the brass, the silver, (and) the gold broken, and became like the chaff from the summer threshing-floor; and the strength (fulness) of the wind carried them away, and there was no place found for them. And the stone that smote the image became a great mountain, and filled the whole earth."[1]

20. Now if we set Daniel's own visions also side by side with this, we shall have one exposition to give of the two together, and shall (be able to) show how concordant with each other they are, and how true. For he speaks thus: "I Daniel saw, and behold the four winds of the heaven strove upon the great sea. And four great beasts came up from the sea, diverse one from another. The first (was) like a lioness, and had wings as of an eagle. I beheld till the wings thereof were plucked, and it was lifted up from the earth, and made stand upon the feet as a man, and a man's heart was given to it. And behold a second beast like to a bear, and it was made stand on one part, and it had three ribs in the mouth of it.[2] I beheld, and lo a beast like a leopard, and it had upon the back of it four wings of a fowl, and the beast had four heads. After this I saw, and behold a fourth beast, dreadful and terrible, and strong exceedingly; it had iron teeth [and claws of brass[3]], which devoured and brake in pieces, and it stamped the residue with the feet of it; and it was diverse from all the beasts that were before it, and it had ten horns. I considered its horns, and behold there came up among them another little horn, and before it there were three of the first horns plucked up by the roots; and behold in this horn

---

[1] Dan. ii. 31-35.

[2] Combefisius adds, "between the teeth of it: and they said thus to it, Arise, devour much flesh."

[3] Combefisius inserted these words, because he thought that they must have been in the vision, as they occur subsequently in the explanation of the vision (v. 19).

were eyes like the eyes of man, and a mouth speaking great things."¹

21. "I beheld till the thrones were set, and the Ancient of days did sit: and His garment was white as snow, and the hair of His head like pure wool: His throne was a flame of fire, His wheels were a burning fire. A stream of fire flowed before Him. Thousand thousands ministered unto Him, and ten thousand times ten thousand stood around Him: the judgment was set, and the books were opened. I beheld then, because of the voice of the great words which the horn spake, till the beast was slain and perished, and his body given to the burning of fire. And the dominion of the other beasts was taken away."²

22. "I saw in the night vision, and, behold, one like the Son of man was coming with the clouds of heaven, and came to the Ancient of days, and was brought near before Him. And there was given Him dominion, and honour, and the kingdom; and all peoples, tribes, and tongues shall serve Him: His dominion is an everlasting dominion, which shall not pass away, and His kingdom shall not be destroyed."³

23. Now since these things, spoken as they are with a mystical meaning, may seem to some hard to understand, we shall keep back nothing fitted to impart an intelligent apprehension of them to those who are possessed of a sound mind. He said, then, that a "lioness came up from the sea," and by that he meant the kingdom of the Babylonians in the world, which also was the head of gold on the image. In saying that "it had wings as of an eagle," he meant that Nebuchadnezzar the king was lifted up and was exalted against God. Then he says, "the wings thereof were plucked," that is to say, his glory was destroyed; for he was driven out of his kingdom. And the words, "a man's heart was given to it, and it was made stand upon the feet as a man," refer to the fact that he repented and recognised himself to be only a man, and gave the glory to God.

24. Then, after the lioness, he sees a "second beast like a bear," and that denoted the Persians. For after the Baby-

¹ Dan. vii. 2-8.   ² Dan. vii. 9-12.   ³ Dan. vii. 13, 14.

Ionians, the Persians held the sovereign power. And in saying that there were "three ribs in the mouth of it," he pointed to three nations, viz. the Persians, and the Medes, and the Babylonians; which were also represented on the image by the silver after the gold. Then (there was) "the third beast, a leopard," which meant the Greeks. For after the Persians, Alexander of Macedon obtained the sovereign power on subverting Darius, as is also shown by the brass on the image. And in saying that it had "four wings of a fowl," he taught us most clearly how the kingdom of Alexander was partitioned. For in speaking of "four heads," he made mention of four kings, viz. those who arose out of that (kingdom).[1] For Alexander, when dying, partitioned out his kingdom into four divisions.

25. Then he says: "A fourth beast, dreadful and terrible; it had iron teeth and claws of brass." And who are these but the Romans? which (kingdom) is meant by the iron—the kingdom which is now established; for the legs of that (image) were of iron. And after this, what remains, beloved, but the toes of the feet of the image, in which part is iron and part clay, mixed together? And mystically by the toes of the feet he meant the kings who are to arise from among them; as Daniel also says (in the words), "I considered the beast, and lo there were ten horns behind it, among which shall rise another (horn), an offshoot, and shall pluck up by the roots the three (that were) before it." And under this was signified none other than Antichrist, who is also himself to raise the kingdom of the Jews. He says that three horns are plucked up by the root by him, viz. the three kings of Egypt, and Libya, and Ethiopia, whom he cuts off in the array of battle. And he, after gaining terrible power over all, being nevertheless a tyrant,[2] shall stir up tribulation and persecution against men, exalting himself against them. For Daniel says: "I considered the horn, and behold that horn made war with the saints, and prevailed against them,

---

[1] See Curtius, x. 10. That Alexander himself divided his kingdom is asserted by Josephus Gorionides (iii.) and Cyril of Jerusalem (*Catech.* 4, *De Sacra Scriptura*), and others.

[2] For ὅμως = *nevertheless*, Gudius suggests ὠμός = savage.

till the beast was slain and perished, and its body was given to the burning of fire."[1]

26. After a little space the stone[2] will come from heaven which smites the image and breaks it in pieces, and subverts all the kingdoms, and gives the kingdom to the saints of the Most High. This is the stone which becomes a great mountain, and fills the whole earth, of which Daniel says: "I saw in the night visions, and behold one like the Son of man came with the clouds of heaven, and came to the Ancient of days, and was brought near before Him. And there was given Him dominion, and glory, and a kingdom; and all peoples, tribes, and languages shall serve Him: and His dominion is an everlasting dominion, which shall not pass away, and His kingdom shall not be destroyed."[3] He showed all power given by the Father to the Son,[4] who is ordained Lord of things in heaven, and things on earth, and things under the earth, and Judge of all:[5] of things in heaven, because He was born, the Word of God, before all (ages): and of things on earth, because He became man in the midst of men, to re-create our Adam through Himself; and of things under the earth, because He was also reckoned among the dead, preaching the gospel to the souls of the saints,[6] (and) by death overcoming death.

27. As these things, then, are in the future, and as the ten toes of the image are equivalent to (so many) democracies, and the ten horns of the fourth beast are distributed over ten kingdoms, let us look at the subject a little more closely, and consider these matters as in the clear light of a personal survey (ὀφθαλμοφανῶς).

28. The golden head of the image and the lioness denoted the Babylonians; the shoulders and arms of silver, and the bear, represented the Persians and Medes; the belly and thighs of brass, and the leopard, meant the Greeks, who held the sovereignty from Alexander's time; the legs of iron, and the beast dreadful and terrible, expressed the Romans, who hold the sovereignty at present; the toes of the feet which

---

[1] Dan. vii. 21, 11.   [2] Dan. ii. 34, 45.   [3] Dan. vii. 13, 14.
[4] Matt. xxviii. 18.   [5] Phil. ii. 10.   [6] 1 Pet. iii. 19.

were part clay and part iron, and the ten horns, were emblems of the kingdoms that are yet to rise; the other little horn that grows up among them meant the Antichrist in their midst; the stone that smites the earth and brings judgment upon the world was Christ.

29. These things, beloved, we impart to you with fear, and yet readily, on account of the love of Christ, which surpasseth all. For if the blessed prophets who preceded us did not choose to proclaim these things, though they knew them, openly and boldly, lest they should disquiet the souls of men, but recounted them mystically in parables and dark sayings, speaking thus, "Here is the mind which hath wisdom,"[1] how much greater risk shall we run in venturing to declare openly things spoken by them in obscure terms! Let us look, therefore, at the things which are to befall this unclean harlot in the last days; and (let us consider) what and what manner of tribulation is destined to visit her in the wrath of God before the judgment as an earnest of her doom.

30. Come, then, O blessed Isaiah; arise, tell us clearly what thou didst prophesy with respect to the mighty Babylon. For thou didst speak also of Jerusalem, and thy word is accomplished. For thou didst speak boldly and openly: "Your country is desolate, your cities are burned with fire; your land, strangers devour it in your presence, and it is desolate as overthrown by many strangers.[2] The daughter of Sion shall be left as a cottage in a vineyard, and as a lodge in a garden of cucumbers, as a besieged city."[3] What then? Are not these things come to pass? Are not the things announced by thee fulfilled? Is not their country, Judea, desolate? Is not the holy place burned with fire? Are not their walls cast down? Are not their cities destroyed? Their land, do not strangers devour it? Do not the Romans rule the country? And indeed these impious people hated thee, and did saw thee asunder, and they crucified Christ. Thou art dead in the world, but thou livest in Christ.

[1] Rev. xvii. 9.
[2] For ὑπὸ πολλῶν Combefisius has ὑπὸ λαῶν = by peoples.
[3] Isa. i. 7, 8.

31. Which of you, then, shall I esteem more than thee? Yet Jeremiah, too, is stoned. But if I should esteem Jeremiah most, yet Daniel too has his testimony. Daniel, I commend thee above all; yet John too gives no false witness. With how many mouths and tongues would I praise you; or rather the Word who spake in you! Ye died with Christ; and ye will live with Christ. Hear ye, and rejoice; behold the things announced by you have been fulfilled in their time. For ye saw these things yourselves first, and then ye proclaimed them to all generations. Ye ministered the oracles of God to all generations. Ye prophets were called, that ye might be able to save all. For then is one a prophet indeed, when, having announced beforetime things about to be, he can afterwards show that they have actually happened. Ye were the disciples of a good Master. These words I address to you as if alive, and with propriety. For ye hold already the crown of life and immortality which is laid up for you in heaven.[1]

32. Speak with me, O blessed Daniel. Give me full assurance, I beseech thee. Thou dost prophesy concerning the lioness in Babylon;[2] for thou wast a captive there. Thou hast unfolded the future regarding the bear; for thou wast still in the world, and didst see the things come to pass. Then thou speakest to me of the leopard; and whence canst thou know this, for thou art already gone to thy rest? Who instructed thee to announce these things, but He who formed[3] thee in (from) thy mother's womb?[4] That is God, thou sayest. Thou hast spoken indeed, and that not falsely. The leopard has arisen; the he-goat is come; he hath smitten the ram; he hath broken his horns in pieces; he hath stamped upon him with his feet. He has been exalted by his fall; (the) four horns have come up from under that one.[5] Rejoice, blessed Daniel! thou hast not been in error: all these things have come to pass.

33. After this again thou hast told me of the beast dread-

---

[1] 2 Tim. iv. 8.   [2] Dan. vii. 4.
[3] For πλάσας Gudius proposes ἀγιάσας (sanctified) or καλίσας (called).
[4] Jer. i. 5.   [5] Dan. viii. 2-8.

ful and terrible. "It had iron teeth and claws of brass: it devoured and brake in pieces, and stamped the residue with the feet of it."[1] Already the iron rules; already it subdues and breaks all in pieces; already it brings all the unwilling into subjection; already we see these things ourselves. Now we glorify God, being instructed by thee.

34. But as the task before us was to speak of the harlot, be thou with us, O blessed Isaiah. Let us mark what thou sayest about Babylon. "Come down, sit upon the ground, O virgin daughter of Babylon; sit, O daughter of the Chaldeans; thou shalt no longer be called tender and delicate. Take the millstone, grind meal, draw aside thy veil,[2] shave the grey hairs, make bare the legs, pass over the rivers. Thy shame shall be uncovered, thy reproach shall be seen: I will take justice of thee, I will no more give thee over to men. As for thy Redeemer, (He is) the Lord of hosts, the Holy One of Israel is his name. Sit thou in compunction, get thee into darkness, O daughter of the Chaldeans: thou shalt no longer be called the strength of the kingdom.

35. "I was wroth with my people; I have polluted mine inheritance, I have given them into thine hand: and thou didst show them no mercy; but upon the ancient (the elders) thou hast very heavily laid thy yoke. And thou saidst, I shall be a princess for ever: thou didst not lay these things to thy heart, neither didst remember thy latter end. Therefore hear now this, thou that art delicate; that sittest, that art confident, that sayest in thine heart, I am, and there is none else; I shall not sit as a widow, neither shall I know the loss of children. But now these two things shall come upon thee in one day, widowhood and the loss of children: they shall come upon thee suddenly in thy sorcery, in the strength of thine enchantments mightily, in the hope of thy fornication. For thou hast said, I am, and there is none else. And thy fornication shall be thy shame, because thou hast said in thy heart, I am. And destruction shall come upon thee, and thou shalt not know it. [(And there shall be) a pit, and thou shalt fall into it; and misery shall fall upon thee,

[1] Dan. vii. 6.   [2] For $\dot{a}\nu a\xi\acute{v}\rho\iota\sigma o\nu$ others read $\dot{a}\nu a\kappa\acute{a}\lambda\upsilon\psi a\iota$ = uncover.

and thou shalt not be able to be made clean; and destruction shall come upon thee, and thou shalt not know it.] Stand now with thy enchantments, and with the multitude of thy sorceries, which thou hast learned from thy youth; if so be thou shalt be able to be profited. Thou art wearied in thy counsels. Let the astrologers of the heavens stand and save thee; let the star-gazers announce to thee what shall come upon thee. Behold, they shall all be as sticks for the fire; so shall they be burned, and they shall not deliver their soul from the flame. Because thou hast coals of fire, sit upon them; so shall it be for thy help. Thou art wearied with change from thy youth. Man has gone astray (each one) by himself; and there shall be no salvation for thee."[1] These things does Isaiah prophesy for thee. Let us see now whether John has spoken to the same effect.

36. For he sees, when in the isle Patmos, a revelation of awful mysteries, which he recounts freely, and makes known to others. Tell me, blessed John, apostle and disciple of the Lord, what didst thou see and hear concerning Babylon? Arise, and speak; for it sent thee also into banishment. "And there came one of the seven angels which had the seven vials, and talked with me, saying unto me, Come hither; I will show unto thee the judgment of the great whore that sitteth upon many waters; with whom the kings of the earth have committed fornication, and the inhabitants of the earth have been made drunk with the wine of her fornication. And he carried me away in the spirit into the wilderness: and I saw a woman sit upon a scarlet-coloured beast, full of names of blasphemy, having seven heads and ten horns. And the woman was arrayed in purple and scarlet colour, and decked with gold, and precious stone(s), and pearls, having a golden cup in her hand, full of abominations and filthiness[2] of the fornication of the earth. Upon her forehead was a name written, Mystery, Babylon the Great, the Mother of Harlots and Abominations of the Earth.

37. "And I saw the woman drunken with the blood of the saints, and with the blood of the martyrs of Jesus: and when

---

[1] Isa. xlvii. 1-15. [2] τὰ ἀκάθαρτα, for the received ἀκαθαρτότητος.

I saw her, I wondered with great admiration. And the angel said unto me, Wherefore didst thou marvel? I will tell thee the mystery of the woman, and of the beast that carrieth her, which hath the seven heads and the ten horns. The beast that thou sawest was, and is not; and shall ascend out of the bottomless pit, and go into perdition: and they that dwell on the earth shall wonder (whose name was not written in the book of life from the foundation of the world) when they behold the beast that was, and is not, and yet shall be.[1]

38. "And here is the mind that hath wisdom. The seven heads are seven mountains, on which the woman sitteth. And there are seven kings: five are fallen, and one is, and the other is not yet come; and when he cometh, he must continue a short space. And the beast that was (and) is not, [even he is the eighth], and is of the seven, and goeth into perdition. And the ten horns which thou sawest are ten kings, which have received no kingdom as yet; but receive power as kings one hour with the beast. These have one mind, and shall give their power and strength unto the beast. These shall make war with the Lamb, and the Lamb shall overcome them: for he is Lord of lords, and King of kings; and they that are with Him are called, and chosen, and faithful.

39. "And he saith to me, The waters which thou sawest, where the whore sitteth, are peoples, and multitudes, and nations, and tongues. And the ten horns which thou sawest, and[2] the beast, these shall hate the whore, and shall make her desolate and naked, and shall eat her flesh, and burn her with fire. For God hath put in their hearts to fulfil His will, and to agree, and give their kingdom unto the beast, until the words of God shall be fulfilled. And the woman which thou sawest is that great city, which reigneth over the kings of the earth.

40. "(And) after these things I saw another angel come down from heaven, having great power; and the earth was lightened with his glory. And he cried mightily[3] with a strong voice, saying, Babylon the great is fallen, is fallen,

---

[1] καὶ παρέσται, for the received καίπερ ἐστί.
[2] καί, for the received ἐπί.   [3] ἰσχυρᾷ for ἐν ἰσχύι.

and is become the habitation of devils, and the hold of every foul spirit, [and a cage of every unclean] and hateful bird. For all nations have drunk of the wine of the wrath of her fornication, and the kings of the earth have committed fornication with her, and the merchants of the earth are waxed rich through the abundance of her delicacies. And I heard another voice from heaven, saying, Come out of her, my people, that ye be not partakers of her sins, and that ye receive not of her plagues: for her sins did cleave even unto heaven,[1] and God hath remembered her iniquities.

41. "Reward her even as she rewarded (you), and double unto her double, according to her works: in the cup which she hath filled, fill to her double. How much she hath glorified herself, and lived deliciously, so much torment and sorrow give her: for she saith in her heart, I sit a queen, and am no widow, and shall see no sorrow. Therefore shall her plagues come in one day, death, and mourning, and famine; and she shall be utterly burned with fire: for strong is the Lord God who judgeth her. And the kings of the earth, who have committed fornication, and lived deliciously with her, shall bewail her, and lament for her, when they shall see the smoke of her burning, standing afar off for the fear of her torment, saying, Alas, alas! that great city Babylon, that mighty city! for in one hour is thy judgment come. And the merchants of the earth shall weep and mourn over her; for no man shall buy their merchandise[2] any more. The merchandise of gold, and silver, and precious stones, and of pearls, and fine linen, and purple, and silk, and scarlet, and all thyine wood, and all manner vessels of ivory, and all manner vessels of most precious wood, and of brass, and iron, and marble, and cinnamon, and spices,[3] and odours, and ointments, and frankincense, and wine, and oil, and fine flour, and wheat, and beasts, and sheep, and goats,[4] and horses, and chariots, and slaves (bodies), and souls of men. And the fruits that thy soul lusted after

---

[1] ἐκολλήθησαν, for the received ἠκολούθησαν.
[2] ἀγοράσει, for the received ἀγοράζει.
[3] ἄμωμον, omitted in the received text.
[4] καὶ τράγους, omitted in the received text.

are departed from thee, and all things which were dainty and goodly have perished[1] from thee, and thou shalt find them no more at all. The merchants of these things, which were made rich[2] by her, shall stand afar off for the fear of her torment, weeping and wailing, and saying, Alas, alas! that great city, that was clothed in fine linen, and purple, and scarlet, and decked with gold, and precious stones, and pearls! for in one hour so great riches is come to nought. And every shipmaster, and all the company in ships, and sailors, and as many as trade by sea, stood afar off, and cried, when they saw the smoke of her burning, saying, What city is like unto this great city? And they cast dust on their heads, and cried, weeping and wailing, saying, Alas, alas! that great city, wherein were made rich all that had ships in the sea by reason of her fatness![3] for in one hour is she made desolate.

42. "Rejoice over her, thou heaven, and ye angels,[4] and apostles, and prophets; for God hath avenged you on her. And a mighty angel took up a stone like a great millstone, and cast it into the sea, saying, Thus with violence shall that great city Babylon be thrown down, and shall be found no more at all. And the voice of harpers and musicians, and of pipers and trumpeters, shall be heard no more at all in thee; and no craftsman, of whatsoever craft he be, shall be found any more in thee; and the sound of a millstone shall be heard no more at all in thee; and the light of a candle shall shine no more at all in thee; and the voice of the bridegroom and of the bride shall be heard no more at all in thee: for thy merchants were the great men of the earth; for by thy sorceries were all nations deceived. And in her was found the blood of prophets and of saints, and of all that were slain upon the earth."[5]

43. With respect, then, to the particular judgment in the torments that are to come upon it in the last times by the hand of the tyrants who shall arise then, the clearest statement has been given in these passages. But it becomes us

---

[1] ἀπώλετο, for the received ἀπῆλθεν.
[2] πλουτίσαντες, for the received πλουτήσαντες.
[3] πιότητος, for the received τιμιότητος.
[4] καὶ οἱ ἄγγελοι, which the received omits.   [5] Rev. xvii. xviii.

further diligently to examine and set forth the period at which these things shall come to pass, and how the little horn shall spring up in their midst. For when the legs of iron have issued in the feet and toes, according to the similitude of the image and that of the terrible beast, as has been shown in the above, (then shall be the time) when the iron and the clay shall be mingled together. Now Daniel will set forth this subject to us. For he says, "And one week will make[1] a covenant with many, and it shall be that in the midst (half) of the week my sacrifice and oblation shall cease."[2] By one week, therefore, he meant the last week which is to be at the end of the whole world; of which week the two prophets Enoch and Elias will take up the half. For they will preach 1260 days clothed in sackcloth, proclaiming repentance to the people and to all the nations.

44. For as two advents of our Lord and Saviour are indicated in the Scriptures, the one being His first advent in the flesh, which took place without honour by reason of His being set at nought, as Isaiah spake of Him aforetime, saying, "We saw Him, and He had no form nor comeliness, but His form was despised (and) rejected (lit. = deficient) above all men; a man smitten and familiar with bearing infirmity, [for His face was turned away]; He was despised, and esteemed not."[3] But His second advent is announced as glorious, when He shall come from heaven with the host of angels, and the glory of His Father, as the prophet saith, "Ye shall see the King in glory;"[4] and, "I saw one like the Son of man coming with the clouds of heaven; and he came to the Ancient of days, and he was brought to Him. And there were given Him dominion, and honour, and glory, and the kingdom; all tribes and languages shall serve Him: His dominion is an everlasting dominion, which shall not pass away."[5] Thus also two forerunners were indicated. The first was John the son of Zacharias, who appeared in all things a forerunner and herald of our Saviour, preaching of the heavenly light that had appeared in the world. He first ful-

---
[1] διαθήσει = will *make*; others, δυναμώσει = will *confirm*.
[2] Dan. ix. 27.   [3] Isa. liii. 2-5.   [4] Isa. xxxiii. 17.   [5] Dan. vii. 13, 14.

filled the course of forerunner, and that from his mother's womb, being conceived by Elisabeth, in order that to those, too, who are children from their mother's womb he might declare the new birth that was to take place for their sakes by the Holy Ghost and the Virgin.

45. He, on hearing the salutation addressed to Elisabeth, leaped with joy in his mother's womb, recognising God the Word conceived in the womb of the Virgin. Thereafter he came forward preaching in the wilderness, proclaiming the baptism of repentance to the people, (and thus) announcing prophetically salvation to the nations living in the wilderness of the world. After this, at the Jordan, seeing the Saviour with his own eye, he points Him out, and says, "Behold the Lamb of God, that taketh away the sin of the world!"[1] He also first preached to those in Hades,[2] becoming a forerunner there when he was put to death by Herod, that there too he might intimate that the Saviour would descend to ransom the souls of the saints from the hand of death.

46. But since the Saviour was the beginning of the resurrection of all men, it was meet that the Lord alone should rise from the dead, by whom too the judgment is to enter for the whole world, that they who have wrestled worthily may be also crowned worthily by Him, by the illustrious Arbiter, to wit, who Himself first accomplished the course, and was received into the heavens, and was set down on the right hand of God the Father, and is to be manifested again at the end of the world as Judge. It is a matter of course that His forerunners must appear first, as He says by Malachi and the angel,[3] "I

---

[1] John i. 29.

[2] It was a common opinion among the Greeks, that the Baptist was Christ's forerunner also among the dead. See Leo Allatius, *De libris eccles. Græcorum*, p. 303.

[3] Or it may be, "Malachi, even the messenger." Ἀγγέλου is the reading restored by Combefisius instead of Ἀγγαίου. The words of the angel in Luke i. 17 ("and the disobedient to the wisdom of the just") are thus inserted in the citation from Malachi; and to that Hippolytus may refer in the addition "and the angel." Or perhaps, as Combefisius rather thinks, the addition simply refers to the meaning of the name Malachi, viz. messenger.

will send to you Elias the Tishbite before the day of the Lord, the great and notable day, comes; and he shall turn the hearts of the fathers to the children, and the disobedient to the wisdom of the just, lest I come and smite the earth utterly."[1] These, then, shall come and proclaim the manifestation of Christ that is to be from heaven; and they shall also perform signs and wonders, in order that men may be put to shame and turned to repentance for their surpassing wickedness and impiety.

47. For John says, "And I will give power unto my two witnesses, and they shall prophesy a thousand two hundred and threescore days, clothed in sackcloth."[2] That is the half of the week whereof Daniel spake. "These are the two olive trees and the two candlesticks standing before the Lord of the earth. And if any man will hurt them, fire will proceed out of their mouth, and devour their enemies; and if any man will hurt them, he must in this manner be killed. These have power to shut heaven, that it rain not in the days of their prophecy; and have power over waters, to turn them to blood, and to smite the earth with all plagues as often as [they will. And when] they shall have finished their course and their testimony," what saith the prophet? "the beast that ascendeth out of the bottomless pit shall make war against them, and shall overcome them, and kill them,"[3] because they will not give glory to Antichrist. For this is meant by the little horn that grows up. He being now elated in heart, begins to exalt himself, and to glorify himself as God, persecuting the saints and blaspheming Christ, even as Daniel says, "I considered the horn, and, behold, in the horn were eyes like the eyes of man, and a mouth speaking great things; and he opened his mouth to blaspheme God. And that horn made war against the saints, and prevailed against them until the beast was slain, and perished, and his body was given to be burned."[4]

48. But as it is incumbent on us to discuss this matter of the beast more exactly, and in particular the question how the Holy Spirit has also mystically indicated his name by

[1] Mal. iv. 5, 6. [2] Rev. xi. 3. [3] Rev. xi. 4–6. [4] Dan. vii. 8, 9.

means of a number, we shall proceed to state more clearly what bears upon him. John then speaks thus: "And I beheld another beast coming up out of the earth; and he had two horns, like a lamb, and he spake as a dragon. And he exercised all the power of the first beast before him; and he made the earth and them which dwell therein to worship the first beast, whose deadly wound was healed. And he did great wonders, so that he maketh fire come down from heaven on the earth in the sight of men, and deceiveth them that dwell on the earth by means of those miracles which he had power to do in the sight of the beast, saying to them that dwell on the earth, that they should make an image to the beast which had the wound by a sword and did live. And he had power to give life unto the image of the beast, [that the image of the beast should both speak], and cause that as many as would not worship the image of the beast should be killed. And he caused all, both small and great, rich and poor, free and bond, to receive a mark in their right hand or in their forehead; and that no man might buy or sell, save he that had the mark, the name of the beast, or the number of his name. Here is wisdom. Let him that hath understanding count the number of the beast; for it is the number of a man, and his number is six hundred threescore and six."[1]

49. By the beast, then, coming up out of the earth, he means the kingdom of Antichrist; and by the two horns he means him and the false prophet after him.[2] And in speaking of "the horns being like a lamb," he means that he will make himself like the Son of God, and set himself forward as king. And the terms, "he spake like a dragon," mean that he is a deceiver, and not truthful. And the words, "he exercised all the power of the first beast before him, and caused the earth and them which dwell therein to worship the first beast, whose deadly wound was healed," signify that, after the manner of the law of Augustus, by whom the

---

[1] Rev. xiii. 11–18.
[2] The text is simply καὶ τὸν μετ' αὐτόν = the false prophet after him. Gudius and Combefisius propose as above, καὶ αὐτόν τε καὶ τὸν μετ' αὐτόν, or μετ' αὐτοῦ = him and the false prophet *with* him.

empire of Rome was established, he too will rule and govern, sanctioning everything by it, and taking greater glory to himself. For this is the fourth beast, whose head was wounded and healed again, in its being broken up or even dishonoured, and partitioned into four crowns; and he then (Antichrist) shall with knavish skill heal it, as it were, and restore it. For this is what is meant by the prophet when he says, "He will give life unto the image, and the image of the beast will speak." For he will act with vigour again, and prove strong by reason of the laws established by him; and he will cause all those who will not worship the image of the beast to be put to death. Here the faith and the patience of the saints will appear, for he says: "And he will cause all, both small and great, rich and poor, free and bond, to receive a mark in their right hand or in their forehead; that no man might buy or sell, save he that had the mark, the name of the beast, or the number of his name." For, being full of guile, and exalting himself against the servants of God, with the wish to afflict them and persecute them out of the world, because they give not glory to him, he will order incense-pans[1] to be set up by all everywhere, that no man among the saints may be able to buy or sell without first sacrificing; for this is what is meant by the mark received upon the right hand. And the word "in their forehead" indicates that all are crowned, and put on a crown of fire, and not of life, but of death. For in this wise, too, did Antiochus Epiphanes the king of Syria, the descendant of Alexander of Macedon, devise measures against the Jews. He, too, in the exaltation of his heart, issued a decree in those times, that *all should set up shrines before their doors, and sacrifice, and that they should march in procession to the honour of Dionysus, waving chaplets of ivy;* and that those who refused obedience should be put to death by strangulation and torture. But he also met his due recompense at the hand of the Lord, the righteous Judge and all-searching God; for he died eaten up of worms. And if

---

[1] θυμία = censers, incense-pans, or sacrificial tripods. This offering of incense was a test very commonly proposed by the pagans to those whose religion they suspected.

one desires to inquire into that more accurately, he will find it recorded in the books of the Maccabees.

50. But now we shall speak of what is before us. For such measures will he, too, devise, seeking to afflict the saints in every way. For the prophet and apostle says: "Here is wisdom, Let him that hath understanding count the number of the beast; for it is the number of a man, and his number is six hundred threescore and six." With respect to his name, it is not in our power to explain it exactly, as the blessed John understood it and was instructed about it, but only to give a conjectural account of it;[1] for when he appears, the blessed one will show us what we seek to know. Yet as far as our doubtful apprehension of the matter goes, we may speak. Many names indeed we find,[2] the letters of which are the equivalent of this number: such as, for instance, the word Titan,[3] an ancient and notable name; or Evanthas,[4] for it too makes up the same number; and many others which might be found. But, as we have already said,[5] the wound of the first beast was healed, and he (the second beast) was to make the image speak,[6] that is to say, he should be powerful; and it is manifest to all that those who at present still hold the power are Latins. If, then, we take the name as the name of a single man, it becomes *Latinus*. Wherefore we ought neither to give it out as if this were certainly his name, nor again ignore the fact that he may not be otherwise designated. But having the mystery of God in our heart, we ought in fear to keep faithfully what has been told us by the blessed prophets, in order that when those things come to pass, we may be prepared for them, and not deceived. For when the times advance, he too, of whom these things are said, will be manifested.

---

[1] ὅσον μόνον ὑπονοῆσαι.   [2] ἰσόψηφα.

[3] Τειτάν. Hippolytus here follows his master Irenæus, who in his Contra hæres. v. 30, § 3, has the words, "*Titan . . . et antiquum et fide dignum et regale . . . nomen*" = Titan . . . both an ancient and good and royal . . . name.

[4] Εὐάνθας, mentioned also by Irenæus in the passage already referred to.

[5] προίφθημεν, the reading proposed by Fabricius instead of προίφημεν.

[6] ποιήσει, Combef. ἐποίησι.

51. But not to confine ourselves to these words and arguments alone, for the purpose of convincing those who love to study the oracles of God, we shall demonstrate the matter by many other proofs. For Daniel says, "And these shall escape out of his hand, even Edom, and Moab, and the chief of the children of Ammon."[1] Ammon and Moab[2] are the children born to Lot by his daughters, and their race survives even now. And Isaiah says: "And they shall fly in the boats of strangers, plundering the sea together, and (they shall spoil) them of the east: and they shall lay hands upon Moab first; and the children of Ammon shall first obey them."[3]

52. In those times, then, he shall arise and meet them. And when he has overmastered three horns out of the ten in the array of war, and has rooted these out, viz. Egypt, and Libya, and Ethiopia, and has got their spoils and trappings, and has brought the remaining horns which suffer into subjection, he will begin to be lifted up in heart, and to exalt himself against God as master of the whole world. And his first expedition will be against Tyre and Berytus, and the circumjacent territory. For by storming these cities first he will strike terror into the others, as Isaiah says, "Be thou ashamed, O Sidon; the sea hath spoken, even the strength of the sea hath spoken, saying, I travailed not, nor brought forth children; neither did I nurse up young men, nor bring up virgins. But when the report comes to Egypt, pain shall seize them for Tyre."[4]

53. These things, then, shall be in the future, beloved; and when the three horns are cut off, he will begin to show himself as God, as Ezekiel has said aforetime: "Because thy heart has been lifted up, and thou hast said, I am God."[5] And to the like effect Isaiah says: "For thou hast said in thine heart, I will ascend into heaven, I will exalt my throne above the stars of heaven: I will be like the Most High. Yet now thou shalt be brought down to hell (Hades), to the foundations of the earth."[6] In like manner also Ezekiel:

[1] Dan. xi. 41. [2] Gen. xix. 37, 38. [3] Isa. xi. 14.
[4] Isa. xxiii. 4, 5. [5] Ezek. xxviii. 2. [6] Isa. xiv. 13-15.

"Wilt thou yet say to those who slay thee, I am God? But thou (shalt be) a man, and no God."[1]

54. As his tribe, then, and his manifestation, and his destruction, have been set forth in these words, and as his name has also been indicated mystically, let us look also at his action. For he will call together all the people to himself, out of every country of the dispersion, making them his own, as though they were his own children, and promising to restore their country, and establish again their kingdom and nation, in order that he may be worshipped by them as God, as the prophet says: "He will collect his whole kingdom, from the rising of the sun even to its setting: they whom he summons and they whom he does not summon shall march with him."[2] And Jeremiah speaks of him thus in a parable: "The partridge cried, (and) gathered what he did not hatch, making himself riches without judgment: in the midst of his days they shall leave him, and at his end he shall be a fool."[3]

55. It will not be detrimental, therefore, to the course of our present argument, if we explain the art of that creature, and show that the prophet has not spoken[4] without a purpose in using the parable (or similitude) of the creature. For as the partridge is a vainglorious creature, when it sees near at hand the nest of another partridge with young in it, and with the parent-bird away on the wing in quest of food, it imitates the cry of the other bird, and calls the young to itself; and they taking it to be their own parent, run to it. And it delights itself proudly in the alien pullets as in its own. But when the real parent-bird returns, and calls them with its own familiar cry, the young recognise it, and forsake the deceiver, and betake themselves to the real parent. This thing, then, the prophet has adopted as a simile, applying it in a similar manner to Antichrist. For he will (endeavour to) allure mankind to himself, wishing to gain possession of those who are not his own, and promising deliverance to all, while he is unable to save himself.

---

[1] Ezek. xxviii. 9.
[2] Quoted already in chap. xv. as from one of the prophets.
[3] Jer. xvii. 11.   [4] Reading ἀπεφήνατο for ἀπεκρίνατο.

56. He then, having gathered to himself the unbelieving everywhere throughout the world, comes at their call to persecute the saints, their enemies and antagonists, as the apostle and evangelist says: "There was in a city a judge, which feared not God, neither regarded man: and there was a widow in that city, who came unto him, saying, Avenge me of mine adversary. And he would not for a while: but afterward he said within himself, Though I fear not God, nor regard man; yet because this widow troubleth me, I will avenge her."[1]

57. By the unrighteous judge, who fears not God, neither regards man, he means without doubt Antichrist, as he is a son of the devil and a vessel of Satan. For when he has the power, he will begin to exalt himself against God, neither in truth fearing God, nor regarding the Son of God, who is the Judge of all. And in saying that there was a widow in the city, he refers to Jerusalem itself, which is a widow indeed, forsaken of her perfect, heavenly spouse, God. She calls Him her adversary, and not her Saviour; for she does not understand that which was said by the prophet Jeremiah: "Because they obeyed not the truth, a spirit of error shall speak then to this people and to Jerusalem."[2] And Isaiah also to the like effect: "Forasmuch as the people refuseth to drink the water of Siloam that goeth softly, but chooseth to have Rasin and Romeliah's son as king over you: therefore, lo, the Lord bringeth up upon you the water of the river, strong and full, even the king of Assyria."[3] By the king he means metaphorically Antichrist, as also another prophet saith: "And this man shall be the peace from me, when the Assyrian shall come up into your land, and when he shall tread in your mountains."[4]

58. And in like manner Moses, knowing beforehand that

---

[1] Luke xviii. 2–5.   [2] Jer. iv. 11   [3] Isa. viii. 6, 7.
[4] Mic. v. 5. The Septuagint reads αὐτῇ = And (he) shall be the peace to it. Hippolytus follows the Hebrew, but makes the pronoun feminine, αὕτη referring to the peace. Again Hippolytus reads ὄρη = mountains, where the Septuagint has χώρας = land, and where the Hebrew word = fortresses or palaces.

the people would reject and disown the true Saviour of the world, and take part with error, and choose an earthly king, and set the heavenly King at nought, says: "Is not this laid up in store with me, and sealed up among my treasures? In the day of vengeance I will recompense (them), and in the time when their foot shall slide."[1] They did slide, therefore, in all things, as they were found to be in harmony with the truth in nothing: neither as concerns the law, because they became transgressors; nor as concerns the prophets, because they cut off even the prophets themselves; nor as concerns the voice of the Gospels, because they crucified the Saviour Himself; nor in believing the apostles, because they persecuted them. At all times they showed themselves enemies and betrayers of the truth, and were found to be haters of God, and not lovers of Him; and such they shall be then when they find opportunity: for, rousing themselves against the servants of God, they will seek to obtain vengeance by the hand of a mortal man. And he, being puffed up with pride by their subserviency, will begin to despatch missives against the saints, commanding to cut them all off everywhere, on the ground of their refusal to reverence and worship him as God, according to the word of Esaias: "Woe to the wings of the vessels of the land,[2] beyond the rivers of Ethiopia: (woe to him) who sendeth sureties by the sea, and letters of papyrus (upon the water; for nimble messengers will go) to a nation[3] anxious and expectant, and a people strange and bitter against them; a nation hopeless and trodden down."[4]

59. But we who hope for the Son of God are persecuted and trodden down by those unbelievers. For the *wings of the vessels* are the churches; and the sea is the world, in which the church is set, like a ship tossed in the deep, but not destroyed; for she has with her the skilled Pilot, Christ. And she bears in her midst also the trophy (which is erected) over death; for she carries with her the cross of the Lord.[5]

---

[1] Deut. xxxii. 34, 35.   [2] οὐαὶ γῆς πλοίων πτέρυγες.
[3] μετίωρον.   [4] Isa. xviii. 1, 2.
[5] Wordsworth, reading ὡς ἱστὸν for ὡς τὸν, would add, *like a mast*. See his Commentary on Acts xxvii. 40.

For her prow is the east, and her stern is the west, and her hold[1] is the south, and her tillers are the two Testaments; and the ropes that stretch around her are the love of Christ, which binds the church; and the net[2] which she bears with her is the laver of the regeneration which renews the believing, whence too are these glories. As the wind the Spirit from heaven is present, by whom those who believe are sealed: she has also anchors of iron accompanying her, viz. the holy commandments of Christ Himself, which are strong as iron. She has also mariners on the right and on the left, assessors like the holy angels, by whom the church is always governed and defended. The ladder in her leading up to the sailyard is an emblem of the passion of Christ, which brings the faithful to the ascent of heaven. And the *psephari*[3] (top-sails) aloft[4] upon the yard are the company of prophets, martyrs, and apostles, who have entered into their rest in the kingdom of Christ.

60. Now, concerning the tribulation of the persecution which is to fall upon the church from the adversary, John also speaks thus: "And I saw a great and wondrous sign in heaven; a woman clothed with the sun, and the moon under her feet, and upon her head a crown of twelve stars. And she, being with child, cries, travailing in birth, and pained to be delivered. And the dragon stood before the woman which was ready to be delivered, for to devour her child as soon as it was born. And she brought forth a man-child, who is to rule all the nations: and the child was caught up unto God and to His throne. And the woman fled into the wilderness, where she hath the place prepared of God, that they should feed her there a thousand two hundred and threescore days. And then when the dragon saw (it), he persecuted the woman which brought forth the man (child). And to the woman were given two wings of the great eagle, that she might fly

---

[1] κύτος, a conjecture of Combefisius for κύκλος.
[2] λίνον, proposed by the same for πλοῖον, boat.
[3] ψηφαροί, a term of doubtful meaning. May it refer to the καρχήσια?
[4] The text reads here αἰνούμενοι, for which αἰρούμενοι is proposed, or better, ᾐωρούμενοι.

into the wilderness, where she is nourished for a time, and times, and half a time, from the face of the serpent. And the serpent cast (out of his mouth water as a flood after the woman, that he might cause her to be carried away of the flood. And the earth helped the woman, and opened her mouth, and swallowed up the flood which the dragon cast) out of his mouth. And the dragon was wroth with the woman, and went to make war with the saints of her seed, which keep the commandments of God, and have the testimony of Jesus."[1]

61. By the "woman then clothed with the sun," he meant most manifestly the church, endued with the Father's word,[2] whose brightness is above the sun. And by "the moon under her feet" he referred to her being adorned, like the moon, with heavenly glory. And the words, "upon her head a crown of twelve stars," refer to the twelve apostles by whom the church was founded. And those, "she, being with child, cries, travailing in birth, and pained to be delivered," mean that the church will not cease to bear from her heart ($\gamma\epsilon\nu\nu\hat{\omega}\sigma\alpha$ $\dot{\epsilon}\kappa$ $\kappa\alpha\rho\delta\iota\alpha\varsigma$) the Word that is persecuted by the unbelieving in the world. "And she brought forth," he says, "a man-child, who is to rule all the nations;" by which is meant that the church, always bringing forth Christ, the perfect man-child of God, who is declared to be God and man, becomes the instructor of all the nations. And the words, "her child was caught up unto God and to His throne," signify that he who is always born of her is a heavenly king, and not an earthly; even as David also declared of old when he said, "The Lord said unto my Lord, Sit Thou at my right hand, until I make Thine enemies Thy footstool."[3] "And the dragon," he says, "saw and persecuted the woman which brought forth the man (child). And to the woman were given two wings of the great eagle, that she might fly into the wilderness, where she is nourished for a time, and times, and half a time, from the face of the serpent."[4] That refers to the one thousand two hundred and threescore days (the half of the week) during which the tyrant is to reign and persecute the church, which

---

[1] Rev. xii. 1–6, etc.   [2] τὸν Λόγον τὸν Πατρῷον.
[3] Ps. cx. 1.   [4] Rev. xi. 3.

flees from city to city, and seeks concealment in the wilderness among the mountains, possessed of no other defence than the two wings of the great eagle, that is to say, the faith of Jesus Christ, who, in stretching forth His holy hands on the holy tree, unfolded two wings, the right and the left, and called to Him all who believed upon Him, and covered them as a hen her chickens. For by the mouth of Malachi also He speaks thus: "And unto you that fear my name shall the Sun of righteousness arise with healing in His wings."[1]

62. The Lord also says, "When ye shall see the abomination of desolation stand in the holy place (whoso readeth, let him understand), then let them which be in Judæa flee into the mountains; and let him which is on the housetop not come down to take his clothes; neither let him which is in the field return back to take anything out of his house. And woe unto them that are with child, and to them that give suck, in those days! for then shall be great tribulation, such as was not since the beginning of the world. And except those days should be shortened, there should no flesh be saved."[2] And Daniel says, "And they shall place the abomination of desolation a thousand two hundred and ninety days. Blessed is he that waiteth, and cometh to the thousand two hundred and ninety-five days."[3]

63. And the blessed Apostle Paul, writing to the Thessalonians, says: "Now we beseech you, brethren, concerning the coming of our Lord Jesus Christ, and our gathering together at it,[4] that ye be not soon shaken in mind, or be troubled, neither by spirit, nor by word, nor by letters as from us, as that the day of the Lord is at hand. Let no man deceive you by any means; for (that day shall not come) except there come the falling away first, and that man of sin be revealed, the son of perdition, who opposeth and exalteth himself above all that

---

[1] Mal. iv. 2.

[2] Matt. xxiv. 15-22; Mark xiii. 14-20; Luke xxi. 20-23.

[3] Dan. xi. 31, xii. 11, 12. The Hebrew has 1335 as the number in the second verse.

[4] Hippolytus reads here ἐπ' αὐτῆς instead of ἐπ' αὐτόν, and makes the pronoun therefore refer to the coming.

is called God, or that is worshipped : so that he sitteth in the temple of God, showing himself that he is God. Remember ye not, that when I was yet with you, I told you these things? And now ye know what withholdeth, that he might be revealed in his time. For the mystery of iniquity doth already work; only he who now letteth (will let), until he be taken out of the way. And then shall that wicked be revealed, whom the Lord Jesus shall consume with the Spirit of His mouth, and shall destroy with the brightness of His coming: (even him) whose coming is after the working of Satan, with all power, and signs, and lying wonders, and with all deceivableness of unrighteousness in them that perish ; because they received not the love of the truth. And for this cause God shall send them strong delusion, that they should believe a lie : that they all might be damned who believed not the truth, but had pleasure in unrighteousness."[1] And Esaias says, "Let the wicked be cut off, that he behold not the glory of the Lord."[2]

64. These things, then, being to come to pass, beloved, and the one week being divided into two parts, and the abomination of desolation being manifested then, and the two prophets and forerunners of the Lord having finished their course, and the whole world finally approaching the consummation, what remains but the coming of our Lord and Saviour Jesus Christ from heaven, for whom we have looked in hope? who shall bring the conflagration and just judgment upon all who have refused to believe on Him. For the Lord says, "And when these things begin to come to pass, then look up, and lift up your heads; for your redemption draweth nigh."[3] "And there shall not a hair of your head perish."[4] "For as the lightning cometh out of the east, and shineth even unto the west, so shall also the coming of the Son of man be. For wheresoever the carcase is, there will the eagles be gathered together."[5] Now the fall[6] took place in paradise; for Adam fell there. And He says again,

---

[1] 2 Thess. ii. 1–11.　　[2] Isa. xxvi. 10.　　[3] Luke xxi. 28.
[4] Luke xxi. 18.　　[5] Matt. xxiv. 27, 28.
[6] The word πτῶμα, used in the Greek as = carcase, is thus interpreted by Hippolytus as = fall, which is its literal sense.

"Then shall the Son of man send His angels, and they shall gather together His elect from the four winds of heaven."[1] And David also, in announcing prophetically the judgment and coming of the Lord, says, "His going forth is from the end of the heaven, and His circuit unto the end of the heaven: and there is no one hid from the heat thereof."[2] By the heat he means the conflagration. And Esaias speaks thus: "Come, my people, enter thou into thy chamber, (and) shut thy door: hide thyself as it were for a little moment, until the indignation of the Lord be overpast."[3] And Paul in like manner: "For the wrath of God is revealed from heaven against all ungodliness and unrighteousness of men, who hold the truth of God in unrighteousness."[4]

65. Moreover, concerning the resurrection and the kingdom of the saints, Daniel says, "And many of them that sleep in the dust of the earth shall arise, some to everlasting life, (and some to shame and everlasting contempt)."[5] Esaias says, "The dead men shall arise, and they that are in their tombs shall awake; for the dew from thee is healing to them."[6] The Lord says, "Many in that day shall hear the voice of the Son of God, and they that hear shall live."[7] And the prophet says, "Awake, thou that sleepest, and arise from the dead, and Christ shall give thee light."[8] And John says, "Blessed and holy is he that hath part in the first resurrection: on such the second death hath no power."[9] For the second death is the lake of fire that burneth. And again the Lord says, "Then shall the righteous shine forth as the sun shineth in his glory."[10] And to the saints He will say, "Come, ye blessed of my Father, inherit the kingdom prepared for you from the foundation of the world."[11] But what saith He to the wicked? "Depart from me, ye cursed, into

---

[1] Matt. xxiv. 31.   [2] Ps. xix. 6.   [3] Isa. xxvi. 20.
[4] Rom. i. 17.   [5] Dan. xii. 2.
[6] Isa. xxvi. 19.   [7] John v. 25.
[8] Eph. v. 14. Epiphanius and others suppose that the words thus cited by Paul are taken from the apocryphal writings of Jeremiah; others that they are a free version of Isa. lx. 1.
[9] Rev. xx. 6.   [10] Matt. xiii. 43.   [11] Matt. xxv. 34.

everlasting fire, prepared for the devil and his angels, which my Father hath prepared." And John says, "Without are dogs, and sorcerers, and whoremongers, and murderers, and idolaters, and whosoever maketh and loveth a lie; for your part is in the hell of fire."[1] And in like manner also Esaias: "And they shall go forth and look upon the carcases of the men that have transgressed against me. And their worm shall not die, neither shall their fire be quenched; and they shall be for a spectacle to all flesh."[2]

66. Concerning the resurrection of the righteous, Paul also speaks thus in writing to the Thessalonians: "We would not have you to be ignorant concerning them which are asleep, that ye sorrow not even as others which have no hope. For if we believe that Jesus died and rose again, even so them also which sleep in Jesus will God bring with Him. For this we say unto you by the word of the Lord, that we which are alive (and) remain unto the coming of the Lord, shall not prevent them which are asleep. For the Lord Himself shall descend from heaven with a shout, with the voice and trump of God, and the dead in Christ shall rise first. Then we which are alive (and) remain shall be caught up together with them in the clouds to meet the Lord in the air; and so shall we ever be with the Lord."[3]

67. These things, then, I have set shortly before thee, O Theophilus, drawing them (from Scripture itself), in order that, maintaining in faith what is written, and anticipating the things that are to be, thou mayest keep thyself void of offence both toward God and toward men, "looking for that blessed hope and appearing of our God and Saviour,"[1] when, having raised the saints among us, He will rejoice with them, glorifying the Father. To Him be the glory unto the endless ages of the ages. Amen.

[1] Rev. xxii. 15.
[2] Isa. lxvi. 24.
[3] 1 Thess. iv. 12.
[4] Tit. ii. 13.

EXPOSITORY TREATISE AGAINST THE JEWS.

BY

ST. HIPPOLYTUS, BISHOP AND MARTYR.

---

1. NOW, then, incline thine ear to me, and hear my words, and give heed, thou Jew. Many a time dost thou boast thyself, in that thou didst condemn Jesus of Nazareth to death, and didst give Him vinegar and gall to drink; and thou dost vaunt thyself because of this. Come therefore, and let us consider together whether perchance thou dost not boast unrighteously, O Israel, (and) whether that small portion of vinegar and gall has not brought down this fearful threatening upon thee, (and) whether this is not the cause of thy present condition involved in these myriad troubles.

2. Let him then be introduced before us who speaketh by the Holy Spirit, and saith truth—David the son of Jesse. He, singing a certain strain with prophetic reference to the true Christ, celebrated our God by the Holy Spirit, (and) declared clearly all that befell Him by the hands of the Jews in His passion; in which (strain) the Christ who humbled Himself and took unto Himself the form of the servant Adam, calls upon God the Father in heaven as it were in our person, and speaks thus in the sixty-ninth Psalm: "Save me, O God; for the waters are come in unto my soul. I am sunk in the mire of the abyss," that is to say, in the corruption of Hades, on account of the transgression in paradise; "and there is no substance," that is, help. "Mine eyes failed while I hoped (or, from my hoping) upon my God; when will He come and save me?"[1]

[1] Ps. lxix. 1 ff.

3. Then, in what next follows, Christ speaks, as it were, in His own person: "Then I restored that," says He, "which I took not away;" that is, on account of the sin of Adam I endured the death which was not mine by sinning. "For, O God, Thou knowest my foolishness; and my sins are not hid from Thee," that is, "for I did not sin," as He means it; and for this reason (it is added), "Let not them be ashamed who want to see" my resurrection on the third day, to wit the apostles. "Because for Thy sake," that is, for the sake of obeying Thee, "I have borne reproach," namely the cross, when "they covered my face with shame," that is to say, the Jews; when "I became a stranger unto my brethren after the flesh, and an alien unto my mother's children," meaning (by the mother) the synagogue. "For the zeal of Thine house, Father, hath eaten me up; and the reproaches of them that reproached Thee are fallen on me," and of them that sacrificed to idols. Wherefore "they that sit in the gate spoke against me," for they crucified me without the gate. "And they that drink sang against me," that is, (they who drink wine) at the feast of the passover. "But as for me, in my prayer unto Thee, O Lord, I said, Father, forgive them," namely the Gentiles, because it is the time for favour with Gentiles. "Let not then the hurricane (of temptations) overwhelm me, neither let the deep (that is, Hades) swallow me up: for Thou wilt not leave my soul in hell (Hades); neither let the pit shut her mouth upon me,"[1] that is, the sepulchre. "By reason of mine enemies, deliver me," that the Jews may not boast, saying, Let us consume him.

4. Now Christ prayed all this œconomically[2] as man; being, however, true God. But, as I have already said, it was the "form of the servant"[3] that spake and suffered these things. Wherefore He added, "My soul looked for reproach and trouble," that is, I suffered of my own will, (and) not by any compulsion. Yet "I waited for one to mourn with me, and there was none," for all my disciples forsook me and fled; and for a "comforter, and I found none."

5. Listen with understanding, O Jew, to what the Christ

[1] Ps. xvi. 10.   [2] οἰκονομικῶς.   [3] Phil. ii. 7.

says: "They gave me gall for my meat; and in my thirst they gave me vinegar to drink." And these things He did indeed endure from you. Hear the Holy Ghost tell you also what return He made to you for that little portion of vinegar. For the prophet says, as in the person of God, "Let their table become a snare and retribution." Of what retribution does He speak? Manifestly, of the misery which has now got hold of thee.

6. And then hear what follows: "Let their eyes be darkened, that they see not." And surely ye have been darkened in the eyes of your soul with a darkness utter and everlasting. For now that the true light has arisen, ye wander as in the night, and stumble on places with no roads, and fall headlong, as having forsaken the way that saith, "I am the way."[1] Furthermore, hear this yet more serious word: "And their back do thou bend always;" that means, in order that they may be slaves to the nations, not four hundred and thirty years as in Egypt, nor seventy as in Babylon, but bend them to servitude, he says, "always." In fine, then, how dost thou indulge vain hopes, expecting to be delivered from the misery which holdeth thee? For that is somewhat strange. And not unjustly has he imprecated this blindness of eyes upon thee. But because thou didst cover the eyes of Christ, (and[2]) thus thou didst beat Him, for this reason, too, bend thou thy back for servitude always. And whereas thou didst pour out His blood in indignation, hear what thy recompense shall be: "Pour out Thine indignation upon them, and let Thy wrathful anger take hold of them;" and, "Let their habitation be desolate," to wit, their celebrated temple.

7. But why, O prophet, tell us, and for what reason was the temple made desolate? Was it on account of that ancient fabrication of the calf? Was it on account of the idolatry of the people? Was it for the blood of the prophets? Was it for the adultery and fornication of Israel? By no means, he says; for in all these transgressions they always found pardon open to them, and benignity; but it was because they

---

[1] John xiv. 6.
[2] The text is οὕτως, for which read perhaps ὅτι = when.

killed the Son of their Benefactor, for He is co-eternal with the Father. Whence He saith, "Father, let their temple be made desolate;[1] for they have persecuted Him whom Thou didst of Thine own will smite for the salvation of the world;" that is, they have persecuted me with a violent and unjust death, "and they have added to the pain of my wounds." In former time, as the Lover of man, I had pain on account of the straying of the Gentiles; but to this pain they have added another, by going also themselves astray. Wherefore "add iniquity to their iniquity, and tribulation to tribulation, and let them not enter into Thy righteousness," that is, into Thy kingdom; but "let them be blotted out of the book of the living, and not be written with the righteous," that is, with their holy fathers and patriarchs.

8. What sayest thou to this, O Jew? It is neither Matthew nor Paul that saith these things, but David, thine anointed, who awards and declares these terrible sentences on account of Christ. And like the great Job, addressing you who speak against the righteous and true, he says, "Thou didst barter the Christ like a slave, thou didst go to Him like a robber in the garden."

9. I produce now the prophecy of Solomon, which speaketh of Christ, and announces clearly and perspicuously things concerning the Jews; and those which not only are befalling them at the present time, but those, too, which shall befall them in the future age, on account of the contumacy and audacity which they exhibited toward the Prince of Life; for the prophet says, "The ungodly said, reasoning with themselves, but not aright," that is, about Christ, "Let us lie in wait for the righteous, because he is not for our turn, and he is clean contrary to our doings and words, and upbraideth us with our offending the law, and professeth to have knowledge of God; and he calleth himself the Child of God."[2] And then he says, "He is grievous to us even to behold; for his life is not like other men's, and his ways are of another fashion. We are esteemed of him as counterfeits, and he abstaineth from our ways as from filthiness, and pro-

---

[1] Cf. Matt. xxiii. 38.   [2] Wisd. ii. 1, 12, 13.

nounceth the end of the just to be blessed."[1] And again, listen to this, O Jew! None of the righteous or prophets called himself the Son of God. And therefore, as in the person of the Jews, Solomon speaks again of this righteous one, who is Christ, thus: "He was made to reprove our thoughts, and he maketh his boast that God is his Father. Let us see, then, if his words be true, and let us prove what shall happen in the end of him; for if the just man be the Son of God, He will help him, and deliver him from the hand of his enemies. Let us condemn him with a shameful death, for by his own saying he shall be respected."[2]

10. And again David, in the Psalms, says with respect to the future age, "Then shall He" (namely Christ) "speak unto them in His wrath, and vex them in His sore displeasure."[3] And again Solomon says concerning Christ and the Jews, that "when the righteous shall stand in great boldness before the face of such as have afflicted Him, and made no account of His words, when they see it they shall be troubled with terrible fear, and shall be amazed at the strangeness of His salvation; and they, repenting and groaning for anguish of spirit, shall say within themselves, This is He whom we had sometimes in derision and a proverb of reproach; we fools accounted His life madness, and His end to be without honour. How is He numbered among the children of God, and His lot is among the saints? Therefore have we erred from the way of truth, and the light of righteousness hath not shined unto us, and the sun of righteousness rose not on us. We wearied ourselves in the way of wickedness and destruction; we have gone through deserts where there lay no way: but as for the way of the Lord, we have not known it. What hath our pride profited us? all those things are passed away like a shadow."[4]

[*The conclusion is wanting.*]

[1] Wisd. ii. 15, 16.   [2] Wisd. ii. 14, 16, 17, 20.
[3] Ps. ii. 5.   [4] Wisd. v. 1-9.

FRAGMENT OF THE DISCOURSE OF ST. HIPPOLYTUS AGAINST THE GREEKS,

WHICH HAS THE TITLE,

"AGAINST PLATO, ON THE CAUSE OF THE UNIVERSE."[1]

[Gallandi, *Vet. Patr.* ii. 451.]

1. 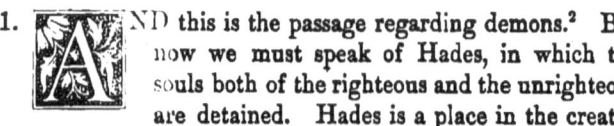AND this is the passage regarding demons.[2] But now we must speak of Hades, in which the souls both of the righteous and the unrighteous are detained. Hades is a place in the created system, rude,[3] a locality beneath the earth, in which the light of the world does not shine; and as the sun does not shine in this locality, there must necessarily be perpetual darkness there. This locality has been destined to be as it were a guardhouse for souls, at which the angels are stationed as guards, distributing according to each one's deeds the temporary[4] punishments for (different) characters. And in this locality there is a certain place[5] set apart by itself, a lake of unquenchable fire, into which we suppose no one has ever yet been cast; for it is prepared against the day determined by God, in which one sentence of righteous judgment shall be justly applied to all. And the unrighteous, and those who believed

---

[1] Two fragments of this discourse are extant also in the *Parallela Damascenica Rupefucaldina*, pp. 755, 789.

[2] The reading in the text is ὁ περὶ δαιμόνων τόπος; others read λόγος for τόπος = thus far the discussion on demons.

[3] ἀκατασκεύαστος.

[4] Or it may be "seasonable," προσκαίρους.

[5] τρόπων. There is another reading, τόπων = of the places.

not God, who have honoured as God the vain works of the hands of men, idols fashioned (by themselves), shall be sentenced to this endless punishment. But the righteous shall obtain the incorruptible and unfading kingdom, who indeed are at present detained in Hades,[1] but not in the same place with the unrighteous. For to this locality there is one descent, at the gate whereof we believe an archangel is stationed with a host. And when those who are conducted by the angels[2] appointed unto the souls have passed through this gate, they do not proceed on one and the same way; but the righteous, being conducted in the light toward the right, and being hymned by the angels stationed at the place, are brought to a locality full of light. And there the righteous from the beginning dwell, not ruled by necessity, but enjoying always the contemplation of the blessings which are in their view, and delighting themselves with the expectation of others ever new, and deeming those ever better than these. And that place brings no toils to them. There, there is neither fierce heat, nor cold, nor thorn;[3] but the face of the fathers and the righteous is seen to be always smiling, as they wait for the rest and eternal revival in heaven which succeed this location. And we call it by the name *Abraham's bosom*. But the unrighteous are dragged toward the left by angels who are ministers of punishment, and they go of their own accord no longer, but are dragged by force as prisoners. And the angels appointed over them send them along,[4] reproaching them and threatening them with an eye of terror, forcing them down into the lower parts. And when they are brought there, those appointed to that service drag them on to the confines of hell

---

[1] Hades, in the view of the ancients, was the general receptacle of souls after their separation from the body, where the good abode happily in a place of light (φωτεινῷ), and the evil all in a place of darkness (σκοτιωτέρῳ). See Colomesii Κειμήλια *litteraria*, 28, and Suicer on ᾅδης. Hence Abraham's bosom and paradise were placed in Hades. See Olympiodorus on *Eccles*. iii. p. 264. The Macedonians, on the authority of Hugo Broughton, prayed in the Lord's words, "Our Father who art in Hades (Πατὴρ ἡμῶν ὁ ἐν ᾅδῃ) (Fabricius).

[2] Cf. *Constitut. Apostol.* viii. 41.   [3] τρίβολος.

[4] In the *Parallela* is inserted here the word ἐπιγελῶντες, *deriding* them.

(γέεννα). And those who are so near hear incessantly the agitation, and feel the hot smoke. And when that vision is so near, as they see the terrible and excessively red[1] spectacle of the fire, they shudder in horror at the expectation of the future judgment, (as if they were) already feeling the power of their punishment. And again, where they see the place of the fathers and the righteous,[2] they are also punished there. For a deep and vast abyss is set there in the midst, so that neither can any of the righteous in sympathy think to pass it, nor any of the unrighteous dare to cross it.

2. Thus far, then, on the subject of Hades, in which the souls of all are detained until the time which God has determined; and then He will accomplish a resurrection of all, not by transferring souls into other bodies,[3] but by raising the bodies themselves. And if, O Greeks, ye refuse credit to this because ye see these (bodies) in their dissolution, learn not to be incredulous. For if ye believe that the soul is originated and is made immortal by God, according to the opinion of Plato,[4] in time, ye ought not to refuse to believe that God is able also to raise the body, which is composed of the same elements, and make it immortal.[5] To be able in one thing, and to be unable in another, is a word which cannot be said of God. We therefore believe that the body also is raised. For if it become corrupt, it is not at least destroyed. For the earth receiving its remains preserves them, and they, becoming as it were seed, and being wrapped up with the richer part of earth, spring up and bloom. And that which is sown is sown indeed bare grain; but at the command of God the Artificer it buds, and is raised arrayed and glorious, but not until it has first died, and been dissolved, and mingled with earth. Not, therefore, without good reason do we believe in

---

[1] According to the reading in *Parallela*, which inserts ξανθήν = red.
[2] The text reads καὶ οὗ, and *where*. But in *Parallela* it is καὶ οὗτοι = and these see, etc. In the same we find ὡς μήτε for καὶ τοὺς δικαίους.
[3] μετινσωματῶν, in opposition to the dogma of metempsychosis.
[4] In the *Timæus*.
[5] The first of the two fragments in the *Parallela* ends here.

the resurrection of the body. Moreover, if it is dissolved in its season on account of the primeval transgression, and is committed to the earth as to a furnace, to be moulded again anew, it is not raised the same thing as it is now, but pure and no longer corruptible. And to every body its own proper soul will be given again; and the soul, being endued again with it, shall not be grieved, but shall rejoice together with it, abiding itself pure with it also pure. And as it now sojourns with it in the world righteously, and finds it in nothing now a traitor, it will receive it again (the body) with great joy. But the unrighteous will receive their bodies unchanged, and unransomed from suffering and disease, and unglorified, and still with all the ills in which they died. And whatever manner of persons they (were when they) lived without faith, as such they shall be faithfully judged.

3.[1] For all, the righteous and the unrighteous alike, shall be brought before God the Word. For the Father hath committed all judgment to Him; and in fulfilment of the Father's counsel, He cometh as Judge whom we call Christ. For it is not Minos and Rhadamanthys that are to judge (the world), as ye fancy, O Greeks, but He whom God the Father hath glorified, of whom we have spoken elsewhere more in particular, for the profit of those who seek the truth. He, in administering the righteous judgment of the Father to all, assigns to each what is righteous according to his works. And being present at His judicial decision, all, both men and angels and demons, shall utter one voice, saying, "Righteous is Thy judgment."[2] Of which voice the justification will be seen in the awarding to each that which is just; since to those who have done well shall be assigned righteously eternal bliss, and to the lovers of iniquity shall be given eternal punishment. And the fire which is unquenchable and without end awaits these latter, and a certain fiery worm which dieth not, and which does not waste the body, but continues bursting forth from the body with unending pain. No sleep will give them rest; no night will soothe them; no death will deliver

---

[1] The second fragment extant in the *Parallela* begins here.
[2] Ps. cxix. 137.

them from punishment; no voice of interceding friends will profit them. For neither are the righteous seen by them any longer, nor are they worthy of remembrance. But the righteous will remember only the righteous deeds by which they reached the heavenly kingdom, in which there is neither sleep, nor pain, nor corruption, nor care,[1] nor night, nor day measured by time; nor sun traversing in necessary course the circle of heaven, which marks the limits of seasons, or the points measured out for the life of man so easily read; nor moon waning or waxing, or inducing the changes of seasons, or moistening the earth; no burning sun, no changeful Bear, no Orion coming forth, no numerous wandering of stars, no painfully-trodden earth, no abode of paradise hard to find; no furious roaring of the sea, forbidding one to touch or traverse it; but this too will be readily passable for the righteous, although it lacks no water. There will be no heaven inaccessible to men, nor will the way of its ascent be one impossible to find; and there will be no earth unwrought, or toilsome for men, but one producing fruit spontaneously in beauty and order; nor will there be generation of wild beasts again, nor the bursting[2] substance of other creatures. Neither with man will there be generation again, but the number of the righteous remains indefectible with the righteous angels and spirits. Ye who believe these words, O men, will be partakers with the righteous, and will have part in these future blessings, which "eye hath not seen nor ear heard, neither have entered into the heart of man the things which God hath prepared for them that love Him."[3] To Him be the glory and the power, for ever and ever. Amen.

[1] The second fragment in the *Parallela* ends here.
[2] ἐκβρασσομένη.
[3] 1 Cor. ii. 9.

AGAINST THE HERESY OF ONE NOETUS.

BY

ST. HIPPOLYTUS, ARCHBISHOP AND MARTYR.

[Gallandi, p. 454.]

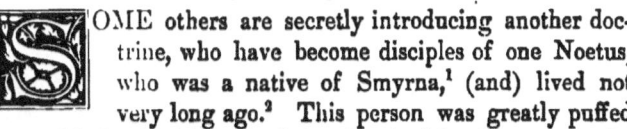OME others are secretly introducing another doctrine, who have become disciples of one Noetus, who was a native of Smyrna,[1] (and) lived not very long ago.[2] This person was greatly puffed up and inflated with pride, being inspired by the conceit of a strange spirit. He alleged that Christ was the Father Himself, and that the Father Himself was born, and suffered, and died. Ye see what pride of heart and what a strange inflated spirit had insinuated themselves into him. From his other actions, then, the proof is already given us that he spoke not with a pure spirit; for he who blasphemes against the Holy Ghost is cast out from the holy inheritance. He alleged that he was himself Moses, and that Aaron was his brother.[3]

---

[1] That Noetus was a native of Smyrna is mentioned also by Theodoret, book iii. *Hæret. fab.* c. iii., and Damascenus, sec. lvii. (who is accustomed to follow Epiphanius); and yet in Epiphanius, *Hæres.* 57, we read that Noetus was an Asian of the city of Ephesus ('Ασιανὸν τῆς 'Εφέσου πόλεως). (Fabricius.)

[2] Epiphanius says that Noetus made his heresy public about 130 years before his time (οὐ πρὸ ἐτῶν πλειόνων ἀλλ' ὡς πρὸ χρόνου τῶν τούτων ἑκατὸν τριάκοντα, πλείω ἢ ἐλάσσω); and as Epiphanius wrote in the year 375, that would make the date of Noetus about 245. He says also that Noetus died *soon after* (ἔναγχος), along with his brother. (Fabricius.)

[3] So also Epiphanius and Damascenus. But Philastrius, *Heresy* 53, puts Elijah for Aaron (hic etiam dicebat se Moysem esse, et fratrem suum Eliam prophetam).

When the blessed presbyters heard this, they summoned him before the church, and examined him. But he denied at first that he held such opinions. Afterwards, however, taking shelter among some, and having gathered round him some others[1] who had embraced the same error, he wished thereafter to uphold his dogma openly as correct. And the blessed presbyters called him again before them, and examined him. But he stood out against them, saying, "What evil, then, am I doing in glorifying Christ?" And the presbyters replied to him, "We too know in truth one God;[2] we know Christ; we know that the Son suffered even as He suffered, and died even as He died, and rose again on the third day, and is at the right hand of the Father, and cometh to judge the living and the dead. And these things which we have learned we allege." Then, after examining him, they expelled him from the church. And he was carried to such a pitch of pride, that he established a school.

2. Now they seek to exhibit the foundation for their dogma by citing the word in the law, "I am the God of your fathers: ye shall have no other gods beside me;"[3] and again in another passage, "I am the first," He saith, "and the last; and beside me there is none other."[4] Thus they say they prove that God is one. And then they answer in this manner: "If therefore I acknowledge Christ to be God, He is the Father Himself, if He is indeed God; and Christ suffered, being Himself God; and consequently the Father suffered, for He was the Father Himself." But the case stands not thus; for the Scriptures do not set forth the matter in this manner. But they make use also of other testimonies, and say, Thus it is written: "This is our God, and there shall none other be accounted of in comparison of Him. He hath found out all the way of knowledge, and hath given it unto Jacob His servant (son), and to Israel His beloved. After-

---

[1] Epiphanius remarks that they were but ten in number.
[2] The following words are the words of the *Symbolum*, as it is extant in Irenæus, i. 10, etc., and iii. 4; and in Tertullian, *contra Praxeam*, ch. ii., and *De Præscript.* ch. xiii., and *De virginibus velandis*, ch. i.
[3] Ex. iii. 6 and xx. 3.   [4] Isa. xliv. 6.

AGAINST THE HERESY OF NOETUS. 53

ward did He show Himself upon earth, and conversed with men."¹ You see, then, he says, that this is God, who is the only One, and who afterwards did show Himself, and conversed with men. And in another place he says, "Egypt hath laboured; and the merchandise of Ethiopia and the Sabeans, men of stature, shall come over unto thee, [and they shall be slaves to thee]; and they shall come after thee bound with manacles, and they shall fall down unto thee, because God is in thee; and they shall make supplication unto thee: and there is no God beside thee. For Thou art God, and we knew not; God of Israel, the Saviour."² Do you see, he says, how the Scriptures proclaim one God? And as this is clearly exhibited, and these passages are testimonies to it, I am under necessity, he says, since one is acknowledged, to make this One the subject of suffering. For Christ was God, and suffered on account of us, being Himself the Father, that He might be able also to save us. And we cannot express ourselves otherwise, he says; for the apostle also acknowledges one God, when he says, "Whose are the fathers, (and) of whom as concerning the flesh Christ came, who is over all, God blessed for ever."³

3. In this way, then, they choose to set forth these things, and they make use only of one class of passages;⁴ just in the same one-sided manner that Theodotus employed when he sought to prove that Christ was a mere man. But neither has the one party nor the other understood the matter rightly, as the Scriptures themselves confute their senselessness, and

¹ Baruch iii. 35-38. ² Isa. xlv. 14. ³ Rom. ix. 5.

⁴ καὶ αὐτοῖς μονοκώλα χρώμενοι, etc. The word μονοκώλα appears to be used adverbially, instead of μονοκώλως and μονοτύπως, which are the terms employed by Epiphanius (p. 481). The meaning is, that the Noetians, in explaining the words of Scripture concerning Christ, looked only to one side of the question—namely, to the divine nature; just as Theodotus, on his part going to the opposite extreme, kept by the human nature exclusively, and held that Christ was a mere man. Besides others, the presbyter Timotheus, in *Cotelerii Monument.* vol. iii. p. 389, mentions Theodotus in these terms: "They say that this Theodotus was the leader and father of the heresy of the Samosatan, having first alleged that Christ was a mere man."

attest the truth. See, brethren, what a rash and audacious dogma they have introduced, when they say without shame, the Father is Himself Christ, Himself the Son, Himself was born, Himself suffered, Himself raised Himself. But it is not so. The Scriptures speak what is right; but Noetus is of a different mind from them. Yet, though Noetus does not understand the truth, the Scriptures are not at once to be repudiated. For who will not say that there is one God? Yet he will not on that account deny the œconomy (*i.e.* the number and disposition of persons in the Trinity). The proper way, therefore, to deal with the question is first of all to refute the interpretation put upon these passages by these men, and then to explain their real meaning. For it is right, in the first place, to expound the truth that the Father is one God, "of whom is every family,"[1] "by whom are all things, of whom are all things, and we in Him."[2]

4. Let us, as I said, see how he is confuted, and then let us set forth the truth. Now he quotes the words, "Egypt has laboured, and the merchandise of Ethiopia and the Sabeans," and so forth on to the words, "For Thou art the God of Israel, the Saviour." And these words he cites without understanding what precedes them. For whenever they wish to attempt anything underhand, they mutilate the Scriptures. But let him quote the passage as a whole, and he will discover the reason kept in view in writing it. For we have the beginning of the section a little above; and we ought, of course, to commence there in showing to whom and about whom the passage speaks. For above, the beginning of the section stands thus: "Ask me concerning my sons and my daughters, and concerning the work of my hands command ye me. I have made the earth, and man upon it: I with my hand have stablished the heaven; I have commanded all the stars. I have raised him up, and all his ways are straight. He shall build my city, and he shall turn back the captivity; not for price nor reward, said the Lord of hosts. Thus said the Lord of hosts, Egypt hath laboured, and the merchandise of Ethiopia and the Sabeans, men of stature, shall come over

[1] Eph. iii. 15.   [2] 1 Cor. viii. 6.

unto thee, and they shall be slaves to thee: and they shall come after thee bound with manacles, and they shall fall down unto thee; and they shall make supplication unto thee, because God is in thee; and there is no God beside thee. For Thou art God, and we knew not; the God of Israel, the Saviour."[1] "In thee, therefore," says he, "God is." But in whom is God except in Christ Jesus, the Father's Word, and the mystery of the œconomy? And again, exhibiting the truth regarding Him, he points to the fact of His being in the flesh when He says, "I have raised Him up in righteousness, and all His ways are straight." For what is this? Of whom does the Father thus testify? It is of the Son that the Father says, "I have raised Him up in righteousness." And that the Father did raise up His Son in righteousness, the Apostle Paul bears witness, saying, "But if the Spirit of Him that raised up Christ Jesus from the dead dwell in you, He that raised up Christ Jesus from the dead shall also quicken your mortal bodies by His Spirit that dwelleth in you."[2] Behold, the word spoken by the prophet is thus made good, "I have raised Him up in righteousness." And in saying, "God is in thee," he referred to the mystery of the œconomy, because when the Word was made incarnate and became man, the Father was in the Son, and the Son in the Father, while the Son was living among men. This, therefore, was signified, brethren, that in reality the mystery of the œconomy by the Holy Ghost and the Virgin was this Word, constituting yet one Son to God.[3] And it is not simply that I say this, but He Himself attests it who came down from heaven; for He speaketh thus: "No man hath ascended up to heaven, but He that came down from heaven, even the Son of man which is in heaven."[4] What then can he seek beside what is thus written? Will he say, forsooth,

---

[1] Isa. xlv. 11-15.   [2] Rom. viii. 11.

[3] Turrian has the following note: "The Word of God constituted (operatum est) one Son to God; *i.e.* the Word of God effected, that He who was the one Son of God was also one Son of man, because as His hypostasis He assumed the flesh. For thus was the Word made flesh."

[4] John iii. 13.

that flesh was in heaven? Yet there is the flesh which was presented by the Father's Word as an offering,—the flesh that came by the Spirit and the Virgin, (and was) demonstrated to be the perfect Son of God. It is evident, therefore, that He offered Himself to the Father. And before this there was no flesh in heaven. Who, then, was in heaven but the Word unincarnate, who was despatched to show that He was upon earth and was also in heaven? For He was Word, He was Spirit, He was Power. The same took to Himself the name common and current among men, and was called from the beginning the Son of man on account of what He was to be, although He was not yet man, as Daniel testifies when he says, "I saw, and behold one like the Son of man came on the clouds of heaven."[1] Rightly, then, did he say that He who was in heaven was called from the beginning by this name, the Word of God, as being that from the beginning.

5. But what is meant, says he, in the other passage: "This is God, and there shall none other be accounted of in comparison of Him?"[2] That said he rightly. For in comparison of the Father who shall be accounted of? But he says: "This is our God; there shall none other be accounted of in comparison of Him. He hath found out all the way of knowledge, and hath given it unto Jacob His servant, and to Israel His beloved." He saith well. For who is Jacob His servant, Israel His beloved, but He of whom He crieth, saying, "This is my beloved Son, in whom I am well pleased: hear ye Him?"[3] Having received, then, all knowledge from the Father, the perfect Israel, the true Jacob, afterward did show Himself upon earth, and conversed with men. And who, again, is meant by Israel[4] but *a man who sees God?* and

---

[1] Dan. vii. 13.   [2] Baruch iii. 36, etc.   [3] Matt. xvii. 5.

[4] The word *Israel* is explained by Philo, *De præmiis et pœnis*, p. 710, and elsewhere, as meaning *seeing God*, ὁρῶν Θεόν, i.e. איש ראה אל. So also in the *Constitutiones Apostol.* vii. 37, viii. 15; Eusebius, *Præparat.* xi. 6, p. 519, and in many others. To the same class may be referred those who make Israel = ὁρατικὸς ἀνὴρ καὶ θεωρητικός, *a man apt to see and speculate*, as Eusebius, *Præparat.* p. 310, or = νοῦς ὁρῶν Θεόν, as

AGAINST THE HERESY OF NOETUS.

there is no one who sees God except the Son alone, the perfect man who alone declares the will of the Father. For John also says, "No man hath seen God at any time; the only-begotten Son, which is in the bosom of the Father, He hath declared[1] Him."[2] And again: "He who came down from heaven testifieth what He hath heard and seen."[3] This, then, is He to whom the Father hath given all knowledge, who did show Himself upon earth, and conversed with men.

6. Let us look next at the apostle's word: "Whose are the fathers, of whom as concerning the flesh Christ came, who is over all, God blessed for ever."[4] This word declares the mystery of the truth rightly and clearly. He who is over all is God; for thus He speaks boldly, "All things are delivered unto me of my Father."[5] He who is over all, God blessed, has been born; and having been made man, He is (yet) God for ever. For to this effect John also has said, "Which is, and which was, and which is to come, the Almighty."[6] And well has he named Christ the Almighty. For in this he has said only what Christ testifies of Himself. For Christ gave this testimony, and said, "All things are delivered unto me of my Father;"[7] and Christ rules all things, and has been appointed Almighty by the Father. And in like manner Paul also, in setting forth the truth that all things are delivered unto Him, said, "Christ the first-fruits; afterwards they that are Christ's at His coming. Then cometh the end, when He shall have delivered up the kingdom to God, even the Father; when He shall have put down all rule, and all authority, and power. For He must reign, till He hath put all enemies under His feet. The last enemy that shall be destroyed is death. For

---

Optatus in the end of the second book; Didymus in Jerome, and Jerome himself in various passages; Maximus, i. p. 284; Olympiodorus on Ecclesiastes, ch. i.; Leontius, *De Sectis*, p. 392; Theophanes, *Ceram. homil.* iv. p. 22, etc. Justin Martyr, *Dialog. cum Tryph.* p. 354, adduces another etymology, ἄνθρωπος νικῶν δύναμιν.

[1] Hippolytus reads διηγήσατο for ἐξηγήσατο.   [2] John i. 18.
[3] John iii. 11, 13.   [4] Rom. ix. 5.   [5] Matt. xi. 27.
[6] Apoc. i. 8.   [7] Matt. xi. 27.

all things are put under Him. But when He saith, All things are put under Him, it is manifest that He is excepted which did put all things under Him. Then shall He also Himself be subject to Him who put all things under Him, that God may be all in all."[1] If, therefore, all things are put under Him with the exception of Him who put them under Him, He is Lord of all, and the Father is Lord of Him, that in all there might be manifested one God, to whom all things are made subject together with Christ, to whom the Father hath made all things subject, with the exception of Himself. And this, indeed, is said by Christ Himself, as when in the Gospel He confessed Him to be His Father and His God. For He speaks thus: "I go to my Father and your Father, and to my God and your God."[2] If, then, Noetus ventures to say that He is the Father Himself, to what father will he say Christ goes away according to the word of the Gospel? But if he will have us abandon the Gospel and give credence to his senselessness, he expends his labour in vain; for "we ought to obey God rather than men."[3]

7. If, again, he allege His own word when He said, "I and the Father are one,"[4] let him attend to the fact, and understand that He did not say, "I and the Father *am one*, but *are one*."[5] For the word *are* (ἐσμὲν) is not said of one person, but it refers to *two persons*, and one power.[6] He has Himself made this clear, when He spake to His Father concerning the disciples, "The glory which Thou gavest me I have given them; that they may be one, even as we are one: I in them, and Thou in me, that they may be made perfect in one; that the world may know that Thou hast sent me."[7] What have the Noetians to say to these things? Are all one body in respect of substance, or is it that we become one in the power and disposition of unity of mind?[8] In the same manner the Son, who was sent and was not known of those who are in the world, confessed that He was in the

---

[1] 1 Cor. xv. 23-28. [2] John xx. 17. [3] Acts v. 29, iv. 19.
[4] John x. 30. [5] ἐγὼ καὶ ὁ πατὴρ ἓν εἰμι—ἓν ἐσμεν.
[6] δύναμιν. [7] John xvii. 22, 23.
[8] ἢ τῇ δυνάμει καὶ τῇ διαθέσει τῆς ὁμοφρονίας ἓν γινόμεθα.

Father in power and disposition. For the Son is the one mind of the Father. We who have the Father's mind believe so (in Him); but they who have it not have denied the Son. And if, again, they choose to allege the fact that Philip inquired about the Father, saying, "Show us the Father, and it sufficeth us," to whom the Lord made answer in these terms: "Have I been so long time with you, and yet hast thou not known me, Philip? He that hath seen me hath seen the Father. Believest thou not that I am in the Father, and the Father in me?"[1] and if they choose to maintain that their dogma is ratified by this passage, as if He owned Himself to be the Father, let them know that it is decidedly against them, and that they are confuted by this very word. For though Christ had spoken of Himself, and showed Himself among all as the Son, they had not yet recognised Him to be such, neither had they been able to apprehend or contemplate His real power. And Philip, not having been able to receive this, as far as it was possible to see it, requested to behold the Father. To whom then the Lord said, "Philip, have I been so long time with you, and yet hast thou not known me? He that hath seen me hath seen the Father." By which He means, If thou hast seen me, thou mayest know the Father through me. For through the image, which is like (the original), the Father is made readily known. But if thou hast not known the image, which is the Son, how dost thou seek to see the Father? And that this is the case is made clear by the rest of the chapter, which signifies that the Son who "has been set forth[2] was sent from the Father,[3] and goeth to the Father."[4]

8. Many other passages, or rather all of them, attest the truth. A man, therefore, even though he will it not, is compelled to acknowledge God the Father Almighty, and Christ Jesus the Son of God, who, being God, became man, to whom also the Father made all things subject, Himself excepted, and the Holy Spirit; and that these, therefore, are three. But if he desires to learn how it is shown still that

[1] John xiv. 8, 9.
[2] Rom. iii. 25.
[3] John v. 30, vi. 29, viii. 16, 18, etc.
[4] John xiii. 1, xiv. 12.

there is one God, let him know that His power (δύναμις) is one. As far as regards the power, therefore, God is one. But as far as regards the œconomy there is a threefold manifestation, as shall be proved afterwards when we give account of the true doctrine. In these things, however, which are thus set forth by us, we are at one. For there is one God in whom we must believe, but unoriginated, impassible, immortal, doing all things as He wills, in the way He wills, and when He wills. What, then, will this Noetus, who knows[1] nothing of the truth, dare to say to these things? And now, as Noetus has been confuted, let us turn to the exhibition of the truth itself, that we may establish the truth, against which all these mighty heresies[2] have arisen without being able to state anything to the purpose.

9. There is, brethren, one God, the knowledge of whom we gain from the holy Scriptures, and from no other source. For just as a man, if he wishes to be skilled in the wisdom of this world, will find himself unable to get at it in any other way than by mastering the dogmas of philosophers, so all of us who wish to practise piety will be unable to learn its practice from any other quarter than the oracles of God. Whatever things, then, the holy Scriptures declare, at these let us look; and whatsoever things they teach, these let us learn; and as the Father wills our belief to be, let us believe; and as He wills the Son to be glorified, let us glorify Him; and as He wills the Holy Spirit to be bestowed, let us receive Him. Not according to our own will, nor according to our own mind, nor yet as using violently those things which are given by God, but even as He has chosen to teach them by the holy Scriptures, so let us discern them.

10. God, subsisting alone, and having nothing contemporaneous with Himself, determined to create the world. And conceiving the world in mind, and willing and uttering the word, He made it; and straightway it appeared, formed as it

---

[1] There is perhaps a play on the words here—Νόητος μὴ νοῶν.

[2] *i.e.* the other thirty-one heresies, which Hippolytus had already attacked. From these words it is apparent also that this treatise was the closing portion of a book against the heresies (Fabricius).

had pleased Him. For us, then, it is sufficient simply to know that there was nothing contemporaneous with God. Beside Him there was nothing; but[1] He, while existing alone, yet existed in plurality.[2] For He was neither without reason, nor wisdom, nor power, nor counsel.[3] And all things were in Him, and He was the All. When He willed, and as He willed,[4] He manifested His word in the times determined by Him, and by Him He made all things. When He wills, He does; and when He thinks, He executes; and when He speaks, He manifests; when He fashions, He contrives in wisdom. For all things that are made He forms by reason and wisdom—creating them in reason, and arranging them in wisdom. He made them, then, as He pleased, for He was God. And as the Author, and fellow-Counsellor, and Framer[5] of the things that are being made, He begat[6] the Word; and as He bears this Word in Himself, and that, too, as (yet) invisible to the world which is created, He makes Him visible; (and) uttering the voice first, and begetting Him as Light of Light,[7] He set Him forth to the world as its Lord, (and) His own mind ($\nu o\hat{\nu}\nu$); and whereas He was visible formerly to Himself alone, and invisible to the world which is made, He makes Him visible in order that the world

---

[1] See, on this passage, Bull's *Defens. fid. Nic.* sec. iii. cap. viii. § 2, p. 219.

[2] πολὺς ἦν.   [3] ἄλογος, ἄσοφος, ἀδύνατος, ἀβούλευτος.

[4] On these words see Bossuet's explanation and defence, *Avertiss.* vi. § 68, *sur les lettres de M. Jurieu.*

[5] ἀρχηγόν, καὶ σύμβουλον, καὶ ἐργάτην.

[6] The "begetting" of which Hippolytus speaks here is not the generation, properly so called, but that manifestation and bringing forth of the Word co-existing from eternity with the Father, which referred to the creation of the world. So at least Bull and Bossuet, as cited above; also Maranus, *De Divinit. J. C.*, lib. iv. cap. xiii. § 3, p. 458.

[7] φῶς ἐκ φωτός. This phrase, adopted by the Nicene fathers, occurs before their time not only here, but also in Justin Martyr, Tatian, and Athenagoras, as is noticed by Grabe, *ad Irenæum,* lib. ii. c. xxiii. Methodius also, in his *Homily on Simeon and Anna,* p. 152, has the expression, σὺ εἶ φῶς ἀληθινὸν ἐκ φωτὸς ἀληθινοῦ Θεὸς ἀληθινὸς ἐκ Θεοῦ ἀληθινοῦ. Athanasius himself also uses the phrase λύχνον ἐκ λύχνου, vol. i. p. 881, ed. Lips.

might see Him in His manifestation, and be capable of being saved.

11. And thus there appeared another beside Himself. But when I say *another*,[1] I do not mean that there are two Gods, but that it is only as light of light, or as water from a fountain, or as a ray from the sun. For there is but one power, which is from the All (ἐκ τοῦ παντός); and the Father is the All, from whom cometh this Power, the Word. And this is the mind (or reason) which came forth into the world, and was manifested as the Son (παῖς) of God. All things, then, are by Him, and He alone is of the Father. Who then adduces a multitude of gods brought in, time after time? For all are shut up, however unwillingly, to admit this fact, that the All runs up into one. If, then, all things run up into one, even according to Valentinus, and Marcion, and Cerinthus, and all their fooleries, they are also reduced, however unwillingly, to this position, that they must acknowledge that the One is the cause of all things. Thus, then, these too, though they wish it not, fall in with the truth, and admit that one God made all things according to His good pleasure. And He gave the law and the prophets; and in giving them, He made them speak by the Holy Ghost, in order that, being gifted with the inspiration of the Father's power, they might declare the Father's counsel and will.

12. Acting then in these (prophets), the Word spoke of Himself. For already He became His own herald, and showed that the Word would be manifested among men. And for this reason He cried thus: "I am made manifest to them that sought me not; I am found of them that asked not for me."[2] And who is He that is made manifest but the Word of the Father?—whom the Father sent, and in whom He showed to men the power proceeding from Him. Thus, then, was the Word made manifest, even as the blessed John

---

[1] Justin Martyr also says that the Son is ἕτερόν τι, *something other*, from the Father; and Tertullian affirms, *Filium et Patrem esse aliud ab alio*, with the same intent as Hippolytus here, viz. to express the distinction of persons.

[2] Isa. lxv. 1.

says. For he sums up the things that were said by the prophets, and shows that this is the Word, by whom all things were made. For he speaks to this effect: " In the beginning was the Word, and the Word was with God, and the Word was God. All things were made by Him, and without Him was not anything made."[1] And beneath He says, "The world was made by Him, and the world knew Him not; He came unto His own, and His own received Him not."[2] If, then, said he, the world was made by Him, according to the word of the prophet, "By the Word of the Lord were the heavens made,"[3] then this is the Word that was also made manifest. We accordingly see the Word incarnate, and we know the Father by Him, and we believe in the Son, (and) we worship the Holy Spirit. Let us then look at the testimony of Scripture with respect to the announcement of the future manifestation of the Word.

13. Now Jeremiah says, "Who hath stood in the counsel[4] of the Lord, and hath perceived His Word?"[5] But the Word of God alone is visible, while the word of man is audible. When he speaks of seeing the Word, I must believe that this visible (Word) has been sent. And there was none other (sent) but the Word. And that He was sent Peter testifies, when he says to the centurion Cornelius: "God sent His Word unto the children of Israel by the preaching of Jesus Christ. This is the God who is Lord of all."[6] If, then, the Word is sent by Jesus Christ, the will[7] of the Father is Jesus Christ.

[1] John i. 1-3. Hippolytus evidently puts the full stop at the οὐδὲ ἕν, attaching the ὃ γέγονεν to the following. So also Irenæus, Clemens Alex., Origen, Theophilus of Antioch, and Eusebius, in several places; so, too, of the Latin fathers—Tertullian, Lactantius, Victorinus, Augustine; and long after these, Honorius Augustodunensis, in his *De imagine Mundi*. This punctuation was also adopted by the heretics Valentinus, Heracleon, Theodotus, and the Macedonians and Eunomians; and hence it is rejected by Epiphanius, ii. p. 80, and Chrysostom. (Fabricius.)
[2] John i. 10, 11.　　　　[3] Ps. xxxiii. 6.
[4] ὑποστήματι, foundation. Victor reads ἐν τῇ ὑποστάσει, in the substance, nature; Symmachus has ἐν τῇ ὁμιλίᾳ, in the fellowship.
[5] Jer. xxiii. 18.　　　　[6] Acts x. 36.
[7] τὸ θέλημα. Many of the patristic theologians called the Son the

14. These things then, brethren, are declared by the Scriptures. And the blessed John, in the testimony of his Gospel, gives us an account of this œconomy (disposition), and acknowledges this Word as God, when he says, "In the beginning was the Word, and the Word was with God, and the Word was God." If, then, the Word was with God, and was also God, what follows? Would one say that he speaks of two Gods?[1] I shall not indeed speak of two Gods, but of one; of two Persons however, and of a third œconomy (disposition), viz. the grace of the Holy Ghost. For the Father indeed is One, but there are two Persons, because there is also the Son; and then there is the third, the Holy Spirit. The Father decrees, the Word executes, and the Son is manifested, through whom the Father is believed on. The œconomy[2] of harmony is led back to one God; for God is One. It is the Father who commands,[3] and the Son who obeys, and the Holy Spirit who gives understanding (συνέτιζον): the Father who is *above all*,[4] and the Son who is

Father's βούλησις or θέλημα. See the passages in Petavius, *De S. S. Trinitate*, lib. vi. c. 8, § 21, and vii. 12, § 12.

[1] From this passage it is clear that Hippolytus taught the doctrine of one God alone and three Persons. A little before, in the eighth chapter, he said that there is one God, according to substance or divine essence, which one substance is in three Persons; and that, according to disposition or œconomy, three are three Persons manifested. By the term *œconomy*, therefore, he understands, with Tertullian, *adversus Praxeam*, ch. iii., the number and disposition of the Trinity (*numerum et dispositionem Trinitatis*). Here he also calls the grace of the Holy Spirit the *third œconomy*, but in the same way as Tertullian, who calls the Holy Spirit the *third grade* (*tertium gradum*). For the terms *gradus*, *forma*, *species*, *dispositio*, and *œconomia* mean the same in Tertullian. (Maranus.)

[2] οἰκονομία συμφωνίας συνάγεται εἰς ἕνα Θεόν, perhaps = the œconomy as being one of harmony, leads to one God.

[3] This mode of speaking of the Father's *commanding* and the Son's *obeying*, was used without any offence, not only by Irenæus, Hippolytus, Origen, and others before the Council of Nicæa, but also after that council by the keenest opponents of the Arian heresy—Athanasius, Basil, Marius Victorinus, Hilary, Prosper, and others. See Petavius, *De Trin.* i. 7, § 7; and Bull, *Defens. fid. Nic.* pp. 138, 164, 167, 170. (Fabricius.)

[4] Referring probably to Eph. iv. 6.

through all, and the Holy Spirit who is *in all*. And we cannot otherwise think of one God,[1] but by believing in truth in Father and Son and Holy Spirit. For the Jews glorified (or gloried in) the Father, but gave Him not thanks, for they they did not recognise the Son. The disciples recognised the Son, but not in the Holy Ghost; wherefore they also denied Him.[2] The Father's Word, therefore, knowing the œconomy (disposition) and the will of the Father, to wit, that the Father seeks to be worshipped in none other way than this, gave this charge to the disciples after He rose from the dead: "Go ye and teach all nations, baptizing them in the name of the Father, and of the Son, and of the Holy Ghost."[3] And by this He showed, that whosoever omitted any one of these, failed in glorifying God perfectly. For it is through this Trinity ($Τριάδος$) that the Father is glorified. For the Father willed, the Son did, the Spirit manifested. The whole Scriptures, then, proclaim this truth.

15. But some one will say to me, You adduce a thing strange to me, when you call the Son the Word. For John indeed speaks of the Word, but it is by a figure of speech. [Nay, it is by no figure of speech.][4] For while thus presenting this Word that was from the beginning, and has now been sent forth, he said below in the Apocalypse, "And I saw heaven opened, and behold a white horse; and He that sat upon him (was) Faithful and True; and in righteousness He doth judge and make war. And His eyes (were) as flame of fire, and on His head were many crowns; and He had a name written that no man knew but He Himself. And He (was) clothed in a vesture dipped in blood: and His name is called

---

[1] The Christian doctrine, Maranus remarks, could not be set forth more accurately; for he contends not only that the number of Persons in no manner detracts from the unity of God, but that the unity of God itself can neither consist nor be adored without this number of Persons.

[2] This is said probably with reference to Peter's denial.

[3] Matt. xxviii. 19.

[4] $ἀλλ'$ $ἄλλως$ $ἀλληγορεῖ$. The words in brackets are given only in the Latin. They may have dropped from the Greek text. At any rate, some such addition seems necessary for the sense.

the Word of God."[1] See then, brethren, how the vesture sprinkled with blood denoted in symbol the flesh, through which the impassible Word of God came under suffering, as also the prophets testify to me. For thus speaks the blessed Micah: "The house of Jacob provoked the Spirit of the Lord to anger. These are their pursuits. Are not His words good with them, and do they walk rightly? And they have risen up in enmity against His countenance of peace, and they have stripped off His glory."[2] That means His suffering in the flesh. And in like manner also the blessed Paul says, "For what the law could not do, in that it was weak, God, sending His own Son in the likeness of sinful flesh, condemned sin in the flesh, that the righteousness of the law might be shown in us, who walk not after the flesh, but after the Spirit."[3] What Son of His own, then, did God send through the flesh but the Word,[4] whom He addressed as Son because He was to become such (or be begotten) in the future? And He takes the common name for tender affection among men in being called the Son. For neither was the Word, prior to incarnation and when by Himself,[5] yet perfect Son, although He was perfect Word, only-begotten. Nor could the flesh subsist by itself apart from the Word, because it has its subsistence (τὴν σύστασιν) in the Word.[6] Thus, then, one perfect Son of God was manifested.

[1] Apoc. xix. 11-13.
[2] Mic. ii. 7, 8. δόξαν: In the present text of the Septuagint it is δοράν, skin.
[3] Hippolytus omits the words διὰ τῆς σαρκός and καὶ περὶ ἁμαρτίας, and reads φανερωθῇ for πληρωθῇ.
[4] ὃν Υἱὸν προσηγόρευε διὰ τὸ μέλλειν αὐτὸν γενέσθαι.
[5] Hippolytus thus gives more definite expression to this temporality of the Sonship, as Dorner remarks, than even Tertullian. See Dorner's *Doctrine of the Person of Christ* (T. & T. Clark), Div. i. vol. ii. p. 88, etc.
[6] "Σύστασις," says Dorner, "be it observed, is not yet equivalent to personality. The sense is, it had its subsistence in the Logos; He was the connective and vehicular force. This is thoroughly unobjectionable. He does not thus necessarily pronounce the humanity of Christ impersonal; although in view of what has preceded, and what remains to be adduced, there can be no doubt that Hippolytus would have defended

16. And these indeed are testimonies bearing on the incarnation of the Word; and there are also very many others. But let us also look at the subject in hand,—namely, the question, brethren, that in reality the Father's Power, which is the Word, came down from heaven, and not the Father Himself. For thus He speaks: "I came forth from the Father, and am come."[1] Now what subject is meant in this sentence, "I came forth from the Father,"[2] but just the Word? And what is it that is begotten of Him, but just the Spirit,[3] that is to say, the Word? But you will say to me, How is He begotten? In your own case you can give no explanation of the way in which you were begotten, although you see every day the cause according to man; neither can you tell with accuracy the œconomy in His case (τὴν περὶ τούτον οἰκονομίαν). For you have it not in your power to acquaint yourself with the practised and indescribable art[4] (method) of the Maker, but only to see, and understand, and believe that man is God's work. Moreover, you are asking an account of the generation of the Word, whom God the Father in His good pleasure begat as He willed. Is it not enough for you to learn that God made the world, but do you also venture to ask whence He made it? Is it not enough for you to learn that the Son of God has been manifested to you for salvation if you believe, but do you also inquire curiously how He was begotten after the Spirit? No more than two,[5] in sooth, have been put in trust to give the account of His generation after the flesh; and are you then so bold as to seek the account (of His generation) after the Spirit, which the Father keeps with Himself, intending to reveal it then to the holy ones and

the impersonality, had the question been agitated at the period at which he lived." See Dorner, as above, i. 95.

[1] John xvi. 28.

[2] Reading ἐξῆλθον. The Latin interpreter seems to read ἐξελθών = what is this that came forth.

[3] πνεῦμα. The divine in Christ is thus designated in the Ante-Nicene fathers generally. See Grotius on Mark ii. 8; and for a full history of the term in this use, Dorner's *Person of Christ*, i. p. 390, etc. (Clark).

[4] τὴν τοῦ δημιουργήσαντος ἔμπειρον καὶ ἀνεκδιήγητον τέχνην.

[5] i.e. Matthew and Luke in their Gospels.

those worthy of seeing His face? Rest satisfied with the word spoken by Christ, viz., "That which is born of the Spirit is spirit,"[1] just as, speaking by the prophet of the generation of the Word, He shows the fact that He is begotten, but reserves the question of the manner and means, to reveal it only in the time determined by Himself. For He speaks thus: "From the womb, before the morning star, I have begotten Thee."[2]

17. These testimonies are sufficient for the believing who study truth, and the unbelieving credit no testimony. For the Holy Spirit, indeed, in the person of the apostles, has testified to this, saying, "And who has believed our report?"[3] Therefore let us not prove ourselves unbelieving, lest the word spoken be fulfilled in us. Let us believe then, dear ($\mu\alpha\kappa\acute{\alpha}\rho\iota\omicron\iota$) brethren, according to the tradition of the apostles that God the Word came down from heaven, (and entered) into the holy Virgin Mary, in order that, taking the flesh from her, and assuming also a human, by which I mean a rational soul, and becoming thus all that man is with the exception of sin, He might save fallen man, and confer immortality on men who believe on His name. In all, therefore, the word of truth is demonstrated to us, to wit, that the Father is One, whose word is present (with Him), by whom He made all things; whom also, as we have said above, the Father sent forth in later times for the salvation of men. This (Word) was preached by the law and the prophets as destined to come into the world. And even as He was preached then, in the same manner also did He come and manifest Himself, being by the Virgin and the Holy Spirit made a new man; for in that He had the heavenly (nature) of the Father, as the Word and the earthly (nature), as taking to Himself the flesh from the old Adam by the medium of the Virgin, He now, coming forth into the world, was manifested as God in a body, coming forth too as a perfect man. For it was not in mere appearance or by conversion ($\kappa\alpha\tau\grave{\alpha}$ $\phi\alpha\nu\tau\alpha\sigma\acute{\iota}\alpha\nu$ $\mathring{\eta}$ $\tau\rho\omicron\pi\acute{\eta}\nu$), but in truth, that He became man.

18. Thus then, too, though demonstrated as God, He does

[1] John iii. 6. [2] Ps. cx. 3. [3] Isa. liii. 1.

not refuse the conditions proper to Him as man,¹ since He hungers and toils and thirsts in weariness, and flees in fear, and prays in trouble. And He who as God has a sleepless nature, slumbers on a pillow. And He who for this end came into the world, begs off from the cup of suffering. And in an agony He sweats blood, and is strengthened by an angel, who Himself strengthens those who believe on Him, and taught men to despise death by His work (or, in deed, ἔργῳ). And He who knew what manner of man Judas was, is betrayed by Judas. And He, who formerly was honoured by him as God, is contemned by Caiaphas.² And He is set at nought by Herod, who is Himself to judge the whole earth. And He is scourged by Pilate, who took upon Himself our infirmities. And by the soldiers He is mocked, at whose behest stand thousands of thousands and myriads of myriads of angels and archangels. And He who fixed the heavens like a vault is fastened to the cross by the Jews. And He who is inseparable from the Father cries to the Father, and commends to Him His spirit; and bowing His head, He gives up the ghost, who said, "I have power to lay down my life, and I have power to take it again;"³ and because He was not overmastered by death, as being Himself Life, He said this: "I lay it down of myself."³ And He who gives life bountifully to all, has His side pierced with a spear. And He who raises the dead is wrapped in linen and laid in a sepulchre, and on the third day He is raised again by the Father, though Himself the Resurrection and the Life. For all these things has He finished for us, who for our sakes was made as we are. For "Himself hath borne our infirmities, and carried our diseases; and for our sakes He was afflicted,"⁴ as Isaiah the prophet has said. This is He who was hymned by the angels, and seen by the shepherds, and waited for by Simeon, and witnessed to by Anna. This is

---

¹ The following passage agrees almost word for word with what is cited as from the *Memoria hæresium* of Hippolytus by Gelasius, in the *De duabus naturis Christi*, vol. viii. *Bibl. Patr.* edit. Lugd. p. 704.

² ἱερατευόμενος, referring to John xi. 51, 52.

³ John x. 18. ⁴ Isa. liii. 4.

He who was inquired after by the wise men, and indicated by the star; He who was engaged in His Father's house, and pointed to by John, and witnessed to by the Father from above in the voice, "This is my beloved Son; hear ye Him."[1] He is crowned victor against the devil ($\sigma\tau\epsilon\phi\alpha\nu o\hat{\nu}\tau\alpha\iota$ $\kappa\alpha\tau\grave{\alpha}$ $\delta\iota\alpha\beta\acute{o}\lambda ov$[2]). This is Jesus of Nazareth, who was invited to the marriage-feast in Cana, and turned the water into wine, and rebuked the sea when agitated by the violence of the winds, and walked on the deep as on dry land, and caused the man blind from birth to see, and raised Lazarus to life after he had been dead four days, and did many mighty works, and forgave sins, and conferred power on the disciples, and had blood and water flowing from His sacred side when pierced with the spear. For His sake the sun is darkened, the day has no light, the rocks are shattered, the veil is rent, the foundations of the earth are shaken, the graves are opened, and the dead are raised, and the rulers are ashamed when they see the Director of the universe upon the cross closing His eye and giving up the ghost. Creation saw, and was troubled; and, unable to bear the sight of His exceeding glory, shrouded itself in darkness. This (is He who) breathes upon the disciples, and gives them the Spirit, and comes in among them when the doors are shut, and is taken up by a cloud into the heavens while the disciples gaze at Him, and is set down on the right hand of the Father, and comes again as the Judge of the living and the dead. This is the God who for our sakes became man, to whom also the Father hath put all things in subjection. To Him be the glory and the power, with the Father and the Holy Spirit, in the holy church both now and ever, and even for evermore. Amen.

[1] Matt. xvii. 5.   [2] Matt. xxvii. 29.

AGAINST BERON AND HELIX.

BY

HIPPOLYTUS, BISHOP OF PORTUS, AND MARTYR.

Fragments of a Discourse, alphabetically divided,[1] on the Divine Nature[2] and the Incarnation, against the heretics Beron and Helix,[3] the beginning of which was in these words, "Holy, holy, holy, Lord God of Sabaoth, with voice never silent the seraphim exclaim and glorify God."

FRAGMENT I.

BY the omnipotent will of God all things are made, and the things that are made are also preserved, being maintained according to their several principles in perfect harmony by Him who is in His nature the omnipotent God and maker of all things,[4] His divine will remaining unalterable by which He has made and moves all things, sustained as they severally are by their own natural laws.[5] For the infinite cannot in any manner or by any account be susceptible of movement, inasmuch as it has nothing towards which and nothing around which it shall be

---

[1] κατὰ στοιχεῖον. The Latin title in the version of Anastasius renders it "ex sermone qui est per elementum."

[2] περὶ θεολογίας.

[3] For Ἥλικος the Codex Regius et Colbertinus of Nicephorus prefers Ἡλικίωνος. Fabricius conjectures that we should read ἡλικιωτῶν αἱρετικῶν, so that the title would be, Against Beron and his fellow-heretics.

[4] αὐτῷ τῷ ... Θεῷ.

[5] τοῖς ἕκαστα φυσικοῖς διεξαγόμενα νόμοις. Anastasius makes it naturalibus producta legibus; Capperonnier, suis quæque legibus temperata vel ordinata.

moved. For in the case of that which is in its nature infinite, and so incapable of being moved, movement would be conversion.[1] Wherefore also the Word of God being made truly man in our manner, yet without sin, and acting and enduring in man's way such sinless things as are proper to our nature, and assuming the circumscription of the flesh of our nature on our behalf, sustained no conversion in that aspect in which He is one with the Father, being made in no respect one with the flesh through the exinanition.[2] But as He was without flesh,[3] He remained without any circumscription. And through the flesh He wrought divinely (θεϊκῶς) those things which are proper to divinity, showing Himself to have both those natures in both of which He wrought, I mean the divine and the human, according to that veritable and real and natural subsistence,[4] (showing Himself thus) as both being in reality and as being understood to be at one and the same time infinite God and finite man, having the nature (οὐσίαν) of each in perfection, with the same activity (ἐνεργείας), that is to say, the same natural properties (φυσικῆς ἰδιότητος); whence we know that their distinction abides always according to the nature of each, and without conversion. But it is not (i.e. the distinction between deity and humanity), as some say, a merely comparative (or relative) matter (κατὰ σύγκρισιν[5]), that we may not speak in an unwarrantable manner of a

[1] τροπὴ γὰρ τοῦ κατὰ φύσιν ἀπείρου, κινεῖσθαι μὴ πεφυκότος, ἡ κίνησις; or may the sense be, "for a change in that which is in its nature infinite would just be the moving of that which is incapable of movement?"

[2] μηδ' ἑνὶ παντελῶς ὁ ταυτόν ἐστι τῷ Πατρὶ γενόμενος ταυτὸν τῇ σαρκὶ διὰ τὴν κένωσιν. Thus in effect Combefisius, correcting the Latin version of Anastasius. Baunius adopts the reading in the Greek Codex Nicephori, viz. ἕνωσιν for κένωσιν, and renders it, "In nothing was the Word, who is the same with the Father, made the same with the flesh through the union" (nulla re Verbum quod idem est cum Patre factum est idem cum carne propter unionem).

[3] δίχα σαρκὸς, i.e. what He was before assuming the flesh, that He continued to be in Himself, viz. independent of limitation.

[4] Or existence, ὕπαρξιν. Anastasius makes it *substantia*.

[5] Migne follows Capperonnier in taking σύγκρισις in this passage to mean not "comparison" or "relation," but "commixture," the "concretion and commixture" of the divine and human, which was the error

greater and a less in one who is ever the same in Himself.[1] For comparisons can be instituted only between objects of like nature, and not between objects of unlike nature. But between God the Maker of all things and that which is made, between the infinite and the finite, between infinitude and finitude, there can be no kind of comparison, since these differ from each other not in mere comparison (or relatively), but absolutely in essence. And yet at the same time there has been effected a certain inexpressible and irrefragable union of the two into one subsistence (ὑπόστασιν), which entirely passes the understanding of anything that is made. For the divine is just the same after the incarnation that it was before the incarnation; in its essence infinite, illimitable, impassible, incomparable, unchangeable, inconvertible, self-potent (αὐτοσθενές), and, in short, subsisting in essence alone the infinitely worthy good.

FRAGMENT II.

The God of all things therefore became truly, according to the Scriptures, without conversion, sinless man, and that in a manner known to Himself alone, as He is the natural Artificer of things which are above our comprehension. And by that same saving act of the incarnation (σωτήριον σάρκωσιν) He introduced into the flesh the activity of His proper divinity, yet without having it (that activity) either circumscribed by the flesh through the exinanition, or growing naturally out of the flesh as it grew out of His divinity,[2] but manifested through it in the things which He wrought in a divine manner in His incarnate state. For the flesh did not become divinity in nature by a transmutation of nature, as though it became essentially flesh of divinity. But what it was before, that also it continued to be in nature and activity

of Apollinaris and Eutyches in their doctrine of the incarnation, and which had been already refuted by Tertullian, *Contra Praxeam*, c. xxvii.

[1] Or, "for that would be to speak of the same being as greater and less than Himself."

[2] οὐδ᾽ ὥσπερ τῆς αὐτοῦ θεότητος οὕτω καὶ αὐτῆς φυσικῶς ἐκφυομένην.

when united with divinity, even as the Saviour said, "The spirit indeed is willing, but the flesh is weak."[1] And working and enduring in the flesh things which were proper to sinless flesh, He proved the evacuation of divinity (to be) for our sakes, confirmed as it was by wonders and by sufferings of the flesh naturally. For with this purpose did the God of all things become man, viz. in order that by suffering in the flesh, which is susceptible of suffering, He might redeem our whole race, which was sold to death; and that by working wondrous things by His divinity, which is unsusceptible of suffering, through the medium of the flesh He might restore it to that incorruptible and blessed life from which it fell away by yielding to the devil; and that He might establish the holy orders of intelligent existences in the heavens in immutability by the mystery of His incarnation ($\sigma\omega\mu\alpha\tau\omega\sigma\epsilon\omega\varsigma$), the doing of which is the recapitulation of all things in Himself.[2] He remained therefore, also, after His incarnation, according to nature, God infinite, and more ($\dot{\upsilon}\pi\epsilon\rho\dot{\alpha}\pi\epsilon\iota\rho\sigma\varsigma$), having the activity proper and suitable to Himself,—an activity growing out of His divinity essentially, and manifested through His perfectly holy flesh by wondrous acts œconomically, to the intent that He might be believed in as God, while working out of Himself ($\alpha\dot{\upsilon}\tau\sigma\upsilon\rho\gamma\hat{\omega}\nu$) by the flesh, which by nature is weak, the salvation of the universe.

FRAGMENT III.

Now, with the view of explaining, by means of an illustration, what has been said concerning the Saviour, (I may say that) the power of thought ($\lambda\dot{o}\gamma\sigma\varsigma$) which I have by nature is proper and suitable to me, as being possessed of a rational and intelligent soul; and to this soul there pertains, according to nature, a self-moved energy and first power, ever-moving, to wit, the thought that streams from it naturally. This thought I utter, when there is occasion, by fitting it to words, and expressing it rightly in signs, using the tongue as an organ, or artificial characters, showing that it is heard,

[1] Matt. xxvi. 41.   [2] Referring probably to Eph. i. 10.

though it comes into actuality by means of objects foreign to itself, and yet is not changed itself by those foreign objects.[1] For my natural thought does not belong to the tongue or the letters, although I effect its utterance by means of these; but it belongs to me, who speak according to my nature, and by means of both these express it as my own, streaming as it does always from my intelligent soul according to its nature, and uttered by means of my bodily tongue organically, as I have said, when there is occasion. Now, to institute a comparison with that which is utterly beyond comparison, just as in us the power of thought that belongs by nature to the soul is brought to utterance by means of our bodily tongue without any change in itself, so, too, in the wondrous incarnation (σωματώσεως) of God is the omnipotent and all-creating energy of the entire deity (τῆς ὅλης θεότητος) manifested without mutation in itself, by means of His perfectly holy flesh, and in the works which He wrought after a divine manner, (that energy of the deity) remaining in its essence free from all circumscription, although it shone through the flesh, which is itself essentially limited. For that which is in its nature unoriginated cannot be circumscribed by an originated nature, although this latter may have grown into one with it (συνέφυ) by a conception which circumscribes all understanding:[2] nor can this be ever brought into the same nature and natural activity with that, so long as they remain each within its own proper and inconvertible nature.[3] For it is only in objects of the same nature that there is the motion that works the same works, showing that the being (οὐσίαν) whose power is natural is incapable in any manner of being or becoming the possession of a being of a different nature without mutation.[4]

---

[1] The text is, διὰ τῶν ἀνομοίων μὲν ὑπάρχοντα. Anastasius reads μὴ for μέν.

[2] Κατὰ σύλληψιν πάντα περιγράφουσαν νοῦν

[3] οὔτε μὴν εἰς τ' αὐτὸν αὐτῷ φέρεσθαι φύσιός ποτε καὶ φυσικῆς ἐνεργείας, ἕως ἂν ἑκάτερον τῆς ἰδίας ἐντὸς μένει φυσικῆς ἀτρεψίας. To φέρεσθαι we supply again πέφυκε.

[4] The sense is extremely doubtful here. The text runs thus: ὁμοφυῶν

FRAGMENT IV.

For, in the view of apostles and prophets and teachers, the mystery of the divine incarnation has been distinguished as having two points of contemplation natural to it,[1] distinct in all things, inasmuch as on the one hand it is the subsistence of perfect deity, and on the other is demonstrative of full humanity. As long, therefore,[2] as the Word is acknowledged to be in substance one, of one energy, there shall never in any way be known a movement (change, κίνησις) in the two. For while God, who is essentially ever-existent, became by His infinite power, according to His will, sinless man, He is what He was, in all wherein God is known; and what He became, He is in all wherein man is known and can be recognised. In both aspects of Himself He never falls out of Himself (μένει ἀνέκπτωτος), in His divine activities and in His human alike, preserving in both relations His own essentially unchangeable perfection.

FRAGMENT V.

For lately a certain person, Beron, along with some others, forsook the delusion of Valentinus, only to involve themselves in deeper error, affirming that the flesh assumed to Himself by the Word became capable of working like works with the deity (γενέσθαι ταυτουργὸν τῇ θεότητι) by virtue of its assumption, and that the deity became susceptible of suffering in the same way with the flesh (ταυτοπαθῆ τῇ σαρκί) by virtue of the exinanition (κένωσιν); and thus they assert the doctrine that there was at the same time a conversion and a

γὰρ μόνων ἡ ταυτουργός ἐστι κίνησις σημαίνουσα τὴν οὐσίαν, ἧς φυσικὴ καθίστηκε δύναμις, ἑτεροφυοῦς ἰδιότητος οὐσίας εἶναι κατ' οὐδένα λόγον, ἢ γενέσθαι δίχα τροπῆς δυναμένην. Anastasius renders it: Connaturalium enim tantum per se operans est motus, manifestans substantiam, cujus naturalem constat esse virtutem: diversæ naturæ proprietatis substantia nulla naturæ esse vel fieri sine convertibilitate valente.

[1] ὀπτὴν καὶ διαφορὰν ἔχον διέγνωσται τὴν ἐν πᾶσι φυσικὴν θεωρίαν.
[2] The text goes, ἕως ἂν οὐχ, which is adopted by Combefisius. But Capperonnier and Migne read οὖν for οὐχ, as we have rendered it.

mixing and a fusing (σύγχυσιν) of the two aspects one with the other. For if the flesh that was assumed became capable of working like works with the deity, it is evident that it also became God in essence in all wherein God is essentially known. And if the deity by the exinanition became susceptible of the same sufferings with the flesh, it is evident that it also became in essence flesh in all wherein flesh essentially can be known. For objects that act in like manner (ὁμοεργῆ), and work like works, and are altogether of like kind, and are susceptible of like suffering with each other, admit of no difference of nature; and if the natures are fused together (συγκεχυμένων), Christ will be a duality (δυάς); and if the persons (προσώπων) are separated, there will be a quaternity (τετράς[1]),—a thing which is altogether to be avoided. And how will they conceive of the one and the same Christ, who is at once God and man by nature? And what manner of existence will He have according to them, if He has become man by a conversion of the deity, and if He has become God by a change of the flesh? For the mutation (μετάπτωσις) of these, the one into the other, is a complete subversion of both. Let the discussion, then, be considered by us again in a different way.

FRAGMENT VI.

Among Christians it is settled as the doctrine of piety, that, according to nature itself, and to the activity and to whatever else pertains thereunto, God is equal and the same with Himself (ἴσον ἑαυτῷ καὶ ταυτόν), having nothing that is His unequal to Himself at all and heterogeneous (ἀκατάλληλον). If, then, according to Beron, the flesh that He assumed to Himself became possessed of the like natural energy with them, it is evident that it also became possessed of the like nature with Him in all wherein that nature consists,—to wit, non-origination, non-generation, infinitude, eternity, incomprehensibility, and whatever else in the way of the transcendent the theological mind discerns in deity; and thus they

[1] *i.e.* instead of Trinity.

both underwent conversion, neither the one nor the other preserving any more the substantial relation of its own proper nature (τῆς ἰδίας φύσεως οὐσιώδη λόγον). For he who recognises an identical operation (ταυτουργίαν) in things of unlike nature, introduces at the same time a fusion of natures and a separation of persons (διαίρεσιν προσωπικήν), their natural existence (ὑπάρξεως) being made entirely undistinguishable by the transference of properties (ἰδιωμάτων).

FRAGMENT VII.

But if it (the flesh) did not become of like nature with that (the deity), neither shall it ever become of like natural energy with that; that He may not be shown to have His energy unequal with His nature, and heterogeneous, and, through all that pertains to Himself, to have entered on an existence outside of His natural equality and identity (φυσικῆς ἔξω γεγονὼς ἰσότητος καὶ ταυτότητος), which is an impious supposition.

FRAGMENT VIII.

Into this error, then, have they been carried, by believing, unhappily, that that divine energy was made the property of the flesh which was only manifested through the flesh in His miraculous actions; by which energy Christ, in so far as He is apprehended as God, gave existence to the universe, and now maintains and governs it. For they did not perceive that it is impossible for the energy of the divine nature to become the property (ἰδίωμα) of a being of a different nature (ἑτεροφανοῦς οὐσίας) apart from conversion; nor did they understand that that is not by any means the property of the flesh which is only manifested through it, and does not spring out of it according to nature; and yet the proof thereof was clear and evident to them. For I, by speaking with the tongue and writing with the hand, reveal through both these one and the same thought of my intelligent soul, its energy (or operation) being natural; in no way showing it as springing naturally out of tongue or hand; nor yet (showing) even the spoken thought as made to belong to them in virtue of its revelation by their means. For no intelligent person ever recognised tongue or hand as capable of thought, just as also no one ever recognised the perfectly holy flesh of God, in virtue of its assumption, and in virtue of the revelation of the divine energy through its medium, as becoming in nature creative (δημιουργόν). But the pious confession of the believer is that, with a view to our salvation, and in order to connect the universe with unchangeableness, the Creator of all things incorporated with Himself (ἐνουσιώσας) a rational soul and a sensible (or sensitive, αἰσθητικοῦ) body from the all-holy Mary, ever-virgin, by an undefiled conception, without conversion, and was made man in nature, but separate from wickedness: the same was perfect God, and the same was perfect man; the same was in nature at once perfect God and man. In His deity He wrought divine things through His all-holy flesh,—such things, namely, as did not pertain to the flesh by nature; and in His humanity He suffered human things,—such things, namely, as did not pertain to deity by nature, by the upbearing of the deity (ἀνοχῇ πάσχων θεότητος). He wrought nothing divine without the body (γυμνὸν σώματος); nor did the same do anything human without the participation of deity (ἄμοιρον δράσας θεότητος). Thus He preserved for Himself a new and fitting method (καινοπρεπῆ τρόπον) by which He wrought (according to the manner of) both, while that which was natural to both remained unchanged (τὸ κατ᾽ ἄμφω φυσικῶς ἀναλλοίωτον); to the accrediting (εἰς πίστωσιν) of His perfect incarnation (ἐνανθρωπήσεως), which is really genuine, and has nothing lacking in it (μηδὲν ἐχούσης φαυλότητος). Beron, therefore, since the case stands with him as I have already stated, confounding together in nature the deity and the humanity of Christ in a single energy (ἐνεργείας μονάδι), and again separating them in person, subverts the life, not knowing that identical operation (ταυτουργίαν) is indicative of the connatural identity only of connatural persons (μόνης τῆς τῶν ὁμοφυῶν προσώπων ὁμοφυοῦς ταυτότητος).

THE DISCOURSE ON THE HOLY THEOPHANY.

BY

HIPPOLYTUS, BISHOP AND MARTYR.

---

1. GOOD, yea, very good, are all the works of our God and Saviour—all of them that eye seeth and mind perceiveth, all that reason interprets and hand handles, all that intellect comprehends and human nature understands. For what richer beauty can there be than that of the circle (δίσκου) of heaven? And what form of more blooming fairness than that of earth's surface? And what is there swifter in the course than the chariot of the sun? And what more graceful car than the lunar orb (σεληνιακοῦ στοιχείου)? And what work more wonderful than the compact mosaic of the stars?[1] And what more productive of supplies than the seasonable winds? And what more spotless mirror than the light of day? And what creature more excellent than man? Very good, then, are all the works of our God and Saviour. And what more requisite gift, again, is there than the element (φύσεως) of water? For with water all things are washed and nourished, and cleansed and bedewed. Water bears the earth, water produces the dew, water exhilarates the vine; water matures the corn in the ear, water ripens the grape-cluster, water softens the olive, water sweetens the palm-date, water reddens the rose and decks the violet, water makes the lily bloom with its brilliant cups. And why should I speak at length? Without the element of water, none of the present order of things can subsist. So necessary is the element of water; for

[1] πολυπηγήτου τῶν ἄστρων μουσίου.

the other elements (στοιχεῖα) took their places beneath the highest vault of the heavens, but the nature of water obtained a seat also above the heavens. And to this the prophet himself is a witness, when he exclaims, " Praise the Lord, ye heavens of heavens, and the water that is above the heavens."[1]

2. Nor is this the only thing that proves the dignity (ἀξιοπιστίαν) of the water. But there is also that which is more honourable than all—the fact that Christ, the Maker of all, came down as the rain,[2] and was known as a spring,[3] and diffused Himself as a river,[4] and was baptized in the Jordan.[5] For you have just heard how Jesus came to John, and was baptized by him in the Jordan. Oh things strange beyond compare! How should the boundless River[6] that makes glad the city of God have been dipped in a little water! The illimitable Spring that bears life to all men, and has no end, was covered by poor and temporary waters! He who is present everywhere, and absent nowhere—who is incomprehensible to angels and invisible to men—comes to the baptism according to His own good pleasure. When you hear these things, beloved, take them not as if spoken literally, but accept them as presented in a figure (œconomically). Whence also the Lord was not unnoticed by the watery element in what He did in secret, in the kindness of His condescension to man. "For the waters saw Him, and were afraid."[7] They well-nigh broke from their place, and burst away from their boundary. Hence the prophet, having this in his view many generations ago, puts the question, "What aileth thee, O sea, that thou fleddest; and thou, Jordan, that thou wast driven back?"[8] And they in reply said, We have seen the Creator of all things in the "form of a servant,"[9] and being ignorant of the mystery of the œconomy, we were lashed with fear.

3. But we, who know the œconomy, adore His mercy, because He hath come to save and not to judge the world. Wherefore John, the forerunner of the Lord, who knew

[1] Ps. cxlviii. 4. [2] Hos. vi. 3. [3] John iv. 14.
[4] John vii. 38. [5] Matt. iii. 13. [6] Ps. xlvi. 4.
[7] Ps. lxxvii. 16. [8] Ps. cxiv. 5. [9] Phil. ii. 7.

not this mystery (before), on learning that He is Lord in truth, cried out, and spake to those who came to be baptized of him, " O generation of vipers,"[1] why look ye so earnestly at me ? "I am not the Christ ;"[2] I am the servant, and not the lord; I am the subject, and not the king; I am the sheep, and not the shepherd; I am a man, and not God. By my birth I loosed the barrenness of my mother; I did not make virginity barren.[3] I was brought up from beneath; I did not come down from above. I bound the tongue of my father;[4] I did not unfold divine grace. I was known by my mother, and I was not announced by a star.[5] I am worthless, and the least; but " after me there comes One who is before me"[6]—after me, indeed, in time, but before me by reason of the inaccessible and unutterable light of divinity. "There comes One mightier than I, whose shoes I am not worthy to bear: He shall baptize you with the Holy Ghost, and with fire."[7] I am subject to authority, but He has authority in Himself. I am bound by sins, but He is the Remover of sins. I apply ($\pi\alpha\rho\acute{a}\pi\tau\omega$) the law, but He bringeth grace to light. I teach as a slave, but He judgeth as the Master. I have the earth as my couch, but He possesses heaven. I baptize with the baptism of repentance, but He confers the gift of adoption : " He shall baptize you with the Holy Ghost, and with fire." Why give ye attention to me ? I am not the Christ.

4. As John says these things to the multitude, and as the people watch in eager expectation of seeing some strange spectacle with their bodily eyes, and the devil[8] is struck with amazement at such a testimony from John, lo, the Lord appears, plain, solitary, uncovered ($\gamma \upsilon \mu \nu \acute{o} \varsigma$), without escort ($\dot{a}\pi\rho o$-

---

[1] Matt. iii. 7.   [2] John i. 20.

[3] οὐ παρθενίαν ἐστείρωσα. So Gregory Thaumaturgus, *Sancta Theophania*, p. 106, edit. Vossii : " Thou, when born of the Virgin Mary, ... didst not loose her virginity ; but didst preserve it, and gifted her with the name of mother."

[4] Luke i. 20.   [5] Matt. ii. 9.   [6] John i. 27.   [7] Matt. iii. 11.

[8] It was a common opinion among the ancient theologians that the devil was ignorant of the mystery of the œconomy, founding on such passages as Matt. iv. 3, 1 Cor. ii. 8. (Fabricius.)

στάτευτος), having on Him the body of man like a garment, and hiding the dignity of the Divinity, that He may elude the snares of the dragon. And not only did He approach John as Lord without royal retinue; but even like a mere man, and one involved in sin, He bent His head to be baptized by John. Wherefore John, on seeing so great a humbling of Himself, was struck with astonishment at the affair, and began to prevent Him, saying, as ye have just heard, "I have need to be baptized of Thee, and comest Thou to me?"[1] What doest Thou, O Lord? Thou teachest things not according to rule.[2] I have preached one thing (regarding Thee), and Thou performest another; the devil has heard one thing, and perceives another. Baptize me with the fire of Divinity; why waitest Thou for water? Enlighten me with the Spirit; why dost Thou attend upon a creature? Baptize me, the Baptist, that Thy pre-eminence may be known. I, O Lord, baptize with the baptism of repentance, and I cannot baptize those who come to me unless they first confess fully their sins. Be it so then that I baptize Thee, what hast Thou to confess? Thou art the Remover of sins, and wilt Thou be baptized with the baptism of repentance? Though I should venture to baptize Thee, the Jordan dares not to come near Thee. "I have need to be baptized of Thee, and comest Thou to me?"

5. And what saith the Lord to him? "Suffer it to be so now, for thus it becometh us to fulfil all righteousness."[3] "Suffer it to be so now," John; thou art not wiser than I. Thou seest as man; I foreknow as God. It becomes me to do this first, and thus to teach. I engage in nothing unbecoming, for I am invested with honour. Dost thou marvel, O John, that I am not come in my dignity? The purple robe of kings suits not one in private station, but military splendour suits a king: am I come to a prince, and not to a friend? "Suffer it to be so now, for thus it becometh us to fulfil all righteousness:" I am the Fulfiller of the law; I seek to leave nothing wanting to its whole fulfilment, that so after me Paul may exclaim, "Christ is the fulfilling of the law

[1] Matt. iii. 14.   [2] ἀκανόνιστα δογματίζεις.   [3] Matt. iii. 15.

for righteousness to every one that believeth."[1] "Suffer it to be so now, for thus it becometh us to fulfil all righteousness." Baptize me, John, in order that no one may despise baptism. I am baptized by thee, the servant, that no one among kings or dignitaries may scorn to be baptized by the hand of a poor priest. Suffer me to go down into the Jordan, in order that they may hear my Father's testimony, and recognise the power of the Son. "Suffer it to be so now, for thus it becometh us to fulfil all righteousness." Then at length John suffers Him. "And Jesus, when He was baptized, went up straightway out of the water: and the heavens were opened unto Him; and, lo, the Spirit of God descended like a dove, and rested upon Him. And a voice (came) from heaven, saying, This is my beloved Son, in whom I am well pleased."[2]

6. Do you see, beloved, how many and how great blessings we would have lost, if the Lord had yielded to the exhortation of John, and declined baptism? For the heavens were shut before this; the region above was inaccessible. We would in that case descend to the lower parts, but we would not ascend to the upper. But was it only that the Lord was baptized? He also renewed the old man, and committed to him again the sceptre of adoption. For straightway "the heavens were opened to Him." A reconciliation took place of the visible with the invisible; the celestial orders were filled with joy; the diseases of earth were healed; secret things were made known; those at enmity were restored to amity. For you have heard the word of the evangelist, saying, "The heavens were opened to Him," on account of three wonders. For when Christ the Bridegroom was baptized, it was meet that the bridal-chamber of heaven should open its brilliant gates. And in like manner also, when the Holy Spirit descended in the form of a dove, and the Father's voice spread everywhere, it was meet that "the gates of heaven should be lifted up."[3] "And, lo, the heavens were opened to Him; and a voice was heard, saying, This is my beloved Son, in whom I am well pleased."

[1] Rom. x. 4.   [2] Matt. iii. 16, 17.   [3] Ps. xxiv. 7.

DISCOURSE ON THE HOLY THEOPHANY. 85

7. The beloved generates love, and the light immaterial the light inaccessible.[1] "This is my beloved Son," He who, being manifested on earth and yet unseparated from the Father's bosom, was manifested, and yet did not appear.[2] For the appearing is a different thing, since in appearance the baptizer here is superior to the baptized. For this reason did the Father send down the Holy Spirit from heaven upon Him who was baptized. For as in the ark of Noah the love of God toward man is signified by the dove, so also now the Spirit, descending in the form of a dove, bearing as it were the fruit of the olive, rested on Him to whom the witness was borne. For what reason? That the faithfulness of the Father's voice might be made known, and that the prophetic utterance of a long time past might be ratified. And what utterance is this? "The voice of the Lord (is) on the waters, the God of glory thundered; the Lord (is) upon many waters."[3] And what voice? "This is my beloved Son, in whom I am well pleased." This is He who is named the son of Joseph, and (who is) according to the divine essence my Only-begotten. "This is my beloved Son"—He who is hungry, and yet maintains myriads; who is weary, and yet gives rest to the weary; who has not where to lay His head,[4] and yet bears up all things in His hand; who suffers, and yet heals sufferings; who is smitten,[5] and yet confers liberty on the world;[6] who is pierced in the side,[7] and yet repairs the side of Adam.[8]

8. But give me now your best attention, I pray you, for I wish to go back to the fountain of life, and to view the fountain

---

[1] φῶς ἄυλον γεννᾷ φῶς ἀπρόσιτον. The Son is called "Light of Light" in the Discourse against Noetus, ch. x. In φῶς ἀπρόσιτον the reference is to 1 Tim. vi. 16.

[2] ἐπιφάνη οὐκ ἐφάνη. See Dorner's *Doctrine of the Person of Christ*, Div. i. vol. ii. p. 97 (Clark).

[3] Ps. xxix. 3.   [4] Luke ix. 5.

[5] ῥαπιζόμενος, referring to the slap in the process of manumitting slaves.

[6] Heb. i. 3.   [7] Matt. xxvi. 67.

[8] That is, the sin introduced by Eve, who was formed by God out of Adam's side. (Fabricius.)

that gushes with healing. The Father of immortality sent the immortal Son and Word into the world, who came to man in order to wash him with water and the Spirit; and He, begetting us again to incorruption of soul and body, breathed into us the breath (spirit) of life, and endued us with an incorruptible panoply. If, therefore, man has become immortal, he will also be God.[1] And if he is made God by water and the Holy Spirit after the regeneration of the laver (κολυμβήθρας), he is found to be also joint-heir with Christ[2] after the resurrection from the dead. Wherefore I preach to this effect: Come, all ye kindreds of the nations, to the immortality of the baptism. I bring good tidings of life to you who tarry in the darkness of ignorance. Come into liberty from slavery, into a kingdom from tyranny, into incorruption from corruption. And how, saith one, shall we come? How? By water and the Holy Ghost. This is the water in conjunction with the Spirit, by which paradise is watered, by which the earth is enriched, by which plants grow, by which animals multiply, and (to sum up the whole in a single word) by which man is begotten again and endued with life, in which also Christ was baptized, and in which the Spirit descended in the form of a dove.

9. This is the Spirit that at the beginning "moved upon the face of the waters;"[3] by whom the world moves; by whom creation consists, and all things have life; who also wrought mightily in the prophets,[4] and descended in flight upon Christ.[5] This is the Spirit that was given to the apostles in the form of fiery tongues.[6] This is the Spirit that David sought when he said, "Create in me a clean heart, O God, and renew a right spirit within me."[7] Of this Spirit Gabriel also spoke to the Virgin, "The Holy Ghost shall come upon thee, and the power of the Highest shall overshadow thee."[8] By this Spirit

---

[1] ἔσται καὶ Θεός, referring probably to 2 Pet. i. 4, ἵνα διὰ τούτων γένησθε θείας κοινωνοὶ φύσεως, "that by these ye might be partakers of the divine nature."

[2] Rom. viii. 17.　　[3] Gen. i. 2.　　[4] Acts xxviii. 25.
[5] Matt. iii. 16.　　[6] Acts ii. 3.　　[7] Ps. li. 10.
[8] Luke i. 35.

Peter spake that blessed word, "Thou art the Christ, the Son of the living God."¹ By this Spirit the rock of the church was stablished.² This is the Spirit, the Comforter, that is sent because of thee,³ that He may show thee to be the son (τέκνον) of God.

10. Come then, be begotten again, O man, into the adoption of God. And how? says one. If thou practisest adultery no more, and committest not murder, and servest not idols; if thou art not overmastered by pleasure; if thou dost not suffer the feeling of pride to rule thee; if thou cleansest off the filthiness of impurity, and puttest off the burden of sin; if thou castest off the armour of the devil, and puttest on the breastplate of faith, even as Isaiah saith, "Wash you, and seek judgment, relieve the oppressed, judge the fatherless, and plead for the widow. And come and let us reason together, saith the Lord. Though your sins be as scarlet, I shall make them white as snow; and though they be like crimson, I shall make them white as wool. And if ye be willing, and hear my voice, ye shall eat the good of the land."⁴ Do you see, beloved, how the prophet spake beforetime of the purifying power of baptism? For he who comes down in faith to the laver of regeneration, and renounces the devil, and joins himself to Christ; who denies the enemy, and makes the confession that Christ is God; who puts off the bondage, and puts on the adoption,—he comes up from the baptism brilliant as the sun,⁵ flashing forth the beams of righteousness, and, which is indeed the chief thing, he returns a son of God and joint-heir with Christ. To Him be the glory and the power, together with His most holy, and good, and quickening Spirit, now and ever, and to all the ages of the ages. Amen.

¹ Matt. xvi. 16. ² Matt. xvi. 18.
³ John xvi. 26. ⁴ Isa. i. 16–19.
⁵ This seems to refer to what the poets sing as to the sun rising out of the waves of ocean. (Fabricius.)

FRAGMENTS

OF

DISCOURSES OR HOMILIES BY HIPPOLYTUS.

I.

[From a Discourse on the Resurrection,[1] in Anastasius Sinaita, Hodegus, p. 350.]

From the Discourse of Hippolytus, Bishop of Rome, on the Resurrection and Incorruption.

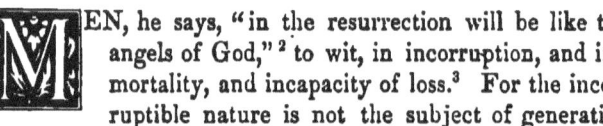MEN, he says, "in the resurrection will be like the angels of God,"[2] to wit, in incorruption, and immortality, and incapacity of loss.[3] For the incorruptible nature is not the subject of generation ($\gamma\epsilon\nu\nu\hat{a}\tau ai$); it grows not, sleeps not, hungers not, thirsts not, is not wearied, suffers not, dies not, is not pierced by nails and spear, sweats not, drops not with blood. Of such kind are the natures of the angels and of souls released from the body. For both these are of another kind, and different from these creatures of our world, which are visible and perishing.

II.

[From the Discourse on the Theology or the Doctrine of Christ's Divine Nature, extant in the *Acts of the Lateran Council*, under Martinus I., ann. 649, secret. v. p. 287, vol. vii. edit. Veneto-Labb.]

From the Discourse of St Hippolytus, Bishop and Martyr, on the Divine Nature ($\pi\epsilon\rho\grave{i}\ \theta\epsilon o\lambda o\gamma\acute{i}a\varsigma$).

God is capable of willing, but not of not willing (οὐ τὸ μὴ θέλειν), for that pertains only to one that changes and makes

---

[1] This treatise is mentioned in the list of his works given on the statue, and also by Jerome, Sophronius, Nicephorus, Honorius, etc.

[2] Matt. xxii. 30.   [3] ἀφευσίᾳ.

choice (τρεπτοῦ καὶ προαιρετοῦ); for things that are being made follow the eternal will of God, by which also things that are made abide sustained.

III.

[From a Homily on the Lord's Paschal Supper, *ibid.* p. 293.]

St. Hippolytus, Bishop and Martyr, in his Homily on the Paschal Supper.

He was altogether (ὅλος) in all, and everywhere; and though He filleth the universe up to all the principalities of the air, He stripped Himself again. And for a brief space He cries that the cup might pass from Him, with a view to show truly that He was also man.[1] But remembering, too, the purpose for which He was sent, He fulfils the dispensation (œconomy) for which He was sent, and exclaims, "Father, not my will,"[2] and, "The spirit is willing, but the flesh is weak."[3]

IV.

[From a Discourse on Elkanah and Hannah. In Theodoret, Dial. i., bearing the title " Unchangeable " (ἄτρεπτος); *Works*, vol. iv. p. 36.]

Take me, O Samuel, the heifer brought tó Bethlehem, in order to show the king begotten of David, and him who is anointed to be king and priest by the Father.

[From the same Discourse.]

Tell me, O blessed Mary, what that was that was conceived by thee in the womb, and what that was that was born by thee in thy virgin matrix. For it was the first-born Word of God that descended to thee from heaven, and was formed as a first-born man in the womb, in order that the first-born Word of God might be shown to be united with a first-born man.

[From the same Discourse.]

And in the second (form),—to wit, by the prophets, as by Samuel, calling back and delivering the people from the

---
[1] καὶ ἄνθρωπος, also man. See Grab. Bull's *Defens. fid. Nic.* p. 108.
[2] Luke xxii. 42.   [3] Matt. xxvi. 41.

slavery of the aliens. And in the third (form), that in which He was incarnate, taking to Himself humanity from the Virgin, in which character also He saw the city, and wept over it.

V.

[From the same Discourse. From Theodoret's Second Dialogue, bearing the title "Unmixed," ἀσύγχυτος; *Works*, vol. iv. p. 88.]

And for this reason three seasons of the year prefigured the Saviour Himself, so that He should fulfil the mysteries prophesied of Him. In the Passover season, so as to exhibit Himself as one destined to be sacrificed like a sheep, and to prove Himself the true Paschal-lamb, even as the apostle says, "Even Christ," who is God, "our passover was sacrificed for us."[1] And at Pentecost so as to presignify the kingdom of heaven, as He Himself first ascended to heaven and brought man as a gift to God.

VI.

[From an Oration on "The Lord is my Shepherd." In Theodoret, Dial. i. p. 36.]

And an ark of imperishable wood was the Saviour Himself. For by this was signified the imperishable and incorruptible tabernacle (of His body), which engendered no corruption of sin. For the man who has sinned also has this confession to make: "My wounds stank, and were corrupt, because of my foolishness."[2] But the Lord was without sin, being of imperishable wood in respect of His humanity,—that is to say, being of the Virgin and the Holy Spirit, covered, as it were, within and without with the purest gold of the Word of God.

VII.

[From a Discourse on the "Great Song." In Theodoret, Dial. ii. pp. 88, 89.]

He who rescued from the lowest hell the first-formed man of earth when he was lost and bound with the chains of

[1] 1 Cor. v. 7.   [2] Ps. xxxviii. 5.

death; He who came down from above, and raised the earthy on high (τὸν κάτω εἰς τὰ ἄνω); He who became the evangelist of the dead, and the redeemer of the souls, and the resurrection of the buried,—He was constituted the helper of vanquished man, being made like him Himself, (so that) the first-born Word acquainted Himself with the first-formed Adam in the Virgin; He who is spiritual sought out the earthy in the womb; He who is the ever-living One sought out him who, through disobedience, is subject to death; He who is heavenly called the terrene to the things that are above; He who is the nobly-born sought, by means of His own subjection, to declare the slave free; He transformed the man into adamant who was dissolved into dust and made the food of the serpent, and declared Him who hung on the tree to be Lord over the conqueror, and thus through the tree He is found victor.

[From the same Discourse.]

For they who know not now the Son of God incarnate, shall know in Him who comes as Judge in glory, Him who is now despised in the body of His humiliation.

[From the same Discourse.]

And the apostles, when they came to the sepulchre on the third day, did not find the body of Jesus; just as the children of Israel went up the mount and sought for the tomb of Moses, but did not find it.

VIII.

[From a Discourse on the beginning of Isaiah. In Theodoret, Dial. i. p. 36.]

Under the figure of Egypt he described the world; and under things made with hands, idolatry; and under the earthquake, the subversion and dissolution of the earth itself. And he represented the Lord the Word as a light cloud, the purest tabernacle, enthroned on which our Lord Jesus Christ entered into this life in order to subvert error.

IX.

[From a second Oration on Daniel. In the tractate of Eustratius, a presbyter of the Church of Constantinople, "Against those who allege that souls, as soon as they are released from the body, cease to act," ch. xix., as edited by Allatius in his work on the *Continuous Harmony of the Western and the Eastern Church on the Dogma of Purgatory*, p. 492.]

Now Hippolytus, the martyr and bishop of Rome, in his second discourse on Daniel, speaks thus :—

Then indeed Azarias, standing along with the others, made their acknowledgments to God with song and prayer in the midst of the furnace. Beginning thus with His holy and glorious and honourable name, they came to the works of the Lord themselves, and named first of all those of heaven, and glorified Him, saying, "Bless the Lord, all ye works of the Lord." Then they passed to the sons of men, and taking up their hymn in order, they then named the spirits that people Tartarus beneath the earth, and the souls of the righteous, in order that they might praise God together with them.

X.

[From an Oration on the Distribution of Talents. In Theodoret, Dial. ii. p. 88.]

Now a person might say that these men, and those who hold a different opinion, are yet near neighbours, being involved in like error. For those men, indeed, either profess that Christ came into our life a mere man, and deny the talent of His divinity, or else, acknowledging Him to be God, they deny, on the other hand, His humanity, and teach that His appearances to those who saw Him as man were illusory, inasmuch as He did not bear with Him true manhood, but was rather a kind of phantom manifestation. Of this class are, for example, Marcion and Valentinus, and the Gnostics, who sunder the Word from the flesh, and thus set aside the one talent, viz. the incarnation.

XI.

[From a Discourse on "The two Robbers." In Theodoret's third Dialogue, bearing the title "Impassible" (ἀπαθής), p. 156.]

The body of the Lord presented both these to the world, the sacred blood and the holy water.

[From the same Discourse.]

And His body, though dead after the manner of man, possesses in it great power of life. For streams which flow not from dead bodies flowed forth from Him, viz. blood and water; in order that we might know what power for life is held by the virtue that dwelt in His body, so as that it appears not to be dead like others, and is able to shed forth for us the springs of life.

[From the same Discourse.]

And not a bone of the Holy Lamb is broken, this figure showing us that suffering toucheth not His strength. For the bones are the strength of the body.

FRAGMENTS FROM OTHER WRITINGS OF HIPPOLYTUS.

I.

[Preserved by the author of the *Chronicon Paschale*, ex ed. Cangii, p. 6.]

NOW Hippolytus, a martyr for piety, who was bishop of the place called Portus, near Rome, in his book *Against all Heresies*, wrote in these terms:—

I perceive, then, that the matter is one of contention. For he[1] speaks thus: Christ kept the supper, then, on that day, and then suffered; whence it is needful that I, too, should keep it in the same manner as the Lord did. But he has fallen into error by not perceiving that at the time when Christ suffered He did not eat the passover of the law. For He was the passover that had been of old proclaimed, and that was fulfilled on that determinate day.

II.

[In the same.]

And again the same (authority), in the first book of his treatise on the Holy Supper, speaks thus:—

Now that neither in the first nor in the last there was anything false is evident; for he who said of old, "I will not any more eat the passover,"[2] probably partook of supper before the passover. But the passover He did not eat, but He suffered; for it was not the time for Him to eat.

---

[1] *i.e.* the opponent of Hippolytus, one of the forerunners of the Quartodecimans.

[2] Luke xxii. 16.

III.

[From a Letter of Hippolytus to a certain queen. In Theodoret's Dial. ii., bearing the title "Unmixed" (ἀσύγχυτος), p. 82; and Dial. iii., entitled "Impassible" (ἀπαθής), p. 155.]

Hippolytus, bishop and martyr, in a letter to a certain queen.[1]

He calls Him, then, "the first-fruits of them that sleep,"[2] as the "first-begotten of the dead."[3] For He, having risen, and being desirous to show that that same (body) had been raised which had also died, when His disciples were in doubt, called Thomas to Him, and said, "Reach hither; handle me, and see: for a spirit hath not bone and flesh, as ye see me have."[4]

[From the same Letter.]

In calling Him *the first-fruits*, he testified to that which we have said, viz. that the Saviour, taking to Himself the flesh out of the same lump, raised this same flesh, and made it the first-fruits of the flesh of the righteous, in order that all we who have believed in the hope of the Risen One may have the resurrection in expectation.

THE STORY OF A MAIDEN OF CORINTH, AND A CERTAIN PERSON MAGISTRIANUS.

[Extract in Palladius, *Historia Lausiaca*, chap. cxlviii.; Gallandi, *Biblioth.* ii. 513.]

The account given by Hippolytus, the friend of the apostles.

In another little book bearing the name of Hippolytus, the friend of the apostles, I found a story of the following nature:—

---

[1] On the question as to who this queen was, see Stephen le Moyne, in notes to the *Varia Sacra*, pp. 1103, 1112. In the marble monument mention is made of a letter of Hippolytus to Severina.

[2] 1 Cor. xv. 20.   [3] Col. i. 18.

[4] John xx. 27; Luke xxiv. 39.

There lived a certain most noble and beautiful maiden[1] in the city of Corinth, in the careful exercise of a virtuous life. At that time some persons falsely charged her before the judge there, who was a Greek, with cursing the times, and the princes, and the images. Now those who trafficked in such things, brought her beauty under the notice of the impious judge, who lusted after women. And he gladly received the accusation with his equine ears and lascivious thoughts. And when she was brought before the bloodstained (judge), he was driven still more frantic with profligate passion. But when, after bringing every device to bear upon her, the profane man could not gain over this woman of God, he subjected the noble maiden to various outrages. And when he failed in these too, and was unable to seduce her from her confession of Christ, the cruel judge became furious against her, and gave her over to a punishment of the following nature : Placing the chaste maiden in a brothel, he charged the manager, saying, Take this woman, and bring me three nummi by her every day. And the man, exacting the money from her by her dishonour, gave her up to any who sought her in the brothel. And when the women-hunters knew that, they came to the brothel, and, paying the price put upon their iniquity, sought to seduce her. But this most honourable maiden, taking counsel with herself to deceive them, called them to her, and earnestly besought them, saying : I have a certain sore in my secret parts, which has an extremely hateful stench ; and I am afraid that ye might come to hate me on account of the abominable sore. Grant me therefore a few days, and then ye may have me even for nothing. With these words the blessed maiden gained over the profligates, and dismissed them for a time. And with most fitting prayers she importuned God, and with contrite supplications she sought to turn Him to compassion. God, therefore, who knew her thoughts, and understood how the chaste maiden was distressed in heart for her purity, gave ear to her ; and the Guardian of the safety of all men in those days interposed with His arrangements in the following manner :

[1] Nicephorus also mentions her in his *Hist. Eccl.* vii. 13.

[In the same, chap. cxlix.]

Of a certain person Magistrianus.

There was a certain young man, Magistrianus,[1] comely in his personal appearance, and of a pious mind, whom God had inspired with such a burning spiritual zeal, that he despised even death itself. He, coming under the guise of profligacy, goes in, when the evening was far gone, to the fellow who kept the women, and pays him five nummi, and says to him, Permit me to spend this night with this damsel. Entering then with her into the private apartment, he says to her, Rise, save thyself. And taking off her garments, and dressing her in his own attire, his night-gown, his cloak, and all the habiliments of a man, he says to her, Wrap yourself up with the top of your cloak, and go out; and doing so, and signing herself entirely with the mystery of the cross, she went forth uncorrupted from that place, and was preserved perfectly stainless by the grace of Christ, and by the instrumentality of the young man, who by his own blood delivered her from dishonour. And on the following day the matter became known, and Magistrianus was brought before the infuriated judge. And when the cruel tyrant had examined the noble champion of Christ, and had learned all, he ordered him to be thrown to the wild beasts,—that in this, too, the honour-hating demon might be put to shame. For, whereas he thought to involve the noble youth in an unhallowed punishment, he exhibited him as a double martyr for Christ, inasmuch as he had both striven nobly for his own immortal soul, and persevered manfully in labours also in behalf of that noble and blessed maiden. Wherefore also he was deemed worthy of double honour with Christ, and of the illustrious and blessed crowns by His goodness.

[1] Nicephorus gives this story also, *Hist. Eccl.* vii. 13.

APPENDIX TO PART II.

OF

THE WORKS OF HIPPOLYTUS.

CONTAINING DUBIOUS AND SPURIOUS PIECES.

[Fabricius, *Works of Hippolytus*, vol. ii.]

A Discourse[1] *by the most blessed Hippolytus, Bishop and Martyr, on the End of the World, and on Antichrist, and on the Second Coming of our Lord Jesus Christ.*

I.

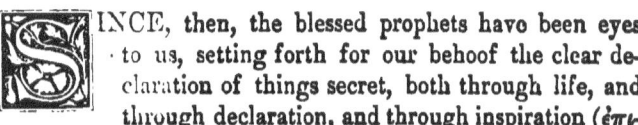SINCE, then, the blessed prophets have been eyes to us, setting forth for our behoof the clear declaration of things secret, both through life, and through declaration, and through inspiration (ἐπιφοιτήσεως) of the Holy Spirit, and discoursing, too, of things not yet come to pass,[2] in this way also[3] to all generations they have pictured forth the grandest subjects for contemplation and for action. Thus, too, they preached of the advent of God[4] in the flesh to the world, His advent by the spotless and God-bearing (θεοτόκου[5]) Mary in the way of birth and

---

[1] This discourse seems to have been a homily addressed to the people.
[2] γεγονότα. Codex Baroccianus gives εὑρηκότα. [3] ὅθεν καί, etc.
[4] Others, τοῦ υἱοῦ τοῦ Θεοῦ, of the Son of God.
[5] This is one of those terms which some allege not to have been yet in use in the time of Hippolytus. But, as Migne observes, if there were no other argument than this against the genuineness of this discourse, this would not avail much, as the term is certainly used by Origen, Methodius, and Dionysius Alex., who were nearly coeval with Hippolytus.

growth, and the manner of His life and conversation with men, and His manifestation by baptism, and the new birth that was to be to all men, and the regeneration by the laver; and the multitude of His miracles, and His blessed passion on the cross, and the insults which He bore at the hands of the Jews, and his burial, and His descent to Hades, and His ascent again, and redemption of the spirits that were of old (ἀπ' αἰώνων), and the destruction of death, and His life-giving awaking from the dead, and His re-creation of the whole world, and His assumption and return to heaven, and His reception of the Spirit, of which the apostles were deemed worthy, and again the second coming, that is destined to declare all things. For as being designated *seers* (βλέποντες), they of necessity signified and spake of these things beforetime.

II.

Hence, too, they indicated the day of the consummation to us, and signified beforehand the day of the apostate that is to appear and deceive men at the last times, and the beginning and end of his kingdom, and the advent of the Judge, and the life of the righteous, and the punishment of the sinners, in order that we all, bearing these things in mind day by day and hour by hour, as children of the Church, might know that " not one jot nor one tittle of these things shall fail,"[1] as the Saviour's own word announced. Let all of you, then, of necessity, open the eyes of your hearts and the ears of your soul, and receive the word which we are about to speak. For I shall unfold to you to-day a narration full of horror and fear, to wit, the account of the consummation, and in particular, of the seduction of the whole world by the enemy and devil; and after these things, the second coming of our Lord Jesus Christ.

III.

Where, then, ye friends of Christ, shall I begin? and with what shall I make my commencement, or what shall I ex-

[1] Matt. v. 18.

pound? and what witness shall I adduce for the things spoken? But let us take those (viz. the prophets) with whom we began this discourse, and adduce them as credible witnesses, to confirm our exposition of the matters discussed; and after them the teaching, or rather the prophecy, of the apostles, [so as to see] how throughout the whole world they herald the day of the consummation. Since these, then, have also shown beforetime things not yet come to pass, and have declared the devices and deceits of wicked men, who are destined to be made manifest, come and let us bring forward Isaiah as our first witness, inasmuch as he instructs us in the times of the consummation. What, then, does he say? "Your country is desolate, your cities are burned with fire: your land, strangers devour it in your presence: the daughter of Zion shall be left as a cottage in a vineyard, and as a lodge in a garden of cucumbers, as a besieged city."[1] You see, beloved, the prophet's illumination, whereby he announced that time so many generations before. For it is not of the Jews that he spake this word of old, nor of the city of Zion, but of the church. For all the prophets have declared Sion to be the bride brought from the nations.

IV.

Wherefore let us direct our discourse to a second witness. And of what sort is this one? Listen to Osea, as he speaks thus grandly: "In those days the Lord shall bring on a burning wind from the desert against them, and shall make their veins dry, and shall make their springs desolate; and all their goodly vessels shall be spoiled. Because they rose up against God, they shall fall by the sword, and their women with child shall be ripped up."[2] And what else is this burning wind from the east, than the Antichrist that is to destroy and dry up the veins of the waters and the fruits of the trees in his times, because men set their hearts on his works? For which reason he shall indeed destroy them, and they shall serve him in his pollution.

[1] Isa. i. 7.   [2] Hos. xiii. 15.

V.

Mark the agreement of prophet with prophet. Acquaint yourself also with another prophet who expresses himself in like manner. For Amos prophesied of the same things in a manner quite in accordance: "Thus saith the Lord, Forasmuch therefore as ye have beaten the poor with the fist,[1] and taken choice gifts from him: ye have built houses, but ye shall not dwell in them: ye have planted pleasant vineyards, but ye shall not drink wine of them. For I know your manifold transgressions, in trampling justice beneath your foot, and taking a bribe, and turning aside the poor in the gate from their right. Therefore the prudent shall keep silence in that time, for it is an evil time."[2] Learn, beloved, the wickedness of the men of that time, how they spoil houses and fields, and take even justice from the just; for when these things come to pass, ye may know that it is the end. For this reason art thou instructed in the wisdom of the prophet, and the revelation that is to be in those days. And all the prophets, as we have already said, have clearly signified the things that are to come to pass in the last times, just as they also have declared things of old.

VI.

But not to expend our argument entirely in going over the words of all the prophets,[3] after citing one other, let us revert to the matter in hand. What is it, then, that Micah says in his prophecy? "Thus saith the Lord concerning the prophets that make my people err, that bite with their teeth, and cry to him, Peace; and if it was not put into their mouth,[4] they prepared[5] war against him. Therefore night shall be

---

[1] κατηγκονδυλίσιτι in the text, for which read κατικονδυλίσατι.

[2] Amos v. 11, 12, 13.

[3] Manuscript E gives the better reading, λόγον ἄπαντα τοῖς τῶν προφητῶν ῥήμασι, "our whole argument on the words of the prophets."

[4] εἰ οὐκ ἰδόθη. Manuscript B omits εἰ = and it was not put into their mouth.

[5] The text reads ἡγίασαν. Manuscript B reads ἤγγισαν. Migne suggests ἤγειραν.

unto you, that ye shall not have a vision;[1] and it shall be dark unto you, that ye shall not divine; and the sun shall not go down over the prophets, and the day shall be dark over them. And the seers shall be ashamed, and the diviners confounded."[2] These things we have recounted beforehand, in order that ye may know the pain that is to be in the last times, and the perturbation, and the manner of life on the part of all men toward each other,[3] and their envy, and hate, and strife, and the negligence of the shepherds toward the sheep, and the unruly disposition of the people toward the priests.[4]

VII.

Wherefore all shall walk after their own will. And the children will lay hands on their parents. The wife will give up her own husband to death, and the husband will bring his own wife to judgment like a criminal. Masters will lord it over their servants savagely,[5] and servants will assume an unruly demeanour toward their masters. None will reverence the grey hairs of the elderly, and none will have pity upon the comeliness of the youthful. The temples of God will be like houses, and there will be overturnings of the churches everywhere. The Scriptures will be despised, and everywhere they will sing the songs of the adversary.[6] Fornications, and adulteries, and perjuries will fill the land; sorceries, and incantations, and divinations will follow after these with all force and zeal. And, on the whole, from among those who profess to be Christians will rise up then false prophets, false apostles, impostors, mischief-makers, evil-doers, liars against

---

[1] ἐξ ὁράσεως.   [2] Mic. iii. 5-7.

[3] For τὴν πρὸς ἀλλήλους ἀναστροφήν, Codex B reads διαστροφὴν καὶ φθοράν.

[4] For ἀνυπότακτον διάθεσιν, Codex B reads ἀταξίαν = unruliness, and adds, καὶ γονεῖς τὰ τέκνα μισήσουσι, καὶ τέκνα τοῖς γονεῦσιν ἐπιβάλλονται χεῖρας, "and parents shall hate their children, and children lay hands on their parents."

[5] For εἰς τοὺς δούλους ἀπάνθρωποι αὐθεντήσονται, Codex B reads, πρὸς τοὺς δούλους ἀπανθρωπίαν κτήσονται.

[6] For ἐχθροῦ, Codex B reads διαβόλου, the devil.

each other, adulterers, fornicators, robbers, grasping, perjured, mendacious, hating each other. The shepherds will be like wolves; the priests will embrace falsehood; the monks[1] will lust after the things of the world; the rich will assume hardness of heart; the rulers will not help the poor; the powerful will cast off all pity; the judges will remove justice from the just, and, blinded with bribes, they will call in unrighteousness.

VIII.

And what am I to say with respect to men,[2] when the very elements themselves will disown their order? There will be earthquakes in every city, and plagues in every country; and monstrous[3] thunderings and frightful lightnings will burn up both houses and fields. Storms of winds will disturb both sea and land excessively; and there will be unfruitfulness on the earth, and a roaring in the sea, and an intolerable agitation on account of souls and the destruction of men.[4] There will be signs in the sun, and signs in the moon, deflections in the stars, distresses of nations, intemperateness in the atmosphere, discharges of hail upon the face of the earth, winters of excessive severity, different[5] frosts, inexorable scorching winds, unexpected thunderings, unlooked-for conflagrations; and in general, lamentation and mourning in the whole earth, without consolation. For, "because iniquity shall abound, the love of many shall wax cold."[6] By reason of the agitation and confusion of all these, the Lord of the universe cries in the Gospel, saying, "Take heed that ye be not deceived; for many shall come in my name, saying, I am

---

[1] This does not agree with the age of Hippolytus.

[2] περὶ ἀνθρώπων, which is the reading of Codex B, instead of ἀπὸ ἀνθρώπων.

[3] ἄμετροι, the reading of Codex B instead of ἄνεμοι.

[4] The text is, ἀπὸ ψυχῶν καὶ ἀπωλείας ἀνθρώπων. We may suggest some such correction as ἀποψυχόντων κατ' ἀπωλείας ἀνθρώπων = "men's hearts failing them concerning the destruction."

[5] διάφοροι. Better with B, ἀδιάφοροι = *promiscuous, without distinction*, and so perhaps *continuous* or *unseasonable*.

[6] Matt. xxiv. 12.

Christ, and the timeth draweth near : go ye not therefore
after them. But when ye shall hear of wars and commotions,
be not terrified: for these things must first come to pass; but
the end is not yet by and by."[1] Let us observe the Word of
the Saviour, how He always admonished us with a view to
our security : "Take heed that ye be not deceived: for many
shall come in my name, saying, I am Christ."

IX.

Now after He was taken up again to the Father, there arose
some, saying, "I am Christ," like Simon Magus and the rest,
whose names we have not time at present to mention. Wherefore also in the last day of the consummation, it must needs
be that false Christs will arise again, saying, "I am Christ,"
and they will deceive many. And multitudes of men will
run from the east even to the west, and from the north even
to the sea, saying, Where is Christ here? where is Christ
there? But being possessed of a vain conceit, and failing to
read the Scriptures carefully, and not being of an upright
mind, they will seek for a name which they shall be unable
to find. For these things must first be ; and thus the son of
perdition—that is to say, the devil—must be seen.

X.

And the apostles, who speak of God,[2] in establishing the
truth of the advent of the Lord Jesus Christ, have each of
them indicated the appearing of these abominable and ruin-
working men, and have openly announced their lawless deeds.
First of all Peter, the rock of the faith, whom Christ our
God called blessed, the teacher of the church, the first disciple, he who has the keys of the kingdom, has instructed us
to this effect: "Know this first, children, that there shall
come in the last days scoffers, walking after their own lusts.[3]
And there shall be false teachers among you, who privily
shall bring in damnable heresies."[4] After him, John the
theologian,[5] and the beloved of Christ, in harmony with him,

---

[1] Luke xxi. 8, 9.   [2] θηγόροι. Codex B gives θιολόγοι.
[3] 2 Pet. iii. 3.   [4] 2 Pet. ii. 1.   [5] θεολόγος.

cries, "The children of the devil are manifest;[1] and even now are there many antichrists;[2] but go not after them.[3] Believe not every spirit, because many false prophets are gone out into the world."[4] And then Jude, the brother of James, speaks in like manner: "In the last times there shall be mockers, walking after their own ungodly lusts. There be they who, without fear, feed[5] themselves."[6] You have observed the concord of the theologians and apostles, and the harmony of their doctrine.

XI.

Finally, hear Paul as he speaks boldly, and mark how clearly he discovers these: "Beware of evil workers, beware of the concision.[7] Beware lest any man spoil you through philosophy and vain deceit.[8] See that ye walk circumspectly, because the days are evil."[9] In fine, then, what man shall have any excuse who hears these things in the church from prophets and apostles, and from the Lord Himself, and yet will give no heed to the care of his soul, and to the time of the consummation, and to that approaching hour when we shall have to stand at the judgment-seat of Christ?

XII.

But being done now with this account of the consummation, we shall turn our exposition to those matters which fall to be stated by us next in order. I adduce, therefore, a witness altogether worthy of credit,—namely, the prophet Daniel, who interpreted the vision of Nabuchodonosor, and from the beginning of the kings down to their end indicated the right (unchangeable, ἀπαράτροπον) way to those who seek to walk therein—to wit, the manifestation of the truth. For

---

[1] 1 John iii. 10. [2] 1 John ii. 18.
[3] Luke xxi. 8. [4] 1 John iv. 1.
[5] οἱ ἀφόβως ἑαυτοὺς ποιμαίνοντες, instead of the received οἱ ἀποδιορίζοντες ἑαυτούς.
[6] Jude 18, 19. [7] Phil. iii. 2.
[8] Col. ii. 8. [9] Eph. v. 15, 16.

what saith the prophet? He presignified the matter clearly to Nabuchodonosor in the following terms: "Thou, O king, sawest, and behold a great image standing before thee, whose head was of gold, its arms and shoulders of silver, its belly and thighs of brass, its legs of iron, its feet part of iron and part of clay. Thou sawest till that a stone was cut out without hand; and it smote the image upon its feet, which were part of iron and part of clay, and brake them to pieces. Then was the clay, and the iron, and the brass, and the silver, and the gold broken to pieces together, and became like the chaff of the summer threshing-floor; and the stone that smote the image became a great mountain, and filled the whole earth."[1]

XIII.

Wherefore, bringing the visions of Daniel into conjunction with these, we shall make one narrative of the two, and show how true and consistent were the things seen in vision by the prophet with those which Nabuchodonosor saw beforehand. For the prophet speaks thus: "I Daniel saw, and, behold, the four winds of the heaven strove upon the great sea. And four great beasts came up from the sea, diverse one from another. The first was like a lioness, and had eagle's wings: I beheld till the wings thereof were plucked, and it was lifted up from the earth, and made stand upon the feet as a man, and a man's heart was given it. And behold a second beast, like to a bear, and it raised up itself on one side, and it had three ribs in the mouth of it between the teeth of it: and they said thus unto it, Arise, devour much flesh. After this I beheld, and lo a third beast, like a leopard, which had upon the back of it four wings of a fowl: the beast had also four heads. After this I saw, and behold a fourth beast, dreadful and terrible, and strong exceedingly; its great iron teeth and its claws of brass[2] devoured and brake in pieces, and it stamped the residue

---

[1] Dan. ii. 31-35.

[2] These words, καὶ οἱ ὄνυχες αὐτοῦ χαλκοῖ, are strange both to the Greek and the Hebrew text of Daniel.

with the feet of it: and it was diverse exceedingly from all the beasts that were before it; and it had ten horns. I considered its horns, and, behold, there came up among them a little horn, and before it there were three of the first horns plucked up by the roots: and, behold, in this horn were eyes like the eyes of man, and a mouth speaking great things."[1]

XIV.

Now, since these things which are thus spoken mystically by the prophet seem to all to be hard to understand, we shall conceal none of them from those who are possessed of sound mind. By mentioning the first beast, namely the *lioness* that comes up out of the sea, Daniel means the kingdom of the Babylonians which was set up in the world; and that same is also the "golden head" of this image. And by speaking of its "wings like an eagle," he shows that king Nabuchodonosor was elevated and exalted himself against God. Then he says that its "wings were plucked out," and means by this that his glory was subverted: for he was driven from his kingdom. And in stating that a "man's heart was given it, and it was made stand upon the feet like a man," he means that he repented, and acknowledged that he was himself but a man, and gave the glory to God. Lo, I have thus unfolded the similitude of the first beast.

XV.

Then after the lioness, the prophet sees a second beast like a bear, which denoted the Persians; for after the Babylonians the Persians had the sovereignty. And in saying, "I saw three ribs in the mouth of it," he referred to three nations, the Persians, Medes, and Babylonians, which were also expressed by the silver that came after the gold in the image. Behold, we have explained the second beast too. Then the third was the leopard, by which were meant the Greeks. For after the Persians, Alexander king of the Macedonians held the sovereignty, when he had destroyed Darius; and this is

[1] Dan. vii. 2-8.

expressed by the brass in the image. And in speaking of "four wings of a fowl, and four heads in the beast," he showed most clearly how the kingdom of Alexander was divided into four parts. For it had four heads,—namely, the four kings that rose out of it. For on his death-bed [1] Alexander divided his kingdom into four parts. Behold, we have discussed the third also.

XVI.

Next he tells us of the "fourth beast, dreadful and terrible; its teeth were of iron, and its claws of brass." And what is meant by these but the kingdom of the Romans, which also is meant by the iron, by which it will crush all the seats of empire that were before it, and will lord it over the whole earth? After this, then, what is left for us to interpret of all that the prophet saw, but the "toes of the image, in which part was of iron and part of clay, mingled together in one?" For by the ten toes of the image he meant figuratively the ten kings who sprang out of it, as Daniel also interpreted the matter. For he says, "I considered the beast, namely the fourth; and behold ten horns after it, among which another horn arose like an offshoot; and it will pluck up by the root three of those before it." And by this offshoot horn none other is signified than the Antichrist, that is to restore the kingdom of the Jews. And the three horns which are to be rooted out by it signify three kings, namely those of Egypt, Libya, and Ethiopia, whom he will destroy in the array of war; [and] when he has vanquished them all, being a savage tyrant, he will raise tribulation and persecution against the saints, exalting himself against them.

XVII.

You see how Daniel interpreted to Nabuchodonosor the dominion of the kingdoms; you see how he explained the form of the image in all its parts ($\pi\hat{a}\sigma\iota$ $\tau o\hat{\iota}\varsigma$ $\pi\acute{\epsilon}\rho a\sigma\iota\nu$); you have observed how he indicated prophetically the meaning of the coming up of the four beasts out of the sea. It remains

---

[1] See Hippolytus on Antichrist, ch. xxiv.

that we open up to you the things done by the Antichrist in particular; and, as far as in our power, declare to you by means of the Scriptures and the prophets, his wandering over the whole earth, and his lawless advent.

XVIII.

As the Lord Jesus Christ made His sojourn with us in the flesh [which he received] from the holy, immaculate Virgin, and took to Himself the tribe of Judah, and came forth from it, the Scripture declared His royal lineage in the word of Jacob, when in his benediction he addressed himself to his son in these terms : "Judah, thou art he whom thy brethren shall praise : thy hands shall be on the neck of thine enemies; thy father's children shall bow down before thee. Judah is a lion's whelp; from a sprout (βλαστοῦ), my son, thou art gone up : he stooped down, he couched as a lion, and as a lion's whelp (σκύμνος) : who shall rouse him up? A ruler (ἄρχων) shall not depart from Judah, nor a leader (ἡγούμενος) from his thighs (ἐκ τῶν μηρῶν), until what is in store for him (τὰ ἀποκείμενα) shall come, and he is the expectation (καὶ αὐτὸς προσδοκία) of the nations."[1] Mark these words of Jacob which were spoken to Judah, and are fulfilled in the Lord. To the same effect, moreover, does the patriarch express himself regarding Antichrist. Wherefore, as he prophesied with respect to Judah, so did he also with respect to his son Dan. For Judah was his fourth son; and Dan, again, was his seventh son. And what, then, did he say of him? "Let Dan be a serpent sitting by the way, that biteth the horse's heel?"[2] And what serpent was there but the deceiver from the beginning, he who is named in Genesis, he who deceived Eve, and bruised Adam in the heel (πτερνίσας)?

XIX.

But seeing now that we must make proof of what is alleged at greater length, we shall not shrink from the task. For it is certain that he is destined to spring from the tribe

[1] Gen. xlix. 8-10. [2] Gen. xlix. 17.

of Dan,[1] and to range himself in opposition like a princely tyrant, a terrible judge and accuser (διάβολος), as the prophet testifies when he says, "Dan shall judge his people, as one tribe in Israel."[2] But some one may say that this was meant of Samson, who sprang from the tribe of Dan, and judged his people for twenty years. That, however, was only partially made good in the case of Samson; but this shall be fulfilled completely in the case of Antichrist. For Jeremiah, too, speaks in this manner: "From Dan we shall hear the sound of the sharpness[3] of his horses; at the sound of the neighing (χρεμετισμοῦ) of his horses the whole land trembled."[4] And again, Moses says: "Dan is a lion's whelp, and he shall leap from Bashan."[5] And that no one may fall into the mistake of thinking that this is spoken of the Saviour, let him attend to this. "Dan," says he, "is a lion's whelp;" and by thus naming the tribe of Dan as the one whence the accuser is destined to spring, he made the matter in hand quite clear. For as Christ is born of the tribe of Judah, so Antichrist shall be born of the tribe of Dan. And as our Lord and Saviour Jesus Christ, the Son of God, was spoken of in prophecy as a *lion* on account of His royalty and glory, in the same manner also has the Scripture prophetically described the accuser as a lion, on account of his tyranny and violence.

XX.

For in every respect that deceiver seeks to make himself appear like the Son of God. Christ is a lion, and Antichrist is a lion. Christ is King of things celestial and things terrestrial, and Antichrist will be king upon earth. The Saviour was manifested as a lamb; and he, too, will appear as a lamb, while he is a wolf within. The Saviour was circumcised, and he in like manner will appear in circumcision. The Saviour sent the apostles unto all the nations, and he in

---

[1] After Irenæus, book v. ch. xxx., many of the ancients express this opinion. See too Bellarmine, *De Pontifice Rom.* iii. 12.
[2] Gen. xlix. 16.
[3] φωνὴν ἐξύτητος. There is another reading, σπουδήν = haste.
[4] Jer. viii. 16.   [5] Deut. xxxiii. 22.

like manner will send false apostles. Christ gathered together the dispersed sheep, and he in like manner will gather together the dispersed people of the Hebrews. Christ gave to those who believed on Him the honourable and life-giving cross, and he in like manner will give his own sign. Christ appeared in the form of man, and he in like manner will come forth in the form of man. Christ arose from among the Hebrews, and he will spring from among the Jews. Christ displayed His flesh like a temple, and raised it up the third day; and he too will raise up again the temple of stone in Jerusalem. And these deceits fabricated by him will become quite intelligible to those who listen to us attentively, from what shall be set forth next in order.

XXI.

For through the Scriptures we are instructed in two advents of the Christ and Saviour. And the first after the flesh was in humiliation, because He was manifested in lowly estate. So then His second advent is declared to be in glory; for He comes from heaven with power, and angels, and the glory of His Father. His first advent had John the Baptist as its forerunner; and His second, in which He is to come in glory, will exhibit Enoch, and Elias, and John the theologian.[1] Behold, too, the Lord's kindness to man; how even in the last times He shows His care for mortals, and pities them. For He will not leave us even then without prophets, but will send them to us for our instruction and assurance, and to make us give heed to the advent of the adversary, as He intimated also of old in this Daniel. For he says, "I

[1] The Apocalypse (xi. 3) mentions only two witnesses, who are understood by the ancients in general as Enoch and Elias. The author of the *Chronicon Paschale*, p. 21, on Enoch, says: "This is he who, along with Elias, is to withstand Antichrist in the last days, and to confute his deceit, according to the tradition of the church." This addition as to the return of John the Evangelist is somewhat more uncommon. And yet Ephraem of Antioch, in Photius, cod. ccxxix., states that this too is supported by ancient ecclesiastical tradition, Christ's saying in John xxi. 22 being understood to that effect. See also Hippolytus, *De Antichristo*, ch. 1.—MIGNE.

shall make a covenant of one week, and in the midst of the week my sacrifice and libation will be removed."[1] For by one week he indicates the showing forth of the seven years which shall be in the last times. And the half of the week the two prophets, along with John, will take for the purpose of proclaiming to all the world the advent of Antichrist, that is to say, for a "thousand two hundred and sixty days clothed in sackcloth;"[2] and they will work signs and wonders with the object of making men ashamed and repentant, even by these means, on account of their surpassing lawlessness and impiety. "And if any man will hurt them, fire will proceed out of their mouth, and devour their enemies. These have power to shut heaven, that it rain not in the days of the advent of Antichrist, and to turn waters into blood, and to smite the earth with all plagues as often as they will."[3] And when they have proclaimed all these things they will fall on the sword, cut off by the accuser (παρὰ τοῦ διαβόλου). And they will fulfil their testimony, as Daniel also says; for he foresaw that the beast that came up out of the abyss would make war with them, namely with Enoch, Elias, and John, and would overcome them, and kill them, because of their refusal to give glory to the accuser. That is the little horn that sprang up.[4] And he being lifted up in heart, begins in the end to exalt himself and glorify himself as God, persecuting the saints and blaspheming Christ.

XXII.

But as, in accordance with the train of our discussion, we have been constrained to come to the matter of the days of the dominion of the adversary, it is necessary to state in the first place what concerns his nativity and growth; and then we must turn our discourse, as we have said before, to the expounding of this matter, viz. that in all respects the accuser and son of lawlessness[5] is to make himself like our Saviour.

---

[1] Dan. ix. 27.   [2] Rev. xi. 3.
[3] Rev. v. 6.   [4] ἀναφανίν. But Cod. B reads ἀναφυίν.
[5] ἀνομίας. Cod. B gives ἀπωλείας, perdition; and for μέλλει = is to, it reads θέλει = wishes.

Thus also the demonstration makes the matter clear to us. Since the Saviour of the world, with the purpose of saving the race of men, was born of the immaculate and virgin[1] Mary, and in the form of the flesh trod the enemy under foot, in the exercise of the power of His own proper divinity; in the same manner also will the accuser come forth from an impure woman upon the earth, but shall be born of a virgin spuriously[2] (ἐν πλάνῃ). For our God sojourned with us in the flesh, after that very flesh of ours which He made for Adam and all Adam's posterity, yet without sin. But the accuser, though he take up the flesh, will do it only in appearance; for how should he wear that flesh which he did not make himself, but against which he warreth daily? And it is my opinion, beloved, that he will assume this phenomenal kind of flesh[3] as an instrument (organ, ὄργανον). For this reason also is he [to be] born of a virgin, as if a spirit, and then to the rest he will be manifested as flesh. For as to a virgin bearing, this we have known only in the case of the all-holy [Virgin], who bore the Saviour clothed in flesh really.[4] For Moses says, "Every male that openeth the womb shall be called holy unto the Lord."[5] This is by no means the case with him (οὐ μὴν οὐδαμῶς); but as the adversary will not open the womb, so neither will he take to himself real flesh, and be circumcised as Christ was circumcised. And even as Christ chose His apostles, so will he too assume a whole people of disciples like himself in wickedness.

XXIII.

Above all, moreover, he will love the nation of the Jews. And with all these he will work signs and terrible wonders,

[1] Cod. B gives ἀειπαρθένου, ever-virgin.
[2] Cod. B reads ἀκριβῶς, exactly. Many of the ancients hold that Antichrist will be a demon in human figure. See Augustine, Sulpicius Severus, in Dialogue ii., and Philippus Dioptra, iii. 11, etc.
[3] φαντασιτικὴν τῆς σαρκὸς αὐτοῦ οὐσίαν.
[4] Cod. B reads τὴν θεοτόκον ἐγνωμεν σαρκικῶς καὶ ἀπλανῶς, instead of the text, σαρκοφόρον ἀπλανῶς, etc.
[5] Ex. xxxiv. 19; Num. viii. 16; Luke ii. 23.

false wonders and not true, in order to deceive his impious equals. For if it were possible, he would seduce even the elect[1] from the love of Christ. But in his first steps he will be gentle, loveable, quiet, pious, pacific, hating injustice, detesting gifts, not allowing idolatry; loving, says he, the Scriptures, reverencing priests, honouring his elders, repudiating fornication, detesting adultery, giving no heed to slanders, not admitting oaths, kind to strangers, kind to the poor, compassionate. And then he will work wonders, cleansing lepers, raising paralytics, expelling demons, proclaiming things remote just as things present, raising the dead, helping widows, defending orphans, loving all, reconciling in love men who contend, and saying to such, "Let not the sun go down upon your wrath;"[2] and he will not acquire gold, nor love silver, nor seek riches.

XXIV.

And all this he will do corruptly and deceitfully, and with the purpose of deluding all to make him king. For when the peoples and tribes see so great virtues and so great powers in him, they will all with one mind meet together to make him king. And above all others shall the nation of the Hebrews be dear to the tyrant himself, while they say one to another, Is there found indeed in our generation such a man, so good and just? That shall be the way with the race of the Jews pre-eminently, as I said before, who, thinking, as they do, that they shall behold the king himself in such power, will approach him to say, We all confide in thee, and acknowledge thee to be just upon the whole earth; we all hope to be saved by thee; and by thy mouth we have received just and incorruptible judgment.

XXV.

And at first, indeed, that deceitful and lawless one, with crafty deceitfulness, will refuse such glory; but the men persisting, and holding by him, will declare him king. And thereafter he will be lifted up in heart, and he who was formerly

---

[1] Matt. xxiv. 24.   [2] Eph. iv. 26.

gentle will become violent, and he who pursued love will become pitiless, and the humble in heart will become haughty and inhuman, and the hater of unrighteousness will persecute the righteous. Then, when he is elevated to his kingdom, he will marshal war; and in his wrath he will smite three mighty kings,—those, namely, of Egypt, Libya, and Ethiopia. And after that he will build the temple in Jerusalem, and will restore it again speedily, and give it over to the Jews. And then he will be lifted up in heart against every man; yea, he will speak blasphemy also against God, thinking in his deceit that he shall be king upon the earth hereafter for ever; not knowing, miserable wretch, that his kingdom is to be quickly brought to naught, and that he will quickly have to meet the fire which is prepared for him, along with all who trust him and serve him. For when Daniel said, "I shall make my covenant for one week,"[1] he indicated seven years; and the one half of the week is for the preaching of the prophets, and for the other half of the week—that is to say, for three years and a half—Antichrist will reign upon the earth. And after this his kingdom and his glory shall be taken away. Behold, ye who love God, what manner of tribulation there shall rise in those days, such as has not been from the foundation of the world, no, nor ever shall be, except in those days alone. Then the lawless one, being lifted up in heart, will gather together his demons in man's form, and will abominate those who call him to the kingdom, and will pollute many souls.

XXVI.

For he will appoint princes over them from among the demons. And he will no longer seem to be pious, but altogether and in all things he will be harsh, severe, passionate, wrathful, terrible, inconstant, dread, morose, hateful, abominable, savage, vengeful, iniquitous. And, bent on casting the whole race of men into the pit of perdition, he will multiply false signs. For when all the people greet him with their acclamations at his displays, he will shout with a strong voice, so

[1] Dan. ix. 27.

that the place shall be shaken in which the multitudes stand by him: "Ye peoples, and tribes, and nations, acquaint yourselves with my mighty authority and power, and the strength of my kingdom. What prince is there so great as I am? What great God is there but I? Who will stand up against my authority?" Under the eye of the spectators he will remove mountains from their places, he will walk on the sea with dry feet, he will bring down fire from heaven, he will turn the day into darkness and the night into day, he will turn the sun about wheresoever he pleases; and, in short, in presence of those who behold him, he will show all the elements of earth and sea to be subject to him in the power of his specious manifestation. For if, while as yet he does not exhibit himself as the son of perdition, he raises and excites against us open war even to battles and slaughters, at that time when he shall come in his own proper person, and men shall see him as he is in reality, what machinations and deceits and delusions will he not bring into play, with the purpose of seducing all men, and leading them off from the way of truth, and from the gate of the kingdom?

XXVII.

Then, after all these things, the heavens will not give their dew, the clouds will not give their rain, the earth will refuse to yield its fruits, the sea shall be filled with stench, the rivers shall be dried up, the fish of the sea shall die, men shall perish of hunger and thirst; and father embracing son, and mother embracing daughter, will die together, and there will be none to bury them. But the whole earth will be filled with the stench arising from the dead bodies cast forth. And the sea, not receiving the floods of the rivers, will become like mire, and will be filled with an unlimited smell and stench. Then there will be a mighty pestilence upon the whole earth, and then, too, inconsolable lamentation, and measureless weeping, and unceasing mourning. Then men will deem those happy who are dead before them, and will say to them, "Open your sepulchres, and take us miserable beings in; open your receptacles for the reception of your wretched kinsmen and acquaintances. Happy are ye, in that ye have not seen our days. Happy are ye, in that ye have not had to witness this painful life of ours, nor this irremediable pestilence, nor these straits that possess our souls."

XXVIII.

Then that abominable one will send his commands throughout every government by the hand at once of demons and of visible men, who shall say, "A mighty king has arisen upon the earth; come ye all to worship him; come ye all to see the strength of his kingdom: for, behold, he will give you corn; and he will bestow upon you wine, and great riches, and lofty honours. For the whole earth and sea obeys his command. Come ye all to him." And by reason of the scarcity of food, all will go to him and worship him; and he will put his mark on their right hand and on their forehead, that no one may put the sign of the honourable cross upon his forehead with his right hand; but his hand is bound. And from that time he shall not have power to seal any one of his members, but he shall be attached to the deceiver, and shall serve him; and in him there is no repentance. But such an one is lost at once to God and to men, and the deceiver will give them scanty food by reason of his abominable seal. And his seal upon the forehead and upon the right hand is the number, "Six hundred three score and six."[1] And I have an opinion as to this number, though I do not know the matter for certain; for many names have been found in this number when it is expressed in writing (ἐν τῇ γραφῇ). Still we say that perhaps the scription of this same seal will give us the word *I deny* (ἀρνοῦμαι[2]). For even in recent days, by means of his ministers—that is to say, the idolaters—that bitter adversary took up the word *deny*, when the lawless

---

[1] Rev. xiii. 18.
[2] The letters of the word ἀρνοῦμαι in their numerical value will not give the number 666 unless it is written ἀρνοῦμε. See Haymo on the Apocalypse, book iv.

pressed upon the witnesses of Christ, with the adjuration, "Deny thy God, the crucified One."[1]

XXIX.

Of such kind, in the time of that hater of all good, will be the seal, the tenor of which will be this: I deny the Maker of heaven and earth, I deny the baptism, I deny my (former) service, and attach myself to thee, and I believe in thee. For this is what the prophets Enoch and Elias will preach: Believe not the enemy who is to come and be seen; for he is an adversary[2] and corrupter and son of perdition, and deceives you;[3] and for this reason he will kill you, and smite them with the sword. Behold the deceit of the enemy, know the machinations of the beguiler, how he seeks to darken the mind of men utterly. For he will show forth his demons brilliant like angels, and he will bring in hosts of the incorporeal without number. And in the presence of all he exhibits himself as taken up into heaven with trumpets and sounds, and the mighty shouting of those who hail him with indescribable hymns; the heir of darkness himself shining like light, and at one time soaring to the heavens, and at another descending to the earth with great glory, and again charging the demons, like angels, to execute his behests with much fear and trembling. Then will he send the cohorts of the demons among mountains and caves and dens of the earth, to track out those who have been concealed from his eyes, and to bring them forward to worship him. And those who yield to him he will seal with his seal; but those who refuse to submit to him he will consume with incomparable pains and bitterest torments and machinations, such as never have been, nor have reached the ear of man, nor have been seen by the eye of mortals.

---

[1] The text is in confusion: ἐπειδὴ καὶ πρώην διὰ τῶν ὑπηρετῶν αὐτοῦ ὁ ἀντίδικος ἐχθρός, ἢ γοῦν τῶν εἰδωλολατρῶν, τοῖς μάρτυσι τοῦ Χριστοῦ προίτρεπον οἱ ἄνομοι, etc.

[2] ἀντίδικος. In B, πλάνος = deceiver.

[3] B reads τὸν κόσμον, the world.

XXX.

Blessed shall they be who overcome the tyrant then. For they shall be set forth as more illustrious and loftier than the first witnesses; for the former witnesses overcame his minions only, but these overthrow and conquer the accuser himself, the son of perdition. With what eulogies and crowns, therefore, will they not be adorned by our King, Jesus Christ!

XXXI.

But let us revert to the matter in hand. When men have received the seal, then, and find neither food nor water, they [will] approach him with a voice of anguish, saying, Give us to eat and drink, for we all faint with hunger and all manner of straits;[1] and bid the heavens yield us water, and drive off from us the beasts that devour men. Then will that crafty one make answer, mocking them with absolute inhumanity, and saying, The heavens refuse to give rain, the earth yields not again its fruits; whence then can I give you food? Then, on hearing the words of this deceiver, these miserable men will perceive that this is the wicked accuser, and will mourn in anguish, and weep vehemently, and beat their face with their hands, and tear their hair, and lacerate their cheeks with their nails, while they say to each other: Woe for the calamity! woe for the bitter contract! woe for the deceitful covenant! woe for the mighty mischance! How have we been beguiled by the deceiver! how have we been joined to him! how have we been caught in his toils! how have we been taken in his abominable net! how have we heard the Scriptures, and understood them not! For truly those who are engrossed with the affairs of life, and with the lust of this world, will be easily brought over to the accuser then, and sealed by him.

XXXII.

But many who are hearers of the divine Scriptures, and have them in their hand, and keep them in mind with under-

---
[1] B reads ὀδύνης, pain.

standing, will escape his imposture. For they will see clearly through his insidious appearance and his deceitful imposture, and will flee from his hands, and betake themselves to the mountains, and hide themselves in the caves of the earth; and they will seek after the Friend of man with tears and a contrite heart; and He will deliver them out of his toils, and with His right hand He will save those from his snares who in a worthy and righteous manner make their supplication to Him.

XXXIII.

You see in what manner of fasting and prayer the saints will exercise themselves at that time. Observe, also, how hard the season and the times will be that are to come upon those in city and country alike. At that time they will be brought from the east even unto the west; and they will come up from the west even unto the east, and will weep greatly and wail vehemently. And when the day begins to dawn they will long for the night, in order that they may find rest from their labours; and when the night descends upon them, by reason of the continuous earthquakes and the tempests in the air, they will desire even to behold the light of the day, and will seek how they may hereafter meet a bitter death. At that time the whole earth will bewail the life of anguish, and the sea and air in like manner will bewail it; and the sun, too, will wail; and the wild beasts, together with the fowls, will wail: mountains and hills, and the trees of the plain, will wail on account of the race of man, because all have turned aside from the holy God, and obeyed the deceiver, and received the mark of that abominable one, the enemy of God, instead of the quickening cross of the Saviour.

XXXIV.

And the churches, too, will wail with a mighty lamentation, because neither oblation nor incense is attended to, nor a service acceptable to God; but the sanctuaries of the churches will become like a garden-watcher's hut, and the holy body and blood of Christ will not be shown in those days. The public service of God shall be extinguished, psalmody shall cease, the reading of the Scriptures shall not be heard; but for men there shall be darkness, and lamentation on lamentation, and woe on woe. At that time silver and gold shall be cast out in the streets, and none shall gather them; but all things shall be held an offence. For all shall be eager to escape and to hide themselves, and they shall not be able anywhere to find concealment from the woes[1] of the adversary; but as they carry his mark about them, they shall be readily recognised and declared to be his. Without there shall be fear, and within trembling, both by night and by day. In the street and in the houses there shall be the dead; in the streets and in the houses there shall be hunger and thirst; in the streets there shall be tumults, and in the houses lamentations. And beauty of countenance shall be withered, for their forms shall be like those of the dead; and the beauty of women shall fade, and the desire of all men shall vanish.

XXXV.

Notwithstanding, not even then will the merciful and benignant God leave the race of men without all comfort; but He will shorten even those days and the period of three years and a half, and He will curtail those times on account of the remnant of those who hide themselves in the mountains and caves, that the phalanx of all those saints fail not utterly. But these days shall run their course rapidly; and the kingdom of the deceiver and Antichrist shall be speedily removed. And then, in fine, in the glance of an eye shall the fashion of this world pass away, and the power of men[2] shall be brought to naught, and all these visible things shall be destroyed.

XXXVI.

As these things, therefore, of which we have spoken before are in the future, beloved, when the one week is divided into parts, and the abomination of desolation has arisen then, and the forerunners of the Lord have finished their proper course, and the whole world, in fine, comes to the consumma-

[1] παθῶν. B reads παγίδων, snares. [2] B reads δαιμόνων, demons.

tion, what remains but the manifestation (ἐπιφάνεια) of our Lord and Saviour Jesus Christ, the Son of God, from heaven, for whom we have hoped; who shall bring forth fire and all just judgment against those who have refused to believe in Him? For the Lord says, "For as the lightning cometh out of the east, and shineth even unto the west, so shall also the coming of the Son of man be; for wheresoever the carcase is, there will the eagles be gathered together."[1] For the sign of the cross[2] shall arise from the east even unto the west, in brightness exceeding that of the sun, and shall announce the advent and manifestation of the Judge, to give to every one according to his works. For concerning the general resurrection and the kingdom of the saints, Daniel says: "And many of them that sleep in the dust of the earth shall awake, some to everlasting life, and some to shame and everlasting contempt."[3] And Isaiah says: "The dead shall rise, and those in the tombs shall awake, and those in the earth shall rejoice."[4] And our Lord says: "Many[5] in that day shall hear the voice of the Son of God, and they that hear shall live."[6]

XXXVII.

For at that time the trumpet shall sound,[7] and awake those that sleep from the lowest parts of the earth, righteous and sinners alike. And every kindred, and tongue, and nation, and tribe shall be raised in the twinkling of an eye;[8] and they shall stand upon the face of the earth, waiting for the coming of the righteous and terrible Judge, in fear and trembling unutterable. For the river of fire shall come forth in fury like an angry sea, and shall burn up mountains and hills, and shall make the sea vanish, and shall dissolve the atmosphere with its heat like wax.[9] The stars of heaven shall fall,[10] the sun shall be turned into darkness, and the

---

[1] Matt. xxiv. 27, 28.　　[2] See Jo. Voss, *Theses Theolog.* p. 228.
[3] Dan. xii. 2.　　[4] Isa. xxvi. 19.
[5] πολλοί, for the received οἱ νεκροί.　　[6] John v. 25.
[7] 1 Thess. iv. 16.　　[8] 1 Cor. xv. 52.　　[9] 2 Pet. iii. 12.
[10] Matt. xxiv. 29

moon into blood.[1] The heaven shall be rolled together like a scroll:[2] the whole earth shall be burnt up by reason of the deeds done in it, which men did corruptly,[3] in fornications, in adulteries, and in lies and uncleanness, and in idolatries, and in murders, and in battles. For there shall be the new heaven and the new earth.[4]

XXXVIII.

Then shall the holy angels run on their commission to gather together all the nations, whom that terrible voice of the trumpet shall awake out of sleep. And before the judgment-seat of Christ shall stand those who once were kings and rulers, chief priests and priests; and they shall give an account of their administration, and of the fold, whoever of them through their negligence have lost one sheep out of the flock. And then shall be brought forward soldiers who were not content with their provision,[5] but oppressed widows and orphans and beggars. Then shall be arraigned the collectors of tribute, who despoil the poor man of more than is ordered, and who make real gold like adulterate, in order to mulct the needy, in fields and in houses and in the churches. Then shall rise up the lewd with shame, who have not kept their bed undefiled, but have been ensnared by all manner of fleshly beauty, and have gone in the way of their own lusts. Then shall rise up those who have not kept the love of the Lord, mute and gloomy, because they contemned the light commandment of the Saviour, which says, Thou shalt love thy neighbour as thyself. Then they, too, shall weep who have possessed the unjust balance, and unjust weights and measures, and dry measures, as they wait for the righteous Judge.

XXXIX.

And why should we add many words concerning those who are sisted before the bar? Then the righteous shall shine

---

[1] Acts ii. 20.
[2] Rev. vi. 14.
[3] διϕθειραν. B reads ἐπραξαν, did.
[4] Rev. xxi. 1.
[5] Luke iii. 14.

forth like the sun, while the wicked shall be shown to be mute and gloomy. For both the righteous and the wicked shall be raised incorruptible: the righteous, to be honoured eternally, and to taste immortal joys; and the wicked, to be punished in judgment eternally. Each ponders[1] the question as to what answer he shall give to the righteous Judge for his deeds, whether good or bad. With all men each one's actions shall environ him, whether he be good or evil. For the powers of the heavens shall be shaken,[2] and fear and trembling shall consume all things, both heaven and earth and things under the earth. And every tongue shall confess Him openly,[3] and shall confess Him who comes to judge righteous judgment, the mighty God and Maker of all things. Then with fear and astonishment shall come angels, thrones, powers, principalities, dominions,[4] and the cherubim and seraphim with their many eyes and six wings, all crying aloud with a mighty voice, "Holy, holy, holy is the Lord of hosts, omnipotent; the heaven and the earth are full of Thy glory."[5] And the King of kings and Lord of lords, the Judge who accepts no man's person, and the Jurist who distributes justice to every man, shall be revealed upon His dread and lofty throne; and all the flesh of mortals shall see His face with great fear and trembling, both the righteous and the sinner.

XL.

Then shall the son of perdition be brought forward, to wit the accuser, with his demons and with his servants, by angels stern and inexorable. And they shall be given over to the fire that is never quenched, and to the worm that never sleepeth, and to the outer darkness. For the people of the Hebrews shall see Him in human form, as He appeared to them [when He came] by the holy Virgin in the flesh, and as they crucified Him. And He will show them the [prints of the] nails in His hands and feet, and His side pierced with the spear, and His head crowned with thorns,

---

[1] The text gives ἐνθυμηθῇ τι, for which B reads ἐνθυμεῖται.
[2] Matt. xxiv. 29.   [3] Phil. ii. 11.
[4] Col. i. 16.   [5] Isa. vi. 3.

and His honourable cross. And once for all shall the people of the Hebrews see all these things, and they shall mourn and weep, as the prophet exclaims, "They shall look on Him whom they have pierced;"[1] and there shall be none to help them or to pity them, because they repented not, neither turned aside from the wicked way. And these shall go away into everlasting punishment with the demons and the accuser.

XLI.

Then He shall gather together all nations, as the holy Gospel so strikingly declares. For what says Matthew the evangelist, or rather the Lord Himself, in the Gospel? "When the Son of man shall come in His glory, and all the holy angels with Him, then shall He sit upon the throne of His glory: and before Him shall be gathered all nations; and He shall separate them one from another, as a shepherd divideth his sheep from the goats: and He shall set the sheep on His right hand, but the goats on the left. Then shall the King say unto them on His right hand, Come, ye blessed of my Father, inherit the kingdom prepared for you from the foundation of the world."[2] Come, ye prophets, who were cast out for my name's sake. Come, ye patriarchs, who before my advent were obedient to me, and longed for my kingdom. Come, ye apostles, who were my fellows in my sufferings in my incarnation, [and suffered with me] in the Gospel. Come, ye martyrs, who confessed me before despots, and endured many torments and pains. Come, ye hierarchs, who did me sacred service blamelessly day and night, and made the oblation of my honourable body and blood daily.

XLII.

Come, ye saints, who disciplined yourselves in mountains and caves and dens of the earth, who honoured my name by continence and prayer and virginity. Come, ye maidens, who desired my bride-chamber, and loved no other bridegroom than me, who by your testimony and habit of life were wedded to me, the immortal and incorruptible Bride-

[1] Zech. xii. 10; John xix. 37.   [2] Matt. xxv. 31-34.

groom. Come, ye friends of the poor and the stranger. Come, ye who kept my love, as I am love. Come, ye who possess peace, for I own that peace. Come, ye blessed of my Father, inherit the kingdom prepared for you, ye who esteemed not riches, ye who had compassion on the poor, who aided the orphans, who helped the widows, who gave drink to the thirsty, who fed the hungry, who received strangers, who clothed the naked, who visited the sick, who comforted those in prison, who helped the blind, who kept the seal of the faith inviolate, who assembled yourselves together in the churches, who listened to my Scriptures, who longed for my words, who observed my law day and night, who endured hardness with me like good soldiers, seeking to please me, your heavenly King. Come, inherit the kingdom prepared for you from the foundation of the world. Behold, my kingdom is made ready; behold, paradise is opened; behold, my immortality is shown in its beauty (κεκαλλώπισται). Come all, inherit the kingdom prepared for you from the foundation of the world.

XLIII.

Then shall the righteous answer, astonished at the mighty and wondrous fact that He, whom the hosts of angels cannot look upon openly, addresses them as friends, and shall cry out to Him, Lord, when saw we Thee an hungered, and fed Thee? Master (δέσποτα), when saw we Thee thirsty, and gave Thee drink? Thou Terrible One (φοβερέ), when saw we Thee naked, and clothed Thee? Immortal (ἀθάνατε), when saw we Thee a stranger, and took Thee in? Thou Friend of man (φιλάνθρωπε), when saw we Thee sick or in prison, and came unto Thee?[1] Thou art the ever-living One. Thou art without beginning, like the Father (συνάναρχος), and co-eternal with the Spirit. Thou art He who made all things out of nothing. Thou art the prince of the angels. Thou art He at whom the depths tremble.[2] Thou art He who is covered with light as with a garment.[3] Thou art He who made us, and fashioned us of earth. Thou art He who

[1] Matt. xxv. 37, etc.   [2] 4 Esdr. iii. 8.   [3] Ps. civ. 2.

formed (δημιουργήσας) things invisible.¹ From Thy presence the whole earth fleeth away,² and how have we received hospitably Thy kingly power and lordship?

XLIV.

Then shall the King of kings make answer again, and say to them, Inasmuch as ye have done it unto one of the least of these my brethren, ye have done it unto me. Inasmuch as ye have received those of whom I have already spoken to you, and clothed them, and fed them, and gave them to drink, I mean the poor who are my members, ye have done it unto me. But come ye into the kingdom prepared for you from the foundation of the world; enjoy for ever and ever that which is given you by my Father in heaven, and the holy and quickening Spirit. And what mouth then will be able to tell out those blessings which eye hath not seen, nor ear heard, neither have entered into the heart of man, the things which God hath prepared for them that love Him?³

XLV.

Ye have heard of the ceaseless joy, ye have heard of the immoveable kingdom, ye have heard of the feast of blessings without end. Learn now, then, also the address of anguish with which the just Judge and the benignant God shall speak to those on the left hand in unmeasured anger and wrath, Depart from me, ye cursed, into everlasting fire, prepared for the devil and his angels. Ye have prepared these things for yourselves; take to yourselves also the enjoyment of them. Depart from me, ye cursed, into the outer darkness, and into the unquenchable fire, prepared for the devil and his angels. I made you, and ye gave yourselves to another. I am He who brought you forth from your mother's womb, and ye rejected me. I am He who fashioned you of earth by my word of command, and ye gave yourselves to another. I am He who nurtured you, and ye served another. I ordained the earth and the sea for your maintenance and the

[1] Col. i. 16. [2] Rev. xx. 11. [3] Isa. lxiv. 4; 1 Cor. ii. 9.

bound (συμπέρασμα) of your life, and ye listened not to my commandments. I made the light for you, that ye might enjoy the day, and the night also, that ye might have rest; and ye vexed me, and set me at naught with your wicked words, and opened the door to the passions. Depart from me, ye workers of iniquity. I know you not, I recognise you not: ye made yourselves the workmen of another lord—namely, the devil. With him inherit ye the darkness, and the fire that is not quenched, and the worm that sleepeth not, and the gnashing of teeth.

XLVI.

For I was an hungered, and ye gave me no meat: I was thirsty, and ye gave me no drink: I was a stranger, and ye took me not in; naked, and ye clothed me not; sick, and ye visited me not: I was in prison, and ye came not unto me. I made your ears that ye might hear the Scriptures; and ye prepared them for the songs of demons, and lyres, and jesting. I made your eyes that you might see the light of my commandments, and keep them; and ye called in fornication and wantonness, and opened them to all other manner of uncleanness. I prepared your mouth for the utterance of adoration, and praise, and psalms, and spiritual odes, and for the exercise of continuous reading; and ye fitted it to railing, and swearing, and blasphemies, while ye sat and spake evil of your neighbours. I made your hands that ye might stretch them forth in prayers and supplications, and ye put them forth to robberies, and murders, and the killing of each other. I ordained your feet to walk in the preparation of the Gospel of peace, both in the churches and the houses of my saints; and ye taught them to run to adulteries, and fornications, and theatres, and dancings, and elevations (tossings, μετεωρισμούς).

XLVII.

At last the assembly is dissolved, the spectacle of this life ceaseth: its deceit and its semblance are passed away. Cleave to me, to whom every knee boweth, of things in heaven, and things on earth, and things under the earth. For all who have been negligent, and have not shown pity in well-doing there, have nothing else due them than the unquenchable fire. For I am the friend of man, but yet also a righteous Judge to all. For I shall award the recompense according to desert; I shall give the reward to all, according to each man's labour; I shall make return to all, according to each man's conflict. I wish to have pity, but I see no oil in your vessels. I desire to have mercy, but ye have passed through life entirely without mercy. I long to have compassion, but your lamps are dark by reason of your hardness of heart. Depart from me. For judgment is without mercy to him that hath showed no mercy.[1]

XLVIII.

Then shall they also make answer to the dread Judge, who accepteth no man's person: Lord, when saw we Thee an hungered, or athirst, or a stranger, or naked, or sick, or in prison, and ministered not unto Thee? Lord, dost Thou know us not? Thou didst form us, Thou didst fashion us, Thou didst make us of four elements, Thou didst give us spirit and soul. On Thee we believed; Thy seal we received, Thy baptism we obtained; we acknowledged Thee to be God, we knew Thee to be Creator; in Thee we wrought signs, through Thee we cast out demons, for Thee we mortified the flesh, for Thee we preserved virginity, for Thee we practised chastity, for Thee we became strangers on the earth; and Thou sayest, I know you not, depart from me! Then shall He make answer to them, and say, Ye acknowledged me as Lord, but ye kept not my words. Ye were marked with the seal of my cross, but ye deleted it by your hardness of heart. Ye obtained my baptism, but ye observed not my commandments. Ye subdued your body to virginity, but ye kept not mercy, but ye did not cast the hatred of your brother out of your souls. For not every one that saith to me, Lord, Lord, shall be saved, but he that doeth my will.[2] And these shall go away into everlasting punishment, but the righteous into life eternal.[3]

[1] Jas. ii. 13.   [2] Matt. vii. 23.   [3] Matt. xxv. 46.

XLIX.

Ye have heard, beloved, the answer of the Lord; ye have learned the sentence of the Judge; ye have been given to understand what kind of awful scrutiny awaits us, and what day and what hour are before us. Let us therefore ponder this every day; let us meditate on this both day and night, both in the house, and by the way, and in the churches, that we may not stand forth at that dread and impartial judgment condemned, abased, and sad, but with purity of action, life, conversation, and confession; so that to us also the merciful and benignant God may say, "Thy faith hath saved thee, go in peace;"[1] and again, "Well done, good and faithful servant; thou hast been faithful over a few things, I will make thee ruler over many things: enter thou into the joy of thy Lord."[2] Which joy may it be ours to reach, by the grace and kindness of our Lord Jesus Christ, to whom pertain glory, honour, and adoration, with His Father, who is without beginning, and His holy, and good, and quickening Spirit, now and ever, and to the ages of the ages. Amen.

"Be thou faithful unto death, and I will give thee the crown of life" (Apoc. ii.).

HIPPOLYTUS ON THE TWELVE APOSTLES:

WHERE EACH OF THEM PREACHED, AND WHERE HE MET HIS END.

Peter preached the gospel in Pontus, and Galatia, and Cappadocia, and Betania, and Italy, and Asia, and was afterwards crucified by Nero in Rome with his head downward, as he had himself desired to suffer in that manner.

Andrew preached to the Scythians and Thracians, and was crucified, suspended on an olive tree, at Patræ, [a town] of Achaia; and there too he was buried.

John, again, in Asia, was banished by Domitian the king to the isle of Patmos, in which also he wrote his Gospel and

[1] Luke vii. 50.   [2] Matt. xxv. 23.

saw the apocalyptic vision; and in Trajan's time he fell asleep at Ephesus, where his remains were sought for; but could not be found.

James, his brother, when preaching in Judea, was cut off with the sword by Herod the tetrarch, and was buried there.

Philip preached in Phrygia, and was crucified in Hierapolis with his head downward in the time of Domitian, and was buried there.

Bartholomew, again, [preached] to the Indians, to whom also he gave the Gospel according to Matthew, [and] was crucified with his head downward, and was buried in Allanum (or Albanum), [a town] of the great Armenia.

And Matthew wrote the Gospel in the Hebrew tongue, and published it at Jerusalem, and fell asleep at Hierees, [a town] of Parthia.

And Thomas preached to the Parthians, Medes, Persians, Hyrcanians, Bactrians, and Margians,[1] and was thrust through in the four members of his body with a pine spear[2] at Calamene,[3] the city of India, and was buried there.

And James the son of Alphæus, when preaching in Jerusalem, was stoned to death by the Jews, and was buried there beside the temple.

Judas, who is also [called] Lebbæus, preached to the people of Edessa (Αἰδεσινοῖς), and to all Mesopotamia, and fell asleep at Berytus, and was buried there.

Simon the Zealot (ὁ Κανανίτης), the son of Clopas, who is also [called] Judas, became bishop of Jerusalem after James the Just, and fell asleep and was buried there at the age of 120 years.

And Matthias, who was one of the seventy, was numbered along with the eleven apostles, and preached in Jerusalem, and fell asleep and was buried there.

And Paul entered into the apostleship a year after the assumption of Christ; and beginning at Jerusalem, he advanced as far as Illyricum, and Italy, and Spain, preaching

---

[1] Μάργοις. Combefisius proposes Μάρδοις. Jerome has "Magis."
[2] The text is ἱλακήδη ἐλογχιάσθη, ἱλακήδη being probably for ἐλάτῃ.
[3] Καλαμύνη. Steph. le Moyne reads Καραμήνη.

the gospel for five-and-thirty years. And in the time of Nero he was beheaded at Rome, and was buried there.

THE SAME HIPPOLYTUS ON THE SEVENTY APOSTLES.

In the Codex Baroccian. 206.

[This is found also, along with the former piece, *On the Twelve Apostles*, in two codices of the Coislinian or Seguierian Library, as Montfaucon states in his recension of the Greek manuscripts of that library. He mentions also a third codex of Hippolytus, *On the Twelve Apostles*.]

1. James the Lord's brother (ἀδελφόθεος), bishop of Jerusalem.
2. Cleopas, bishop of Jerusalem.
3. Matthias, who supplied the vacant place in the number of the twelve apostles.
4. Thaddeus, who conveyed the epistle to Augarus.
5. Ananias, who baptized Paul, [and was] bishop of Damascus.
6. Stephen, the first martyr.
7. Philip, who baptized the eunuch.
8. Prochorus, bishop of Nicomedia, who also was the first that departed (ἐξελθών), believing together with his daughters.
9. Nicanor died when Stephen was martyred.
10. Timon, bishop of Bostra.
11. Parmenas, bishop of Soli.
12. Nicolaus, bishop of Samaria.
13. Barnabas, bishop of Milan.
14. Mark the evangelist, bishop of Alexandria.
15. Luke the evangelist.
    These two belonged to the seventy disciples who were scattered[1] by the offence of the word which Christ spake, "Except a man eat my flesh, and drink my

[1] The text is, οὗτοι οἱ β΄ τῶν ὁ τυγχανόντων διασκορπισθέντων. It may be meant for, "these two of the seventy were scattered," etc.

APPENDIX TO PART II. 133

blood, he is not worthy of me."[1] But the one being induced to return to the Lord by Peter's instrumentality, and the other by Paul's, they were honoured to preach that gospel[2] on account of which they also suffered martyrdom, the one being burned, and the other being crucified on an olive tree.

16. Silas, bishop of Corinth.
17. Silvanus, bishop of Thessalonica.
18. Crisces (Crescens), bishop of Carchedon in Gaul.
19. Epænetus, bishop of Carthage.
20. Andronicus, bishop of Pannonia.
21. Amplias, bishop of Odyssus.
22. Urban, bishop of Macedonia.
23. Stachys, bishop of Byzantium
24. Barnabas, bishop of Heraclea.
25. Phygellus, bishop of Ephesus. He was of the party also of Simon [Magus].
26. Hermogenes. He, too, was of the same mind with the former.
27. Demas, who also became a priest of idols.
28. Apelles, bishop of Smyrna.
29. Aristobulus, bishop of Britain.
30. Narcissus, bishop of Athens.
31. Herodion, bishop of Tarsus.
32. Agabus the prophet.
33. Rufus, bishop of Thebes.
34. Asyncritus, bishop of Hyrcania.
35. Phlegon, bishop of Marathon.
36. Hermes, bishop of Dalmatia.
37. Patrobulus,[3] bishop of Puteoli.
38. Hermas, bishop of Philippi.
39. Linus, bishop of Rome.
40. Caius, bishop of Ephesus.
41. Philologus, bishop of Sinope.

---

[1] John vi. 53, 66.

[2] εὐαγγελίζεσθαι, perhaps = *write* of that gospel, as the Latin version puts it.

[3] Rom. xvi. 14, Πατρόβας.

42, 43. Olympus and Rhodion were martyred in Rome.
44. Lucius, bishop of Laodicea in Syria.
45. Jason, bishop of Tarsus.
46. Sosipater, bishop of Iconium.
47. Tertius, bishop of Iconium.
48. Erastus, bishop of Panellas.
49. Quartus, bishop of Berytus.
50. Apollo, bishop of Cæsarea.
51. Cephas. (In the manuscript there is a lacuna here.)
52. Sosthenes, bishop of Colophonia.
53. Tychicus, bishop of Colophonia.
54. Epaphroditus, bishop of Andriace.
55. Cæsar, bishop of Dyrrachium.
56. Mark, cousin to Barnabas, bishop of Apollonia.
57. Justus, bishop of Eleutheropolis.
58. Artemas, bishop of Lystra.
59. Clement, bishop of Sardinia.
60. Onesiphorus, bishop of Corone.
61. Tychicus, bishop of Chalcedon.
62. Carpus, bishop of Berytus in Thrace.
63. Evodus, bishop of Antioch.
64. Aristarchus, bishop of Apamea.
65. Mark, who is also John, bishop of Bibloupolis.
66. Zenas, bishop of Diospolis.
67. Philemon, bishop of Gaza.
68, 69. Aristarchus and Pudes.
70. Trophimus, who was martyred along with Paul.

HEADS OF THE CANONS OF ABULIDES OR HIPPOLYTUS,

WHICH ARE USED BY THE ÆTHIOPIAN CHRISTIANS.

[These were first published in French by Jo. Michael Wanslebius in his book *De Ecclesia Alexandrina*, Paris 1677, p. 12; then in Latin, by Job Ludolfus, in his *Commentar. ad historiam Æthiopicam*, Frankfort 1691, p. 333; and by William Whiston, in vol. iii. of his *Primitive Christianity Revived*, published in English at London, 1711, p. 543. He has also noted the passages in the *Constitutiones Apostolicæ*, treating the same matters.]

1. Of the holy faith of Jesus Christ.[1]
2. Of bishops.[2]
3. Of prayers spoken on the ordination of bishops, and of the order of the Mass.[3]
4. Of the ordination of presbyters.
5. Of the ordination of deacons.
6. Of those who suffer persecution for the faith.[4]
7. Of the election of reader and sub-deacon.[5]
8. Of the gift of healing.[6]
9. Of the presbyter who abides in a place inconvenient for his office.[7]
10. Of those who are converted to the Christian religion.
11. Of him who makes idols.[8]
12. Various pursuits (*studia*) are enumerated, the followers of which are not to be admitted to the Christian religion until repentance is exhibited.[9]
13. Of the place which the highest kings or princes shall occupy in the temple.[10]
14. That it is not meet for Christians to bear arms.[11]
15. Of works which are unlawful to Christians.[12]
16. Of the Christian who marries a slave-woman.[13]

---

[1] *Constit. Apostol.* lib. vi. ch. 11, etc.
[2] Lib. vii. ch. 41.
[3] Lib. vii. ch. 4, 5, 10.
[4] Lib. viii. ch. 17, 18, 19, 20, 23, 45.
[5] Lib. viii. ch. 21, 22.
[6] Lib. viii. ch. 1, 2.
[7] Lib. viii. ch. 46, 32.
[8] Lib. viii. ch. 46, 32.
[9] Lib. viii. ch. 46, 32.
[10] Wanting.
[11] Lib. viii. ch. 32.
[12] Lib. viii. ch. 32.
[13] Lib. viii. ch. 32.

17. Of the free woman.[1]
18. Of the midwife; and that the women ought to be separate from the men in prayer.[2]
19. Of the catechumen who suffers martyrdom before baptism.[3]
20. Of the fast of the fourth and sixth holiday; and of Lent.[4]
21. That presbyters should assemble daily with the people in church.[5]
22. Of the week of the Jews' passover; and of him who knows not passover (Easter).[6]
23. That every one be held to learn doctrine.[7]
24. Of the care of the bishop over the sick.[8]
25. Of him on whom the care of the sick is enjoined; and of the time at which prayers are to be made.[9]
26. Of the time at which exhortations are to be heard.[10]
27. Of him who frequents the temple every day.[11]
28. That the faithful ought to eat nothing before the holy communion.[12]
29. That care is to be well taken that nothing fall from the chalice to the ground.[13]
30. Of catechumens.[14]
31. That a deacon may dispense the Eucharist to the people with permission of a bishop or presbyter.[15]
32. That widows and virgins ought to pray constantly.[16]
33. That commemoration should be made of the faithful dead every day, with the exception of the Lord's day.[17]
34. Of the sober behaviour of the secular [laymen] in church.[18]

[1] Lib. viii. ch. 32.
[2] Lib. ii. ch. 57.
[3] Lib. v. ch. 6.
[4] Lib. v. ch. 13, 15.
[5] Lib. ii. ch. 36.
[6] Lib. v. ch. 15, etc.
[7] Lib. vii. ch. 39, 40, 41.
[8] Lib. iv. ch. 2.
[9] Lib. iii. ch. 19, viii. ch. 34.
[10] Lib. viii. ch. 32.
[11] Lib. ii. ch. 59.
[12] Wanting.
[13] Wanting.
[14] Lib. vii. ch. 39, etc.
[15] Lib. viii. ch. 28.
[16] Lib. iii. ch. 6, 7, 13.
[17] Lib. iv. ch. 14, viii. ch. 41-44.
[18] Lib. ii. ch. 57.

35. That deacons may pronounce the benediction and thanksgiving at the love-feasts when a bishop is not present.[1]
36. Of the first-fruits of the earth, and of vows [2] (or offerings).
37. When a bishop celebrates the holy communion (Synaxis), the presbyters who stand by him should be clothed in white.[3]
38. That no one ought to sleep on the night of the resurrection of our Lord Jesus Christ.[4]

CANONS OF THE CHURCH OF ALEXANDRIA.
WRONGLY ASCRIBED TO HIPPOLYTUS.

[*De Magistris, Acta Martyrum ad Ostia Tiberina*, Rome 1795, fol. Append. p. 478.]

In the name of the Father, and the Son, and the Holy Spirit, Amen. Those are the canons of the church, ordinances which Hippolytus wrote, by whom [the church] speaketh; and the number of them is thirty-eight canons. Greeting from the Lord.

Canon First. Of the Catholic faith. Before all things should we speak of the faith, holy and right, regarding our Lord Jesus Christ, the Son of the living God; and we have [consequently] placed that canon in the faith (the symbol); and we agree in this with all reasonable certitude, that the Trinity is equal perfectly in honour, and equal in glory, and has neither beginning nor end. The Word [is] the Son of God, and is Himself the Creator of every creature, of things visible and invisible. This we lay down with one accord, in opposition to those who have said boldly, that it is not right [to speak] of the Word of God as our Lord Jesus Christ spake. We come together chiefly to bring out the holy truth (*ad proferendum sancte*) regarding God; and we have separated them, because

---
[1] Wanting.
[2] Lib. ii. ch. 25.
[3] Lib. vii. ch. 29, viii. 30, 31.
[4] Lib. viii. ch. 12, v. ch. 19.

they do not agree with the church in theology, nor with us the sons of the Scriptures. On this account we have sundered them from the church, and have left what concerns them to God, who will judge His creatures with justice. To those, moreover, who are not cognisant of them, we make this known without ill-will, in order that they may not rush into an evil death, like heretics, but may gain eternal life, and teach their sons and their posterity this one true faith.

Canon Second. Of bishops. A bishop should be elected by all the people, and he should be unimpeachable, as it is written of him in the apostle; in the week in which he is ordained, the whole people should also say, We desire him; and there should be silence in the whole hall, and they should all pray in his behalf, and say, O God, stablish him whom Thou hast prepared for us, etc.

Canon Third. Prayer in behalf of him who is made bishop, and the ordinance of the Mass (*ordinatio missæ*). O God, the Father of our Lord Jesus Christ, the Father of mercies, and the God of all consolation, etc.

Canon Fourth. Of the ordination of a presbyter.

Canon Fifth. Of the constituting a deacon.

Canon Sixth. Of those who have suffered for the faith.

Canon Seventh. Of him who is elected reader and sub-deacon.

Canon Eighth. Of the gift of healings.

Canon Ninth. That a presbyter should not dwell in unbefitting places; and of the honour of widows.

Canon Tenth. Of those who wish to become Nazarenes (Christians).

Canon Eleventh. Of him who makes idols and images, or the artificer.

Canon Twelfth. Of the prohibition of those works, the authors of which are not to be received but on the exhibition of repentance.

Canon Thirteenth. Of a prince or a soldier, that they be not received indiscriminately.

Canon Fourteenth. That a Nazarene may not become a soldier unless by order.

Canon Fifteenth. Enumeration of works which are unlawful.

Canon Sixteenth. Of him who has a lawful wife, and takes another beside her.

Canon Seventeenth. Of a free-born woman, and her duties. Of midwives, and of the separation of men from women. Of virgins, that they should cover their faces and their heads.

Canon Eighteenth. Of women in childbed, and of midwives again.

Canon Nineteenth. Of catechumens, and the ordinance of Baptism and the Mass.

Canon Twentieth. Of the fast [the six days], and of that of Lent.

Canon Twenty-first. Of the daily assembling of priests and people in the church.

Canon Twenty-second. Of the week of the Jews' passover, wherein joy shall be put away, and of what is eaten therein; and of him who, being brought up abroad, is ignorant of the connection (*textum*, Calendar).

Canon Twenty-third. Of doctrine, that it should be continuous (greater than the sea), and that its words ought to be fulfilled by deeds.

Canon Twenty-fourth. Of the bishop's visitation of the sick; and that if an infirm man has prayed in the church, and has a house, he should go to him.

Canon Twenty-fifth. Of the procurator appointed for the sick, and of the bishop, and the times of prayer.

Canon Twenty-sixth. Of the hearing of the word in church, and of praying in it.

Canon Twenty-seventh. Of him who does not come to church daily,—let him read books; and of prayer at midnight and cock-crowing, and of the washing of hands at the time of any prayer.

Canon Twenty-eighth. That none of the believers should

taste anything, but after he has taken the sacred mysteries, especially in the days of fasting.

Canon Twenty-ninth. Of the keeping of oblations which are laid upon the altar,—that nothing fall into the sacred chalice, and that nothing fall from the priests, nor from the boys when they take communion; that an evil spirit rule them not, and that no one speak in the protection (sanctuary), except in prayer; and when the oblations of the people cease, let psalms be read with all attention, even to the signal of the bell; and of the sign of the cross, and the casting of the dust of the altar into the pool.

Canon Thirtieth. Of catechumens and the like.

Canon Thirty-first. Of the bishop and presbyter bidding the deacons present the communion.

Canon Thirty-second. Of virgins and widows, that they should pray and fast in the church. Let those who are given to the clerical order pray according to their judgment. Let not a bishop be bound to fasting but with the clergy. And on account of a feast or supper, let him prepare for the poor (and of the preparing a table for the poor).

Canon Thirty-third. Of the *Atalmsas* (the oblation), which they shall present for those who are dead, that it be not done on the Lord's day.

Canon Thirty-fourth. That no one speak much, nor make a clamour; and of the entrance of the saints into the mansions of the faithful.

Canon Thirty-fifth. Of a deacon present at a feast at which there is a presbyter present,—let him do his part in prayer and the breaking of bread for a blessing, and not for the body; and of the discharge of widows.

Canon Thirty-sixth. Of the first-fruits of the earth, and the first dedication of them; and of presses, oil, honey, milk, wool, and the like, which may be offered to the bishop for his blessing.

Canon Thirty-seventh. As often as a bishop takes of the sacred mysteries, let the deacons and presbyters be gathered together, clothed in white robes, brilliant in the view of all the people; and in like manner with a reader.

Canon Thirty-eighth. Of the night on which our Lord Jesus Christ rose. That no one shall sleep on that night, and wash himself with water; and a declaration concerning such an one; and a declaration concerning him who sins after baptism, and of things lawful and unlawful.

The sacred canons of the holy patriarch Hippolytus, the first patriarch of the great city of Rome, which he composed, are ended; and the number of them is thirty-eight canons. May the Lord help us to keep them. And to God be glory for ever, and on us be His mercy for ever. Amen.

FRAGMENTS.

THE EPISTLES OF POPE ZEPHYRINUS.

INTRODUCTORY NOTICE.

THE little that is known of Zephyrinus is derived from Eusebius. That historian states that Zephyrinus succeeded Victor in the presidency of the Roman Church "about the ninth year of the reign of Severus"[1] (A.D. 201), and that he died in the first year of the reign of Antoninus[2] (Heliogabalus, A.D. 218). He is several times alluded to in the fragments ascribed to Caius, or in connection with them.

The two letters bearing his name are forgeries. They belong to the famous collection of False Decretals forged in the ninth century. In regard to these Decretals, Dean Milman says: " Up to this period the Decretals, the letters or edicts of the Bishops of Rome, according to the authorized or common collection of Dionysius, commenced with Pope Siricius, towards the close of the fourth century. To the collection of Dionysius was added that of the authentic councils, which bore the name of Isidore of Seville. On a sudden was promulgated, unannounced, without preparation, not absolutely unquestioned, but apparently overawing at once all doubt, a new code, which to the former authentic documents added fifty-nine letters and decrees of the twenty oldest popes from Clement to Melchiades, and the donation of Constantine; and in the third part, among the decrees of the popes and of the councils from Sylvester to Gregory II., thirty-nine false decrees, and the acts of several unauthentic councils."[3]

In regard to the authorship and date of the False Decretals, Dean Milman says: "The author or authors of this most

[1] *Hist. Eccl.* v. 28. [2] *Hist. Eccl.* vi. 21.
[3] *History of Latin Christianity*, voL iii. p. 191.

audacious and elaborate of pious frauds are unknown; the date and place of its compilation are driven into such narrow limits that they may be determined within a few years, and within a very circumscribed region. The False Decretals came not from Rome; the time of their arrival at Rome, after they were known beyond the Alps, appears almost certain. In one year Nicolas I. is apparently ignorant of their existence; the next he speaks of them with full knowledge. They contain words manifestly used at the Council of Paris, A.D. 829, consequently are of later date. They were known to the Levite Benedict of Mentz, who composed a supplement to the collection of capitularies by Ansegise, between A.D. 840-847. The city of Mentz is designated with nearly equal certainty as the place in which, if not actually composed, they were first promulgated as the canon law of Christendom."[1]

THE FIRST EPISTLE.

TO ALL THE BISHOPS OF SICILY.

Of the Final Decision of the Trials of Bishops, and graver Ecclesiastical Cases in the Seat of the Apostles.

ZEPHYRINUS, archbishop of the city of Rome, to all the bishops settled in Sicily, in the Lord, greeting.

We ought to be mindful of the grace of God to us, which in His own merciful regard has raised us for this purpose to the summit of priestly honour, that, abiding by His commandments, and appointed in a certain supervision of His priests, we may prohibit things unlawful, and teach those that are to be followed. As night does not extinguish the stars of heaven, so the unrighteousness of the world does not blind the minds of the faithful that hold by the sure support of Scripture. Therefore we ought to consider well and attend carefully to the Scriptures, and the divine precepts which are contained

[1] *History of Latin Christianity,* vol. iii. p. 193.

in these Scriptures, in order that we may show ourselves not transgressors, but fulfillers of the law of God.

Now patriarchs and primates, in investigating the case of an accused bishop, should not pronounce a final decision until, supported by the authority of the apostles, they find that the person either confesses himself guilty, or is proved so by witnesses trustworthy and regularly examined, who should not be fewer in number than were those disciples whom the Lord directed to be chosen for the help of the apostles—that is, seventy-two. Detractors also, who are to be rooted out by divine authority, and the advisers of enemies (*auctores inimicorum*), we do not admit in the indictment of bishops or in evidence against them; nor should any one of superior rank be indicted or condemned on the accusations of inferiors. Nor in a doubtful case should a decisive judgment be pronounced; nor should any trial be held valid unless it has been conducted according to order. No one, moreover, should be judged in his absence, because both divine and human laws forbid that. The accusers of those persons should also be free of all suspicion, because the Lord has chosen that His pillars should stand firm, and not be shaken by any one who will. For a sentence should not bind any of them if it is not given by their proper judge, because even the laws of the world ordain that that be done. For any accused bishop may, if it be necessary, choose twelve judges by whom his case may be justly judged. Nor should he be heard or excommunicated or judged until these be chosen by him; and on his being regularly summoned at first to a council of his own bishops, his case should be justly heard by them, and investigated on sound principles. The end of his case, however, should be remitted to the seat of the apostles, that it may be finally decided there. Nor should it be finished, as has been decreed of old by the apostles or their successors, until it is sustained by its authority. To it also all, and especially the oppressed, should appeal and have recourse as to a mother, that they may be nourished by her breasts, defended by her authority, and relieved of their oppressions, because "a mother cannot," and should

not, "forget her son."¹ For the trials of bishops and
graver ecclesiastical cases, as the apostles and their holy
successors have decreed, are to be finally decided along with
other bishops² by the seat of the apostles, and by no other;
because, although they may be transferred to other bishops,
it was yet to the blessed Apostle Peter these terms were
addressed : "Whatsoever thou shalt bind on earth shall be
bound in heaven, and whatsoever thou shalt loose on earth
shall be loosed in heaven."³ And the other privileges which
have been granted to this holy seat alone are found embodied
both in the constitutions of the apostles⁴ and their successors,
and in very many others in harmony with these. For the
apostles have prefixed seventy⁵ decrees, together with very
many other bishops, and have appointed them to be kept. For
to judge rashly of the secrets of another's heart is sin ; and it
is unjust to reprove him on suspicion whose works seem not
other than good, since God alone is Judge of those things which
are unknown to men. He, however, "knoweth the secrets of
the heart,"⁶ and not another. For unjust judgments are to
be guarded against by all, especially however by the servants
of God. "And the servant of the Lord must not strive,"⁷
nor harm any one. For bishops are to be borne by laity and
clergy, and masters by servants, in order that, under the
exercise of endurance, things temporal may be maintained,
and things eternal hoped for. For that increases the worth of
virtue, which does not violate the purpose of religion. You
should be earnestly intent that none of your brothers be

¹ Isa. xlix. 15.   ² The word "bishops" is omitted in MS.
³ Matt. xvi. 19.
⁴ He means the seventy-third apostolic canon, in which it is ordained
that episcopal cases be not decided but by superior bishops, councils, or
the Roman pontiff.
⁵ Another reading has sixty, and another fifty. Whatever be the
reading, it is true that by these decrees he means the apostolic canons ;
and although their number was only fifty, yet, because sometimes
several decrees are comprehended in one canon, there would be no
inconsistency between the number of sixty or seventy apostolic decrees
and the number of fifty apostolic canons (Sev. Bin.).
⁶ Ps. xliv. 21.   ⁷ 2 Tim. ii. 24.

grievously injured or undone. Therefore you ought to succour the oppressed, and deliver them from the hand of their persecutors, in order that with the blessed Job you may say : "The blessing of him that was ready to perish will come upon me, and I consoled the widow's heart. I put on righteousness, and clothed myself with a robe and a diadem, my judgment. I was eye to the blind, and foot to the lame. I was a father to the poor, and the cause which I knew not I searched out most carefully. I brake the grinders of the wicked, and plucked the spoil out of his teeth;"[1] and so forth. You, therefore, who have been placed in eminence by God, ought with all your power to check and repel those who prepare snares for brethren, or raise seditions and offences against them. For it is easy by word to deceive man, not however God. Therefore you ought to keep these off, and be on your guard against them, until such darkness is done away utterly, and the morning star shines upon them, and gladness arises, most holy brethren. Given on the 20th September, in the consulship of the most illustrious Saturninus and Gallicanus.[2]

THE SECOND EPISTLE.

TO THE BISHOPS OF THE PROVINCE OF EGYPT.

Zephyrinus, archbishop of the city of Rome, to the most beloved brethren who serve the Lord in Egypt.

So great trust have we received from the Lord, the Founder of this holy seat and of the apostolic church, and from the blessed Peter, chief of the apostles, that we may labour with unwearied affection[3] for the universal church which has been redeemed by the blood of Christ, and aid all who serve the Lord, and give help to all who live piously by apostolic authority. All who will live[4] piously in Christ must

---

[1] Job xxix. 13-17, according to the Vulgate version.

[2] Or, Gallus. Saturninus and Gallus were consuls in the year 198, while Victor was yet alive.

[3] Or, diligence.   [4] 2 Tim. ii. 24.

needs endure reproaches from the impious and aliens, and be despised as fools and madmen, that they may be made better and purer who lose the good things of time that they may gain those of eternity. But the contempt and ridicule of those who afflict and scorn them will be cast back upon themselves, when their abundance shall change to want, and their pride to confusion.

I.

On the Spoliation or Expulsion of certain Bishops.

It has been reported at the seat of the apostles by your delegates,[1] that certain of our brethren, bishops to wit, are being expelled from their churches and seats, and deprived of their goods, and summoned, thus destitute and spoiled, to trial; a thing which is void of all reason, since the constitutions of the apostles and their successors, and the statutes of emperors, and the regulations of laws, prohibit it, and the authority of the seat of the apostles forbids it to be done. It has been ordained, indeed, in the ancient statutes, that bishops who have been ejected and spoiled of their property should recover their churches, and, in the first place, have all their property restored to them; and then, in the second place, that if any one may desire to accuse them justly, he should do so at the like risk; that the judges should be discreet, the bishops right-minded and harmonious in the church, where they should be witnesses for every one who seemed to be oppressed; and that they should not answer till all that belonged to them was restored to them, and to their churches by law without detriment. Nor is it strange, brethren, if they persecute you, when they persecuted even to death your Head, Christ our Lord. Yet even persecutions are to be endured patiently, that ye may be known to be His disciples,

---

[1] By these *apocrisarii* are meant the deputies of the bishops, and their *locum tenentes*, as it were, who manage the affairs of the church, hear the cases of individuals, and refer them to the bishops. They are therefore called *apocrisarii*, i.e. responders, from ἀποκρίνομαι, to respond. Mention is made of them in Justinian Novell. *Quomodo oporteat Episcopos*, chap. xii. Albericus understands by them the legates of the Pope.

for whom also ye suffer. Whence, too, he says Himself, "Blessed are they which are persecuted for righteousness' sake."[1] Sustained by these testimonies, we ought not greatly to fear the reproach of men, nor be overcome by their upbraidings, since the Lord gives us this command by Isaiah the prophet, saying, "Hearken unto me, ye that know righteousness, my people, in whose heart is my law; fear ye not the reproach of men, neither be ye afraid of their revilings;"[2] considering what is written in the Psalm, "Shall not God search this out? for He knoweth the secrets of the heart,[3] and the thoughts of such men, that they are vanity."[4] "They spoke vanity every one with his neighbour: with deceitful lips in their heart, and with an evil heart they spoke. But the Lord shall cut off all deceitful lips, and the tongue that speaketh proud things; who have said, Our lips are our own; who is Lord over us?"[5] For if they kept these things in memory, they would by no means break forth into so great wickedness. For they do not this by laudable and paternal instruction (*probabili et paterna doctrina*), but that they may wreak their vengeful feeling against the servants of God. For it is written, "The way of a fool is right in his eyes;"[6] and, "There are ways which seem right unto a man, but the end thereof leads to death."[7] Now we who suffer these things ought to leave them to the judgment of God, who will render to every man according to his works;[8] who also has thundered through His servants, saying, "Vengeance is mine, I will repay."[9] Assist ye, therefore, one another in good faith, and by deed and with a hearty will; nor let any one remove his hand from the help of a brother, since "by this," saith the Lord, "shall all men know that ye are my disciples, if ye have love one to another."[10] Whence, too, He speaks by the prophet, saying, "Behold how good and how pleasant it is for brethren to dwell together in unity!"[11] In a spiritual dwelling, I interpret it, and in a concord which is in God,

[1] Matt. v. 10.   [2] Isa. li. 7.   [3] Ps. xliv. 21.
[4] Ps. xciv. 11.   [5] Ps. xii. 2–4.   [6] Prov. xii. 15.
[7] Prov. xiv. 12.   [8] Matt. xvi. 27.   [9] Rom. xii. 19.
[10] John xiii. 35.   [11] Ps. cxxxiii. 1.

and in the unity of the faith which distinguishes this pleasant dwelling according to truth, which indeed was more beauteously illustrated in Aaron and the priests[1] clothed with honour, as ointment upon the head, nurturing the highest understanding, and leading even to the end of wisdom. For in this dwelling the Lord has promised blessing and eternal life. Apprehending, therefore, the importance of this utterance of the prophet, we have spoken this present brotherly word for love's sake, and by no means seeking, or meaning to seek, our own things. For it is not good to repay detraction with detraction, or (according to the common proverb) to cast out a beam with a beam (*excutere palum palo*). Be it far from us. Such manners are not ours. May the Godhead indeed forbid it. By the just judgment of God, power is given sometimes to sinners to persecute His saints, in order that they who are aided and borne on by the Spirit of God may become more glorious through the discipline of sufferings. But to those very persons who persecute, and reproach, and injure them, there will doubtless be woe. Woe, woe to those who injure the servants of God; for injury done to them concerns Him whose service they discharge, and whose function they execute. But we pray that a door of enclosure be placed upon their mouths, as we desire that no one perish or be defiled by their lips, and that they think or publish with their mouth no hurtful word. Whence also the Lord speaks by the prophet, "I said I will take heed to my ways, that I sin not with my tongue."[2] May the Lord Almighty, and His only-begotten Son and our Saviour Jesus Christ, give you this incitement, that with all means in your power you aid all the brethren under whatsoever tribulations they labour, and esteem, as is meet, their sufferings your own. Afford them the utmost assistance by word and deed, that ye may be found His true disciples, who enjoined all to love the brethren as themselves.

[1] The MS. reads, "and those wearing the priestly dignity."
[2] Ps. xxxix. 1.

II.

On the Ordination of Presbyters and Deacons.

Ordinations of presbyters and Levites, moreover, solemnly perform on a suitable occasion, and in the presence of many witnesses; and to this duty advance tried and learned men, that ye may be greatly gladdened by their fellowship and help. Place the confidence of your hearts without ceasing on the goodness of God, and declare these and the other divine words to succeeding generations: "For this is our God for ever and ever, and He will guide us to eternity."[1] Given on the 7th November, in the consulship of the most illustrious Saturninus and Gallicanus.[2]

[1] Ps. xlviii. 14.　　　[2] Or, Gallus.

FRAGMENTS OF CAIUS,

A PRESBYTER OF ROME.

INTRODUCTORY NOTICE.

EUSEBIUS states that Caius lived in the time of Zephyrinus.[1] He speaks of him as a member of the Catholic Church (ἐκκλησιαστικὸς ἀνήρ), and as being most learned. And he mentions that a dialogue of his was extant in his time, in which he argued with Proclus, the leader of the Cataphrygian heresy; and that Caius in this dialogue spoke of only thirteen epistles of the Apostle Paul, " not counting the Epistle to the Hebrews with the rest." [2]

Eusebius mentions no other work of Caius. He makes extracts from a work against the heresy of Artemon in the fifth book of his *Ecclesiastical History*, but he states distinctly that the work was anonymous. He evidently did not know who was the author. Theodoret and Nicephorus affirm that the work from which Eusebius made these extracts bore the title of *The Little Labyrinth*. Photius has the following notice of Caius: " Read the work of Josephus on the universe, bearing in some manuscripts the inscription *On the Cause of the Universe*, and in others, *On the Substance of the Universe*. . . . But I found that this treatise is not the work of Josephus, but of one Gaius a presbyter, who lived in Rome, who they say composed *The Labyrinth* also, and whose dialogue with Proclus, the champion of the Montanistic heresy, is in circulation. . . . They say also that he composed another treatise specially directed against the heresy of Artemon."[3] Photius here ascribes four works to Caius : 1. *On the Universe* ; 2. *The*

[1] *Hist. Eccl.* ii. 25, vi. 20.   [2] *Hist. Eccl.* vi. 20.   [3] Cod. 48.

Labyrinth; 3. *The Dialogue between himself and Proclus;* 4. *The Treatise against the Heresy of Artemon.* He does not say that he read any of them but the first. This treatise is now assigned to Hippolytus. The information of Photius in regard to the other three, derived as it is from the statements of others, cannot be trusted.

The very important fragment, called *Canon Muratorius,* was discovered by Muratori in the Ambrosian Library at Milan, and published by him in his *Antiquitates Italicæ* in 1740. This manuscript belongs to the seventh or eighth century. Muratori ascribed it to Caius, Bunsen to Hegesippus; but there is no clue whatever to the authorship. From internal evidence the writer of the fragment is believed to belong to the latter half of the second century. The fragment has been much discussed. For a full account of it, see Westcott's *General Survey of the History of the Canon of the New Testament,* 2d ed. p. 184 ff., and Tregelles' *Canon Muratorianus.*

I. FROM A DIALOGUE OR DISPUTATION AGAINST PROCLUS, A DEFENDER OF THE SECT OF THE CATAPHRYGIANS.

I.

[Preserved in Eusebius' *Eccles. Hist.* ii. 25.]

AND I can show the trophies of the apostles.[1] For if you choose to go to the Vatican or to the Ostian Road,[2] you will find the trophies of those who founded this church.

[1] So Jerome, in the Epistle to Marcellus, says: "There, too, is a holy church; there are the trophies of the apostles and martyrs."

[2] The MSS. and the *Chronicon* of Georgius Syncellus read *Vasican,* Βασικανόν. The reference is to the Vatican as the traditional burial place of Peter, and to the Ostian Road as that of Paul.

II.

[In the same, iii. 28.]

But Cerinthus, too, through revelations written, as he would have us believe, by a great apostle, brings before us marvellous things, which he pretends were shown him by angels; alleging that after the resurrection the kingdom of Christ is to be on earth, and that the flesh[1] dwelling in Jerusalem is again to be subject to desires and pleasures. And being an enemy to the Scriptures of God, wishing to deceive men, he says that there is to be a space of a thousand years for marriage festivals.

III.

[In the same, iii. 31.]

And after this there were four prophetesses, daughters of Philip, at Hierapolis in Asia. Their tomb is there, and that, too, of their father.[2]

II. FRAGMENTS OF AN ANONYMOUS WORK AGAINST THE HERESY OF ARTEMON, ASCRIBED BY SOME TO CAIUS.

I.

[In Eusebius' *Eccl. Hist.* v. 28.]

For they say that all those of the first age, and the apostles themselves, both received and taught those things which these now maintain;[3] and that the truth of gospel preaching was preserved until the times of Victor, who was the thirteenth bishop in Rome from Peter, and that from his successor Zephyrinus the truth was falsified. And perhaps what they

---

[1] *i.e.* men.

[2] This extract is taken from the Disputation of Caius, but the words are those of Proclus, as is shown by the citation in Eusebius.

[3] Artemon and his followers maintained that Christ was mere (ψιλόν) man.

allege might be credible, did not the holy Scriptures, in the
first place, contradict them. And then, besides, there are
writings of certain brethren older than the times of Victor,
which they wrote against the heathen in defence of the truth,
and against the heresies of their time: I mean Justin and
Miltiades, and Tatian and Clement, and many others, in all
which divinity is ascribed to Christ. For who is ignorant of
the books of Irenæus and Melito, and the rest, which declare
Christ to be God and man? All the psalms, too, and hymns[1]
of brethren, which have been written from the beginning by
the faithful, celebrate Christ the Word of God, ascribing
divinity to Him. Since the doctrine of the church, then, has
been proclaimed so many years ago, how is it possible that
men have preached, up to the time of Victor, in the manner
asserted by these? And how are they not ashamed to utter
these calumnies against Victor, knowing well that Victor excommunicated Theodotus the tanner, the leader and father of
this God-denying apostasy, who first affirmed that Christ was
a mere man? For if, as they allege, Victor entertained the
very opinions which their blasphemy teaches, how should he
have cast off Theodotus, the author of this heresy?

II.

[In Eusebius, as above.]

I shall, at any rate, remind many of the brethren of an
affair that took place in our own time,—an affair which, had
it taken place in Sodom, might, I think, have been a warning
even to them. There was a certain confessor, Natalius,[2] who

[1] From this it appears that it was a very ancient custom in the church
to compose hymns and psalms in honour of Christ. Pliny, in his letter
to Trajan, also states that the Christians were accustomed to meet
together and sing hymns to Christ. Hippolytus also may be understood
to refer to these hymns and psalms towards the close of his oration on
the end of the world, where he says: "Your mouth I made to give
glory and praise, and to utter psalms and spiritual songs." A hymn of
this kind in honour of Jesus Christ, composed by Clement of Alexandria,
is extant at the end of his books entitled *Pædagogi*.

[2] This *may*, perhaps, be the Cæcilius Natalis who appears in the

lived not in distant times, but in our own day. He was
deluded once by Asclepiodotus, and another Theodotus, a
banker. And these were both disciples of Theodotus the
tanner, the first who was cut off from communion on account
of this sentiment, or rather senselessness, by Victor, as I said,
the bishop of the time. Now Natalius was persuaded by
them to let himself be chosen[1] bishop of this heresy, on the
understanding that he should receive from them a salary of
150 denarii a month. Connecting himself, therefore, with
them, he was on many occasions admonished by the Lord
in visions. For our merciful God and Lord Jesus Christ
was not willing that a witness of His own sufferings should
perish, being without the church. But as he gave little heed
to the visions, being ensnared by the dignity of presiding
among them, and by that sordid lust of gain which ruins very
many, he was at last scourged by holy angels, and severely
beaten through a whole night, so that he rose early in the
morning, and threw himself, clothed with sackcloth and
covered with ashes, before Zephyrinus the bishop, with great
haste and many tears, rolling beneath the feet not only of
the clergy, but even of the laity, and moving the pity of the
compassionate church of the merciful Christ by his weeping.
And after trying many a prayer, and showing the weals left
by the blows which he had received, he was at length with
difficulty admitted to communion.

III.

[In Eusebius, as above.]

The sacred Scriptures they have boldly falsified, and the
canons of the ancient faith they have rejected, and Christ
they have ignored, not inquiring what the sacred Scriptures
say, but laboriously seeking to discover what form of syllo-

Octavius of Minucius Felix, as maintaining the cause of paganism
against Octavius Januarius, and becoming a convert to the truth
through the discussion. Name, time, and profession at least suit.

[1] There is another reading—*named* (κληθῆναι) instead of *chosen* or
elected (κληρωθῆναι).

gism might be contrived to establish their impiety. And
should any one lay before them a word of divine Scripture,
they examine whether it will make a connected or disjoined
form of syllogism;[1] and leaving the holy Scriptures of God,
they study geometry, as men who are of the earth, and speak
of the earth, and are ignorant of Him who cometh from
above. Euclid, indeed, is laboriously measured[2] by some of
them, and Aristotle and Theophrastus are admired; and
Galen,[3] forsooth, is perhaps even worshipped by some of
them. But as to those men who abuse the arts of the unbelievers to establish their own heretical doctrine, and by the
craft of the impious adulterate the simple faith of the divine
Scriptures, what need is there to say that these are not near
the faith? For this reason is it they have boldly laid their
hands upon the divine Scriptures, alleging that they have
corrected them. And that I do not state this against them
falsely, any one who pleases may ascertain. For if any one
should choose to collect and compare all their copies together,
he would find many discrepancies among them. The copies
of Asclepiades,[4] at any rate, will be found at variance with
those of Theodotus. And many such copies are to be had,
because their disciples were very zealous in inserting the
corrections, as they call them, *i.e.* the corruptions made by
each of them. And again, the copies of Hermophilus do not
agree with these; and as for those of Apollonius,[5] they are
not consistent even with themselves. For one may compare

[1] The *connected* form here is the *hypothetical*, as *e.g.*, "If it is day, it is light." The *disjoined* is the *disjunctive*, as *e.g.*, "It is either day or night." The words admit another rendering, viz., "Whether it, when connected or disjoined, will make the form of a syllogism."

[2] There is a play in the original on the word *geometry*.

[3] Galen composed treatises on the figures of syllogisms, and on philosophy in general. This is also a notable testimony, as proceeding from
a very ancient author, almost contemporary with Galen himself. And
from a great number of other writers, as well as this one, it is evident
that Galen was ranked as the equal of Aristotle, Theophrastus, and even
Plato.

[4] In Nicephorus it is *Asclepiodotus*, which is also the reading of Rufinus.

[5] It appears from Theodoret (*Hæret. Fab.* book ii. ch. v.), as well as from
Nicephorus and Rufinus, that we should read *Apollonides* for Apollonius.

those which were formerly prepared by them[1] with those which have been afterwards corrupted with a special object, and many discrepancies will be found. And as to the great audacity implied in this offence, it is not likely that even they themselves can be ignorant of that. For either they do not believe that the divine Scriptures were dictated by the Holy Spirit, and are thus infidels; or they think themselves wiser than the Holy Spirit, and what are they then but demoniacs? Nor can they deny that the crime is theirs, when the copies have been written with their own hand; nor[2] did they receive such copies of the Scriptures from those by whom they were first instructed in the faith, and they cannot produce copies from which these were transcribed. And some of them did not even think it worth while to corrupt them; but simply denying the law and the prophets for the sake of their lawless and impious doctrine, under pretext of grace, they sunk down to the lowest abyss of perdition.

III. CANON MURATORIANUS—AN ACEPHALOUS FRAGMENT ON THE CANON OF THE SACRED SCRIPTURES, ASCRIBED BY SOME TO CAIUS.

[In Muratori, *V. C. Antiq. Ital. Med. æv.* vol. iii. col. 854.]

1. . . . . . those things at which he was present he placed thus.[3] The third book of the Gospel, that according to Luke, the well-known physician Luke wrote in his own name[4] in order after the ascension of Christ, and when

[1] There is another reading—*by him*.
[2] This paragraph, down to the word "transcribed," is wanting in the Codex Regius.
[3] The text is, "quibus tamen interfuit et ita posuit." Westcott omits the "et." Bunsen proposes "*ipse non interfuit*." The reference probably is to the statement of Papias (Euseb. *Histor.* *Eccles.* iii. 39) as to Mark's Gospel being a narrative not of what he himself witnessed, but of what he heard from Peter.
[4] The text gives "numine suo ex opinione concriset," for which we read "nomine suo ex ordine conscripsit" with Westcott.

Paul had associated him with himself[1] as one studious of right.[2] Nor did he himself see the Lord in the flesh; and he, according as he was able to accomplish it, began[3] his narrative with the nativity of John. The fourth Gospel is that of John, one of the disciples. When his fellow-disciples and bishops entreated him, he said, "Fast ye now with me for the space of three days, and let us recount to each other whatever may be revealed to each of us." On the same night it was revealed to Andrew, one of the apostles, that John should narrate all things in his own name as they called them to mind (or as they revised them, *recognoscentibus*). And hence, although different points (*principia*) are taught us in the several books of the Gospels, there is no difference as regards the faith of believers, inasmuch as in all of them all things are related under one imperial (*principali*, leading) spirit, which concern the [Lord's] nativity, His passion, His resurrection, His conversation with His disciples, and His twofold advent,—the first in the humiliation of rejection, which is now past, and the second in the glory of royal power, which is yet in the future. What marvel is it, then, that John brings forward these several things (*singula*) so constantly in his epistles also, saying in his own person, "What we have seen with our eyes, and heard with our ears, and our hands have handled, that have we written."[4] For thus he professes himself to be not only the eye-witness, but also the hearer; and besides that, the historian of all the wondrous facts concerning the Lord in their order.

2. Moreover, the acts of all the apostles are comprised by Luke in one book, and addressed to the most excellent Theophilus, because these different events took place when he was present himself; and he shows this clearly (*i.e.* that the principle on which he wrote was to give only what fell under his

---

[1] Reading "secum" for "secundum."
[2] The text gives "quasi ut juris studiosum," for which "quasi et virtutis studiosum," = "as one devoted to virtue," has been proposed. Bunsen reads "itineris socium" = "as his companion in the way."
[3] "Incepit" for "incipet."
[4] 1 John i. 1.

own notice) by the omission[1] of the passion of Peter, and also of the journey of Paul, when he went from the city (Rome) to Spain.

3. As to the epistles[2] of Paul, again, to those who will understand the matter, they indicate of themselves what they are, and from what place or with what object they were directed. He wrote first of all, and at considerable length, to the Corinthians, to check the schism of heresy; and then to the Galatians, to forbid circumcision; and then to the Romans on the rule of the [Old Testament] Scriptures, and also to show them that Christ is the first object (*principium*) in these;—which it is needful for us to discuss severally,[3] as the blessed Apostle Paul, following the rule of his predecessor John, writes to no more than seven churches by name, in this order: the first to the Corinthians, the second to the Ephesians, the third to the Philippians, the fourth to the Colossians, the fifth to the Galatians, the sixth to the Thessalonians, the seventh to the Romans. Moreover, though he writes twice to the Corinthians and Thessalonians for their correction, it is yet shown (*i.e.* by this sevenfold writing) that there is one church spread abroad through the whole world. And John too, indeed, in the Apocalypse, although he writes only to seven churches, yet addresses all. He wrote, besides these, one to Philemon, and one to Titus, and two to Timothy, in simple personal affection and love indeed; but yet these are hallowed in the esteem of the catholic church, [and] in the regulation of ecclesiastical discipline. There are also in circulation one to the Laodiceans, and another to the Alexandrians, forged under the name of Paul, [and] addressed against the heresy of Marcion; and there are also several others which cannot be received into the catholic church, for it is not suitable for gall to be mingled with honey.

[1] The text is, "semote passionem Petri," etc., for which Westcott reads "semotâ."

[2] Reading "epistolæ" and "directæ" instead of "epistola" and "directe," and "volentibus" for "voluntatibus."

[3] The text is, "de quibus singulis necesse est a nobis disputari cum," etc. Bunsen reads, "de quibus non necesse est a nobis disputari cur" = "on which we need not discuss the reason why."

4. The Epistle of Jude, indeed (*sane*), and two belonging to the above-named John (or bearing the name of John), are reckoned among the catholic [epistles].[1] And the [book of] Wisdom, written by the friends of Solomon in his honour, [is admitted]. We receive also the Apocalypse of John and [that of] Peter, though some amongst us will not have this latter read in the church. The *Pastor*, moreover, did Hermas write very recently in our times in the city of Rome, while his brother bishop Pius sat in the chair of the church of Rome. And therefore it also ought to be read; but it cannot be made public[2] in the church to the people, nor [placed] among the prophets, as their number is complete, nor among the apostles to the end of time. Of [the writings of] Arsinous, called also Valentinus, or of Miltiades, we receive nothing at all. Those too who wrote the new *Book of Psalms* for Marcion, together with Basilides and the founder of the Asian Cataphrygians, [are rejected].

[1] The text is "in catholica," which may be "in the catholic church." Bunsen, Westcott, etc., read "in catholicis."

[2] Reading " sed publicari " for " se publicare."

THE EXTANT WRITINGS OF JULIUS AFRICANUS.

INTRODUCTORY NOTICE.

THE principal facts known to us in the life of Africanus are derived from himself and the *Chronicon* of Eusebius. He says of himself that he went to Alexandria on account of the fame of Heraclas. In the *Chronicon*, under the year 226, it is stated that "Nicopolis in Palestine, which formerly bore the name of Emmaus, was built, Africanus, the author of the *Chronology*, acting as ambassador on behalf of it, and having the charge of it." Dionysius Bar-Salibi speaks of Africanus as bishop of Emmaus.

Eusebius describes Africanus as being the author of a work called κεστοί.[1] Suidas says that this book detailed various kinds of cures, consisting of charms and written forms, and such like. Some have supposed that such a work is not likely to have been written by a Christian writer: they appeal also to the fact that no notice is taken of the κεστοί by Jerome in his notice of Africanus, nor by Rufinus in his translation of Eusebius. They therefore deem the clause in Eusebius an interpolation, and they suppose that two bore the name of Africanus,—one the author of the κεστοί, the other the Christian writer. Suidas identifies them, says that he was surnamed Sextus, and that he was a Libyan philosopher.

The works ascribed to Africanus, beside the *Cesti*, are the following:

1. *Five Books of Chronology.* Photius[2] says of this work, that it was concise, but omitted nothing of importance. It

[1] *Hist. Eccl.* vi. 31.   [2] Cod. 34.

began with the cosmogony of Moses, and went down to the advent of Christ. It summarized also the events from the time of Christ to the reign of the Emperor Macrinus.

2. A very famous letter to Aristides, in which he endeavoured to reconcile the apparent discrepancies in the genealogies of Christ given by Matthew and Luke.

3. A letter to Origen, in which he endeavoured to prove that the story of Susanna in Daniel was a forgery. A translation of this letter will be given in the *Works of Origen*.

4. *The Acts of Symphorosa and her Seven Sons* are attributed in the MSS. to Africanus; but no ancient writer speaks of him as the author of this work.

I. THE EPISTLE OF AFRICANUS TO ARISTIDES.

[This letter, as given by Eusebius, is acephalous. A large portion of it is supplied by Cardinal Angelo Mai in the *Bibliotheca nova Patrum*, vol. iv. pp. 231 and 273. We enclose in brackets the parts wanting in Gallandi, who copied Eusebius (*Hist. Eccl.* i. 7).]

I.

FRICANUS ON THE GENEALOGY IN THE HOLY GOSPELS.[1]—Some indeed incorrectly allege that this discrepant enumeration and mixing of the names both of priestly men, as they think, and royal, was made properly (δικαίως), in order that Christ might be shown rightfully to be both Priest and King; as if any one disbelieved this, or had any other hope than this, that Christ is the High Priest of His Father, who presents our prayers to Him, and a supramundane King, who rules by the Spirit those whom He has delivered, a co-operator in the government of all things. And this is announced to us not by the catalogue of the tribes, nor by the mixing of the registered generations, but by the patriarchs and prophets.

---

[1] On this celebrated letter of Africanus to Aristides, consult especially Eusebius (*Hist. Eccl.* i. 7); also Jerome, comm. on Matt. i. 16; Augustine, *Retract.* ii. 7; Photius, cod. xxxiv. p. 22; and in addition to these, Zacharias Chrysopol. in *Bibl. P. P. Lugd.* vol. xix. p. 751.

Let us not therefore descend to such religious trifling as to establish the kingship and priesthood of Christ by the interchanges of the names. For the priestly tribe of Levi, too, was allied with the kingly tribe of Juda, through the circumstance that Aaron married Elizabeth the sister of Naasson,[1] and that Eleazar again married the daughter of Phatiel,[2] and begat children. The evangelists, therefore, would thus have spoken falsely, affirming what was not truth, but a fictitious commendation. And for this reason the one traced the pedigree of Jacob the father of Joseph from David through Solomon; the other traced that of Heli also, though in a different way, the father of Joseph, from Nathan the son of David. And they ought not indeed to have been ignorant that both orders of the ancestors enumerated are the generation of David, the royal tribe of Juda. For if Nathan was a prophet, so also was Solomon, and so too the father of both of them; and there were prophets belonging to many of the tribes, but priests belonging to none of the tribes, save the Levites only. To no purpose, then, is this fabrication of theirs. Nor shall an assertion of this kind prevail in the church of Christ against the exact truth, so as that a lie should be contrived for the praise and glory of Christ. For who does not know that most holy word of the apostle also, who, when he was preaching and proclaiming the resurrection of our Saviour, and confidently affirming the truth, said with great fear, "If any say that Christ is not risen, and we assert and have believed this, and both hope for and preach that very thing, we are false witnesses of God, in alleging that He raised up Christ, whom He raised not up?"[3] And if he who glorifies God the Father is thus afraid lest he should seem a false witness in narrating a marvellous fact, how should not he be justly afraid, who tries to establish the truth by a false statement, preparing an untrue opinion? For if the generations are different, and trace down no genuine seed to Joseph, and if all has been stated only with the view of establishing the position of Him who was to be born—to confirm the truth, namely, that He who was to be would be king and priest,

[1] Ex. vi. 23.   [2] Ex. vi. 25.   [3] 1 Cor. xv. 12, etc.

there being at the same time no proof given, but the dignity of the words being brought down to a feeble hymn,—it is evident that no praise accrues to God from that, since it is a falsehood, but rather judgment returns on him who asserts it, because he vaunts an unreality as though it were reality. Therefore, that we may expose the ignorance also of him who speaks thus, and prevent any one from stumbling at this folly, I shall set forth the true history of these matters.]

II.

For[1] whereas in Israel the names of their generations were enumerated either according to nature or according to law,—according to nature, indeed, by the succession of legitimate offspring, and according to law whenever another raised up children to the name of a brother dying childless; for because no clear hope of resurrection was yet given them, they had a representation of the future promise in a kind of mortal resurrection, with the view of perpetuating the name of one deceased;—whereas, then, of those entered in this genealogy, some succeeded by legitimate descent as son to father, while others begotten in one family were introduced to another in name, mention is therefore made of both—of those who were progenitors in fact, and of those who were so only in name. Thus neither of the evangelists is in error; as the one reckons by nature and the other by law. For the several generations, viz. those descending from Solomon and those from Nathan, were so intermingled[2] by the raising up of children to the childless,[3] and by second marriages, and the raising up of seed, that the same persons are quite justly reckoned to belong at one time to the one, and at another to the other, *i.e.* to their reputed or to their actual fathers. And

---

[1] Here what is given in Eusebius begins.

[2] Reading συνεπιπλάκη. Migne would make it equivalent to "super-implexum est." Rufinus renders it, "Reconjunctum namque est sibi invicem genus, et illud per Salomonem et illud quod per Nathan deducitur," etc.

[3] ἀναστάσεσιν ἀτέκνων. Rufinus and Damascenus omit these words in their versions of the passage.

hence it is that both these accounts are true, and come down to Joseph, with considerable intricacy indeed, but yet quite accurately.

III.

But in order that what I have said may be made evident, I shall explain the interchange[1] of the generations. If we reckon the generations from David through Solomon, Matthan is found to be the third from the end, who begat Jacob the father of Joseph. But if, with Luke, we reckon them from Nathan the son of David, in like manner the third from the end is Melchi, whose son was Heli the father of Joseph. For Joseph was the son of Heli, the son of Melchi.[2] As Joseph, therefore, is the object proposed to us, we have to show how it is that each is represented as his father, both Jacob as descending from Solomon, and Heli as descending from Nathan: first, how these two, Jacob and Heli, were brothers; and then also how the fathers of these, Matthan and Melchi, being of different families, are shown to be the grandfathers of Joseph. Well, then, Matthan and Melchi, having taken the same woman to wife in succession, begat children who were uterine brothers, as the law did not prevent a widow,[3] whether such by divorce or by the death of her husband, from marrying another. By Estha, then—for such is her name according to tradition—Matthan first, the descendant of Solomon, begets Jacob; and on Matthan's death, Melchi, who traces his descent back to Nathan, being of the same tribe but of another family, having married her, as has been already said, had a son Heli. Thus, then, we shall find Jacob and Heli uterine brothers, though of different families. And of these, the one Jacob having taken the wife of his

---

[1] The reading of the Codex Regius is ἀκολουθίαν, i.e. succession; the other leading MSS. give ἐπαλλαγήν, i.e. interchange or confusion.

[2] But in our text in Luke iii. 23, 24, and so, too, in the Vulgate, Matthat and Levi are inserted between Heli and Melchi. It may be that these two names were not found in the copy used by Africanus.

[3] Here Africanus applies the term "widow" (χηρεύουσαν) to one divorced as well as to one bereaved.

brother Heli, who died childless, begat by her the third, Joseph—his son by nature and by account (κατὰ λόγον). Whence also it is written, "And Jacob begat Joseph." But according to law he was the son of Heli, for Jacob his brother raised up seed to him. Wherefore also the genealogy deduced through him will not be made void, which the Evangelist Matthew in his enumeration gives thus: "And Jacob begat Joseph." But Luke, on the other hand, says, "Who was the son, as was supposed[1] (for this, too, he adds), of Joseph, the son of Heli, the son of Melchi." For it was not possible more distinctly to state the generation according to law; and thus in this mode of generation he has entirely omitted the word "begat" to the very end, carrying back the genealogy by way of conclusion to Adam and to God.[2]

IV.

Nor indeed is this incapable of proof, neither is it a rash conjecture. For the kinsmen of the Saviour after the flesh, whether to magnify their own origin or simply to state the fact, but at all events speaking truth, have also handed down the following account: Some Idumean robbers attacking Ascalon, a city of Palestine, besides other spoils which they took from a temple of Apollo, which was built near the walls, carried off captive one Antipater, son of a certain Herod, a servant of the temple. And as the priest[3] was not able to pay the ransom for his son, Antipater was brought up in the customs

---

[1] Two things may be remarked here: first, that Africanus refers the phrase "as was supposed" not only to the words "son of Joseph," but also to those that follow, "the son of Heli;" so that Christ would be the son of Joseph by legal adoption, just in the same way as Joseph was the son of Heli, which would lead to the absurd and impious conclusion that Christ was the son of Mary and a brother of Joseph married by her after the death of the latter. And second, that in the genealogy here assigned to Luke, Melchi holds the *third* place; whence it would seem either that Africanus's memory had failed him, or that in his copy of the Gospel Melchi stood in place of Matthat, as Bede conjectures (Migne).

[2] Other MSS. read, "Adam the son of God."

[3] The word "priest" is used here perhaps improperly for "servant of the temple," i.e. ἱερεύς for ἱερόδουλος.

of the Idumeans, and afterwards enjoyed the friendship of
Hyrcanus, the high priest of Judea. And being sent on an
embassy to Pompey on behalf of Hyrcanus, and having
restored to him the kingdom which was being wasted by
Aristobulus his brother, he was so fortunate as to obtain the
title of procurator of Palestine.[1] And when Antipater was
treacherously slain through envy of his great good fortune,
his son Herod succeeded him, who was afterwards appointed
king of Judea under Antony and Augustus by a decree of
the senate. His sons were Herod and the other tetrarchs.
These accounts are given also in the histories of the Greeks.[2]

V.

But as up to that time the genealogies of the Hebrews had
been registered in the public archives, and those, too, which
were traced back to the proselytes[3]—as, for example, to Achior
the Ammanite, and Ruth the Moabitess, and those who left
Egypt along with the Israelites, and intermarried with them—
Herod, knowing that the lineage of the Israelites contributed
nothing to him, and goaded by the consciousness of his
ignoble birth, burned the registers of their families. This
he did, thinking that he would appear to be of noble birth, if
no one else could trace back his descent by the public register
to the patriarchs or proselytes, and to that mixed race called
georæ.[4] A few, however, of the studious, having private

---

[1] So Josephus styles him "procurator of Judea, and viceroy" (ἐπι-
μελητὴς τῆς Ἰουδαίας, and ἐπίτροπος).

[2] This whole story about Antipater is fictitious. Antipater's father
was not Herod, a servant in the temple of Apollo, but Antipater an
Idumean, as we learn from Josephus (xiv. 2). This Antipater was made
prefect of Idumea by Alexander king of the Jews, and laid the foundation of the power to which his descendants rose. He acquired great
wealth, and was on terms of friendship with Ascalon, Gaza, and the
Arabians.

[3] Several MSS. read ἀρχιπροσηλύτων for ἄχρι προσηλύτων, whence some
conjecture that the correct reading should be ἄχρι τῶν ἀρχιπροσηλύτων,
i.e. back to the "chief proselytes,"—these being, as it were, patriarchs
among the proselytes, like Achior, and those who joined the Israelites
on their flight from Egypt.

[4] This word occurs in the Septuagint version of Ex. xii. 19, and

records of their own, either by remembering the names or by getting at them in some other way from the archives, pride themselves in preserving the memory of their noble descent; and among these happen to be those already mentioned, called *desposyni*,[1] on account of their connection with the family of the Saviour. And these coming from Nazara and Cochaba, Judean villages, to other parts of the country, set forth the above-named genealogy[2] as accurately as possible from the Book of Days.[3] Whether, then, the case stand thus or not, no one could discover a more obvious explanation, according to my own opinion and that of any sound judge. And let this suffice us for the matter, although it is not supported by testimony, because we have nothing more satisfactory or true to allege upon it. The Gospel, however, in any case states the truth.

refers to the *strangers* who left Egypt along with the Israelites. For Israel was accompanied by a mixed body, consisting on the one hand of native Egyptians, who are named αὐτόχθονες in that passage of Exodus, and by the resident aliens, who are called γειῶραι. Justin Martyr has the form γηόραν in *Dialogue with Trypho*, ch. cxxii. The root of the term is evidently the Hebrew גר, "stranger."

[1] The word δεσπόσυνοι was employed to indicate the Lord's relatives, as being His according to the flesh. The term means literally, "those who belong to a master," and thence it was used also to signify "one's heirs."

[2] προειρημένην. Nicephorus reads προκειμένην.

[3] ἐκ τι τῆς βίβλου τῶν ἡμερῶν. By this "Book of Days" Africanus understands those "day-books" which he has named, a little before this, ἰδιωτικὰς ἀπογραφάς. For among the Jews, most persons setting a high value on their lineage were in the habit of keeping by them private records of their descent copied from the public archives, as we see it done also by nobles among ourselves. Besides, by the insertion of the particle τι, which is found in all our codices, and also in Nicephorus, it appears that something is wanting in this passage. Wherefore it seems necessary to supply these words, καὶ ἀπὸ μνήμης ἐς ὅσον ἐξικνοῦντο, "and from memory," etc. Thus at least Rufinus seems to have read the passage, for he renders it: Ordinem supradictae generationis partim memoriter, partim etiam ex dierum libris, in quantum erat possibile, perdocebant (Migne).

VI.

Matthan, descended from Solomon, begat Jacob. Matthan dying, Melchi, descended from Nathan, begat Heli by the same wife. Therefore Heli and Jacob are uterine brothers. Heli dying childless, Jacob raised up seed to him and begat Joseph, his own son by nature, but the son of Heli by law. Thus Joseph was the son of both.

II. THE EXTANT FRAGMENTS OF THE FIVE BOOKS OF THE CHRONOGRAPHY OF JULIUS AFRICANUS.

I.

[In Georgius Syncellus, *Chron.* p. 17, ed. Paris, 14 Venet.]

On the Mythical Chronology of the Egyptians and Chaldeans.

THE Egyptians, indeed, with their boastful notions of their own antiquity, have put forth a sort of account of it by the hand of their astrologers in cycles and myriads of years; which some of those who have had the repute of studying such subjects profoundly have in a summary way called lunar years; and inclining no less than others to the mythical, [they think they] fall in with the eight or nine thousands of years which the Egyptian priests in Plato falsely reckon up to Solon.[1]

(And after some other matter :)

For why should I speak of the three myriad years of the Phœnicians, or of the follies of the Chaldeans, their forty-eight myriads? For the Jews, deriving their origin from them as descendants of Abraham, having been taught a modest mind, and one such as becomes men, together with the truth by the spirit of Moses, have handed down to us, by

[1] The text is : . . . συμπίπτουσι ταῖς ὀκτὼ καὶ ἐννέα χιλιάσιν ἐτῶν, ἃς Αἰγυπτίων οἱ παρὰ Πλάτωνι ἱερεῖς εἰς Σόλωνα καταριθμοῦντες οὐκ ἀπ.η θεύουσι.

their extant Hebrew histories, the number of 5500 years as the period up to the advent of the Word of salvation, that was announced to the world in the time of the sway of the Cæsars.

II.

[In the same, p. 19, al. 15.]

When men multiplied on the earth, the angels of heaven came together with the daughters of men. In some copies I found "the sons of God." What is meant by the Spirit, in my opinion, is that the descendants of Seth are called the sons of God on account of the righteous men and patriarchs who have sprung from him, even down to the Saviour Himself; but that the descendants of Cain are named the seed of men, as having nothing divine in them, on account of the wickedness of their race and the inequality of their nature, being a mixed people, and having stirred the indignation of God.[1] But if it is thought that these refer to angels, we must take them to be those who deal with magic and jugglery, who taught the women the motions of the stars and the knowledge of things celestial, by whose power they conceived the giants as their children, by whom wickedness came to its height on the earth, until God decreed that the whole race of the living should perish in their impiety by the deluge.

III.

[In the same, p. 81, al. 65.]

Adam, when 230 years old, begets Seth; and after living other 700 years he died, that is, a second death.

Seth, when 205 years old, begat Enos; from Adam therefore to the birth of Enos there are 435 years in all.

Enos, when 190 years old, begets Cainan.

Cainan again, when 170 years old, begts Malaleel;

And Malaleel, when 165 years old, begets Jared;

---

[1] The text here is manifestly corrupt: ἐπιμιχθέντων αὐτῶν, τὴν ἀγανάκτησιν ποιήσασθαι τὸν Θεόν.

And Jared, when 162 years old, begets Enoch;
And Enoch, when 165 years old, begets Mathusala; and having pleased God, after a life of other 200 years, he was not found.
Mathusala, when 187 years old, begat Lamech.
Lamech, when 188 years old, begets Noe.

IV.

[In the same, p. 21, al. 17.]

On the Deluge.

God decreed to destroy the whole race of the living by a flood, having threatened that men should not survive beyond 120 years. Nor let it be deemed a matter of difficulty, because some lived afterwards a longer period than that. For the space of time meant was 100 years up to the flood in the case of the sinners of that time; for they were 20 years old. God instructed Noe, who pleased him on account of his righteousness, to prepare an ark; and when it was finished, there entered it Noe himself and his sons, his wife and his daughters-in-law, and firstlings of every living creature, with a view to the duration of the race. And Noe was 600 years old when the flood came on. And when the water abated, the ark settled on the mountains of Ararat, which we know to be in Parthia;[1] but some say that they are at Celænæ[2] of Phrygia, and I have seen both places. And the flood prevailed for a year, and then the earth became dry. And they came out of the ark in pairs, as may be found, and not in the manner in which they had entered, viz. distinguished according to their species, and were blessed by God. And each of these things indicates something useful to us.

[1] That is, in Armenia.
[2] For there was a hill Ararat in Phrygia, from which the Marsyas issued, and the ark was declared to have rested there by the Sibylline oracles.

V.

[In the same, p. 83, al. 67.]

Noe was 600 years old when the flood came on. From Adam, therefore, to Noe and the flood, are 2262 years.

VI.

[In the same, p. 86, al. 68.]

And after the flood, Sem begat Arphaxad.

Arphaxad, when 135 years old, begets Sala in the year 2397.

Sala, when 130 years old, begets Heber in the year 2527.

Heber, when 134 years old, begets Phalec in the year 2661, so called because the earth was divided in his days.

Phalec, when 130 years old, begat Ragan, and after living other 209 years died.

VII.

[In the same, p. 93, al. 74.]

In the year of the world 3277, Abraham entered the promised land of Canaan.

VIII.

[In the same, p. 99, al. 79.]

Of Abraham.

From this rises the appellation of the *Hebrews*. For the word *Hebrews* is interpreted to mean *those who migrate across*, viz. who crossed the Euphrates with Abraham; and it is not derived, as some think, from the fore-mentioned Heber. From the flood and Noe, therefore, to Abraham's entrance into the promised land, there are in all 1015 years; and from Adam, in 20 generations, 3277 years.

IX.

[In the same, p. 100, al. 80.]

Of Abraham and Lot.

When a famine pressed the land of Canaan, Abraham came down to Egypt; and fearing lest he should be put out of the way on account of the beauty of his wife, he pretended that he was her brother. But Pharaoh took her to himself when she was commended to him; for this is the name the Egyptians give their kings. And he was punished by God; and Abraham, along with all pertaining to him, was dismissed enriched. In Canaan, Abraham's shepherds and Lot's contended with each other; and with mutual consent they separated, Lot choosing to dwell in Sodom on account of the fertility and beauty of the land, which had five cities, Sodom, Gomorrah, Adama, Seboim, Segor, and as many kings. On these their neighbours the four Syrian kings made war, whose leader was Chodollogomor king of Ælam. And they met by the Salt Sea, which is now called the Dead Sea. In it I have seen very many wonderful things. For that water sustains no living thing, and dead bodies are carried beneath its depths, while the living do not readily even dip under it. Lighted torches are borne upon it, but when extinguished they sink. And there are the springs of bitumen; and it yields alum and salt a little different from the common kinds, for they are pungent and transparent. And wherever fruit is found about it, it is found full of a thick, foul smoke. And the water acts as a cure to those who use it, and it is drained in a manner contrary to any other water.[1] And if it had not the river Jordan feeding it like a shell,[2] and to a great extent withstanding its tendency, it would have failed more rapidly than appears. There is also by it a great quantity of the balsam plant; but it is supposed to have been destroyed by God on account of the impiety of the neighbouring people.

---

[1] λήγει τε παντὶ ὕδατι πάσχων τἀινάντια.
[2] ὡς πορφύραν.

X.

[In the same, p. 107, al. 86.]

Of the Patriarch Jacob.

1. The shepherd's tent belonging to Jacob, which was preserved at Edessa to the time of Antonine Emperor of the Romans, was destroyed by a thunderbolt.[1]

2. Jacob, being displeased at what had been done by Symeon and Levi at Shecem against the people of the country, on account of the violation of their sister, buried at Shecem the gods which he had with him near a rock under the wonderful terebinth,[2] which up to this day is reverenced by the neighbouring people in honour of the patriarchs, and removed thence to Bethel. By the trunk of this terebinth there was an altar on which the inhabitants of the country offered *ectenæ*[3] in their general assemblies; and though it seemed to be burned, it was not consumed. Near it is the tomb of Abraham and Isaac. And some say that the staff of one of the angels who were entertained by Abraham was planted there.

XI.

[In the same, p. 106, al. 85.]

From Adam, therefore, to the death of Joseph, according to this book, are 23 generations, and 3563 years.

---

[1] Heliogabalus is probably intended, in whose time Africanus flourished. At least so thinks Syncellus.

[2] On this terebinth, see Scaliger (*ad Græca Euseb.* p. 414); Franciscus Quaresimus, in *Elucid. terræ sanctæ;* Eugenius Rogerius, etc.; and also Valesius, *ad Euseb. De Vit. Constant.* iii. 53, notes 3 and 5.

[3] Scaliger acknowledges himself ignorant of this word ἐκτενάς. In the Eastern Church it is used to denote protracted prayers (*preces protensiores*) offered by the deacon on behalf of all classes of men, and the various necessities of human life. See Suicer, *sub voce.* Allatius thinks the text corrupt, and would read, ἐφ' ὃν τά τε ὁλοκαυτώματα καὶ τὰς ἑκατόμβας ἀνέφερον = on which they offered both holocausts and hecatombs.

XII.

[In the same, p. 148, al. 118, from the Third Book of the *Chron.* of Africanus.]

From this record (συντάγματος), therefore, we affirm that Ogygus,[1] from whom the first flood [in Attica] derived its name,[2] and who was saved when many perished, lived at the time of the exodus of the people from Egypt along with Moses.[3] (*After a break*): And after Ogygus, on account of the vast destruction caused by the flood, the present land of Attica remained without a king till the time of Cecrops, 189 years.[4] Philochorus, however, affirms that Ogygus, Actæus, or whatever other fictitious name is adduced, never existed. (*After another break*): From Ogygus to Cyrus, as from Moses to his time, are 1235 years.

XIII.

[From the same Third Book. In Euseb. *Præpar.* x. 40.]

1. Up to the time of the Olympiads there is no certain history among the Greeks, all things before that date being confused, and in no way consistent with each other. But these [Olympiads] were thoroughly investigated (ἠκριβῶντο) by many, as the Greeks made up the records of their history not according to long spaces, but in periods of four years. For which reason I shall select the most remarkable of the mythical narratives before the time of the first Olympiad, and rapidly run over them. But those after that period, at least those that are notable, I shall take together, Hebrew

---

[1] Others write Ogyges. Josephus (*in Apionem*), Euseb. (*de Præpar.*), Tatian (*Orat. adv. gent.*), Clemens (*Strom.*), and others, write Ogygus.

[2] The text is, ὅς τοῦ πρωτοῦ κατακλυσμοῦ γέγονεν ἐπώνυμος. The word ἐπώνυμος is susceptible of two meanings, either "taking the name from" or "giving the name to." 'Ωγύγια κακά was a proverbial expression for primeval ills.

[3] The text is here, κατὰ τὴν Αἴγυπτον τοῦ λαοῦ μετὰ Μωϋσέως ἔξοδον γενέσθαι, for which we may read κατὰ τὴν ἐξ Αἰγύπτου, etc.

[4] "Ωγυγον 'Ακταῖον ἢ τὰ πλασσόμενα τῶν ὀνομάτων. Compare xiii. 6, where we have τὸν γὰρ μετὰ "Ωγυγον 'Ακταῖον, etc.

events in connection with Greek, according to their dates, examining carefully the affairs of the Hebrews, and touching more cursorily on those of the Greeks; and my plan will be as follows: Taking up some single event in Hebrew history synchronous with another in Greek history, and keeping by it as the main subject, subtracting or adding as may seem needful in the narrative, I shall note what Greek or Persian of note, or remarkable personage of any other nationality, flourished at the date of that event in Hebrew history; and thus I may perhaps attain the object which I propose to myself.

2. The most famous exile that befell the Hebrews, then— to wit, when they were led captive by Nabuchodonosor king of Babylon—lasted 70 years, as Jeremias had prophesied. Berosus the Babylonian, moreover, makes mention of Nabuchodonosor. And after the 70 years of captivity, Cyrus became king of the Persians at the time of the 55th Olympiad, as may be ascertained from the *Bibliothecæ* of Diodorus and the histories of Thallus and Castor, and also from Polybius and Phlegon, and others besides these, who have made the Olympiads a subject of study. For the date is a matter of agreement among them all. And Cyrus then, in the first year of his reign, which was the first year of the 55th Olympiad, effected the first partial restoration of the people by the hand of Zorobabel, with whom also was Jesus the son of Josedec, since the period of 70 years was now fulfilled, as is narrated in Esdra the Hebrew historian. The narratives of the beginning of the sovereignty of Cyrus and the end of the captivity accordingly coincide. And thus, according to the reckoning of the Olympiads, there will be found a like harmony of events even to our time. And by following this, we shall also make the other narratives fit in with each other in the same manner.

3. But if the Attic time-reckoning is taken as the standard for affairs prior to these, then from Ogygus, who was believed by them to be an autochthon, in whose time also the first great flood took place in Attica, while Phoroneus reigned over the Argives, as Acusilaus relates, up to the date of the

first Olympiad, from which period the Greeks thought they could fix dates accurately, there are altogether 1020 years; which number both coincides with the above-mentioned, and will be established by what follows. For these things are also recorded by the Athenian[1] historians Hellanicus and Philochorus, who record Attic affairs; and by Castor and Thallus, who record Syrian affairs; and by Diodorus, who writes a universal history in his *Bibliothecæ*; and by Alexander Polyhistor, and by some of our own time, yet more carefully, and[2] by all the Attic writers. Whatever narrative of note, therefore, meets us in these 1020 years, shall be given in its proper place.

4. In accordance with this writing, therefore, we affirm that Ogygus, who gave his name to the first flood, and was saved when many perished, lived at the time of the exodus of the people from Egypt along with Moses.[3] And this we make out in the following manner. From Ogygus up to the first Olympiad already mentioned, it will be shown that there are 1020 years; and from the first Olympiad to the first year of the 55th, that is the first year of King Cyrus, which was also the end of the captivity, are 217 years. From Ogygus, therefore, to Cyrus are 1237. And if one carries the calculation backwards from the end of the captivity, there are 1237 years. Thus, by analysis, the same period is found to the first year of the exodus of Israel under Moses from Egypt, as from the 55th Olympiad to Ogygus, who founded Eleusis. And from this point we get a more notable beginning for Attic chronography.

5. So much, then, for the period prior to Ogygus. And at his time Moses left Egypt. And we demonstrate in the following manner how reliable is the statement that this happened at that date. From the exodus of Moses up to

---

[1] There is a difficulty in the text; Viger omits "Athenian."

[2] The Latin translator expunges the "and" (καί), and makes it more careful *than* all the Attic writers.

[3] The original here, as in the same passage above, is corrupt. It gives κατὰ τὴν Αἴγυπτον, which Migne would either omit entirely or replace by ἀπ' Αἰγύπτου.

Cyrus, who reigned after the captivity, are 1237 years. For the remaining years of Moses are 40. The years of Jesus, who led the people after him, are 25; those of the elders, who were judges after Jesus, are 30; those of the judges, whose history is given in the book of Judges, are 490; those of the priests Eli and Samuel are 90; those of the successive kings of the Hebrews are 490. (Then come the 70 years of the captivity[1]), the last year of which was the first year of the reign of Cyrus, as we have already said.

6. And from Moses, then, to the first Olympiad there are 1020 years, as to the first year of the 55th Olympiad from the same are 1237, in which enumeration the reckoning of the Greeks coincides with us. And after Ogygus, by reason of the vast destruction caused by the flood, the present land of Attica remained without a king up to Cecrops, a period of 189 years. For Philochorus asserts that the Actæus who is said to have succeeded Ogygus, or whatever other fictitious names are adduced, never existed. *And again:* From Ogygus, therefore, to Cyrus, *says he,* the same period is reckoned as from Moses to the same date, viz. 1237 years; and some of the Greeks also record that Moses lived at that same time. Polemo, for instance, in the first book of his *Greek History,* says: In the time of Apis, son of Phoroneus, a division of the army of the Egyptians left Egypt, and settled in the Palestine called Syrian, not far from Arabia: these are evidently those who were with Moses. And Apion the son of Poseidonius, the most laborious of grammarians, in his book *Against the Jews,* and in the fourth book of his *History,* says that in the time of Inachus king of Argos, when Amosis reigned over Egypt, the Jews revolted under the leadership of Moses. And Herodotus also makes mention of this revolt, and of Amosis, in his second book, and in a certain way also of the Jews themselves, reckoning them among the circumcised, and calling them the Assyrians of Palestine, perhaps through Abraham. And Ptolemy the Mendesian, who narrates the history of the Egyptians from the earliest times, gives

[1] The words in parenthesis are inserted according to Viger's proposal, as there is a manifest omission in the text.

the same account of all these things; so that among them in general there is no difference worth notice in the chronology.

7. It should be observed, further, that all the legendary accounts which are deemed specially remarkable by the Greeks by reason of their antiquity, are found to belong to a period posterior to Moses; such as their floods and conflagrations, Prometheus, Io, Europa, the Sparti, the abduction of Proserpine, their mysteries, their legislations, the deeds of Dionysus, Perseus, the Argonauts, the Centaurs, the Minotaur, the affairs of Troy, the labours of Hercules, the return of the Heraclidæ, the Ionian migration and the Olympiads. And it seemed good to me to give an account especially of the before-noted period of the Attic sovereignty, as I intend to narrate the history of the Greeks side by side with that of the Hebrews. For any one will be able, if he only start from my position, to make out the reckoning equally well with me. Now, in the first year of that period of 1020 years, stretching from Moses and Ogygus to the first Olympiad, the passover and the exodus of the Hebrews from Egypt took place, and also in Attica the flood of Ogygus. And that is according to reason. For when the Egyptians were being smitten in the anger of God with hail and storms, it was only to be expected that certain parts of the earth should suffer with them; and, in especial, it was but to be expected that the Athenians should participate in such calamity with the Egyptians, since they were supposed to be a colony from them, as Theopompus alleges in his *Tricarenus*, and others besides him. The intervening period has been passed by, as no remarkable event is recorded during it among the Greeks. But after 94 years Prometheus arose, according to some, who was fabulously reported to have formed men; for being a wise man, he transformed them from the state of extreme rudeness to culture.

XIV.

[From the same Third Book. In the *Chron. Paschal.* p. 104, ed. Paris, 84 Venet.]

Æschylus, the son of Agamestor, ruled the Athenians

twenty-three years, in whose time Joatham reigned in Jerusalem.

And our canon brings Joatham king of Juda within the first Olympiad.

XV.

[From the same, Book III., and from Book IV. In Syncellus, p. 197, al. 158.]

And Africanus, in the third book of his History, writes: Now the first Olympiad recorded—which, however, was really the fourteenth—was the period when Corœbus was victor;[1] at that time Ahaz was in the first year of his reign in Jerusalem. *Then in the fourth book he says:* It is therefore with the first year of the reign of Ahaz that we have shown the first Olympiad to fall in.

XVI.

[From Book v. In Eusebius, *Demonst. Evang.* Book VIII. ch. ii. p. 389, etc.[2]]

On the Seventy Weeks of Daniel.

1. This passage, therefore, as it stands thus, touches on many marvellous things. At present, however, I shall speak only of those things in it which bear upon chronology, and matters connected therewith. That the passage speaks then of the advent of Christ, who was to manifest Himself after seventy weeks, is evident. For in the Saviour's time, or from Him, are transgressions abrogated, and sins brought to an end. And through remission, moreover, are iniquities, along with offences, blotted out by expiation; and an everlasting righteousness is preached, different from that which is by the law, and visions and prophecies [are] until John, and the Most Holy is anointed. For before the advent of the

---

[1] The text is, ἀναγραφῆναι δὲ πρώτην τὴν τεσσαρισκαιδεκάτην, etc.

[2] The Latin version of this section is by Bernardinus Donatus of Verona. There is also a version by Jerome given in his commentary on Dan. ix. 24.

Saviour these things were not yet, and were therefore only looked for. And the beginning of the numbers, that is, of the seventy weeks, which make up 490 years, the angel instructs us to take from the going forth of the commandment to answer and to build Jerusalem. And this happened in the twentieth year of the reign of Artaxerxes king of Persia. For Nehemiah his cup-bearer besought him, and received the answer that Jerusalem should be built. And the word went forth commanding these things; for up to that time the city was desolate. For when Cyrus, after the seventy years' captivity, gave free permission to all to return who desired it, some of them under the leadership of Jesus the high priest and Zorobabel, and others after these under the leadership of Esdra, returned, but were prevented at first from building the temple, and from surrounding the city with a wall, on the plea that that had not been commanded.

2. It remained in this position, accordingly, until Nehemiah and the reign of Artaxerxes, and the 115th year of the sovereignty of the Persians. And from the capture of Jerusalem that makes 185 years. And at that time King Artaxerxes gave order that the city should be built; and Nehemiah being despatched, superintended the work, and the street and the surrounding wall were built, as had been prophesied. And reckoning from that point, we make up seventy weeks to the time of Christ. For if we begin to reckon from any other point, and not from this, the periods will not correspond, and very many odd results will meet us. For if we begin the calculation of the seventy weeks from Cyrus and the first restoration, there will be upwards of one hundred years too many, and there will be a larger number if we begin from the day on which the angel gave the prophecy to Daniel, and a much larger number still if we begin from the commencement of the captivity. For we find the sovereignty of the Persians comprising a period of 230 years, and that of the Macedonians extending over 370 years, and from that to the 16th[1] year of Tiberius Cæsar is a period of about 60 years.

3. It is by calculating from Artaxerxes, therefore, up to the

[1] Jerome in his version gives the 15th (*quintum decimum*).

time of Christ that the seventy weeks are made up, according to the numeration of the Jews. For from Nehemiah, who was despatched by Artaxerxes to build Jerusalem in the 115th year of the Persian empire, and the 20th year of the reign of Artaxerxes himself, and the 4th year of the 83d Olympiad, up to this date, which was the second year of the 202d Olympiad, and the 16th year of the reign of Tiberius Cæsar, there are reckoned 475 years, which make 490 according to the Hebrew numeration, as they measure the years by the course of the moon; so that, as is easy to show, their year consists of 354 days, while the solar year has $365\frac{1}{4}$ days. For the latter exceeds the period of twelve months, according to the moon's course, by $11\frac{1}{4}$ days. Hence the Greeks and the Jews insert three intercalary months every 8 years. For 8 times $11\frac{1}{4}$ days makes up 3 months. Therefore 475 years make 59 periods of 8 years each, and 3 months besides. But since thus there are 3 intercalary months every 8 years, we get thus 15 years *minus* a few days; and these being added to the 475 years, make up in all the 70 weeks.

XVII.

[In Syncellus, p. 307, al. 244.]

On the Fortunes of Hyrcanus and Antigonus, and on Herod, Augustus, Antony, and Cleopatra, in abstract.

1. Octavius Sebastus, or, as the Romans call him, Augustus, the adopted son of Caius, on returning to Rome from Apollonias in Epirus, where he was educated, possessed himself of the first place in the government. And Antony afterwards obtained the rule of Asia and the districts beyond. In his time the Jews accused Herod; but he put the deputies to death, and restored Herod to his government. Afterwards, however, along with Hyrcanus and Phasælus his brother, he was driven out, and betook himself in flight to Antony. And as the Jews would not receive him, an obstinate battle took place; and in a short time after, as he had conquered in battle, he also drove out Antigonus, who had returned. And

Antigonus fled to Herod the Parthian king, and was restored by the help of his son Pacorus, which help was given on his promising to pay 1000 talents of gold. And Herod then in his turn had to flee, while Phasælus was slain in battle, and Hyrcanus was surrendered alive to Antigonus. And after cutting off his ears, that he might be disqualified for the priesthood, he gave him to the Parthians to lead into captivity; for he scrupled to put him to death, as he was a relation of his own. And Herod, on his expulsion, betook himself first to Malichus king of the Arabians; and when he did not receive him, through fear of the Parthians, he went away to Alexandria to Cleopatra. That was in the 185th Olympiad. Cleopatra having put to death her brother, who was her consort in the government, and being then summoned by Antony to Cilicia to make her defence, committed the care of the sovereignty to Herod; and as he requested that he should not be entrusted with anything until he was restored to his own government,[1] she took him with her and went to Antony. And as he was smitten with love for the princess, they despatched Herod to Rome to Octavius Augustus, who, on behalf of Antipater, Herod's father, and on behalf of Herod himself, and also because Antigonus was established as king by the help of the Parthians, gave a commission to the generals in Palestine and Syria to restore him to his government. And in concert with Sosius he waged war against Antigonus, for a long time, and in manifold engagements. At that time also, Josephus, Herod's brother, died in his command. And Herod coming to Antony[2] . . .

2. For three years they besieged Antigonus, and then brought him alive to Antony. And Antony himself also proclaimed Herod as king, and gave him, in addition, the cities Hippus, Gadara, Gaza, Joppa, Anthedon, and a part of Arabia, Trachonitis, and Auranitis, and Sacia, and Gaulanitis;[3] and besides these, also the procuratorship of Syria.

[1] The sense is doubtful here: καὶ ὡς οὐδὲν ἤξίου πιστεύεσθαι ἔστ' ἂν καταχθῇ εἰς τὴν ἑαυτοῦ ἀρχήν, etc.

[2] There is a break here in the original.

[3] This is according to the rendering of the Latin version.

Herod was declared king of the Jews by the senate and Octavius Augustus, and reigned 34 years. Antony, when about to go on an expedition against the Parthians, slew Antigonus the king of the Jews, and gave Arabia to Cleopatra; and passing over into the territory of the Parthians, sustained a severe defeat, losing the greater part of his army. That was in the 186th Olympiad. Octavius Augustus led the forces of Italy and all the West against Antony, who refused to return to Rome through fear, on account of his failure in Parthia, and through his love for Cleopatra. And Antony met him with the forces of Asia. Herod, however, like a shrewd fellow, and one who waits upon the powerful, sent a double set of letters, and despatched his army to sea, charging his generals to watch the issue of events. And when the victory was decided, and when Antony, after sustaining two naval defeats, had fled to Egypt along with Cleopatra, they who bore the letters delivered to Augustus those which they had been keeping secretly for Antony. And on Herod falls[1] . . .

3. Cleopatra shut herself up in a mausoleum,[2] and made away with herself, employing the wild asp as the instrument of death. At that time Augustus captured Cleopatra's sons, Helios and Selene,[3] on their flight to the Thebaid. Nicopolis was founded opposite Actium, and the games called Actia were instituted. On the capture of Alexandria, Cornelius Gallus was sent as first governor of Egypt, and he destroyed the cities of the Egyptians that refused obedience. Up to this time the Lagidæ ruled; and the whole duration of the Macedonian empire after the subversion of the Persian power was 298 years. Thus is made up the whole period from the foundation of the Macedonian empire to its subversion in the time of the Ptolemies, and under Cleopatra, the last of these, the date of which event is the 11th year of the monarchy

---

[1] Here again there is a blank in the original.
[2] The text is corrupt here. It gives, ἐν τῷ μισαιολίῳ, a word unknown in Greek. Scaliger reads Μαισαιόλιον. Goarus proposes Μαυσωλαῖον, which we adopt in the translation.
[3] i.e. *sun* and *moon*.

and empire of the Romans, and the 4th year of the 187th Olympiad. Altogether, from Adam 5472 years are reckoned.

4. After the taking of Alexandria the 188th Olympiad began. Herod founded anew the city of the Gabinii,[1] the ancient Samaria, and called it Sebaste; and having erected its seaport, the tower of Strato, into a city, he named it Cæsarea after the same, and raised in each a temple in honour of Octavius. And afterwards he founded Antipatris in the Lydian plain, so naming it after his father, and settled in it the people about Sebaste, whom he had dispossessed of their land. He founded also other cities; and to the Jews he was severe, but to other nations most urbane.

It was now the 189th Olympiad, which [Olympiad] in the year that had the bissextile day, the 6th day before the Calends of March (*i.e.* the 24th of February), corresponded with the 24th year of the era of Antioch, whereby the year was determined in its proper limits.[2]

XVIII.

[In the same, p. 322 or 256.]

On the Circumstances connected with our Saviour's Passion and His Life-giving Resurrection.

1. As to His works severally, and His cures effected upon body and soul, and the mysteries of His doctrine, and the resurrection from the dead, these have been most authori-

[1] Samaria was so named in reference to its restoration by Gabinius, the proconsul of Syria. See Josephus (*Antiq.* book xiv. ch. x.), who states that Gabinius traversed Judea, and gave orders for the rebuilding of such towns as he found destroyed; and that in this way Samaria, Azotus, Scythopolis, Antedon, Raphia, Dora, Marissa, and not a few others, were restored.

[2] The text is: ἦν Ὀλυμπιὰς ρπθ, ἥτις πρὸ ϛ' καλανδῶν Μαρτίων κατὰ Ἀρτιοχεῖς κδ' ἔτει ἤχθη, δι' ἧς ἐπὶ τῶν ἰδίων ὁρίων ἴστη ὁ ἐνιαυτός. In every fourth year the 24th day of February (= vi. Cal. Mart.) was reckoned twice. There were three different eras of Antioch, of which the one most commonly used began in November 49 B.C. Migne refers the reader to the notes of Goarus on the passage, which we have not seen. The sense of this obscure passage seems to be, that that period formed another fixed point in chronology.

tatively set forth by His disciples and apostles before us. On the whole world there pressed a most fearful darkness; and the rocks were rent by an earthquake, and many places in Judea and other districts were thrown down. This darkness Thallus, in the third book of his *History*, calls, as appears to me without reason, an eclipse of the sun. For the Hebrews celebrate the passover on the 14th day according to the moon, and the passion of our Saviour falls on the day before the passover; but an eclipse of the sun takes place only when the moon comes under the sun. And it cannot happen at any other time but in the interval between the first day of the new moon and the last of the old, that is, at their junction: how then should an eclipse be supposed to happen when the moon is almost diametrically opposite the sun? Let that opinion pass however; let it carry the majority with it; and let this portent of the world be deemed an eclipse of the sun, like others a portent only to the eye (ἔν τι κατὰ τὴν ὄψιν). Phlegon records that, in the time of Tiberius Cæsar, at full moon, there was a full eclipse of the sun from the sixth hour to the ninth—manifestly that one of which we speak. But what has an eclipse in common with an earthquake, the rending rocks, and the resurrection of the dead, and so great a perturbation throughout the universe? Surely no such event as this is recorded for a long period. But it was a darkness induced by God, because the Lord happened then to suffer. And calculation makes out that the period of 70 weeks, as noted in Daniel, is completed at this time.

2. From Artaxerxes, moreover, 70 weeks are reckoned up to the time of Christ, according to the numeration of the Jews. For from Nehemiah, who was sent by Artaxerxes to people Jerusalem, about the 120th year of the Persian empire, and in the 20th year of Artaxerxes himself, and the 4th year of the 83d Olympiad, up to this time, which was the 2d year of the 102d Olympiad, and the 16th year of the reign of Tiberius Cæsar, there are given 475 years, which make 490 Hebrew years, since they measure the years by the lunar month of $29\frac{1}{2}$ days, as may easily be explained, the annual period according to the sun consisting of $365\frac{1}{4}$ days, while

CHRONOGRAPHY OF JULIUS AFRICANUS. 189

the lunar period of 12 months has 11¼ days less. For which reason the Greeks and the Jews insert three intercalary months every eight years. For 8 times 11¼ days make 3 months. The 475 years, therefore, contain 59 periods of 8 years and three months over : thus, the three intercalary months for every 8 years being added, we get 15 years, and these together with the 475 years make 70 weeks. Let no one now think us unskilled in the calculations of astronomy, when we fix without further ado the number of days at 365¼. For it is not in ignorance of the truth, but rather by reason of exact study (διὰ τὴν λεπτολογίαν), that we have stated our opinion so shortly. But let what follows also be presented as in outline (or in a table, ὡς ἐν γραφῇ) to those who endeavour to inquire minutely into all things.

3. Each year in the general consists of 365 days; and the space of a day and night being divided into nineteen parts, we have also, five of these. And in saying that the year consists of 365¼ days, and there being the five nineteenth parts .... to the 475 there are 6¼ days. Furthermore, we find, according to exact computation, that the lunar month has 29½ days ....[1] And these come to (καταγίνεται) a little time. Now it happens that from the 20th year of the reign of Artaxerxes (as it is given in Ezra among the Hebrews), which, according to the Greeks, was the 4th year of the 80th Olympiad, to the 16th year of Tiberius Cæsar, which was the second year of the 102d Olympiad, there are in all the 475 years already noted, which in the Hebrew system make 490 years, as has been previously stated, that is, 70 weeks, by which period the time of Christ's advent was measured in the announcement made to Daniel by Gabriel. And if any

[1] The text in the beginning of this section is hopelessly corrupt. Scaliger declares that neither could he follow these things, nor did the man that dreamt them understand them. We may subjoin the Greek text as it stands in Migne : Μεταξὺ δὲ τοῦ λέγειν τὸν ἐνιαυτὸν ἡμιρῶν τξι, καὶ τετραμορίου, καὶ τῶν ἀπὸ ιθ' τῆς νυχθημέρου, μερῶν ἱ .... εἰς τὰ ὑαί, ἡμέραι τὸ παράλληλον εἰσί σ', καὶ τετραμόριον. Ἔτι γε μὴν τὸν τῆς σιζ ἡμης μῆνα κατὰ τὴν ἀκριβῆ λεπτολογίαν εὑρίσκομεν κθ, καὶ ἡμισείας ἡμέρας ἐν νυκτὸς διαιρεθείσης εἰς μέρη σὶ, τούτων τὰ ο', καὶ ἥμισυ ... ἃ γίνεται ἐν κοστοτέταρτα τρία.

one thinks that the 15 Hebrew years added to the others involve us in an error of 10, nothing at least which cannot be accounted for has been introduced. And the 1½ week which we suppose must be added to make the whole number, meets the question about the 15 years, and removes the difficulty about the time; and that the prophecies are usually put forth in a somewhat symbolic form, is quite evident.

4. As far, then, as is in our power, we have taken the Scripture, I think, correctly; especially seeing that the preceding section about the vision seems to state the whole matter shortly, its first words being, "In the third year of the reign of Belshazzar,"[1] where he prophesies of the subversion of the Persian power by the Greeks, which empires are symbolized in the prophecy under the figures of the ram and the goat respectively.[2] "The sacrifice," he says, "shall be abolished, and the holy places shall be made desolate, so as to be trodden under foot; which things shall be determined within 2300 days."[2] For if we take the day as a month, just as elsewhere in prophecy days are taken as years, and in different places are used in different ways, reducing the period in the same way as has been done above to Hebrew months, we shall find the period fully made out to the 20th year of the reign of Artaxerxes, from the capture of Jerusalem. For there are given thus 185 years, and one year falls to be added to these—the year in which Nehemiah built the wall of the city. In 186 years, therefore, we find 2300 Hebrew months, as 8 years have in addition 3 intercalary months. From Artaxerxes, again, in whose time the command went forth that Jerusalem should be built, there are 70 weeks. These matters, however, we have discussed by themselves, and with greater exactness, in our book *On the Weeks and this Prophecy*. But I am amazed that the Jews deny that the Lord has yet come, and that the followers of Marcion refuse to admit that His coming was predicted in the prophecies when the Scriptures display the matter so openly to our view. (*And after something else*): The period, then, to the advent of the Lord from Adam and the creation is 5531 years, from which epoch to

---

[1] Dan. viii. 1.   [2] Dan. viii. 13, 14.

the 250th Olympiad there are 192 years, as has been shown above.

XIX.

[In Basil, *De Spiritu Sancto*, ch. xxix. § 73; *Works*, vol. iii. p. 61, edit. Paris.]

For we who both know the measure of those words,[1] and are not ignorant of the grace of faith, give thanks to the Father,[2] who has bestowed on us His creatures Jesus Christ the Saviour of all, and our Lord;[3] to whom be glory and majesty, with the Holy Spirit, for ever.

THE PASSION OF ST. SYMPHOROSA AND HER SEVEN SONS.

[Gallandi, *Bibl. Patrum*, vol. i. Proleg. p. lxxi. and p. 329.]

[The text is given from the edition of Ruinart. His preface, which Migne also cites, is as follows: "The narrative of the martyrdom of St. Symphorosa and her seven sons, which we here publish, is ascribed in the MSS. to Julius Africanus, a writer of the highest repute. And it may perhaps have been inserted in his books on *Chronography*,—a work which Eusebius (*Hist. Eccles.* vi. 31) testifies to have been written with the greatest care, since in these he detailed the chief events in history from the foundation of the world to the times of the Emperor Heliogabalus. As that work, however, is lost, that this narrative is really to be ascribed to Africanus, I would not venture positively to assert, although at the same time there seems no ground for doubting its genuineness. We print it, moreover, from the editions of Mombritius, Surius, and Cardulus, collated with two Colbert MSS. and one in the library of the Sorbonne. The occasion for

---

[1] For ῥημάτων, words, three MSS. give ῥητῶν, sayings.
[2] For ἡμῖν Πατρί there is another reading, ἡμῶν πατράσι = to Him who gave to our fathers.
[3] These words, "and our Lord," are wanting in three MSS.

the death of these saints was found in the vicinity of that most famous palace which was built by Adrian at his country seat at Tiber, according to Spartianus. For when the emperor gave orders that this palace, which he had built for his pleasure, should be purified by some piacular ceremonies, the priests seized this opportunity for accusing Symphorosa, alleging that the gods would not be satisfied until Symphorosa should either sacrifice to them or be herself sacrificed; which last thing was done by Hadrian, whom, from many others of his deeds, we know to have been exceedingly superstitious, about the year of Christ 120, that is, about the beginning of his reign, at which period indeed, as Dio Cassius observes, that emperor put a great number to death. The memory of these martyrs, moreover, is celebrated in all the most ancient martyrologies, although they assign different days for it. The Roman, along with Notker, fixes their festival for the 18th July, Rabanus for the 21st of the same month, Usuardus and Ado for the 21st June. In the Tiburtine road there still exists the rubbish of an old church, as Aringhi states (*Rom. Subter.* iv. 17), which was consecrated to God under their name, and which still retains the title, *To the Seven Brothers.* I have no doubt that it was built in that place to which the pontiffs in the *Acta*, sec. iv., gave the name, *To the Seven Biothanati*, *i.e.* those cut off by a violent death, as Baronius remarks, at the year 138." So far Ruinart : see also Tillemont, *Mém. Eccles.* ii. pp. 241 and 595; and the Bollandists, *Act. S.S. Junii*, vol. iv. p. 350.]

1. When Adrian had built a palace, and wished to dedicate it by that wicked ceremonial, and began to seek responses by sacrifices to idols, and to the demons that dwell in idols, they replied,[1] and said : " The widow Symphorosa, with her seven sons, wounds us day by day in invoking her God. If she therefore, together with her sons, shall offer sacrifice, we promise to make good all that you ask." Then Adrian ordered her to be seized, along with her sons, and advised them in courteous terms to consent to offer sacrifice to the

[1] See Eusebius, *Life of Constantine*, ii. 50.

idols. To him, however, the blessed Symphorosa answered: "My husband Getulius,[1] together with his brother Amantius, when they were tribunes in thy service, suffered different punishments for the name of Christ, rather than consent to sacrifice to idols, and, like good athletes, they overcame thy demons in death. For, rather than be prevailed on, they chose to be beheaded, and suffered death; which death, being endured for the name of Christ, gained them temporal ignominy indeed among men of this earth, but everlasting honour and glory among the angels; and moving now among them, and exhibiting[2] the trophies of their sufferings, they enjoy eternal life with the King eternal in the heavens."

2. The Emperor Adrian said to the holy Symphorosa: "Either sacrifice thou along with thy sons to the omnipotent gods, or else I shall cause thee to be sacrificed thyself, together with thy sons." The blessed Symphorosa answered: "And whence is this great good to me, that I should be deemed worthy along with my sons to be offered as an oblation to God?"[3] The Emperor Adrian said: "I shall cause thee to be sacrificed to my gods." The blessed Symphorosa replied: "Thy gods cannot take me in sacrifice; but if I am burned for the name of Christ, my God, I shall rather consume those demons of thine." The Emperor Adrian said: "Choose thou one of these alternatives: either sacrifice to my gods, or perish by an evil death." The blessed Symphorosa replied: "Thou thinkest that my mind can be altered by some kind of terror; whereas I long to rest with my husband Getulius,[4] whom thou didst put to death for Christ's name." Then the Emperor Adrian ordered her to be led away to the temple of Hercules, and there first to be beaten with blows on the cheek, and afterwards to be suspended by the hair. But when by no argument and by no terror could he divert her from her good

---

[1] The Martyrologies celebrate their memory on the 10th June: one of the Colbert MSS. gives *Zoticus* for *Getulius*.

[2] A Colbert MS. gives "laudantes" = praising.

[3] This response, along with the next interrogation, is wanting in the Colbert manuscript.

[4] Sur., Card., and the Colbert Codex give "Zoticus."

resolution, he ordered her to be thrown into the river with a large stone fastened to her neck. And her brother Eugenius, principal of the district of Tiber, picked up her body, and buried it in a suburb of the same city.

3. Then, on another day, the Emperor Adrian ordered all her seven sons to be brought before him in company; and when he had challenged them to sacrifice to idols, and perceived that they yielded by no means to his threats and terrors, he ordered seven stakes to be fixed around the temple of Hercules, and commanded them to be stretched on the blocks there. And he ordered Crescens, the first, to be transfixed in the throat; and Julian, the second, to be stabbed in the breast; and Nemesius, the third, to be struck through the heart; and Primitivus, the fourth, to be wounded in the navel; and Justin, the fifth, to be struck through in the back with a sword; and Stracteus,[1] the sixth, to be wounded in the side; and Eugenius, the seventh, to be cleft in twain from the head downwards.

4. The next day again the Emperor Adrian came to the temple of Hercules, and ordered their bodies to be carried off together, and cast into a deep pit; and the pontiffs gave to that place the name, *To the Seven Biothanati*.[2] After these things the persecution ceased for a year and a half, in which period the holy bodies of all the martyrs were honoured, and consigned with all care to tumuli erected for that purpose, and their names are written in the book of life. The natal day, moreover, of the holy martyrs of Christ, the blessed Symphorosa and her seven sons, Crescens, Julian, Nemesius, Primitivus, Justin, Stracteus, and Eugenius, is held on the 18th July. Their bodies rest on the Tiburtine road, at the eighth mile-stone from the city, under the kingship of our Lord Jesus Christ, to whom is honour and glory for ever and ever. Amen.

[1] The Colbert Codex reads "Extacteus;" Cardulus gives "Stacteus," by which name he is designated beneath by them all.

[2] In one of the Colbert codices, and in another from the Sorbonne, there is a passage inserted here about the death of Adrian, which is said to have happened a little after that of these martyrs.

AFRICANUS' NARRATIVE OF EVENTS HAPPENING IN PERSIA ON THE BIRTH OF CHRIST.

[Edited from two Munich codices by J. Chr. von. Aretin, in his *Beiträge zur Geschichte und Literatur*, anno 1804, p. ii. p. 49.]

[The best introduction to this production will be the following preface, as given in Migne:—Many men of learning thus far have been of opinion that the narrative by Africanus of events happening in Persia on Christ's birth, which is extant in two MSS. in the Electoral Library of Munich, and in one belonging to the Imperial Library of Vienna, is a fragment of that famous work which Sextus Julius Africanus, a Christian author of the third century after Christ, composed on the history of the world in the chronological order of events up to the reign of Macrinus, and presented in five books to Alexander, son of Mammæa, with the view of obtaining the restoration of his native town Emmaus. With the same expectation which I see incited Lambecius and his compendiator Nesselius, I, too, set myself with the greatest eagerness to go over the codices of our Electoral Library.... But, as the common proverb goes, I found coals instead of treasure. This narrative, so far from its being to be ascribed to a writer well reputed by the common voice of antiquity, does not contain anything worthy of the genius of the chronographer Africanus. Wherefore, since by the unanimous testimony of the ancients he was a man of consummate learning and sharpest judgment, while the author of the *Cesti*, which also puts forward the name of Africanus, has been long marked by critics with the character either of anile credulity, or of a marvellous propensity to superstitious fancies, I can readily fall in with the opinion of those who think that he is a different person from the chronographer, and would ascribe this wretched production also to him. But, dear reader, on perusing these pages, if your indignation is not stirred against the man's rashness, you will at least join with me in laughing at his prodigious follies, and will learn, at the same time, that the testimonies of men most distinguished for learning are not to be rated so highly as to supersede personal examination when opportunity permits.]

AFRICANUS' NARRATIVE OF EVENTS HAPPENING IN PERSIA ON THE INCARNATION OF OUR LORD AND GOD AND SAVIOUR JESUS CHRIST.

Christ first of all became known from Persia. For nothing escapes the learned jurists of that country, who investigate all things with the utmost care. The facts,[1] therefore, which are inscribed upon the golden plates,[2] and laid up in the royal temples, I shall record; for it is from the temples there, and the priests connected with them, that the name of Christ has been heard of. Now there is a temple there to Juno, surpassing even the royal palace, which temple Cyrus, that prince instructed in all piety, built, and in which he dedicated in honour of the gods golden and silver statues, and adorned them with precious stones,—that I may not waste words in a profuse description of that ornamentation. Now about that time (as the records on the plates testify), the king having entered the temple, with the view of getting an interpretation of certain dreams, was addressed by the priest Prupupius thus: I congratulate thee, master: Juno has conceived. And the king, smiling, said to him, Has she who is dead conceived? And he said, Yes, she who was dead has come to life again, and begets life. And the king said, What is this? explain it to me. And he replied, In truth, master, the time for these things is at hand. For during the whole night the images, both of gods and goddesses, continued beating the ground, saying to each other, Come, let us congratulate Juno. And they say to me, Prophet, come forward; congratulate Juno, for she has been embraced. And I said, How can she be embraced who no longer exists? To which they reply, She has come to life again, and is no longer

---

[1] The MSS. read γάρ, for.
[2] The term in the original (ἀλκλαρίαις) is one altogether foreign to Greek, and seems to be of Arabic origin. The sense, however, is evident from the use of synonymous terms in the context.

called Juno,[1] but Urania. For the mighty Sol has embraced her. Then the goddesses say to the gods, making the matter plainer, *Pege*[2] is she who is embraced; for did not Juno espouse an artificer? And the gods say, That she is rightly called *Pege*, we admit. Her name, moreover, is *Myria*; for she bears in her womb, as in the deep, a vessel of a myriad talents' burden. And as to this title Pege, let it be understood thus: This stream of water sends forth the perennial stream of spirit,—a stream containing but a single fish,[3] taken with the hook of Divinity, and sustaining the whole world with its flesh as though it were in the sea. You have well said, She has an artificer [in espousal]; but by that espousal she does not bear an artificer on an equality with herself. For this artificer who is born, the son of the chief artificer, framed by his excellent skill the roof of the third heavens, and established by his word this lower world, with its threefold sphere[4] of habitation.

Thus, then, the statues disputed with each other concerning Juno and Pege, and [at length] with one voice they said: When the day is finished, we all, gods and goddesses, shall know the matter clearly. Now, therefore, master, tarry for the rest of the day. For the matter shall certainly come to pass. For that which emerges is no common affair.

And when the king abode there and watched the statues, the harpers of their own accord began to strike their harps, and the muses to sing; and whatsoever creatures were within, whether quadruped or fowl, in silver and gold, uttered their several voices. And as the king shuddered, and was filled

---

[1] There is a play upon the words, perhaps, in the original. The Greek term for Juno ("Ηρα) may be derived from ἔρα, *terra*, so that the antithesis intended is, "She is no longer called *Earthly*, but *Heavenly*."

[2] *i.e.* Fountain, Spring, or Stream.

[3] The initial letters of the Greek 'Ιησοῦς Χριστός Θεοῦ Υἱός Σωτήρ, *i.e.* "Jesus Christ the Son of God the Saviour," when joined together, make the word ἰχθύς, *i.e.* fish; and the fathers used the word, therefore, as a mystic symbol of Christ, who could live in the depth of our mortality as in the abyss of the sea.

[4] *i.e.* as sea, land, and sky.

with great fear, he was about to retire. For he could not endure the spontaneous tumult. The priest therefore said to him, Remain, O king, for the full revelation is at hand which the God of gods has chosen to declare to us.

And when these things were said, the roof was opened, and a bright star descended and stood above the pillar of Pege, and a voice was heard to this effect: Sovereign Pege, the mighty Sun has sent me to make the announcement to you, and at the same time to do you service in parturition, designing blameless nuptials with you, O mother of the chief of all ranks of being, bride of the triune Deity. And the child begotten by extraordinary generation is called the *Beginning* and the *End*,—the beginning of salvation, and the end of perdition.

And when this word was spoken, all the statues fell upon their faces, that of Pege alone standing, on which also a royal diadem was found placed, having on its upper side a star set in a carbuncle and an emerald. And on its lower side the star rested.

And the king forthwith gave orders to bring in all the interpreters of prodigies, and the sages who were under his dominion. And when all the heralds sped with their proclamations, all these assembled in the temple. And when they saw the star above Pege, and the diadem with the star and the stone, and the statues lying on the floor, they said: O king, a root (offspring) divine and princely has risen, bearing the image of the King of heaven and earth. For Pege-Myria is the daughter of the Bethlehemite Pege. And the diadem is the mark of a king, and the star is a celestial announcement of portents to fall on the earth. But of Judah has arisen a kingdom which shall subvert all the memorials of the Jews. And the prostration of the gods upon the floor prefigured the end of their honour. For he who comes, being of more ancient dignity, shall displace all the recent. Now therefore, O king, send to Jerusalem. For you will find the Christ of the Omnipotent God borne in bodily form in the bodily arms of a woman. And the star remained above the statue of Pege, called the

Celestial, until the wise men came forth, and then it went with them.

And then, in the depth of evening, Dionysus appeared in the temple, unaccompanied by the Satyrs, and said to the images: Pege is not one of us, but stands far above us, in that she gives birth to a man whose conception is in divine fashion (θείας τύχης σύλλημμα). O priest Prupupius! what dost thou tarrying here? An action, indicated in writings of old (ἔγγραφος), has come upon us, and we shall be convicted as false by a person of power and energy (ἐμπράκτου). Wherein we have been deceivers, we have been deceivers; and wherein we have ruled, we have ruled. No longer give we oracular responses. Gone from us is our honour. Without glory and reward are we become. There is One, and One only, who receives again at the hands of all His proper honour. For the rest, be not disturbed.[1] No longer shall the Persians exact tribute of earth and sky. For He who established these things is at hand, to bring practical tribute (πρακτικοὺς φόρους) to Him who sent Him, to renew the ancient image, and to put image with image, and bring the dissimilar to similarity. Heaven rejoices with earth, and earth itself exults at receiving matter of exultation from heaven. Things which have not happened above, have happened on earth beneath. He whom the order of the blessed has not seen, is seen by the order of the miserable. Flame threatens those; dew attends these. To Myria is given the blessed lot of bearing Pege in Bethlehem, and of conceiving grace of grace. Judæa has seen its bloom, and this country is fading. To Gentiles and aliens, salvation is come; to the wretched, relief is ministered abundantly. With right do women dance, and say, Lady Pege, Spring-bearer, thou mother of the heavenly constellation. Thou cloud that bringest us dew after heat, remember thy dependants, O mistress.

The king then, without delay, sent some of the Magi under his dominion with gifts, the star showing them the way. And when they returned, they narrated to the men of

[1] The text gives θροβαδεῖ, for which Migne proposes θορύβηθι.

that time those same things which were also written on the plates of gold, and which were to the following effect:

When we came to Jerusalem, the sign, together with our arrival, roused all the people. How is this, say they, that wise men of the Persians are here, and that along with them there is this strange stellar phenomenon? And the chief of the Jews interrogated us in this way: What is this that attends you,[1] and with what purpose are you here? And we said: He whom ye call Messias is born. And they were confounded, and dared not withstand us. But they said to us, By the justice of Heaven, tell us what ye know of this matter. And we made answer to them: Ye labour under unbelief; and neither without an oath nor with an oath do ye believe us, but ye follow your own heedless counsel. For the Christ, the Son of the Most High, is born, and He is the subverter of your law and synagogues. And therefore is it that, struck with this most excellent response as with a dart,[2] ye hear in bitterness this name which has come upon you suddenly. And they then, taking counsel together, urged us to accept their gifts, and tell to none that such an event had taken place in that land of theirs, lest, as they say, *a revolt rise against us*. But we replied: We have brought gifts in His honour, with the view of proclaiming those mighty things which we know to have happened in our country on occasion of His birth; and do ye bid us take your bribes, and conceal the things which have been communicated to us by the Divinity who is above the heavens, and neglect the commandments of our proper King? And after urging many considerations on us, they gave the matter up. And when the king of Judea sent for us and had some converse with us, and put to us certain questions as to the statements we made to him, we acted in the same manner, until he was thoroughly enraged at our replies. We left him accordingly, without giving any greater heed to him than to any common person.

And we came to that place then to which we were sent,

---

[1] τί τὸ ἑπόμενον, perhaps meant for, What business brings you?
[2] ὑπὲρ μαντείας ἀρίστης ὥσπερ κατατοξευόμενοι.

and saw the mother and the child, the star indicating to us the royal babe. And we said to the mother: What art thou named, O renowned mother? And she says: Mary, masters. And we said to her: Whence art thou sprung (ὁρμωμένη)? And she replies: From this district of the Bethlehemites (Βηθλεωτῶν). Then said we: Hast thou not had a husband? And she answers: I was only betrothed with a view to the marriage convenant, my thoughts being far removed from this. For I had no mind to come to this. And while I was giving very little concern to it, when a certain Sabbath dawned, and straightway at the rising of the sun, an angel appeared to me bringing me suddenly the glad tidings of a son. And in trouble I cried out, Be it not so to me, Lord, for I have not a husband. And he persuaded me to believe, that by the will of God I should have this son.

Then said we to her: Mother, mother, all the gods of the Persians have called thee blessed. Thy glory is great; for thou art exalted above all women of renown, and thou art shown to be more queenly than all queens.

The child, moreover, was seated on the ground, being, as she said, in His second year, and having in part the likeness of His mother. And she had long hands,[1] and a body somewhat delicate; and her colour was like that of ripe wheat (σιτόχροος); and she was of a round face, and had her hair bound up. And as we had along with us a servant skilled in painting from the life, we brought with us to our country a likeness of them both; and it was placed by our hand in the sacred (διοπετεῖ) temple, with this inscription on it: To Jove the Sun, the mighty God, the King of Jesus, the power of Persia dedicated this.

And taking the child up, each of us in turn, and bearing Him in our arms, we saluted Him and worshipped Him, and presented to Him gold, and myrrh, and frankincense, addressing Him thus: We gift Thee with Thine own, O Jesus, Ruler of heaven. Ill would things unordered be ordered, wert Thou not at hand. In no other way could things

[1] μακρὰς τὰς χεῖρας according to Migne, instead of the reading of the manuscripts, μακρὶν τὴν χῆραν ἔχουσα.

heavenly be brought into conjunction with things earthly, but by Thy descent. Such service cannot be discharged, if only the servant is sent us, as when the Master Himself is present; neither can so much be achieved when the king sends only his satraps to war, as when the king is there himself. It became the wisdom of Thy system, that Thou shouldst deal in this manner with men.[1]

And the child leaped and laughed at our caresses and words. And when we had bidden the mother farewell (συν-ταξάμενοι), and when she had shown us honour, and we had testified to her the reverence which became us, we came again to the place in which we lodged. And at eventide there appeared to us one of a terrible and fearful countenance, saying: Get ye out quickly, lest ye be taken in a snare. And we in terror said: And who is he, O divine leader, that plotteth against so august an embassage? And he replied: Herod; but get you up straightway and depart in safety and peace.

And we made speed to depart thence in all earnestness; and we reported in Jerusalem all that we had seen. Behold, then, the great things that we have told you regarding Christ; and we saw Christ our Saviour, who was made known as both God and man. To Him be the glory and the power unto the ages of the ages. Amen.

[1] The manuscripts give ἀντάρτας, for which Migne proposes ἀνθρώπους or ἀντεργάτας.

THE EPISTLES OF POPE CALLISTUS.

CALLISTUS succeeded Zephyrinus in the bishopric of Rome, and discharged the duties of that office for five years. This is all the information which Eusebius[1] gives us in regard to Callistus. Later writers make many other statements.

The letters attributed to him form part of the False Decretals of the pseudo-Isidorus, mentioned in the notice of Zephyrinus.

[Mansi, *Concil.* i. 737.]

THE FIRST EPISTLE.

TO BISHOP BENEDICTUS.

On the Fasts of the Four Seasons, and that no one should take up an Accusation against a Doctor (teacher).

CALLISTUS, archbishop of the church catholic in the city of Rome, to Benedictus, our brother and bishop, greeting in the Lord.

By the love of the brotherhood we are bound, and by our apostolic rule we are constrained, to give answer to the inquiries of the brethren, according to what the Lord has given us, and to furnish them with the authority of the seal of the apostles.

I.

[Of the seasons for fasting.]

Fasting, which ye have learned to hold three times in the year among us, we decree now to take place, as more suitable, in four seasons; so that even as the year revolves through four seasons, we too may keep a solemn fast quarterly in

---

[1] In his *Chronicon* and *Hist. Eccl.* vi. 21.

the four seasons of the year. And as we are replenished with corn, and wine, and oil for the nourishment of our bodies, so let us be replenished with fasting for the nourishment of our souls, in accordance with the word of the prophet Zechariah, who says, "The word of the Lord came to me, saying, Thus saith the Lord of hosts, As I thought to punish you, when your fathers provoked me to wrath, and I repented not; so again have I thought in these days to do well unto Jerusalem, and to the house of Judah: fear ye not. These are the things that ye shall do: Speak ye every man the truth to his neighbour; judge the truth and the judgment of peace in your gates; and let none of you imagine evil in your hearts against his neighbour, and love no false oath: for all these are things that I hate, saith the Lord of hosts. And the word of the Lord of hosts came unto me, saying, Thus saith the Lord of hosts, The fast of the fourth month, and the fast of the fifth, and the fast of the seventh, and the fast of the tenth, shall be to the house of the Lord joy and gladness, and cheerful feasts; only love the truth and peace, saith the Lord of hosts."[1] In this, then, we ought to be all of one mind, so that, according to apostolic teaching, we may all say the same thing, and that there be no divisions among us. Let us then be perfect in the same mind, and in the same judgment;[2] in ready zeal for which work we congratulate ourselves on having your affection as our partner. For it is not meet for the members to be at variance with the head; but, according to the testimony of sacred Scripture,[3] all the members should follow the head. It is matter of doubt, moreover, to no one, that the church of the apostles is the mother of all the churches, from whose ordinances it is not right that you should deviate to any extent. And as the Son of God came to do the Father's will, so shall ye fulfil the will of your mother, which is the church, the head of which, as has been stated already, is the church of Rome. Wherefore, whatsoever may be done against the discipline of this church, without the decision of justice, cannot on any account be permitted to be held valid.

[1] Zech. viii. 1-19. [2] 1 Pet. iii. [3] 1 Cor. xii.

II.

[Of accusations against doctors.]

Moreover, let no one take up an accusation against a doctor (teacher), because it is not right for sons to find fault with fathers, nor for slaves to wound their masters. Now, all those whom they instruct are sons of doctors; and as sons ought to love their fathers after the flesh, so ought they to love their spiritual fathers. For he does not live rightly who does not believe rightly, or who reprehends fathers, or calumniates them. Doctors therefore, who are also called fathers, are rather to be borne with than reprehended, unless they err from the true faith. Let no one, consequently, accuse a doctor by writing (*per scripta*); neither let him answer to any accuser, unless he be one who is trustworthy and recognised by law, and who leads also a life and conversation free from reproach. For it is a thing unworthy that a doctor should reply to a foolish and ignorant person, and one who leads a reprehensible life, according to the man's folly; as Scripture says, Answer not a fool according to his folly.[1] He does not live rightly who does not believe rightly. He means nothing evil who is faithful. If any one is faithful (a believer), let him see to it that he make no false allegations, nor lay a snare for any man. The faithful man acts always in faith; and the unfaithful man plots cunningly, and strives to work the ruin of those who are faithful, and who live in piety and righteousness, because like seeks like. The unfaithful man is one dead in the living body. And on the other hand, the discourse of the man of faith guards the life of his hearers. For as the catholic doctor, and especially the priest of the Lord, ought to be involved in no error, so ought he to be wronged by no machination or passion. Holy Scripture indeed says, Go not after thy lusts, but refrain thyself from thine appetites;[2] and we must resist many allurements of this world, and many vanities, in order that the integrity of a true continence may be obtained, whereof the first blemish is pride, the beginning of transgression and

[1] Prov. xxvi. 4.   [2] Ecclus. xviii. 30.

the origin of sin; for the mind with lustful will knows neither to abstain nor to give itself to piety. No good man has an enemy except in the wicked, who are permitted to be such only in order that the good man may be corrected or exercised through their means. Whatever, therefore, is faultless is defended by the church catholic. Neither for prince, nor for any one who observes piety, is it lawful to venture anything contrary to the divine injunctions. Consequently an unjust judgment, or an unjust decision (*diffinitio*), instituted or enforced by judges under the fear or by the command of a prince, or any bishop or person of influence, cannot be valid. The religious man ought not to hold it enough merely to refrain from entering into the enmities of others, or increasing them by evil speech, unless he also make it his study to extinguish them by good speech.[1] Better is a humble confession in evil deeds, than a proud boasting in good deeds.[2] Moreover, all who live the blessed life, choose rather to run that course in the proper estate of peace and righteousness, than to involve themselves in the avenging pains of our sins.[3] For I am mindful that I preside over the church under the name of him whose confession was honoured by our Lord Jesus Christ, and whose faith ever destroys all errors. And I understand that I am not at liberty to act otherwise than to expend all my efforts on that cause in which the well-being of the universal church is at stake (*infestatur*). I hope, too, that the mercy of God will so favour us, that, with the help of His clemency, every deadly disease may be removed, God Himself expelling it, and that whatever may be done wholesomely, under His inspiration and help, may be accomplished to the praise of thy faith and devotion. For all things cannot otherwise be safe, unless, as far as pertains to the service of the divine office, sacerdotal authority upholds them. Given on the 21st day of November, in the consulship of the most illustrious Antoninus and Alexander.[4]

---

[1] See Augustine's *Confessions*, book ix. ch. ix.
[2] See Augustine on Ps. xciii.
[3] See Ambrose, Epistle xxi.
[4] In the year 222.

THE SECOND EPISTLE.

TO ALL THE BISHOPS OF GAUL.

[Of conspiracies and other illicit pursuits, that they be not engaged in, and of the restoration of the lapsed after penitence.] :

Callistus to our most dearly beloved brethren, all the bishops settled throughout Gaul.

By the report of very many, we learn that your love, by the zeal of the Holy Spirit, holds and guides the helm of the church so firmly in the face of all assaults, that by God's will it is conscious neither of shipwreck nor of the losses of shipwreck. Rejoicing, therefore, in such testimonies, we beg you not to permit anything to be done in those parts contrary to the apostolic statutes; but, supported by our authority, do ye check what is injurious, and prohibit what is unlawful.

I.

[Of those who conspire against bishops, or who take part with such.]

Now we have heard that the crime of conspiracies prevails in your parts, and it has been shown us that the people are conspiring against their bishops; of which crime the craft is hateful, not only among Christians, but even among the heathen, and it is forbidden by foreign laws. And therefore the laws not only of the church, but of the world, condemn those who are guilty of this crime; and not only those indeed who actually conspire, but those also who take part with such.[1] Our predecessors, moreover, together with a very numerous body of bishops, ordained that any (guilty of this offence) among those who are set in the honour of the priesthood, and who belong to the clergy, should be deprived of the honour which they enjoy; and they ordered that others should be cut off from communion, and expelled from the church; and they decreed, at the same time, that all men of both orders should be infamous (*infames*); and that, too,

[1] Cf. Rom. i. 32.

not only for those who did the deed, but for those also who took part with such. For it is but equitable that those who despise the divine mandates, and prove themselves disobedient to the ordinances of the fathers, should be chastised with severer penalties, in order that others may fear to do such things, and that all may rejoice in brotherly concord, and all take to themselves the example of severity and goodness. For if (which may God forbid) we neglect the care of the church, and are regardless of its strength, our slothfulness will destroy discipline, and injury will be done assuredly to the souls of the faithful. Such persons, moreover, are not to be admitted to accuse any one: neither can their voice, nor that of those who are under the ban, injure or criminate any man.

II.

[Of those who have intercourse with excommunicated persons, or with unbelievers.]

Those, too, who are excommunicated by the priests, let no one receive previous to the just examination of both sides; nor let him have any intercourse with such in speech, or in eating or drinking, or in the salutation with the kiss, nor let him greet such; because, whosoever wittingly holds intercourse with the excommunicated in these or other prohibited matters, will subject himself, according to the ordinance of the apostles,[1] to like excommunication. From these, therefore, let clergy and laity keep themselves, if they would not have the same penalty to endure. Also do not join the unbelievers, neither have any fellowship with them. They who do such things, indeed, are judged not as believers, but as unbelievers. Whence the apostle says: "What part hath he that believeth with an infidel? or what fellowship hath righteousness with unrighteousness?"[2]

[1] The reference is to the 11th and 12th of the canons of the apostles.
[2] 2 Cor. vi. 14, 15.

III.

[That no bishop should presume in anything pertaining to another's parish, and of the transference of bishops.]

Let no one, again, trespass upon the boundaries of another, nor presume to judge or excommunicate one belonging to another's parish; because such judgment or ordination, or excommunication or condemnation, shall neither be ratified nor have any virtue; since no one shall be bound by the decision of another judge than his own, neither shall he be condemned by such. Whence also the Lord speaks to this effect: "Pass not the ancient landmarks which thy fathers have set."[1] Moreover, let no primate or metropolitan [invade] the church or parish of a diocesan (*diœcesani*), or presume to excommunicate or judge any one belonging to his parish, or do anything without his counsel or judgment; but let him observe this law, which has been laid down by the apostles[2] and fathers, and our predecessors, and has been ratified by us: to wit, that if any metropolitan bishop, except in that which pertains to his own proper parish alone, shall attempt to do anything without the counsel and good-will of all the con-provincial bishops, he will do it at the risk of his position, and what he does in this manner shall be held null and void; but whatever it may be necessary to do or to arrange with regard to the cases of the body of provincial bishops, and the necessities of their churches and clergy and laity, this should be done by consent of all the pontiffs of the same province, and that too without any pride of lordship, but with the most humble and harmonious action, even as the Lord says: "I came not to be ministered unto, but to minister."[3] And in another passage he says: "And whosoever of you is the greater, shall be your servant,"[4] and so forth. And in like manner the bishops of the same province themselves should do all things in counsel with him, except so much as pertains to their own proper parishes, in accordance with the statutes of the holy fathers (who, although

[1] Prov. xxii. 28.
[2] Canons 35 and 36.
[3] Matt. xx. 28.
[4] Mark x. 44.

they have preceded us by a certain interval of time, have yet drawn the light of truth and faith from one and the same fountain of purity, and have sought the prosperity of the church of God and the common advantage of all Christians by the same enlightening and guiding Spirit), that with one mind, and one mouth, and one accord, the Holy Trinity may be glorified for ever. No primate, no metropolitan, nor any of the other bishops, is at liberty to enter the seat of another, or to occupy a possession which does not pertain to him, and which forms part of the parish of another bishop, at the direction of any one, unless he is invited by him to whose jurisdiction it is acknowledged to belong; nor can he set about any arrangement or ordinance, or judgment there, if he wishes to keep the honour of his station. But if he presume to do otherwise, he shall be condemned; and not only he, but those who co-operate and agree with him: for just as the power of making appointments (*ordinatio*) is interdicted in such circumstances, so also is the power of judging or of disposing of other matters. For if a man has no power to appoint, how shall he judge? Without doubt, he shall in no wise judge or have power to judge: for just as another man's wife cannot intermarry with any one (*adulterari*), nor be judged or disposed of by any one but by her own husband so long as he liveth; so neither can it in anywise be allowed that the wife of a bishop, by whom undoubtedly is meant his church or parish, should be judged or disposed of by another without his (the bishop's) judgment and good-will so long as he liveth, or enjoy another's embrace, that is, his ordaining. Wherefore the apostle says: "The wife is bound by the law so long as her husband liveth; but if he be dead, she is loosed from the law of her husband."[1] In like manner also, the spouse of a bishop (for the church is called his spouse and wife) is bound to him while he liveth; but when he is dead she is loosed, and may be wedded to whomsoever she will, only in the Lord, that is, according to order. For if, while he is alive, she marry another, she shall be judged to be an adulteress. And in the same manner, he too, if he

[1] Rom. vii. 2.

marry another of his own will, shall be held to be an adulterer, and shall be deprived of the privilege of communion. If, however, he is persecuted in his own church, he must flee to another, and attach himself to it, as the Lord says: "If they persecute you in one city, flee ye into another."[1] If, however, the change be made for the sake of the good [of the church], he may not do this of himself, but only on the invitation of the brethren, and with the sanction of this holy seat, and not for ambition's sake, but for the public good.

IV.

[Of marriages among blood-relations, and of those who are born of them; and of accusations which the laws reject.]

Moreover, marriages among blood-relations are forbidden, since all laws, both sacred and secular, forbid such. Wherefore the divine laws not only expel, but even anathematize those who do so, and those who spring from them. Secular laws, again, call such persons infamous, and interdict them from inheriting. And we too, following our fathers, and keeping close by their footsteps, brand such with infamy, and hold them to be infamous, because they are sprinkled with the stains of infamy. Neither ought we to admit those men or their accusations, that secular laws reject. (For who doubts that human laws, when they are not inconsistent with reason and honour, are to be embraced, especially when they either further the public good or defend the authority of the ecclesiastical office, and uphold it as a help?) And we call those blood-relations whom divine laws, and those of the emperors, both Roman and Greek, name blood-relations, and whom they admit to the right of inheriting, and cannot exclude from that. Marriages, then, between such are neither lawful nor capable of holding good, but are to be rejected. (And if any such are attempted in rash daring, they come to be rescinded by apostolic authority.)

[1] Matt. x. 23.

V.

[Of those who ought not to be admitted to prefer an accusation, or to bear witness; and that evidence is not to be given but on things happening in the person's presence.]

Whosoever, therefore, has not been lawfully married, or has been united without the dotal title (*dotali titulo*) and the blessing of a priest, cannot by any means bring a charge against priests, or those who are lawfully married, or bear witness against them, since every one who is polluted with the stain of incest is infamous, and is not allowed to accuse the above-named. And consequently not only they, but all those too who agree with them, are to be rejected, and are rendered infamous. We hold that the same should also be the case with robbers, or with those who assault the elderly. The laws of the world, indeed, put such persons to death; but we, with whom mercy has the first place, receive them under the mark of infamy to repentance. That infamy also with which they are stained, we are not able to remove; but our desire is to heal their souls by public penitence, and by satisfaction made to the church: for public sins are not to be purged by secret correction. Those, again, who are suspected in the matter of the right faith, should by no means be admitted to prefer charges against priests, and against those of whose faith there is no doubt; and such persons should be held of doubtful authority in matters of human testimony. Their voice, consequently, should be reckoned invalid whose faith is doubted; and no credit should be given to those who are ignorant of the right faith. Accordingly, in judgment, inquiry should be made as to the conversation and faith of the person who accuses, and of him who is accused; since those who are not of correct conversation and faith, and whose life is open to impeachment, are not allowed to accuse their elders, neither can such permission be given to those whose faith and life and liberty are unknown. Nor should vile persons be admitted to accuse them. But a clear examination is to be made as to what kind of persons the accusers are (*rimandæ sunt enucleatim personæ accusatorum*); for they are not to be admitted readily without writing, and are never to be admitted (as accusers) on mere writing. For no one may either accuse or be accused by mere writing, but with the living voice; and every one must lay his accusation in the presence of him whom he seeks to accuse. And no credit should be given to any accuser in the absence of him whom he seeks to accuse. In like manner, witnesses must not prefer their evidence by writing only ; but they must give their testimony truthfully in their own persons, and in matters which they have seen and do know. And they are not to give evidence in any other cases or matters but in those which are known to have happened in their presence. Accusers, moreover, of one blood, are not to bear witness against those who are not related to the family, nor is that to be the case with domestics (*familiares*) or those proceeding from the house; but if it is their wish, and they agree among themselves, the parents only should give evidence in such cases, and not others. Neither accusers nor witnesses should be admitted who are open to any suspicion; for the feeling of relationship, or friendship, or lordship, is wont to impede the truth. Carnal love, and fear, and avarice, commonly blunt the perceptions of men, and pervert their opinions; so that they look on gain as godliness, and on money as the reward of prudence. Let no one, then, speak deceitfully to his neighbour.[1] The mouth of the malevolent is a deep pit. The innocent man, while he believes easily, falls readily; but though he falls, he rises; and the shuffler, with all his arts, goes headlong to ruin, whence he can never rise or escape. Therefore let every one weigh well his words, and let him not say to another what he would not say to himself. Whence the sacred Scripture says well: "Do not that to another which thou wouldest not have done to thyself."[2] For we need time to do anything perfectly (*maturius*); and let us not be precipitate in our counsels or our works, neither let us violate order. But if any one has fallen in anything, let us not consign him to ruin; but let us reprove him with brotherly affection, as the blessed apostle says: "If a man be overtaken in any

[1] Ps. xxiv. 4.   [2] Cf. Tobit iv. 15.

fault, ye which are spiritual restore such an one in the spirit of meekness; considering thyself, lest thou also be tempted. Bear ye one another's burden, and so will ye fulfil the law of Christ."[1] Furthermore, the sainted David had deadly crimes to repent of, and yet he was continued in honour. The blessed Peter also shed the bitterest tears when he repented of having denied the Lord; but still he abode an apostle. And the Lord by the prophet makes this promise to the sinning: "In the day that the sinner is converted, and repenteth, I will not mention any more against him all his transgressions."[2]

VI.

[As to whether a priest may minister after a lapse.]

For those are in error who think that the priests of the Lord, after a lapse, although they may have exhibited true repentance, are not capable of ministering to the Lord, and engaging their honourable offices, though they may lead a good life thereafter, and keep their priesthood correctly. And those who hold this opinion are not only in error, but also seem to dispute and act in opposition to (the power of) the keys committed to the church, whereof it is said: "Whatsoever ye shall loose on earth, shall be loosed in heaven."[3] And in short, this opinion either is not the Lord's, or it is true. But (be that as it may) we believe without hesitation, that both the priests of the Lord and other believers may return to their honours after a proper satisfaction for their error, as the Lord Himself testifies by His prophet: "Shall he who falls not also rise again? and shall he who turns away not return?"[4] And in another passage the Lord says: "I desire not the death of the sinner, but that he may turn, and live."[5] And the prophet David, on his repentance, said: "Restore unto me the joy of Thy salvation, and uphold me with Thy free Spirit."[6] And he indeed, after his repentance, taught others also, and offered

[1] Gal. vi. 1, 4.   [2] Ezek. xviii. 21, 22.   [3] Matt. xviii. 18.
[4] Jer. viii. 4.   [5] Ezek. xviii. 32 and xxxiii. 11.
[6] Ps. li. 12.

sacrifice to God, giving thereby an example to the teachers of the holy church, that if they have fallen, and thereafter have exhibited a right repentance to God, they may do both things in like manner. For he taught when he said: "I will teach transgressors Thy ways, and sinners shall be converted unto Thee."[1] And he offered sacrifice for himself, while he said: "The sacrifice for God is a broken spirit."[2] For the prophet, seeing his own transgressions purged by repentance, had no doubt as to healing those of others by preaching, and by making offering to God. Thus the shedding of tears moves the mind's feeling (*passionem*). And when the satisfaction is made good, the mind is turned aside from anger. For how does that man think that mercy will be shown to himself, who does not forgive his neighbour? If offences abound, then, let mercy also abound; for with the Lord there is mercy, and with Him is plenteous redemption.[3] In the Lord's hand there is abundance of all things, because He is the Lord of powers (*virtutum*) and the King of glory.[4] For the apostle says: "All have sinned, and come short of the glory of God; being justified freely by His grace, through the redemption that is in Jesus Christ: whom God hath set forth to be a propitiation through faith in His blood, to declare His righteousness for the remission of sins that are past, through the forbearance of God; to declare, *I say*, at this time His righteousness, that He might be just, and the justifier of him which believeth in Jesus."[5] And David says: "Blessed are they whose iniquities are forgiven, and whose sins are covered."[6] Man, therefore, is cleansed of his sin, and rises again by the grace of God though he has fallen, and abides in his first position, according to the above-cited authorities. Let him see to it that he sin no more, that the sentence of the Gospel may abide in him: "Go, and sin no more."[7] Whence the apostle says: "Let not sin therefore reign in your mortal body, that ye should obey the lusts thereof: neither yield ye your members as instruments of unrighteous-

---

[1] Ps. li. 13.   [2] Ps. li. 17.   [3] Ps. cxxx. 7.
[4] Ps. xxiv. 10.   [5] Rom. iii. 23—26.   [6] Ps. xxxii. 1.
[7] John viii. 11.

ness unto sin: but yield yourselves unto God, as those tnat are alive from the dead, and your members as instruments of righteousness unto God. For sin shall not have dominion over you: for ye are not under the law, but under grace. What then? shall we sin because we are not under the law, but under grace? God forbid. Know ye not, that to whom ye yield yourselves servants to obey, his servants ye are to whom ye obey; whether of sin unto death, or of obedience unto righteousness? But God be thanked, that ye were the servants of sin; but ye have obeyed from the heart that form of doctrine which was delivered you. Being then made free from sin, ye became the servants of righteousness. I speak after the manner of men."[1] For greater is the sin of him who judgeth, than of him who is judged. "Thinkest thou," says the apostle, "O man, that judgest them that do such things, and doest the same, that thou shalt escape the judgment of God? or despisest thou the riches of His goodness, and forbearance, and long-suffering? Dost thou not know that the goodness of God leadeth thee to repentance? But, after thy hardness and impenitent heart, thou treasurest up unto thyself wrath against the day of wrath and revelation of the righteous judgment of God; who will render to every man according to his deeds: to them who, by patient continuance in well-doing, seek for glory, and honour, and immortality, eternal life; but unto them that are contentious, and do not obey the truth, but obey unrighteousness, indignation and wrath, tribulation and anguish, upon every soul of man that doeth evil, of the Jew first, and (also) of the Greek: but glory, honour, and peace, to every man that worketh good."[2] My brethren, shun not only the holding, but even the hearing, of the judgment that bans mercy; for better is mercy than all whole burnt-offerings and sacrifices.[3] We have replied to your interrogations shortly, because your letter found us burdened overmuch, and preoccupied with other judgments. Given on the 8th day of October, in the consulship of the most illustrious Antonine and Alexander."[4]

[1] Rom. vi. 12-19.
[2] Rom. iii. 8-10.
[3] Mark xii. 33.
[4] In the year 222.

THE EPISTLE OF POPE URBAN FIRST.

TO ALL CHRISTIANS.

URBAN was the successor of Callistus. The letter ascribed to him is one of the pseudo-Isidorian forgeries.

[Mansi, *Concil. Collect.* i. p. 748.]

Of the church's receiving only the property of the faithful, and not the price of the same, as in the times of the apostles; and as to why elevated seats should be prepared in the churches for the bishops; and as to the fact that no one should have intercourse with those whom the bishops excommunicate, and that no one should receive those whom they have cast out in any manner whatever.

1. Of the life in common, and of the reason why the church has begun to hold property.
2. Of the persons by whom, and the uses for which, ecclesiastical property should be managed, and of the invaders thereof.
3. As to any one's attempting to take from the church the right of holding property.
4. Of the seats of the bishops.
5. That no one should have intercourse with those with whom the bishop has no intercourse, or receive those whom he rejects.
6. Of the engagement made in baptism, and of those who have given themselves to the life in common.
7. Of the imposition of the bishop's hand.

URBAN, bishop, to all Christians, in sanctification of the spirit, in obedience and sprinkling of the blood of Jesus Christ our Lord, greeting.

It becomes all Christians, most dearly beloved, to imitate Him whose name they have received. "What doth it profit, my brethren," says the Apostle James, "though a man say he hath faith, and have not works?"[1] "My brethren, be not many masters, knowing that ye receive (*sumitis*) the greater condemnation; for in many things we offend all."[2] "Let him who is a wise man, and endued with knowledge among you, show out of a good conversation his works with meekness of wisdom."[3]

I.

We know that you are not ignorant of the fact that hitherto the principle of living with all things in common has been in vigorous operation among good Christians, and is still so by the grace of God; and most of all among those who have been chosen to the lot of the Lord, that is to say, the clergy, even as we read in the Acts of the Apostles: "And the multitude of them that believed were of one heart and of one soul: neither said any of them that ought of the things which he possessed was his own; but they had all things common. And with great power gave the apostles witness of the resurrection of Jesus Christ: and great grace was upon them all. Neither was there any among them that lacked: for as many as were possessors of lands or houses sold them, and brought the prices of the things that were sold, and laid them down at the apostles' feet: and distribution was made unto every man according as he had need. And Joseph, who by the apostles was surnamed Barnabas (which is, being interpreted, the son of consolation), a Levite, and of the country of Cyprus, having land, sold it, and brought the money, and laid it at the apostles' feet;"[4] and so forth. Accordingly, as the chief priests and others, and the Levites, and the rest of the faithful, perceived that it might be of more advantage if they handed over to the churches over which the bishops presided the heritages and fields which they were in the way of selling, inasmuch as they might furnish a larger and better maintenance for the faithful who hold the common faith, not only in present but also in future times, out of the revenues of such property than out

[1] Jas. ii. 14.
[2] Jas. iii. 1, 2.
[3] Jas. iii. 13.
[4] Acts iv. 32–37.

of the money for which they might at once be sold, they began to consign to the mother churches the property and lands which they were wont to sell, and got into the manner of living on the revenues of these.

II.

The property, moreover, in the possession of the several parishes was left in the hands of the bishops, who hold the place of the apostles; and it is so to this day, and ought to be so in all future time. And out of those possessions the bishops and the faithful as their stewards ought to furnish to all who wish to enter the life in common all necessaries as they best can, so that none may be found in want among them. For the possessions of the faithful are also called oblations, because they are offered to the Lord. They ought not therefore to be turned to any other uses than those of the church, and in behoof of Christian brethren before mentioned, and of the poor; for they are the offerings of the faithful, and they are redemption moneys for sins (*pretia peccatorum*), and the patrimony of the poor, and are given over to the Lord for the purpose already named. But if any one act otherwise (which may God forbid), let him take care lest he meet the condemnation of Ananias and Sapphira, and be found guilty of sacrilege, as those were who lied as to the price of the property designated, of whom we read thus in the beforecited passage of the Acts of the Apostles: "But a certain man named Ananias, with Sapphira his wife, sold land (*agrum*), and kept back part of the price, his wife also being privy to it, and brought a certain part, and laid it at the apostles' feet. But Peter said to Ananias, Why hath Satan tempted (*tentavit*) thine heart to lie to the Holy Ghost, and to keep back part of the price of the land? Whiles it remained, was it not thine own? and after it was sold, was it not in thine own power? Why hast thou conceived this thing in thine heart? Thou hast not lied unto men, but unto the Lord. And Ananias, hearing these words, fell down, and gave up the ghost. And great fear came on all them that heard [these things]. And the young men arose, and removed him (*amoverunt*), and carried him out, and buried him. And it was about the space of three hours after, when his wife, not knowing what was done, came in. And Peter answered unto her, and said, Tell me whether ye sold the land for so much? And she said, Yea, for so much. Then Peter said unto her, How is it that ye have agreed together to tempt the Spirit of the Lord? Behold, the feet of them which have buried thy husband are at the door, and shall carry thee out. Then fell she down straightway at his feet, and yielded up the ghost. And the young men came in, and found her dead, and, carrying her forth, buried her by her husband. And great fear came upon all the church, and upon as many as heard these things."[1] These things, brethren, are carefully to be guarded against, and greatly to be feared. For the property of the church, not being like personal, but like common property, and property offered to the Lord, is to be dispensed with the deepest fear, in the spirit of faithfulness, and for no other objects than the above-named, lest those should incur the guilt of sacrilege who divert it from the hands to which it was consigned, and lest they should come under the punishment and death of Ananias and Sapphira, and lest (which is yet worse) they should become anathema maranatha, and lest, though their body may not fall dead like that of Ananias and Sapphira, their soul, which is nobler than the body, should fall dead, and be cut off from the company of the faithful, and sink into the depths of the pit. Wherefore all must give heed to this matter, and watch in faithfulness, and avert the dishonour of such usurpation, lest possessions dedicated to the uses of things secret (or sacred) and heavenly be spoiled by any parties invading them. And if any one do so, then, after the sharp vengeance which is due to such a crime, and which is justly to be carried out against the sacrilegious, let him be condemned to perpetual infamy, and cast into prison or consigned to life-long exile. For, according to the apostle,[2] we ought to deliver such a man to Satan, that the spirit may be saved in the day of the Lord.

[1] Acts v. 1–11.   [2] 1 Cor. v. 5.

III.

By the increase, therefore, and the mode of life which have been mentioned, the churches over which the bishops preside have grown so greatly with the help of the Lord, and the greater part of them are now in possession of so much property, that among them there is not a man who, selecting the life in common, is kept in poverty; but such an one receives all necessaries from the bishop and his ministers. Therefore, if any one in modern or in future times shall rise up and attempt to divert that property, let him be smitten with the judgment which has been already mentioned.

IV.

Furthermore, as to the fact that in the churches of the bishops there are found elevated seats set up and prepared like a throne, they show by these that the power of inspection and of judging, and the authority to loose and bind, are given to them by the Lord. Whence the Saviour Himself says in the Gospel, "Whatsoever ye shall bind on earth shall be bound in heaven; and whatsoever ye shall loose on earth shall be loosed in heaven."[1] And elsewhere: "Receive ye the Holy Ghost. Whose soever sins ye remit, are remitted unto them; and whose soever sins ye retain, they are retained."[2]

V.

These things, then, we have set before you, most dearly beloved, in order that ye may understand the power of your bishops, and give reverence to God in them, and love them as your own souls; and in order that ye may have no communication with those with whom they have none, and that ye may not receive those whom they have cast out. For the judgment of a bishop is greatly to be feared, although he may bind one unjustly, which, however, he ought to guard against with the utmost care.

[1] Matt. xviii. 18. [2] John xx. 22, 23.

VI.

And in exhorting you, we also admonish all who have embraced the faith of Christ, and who have taken from Christ the name of Christian, that ye make your Christianity vain in no respect, but keep stedfastly the engagement which ye took upon yourselves in baptism, so that ye may be found not reprobate, but worthy in His presence. And if any one of you has entered the life which has all things common, and has taken the vow to hold no private property, let him see to it that he make not his promise vain, but let him keep with all faithfulness this engagement which he has made to the Lord, so that he may acquire for himself not damnation, but a reward; for it is better for a man not to take a vow at all, than not to discharge to the best of his ability the vow that he has made. For they who have made a vow, or taken on them the faith, and have not kept their vow, or have carried out their life in things evil, are punished more severely than those who have carried out their life without a vow, or have died without faith, but not without doing good works. For to this end have we received a reasonable mind by the gift of nature, and the renewal also of the second birth, that, according to the apostle, we may discern (*sapiamus*) rather things above, and not things on the earth;[1] for the wisdom of this world is foolishness with God.[2] For to what, most dearly beloved, does the wisdom of this world urge us, but to seek things that are hurtful, and to love things that are to perish, and to neglect things that are healthful, and to esteem as of no value things that are lasting? It commends the love of money, of which it is said, The love of money is the root of all evil;[3] and which has this evil in especial, that while it obtrudes the transitory, it hides from view the eternal; and while it looks on things that are outside, it does not look in upon things that lurk within; and while it seeks after strange things, it is an evil that makes itself strange to him who does it.[4] Behold, to what does the wisdom of this world urge a

---

[1] Col. iii. 2.
[2] 1 Cor. iii. 19.
[3] 1 Tim. vi. 10.
[4] "Sectatori," for which read "factori."

man? To live in pleasures. Whence it is said: A widow that liveth in pleasure, is dead while she liveth.¹ It urges a man to feed the flesh with the softest delights, with sins, and vices, and flames, to press the soul with intemperance in food and wine, and to check the life of the spirit, and to put into his enemy's hand the sword to be used against himself. Behold, what is the counsel which the wisdom of this world gives? That those who are good should choose rather to be evil, and that in error of mind they should be zealous to be sinners, and should not bethink themselves of that terrible voice of God, when the wicked shall be burned up like grass.²

VII.

For all the faithful ought to receive the Holy Spirit after baptism by imposition of the hand of the bishops, so that they may be found to be Christians fully; because when the Holy Spirit is shed upon them, the believing heart is enlarged for prudence and stedfastness. We receive of the Holy Spirit in order that we may be made spiritual; for the natural man receiveth not the things of the Spirit of God.³ We receive of the Holy Spirit in order that we may be wise to discern between good and evil, to love the just, and to loathe the unjust, so as to withstand malice and pride, and resist luxury and divers allurements, and impure and unworthy lust. We receive of the Holy Spirit in order that, fired with the love of life and the ardour of glory, we may be able to raise our mind from things earthly to things heavenly and divine.—Given on the Nones of September,—that is, on the fifth day of the same month, in the consulship of the most illustrious Antonine and Alexander.

¹ 1 Tim. v. 6.   ² Ps. xcii. 7.   ³ 1 Cor. ii. 14.

THE EXTANT WRITINGS OF ASTERIUS URBANUS:

BEING FRAGMENTS OF THREE BOOKS TO ABERCIUS MARCELLUS AGAINST THE MONTANISTS.

NOTHING is known of Asterius Urbanus. The name occurs in Fragment IV., translated in p. 228; and from the allusion made to him there, some have inferred that he was the author of the work against the Montanists, from which Eusebius has made these extracts. The inference is unfounded. There is no clue to the authorship. It has been attributed by different critics to Apollinaris, Apollonius, and Rhodon.

[Gallandi, vol. iii. p. 273, from Eusebius, *Hist. Eccl.* v. ch. 16, 17.]

I. THE EXORDIUM.

AVING now for a very long and surely a very sufficient period had the charge pressed upon me by thee, my dear Avircius[1] Marcellus, to write some sort of treatise against the heresy that bears the name of Miltiades,[2] I have somehow been very

---

[1] The manuscripts write the name 'Αουίρκιος, Avircius; but Nicephorus (book iv.) gives it as 'Αβίρκιος, Abercius.

[2] Nicephorus adds ἴσον δ' εἰπεῖν Μοντανόν, which seems, however, to be but a scholium. It may appear difficult to account for the fact that the name of Miltiades rather than that of Montanus is associated with the heresy of the Cataphrygians, and some consequently have conjectured that we should read here *Alcibiades*, as that is a name mentioned in con-

doubtfully disposed toward the task up till now; not that I felt any difficulty in refuting the falsehood, and in bearing my testimony to the truth, but that I was apprehensive and fearful lest I should appear to any to be adding some new word or precept[1] to the doctrine of the gospel of the New Testament, with respect to which indeed it is not possible for one who has chosen to have his manner of life in accordance with the gospel itself, either to add anything to it or to take away anything from it. Being recently, however, at Ancyra, a town of Galatia, and finding the church in Pontus[2] greatly agitated[3] by this new prophecy, as they call it, but which should rather be called this false prophecy, as shall be shown presently, I discoursed to the best of my ability, with the help of God, for many days in the church, both on these subjects and on various others[4] which were brought under my notice by them. And this I did in such manner that the church rejoiced and was strengthened in the truth, while the adversaries[5] were forthwith routed, and the opponents put to grief. And the presbyters of the place accordingly requested us to leave behind us some memorandum of the things which we alleged in opposition to the adversaries of the truth, there being present also our fellow-presbyter Zoticus Otrenus.[6] This, however, we did not; but we promised, if the Lord gave us opportunity, to write down the matters here, and send them to them with all speed.

II. FROM BOOK I.

Now the attitude of opposition (ἔνστασις) which they have

cert with Montanus and Theodotus in Euseb. v. 3. In the Muratorian fragment, however, as given above among the writings of Caius, we find again a Miltiades named among the heretics.

[1] ἐπισυγγράφειν ἢ ἐπιδιατάσσεσθαι.
[2] κατὰ πόντον. But the Codex Regius reads κατὰ τόπον, the church of the place, i.e. the church of Ancyra itself. This reading is confirmed by Nicephorus, book iv. 23, and is adopted by the Latin interpreter.
[3] διατεθρυλλημένην, ringing with it, deafened by it.
[4] ἕκαστά τι. Others propose ἑκάστοτε, constantly, daily.
[5] ἀντιθέτους. Others read ἀντιθέους, the enemies of God.
[6] Ζωτικοῦ τοῦ Ὀτρηνοῦ. Nicephorus reads Ὀστρηνοῦ.

assumed, and this new heresy of theirs which puts them in a position of separation from the church, had their origin in the following manner. There is said to be a certain village called Ardaba[1] in the Mysia, which touches Phrygia.[2] There, they say, one of those who had been but recently converted to the faith, a person of the name of Montanus, when Gratus was proconsul of Asia, gave the adversary entrance against himself by the excessive lust of his soul after taking the lead. And this person was carried away in spirit (πνευματοφορηθῆναι); and suddenly being seized with a kind of frenzy and ecstasy, he raved, and began to speak and to utter strange things, and to prophesy in a manner contrary to the custom of the church, as handed down from early times and preserved thenceforward in a continuous succession. And among those who were present on that occasion, and heard those spurious utterances, there were some who were indignant, and rebuked him as one frenzied, and under the power of demons, and possessed by the spirit of delusion, and agitating the multitude, and debarred him from speaking any more; for they were mindful of the Lord's distinction (διαστολῆς) and threatening, whereby He warned them to be on their guard vigilantly against the coming of the false prophets. But there were others too, who, as if elated by the Holy Spirit and the prophetic gift, and not a little puffed up, and forgetting entirely the Lord's distinction, challenged the maddening and insidious and seductive spirit, being themselves cajoled and misled by him, so that there was no longer any checking him (and reducing him) to silence (εἰς τὸ μηκέτι κωλύεσθαι σιωπᾶν). And thus by a kind of artifice, or rather by such a process of craft, the devil having devised destruction against those who were disobedient [to the Lord's warning], and being unworthily honoured by them, secretly

---

[1] 'Αρδαβαῦ. One codex makes it 'Αρδαβᾶβ.
[2] ἐν τῇ κατὰ τὴν Φρυγίαν Μυσίᾳ. Rufinus renders it, *apud Phrygiam Mysiæ civitatem*; others render it, *apud Mysiam Phrygiæ*; Migne takes it as defining this Mysia to be the Asiatic one, in distinction from the European territory, which the Latins called Mœsia, but the Greeks also Μυσία.

excited and inflamed their minds that had already left the faith which is according to truth, in order to play the harlot with error.[1] For he stirred up two others also, women, and filled them with the spurious spirit, so that they too spoke in a frenzy and unseasonably, and in a strange manner, like the person already mentioned, while the spirit called them happy as they rejoiced and exulted proudly at his working, and puffed them up by the magnitude of his promises; while, on the other hand, at times also he condemned them skilfully and plausibly, in order that he might seem to them also to have the power of reproof.[2] And those few who were thus deluded were Phrygians. But the same arrogant spirit taught them to revile the church universal under heaven, because that false spirit of prophecy found neither honour from it nor entrance into it. For when the faithful throughout Asia met together often and in many places of Asia for deliberation on this subject, and subjected those novel doctrines to examination, and declared them to be spurious, and rejected them as heretical, they were in consequence of that expelled from the church and debarred from communion.

III. FROM BOOK II.

Wherefore, since they stigmatized us as slayers of the prophets because we did not receive their loquacious ($\dot{\alpha}\mu\epsilon\tau\rho о\phi\dot{\omega}\nu o\nu\varsigma$[3]) prophets (for they say that these are they whom the Lord promised to send to the people), let them answer us in the name of God, and tell us, O friends, whether there is any one among those who began to speak from Montanus and the women onward that was persecuted by the Jews or

---

[1] τὴν ἀποκεκοιμημένην, etc.; the verb being used literally of the wife who proves false to her marriage vow.

[2] ἐλεγκτικόν. Montanus, that is to say, or the demon that spake by Montanus, knew that it had been said of old by the Lord, that when the Spirit came He would convince or reprove the world of sin; and hence this false spirit, with the view of confirming his hearers in the belief that he was the true Spirit of God, sometimes rebuked and condemned them. See a passage in Ambrose's *Epistle to the Thessal.* ch. v. (Migne).

[3] So Homer in the *Iliad* calls Thersites ἀμετροεπής, unbridled of tongue, and thus also *mendacious*.

put to death by the wicked? There is not one. Not even one of them is there who was seized and crucified for the name[1] [of Christ]. No; certainly not. Neither assuredly was there one of these women who was ever scourged in the synagogues of the Jews, or stoned. No; never anywhere. It is indeed by another kind of death that Montanus and Maximilla are said to have met their end. For the report is, that by the instigation of that maddening spirit both of them hung themselves; not together indeed, but at the particular time of the death of each (κατὰ δὲ τὸν ἑκαστοῦ τελευτῆς καιρόν), as the common story goes. And thus they died, and finished their life like the traitor Judas. Thus, also, the general report gives it that Theodotus—that astonishing person who was, so to speak, the first procurator[2] of their so-called prophecy, and who, as if he were sometime taken up and received into the heavens, fell into spurious ecstasies (παρεκστῆναι), and gave himself wholly over to the spirit of delusion—was at last tossed by him (δισκευθέντα, pitched like a quoit) into the air, and met his end miserably. People say then that this took place in the way we have stated. But as we did not see[3] them ourselves, we do not presume to think that we know any of these things with certainty. And it may therefore have been in this way perhaps, and perhaps in some other way, that Montanus and Theodotus and the woman mentioned above perished.

IV.

And let not the spirit of Maximilla say (as it is found in the same book of Asterius Urbanus[4]), "I am chased like a wolf

---

[1] τοῦ ὀνόματος. Nicephorus reads τοῦ νόμου, for the law.

[2] οἷον ἐπίτροπον. Rufinus renders it, "veluti primogenitum prophetiæ ipsorum." Migne takes it as meaning *steward*, manager of a common fund established among the Montanists for the support of their prophets. Eusebius (v. 18) quotes Apollonius as saying of Montanus, that he *established exactors of money, and provided salaries for those who preached his doctrine*.

[3] The text is, ἀλλὰ μὴν ἄνευ. But in various codices we have the more correct reading, ἀλλὰ μὴ ἄνευ.

[4] These words are apparently a scholium, which Eusebius himself or

from the sheep; I am no wolf. I am word, and spirit, and power." But let him clearly exhibit and prove the power in the spirit. And by the spirit let him constrain to a confession those who were present at that time for the very purpose of trying and holding converse with the talkative spirit—those men so highly reputed as men and bishops— namely, Zoticus of the village of Comana,[1] and Julian of Apamea, whose mouths Themison[2] and his followers bridled, and prevented the false and seductive spirit from being confuted by them.

V.

And has not the falsity of this also been made manifest already? For it is now upwards of thirteen years since the woman died, and there has arisen neither a partial nor a universal war in the world. Nay, rather there has been steady and continued peace to the Christians by the mercy of God.

VI. FROM BOOK III.

But as they have been refuted in all their allegations, and are thus at a loss what to say, they try to take refuge in their martyrs. For they say that they have many martyrs, and that this is a sure proof of the power of their so-called prophetic spirit. But this allegation, as it seems, carries not a whit more truth with it than the others. For indeed some of the other heresies have also a great multitude of martyrs; but yet certainly we shall not on that account agree with

---

some old commentator had written on the margin of his copy. We gather also from them that Asterius Urbanus was credited with the authorship of these three books, and not Apollinaris, as some have supposed.

[1] Comana seems to have been a town of Pamphylia. At least a bishop of Comana is mentioned in the epistle of the bishops of Pamphylia to Leo Augustus, cited in the third part of the *Council of Chalcedon*, p. 391.

[2] Themison was a person of note among the Montanists, who boasted of himself as a confessor and martyr, and had the audacity to write a catholic epistle to the churches like an apostle, with the view of commending the new prophecy to them. See Euseb. v. 18.

them, neither shall we acknowledge that they have truth in them. And those first heretics, who from the heresy of Marcion are called Marcionites, allege that they have a great multitude of martyrs for Christ. But yet they do not confess Christ Himself according to truth.

VII.

Hence, also, whenever those who have been called to martyrdom for the true faith by the church happen to fall in with any of those so-called martyrs of the Phrygian heresy, they always separate from them, and die without having fellowship with them, because they do not choose to give their assent to the spirit of Montanus and the women. And that this is truly the case, and that it has actually taken place in our own times at Apamea, a town on the Mæander, in the case of those who suffered martyrdom with Caius[1] and Alexander, natives of Eumenia, is clear to all.

VIII.

As I found these things in a certain writing of theirs directed against the writing of our brother Alcibiades,[2] in which he proves the impropriety of a prophet's speaking in ecstasy, I made an abridgment of that work.

IX.

But the false prophet falls into a spurious ecstasy, which is accompanied by a want of all shame and fear. For beginning with a voluntary (designed) rudeness, he ends with an involuntary madness of soul, as has been already stated. But they will never be able to show that any one of the Old Testament prophets, or any one of the New, was carried away in spirit after this fashion. Nor will they be able to boast that Agabus, or Judas, or Silas, or the daughters of

---

[1] ἐν τοῖς περὶ Γάιον ... μαρτυρήσασι. It may be intended for, "in the case of the martyrs Caius and Alexander."

[2] Migne is of opinion that there has been an interchange of names between this passage and the Exordium, and that we should read Miltiades here, and Alcibiades there. But see the note to the Exordium.

Philip, or [the woman] Ammia in Philadelphia, or Quadratus, or indeed any of the others who do not in any respect belong to them, were moved in this way.

X.

For if, after Quadratus and the woman Ammia in Philadelphia, as they say, the women who attached themselves to Montanus succeeded to the gift of prophecy, let them show us which of them thus succeeded Montanus and his women. For the apostle deems that the gift of prophecy should abide in all the church up to the time of the final advent. But they will not be able to show the gift to be in their possession even at the present time, which is the fourteenth year only from the death of Maximilla.[1]

[1] This seems to be the sense of the text, which appears to be imperfect here: ἀλλ' οὐκ ἂν ἔχοιεν δεῖξαι τεσσαρισκαιδέκατον ἤδη που τοῦτο ἔτος ἀπὸ τῆς Μαξιμίλλης τελευτῆς.

THE EPISTLES OF POPE PONTIANUS.

EUSEBIUS tells us that Pontianus was bishop of the Roman church five or six years [230-235 A.D.]. He succeeded Urbanus. The letters are the forgeries of the pseudo-Isidorus.

(Mansi, *Concil. Collect.* i. 735.)

THE FIRST EPISTLE.

TO FELIX SUBSCRIBONIUS.

On the honour to be bestowed on priests.

PONTIANUS, bishop, to Felix Subscribonius, greeting.

Our heart is exceedingly rejoiced with your goodness, in that you strive by all means in your power to carry out the practice of holy religion, and strengthen sad and destitute brethren in faith and religion. Wherefore we implore the mercy of our Redeemer, that His grace may support us in all things, and that He may grant us to carry out in effect what He has given us to aspire after. In this good thing, therefore, the benefits of recompense are multiplied just in proportion as our zeal for the work increases. And because in all these things we need the assistance of divine grace, we implore with constant prayers the clemency of Omnipotent God, that He may both grant us the desire for these good works which should ever be wrought by us, and give us power also to perform them, and direct us in that way, for the fruit of well-doing—which [way] the Pastor of pastors declared Himself to be—so that ye may be able to carry out through Him, without whom nothing can be done, those good works which you have begun. Moreover, with respect to the priests of the Lord whom we have heard you aid against the plots of wicked men, and whose cause you sustain, know ye that in so doing ye please God greatly, who has called them to the service of Himself, and has honoured them with so intimate a fellowship with Him, that through them He accepts the oblations of others, and pardons their sins, and reconciles them with Him. They also make the body of the Lord with their own mouth (*proprio ore corpus Domini conficiunt*), and give it to the people. For of them it is said: He that hurteth you, hurteth me; and he that doeth you an injury, shall receive again that which he hath done unrighteously.[1] And elsewhere: He that heareth you, heareth me; and he that despiseth you, despiseth me; and he that despiseth me, despiseth Him that sent me.[2] Hence they are not to be molested, but honoured. And in them the Lord Himself is honoured, whose commission they execute. They accordingly, if they happen to fall, are to be raised up and sustained by the faithful. And again, they are not to be accused by the infamous, or the wicked, or the hostile, or by the members of another sect or religion. If they sin, they are to be arraigned by the other priests; further, they are to be held in check (*constringantur*) by the chief pontiffs, and they are not to be arraigned or restrained by seculars or by men of evil life. Not slight, therefore, is our grief in hearing that you have to sorrow for your brother's passing away (*transitu*). For which reason we beseech Almighty God to console you by the breathing (*aspiratione*) of His grace, and keep you with heavenly guardianship from evil spirits and perverse men. For if ye have to bear any turmoil of certain adversaries after his decease, do not think it strange though ye, who seek to enjoy good in your own country—that is, in the land of the living—have to bear evil things at the hands of men in a strange country. For the present life is a sojourning; and to him who sighs after the true fatherland, the place of his sojourning is a trial, however pleasant it may seem. And as to you who seek the fatherland, among the

[1] Perhaps Zech. ii. 8.   [2] Luke x. 16.

sighs which ye heave I hear the groans also of human oppression rising. And this happens by the wonderful dispensation of Almighty God, in order that, while the truth calls you in love, this present world may cast back your affection from itself through the tribulations which it brings on, and that the mind may be so much the more easily delivered from the love of this world, as it is also impelled while it is called. Therefore, as you have begun, give heed to the duty of hospitality; labour most urgently in prayer and tears; devote yourselves more liberally and freely now to those almsgivings which you have ever loved, in order that in the recompense the profit to you for your work may be greater in proportion as your zeal for the labour has risen to higher degrees here.

Furthermore, hailing your goodness with paternal pleasantness, we beg you not to fail in the good works which ye have begun. And may no one be able to turn you from them; but may the clergy and servants of God, and all Christians who sojourn in those parts, fully discover by the love of Christ and Saint Peter the disposition of your charity in all things, and obtain the comforts of your favour in every necessity that may arise; to the end that all may be defended and helped by your aid, and that we, too, may owe you thanks, and that our Lord Jesus Christ may make good [to you] eternal glory, and that the blessed Apostle Peter, the chief of the apostles, in whose cause you spend yourselves, may open the gate of that same glory.—Given on the 10th day before the kalends of February (the 23d of January), in the consulship of the most illustrious Severus and Quintianus.[1]

THE SECOND EPISTLE.

TO ALL BISHOPS.

On brotherly love, and on avoiding the evil.

PONTIANUS, bishop of the holy and universal church, to all who worship the Lord aright, and love the divine worship, greeting.

Glory to God in the highest, and on earth peace to men of

[1] In the year 235.

good will.[1] These words, most beloved, are not the words of men, but of angels; and they were not devised by human sense, but were uttered by angels at the birth of the Saviour. And from these words it can be understood without doubt by all that peace is given by the Lord, not to men of evil will, but to men of good will. Whence the Lord, speaking by the prophet, says: "How good is God to Israel, even to such as are of a clean heart! But as for me, my feet were almost gone; my steps had well-nigh slipped: for I was envious at the unrighteous, when I saw the prosperity of the wicked."[2] Of the good, however, the Truth says in His own person, "Blessed are the pure in heart, for they shall see God."[3] And they are not the pure in heart who think evil things, or things hurtful to their brethren; for he who is the faithful man devises nothing evil. The faithful man, accordingly, loves rather to hear things which are becoming, than to speak things which are not becoming. And if any one is faithful, let him see to it that he speak no evil, and lay no snares in the way of any one. In this, then, are the children of God distinguished from the children of the devil. For the children of God always think and strive to do things which are of God, and give help unceasingly to their brethren, and wish to injure no one. But, on the other hand, the children of the devil are always meditating things evil and hurtful, because their deeds are evil. And of them the Lord, speaking by the prophet Jeremiah, says: "I will utter my judgments against them touching all their wickedness."[4] "Wherefore I will yet plead with you, saith the Lord; and with your children's children will I plead."[5] "Behold, I frame evil against you, and devise a device against you."[6] These things, brethren, are greatly to be feared, and to be guarded against by all; for the man on whom the judgment of God may fall will not depart unhurt. And therefore let every one see to it carefully that he neither contrive nor do against a brother what he would not wish to have to endure himself. And let not the man of faith come under the suspicion even

[1] Luke ii. 14.   [2] Ps. lxxiii. 1-3.   [3] Matt. v. 8.
[4] Jer. i. 16.   [5] Jer. ii. 9.   [6] Jer. xviii. 11.

of saying or doing what he would not wish to have to endure himself. Wherefore persons suspected, or hostile or litigious, and those who are not of good conversation, or whose life is reprehensible, and those who do not hold and teach the right faith, have been debarred from being either accusers or witnesses by our predecessors with apostolic authority; and we too remove them from that function, and exclude them from it in times to come, lest those lapse wilfully whom we ought to keep in and save; lest not only (which may God forbid!) the predicted judgment of God should fall upon both, but we also should perish (which may God forbid!) through their fault. For it is written, "Have they made thee the master [of a feast]? Take care for them, that thou mayst be merry on their account, and receive as thy crown the ornament of esteem, and find approbation of thine election."[1] For the evil word affects the heart, out of which proceed these four objects, good and evil, life and death; and the tongue in its assiduous action is what determines these. Wherefore the before-named parties are altogether to be avoided; and until the before-noted matters are investigated, and the parties are found to be clear of such, they are not to be received: for the right sacrifice is to give heed to the commandments, and to depart from all iniquity. "To depart from wickedness is a thing pleasing to the Lord, and to forsake unrighteousness is [a sacrifice of] praise."[2] For it is written, "Love thy friend, and be faithful unto him. But if thou bewrayest his secrets, follow no more after him. For as a man who destroyeth his friend, so is he who destroys (loseth) the friendship of his neighbour. And as one that letteth a bird go out of his hand, so art thou that hast let thy neighbour go and shalt not get him again. Follow after him no more, for he is far off. For he has escaped like a roe out of the snare, because his soul is wounded. Thou wilt not be able to bind him any more, and there is reconciliation for the reviled. But to bewray the secrets of a friend is the desperation of a wretched soul. He that winketh with the eye worketh evil, and no one will cast him off. When thou art present, he will

[1] Ecclus. xxxii. 1-3. [2] Ecclus. xxxv. 1-3.

despise his own mouth, and express his wonder at thy discourse; but at the last he will writhe his mouth, and slander thy sayings. I have hated many things, but nothing like him; and the Lord will hate him. Whoso casteth a stone on high, it will fall upon his own head, and a deceitful stroke of the deceitful will make wounds. Whoso diggeth a pit shall fall therein; and he that setteth a stone in his neighbour's way will fall thereon; and he that placeth a snare for another will perish therein. He that worketh mischief, it shall fall upon him, and he shall not know whence it cometh on him. Mockery and reproach are from the proud; and vengeance, as a lion, shall be in wait for them. They that rejoice at the fall of the righteous shall perish in the snare, and anguish shall consume them before they die. Anger and wrath are both abominations, and the sinful man shall have them both."[1] "He that will be avenged shall find vengeance from the Lord, and he will surely keep his sins. Forgive thy neighbour the hurt that he hath done unto thee, and then shall thy sins be forgiven thee when thou prayest. One man beareth hatred against another; and doth he ask redress of God? He showeth no mercy to a man which is like himself; and doth he ask forgiveness of the Most High for his own sins? He, though he is flesh, nourisheth hatred; and doth he ask pardon of God? Who will entreat for his sins? Remember thy end, and let enmity cease; for corruption and death impend on commandments. Remember the fear of God, and bear no malice to thy neighbour. Remember the covenant of the Highest, and look down upon (*despice*) the ignorance of thy neighbour. Abstain from strife, and thou shalt diminish thy sins. For a furious man kindleth strife; and a sinful man will disquiet friends, and make enmity among them that be at peace. For even as the trees of the wood are, so will the fire burn; and as a man's strength is, so will his anger be; and as his riches are, so will he make his anger rise. An hastened contention will kindle a fire, and an hasting quarrel will shed blood, and a testifying (*testificans*) tongue will bring death. If thou blow upon the spark,

[1] Ecclus. xxvii. 17–30.

it will burn like a fire; and if thou spit upon it, it will be extinguished: and both these come out of the mouth. Cursed be the whisperer and double-tongued, for such have troubled many that were at peace. A third (*tertia*) tongue hath disquieted many, and driven them from nation to nation: the fortified cities of the rich it hath pulled down, and overthrown the houses of great men. It has subverted the virtues of peoples, and has destroyed strong nations. A third tongue hath cast out truthful[1] women, and deprived them of their labours. Whoso hearkeneth unto it shall never find rest, and never dwell quietly. The stroke of the whip maketh marks in the flesh, but the stroke of the tongue will break bones. Many have fallen by the edge of the sword, but not in such manner as those who have perished by their tongue. Well is he that is defended from the evil tongue, who hath not passed into the anger thereof, and who hath not drawn the yoke thereof, nor hath been bound with the bands of it; for the yoke thereof is a yoke of iron, and the band thereof is a band of brass. The death thereof is the vilest death, and the grave were better than it. The perseverance thereof shall not abide; but it shall hold the ways of the unrighteous, and its flame shall not burn the righteous. Such as forsake the Lord shall fall into it, and it shall burn in them, and not be quenched; and it shall be sent upon them as a lion, and hurt them as a leopard. Hedge thine ears about with thorns, and listen not to the evil tongue; and make a door for thy mouth, and bars for thine ears. Smelt (*confla*) thy gold and silver, and make a balance for thy words, and right curbs for thy mouth. And beware that thou slide not perchance in thy tongue, and fall before thine enemies that lie in wait for thee, and thy fall be irremediable even to death."[2] "Make no tarrying to turn to the Lord, and put not off from day to day. For suddenly shall His wrath come, and in the time of vengeance He will destroy thee. Set not thine heart upon goods unjustly gotten, for they shall not profit thee in the day of veiling (for execution, *obductionis*) and vengeance. Move not with every wind, and go not into every way; for so is

---

[1] Veridicas. The text reads "viratas."   [2] Ecclus. xxviii.

the sinner proved with the double-tongue. Be stedfast in the way of the Lord, and in the truth of thine understanding, and in knowledge; and let the word of peace and righteousness attend thee. Be courteous in hearing the word, that thou mayest understand it, and with wisdom give a true answer. If thou hast understanding, answer thy neighbour; if not, lay thy hand upon thy mouth, lest thou be caught in a word of folly, and be confounded. Honour and glory are in the talk of the intelligent man; the tongue of the unwise is his fall. Be not called a whisperer, and be not caught in thy tongue, and confounded. For confusion and penitence are upon the thief, and the worst condemnation upon the double-tongued. Moreover, for the whisperer there is hatred, and enmity, and shame. Justify the small and the great alike."[1] "Instead of a friend, become not an enemy to thy neighbour. For the evil man shall inherit reproach and shame, and every sinner in like manner that is envious and double-tongued. Extol not thyself in the counsel of thine own heart as a bull, lest perchance thy virtue be shattered in folly, and it consume thy leaves, and destroy thy fruits, and thou be left as a dry tree in the desert. For a wicked soul shall destroy him that hath it, and makes him to be laughed to scorn by his enemies, and shall bring him down to the lot of the impious."[2] Most dearly beloved, study to lift up the oppressed, and always help the necessitous; for if a man relieves an afflicted brother, delivers a captive, or consoles a mourner, let him have no doubt that that will be recompensed to him by Him on whom he bestows it all, and who says: "Inasmuch as ye have done it unto one of the least of my brethren, ye have done it unto me."[3] Strive, then, unceasingly to do what is good in such wise that ye may both obtain the fruit of good works here, and enjoy the favour of God in the future, to the intent that hereafter ye may be worthy to enter the court of the heavenly kingdom.—Given on the fourth day before the kalends of May (the 28th of April), in the consulship of the most illustrious Severus and Quintianus.

[1] Ecclus. v. 7-18.   [2] Ecclus. vi. 1-4.   [3] Matt. xxv. 40.

POPE ANTERUS.

ANTERUS succeeded Pontianus in the bishopric of the Roman church [235-236 A.D.]. The letter ascribed to him is one of the pseudo-Isidorian forgeries.

THE EPISTLE.
On the transference of bishops (of episcopal seats).

TO the brethren, most dearly beloved, constituted to be bishops in the provinces of Bœtica and Toletana, Bishop Anterus sends greeting in the Lord.

I should wish, my dearest brethren, always to receive the glad account of your sincere love and peace, so that the signs of your welfare might be promoted in turn by the dissemination of our letters among you, if our ancient enemy should give us quiet and deliverance from his attacks; who was a liar from the beginning,[1] the enemy of the truth, the rival of man—in order to deceive whom he first deceived himself,—the adversary of modesty, the master of luxury. He feeds on cruelties; he is punished by abstinence; he hates fasts, and his ministers preach to that effect, as he declares them to be superfluous, having no hope of the future, and echoing that sentence of the apostle, in which he says, "Let us eat and drink, for to-morrow we shall die."[2] O miserable boldness! O subtlety of a desperate mind! For he exhorts to hatred, and puts concord to flight. And because the mind of man is easily drawn over to the worse part, and chooses rather to walk by the broad way than laboriously to take its course by the narrow way, for this reason, brethren most dearly beloved, follow ye the better, and always leave the

[1] John viii. 44.   [2] 1 Cor. xv. 32.

worse behind you. Do good, avoid evil, in order that ye may be found to be the disciples of the Lord in truth.

Now, of the transference of bishops, on which subject it has been your wish to consult the holy seat of the apostles, know ye that that may lawfully be done for the sake of the common good, or when it is absolutely necessary, but not at the mere will or bidding of any individual. Peter, our holy master, and the prince of the apostles, was translated for the sake of the common good from Antioch to Rome, in order that he might be in a position there of doing more service. Eusebius also was transferred from a certain minor city to Alexandria by apostolic authority. In like manner Felix, on account of the doctrine and the good life which he maintained, was translated by the common consent of the bishops and the other priests, and the people from the city in which, on the election of the citizens, he had been ordained, to Ephesus. For that man is not chargeable with shifting from city to city who does not do that of his own inclination or by the force of ambition, but who is transferred for the general good, or in virtue of some necessity, by the counsel and with the consent of the chief parties. Nor can he be said to transfer himself from a smaller city to a larger, who is placed in that position not by his own self-seeking or his own choice, but either as being driven out of his own proper seat by force, or as being compelled by some necessity, and who without pride and in humility has been translated and installed there by others for the good of the place or the people: for man looketh on the countenance, but the Lord seeth the heart. And the Lord, speaking by the prophet, says, "The Lord knows the thoughts of men, that they are vanity."[1] That man, therefore, does not change his seat who does not change his mind. Nor does he change his city who is changed not of his own will, but by the decision and election of others. And accordingly he does not shift from city to city who does not leave his own city for the sake of gain to himself, or of his own choice, but who, as has already been said, has been translated to another city either in consequence of being driven out of his own

[1] Ps. xciv. 11.

seat, or compelled by some necessity, or in virtue of the election and injunction òf the priests and people. For as the bishops have power regularly to ordain bishops and other orders of priests, so, as often as any matter of advantage or necessity constrains them, they have power in the above-mentioned manner both to transfer and to install. As ye have asked our opinion in these matters, though they are not subjects unknown to you, we give you these things in charge to hold them, lest, through the ignorance of some, that which is better and more profitable be avoided, and what is more profitless be taken up, even as we read in the holy Gospel: "Woe unto you, hypocrites! for ye pay tithe of mint, and anise, and cummin, and have omitted the weightier matters of the law, judgment, mercy, and faith: these ought ye to have done, and not to leave the other undone. Ye blind guides, which strain out a gnat and swallow a camel."[1] What is lawful is [with them] not lawful, and what is not lawful is lawful. Even as Jannes and Mambres[2] resisted the truth, so do they, being reprobate in mind, and lovers of pleasure rather than of God, teach that that is unlawful which is lawful, to wit, that bishops should shift from city to city in the manner already noted; and what is unlawful they teach as lawful, to wit, to omit to show mercy to those who endure straits: that is to say, they deny that a bishop belonging to another city should be bestowed for good, or for necessity's sake, upon those who have no bishop, and who want the sacred episcopal ministry; and that another episcopal seat should be assigned to bishops who endure persecution or straits. They contradict the sacred Scripture also, which testifies that God desireth mercy rather than judgment[3] (*judicium*).

What greater charity, I pray you, can there be, or what more profitable service of piety, on the part of any one to another, than to deliver him from the darkness of ignorance and the thick darkness of inexperience, and restore him, in fine, by the nutriment of the doctrine of the true faith, not for gain indeed, or ambition, but for instruction and edification? For he becomes, so to speak, the hand for the maimed,

[1] Matt. xxiii. 23, 24.   [2] 2 Tim. iii. 8.   [3] Hos. vi. 6.

the foot for the lame, the eye for the blind,[1] who unlocks the treasure of wisdom and knowledge to one wrapped in the darkness of ignorance, and opens up to such an one the brightness of the light and the ways of the Lord.][2]

Now for both parties—namely, for those who endure a famine of the word of God, and for bishops who endure straits, when they are installed in other cities for the common good —no small degree of mercy is shown. And they who deny this, although they have the form of godliness, do yet deny the power thereof.[3] For in such a matter I make no recognition of race (*prosapiam*). If, however, any one of the wise, whom the stress of this storm (or season) has allied with other leaders among the unwise, is stained with a participation in their deeds, yet the excellence of the wise man, although he may chance to be privy to their offences, makes him incapable of giving himself as a leader to sinners. The cause of public good and necessity is one thing, and the cause of self-seeking, and presumption, or private inclination, is another thing. On account of self-seeking, or presumption, or private inclination, bishops are not to be transferred from one city to another, but only on account of public good and necessity. And this is a matter which no one denies, except those of whom it is said, "They have erred through wine; they have not known the seer; they have been ignorant of judgment."[4] For if I were constrained to open up in narration things that have been brought to end, I would show you that no comfort comes from the comparison of such deeds. But, most dearly beloved, "stand ye in the ways, and see, and ask for the old paths of the Lord, and see what is the good way and the right, and walk therein, and ye shall find rest for your souls."[5] And, to speak according to the word of Wisdom : " Love righteousness, ye that be judges of the earth. Think of the Lord in goodness, and in simplicity of heart seek Him. For He is found of them that tempt Him not, and showeth Himself unto such as do not distrust Him. For froward

---

[1] Job xxix. 15.
[2] The bracketed passage is wanting in one manuscript.
[3] 2 Tim. iii. 5. [4] Isa. xxviii. 7. [5] Jer. vi. 16.

thoughts separate from God; and His power, when it is tried, reproveth the unwise. For into a malicious soul wisdom shall not enter, nor dwell in the body that is subject unto sin. For the holy spirit of discipline will flee deceit, and remove from thoughts that are without understanding, and will not abide when unrighteousness cometh in. For wisdom is a benign spirit, and will not acquit a blasphemer of His words. For God is witness of his reins, and a true beholder of his heart, and a hearer of his tongue. For the Spirit of the Lord hath filled the world, and that which containeth all things hath knowledge of the voice. Therefore he that speaketh unrighteous things cannot be hid; neither shall vengeance, when it punisheth, pass by him. For inquisition shall be made into the counsels of the ungodly. And the sound of his words shall come unto the Lord, and unto the manifestation of his wicked deeds; for the ear of jealousy heareth all things, and the noise of murmurings shall not be hid. Therefore beware of murmuring, which is unprofitable; and refrain your tongue from backbiting, for there is no word so secret that it shall go for nought. The mouth that belieth slayeth the soul. Seek not death in the error of your life, and pull not upon yourself destruction with the works of your hands; for God made not death, neither hath He pleasure in the destruction of the living. For He created all things that they might have their being, and He wished the nations of the world to be healthful. There is no poison of destruction in them, nor the kingdom of death upon the earth of the living. Righteousness is perpetual and immortal, but unrighteousness is the acquisition of death. And ungodly men with their hands and words called it to them; and when they thought to have it their friend, they consumed to nought, and made a covenant with it; because they are worthy of death who take part with it."[1] "For they said, reasoning with themselves, but not aright, The time of our life is short and tedious; and in the death of a man there is no remedy, neither was there any man known to have returned from the grave. For we are born of nothing, and we shall be hereafter as though we had

[1] Wisd. i.

never been. For the breath in our nostrils is as smoke, and speech is a little spark for the moving of our heart; which being extinguished, our body shall be turned into ashes, and our spirit shall vanish as the soft air. And our life shall pass as the trace of a cloud, and shall be dispersed as a mist that is driven away with the beams of the sun, and overcome with the heat thereof. And our name shall be forgotten in time, and no man shall have our works in remembrance. For our time is a very shadow that passeth away, and after our end there is no returning; for it is fast sealed, and no man shall come again." [1] And for this reason every one must see to it that he keep himself with all care, and watch himself for his own good, so that when his last day and the end of his life come upon him, he may not pass over to everlasting death, but to eternal life. For the deeds of those put under us are judged by us, but our own doth God judge. Sometimes, moreover, bishops are perverted through the fault of the people, to the end that those fall more precipitately who follow them. When the head languisheth, the other members of the body are affected thereby. And viler are those who corrupt the life and morals of the good, than those who spoil the property and goods of others. Let each one take care that he have neither an itching tongue nor itching ears; that is to say, that he neither be a detractor of others himself, nor listen to others in their detractions. "Thou sattest," saith he, "and spakest against thy brother; and thou didst slander thine own mother's son." [2] Let every individual abstain from a detracting tongue, and keep a guard upon his own words, and understand that all that they say of others shall enter into the judgment wherewith they themselves shall be judged. No one readily refers to an unwilling auditor. Let it be the care of all of you, most dearly beloved, to keep not only your eyes, but also your tongue, pure. And let not another house ever know by your means what is done in any man's house. Let all have the simplicity of the dove, that they devise not guile against any one; and the subtlety of the serpent, that they be not overthrown by the crafty designs

[1] Wisd. ii. 1–5.   [2] Ps. l. 20.

of others. It does not belong to my humble station and measure to judge others, and to say anything unfavourable of the ministers of the churches. Far be it from me that I should say anything unfavourable of those who are the successors to the apostolic status, and make the body of Christ with their sacred mouth; by whose instrumentality we too are Christians, and who have the keys of the kingdom of heaven, and exercise judgment before the day of judgment. Moreover, it is contained in the ancient law, that whoever has not given obedience to the priests should either be stoned outside the camp by the people, or with his neck beneath the sword should expiate his presumption by his blood.[1] Now, however, the disobedient is cut off by spiritual chastisement; and being cast out of the church, is torn by the rabid mouth of demons.[2] For it becomes those who have God in their heritage, to serve God free from all the hindrances of the world, so that they may be able to say, "The Lord is the portion of mine inheritance."[3] "O how good and pleasant is Thy Spirit, O Lord, in all things!"[4] "And thou sparest all because they are Thine, O Lord, who lovest souls. *Therefore chastenest Thou them* by little and little that offend, and warnest them of those things wherein they offend, and dost address them, that leaving their wickedness, they may believe on Thee, O Lord."[5] "But Thou, our God, art gracious and true, long-suffering, and in mercy ordering all things. For if we sin, we are Thine, knowing Thy power. And if we sin not, we know that we are counted Thine."[6] "The spirit of those that fear the Lord shall be required of him; and in His regard they shall be blessed."[7] Wherefore, most beloved brethren, "let no corrupt communication proceed out of your mouth, but that which is good to the use of edifying, that it may minister grace to the hearers. And grieve not the Holy Spirit of God, whereby ye are sealed unto the day of redemption. Let all bitterness, and wrath, and anger, and clamour, and evil-speaking, be put away from you, with all

---

[1] Deut. xvii. [2] Thus far Jerome. [3] Ps. xvi. 5.
[4] Wisd. xii. 1. [5] Wisd. xii. 2. [6] Wisd. xv. 1, 2.
[7] Ecclus. xxxiv. 13, 14.

malice. And be ye kind one to another, tender-hearted, forgiving one another, even as God in Christ hath forgiven you."[1] "Be ye therefore followers of God, as dear children; and walk in love, as Christ also hath loved us, and hath given Himself for us an offering and a sacrifice to God for a sweet-smelling savour. But fornication, and all uncleanness, or covetousness, let it not be once named among you, as becometh saints; neither filthiness, nor foolish talking, nor jesting, which are not convenient; but rather giving of thanks. For this know ye, understanding that no whoremonger, nor unclean person, nor covetous man, who is an idolater, hath any inheritance in the kingdom of Christ and of God. Let no man deceive you with vain words: for because of these things cometh the wrath of God upon the children of disobedience. Be not ye therefore partakers with them. For ye were sometimes darkness, but now are ye light in the Lord: walk as children of light (for the fruit of the Spirit is in all goodness, and righteousness, and truth), proving what is acceptable unto the Lord. And have no fellowship with the unfruitful works of darkness, but rather reprove them. For it is a shame even to speak of those things which are done of them in secret. But all things that are reproved are made manifest by the light: for whatsoever is made manifest (*manifestatur*) is light. Wherefore He saith, Awake, thou that sleepest, and arise from the dead, and Christ shall give thee light. See then that ye walk circumspectly, brethren, not as fools, but as wise, redeeming the time, because the days are evil. Wherefore be ye not unwise, but understanding what the will of the Lord is. And be not drunk with wine, wherein is excess; but be filled with the Holy Spirit; speaking to yourselves in psalms, and hymns, and spiritual songs, singing and making melody in your hearts to the Lord; giving thanks always for all things unto God and the Father in the name of our Lord Jesus Christ, submitting yourselves one to another in the fear of Christ."[2] Therefore, brethren, stand fast and hold the tradition of the apostles and the apostolic seat, " that our

[1] Eph. iv. 29-32.　　　　　[2] Eph. v. 1-21.

Lord Jesus Christ and our Father, which hath loved us, and hath given us everlasting consolation and good hope through grace, may comfort your hearts, and stablish you in every good work and word."[1] "Finally, brethren, pray for us, that the word of the Lord may have free course, and be glorified, even as it is with you, and that we may be delivered from unreasonable and wicked men: for all men have not faith. But the Lord is faithful, who shall stablish you, and keep you from evil."[2] Wherefore set your hearts continually in the strength (*virtute*) of God, and always resist the wicked, and tell these things, according to the word of the prophet, "to the generations following; for this God is our God unto eternity, and He will rule us for ever and ever."[3] Hence ye who are set for examples (*in specula*) by the Lord, ought by all means to check and keep back those who devise crafty counsels against the brethren, or excite against them seditions and slanders. For it is an easy thing to deceive man with a word, but it is not so with the Lord. Wherefore ye ought to reprehend such persons, and turn away from them, to the end that, all darkness of this manner being completely done away, the Morning Star may shine upon them, and gladness arise in their hearts. "*And we have* confidence in the Lord touching you, brethren, that ye both do and will do the things which we command you."[4] For the more ye show forth your kindnesses to them, the greater a return have ye to look for from the omnipotent God whom they serve. May the omnipotent God keep you in His protection, and grant you to maintain honour and precept; and may glory and honour be to God the Father Almighty, and to his only-begotten Son our Saviour, with the Holy Spirit, for ever and ever. Amen.

Given on the 12th day before the kalends of April (the 21st of March), in the consulship of the most illustrious Maximianus and Africanus.

[1] 2 Thess. ii. 15-17. [2] 2 Thess. iii. 1-3.
[3] Ps. xlviii. 13, 14. [4] 2 Thess. iii. 4.

THE EPISTLES OF POPE FABIAN.

FABIAN was bishop of Rome from 236 to 250 A.D. The letters ascribed to him are rejected by all as spurious.

THE FIRST EPISTLE.

TO ALL THE MINISTERS OF THE CHURCH CATHOLIC.

Of those who ought not to be admitted to clear themselves, and of the duty of having no fellowship with the excommunicated.

TO the dearly-beloved brethren in the ministry of the church catholic in all regions, Fabian sends greeting in the Lord.

By the divine precepts and the apostolic institutes, we are admonished to watch in behoof of the position of all the churches with unwearied interest. Whence it follows that you ought to know what is being done in things sacred in the church of Rome, in order that, by following her example, ye may be found to be true children of her who is called your mother. Accordingly, as we have received the institution from our fathers, we maintain seven deacons in the city of Rome distributed over seven districts of the state, who attend to the services enjoined on them week by week, and on the Lord's days and the solemn festivals, in concert with the subdeacons, and acolytes, and servants of the succeeding orders, and hold themselves in readiness every hour for religious duty, and for the discharge of all that is enjoined upon them. In like manner ought ye also to do throughout your different cities, as may be convenient, that religious duty may be discharged zealously and regularly, without any delay or negligence. Furthermore, we have ordained in like manner seven subdeacons who shall stand by (*imminerent*) the seven notaries, and bring into one full and accurate account the histories of the martyrs, and lay them before us for our examination. And this, too, we urge you all to do, so that no doubt or questioning of these things may arise in later times; "for whatsoever things were written, were written for our learning."[1] And whatsoever things are written in truth in our times, are directed to the learning of future times. And therefore we enjoin these duties to be put in charge of the most faithful, that nothing false may be found in them, from which an offence (which may God forbid) may arise to the faithful. For this reason also we beg it of your love in paternal benignity, that the holy church may now find the good-will of your love in all things, and obtain the comforts of your favour whenever there is necessity. And as the goodness of your zeal affords us the assurance that we ought to distrust it in nothing, but rather commit these things in all confidence to you as to wise sons of our church; so, small importance being attached to opportune occasions, your virtue ought to exert itself the more strenuously in labours, and keep off reproaches by all possible means, and with all zeal. We exhort you also, according to the word of the apostle, to be "stedfast and immoveable, always abounding in the work of the Lord; forasmuch as ye know that your labour is not vain in the Lord."[2] And in another place: "Watch ye, and pray, and stand fast in the faith. Quit you like men, and be strong. Let all things be done with charity."[3] Furthermore, we desire you to know this, that in our times, as our sins embarrassed us, and that ancient enemy who always goeth about like a roaring lion, seeking whom he may devour,[4] instigated him, Novatus came up out of Africa, and separated Novatianus and certain other confessors of Christ from the church of Christ, and persuaded them into the acceptance of evil doctrine. From such persons, brethren, keep yourselves aloof, and beware of all who hold a faith and

---

[1] Rom. xv. 4.
[2] 1 Cor. xv. 58.
[3] 1 Cor. xvi. 13, 14.
[4] 1 Pet. v. 8.

doctrine different from that which the apostles and their successors have held and taught, lest (which may God forbid) going after him ye fall into the toils of Satan, and be bound with his fetters. Wherefore with most earnest prayers we beg it of your brotherly love, that ye may deem it fit to remember our insignificance in your holy prayers, beseeching and entreating the Lord of heaven that we, as well as our holy mother the church of Christ, redeemed with His precious blood, may be delivered from the toils of Satan, who lieth in wait for us, and from troublesome and wicked men, and that the Word of God may have free course and be glorified, and that the evil doctrine of them, and of all who teach things contrary to the truth, may be overthrown and perish. We beseech you also to be zealous in praying in your pious supplications, that our God and Lord Jesus Christ, who will have all men to be saved, and no one to perish,[1] may, by His vast omnipotence, cause their hearts to turn again to sound doctrine and to the catholic faith, in order that they may be recovered from the toils of the devil who are held captive by him, and be united with the children of our mother the church. Be mindful also of your brethren, and have pity upon them, and labour for them by all means in your power, that they be not lost, but be saved unto the Lord by your prayers, and other efforts of your goodness. So act therefore in these matters that ye may approve yourselves as obedient and faithful children of the holy church of God, and that ye may obtain the recompense of reward. These men, and all else who do not teach the true doctrine, and hold not the true faith, cannot act as accusers of any true believer, because they are branded with infamy, and are cut off from the bosom of our holy mother the church by the sword of the apostles, until their return to correct conversation and belief. Hence by apostolic authority, and in agreement with all the sons of the same apostolic and universal church, we resolve that all who come under suspicion with respect to the catholic faith cannot be admitted as accusers of those who hold the true creed; for suspicions are always to be set aside. Rightly

[1] 1 Tim. ii. 4.

therefore are charges which are preferred by those who are
objects of suspicion in the matter of the true faith, rejected.
Neither are they at all to be credited who are unacquainted
with the faith of the Trinity. In like manner we set aside
and withdraw from all part in the accusing of the faithful,
all those whom the decrees of the holy fathers in times past
and times future alike anathematize. Accordingly, the believing ought always to be kept distinct from the unbelieving,
and the righteous from the unrighteous; since the unbelieving
and evil-minded, by every means in their power, are always
troubling the believing, and striving to undo them; and consequently they are not to be received, but rejected and kept
entirely at a distance, lest they may undo or defame the
believing. For this reason, dearly beloved, beware of the
pit of such persons, into which we know many have fallen.
Beware of the snares (or darts) of such persons, and of the
efforts of the ancient enemy, by which we have seen even
those closely connected with us fall wounded before us.
Watch the nooses of the liers in wait, by which they are
wont to strangle associates and comrades. Follow not such,
but keep them far off from you. Be ye, according to the
voice of Truth, wise as serpents and harmless as doves.[1] See
to it that ye neither run nor labour in vain; but, sustained by
each other's prayers and supplications, strive ye to do the
will of God; and from those persons whom I have mentioned,
if they show themselves incorrigible, keep yourselves separate
in all things. In like manner keep yourselves separate from
all those of whom the apostle makes mention when he says,
" with such persons, no, not to eat;"[2] since these latter, as
well as the former, are to be rejected, and are not to be
admitted before they have given satisfaction to the church.
For those with whom it is not lawful to eat are manifestly
separated from all intercourse with the rest of the brethren
until such satisfaction is given. Wherefore they ought not
and cannot be admitted to the preferring of charges against
the faithful, but they ought to be debarred from their society
until the satisfaction already mentioned is given, lest these

[1] Matt. x. 16.   [2] 1 Cor. v. 11.

too should be made like them, or underlie their excommunication; for to this effect have the apostles decreed, saying, With the excommunicated no fellowship is to be held. And if any one, setting aside the rules wittingly, sings with the excommunicated in his house, or speaks or prays in company with them, that man is to be deprived of the privilege of communion. Such persons, therefore, are in all things to be guarded against, and are not to be received, because, according to the apostle, not only those who commit such things are condemned, but also those who consent with those who do them.[1] Whence also the blessed chief of the apostles, Peter, addressing the people at the ordination of Clement, says this among other things:[2] If this Clement is hostile to any one on account of his deeds, wait not ye for his saying directly to you, Be not on terms of friendship with this man. But mark ye carefully his will as ye ought, and second it without need of direct injunction; and separate yourselves from that man to whom ye perceive him to be inimical, and speak not with those with whom he speaks not, in order that every one who may be in fault, as he desires to possess the friendship of all of you, may be zealous in effecting a reconciliation all the more quickly with him who presides over all, so that he may return to spiritual well-being (*redeat ad salutem*) hereby, when he begins to yield obedience to the charges of the president. If, however, any one is not friendly, and speaks with those with whom he (his chief) speaks not, such an one belongs to those who seek to exterminate the church of God; and though he seems to be with you in body, he is against you in mind and heart. And such an one is a much more dangerous enemy than those who are without, and who are openly hostile. For this man under the guise of friendship acts the part of an enemy, and scatters and ruins the church. And therefore, dearly beloved, in these apostolic institutes we warn and teach you, that your charity, being instructed therein (*effecta certior*), may hereafter study to act with greater care and prudence, so that perverse and unbelieving

---

[1] Rom. i. 32.
[2] *Clementines*: Ep. of Clem. to James, xviii.

men may not have the power of injuring the faithful and well-disposed; for the hope of such, and of all the ungodly, is like dust that is blown away with the wind; and like a thin froth that is driven away with the storm; and like as the smoke which is dispersed here and there with a tempest, and as the remembrance of a guest of a single day that passeth away.[1] With the utmost care, dearly beloved, are such persons to be guarded against, and avoided, and rejected, if they show themselves injurious. For the laws of the world, no less than those of the church, do not admit the injurious, but reject them. Whence it is written, "The mouth of the wicked devoureth iniquity."[2] And the Lord, speaking by the prophet, saith, "With the holy thou wilt show thyself holy; and with the froward thou wilt show thyself froward; and with the excellent thou wilt show thyself excellent (*electus*); and with the innocent man thou wilt show thyself innocent."[3] And the apostle says, "Evil communications corrupt good manners."[4] Wherefore, as has already been indicated, the wicked are always to be avoided and shunned, and the good and rightly-disposed are to be stedfastly followed, in order that, as far as possible, we may avoid the peril of sloth. And lest this pest may be spread abroad more widely, let us cut it off from us with all possible severity; for the temerity of presumption does not intervene where there is the diligence of piety. Let every one of you, sustained by this apostolic representation, act according to his strength, and study in brotherly love and in godly piety to keep his own manners correct, and to help each other, and to abide in charity, and to keep himself in the will of God unceasingly, in order that we may praise the Lord together, and give Him thanks always without wearying. Fare ye well in the Lord, dearly beloved, and with the Lord's help strive to fulfil to the best of your ability the things before mentioned.—Given on the first day of July, in the consulship of the most illustrious Maximinus (or, Maximus) and Africanus.[5]

[1] Wisd. v. 14.   [2] Prov. xix. 28.   [3] Ps. xviii. 25, 26.
[4] 1 Cor. xv. 33.   [5] In the year 236.

THE SECOND EPISTLE.

TO ALL THE BISHOPS OF THE EAST.

That the chrism[1] should be renewed with consecration every year, and that the old supply should be set aside to be burnt in the churches; also concerning the accusing of priests, and on the duty of the sheep not to dare to blame their shepherd unless he errs in the faith.

I. That new chrism should be made every year, and the old be burnt.
II. Of the right of bishops not to be accused or hurt by detraction.

FABIAN, bishop of the city of Rome, to all the bishops of the East, and to the whole body of the faithful, greeting in the Lord.

Your love for the seat of the apostles requires counsels which we neither can nor ought to deny you. It is clear, moreover, that our predecessors did this for the bishops of many districts; and brotherly charity and the debt of obedience impose the duty of so doing also upon us who, by the bountiful goodness of God, are placed in the same seat. Care, therefore, is to be had by your solicitude, that neither remissness may avail to neglect, nor presumption be able to disturb, those things which have been ordained by the apostles and their successors, and established under the inspiration of the Holy Spirit. But as it was proper that that should be defined which the use of right order required, so what has been so defined ought not to be violated.

I.

Now, among other matters, in your letter we find it stated that certain bishops of your district adopt a different practice from yours and ours, and do not prepare the chrism at the Lord's Supper every year, but keep it in use for two or three, making such a supply of the holy chrism once for all. For they say, as we find in the letter referred to, that balsam cannot be got every year; and besides that, even though it

[1] The unguent of oil and balsam used in the so-called sacrament of confirmation.

were got, there would be no necessity for preparing chrism every year, but that, so long as the one preparation of chrism is sufficiently large, they have no need to make another. They are in error, however, who think so; and in making such statements they speak like madmen rather than men in their right senses. For on that day the Lord Jesus, after supping with His disciples, and washing their feet, according to the tradition which our predecessors received from the holy apostles and left to us, taught them to prepare the chrism. That washing of their feet signifies our baptism, as it is completed and confirmed by the unction of the holy chrism. For as the solemn observance of that day is to be kept every year, so the preparing of that holy chrism is to be attended to every year, and it is to be renewed from year to year and given to the faithful. For [the material of] this new sacrament is to be made anew every year, and on the day already named; and the old supply is to be burned in the holy churches. These things we have received from the holy apostles and their successors, and we commit them to your keeping. The holy church of Rome and that of Antioch have been guardians of these things from the times of the apostles: these things also the churches of Jerusalem and Ephesus maintain. Presiding over these churches, the apostles taught these things, and ordained that the old chrism should be burnt, and permitted them to use it no longer than one year, and commanded them thereafter to use the new, and not the old material. If any one, therefore, ventures to go against these things, let him understand that the door of indulgence is barred against him on your part and on that of all right-minded men: for the perverse doctrine of most depraved minds, while it uses the reins too indulgently, slips into the sin of presumption; and it can by no means be cast out, unless it is cleared of all support and correction on the part of the intelligent. And those usages which the holy church throughout the whole world uniformly observes with respect to the divine mysteries, and towards the subjects of baptism, are not to be regarded with indifferent concern, lest we make way for purposeless efforts and superstitions. We ought not, therefore, to bring over the untaught minds of the faithful to such practices as we have named, because they should be instructed rather than played upon. For good deeds make for our happiness, and evil deeds prick us with the stings of sorrow. But here, however we are situated, we are among the hands of robbers and the teeth of raging wolves, and the contumacious are put in the place of the true sheep. And it is by the barking of the dogs and the staff of the shepherd that the fury of the wolves is checked. Those wounds, moreover, which cannot be healed by remedies, must be cut out with the knife. Neither can we keep silence, for, in seeking here to call back some from things unlawful, we are impelled by the instinct of our office, having been set on the watch-towers by the Lord with this object, that we should prove the diligence of our watchfulness by checking things that should be prohibited, and deciding for things that should be observed.

II.

You desired also to consult us, as we find in the above-mentioned letter of yours, on the subject of the accusing of priests,—a thing which, as we learn also from the same epistle, is exceedingly frequent among you. You have intimated, besides, that very many notice that not a few in places of ecclesiastical dignity do not live in a manner conformable to the discourses and sacraments with which the people are served by their means. O miserable men, who in looking at these forget Christ, who long since indeed told us how that the law of God should be obeyed, rather than that those should be looked to for imitation who do not the things which they say; and bearing with the traitor himself even to the end, He sent him also along with the rest to preach the gospel. For the apostles had no such custom, neither did they teach that it was one fit to be had. And to like effect their successors also, foreseeing by the Spirit of God things to come, have determined largely on such subjects. Besides, as you read in the Acts of the Apostles, "There was at that time among them that believed one heart and one soul; neither said any of them that ought of the things which he possessed was his own; but they had all things common."[1] For there was no laying of accusations against each other among them, except what was friendly; neither ought there ever to be such among their followers or among believers: for the Lord says, "Do not that to another which thou wouldst not have done to thyself."[2] And He says also, "Thou shalt love thy neighbour as thyself;"[3] and, "Love worketh no ill to his neighbour."[4] In accordance herewith, the apostles themselves and their successors decreed of old time that those persons should not be admitted to lay accusations who were under suspicion, or who but yesterday, or the day before, or a little time ago, were at enmity, as they come thus under suspicion, or who are not of good conversation, or whose life is reprehensible, or who are doubtful in the matter of the true faith. In like manner is it decided to be with those whose faith and life and liberty are unknown, or who are marked with the stains of infamy, or entangled in the snares of offences. Again, those have neither the right nor the power to accuse the priests or the clergy, who are incapable themselves of being made priests legitimately, and are not of their order; for just as the priests and the other members of the clerical order are debarred from laying accusations against the secular laity, so these latter, too, should be debarred and excluded from the right of bringing charges against the former. And as the former should not be admitted by the latter, so the latter should not be admitted by the former: for as the conversation of the priests of the Lord ought to be something separate from the conversation of these others, so should they be separate from them also in the matter of litigation; "for the servant of the Lord ought not to strive."[5] To the utmost of your power, dearly beloved brethren, do ye prohibit such accusations, and all unrighteous and injurious emulations, because contention is to be avoided by all means. "For a just man will fall seven times in a day, and will rise again; but the wicked shall fall into mischief. Rejoice not when thine

---

[1] Acts iv. 32.   [2] Matt. vii. 12; Luke vi.
[3] Matt. xxii. 39; Mark xii. 31.   [4] Rom. xiii. 10.
[5] 1 Tim. ii. 24.

enemy falleth," saith Solomon, "and let not thine heart be glad when he stumbleth; lest the Lord see it, and it displease Him, and He turn away His wrath from him. Fret not thyself because of evil-doers, neither be thou envious at the wicked: for the evil have not the hope of the future, and the candle of the wicked shall be put out. Envy not evil men, neither be thou desirous to be with them; for their mind meditates rapine, and their lips speak deceits."[1] Dearly beloved, beware of these things. Ponder these things, and minister comfort to the brethren in all things; for, as the Truth says in His own person, " By this shall all men know that ye are my disciples, if ye have love one to another."[2] For if in things secular each man's right and his proper position are kept for him, how much more ought there to be no confusion induced in matters of ecclesiastical order! And this is a right which will be duly observed if no deference is paid to mere power, but all to equity. Whence it is an established duty, that the bishops of each several district should exercise a watchful care over all those who live under their rule, and in the fear of God should dispose of all cases in which they are concerned, and of all matters in which they are interested. It is therefore extremely inequitable that any [bishops] should neglect their own cases, and mix themselves up with those of others. But those whose part it is to ordain such persons to the priesthood, and by whom they have been already ordained, ought to order the life and judgment of such by the exercise of a competent and regular administration; for, as the law says, "Cursed is every one that removeth his neighbour's landmarks. And all the people said Amen."[3] To this therefore, brethren, has God foreordained you, and all who hold the highest office of the priesthood, that ye should put all injustice out of the way, and cut off presumption, and help those who labour in the priesthood, and give no occasion for their reproach and trouble, but bring assistance to him who endures calumny and reproach, and cut off him who works calumny and reproach, and act for the help of the Lord in His priests. The Lord, moreover, has chosen the priests for Himself, that they

[1] Prov. xxiv. 17, etc.   [2] John xiii. 35.   [3] Deut. xxvii. 17.

should sacrifice to Him, and offer oblations to their Lord. He commanded the Levites also to be under them in their ministries. Whence He speaks to Moses in these terms: "And Eleazar the son of Aaron the priest shall be chief over the chief of the Levites, and have the oversight of them that keep the charge of the sanctuary."[1] For of these the Lord spake to Moses in this wise: "Take the Levites instead of the first-born among the children of Israel, and the cattle of the Levites instead of their cattle; and the Levites shall be mine: I am the Lord."[2] If the Lord willed the Levites to be His own, how much more has He taken the priests for Himself! And of these He says: "If any stranger cometh nigh, he shall be put to death."[3] All objects, moreover, that are the Lord's are to be handled carefully, and are not lightly to be injured; for even among men, those are reckoned faithful who attend to the interests of their masters rightly, and deal with them faithfully, and rightly observe the commands of their masters, and transgress them not. And those, on the other hand, are reputed unfaithful who deal with the interests of their masters carelessly and negligently, and despise their commands, and do not observe them as they ought. Accordingly we have set these matters before you, in order that those who now know it not may know this; viz., that the priests, too, whom the Lord has taken to Himself from among all men, and has willed to be His own, are not to be dealt with lightly, nor injured, nor rashly accused or reprehended, save by their masters, seeing that the Lord has chosen to reserve their causes to Himself, and ministers vengeance according to His own judgment. For in these and other precepts of the Lord the faithful are distinguished, and the unfaithful at the same time disapproved. For these are rather to be borne with by the faithful than made subjects of reproach (*exprobrandi*); just as there is chaff with the wheat even to the last winnowing, and as there are bad fish with good even on to their separation, which is yet to be on the shore,—that is to say, at the end of the world. By no means, then, can that man be condemned by a human examination, whom God has re-

[1] Num. iii. 32.   [2] Num. iii. 45.   [3] Num. i. 51.

served for His own judgment, that the purpose of God, according to which He has decreed to save what had perished, may be unalterable. And consequently, as His will suffers no change, let no man presume on matters which are not conceded to him. And herein is the meaning of that word which the apostle speaks: "Now therefore there is utterly a fault among you, because ye go to law one with another. Why do ye not rather take wrong? why do ye not rather suffer yourselves to be defrauded?"[1] To this, too, our Lord's word may refer: "And if any man will take away thy coat, and sue thee at the law, let him have thy cloak also."[2] And in another place: "Of him that taketh away thy goods, ask them not again."[3] Moreover, there are certain things which might be thought most trivial were they not shown in the Scriptures to be of more serious import. Who would ever consider the man who says to his brother "Thou fool" worthy of hell-fire, were it not that the Truth Himself told us so?[4] Those, furthermore, who commit those sins whereof the apostle says, "They who do such things shall not inherit the kingdom of God,"[5] are by all means to be guarded against, and are to be compelled to seek amendment if they do not choose it voluntarily, because they are marked with the stains of infamy, and go down into the pit, unless assistance is brought them by sacerdotal authority. Those also are to be dealt with in like manner of whom he says, "With such persons, no, not to eat;"[6] because such persons are branded with infamy until they are restored by sacerdotal authority, and reinstated in the bosom of our holy mother the church; since those who are outside us cannot communicate with us. And it is manifest that these are outside us, and ought to be separated from us, with whom it is not lawful for us to eat or to take food. In like manner also, all persons who underlie the charge of any manner of turpitude and dishonour, are rendered infamous; and all who arm themselves against fathers are rendered infamous. "Sand, and salt, and a mass of iron, is easier to bear than a man without

---

[1] 1 Cor. vi. 7.   [2] Matt. v. 40.   [3] Luke vi. 30.
[4] Matt. v. 22.   [5] Gal. v. 21.   [6] 1 Cor. v. 11.

understanding, and foolish and impious."[1] "He that wanteth understanding thinks upon vain things; and a foolish and erring man imagineth follies."[2] For their suspicion has overthrown many, and their opinion hath held them in vanity. "A stubborn heart shall fare evil at the last; and he that loveth danger shall perish therein. A heart that entereth two ways shall not have rest; and the evil heart in them shall be made to stumble. A wicked heart shall be laden with sorrows; and the sinner shall heap sin upon sin."[3] The holy apostles and their successors, having such things in mind, and foreseeing, as being filled with the Holy Spirit, the course of wicked men, and having regard to the simple, determined that the accusing of priests should be a matter undertaken with difficulty, or never undertaken, that they might not be ruined or displaced by wicked men. For if this were made an easy matter to secular and wicked men, there would remain no one, or but the scantiest few; seeing that it ever has been and still is the case—and (which is yet worse) that too in growing measure—that the wicked persecute the good, and that the carnal are hostile to the spiritual. For this reason, then, as has been already said, they decreed that such should not be accused at all; or if that could not be avoided, that the accusing of such should be made a matter of great difficulty. And they determined also, as has been stated above, by what persons that function should not be assumed; and they resolved further, that bishops should not be cast out from their own proper seats and churches. But if in any way the matter [of accusation] should be taken in hand before their rightful seat and all their property are restored by those laws, they should by no means be accused or criminated by any one, and should not answer any one on such charges, unless they choose to do so of their own accord. But after they have been reinstated, as has been before noted, and have had all their effects restored to them by those laws, when their affairs are arranged and set in order, they should then have a long period allowed them for the disposing of their case; and thereafter, if need be, they should be

[1] Ecclus. xxii. 15. [2] Ecclus. xvi. 23. [3] Ecclus. iii. 24, etc.

regularly summoned, and so come to the suit; and if the matter seem just, they should answer the propositions of their accusers with the help of their brethren. For so long as their effects, or their churches and property, are held by their adversaries, or by any person, no manner of reason allows that any charge ought to be preferred against them. And no one is at liberty by any means to bring any charge against them, whether superior or inferior, so long as they are dispossessed of their churches, effects, or powers. In like manner also it was decreed, and we too confirm the same statutes and hereby decree, that if any one among the clergy proves an enemy or traducer of his bishops, and seeks to criminate them, or conspires against them, at once, before the consideration of judicial investigation, he should be removed from the clerical order, and given over to the court (*curiæ*), to which he shall devote himself zealously all the days of his life, and shall remain infamous without any hope of restoration. And let no one ever presume to be at once accuser, and judge, or witness; for in every judicial investigation there must always be four persons present: that is, the judges elected, and the accusers, and the defenders, and the witnesses. In like manner we decree and ordain by apostolic authority, that the flock should not dare to bring a charge against their pastor, to whose care they had been consigned, unless he falls into error in the faith; for the deeds of superiors are not to be smitten with the sword of the mouth; neither can the disciple be above the master, as the voice of Truth saith, "The disciple is not above his master, nor the servant above his lord."[1] And pride is hateful before God and men, and all iniquity is execrable. "The Lord hath destroyed the memory of the proud, and hath left the memory of the humble in mind. The seed of men shall be honoured, this [seed] that feareth God. But that seed shall be dishonoured that transgresseth the commandments of the Lord. Among brethren, he that is chief is honourable; and they that fear the Lord shall be in His eyes. My son, saith Solomon, preserve thy soul in meekness, and give honour to him whom honour beseemeth."[2] "Blame not any one before

[1] Matt. x. 24.   [2] Ecclus. x. 7, etc.

thou examinest him; and when thou hast examined him, reprove him justly. Answer not a word before thou hearest the cause; neither interrupt with talk in the midst of thy seniors."[1] After the example of Ham the son of Noah, they are condemned who bring the faults of their fathers into public view, or presume to accuse or calumniate them; even as was the case with Ham, who did not cover the shame of his father Noah, but exhibited it for mockery. And in like manner those are justified by the example of Shem and Japhet, who reverently cover and seek not to display those matters in which they find their fathers to have erred. For if a bishop should happen to err from the faith, he should in the first place be corrected privately by those placed under him (*a subditis suis*). And if he show himself incorrigible (which may God forbid), then an accusation should be laid against him before his primates, or before the seat of the apostles. For his other actings, however, he is rather to be borne with by his flock and those put under him, than accused or made the subject of public detraction; because when any offence is committed in these matters by those put under them, His ordinance is withstood who set them before him, as the apostle says, "Whosoever resisteth the power, resisteth the ordinance of God."[2] But he who fears Almighty God, agrees in no way to do anything contrary to the gospel, or contrary to the apostles, or contrary to the prophets or the institutions of the holy fathers. The priests therefore are to be honoured, and not to be injured or reproached. Thus read we in Ecclesiasticus: "Fear the Lord with all thy soul, and reverence His priests. Love Him that made thee with all thy strength, and forsake not His ministers. Honour God with thy whole soul, and honour the priest, and cleanse thyself beforehand with the shoulders (*propurga te cum brachiis*). Give him his portion, as it is commanded thee, of the first-fruits; and purge thyself concerning negligence with a few things. Thou shalt offer the gift of thy shoulders, and the sacrifice of sanctification, and the first-fruits of the holy things to the Lord. And stretch thine hand unto the poor, that

[1] Ecclus. xi. 7, 8. [2] Rom. xiii. 2.

thine atonement and blessing may be perfected."[1] We desire these things to become known not to you only, but through you to all the brethren, that we may abide in Christ of one accord and one mind, making no claim for ourselves through strife or vainglory, and being pleasers not of men, but of God our Saviour. To Him belongeth honour and glory, for ever and ever. Amen.

THE THIRD EPISTLE.

TO BISHOP HILARY.

That extraneous judgments should be rejected, and that the accused person should carry out his cause in his own locality; and that every one who brings forward a charge should intimate in writing his ability to prove it, and that if he fails to prove what he alleges, he should bear the penalty which he advanced.

I. Of those who ought not to be admitted to the right of accusation.
II. Of extraneous judgments.
III. Of the arraigned.
IV. Of the case of any one bringing forward a charge in passion, or failing to prove his allegations.
V. On the question of an accused bishop appealing to the seat of the apostles.

FABIAN, to my dearly beloved brother Bishop Hilary.

We ought to be mindful of the grace of God to us, who, in the compassion of His own regard, hath raised us for this reason to the summit of sacerdotal dignity, that by cleaving to His commandments, and by being set in a certain eminence as overseers of His priests, we may restrain things unlawful, and inculcate things that are to be followed. For we have heard that in those western parts in which you dwell, the craft of the devil rageth so violently against the people of Christ, and breaketh forth in delusions so manifold, that it oppresseth and troubleth not only the secular laity, but the priests of the Lord themselves also. Wherefore, involved as we are in deep grief, we cannot conceal what we ought

[1] Ecclus. vii. 29-32.

severely to correct. Accordingly a sufficient remedy must be employed for such wounds, lest a hasty facility in the cure may prove of no service for the deadly disease of the head; and lest the trouble, by being too easily dealt with, may involve, through the defect of an illegitimate mode of cure, the hurt and the healers together in its evil.

I. On this account, therefore, we decree and resolve, that those who are not of good conversation, or whose life is impeachable, or whose faith and life and liberty are unknown, should not have the power of accusing the priests of the Lord, lest vile persons should thus be admitted to the liberty of accusing them. In like manner, those who are involved in any matters of accusation, or who are under suspicion, should not have a voice in laying charges against their seniors; for the voice of the suspected and the inimical is wont to oppress the truth.

II. Moreover, by a general ordinance, and without prejudice to the authority of the apostles in all things, we prohibit extraneous judgments, because it is not fit that he should be judged by strangers, who ought to have those of his own province and those elected by himself as his judges, unless an appeal has been made. Wherefore, if any one of the bishops is accused on precise charges, he ought to be heard by all the bishops who are in the province; for it is not right that an accused person should be heard elsewhere than in his own circuit. Again, if any one is of opinion that he has a judge adverse to him, he should claim the right of appeal; and an appellant ought to be injured by no kind of oppression or detention; but an appellant ought to have the liberty of righting his case, when wronged, by the remedy of appeal. There ought also to be liberty of appeal in criminal cases. And the right of appealing ought to be denied to no one whom judgment has destined for punishment.

III. A person arraigned ought to plead his cause before his judge; and an arraigned person may refuse to speak, if he choose so, before one who is not his own proper judge; and indulgence (*induciæ*) should be granted to the arraigned as often as they appeal.

IV. If, then, any one in passion brings a charge rashly against any one, mere abuse is not to be taken for an accusation. But a certain time being allowed for dealing with the matter, the person should profess his ability in writing to prove what he has alleged in passion; so that, if he should happen to think better of the things he uttered in passion, and decline to repeat or write them, the person may not be held as charged with the crime. Every one, therefore, who adduces a charge, ought to state in writing his ability to prove it. And, indeed, a cause should always be dealt with in the place where the charge is admitted; and the man who fails to substantiate his allegation, should himself bear the penalty which he advanced.

V. It is determined, moreover, that, in the case of an accused bishop appealing to the seat of the apostles, that should be held to be a settlement which is the decision of the pontiff of that same seat. On all occasions, however, in cases concerning priests, let this form be maintained, that no one be bound by a decision pronounced by another than his own proper judge. It is the duty also of all the faithful to be ready to help the oppressed and the miserable in their distress, in order that by the manifestation of another manner of recompense (*vindictæ*) they may be able to keep the recompense (vengeance) of God from themselves. For he offers (*libat*) things prosperous to the Lord who keeps off things adverse from the afflicted. Whence it is written, "A brother aiding a brother shall be exalted."[1] For the church of God ought to be without spot or wrinkle, and therefore it ought not to be trodden and defiled by certain persons; for it is written, "My dove, my undefiled, is but one."[2] Hence, again, the Lord says to Moses, "There is a place with me (*penes me*), and thou shalt stand upon a rock."[3] What place is there that belongs not to the Lord, seeing that all things consist in Him by whom they were created? There is a place, however, with God—to wit, the unity of the holy church—in which there is a standing upon a rock, while the perfection of the confession (*confessionis soliditas*) is held in lowliness.

[1] Prov. xviii. 19.   [2] Cant. vi. 9.   [3] Ex. xxxiii. 21.

We admonish thee, our brother, and all our brethren who are rulers in the church of Christ, which He hath purchased with His blood, to keep back, by whatever checks ye possess, all men from that abyss into which some brethren are slipping, in reviling the Lord's pastors, and persecuting them both by word and deed; and we counsel you not to suffer them to be wounded with the hook of passion: for it is written, "For the wrath of man worketh not the righteousness of God."[1] Hence it is said again, "Let every man be swift to hear, but slow to speak, and slow to wrath."[2] Now I doubt not that with God's help you observe all these things; but as an occasion for counsel has arisen, I also secretly attach my word to your good desires and deeds, so that what you are doing of yourselves and independently of admonition you may do presently not by yourselves alone, now that the counsellor himself is added to you. Wherefore, brethren, it becomes you and all the faithful to love each other, and not to calumniate or accuse one another: for it is written, "Love thy neighbour, and be faithful unto him. But if thou bewrayest his secrets, thou shalt follow no more after him. For as a man who destroyeth his friend, so is he that loseth the love of his neighbour. And as one that letteth a bird go out of his hand, so art thou who hast let thy neighbour go, and shalt not get him again. Follow after him no more, for he is far off. For he is as a roe escaped out of the snare, since his soul is wounded. Further thou wilt not be able to bind him up, and after reviling there may be reconcilement; but to bewray the secrets of a friend is the despair of an unhappy mind. He that winketh with the eye worketh evil, and every one will cast him off. When thou art present, he will speak sweetly, and will admire thy words. But at last he will writhe his mouth, and slander thy sayings. I have hated many things, but nothing like him; and the Lord will hate him. Whoso casteth a stone on high, it will fall upon his own head; and a deceitful stroke shall make wounds in the deceiver. Whoso diggeth a pit shall fall therein; and he that placeth a stone in his neighbour's way shall stumble thereon; and he that setteth a trap for another

[1] Jas. i. 20.   [2] Jas. i. 19.

shall perish in it. He that worketh mischief, it shall fall upon him; and he shall not know whence it cometh on him. Mockery and reproach are from the proud; and vengeance, as a lion, shall lie in wait for them. They that rejoice at the fall of the righteous shall be taken in the snare; and anguish shall consume them before they die. Wrath and fury are both abominations, and the sinful man shall have them both."[1]
" He that desireth to be avenged shall find vengeance from the Lord, and He will surely keep his sins [in remembrance]. Forgive thy neighbour the hurt that he hath done thee; so shall thy sins also be forgiven thee when thou prayest. One man beareth hatred against another, and doth he seek pardon from the Lord? He showeth no mercy to a man which is like himself, and doth he ask forgiveness of his own sins from the Most High? He, though he is but flesh, nourishes hatred; and does he implore mercy from God? Who will entreat for pardon of his sins? Remember thy end, and let enmity cease. For corruption and death impend on His commandments. Remember the fear of God, and bear no malice to thy neighbour. Remember the covenant of the Highest, and wink at the ignorance of thy neighbour. Abstain from strife, and thou shalt diminish thy sins. For a furious man will kindle strife, and a sinful man will disquiet friends, and will make debate among them that be at peace. For according to the trees of the wood, so will the fire burn; and according as a man's strength is, so will his wrath be; and according to his riches, his anger will rise. An hasty contention will kindle a fire; and an hasty fighting will shed blood;' and a tale-bearing (*testificans*) tongue will cause death. If thou blow the spark, it shall burn like a fire; and if thou spit upon it, it shall be quenched; and both these come out of thy mouth. The whisperer and double-tongued is cursed; for he has destroyed many that were at peace. A backbiting (*tertia*) tongue hath disquieted many, and driven them from nation to nation. Strong cities of the rich hath it pulled down, and overthrown the houses of great men. It has destroyed the strength of peoples, and has scattered strong

[1] Ecclus. xxvii. 17-30.

nations. A backbiting tongue hath cast out virtuous women (*viratas*, spirited), and deprived them of their labours. Whoso hearkeneth unto it shall never find rest, and shall never have a friend on whom he may repose. The stroke of the whip maketh marks; but the stroke of the tongue will break the bones. Many have fallen by the edge of the sword, but not so many as have fallen by the tongue. Well is he that is defended from the evil tongue, and hath not passed through the venom thereof; who hath not drawn the yoke thereof, nor hath been bound in her bands. For the yoke thereof is a yoke of iron, and the bands thereof are bands of brass. The death thereof is an evil death, and the grave were better than it. Its endurance shall not abide, but it shall possess the ways of the unrighteous. In its flame it shall not burn the righteous. Such as forsake the Lord shall fall into it; and it shall burn in them, and not be quenched; and it shall be sent upon them as a lion, and devour them as a leopard. Hedge thine ears (*sæpi aures*) about with thorns, and refuse to listen to the evil tongue, and make a door for thy mouth and bars for thine ears. Smelt (*confla*) thy gold and thy silver, and make a balance for thy words, and a right bridle for thy mouth. And beware lest thou slide perchance in thy tongue, and fall in the sight of thine enemies that be in wait for thee, and thy fall be irremediable unto death."[1] Let all beware of these things, and "keep thy tongue from evil, and thy lips from speaking guile."[2] "Finally, dearly beloved, be strong in the Lord, and in the power of His might. Put on the armour of God, that ye may be able to stand against the wiles of the devil; for we wrestle not against flesh and blood, but against principalities and powers, against the rulers of the darkness of this world, against spiritual wickedness in heavenly places (*cælestibus*). Wherefore take unto you the armour of God, that ye may be able to withstand in the evil day, and to stand perfect in all (*omnibus perfecti*). Stand therefore, having your loins girt about with truth, and having on the breastplate of righteousness, and your feet shod with the preparation of the gospel of peace; in all (*in omnibus*) taking

[1] Ecclus. xxviii. [2] Ps. xxxiv. 13.

the shield of faith, wherewith ye shall be able to quench all the fiery darts of the wicked one. And take the helmet of salvation, and the sword of the Spirit, which is the word of God."[1] It is our wish, brother, that those things which we have written to you should be made known generally to all, in order that things which touch the others should be made known to all. May Almighty God protect you, brother, and all our brethren everywhere situate, even to the end,—even He who has thought good to redeem the whole world, our Lord Jesus Christ, who is blessed for ever. Amen.—Given on the 16th day of October, in the consulship of the most illustrious Africanus and Decius.

[1] Eph. vi. 10-17.

DECREES OF FABIAN.

TAKEN FROM THE DECRETAL OF GRATIAN.

I.

That the man who refuses to be reconciled to his brother should be reduced by the severest fastings.

[Dist. 90, *Si quis contristatus.* Basil, *in Reg.* c. 74.]

F any injured person refuses to be reconciled to his brother, when he who has injured him offers satisfaction, he should be reduced by the severest fastings, even until he accepts the satisfaction offered him with thankful mind.

II.

The man is rendered infamous who knowingly presumes to forswear himself.

[6, Q. 1, *Quicunque sciens.* Regino in the *Book of Penance.*]

Whosoever has knowingly forsworn himself, should be put for forty days on bread and water, and do penance also for the seven following years; and he should never be without penance; and he should never be admitted to bear witness. After this, however, he may enjoy communion.

III.

A man and a woman subject to madness cannot enter into marriage.

[32, Q. 7, *Neque furiosus.* And in the *Decret. Ivo.* book vi. Regino adduces it from the law of Rome.]

Neither can a mad man nor a mad woman enter into the marriage relation. But if it has been entered, then they shall not be separated.

IV.

Marriage relations in the fifth generation may unite with each other; and in the fourth generation, if they are found, they should not be separated.

[35, Q. 2 and 3, *De propinquis*. From the *Pœnitentials* of Theodorus.]

Concerning relations who enter affinity by the connection of husband and wife, these, on the decease of wife or husband, may form a union in the fifth generation; and in the fourth, if they are found, they should not be separated. In the third degree of relationship, however, it is not lawful for one to take the wife of another on his death. In an equable manner, a man may be united in marriage after his wife's death with those who are his own kinswomen, and with the kinswomen of his wife.

To the immediately preceding notice.

[From the same.]

Those who marry a wife allied by blood, and are separated, shall not be at liberty, as long as both parties are alive, to unite other wives with them in marriage, unless they can plead the excuse of ignorance.

V.

Blood connections alone, or, if offspring entirely fails, the old and trustworthy, should reckon the matter of propinquity in the synod.

[35, Q. 6, *Consanguineos extraneorum*. And in the *Decret. Ivo.* vii.]

No alien should accuse blood connections, or reckon the matter of consanguinity in the synod, but relations to whose knowledge it pertains,—that is, father and mother, sister and brother, paternal uncle, maternal uncle, paternal aunt, maternal aunt, and their children. If, however, offspring entirely fails, the bishop shall make inquiry canonically of the older and more trustworthy persons to whom the same relationship may be known; and if such relationship is found, the parties should be separated.

VI.

Every one of the faithful should communicate three times a year.

[*De Consecr.* dist. 2, *Etsi non.* And in the *Decret. Ivo.* i.]

Although they may not do it more frequently, yet at least three times in the year should the laity communicate, unless one happen to be hindered by any more serious offences,—to wit, at Easter, and Pentecost, and the Lord's Nativity.

VII.

A presbyter should not be ordained younger than thirty years of age.

[Dist. 78, *Si quis*, 30; and in the *Decret. Ivo.* iii.; from Martin Bracar, ch. 20.]

If one has not completed thirty years of age, he should in no way be ordained as presbyter, even although he may be extremely worthy; for even the Lord Himself was baptized only when He was thirty years of age, and at that period He began to teach. It is not right, therefore, that one who is to be ordained should be consecrated until he has reached this legitimate age.

THE DECREES OF THE SAME, FROM THE CODEX OF DECREES IN SIXTEEN BOOKS, FROM THE FIFTH BOOK, AND THE SEVENTH AND NINTH CHAPTERS.

I. That the oblation of the altar should be made each Lord's day.

WE decree that on each Lord's day the oblation of the altar should be made by all men and women in bread and wine, in order that by means of these sacrifices they may be released from the burden of their sins.

II. That an illiterate presbyter may not venture to celebrate mass.

The sacrifice is not to be accepted from the hand of a priest, who is not competent to discharge the prayers or actions (*actiones*) and other observances in the mass according to religious usage.

FRAGMENTS OF THE EPISTLES OF ALEXANDER,

BISHOP, FIRST OF CAPPADOCIA AND THEN OF JERUSALEM, AND MARTYR.

ALEXANDER was at first bishop of a church in Cappadocia, but on his visiting Jerusalem he was appointed to the bishopric of the church there, while the previous bishop Narcissus was alive, in consequence of a vision which was believed to be divine.[1] During the Decian persecution he was thrown into prison at Cæsarea, and died there,[2] A.D. 251. The only writings of his which we know are those from which the extracts are made.

I.

AN EPISTLE TO THE PEOPLE OF ANTIOCH.

[In Eusebius, *Hist. Eccles.* book vi. ch. xi.]

ALEXANDER, a servant and prisoner of Jesus Christ, sends greeting in the Lord to the blessed church of Antioch. Easy and light has the Lord made my bonds to me during the time of my imprisonment, since I have learned that in the providence of God, Asclepiades—who, in regard to the right faith, is most eminently qualified for the office—has undertaken the episcopate of your holy church of Antioch. And this epistle, my brethren and masters, I have sent by the hand of the blessed presbyter Clement,[3] a man virtuous and well tried,

---

[1] Euseb. *Hist. Eccles.* vi. 11.   [2] Euseb. *Hist. Eccles.* vi. 46.
[3] It was the opinion of Jerome in his *Catalogus* that the Clement spoken of by Alexander was Clement of Alexandria. This Clement, at any rate, did live up to the time of the Emperor Severus, and sojourned

whom ye know already, and will know yet better; who also, coming here by the providence and supervision of the Master, has strengthened and increased the church of the Lord.

II.

FROM AN EPISTLE TO THE ANTINOITES.

[In the same.]

Narcissus salutes you, who held the episcopate in this district before me, who is now also my colleague and rival in prayer for you,[1] and who, having now attained to (ἠνυκώς) his hundred and tenth year, unites with me in exhorting you to be of one mind.[2]

III.

FROM AN EPISTLE TO ORIGEN.

[In the same, ch. xiv.]

For this, as thou knowest, was the will of God, that the friendship subsisting between us from our forefathers should be maintained unbroken, yea rather, that it should increase in fervency and strength. For we are well acquainted with those blessed fathers who have trodden the course before us, and to whom we too shall soon go: Pantænus, namely, that man verily blessed, my master; and also the holy Clement, who was once my master and my benefactor; and all the rest who may be like them, by whose means also I have come to know thee, my lord and brother, who excellest all.

in these parts, as he tells us himself in the first book of his *Stromateis*. And he was also the friend of bishop Alexander, to whom he dedicated his book *On the Ecclesiastical Canon, or Against the Jews*, as Eusebius states in his *Eccles. Hist.* book vi. ch. xiii. (Migne.)

[1] συνεξεταζόμενός μοι διὰ τῶν εὐχῶν. Jerome renders it: Salutat vos Narcissus, qui ante me hic tenuit episcopalem locum et nunc mecum eundem orationibus regit.

[2] The text gives ὁμοίως ἐμοὶ φρονῆσαι. Several of the codices and also Nicephorus give the better reading, ὁμοίως ἐμοὶ ὁμοφρονῆσαι, which is confirmed by the interpretations of Rufinus and Jerome.

IV.

FROM AN EPISTLE TO DEMETRIUS, BISHOP OF ALEXANDRIA.

[In the same, ch. xix.]

And he[1] (*i.e.* Demetrius) has added to his letter that this is a matter that was never heard of before, and has never been done now,—namely, that laymen should take part (in public speaking, ὁμιλεῖν) when there are bishops present. But in this assertion he has departed evidently far from the truth by some means. For, indeed, wherever there are found persons capable of profiting the brethren, such persons are exhorted by the holy bishops to address the people. Such was the case at Laranda, where Evelpis was thus exhorted by Neon; and at Iconium, Paulinus was thus exhorted by Celsus; and at Synada, Theodorus also by Atticus, our blessed brethren. And it is probable that this is done in other places also, although we know not the fact.

[1] Demetrius is, for honour's sake, addressed in the third person. Perhaps ἡ σὴ ἁγιότης or some such form preceded.

INDEXES.

I. INDEX OF TEXTS.

	VOL. PAGE		VOL. PAGE
Gen. i. 1,	i. 313	Gen. xlix. 5,	i. 409, 410
i. 2,	i. 203, ii. 86	xlix. 7,	i. 410
i. 3,	i. 276, ii. 10	xlix. 8-10,	ii. 109
i. 4, 5, 7,	i. 313	xlix. 11,	i. 411
i. 5,	i. 407	xlix. 12-15,	i. 411
i. 6,	i. 408	xlix. 16,	ii. 11, 110
i. 6, 7,	i. 193, 408	xlix. 16-20,	i. 413
i. 7,	i. 151	xlix. 17,	ii. 10, 109
i. 26,	i. 289	xlix. 21-26,	i. 416
i. 28,	i. 187	xlix. 27,	i. 420
ii. 2,	i. 203, 233	Ex. iii. 6,	ii. 52
ii. 7,	i. 203, 235, 421	iv. 2-4,	i. 166
ii. 8,	i. 186	vi. 2, 3,	i. 238, 282
ii. 10,	i. 151, 204	vi. 23,	ii. 165
ii. 11-14,	i. 151	vi. 25,	ii. 165
ii. 16, 17,	i. 176, 189	vii.,	i. 320
iii. 8,	i. 408	vii. 1,	i. 468
iii. 15,	i. 415	viii.,	i. 320
iii. 19,	i. 236	viii. 9-13,	i. 166
iii. 24,	i. 208	xii. 19,	ii. 169
iv. 5,	i. 166	xv. 27,	i. 161
iv. 15,	i. 166	xx. 8,	ii. 52
vi.,	i. 493	xx. 13-15,	i. 177
vi. 3,	i. 500	xxv. 10,	i. 448
viii. 1,	i. 494	xxxii. 4,	i. 456
xi. 16,	i. 390	xxxiii. 3,	i. 456
xi. 26,	i. 390	xxxiii. 21,	ii. 267
xii. 1,	i. 177	xxxiv. 19,	ii. 113
xix. 37, 38,	ii. 31	Num. i. 51,	ii. 260
xxiii. 10,	i. 166	iii. 32,	ii. 260
xxv. 23,	i. 422	iii. 45,	ii. 260
xxvii. 1,	i. 166	viii. 16,	ii. 113
xxvii. 9,	i. 422	Deut. iii. 2,	i. 313
xxvii. 20,	i. 422	iv. 24,	i. 198
xxvii. 41,	i. 422	iv. 35,	i. 234
xxviii. 7, 17,	i. 142	v. 17-19,	i. 177
xxx. 37, 39,	i. 168	v. 22,	i. 310
xliv. 2, 5,	i. 140	ix. 3,	i. 233
xlvi. 11,	i. 390	xvii.,	ii. 246
xlviii. 3, 4,	i. 420	xxvii. 17,	ii. 259
xlix. 3,	i. 408	xxxi. 20,	i. 145
xlix. 4,	i. 409	xxxii. 33,	i. 428

INDEX OF TEXTS.

	VOL. PAGE		VOL. PAGE
Deut. xxxii. 34, 35,	ii. 34	Ps. xxxiv. 13,	ii. 270
xxxiii. 8,	i. 410	xxxv. 17,	i. 142
xxxiii. 11,	i. 496	xxxvi. 6,	i. 429
xxxiii. 17,	i. 151	xxxviii. 5,	ii. 90
xxxiii. 18,	i. 412	xxxviii. 6,	i. 426
xxxiii. 22,	ii. 10, 110	xxxix. 1,	ii. 151
Josh. iii. 7-17,	i. 139	xliv. 21,	ii. 147, 150
x. 12,	i. 441	xlv. 2,	i. 438
1 Sam. ii. 35,	i. 451	xlv. 11,	i. 417
ix. 9,	ii. 5	xlv. 17,	i. 414
x. 1,	i. 152	xlvi. 4,	ii. 81
xvi. 13,	i. 152	xlviii. 13, 14,	ii. 248
xvi. 14,	i. 152	xlviii. 14,	ii. 152
xxviii.,	i. 423	l. 3,	i. 233
1 Kings iii. 12,	i. 430	l. 20,	ii. 245
iv. 32,	i. 440	li. 3,	i. 285
2 Kings xxii. 8,	i. 477	li. 10,	ii. 86
xxiv. 10,	i. 443	li. 12,	ii. 214
xxv. 27,	i. 443	li. 13,	ii. 215
1 Chron. iii. 15,	i. 443	li. 17,	ii. 215
Job i. 7,	i. 115	lv. 15,	i. 505
xxi. 1,	i. 433	lviii. 11,	i. 505
xxix. 13-17,	ii. 148	lxii. 6,	i. 506
xxix. 15,	ii. 243	lxviii. 18,	i. 507
xl. 27, LXX.,	i. 142	lxix. 1, etc.,	ii. 41
xli. 8,	i. 142	lxix. 11,	i. 506
Ps. ii.,	i. 425	lxxii. 6,	i. 138
ii. 2,	i. 410	lxxiii. 1-3,	ii. 235
ii. 5,	ii. 45	lxxvii. 16,	ii. 81
ii. 9,	i. 136	lxxviii. 45-47,	i. 427
iii. 5,	ii. 9	lxxviii. 48,	i. 428
viii. 2,	i. 255	lxxxix. 4,	i. 507
xii. 2-4,	ii. 150	xc. 4,	i. 447
xvi. 5,	ii. 246	xciv. 11,	ii. 150, 241
xvi. 10,	ii. 42	xcvi. 11,	i. 507
xix. 1,	i. 255	civ. 2,	ii. 126
xix. 3,	i. 141	cix. 10,	i. 232
xix. 4, 5,	i. 324	cx. 1,	i. 188, 416, ii. 36
xix. 6,	ii. 39	cx. 3,	i. 398, ii. 68
xix. 18, 25, 26,	ii. 254	cx. 4,	i. 183, 193
xxii. 6,	i. 142	cxiv. 5,	ii. 81
xxii. 20, 21,	i. 142	cxvii. 19,	i. 188
xxiii.,	i. 425	cxviii. 20,	i. 188
xxiv.,	i. 426	cxviii. 22,	i. 137
xxiv. 7,	i. 426, ii. 84	cxix. 30-32,	i. 505
xxiv. 7-9,	i. 142	cxix. 137,	ii. 49
xxiv. 8,	i. 142	cxxvii. 7,	i. 508
xxix. 3,	i. 174, 374, ii. 85	cxxx. 1,	ii. 215
xxix. 3-10,	i. 141	cxxxiii. 1,	ii. 150
xxxi. 22,	i. 505	cxxxiii. 2,	i. 278
xxxii. 1,	ii. 215	cxxxix. 15,	i. 508
xxxii. 5,	i. 284	cxlviii. 4,	ii. 81
xxxii. 9,	i. 398	Prov. i. 3,	i. 430
xxxiii. 6,	ii. 63	i. 7,	i. 232, 284
xxxiv. 4,	ii. 213	i. 11,	i. 430
xxxiv. 10,	ii. 215	i. 32,	i. 479

INDEX OF TEXTS.

	VOL. PAGE		VOL. PAGE
Prov. iii. 35,	i. 430	Isa. xiv. 13-15,	ii. 31
iv. 2,	i. 431	xviii. 1, 2,	ii. 34
iv. 8,	i. 431	xix. 1,	i. 441
iv. 14,	i. 431	xxiii. 4, 5,	ii. 31
iv. 25,	i. 431	xxvi. 10,	ii. 38
iv. 27,	i. 431	xxvi. 19,	ii. 39, 122
v. 19,	i. 432	xxvi. 20,	ii. 39
vi. 27,	i. 432	xxvi. 24,	ii. 40
vii. 22,	i. 433	xxviii. 7,	ii. 243
vii. 26,	i. 433	xxviii. 10,	i. 139
viii. 22-24,	i. 203	xxviii. 16,	i. 137
ix. 1,	i. 433, 438	xxix. 11,	i. 453
ix. 10,	i. 232	xxxviii. 5, 7, 8,	i. 441
ix. 12,	i. 433	xl. 6,	i. 331
xi. 30,	i. 434	xl. 15,	i. 152
xii. 2,	i. 434	xli. 8,	i. 142
xii. 15,	ii. 150	xlii. 1,	ii. 5
xiv. 12,	ii. 150	xliii. 1, 2,	i. 142
xvii. 16,	i. 432	xliv. 6,	ii. 52
xvii. 27,	i. 434	xlv. 1,	ii. 62
xviii. 19,	ii. 267	xlv. 5, 14, 18, 21, 22,	i. 234
xix. 28,	ii. 254	xlv. 7,	i. 429
xxii. 28,	ii. 209	xlv. 11-15,	ii. 55
xxiv. 17,	ii. 259	xlv. 14,	ii. 53
xxv. 1,	i. 440	xlvii. 1-15,	ii. 20
xxvi. 4,	ii. 205	xlix. 9,	i. 453
xxvi. 27,	i. 483	xlix. 15,	i. 142, ii. 147
xxvii. 22,	i. 437	li. 7,	ii. 150
xxx. 15,	i. 434	liii. 1,	ii. 68
xxx. 17,	i. 435	liii. 2-5,	ii. 25
xxx. 18, 19,	i. 435	liii. 4,	ii. 69
xxx. 19,	i. 435	liii. 9,	i. 502
xxx. 20,	i. 436	liv. 1,	i. 146
xxx. 21,	i. 437	lviii. 9,	i. 481
xxx. 21-23,	i. 436	lxi. 1,	i. 452, ii. 39
xxx. 24-28,	i. 436	lxiv. 4,	i. 183, 188, ii. 127
xxx. 29,	i. 437	Jer. i. 5,	i. 204, ii. 19
Eccles. xi. 5,	i. 508	i. 16,	ii. 235
Song,	i. 439	ii. 9,	ii. 235
vi. 9,	ii. 267	iv. 11,	ii. 33
Isa. i. 7,	ii. 100	vi. 16,	ii. 243
i. 7, 8,	ii. 18	viii. 4,	ii. 214
i. 16-19,	ii. 87	viii. 16,	ii. 11, 111
i. 21,	ii. 9	xvii. 9,	i. 146
i. 26,	i. 456	xvii. 11,	ii. 32
ii. 4,	i. 206	xviii. 11,	ii. 235
vi. 3,	ii. 124	xxii. 24,	i. 445
vi. 10,	i. 169	xxv. 11,	i. 445, 451
vii. 14,	i. 148	xxxi. 15,	i. 146
viii. 6, 7,	ii. 33	xxxiii. 18,	ii. 63
ix. 27,	ii. 25	xliii. 8,	i. 477
x. 12-17,	ii. 12	xlix. 14,	i. 429
xi. 1,	ii. 9	Ezek. xviii. 2-10,	ii. 13
xi. 2,	ii. 438	xviii. 21, 22,	ii. 214
xi. 14,	i. 461, ii. 31	xviii. 32,	ii. 214
xiv. 4-21,	ii. 13	xxviii. 2,	ii. 31

INDEX OF TEXTS.

	VOL. PAGE		VOL. PAGE
Ezek. xxviii. 9,	ii. 32	Dan. x. 6,	i. 456, 474
xxxiii. 11,	ii. 214	x. 7,	i. 474
Dan. i. 1,	ii. 463	x. 12,	i. 475
i. 2,	i. 463	x. 13,	i. 475
i. 8,	i. 464	x. 16,	i. 475
i. 12,	i. 464	x. 18,	i. 475
ii. 3, 5,	i. 464	x. 20,	i. 475
ii. 10,	i. 465	xi. 31,	ii. 37
ii. 14,	i. 465	xi. 33,	i. 458
ii. 23,	i. 465	xi. 41,	ii. 31
ii. 27,	i. 465	xii. 1,	i. 475
ii. 29,	i. 465	xii. 2,	i. 476, ii. 39, 122
ii. 31,	i. 465, 466	xii. 3,	i. 476
ii. 31-35,	ii. 14, 106	xii. 7,	i. 476
ii. 33,	i. 468	xii. 9,	i. 476
ii. 34,	i. 468	xii. 11,	i. 477
ii. 34, 45,	ii. 17	xii. 11, 12,	ii. 37
ii. 45,	i. 137, 468	Hos. i. 2,	i. 193
ii. 46,	i. 468	vi. 3,	ii. 81
ii. 48,	i. 468	vi. 6,	ii. 241
ii. 49,	i. 468, 469	xiii. 15,	ii. 100
iii. 1,	i. 469	xiv. 9,	i. 465
iii. 7,	i. 469	Amos v. 11, 12, 13,	ii. 101
iii. 16,	i. 469	Mic. ii. 7, 8,	ii. 66
iii. 19,	i. 469, 470	v. 3-7,	ii. 102
iii. 47,	i. 470	v. 5,	ii. 33
iii. 92 (i.e. 25),	i. 470	Zech. ii. 8,	ii. 233
iii. 93 (i.e. 26),	i. 470	vi. 12,	i. 436
iii. 97 (i.e. 30),	i. 470, 471	viii. 1-19,	ii. 204
iv. 10-12,	i. 200	xii. 10,	ii. 25
vii.,	i. 445	Mal. iv. 2,	ii. 27
vii. 1,	i. 471	iv. 5, 6,	ii. 27
vii. 2,	i. 471		
vii. 2-8,	ii. 15, 107	APOCRYPHA.	
vii. 3,	i. 471	4 Esdras iii. 8,	ii. 126
vii. 4,	i. 445, 471, ii. 19	Tobit iii. 17,	i. 483
vii. 5,	i. 471	iv. 15,	ii. 213
vii. 6,	i. 472, ii. 20	Wisd. i.,	ii. 244
vii. 7,	i. 472	ii. 1-5,	ii. 245
vii. 8,	i. 473	ii. 1, 12, 13,	ii. 44
vii. 9-12,	ii. 15	ii. 14, 16, 17, 20,	ii. 45
vii. 9, 13, 22,	i. 232	ii. 15, 16,	ii. 45
vii. 13,	i. 473, 484, ii. 56	v. 1-9,	ii. 45
vii. 13, 14,	ii. 15, 16, 25	xii. 1,	ii. 246
vii. 14,	i. 473	xii. 2,	ii. 246
vii. 17,	i. 473	xv. 1, 2,	ii. 246
vii. 19,	i. 474	Ecclus. i. 26,	i. 502
vii. 21,	ii. 17	iii. 24,	ii. 262
vii. 22,	i. 474	v. 7-18,	ii. 239
vii. 25,	i. 474	vi. 1-4,	ii. 239
viii. 1,	ii. 190	vii. 29-32,	ii. 265
viii. 2-8,	ii. 19	x. 7,	ii. 263
viii. 13, 14,	ii. 190	xi. 78,	ii. 264
ix. 21,	i. 474	xvi. 23,	ii. 262
ix. 24,	449, ii. 182	xviii. 30,	ii. 205
ix. 27,	ii. 25, 112, 115	xxii. 13,	ii. 262

INDEX OF TEXTS. 283

	VOL. PAGE		VOL. PAGE
Ecclus. xxvii. 17-30,	ii. 269	Matt. xiii. 20,	i. 345
xxviii.,	ii. 270	xiii. 31, 32,	i. 149
xxxii. 1-3,	ii. 36	xiii. 33, 34,	i. 140
xxxiv. 13, 14,	ii. 246	xiii. 43,	i. 476, ii. 39
xxxv. 1-3,	ii. 236	xvi. 16,	ii. 87
Baruch iii. 35,	ii. 53	xvi. 18,	ii. 87
iii. 36,	ii. 56	xvi. 19,	ii. 147
Sus. i. 61,	i. 477, 483	xvi. 27,	ii. 150
1 Macc. ii. 33,	i. 438	xvii. 5,	ii. 56, 70
		xviii. 18,	ii. 221
Matt. ii. 1, 2,	i. 287	xix. 17,	i. 134, 299
ii. 9,	ii. 282	xx. 16,	i. 419
ii. 18,	i. 146	xx. 28,	ii. 209
iii. 7,	ii. 82	xxi. 19, 20,	i. 310
iii. 10,	i. 145	xxi. 31,	i. 144, 419
iii. 11,	ii. 82	xxii. 30,	ii. 288
iii. 12,	i. 200	xxii. 39,	ii. 258
iii. 13,	ii. 81	xxiii. 23, 24,	ii. 242
iii. 14, 15,	ii. 83	xxiii. 27,	i. 143
iii. 16,	ii. 86	xxiii. 38,	ii. 44
iii. 16, 17,	ii. 84	xxiv. 12,	i. 463, ii. 103
iv. 3,	ii. 82	xxiv. 15-22,	ii. 37
iv. 15,	i. 417	xxiv. 24,	ii. 114
iv. 15, 16,	i. 412	xxiv. 27,	ii. 122
iv. 17,	i. 417	xxiv. 27, 28,	ii. 38
v. 8,	ii. 235	xxiv. 29,	ii. 122, 124
v. 10,	ii. 150	xxiv. 31,	ii. 39
v. 15,	i. 135	xxv. 21,	i. 397
v. 17,	i. 413	xxv. 23,	i. 397, ii. 130
v. 22,	ii. 261	xxv. 31-34,	ii. 125
v. 18,	i. 218, ii. 99	xxv. 34,	i. 414, ii. 39
v. 40,	ii. 261	xxv. 37,	ii. 126
v. 45,	i. 135	xxv. 40,	ii. 239
vii. 3, 4,	i. 309	xxv. 46,	ii. 129
vii. 6,	i. 145, 350	xxvi. 41,	ii. 74, 89
vii. 11,	i. 169	xxvi. 67,	ii. 85
vii. 12,	ii. 258	xxvii. 29,	ii. 70
vii. 13,	i. 143	xxvii. 52, 53,	i. 143
vii. 13,	i. 148	xxviii. 18,	ii. 17
vii. 13, 14,	i. 148, 480	xxviii. 19,	ii. 69
vii. 18,	i. 383	Mark iv. 3-9,	i. 144, 311
vii. 21,	i. 144	iv. 31, 32,	i. 149
vii. 23,	ii. 129	x. 18,	i. 134, 299
x. 3,	i. 207	x. 38,	i. 141
x. 5,	i. 182	x. 44,	ii. 209
x. 16,	ii. 252	xi. 13, 14, 20, 21,	i. 310
x. 23,	ii. 211	xi. 14, 15,	i. 314
x. 24,	ii. 263	xii. 31,	ii. 258
x. 27,	i. 133, 454	xii. 33,	ii. 216
x. 34,	i. 180	xiii. 14-20,	ii. 37
xi. 27,	i. 227 bis.	Luke i. 17,	ii. 26
xi. 28,	i. 413	i. 20,	ii. 82
xii. 18,	ii. 5	i. 35,	i. 236, ii. 86
xiii. 3-8,	i. 311	i. 36-38,	i. 258
xiii. 3-9,	i. 144	ii. 14,	ii. 235
xiii. 13,	i. 139	ii. 34,	i. 413

INDEX OF TEXTS.

	VOL. PAGE		VOL. PAGE
Luke ii. 38,	ii. 113	John v. 30,	ii. 59, 122
iii. 9,	i. 145, 207	v. 37,	i. 141
iii. 14,	ii. 123	vi. 29,	ii. 59
iii. 17,	i. 20	vi. 35,	i. 416
iii. 23, 24,	ii. 167	vi. 44,	i. 144
iv. 18,	i. 452	vi. 53,	i. 141
vi.,	ii. 258	vi. 53, 66,	ii. 133
vi. 30,	ii. 261	vii. 38,	ii. 81
vi. 35,	i. 138	viii. 9,	i. 143
vi. 41, 42,	i. 309	viii. 11,	ii. 215
vii. 41,	i. 499	viii. 16, 18,	ii. 59
vii. 50,	ii. 130	viii. 44,	i. 169, ii. 240
viii. 5-8,	i. 144, 311	ix. 1,	i. 152
ix. 5,	ii. 85	x. 7,	i. 169
x. 16,	ii. 233	x. 8,	i. 236
xiii. 7,	i. 310	x. 17, 18,	i. 388
xiii. 15, 16,	i. 453	x. 18,	ii. 69
xiii. 19,	i. 148	x. 30,	i. 158
xv. 4-10,	i. 260	x. 34,	i. 138
xvi. 10-12,	i. 397	xi. 51, 52,	ii. 69
xvii. 21,	i. 133, 149	xi. 52,	ii. 8
xviii. 2-5,	ii. 33	xiii. 1,	ii. 59
xviii. 19,	i. 134, 299	xiii. 35,	ii. 150, 259
xxi. 8,	ii. 105	xiv. 6,	ii. 43
xxi. 8, 9,	ii. 104	xiv. 8, 9,	ii. 59
xxi. 18,	ii. 38	xiv. 11,	i. 342
xxi. 20-23,	ii. 37	xiv. 12,	ii. 59
xxi. 28,	ii. 38	xiv. 30,	i. 435
xxii. 16,	ii. 94	xv. 1,	ii. 9
xxii. 41,	ii. 89	xvi. 26,	ii. 87
xxiv. 39,	ii. 95	xvi. 28,	ii. 67
John i. 1-3,	ii. 63	xvii. 5,	i. 418
i. 1-4,	i. 167	xvii. 22, 23,	i. 58
i. 3,	i. 148	xviii. 37,	ii. 7
i. 3, 4,	i. 140	xix. 14,	ii. 448
i. 9,	i. 152, 276	xix. 26,	i. 181
i. 10, 11,	ii. 63	xix. 27,	ii. 125
i. 16,	i. 420	xx. 17,	ii. 58
i. 18,	ii. 57	xx. 22, 23,	ii. 221
i. 20,	ii. 82	Acts ii. 3,	ii. 86
i. 27,	ii. 82	ii. 20,	ii. 123
i. 29,	i. 452, ii. 7, 26	ii. 24,	i. 175
ii. 1-11,	i. 140	iv. 19,	ii. 58
ii. 4,	i. 287	iv. 32-37,	ii. 218, 258
ii. 19,	ii. 8	v. 1-11,	ii. 220
iii. 5, 6,	i. 316	v. 29,	ii. 58
iii. 6,	i. 138, ii. 68	viii. 9-24,	i. 196
iii. 11, 13,	ii. 57	x. 36,	ii. 63
iii. 13,	ii. 55	xvii. 23,	i. 302
iii. 14, 15,	i. 166	xxvii. 10,	ii. 34
iii. 31,	i. 505	xxviii. 25,	ii. 86
iv. 7-14,	i. 176	Rom. i. 17,	ii. 39
iv. 10,	i. 152	i. 32,	ii. 207, 253
iv. 14,	i. 193, ii. 81	i. 20-27,	i. 138
iv. 21,	i. 148	iii. 3-10,	ii. 216
v. 25,	ii. 39	iii. 23-26,	ii. 215

INDEX OF TEXTS. 285

	VOL. PAGE		VOL. PAGE
Rom. iii. 25,	ii. 59	Gal. vi. 1-4,	ii. 214
v. 14,	i. 282	vi. 15,	i. 132, 399
vi. 12-19,	ii. 216	Eph. i. 10,	ii. 74
vii. 2,	ii. 210	i. 21,	i. 283
viii. 11,	ii. 55	ii. 14,	i. 452
viii. 11, 12,	i. 237	ii. 17,	i. 143
viii. 17,	ii. 86	iii. 3-5,	i. 285
viii. 19-22,	i. 182, 286	iii. 14-18,	i. 235
viii. 36,	i. 438	iii. 15,	i. 137, ii. 54
ix. 5,	ii. 53, 57	iv. 6,	ii. 64
x. 4,	ii. 84	iv. 13,	ii. 6
x. 18,	i. 136	iv. 26,	ii. 114
xii. 19,	ii. 150	iv. 29-32,	ii. 247
xiii. 2,	ii. 264	v. 1-21,	ii. 247
xiii. 10,	ii. 258	v. 14,	i. 136, ii. 39
xiv. 4,	i. 344	v. 15, 16,	ii. 105
xv. 4,	ii. 250	vi. 10-17,	ii. 271
xvi. 14,	ii. 133	Phil. ii. 6, 7,	i. 374
1 Cor. i. 2,	i. 183	ii. 7,	i. 175, ii. 42, 81
ii. 8,	ii. 82	ii. 7-9,	i. 418
ii. 9,	i. 188, 193, ii. 50, 127	ii. 10,	ii. 17
ii. 13, 14,	i. 144	ii. 11,	ii. 124
ii. 14,	i. 235, 284, ii. 223	iii. 2,	ii. 105
iii. 19,	ii. 222	iii. 15,	i. 417
v. 5,	ii. 220	Col. i. 16,	ii. 124, 127
v. 7,	i. 399, ii. 90	i. 18,	ii. 95
v. 11,	ii. 252, 261	i. 19,	i. 155, 319
vi. 7,	ii. 261	i. 26,	i. 236
viii. 6,	ii. 54	ii. 8,	ii. 105
x. 11,	i. 144, 480	ii. 9,	i. 155, 372
xi. 32,	i. 204	ii. 11, 14, 15,	i. 315
xii.,	ii. 204	iii. 2,	ii. 222
xv. 12,	ii. 165	1 Thess. iv. 12,	ii. 40
xv. 20,	ii. 95	iv. 16,	ii. 122
xv. 23-28,	ii. 58	2 Thess. ii. 1-11,	ii. 38
xv. 32,	ii. 240	ii. 15-17,	ii. 248
xv. 33,	ii. 254	iii. 1-3,	ii. 248
xv. 47,	i. 419	iii. 2,	ii. 4
xv. 52,	ii. 122	iii. 4,	ii. 248
xv. 58,	ii. 250	1 Tim. ii. 4,	ii. 251
xvi. 13, 14,	ii. 250	ii. 5,	i. 423
2 Cor. ii. 12,	i. 143	ii. 24,	ii. 58
v. 17,	i. 132, 399	iv. 1-5,	i. 326
vi. 14, 15,	ii. 208	iv. 3,	i. 297
xii. 4,	i. 285	v. 6,	ii. 223
xiii. 14,	i. 415	v. 20,	i. 437
Gal. i. 1,	ii. 9	vi. 16,	ii. 85
ii. 4,	i. 479	vi. 20, 21,	ii. 4
iii. 19,	i. 299	2 Tim. ii. 1-3,	ii. 4
iii. 20,	i. 423	ii. 24,	ii. 147, 148
iii. 28,	i. 132	iii. 5,	ii. 243
iv. 26,	i. 138	iii. 8,	ii. 242
iv. 27,	i. 146	iv. 8,	ii. 19
v. 17,	i. 190	Tit. ii. 13,	ii. 40
v. 21,	ii. 261	Heb. i. 3,	ii. 85
v. 22,	i. 429	vii. 21,	i. 183, 193

286   INDEX OF SUBJECTS.

	VOL. PAGE		VOL. PAGE
Heb. ix. 29,	i. 233	Jude 18, 19,	ii. 105
Jas. i. 19,	ii. 268	Rev. i. 8,	i. 207, ii. 57
i. 20,	ii. 268	ii. 6,	i. 305
ii. 13,	ii. 129	iii. 7,	i. 453
ii. 14,	ii. 218	iii. 14,	i. 186
iii. 1, 2,	ii. 218	v.,	i. 454
iii. 13,	ii. 218	v. 5,	ii. 7
1 Pet. i. 24,	i. 200	v. 6,	ii. 112
iii.,	ii. 204	vi. 14,	ii. 123
iii. 19,	ii. 17	xi. 3, i. 461, ii. 27, 36, 111, 112	
v. 8,	ii. 250	xi. 4-6,	ii. 27
2 Pet. i. 18, 19,	i. 398	xii. 1-6,	ii. 36
i. 21,	ii. 5	xiii. 11-18,	ii. 28
ii. 1,	ii. 104	xiii. 18,	i. 115
ii. 4,	i. 401	xvii. 9,	ii. 18
ii. 22,	i. 330	xvii. 10,	i. 447
iii. 3,	ii. 104	xvii. 18,	ii. 24
iii. 12,	ii. 22	xix. 6,	i. 456
1 John i. 1,	ii. 160	xix. 11-13,	ii. 66
ii. 18,	ii. 105	xx. 6,	ii. 39
iii. 10,	ii. 105	xx. 11,	ii. 127
iv. 1,	ii. 105	xxi. 1,	ii. 123
v. 16,	i. 343	xxii. 15,	ii. 40

II.—INDEX OF SUBJECTS INCIDENTALLY OR FORMALLY TREATED OF.

ABOMINATION of desolation, the, i. 477.
Abraham, ii. 174; and Lot, 175.
Abraham's bosom, ii. 47.
Abulides, the Canons of, ii. 135, etc.
Academics, the, i. 58.
Accidents, the, of Aristotle, i. 64.
Accusers, who should not be admitted as, ii. 212, etc., 266.
Acts of the Apostles, the, ii. 160, 161.
Adam, the Naassene doctrine concerning, i. 129, 130, 136, 137.
Adam, Rabbinical ideas respecting the perfection of, 130 note, 139.
Address, the concluding, of Hippolytus to the Gentiles, i. 40-43.
Adrian, the Emperor, and St. Symphorosa and her sons, ii. 191-194.
Advent, the second, of our Lord, ii. 122.
Advents, two, of our Lord, indicated in Scripture, ii. 25, 111.
Æons, doctrines concerning, i. 65;

theory of Valentinus respecting the emanations of, 227, etc., 237, etc.; Secundus' system of, 241; Docetic views of, 309-313.
Æsculapius, the burning of, i. 99.
Æthalides or Thallis, i. 33.
Air, the place it holds in the system of Anaximenes, i. 39.
Alalcomeneus, the, of the Naaseni, i. 129.
Alexander the Great, the he-ram of Daniel, i. 449.
Alexander I. of Syria, i. 459.
Alexandria, the Canons of the church of, ii. 137, etc.
Alpha, why Jesus is so called, according to Marcus, i. 257.
Alphabet, the, Marcus' mystic interpretation of, i. 251.
Altar, the oblation of the, ii. 274.
Ampa, the well of, i. 181.
Amygdalus, i. 148.
Anacreon, i. 148.

INDEX OF SUBJECTS.

Anaxagoras of Clazomene, his theory of mind, theogony, and astronomy, i. 40, etc.
Anaximander, the philosophical system of, i. 37, 38.
Anaximenes, his system, i. 39.
Ancient of Days, the, i. 475, 476.
Andrew the apostle, ii. 130.
Angelology, the, of the heretic Justinus, i. 186, etc.
Angels, the speed of, i. 474.
Angels, evil, i. 429.
Anger of God, the, i. 429.
Anguitenens, i. 117.
Animals, how they originated, according to Archelaus, i. 43.
Anterus, Bishop of Rome, ii. 240.
Antichrist, described by Daniel, i. 460; and Christ, ii. 7, etc.; springs from the tribe of Dan, 10; how foretold and described by the prophets, 11, etc.; a discourse concerning, 109-111; strives to make himself like the Son of God, 110, etc.; his nativity and growth, 112, 113; his seductive and deceiving mode of procedure, 113, 114; his cruelty, 115, 116; wonders wrought by, 116; the miserable results of his reign, 116; followed by the great mass of the people, 117; the number and seal of, 117, 118; the misery of his deluded followers, 119; who shall escape his imposture, 119, 120; the misery of the time of, 120.
Antigonus, the fortunes of, ii. 184, 185.
Antiochus Epiphanes, i. 450, 457.
Ants, conies, and spiders, i. 436.
Apelles, the doctrines of, i. 306; and Philumene, *ibid.*; summary of opinions of, 384.
Apocalypse, the, of John, referred to, ii. 161, 162; of Peter, 162.
Apostasy, the last, ii. 120, etc.
Apostles, the twelve, a brief history of, ii. 130, etc.; the seventy, a list of, 132.
Apparition, mode of managing an, i. 104.
Apsethus the Libyan, i. 197, 198.
Aquarius, type of those born under, i. 92.
Aratus, quoted, i. 114; opinions of the heretics borrowed from, 115,

etc.; on the appearance and position of the stars, 116, etc.
Archelaus, the philosophical system of, i. 43.
Archimedes, his astronomical calculations, i. 177-180.
Archon, the great, of Basilides, i. 279; of the Docetæ, 313, 378.
Aries, the type of those born under, i. 87.
Aristotle, his philosophy, i. 54, 56; the system of Basilides derived from, 267, etc.; sketch of the philosophy of, 268; the general idea of, 168; nonentity as a cause in the system of, 269; substance, according to, *ibid.*; the predicates of, 170; the cosmogony of, 271; the psychology of, 272; followed by Basilides and Isidorus, 273, 274; his "Entelecheia" adopted by Basilides, 280.
Aristoxenus, i. 33.
Arithmeticians, the system of the, i. 82, 86; and geometers, 122.
Ark, the story of Noah's building the, i. 491-494; rested on the top of Mount Kardu, 495; made of imperishable wood, 425, 426, 448, ii. 90.
Armius, author of the *Book of Times*, i. 489.
Arnobius quoted respecting Zoroaster, i. 34.
Asher, i. 415, 416.
Asterius Urbanus, ii. 224.
Astrologers, the systems of, i. 64; the prodigies of, 75, etc.; waste of mental energy in the systems of, 80.
Astrology, the Chaldean, the heresy derived from, 65; the horoscope the foundation of, 66; the folly of, 120; of the Peratæ, 156-160.
Astronomers, the system of, i. 75.
Astronomic calculations, i. 77; distances, 77, 78.
Astronomic system, the, of Pythagoras, i. 223.
Astronomy, the founder of the Greek, i. 30; the, of Anaximander, 37; of Anaximenes, 39; of Anaxagoras, 41, 42.
Astrotheosophists, i. 113.
Atomism, the, of Epicurus, i. 57.
Attis, the hermaphrodite man, of the Naaseni, i. 131, 132.

INDEX OF SUBJECTS.

Azarias, the song of, ii. 92.
Babylon, how spoken of by the prophets, ii. 18-25.
Babylonian captivity, the, i. 443, 444, ii. 179.
Baptism, the engagement made in, ii. 222.
Baptism, the heretical practices of the Marcites in regard to, i. 245.
Baptism, the purifying power of, ii. 87.
Baptism, the, of Jesus, ii. 81-85.
Bartholomew the apostle, ii. 131.
Baruch, the book of, containing the heresy of Justinus, i. 183, 192, 193.
Basilides, the system of, derived from Aristotle, i. 267; and Isidorus, 273; adopts the Aristotelian doctrine of nonentity, 274; origin of the world according to, 275; his account of the Sonship in the creative process, 277; the "great Archon" of, 279; adopts the Entelecheia of Aristotle, 280, 281; a further explanation of the Sonship by, 282; derivation of the gospel according to, 283; number of heavens, according to, 284, 285; the mystery of the birth of Christ, according to, 285; his notion of the inner man and of the gospel, 286-289; his interpretation of the life and sufferings of our Lord, 288, 289; a summary of the opinions of, 377.
Bear, the, of Daniel's vision, i. 471; with the three ribs between his teeth, ii. 107.
Bear, the constellation of, i. 117.
Beast, the, ii. 28; the number of, 30.
Beast, the, with two horns, ii. 28.
Beasts, the four, of Daniel, i. 445, etc., 471-474, ii. 106.
Benjamin, i. 420.
Beron, having escaped from Valentinianism, falls into a new error, ii. 76.
Birth of Christ, events which happened in Persia at the time of the, ii. 195-202.
Bishops, respecting the accusation and trial of, ii. 146; on the spoliation and expulsion of certain, 149; of conspiring against, 207; should not intrude on each other's parish, 209; the seats of, 221; no intercourse to be had with those rejected by, 221; the imposition of the hands of, bestows the Holy Spirit, 223; respecting the transference of, 240, etc.; punishment of the clergyman who traduces, 263; when accused, by whom to be heard, 266; the case of the accused appealing to Rome, 267; admonitions to, respecting reviling pastors, or each other, 268.
Blood and water, the, which flowed from the side of Jesus, ii. 93.
Blood relations, marriage among, ii. 211.
Bone, a, of Christ not broken, ii. 93.
Boreas, i. 432.
Brachmans, the peculiar opinions of the, i. 59, 60.
Brotherly love, ii. 234, etc.
Bythus, i. 242.

Caius, presbyter of Rome, a notice of, ii. 150.
Calculations, predictions by, i. 82, etc.
Callistus, and Zephyrinus, Popes of Rome, implicated in the Noetian heresy, i. 329, 330; the conduct of, in the matter of Noetianism, 336-338; the personal history of, 338; occupation of, as a banker, 338; fraud perpetrated by, on Carpophorus, 338; absconds, attempts suicide, and is condemned to the treadmill, 339; insults the Jews in their synagogue, to secure for himself the honour of martyrdom, 339, 340; is sentenced by the prefect to be banished to Sardinia, 340; artfully obtains his liberty, and returns to Rome, 340, 341; succeeds Zephyrinus as bishop of Rome, 342; the heresy of, his school at Rome, and its shameful practices, 343-345; summary of the views of, 387, 388.
Cancer, type of those born under, i. 89.
Canis, i. 118; the influence of, 119.
Canon, the, of Muratori, ii. 159-162.
Canons, the, of Abulides, ii. 135, etc.
Canons, the, of the church of Alexandria, ii. 137.
Capricorn, the type of those born under, i. 92.

INDEX OF SUBJECTS.

Captivity, the Babylonian, i. 443, 444.
Carpocrates; the heresy of, i. 300; wicked doctrines held by, respecting Jesus Christ, *ibid.*; the doctrine of, respecting souls, 300, 301.
Carpophorus, and Callistus—fraud of the latter on, i. 338-340.
Categories, the, of Aristotle, i. 54; of Pythagoras, 216.
Cauldron, divination by, i. 103.
Cemphus, the bird so named, i. 433.
Cerdo, the heresy of, i. 305; and Marcion, 383.
Cerinthus, the system of, concerning Christ, i. 302, 385; his millenarianism, ii. 155.
Chaldean astrology, i. 65; practical absurdity of the, 73; its doctrine of circles, 75.
Chrism, new, to be made every year, and the old burnt, ii. 255.
Christ, His sinlessness, i. 435; time of His birth, 447; the kingdom of, 473; the purification of, 485; His soul in Hades, *ibid.*; and Antichrist, ii. 7; predicted under the figure of a lion, *ibid.*; two advents of, indicated in Scripture, 25; predictions respecting, 41, etc.; the Judge of all, 49; and the Father, 54; distinct from the Father, 58; an ark of imperishable wood, 90; the Helper of men, 90, 91; the First-fruits, 95; His mighty works foretold by the prophets, 98, 99; His passion, 197, etc.; what happened in Persia at the birth of, 195-202.
Christ, Valentinus' views of, i. 229.
Christ Jesus, the name, in the system of Marcus, i. 251; the life and death of, as explained by the system of Marcus, 253-259; the object of His coming, according to Saturnilus, 290; undoes the work of the Demiurge, according to the Docetæ, 313; Docetic views of His baptism and death, 315; reason why, according to the Docetæ, He lived thirty years on earth, 316.
Chronography, the, of Julius Africanus, ii. 171.
Chronology, Jewish, i. 389-391, ii. 172, etc.; and of the Greeks, 177, etc.
Chronology, mythical, of the Egyptians and Chaldeans, ii. 171.

Church, the, like a ship, i. 435; a further description of, ii. 34, 35.
Circles, the Chaldean doctrine of, i. 75.
Clement of Alexandria, ii. 275.
Cleomenes, a disciple of Noetus, i. 329.
Cleopatra, ii. 186.
Clepsydra, the, used in connection with the horoscope, i. 70-72.
Colarbasus, the heretic, i. 80, 81; and Marcus, refuted by Irenæus, 264.
Communicate, the duty of the faithful to, at least once a year, ii. 274.
Condy, the cup so called, i. 140.
Conflagration of the world, the Stoic doctrine of the, i. 56.
Conies, the figurative meaning of, i. 437.
Constellations, the, according to Aratus, and as worked into the systems of the heretics, i. 115-120.
Corona and Lyra, the constellations of, i. 117.
Corybas, i. 141.
Cosmogony, the, of Hesiod, i. 61; of Justinus, 185; of Pythagoras, 219; of Marcus, 262.
Creation, the, theory of Valentinus respecting the origin of, i. 233.
Cycnus, the bird so named, i. 120.
Cyllenius in the Naassene system, i. 135.
Cynosura, or Cynosuris, in the system of the heretics, i. 118.

Daily bread, i. 484.
Dan, as spoken of in Jacob's blessing, i. 413-415; Antichrist was to spring from, ii. 10, 109, 110.
Daniel, the prophet, i. 443; the visions of, 445, etc.; carried to Babylon, 463; holy resolution of, 464; interprets the king of Babylon's dream, 464, 465; the seventy weeks of, ii. 182, 188, 190.
Darius, i. 457.
David not the author of all the Psalms, i. 498, 504.
Dead Sea, the, ii. 175.
Decalogue, the, according to Monoimus, i. 320.
Decretals, the false, Dean Milman quoted respecting, ii. 144, 145.
Deity, the diversity of opinions re-

INDEX OF SUBJECTS.

specting the, among philosophers and theologians, i. 108-111.
Deluge, the, ii. 173.
Demetrius, bishop of Alexandria, an epistle to, ii. 276.
Demiurge, the work of, perishable, according to Marcus, i. 263; the work of, undone by Christ, according to the Docetæ, 313, 314.
Democritus, the theogony of, i. 45.
Demon, a fiery, produced by magic, i. 103.
Demons, incantations of, i. 94, etc.
Desposyni, the, ii. 170 and note.
Διαψάλμα, i. 503.
Diodorus of Eretria, i. 33, note.
Discord and friendship in the system of Empedocles, i. 292-296.
Divination by means of a cauldron, i. 103.
Docetæ, the, the opinions of, respecting God and Æons, i. 309-311; respecting the incarnation, 311; their notions about a fiery god, 312; hold that the work of the Demiurge was undone by Jesus, 313, 314; their account of the baptism and death of Christ, 315, 316; their notion as to why Christ lived thirty years on earth, 316; the doctrines of, derived from the Greek sophists, 316, 317; summary of the opinions of, 381, etc.
Doctors, of accusations against, ii. 205, 206.
Doctrine of truth, the, a summary of, i. 393-400.
Dragon, the constellation of, i. 119.
Druids, the, i. 61.
Duads, Valentinus' theory of emanation by, i. 224, 227.
Duality of substance, the, according to Pythagoras, i. 216.
Earth, Archelaus' view of the, i. 43.
Earthquakes, how caused, according to Anaximenes, i. 40; according to Anaxagoras, 42.
Ebionæans, the, the doctrine of, i. 303, 385.
Ecphantus, his scepticism, i. 47.
Edem, the, of the Naaseni, i. 151; of Justinus, 185, 379, 380.
Eggs, used in incantations, i. 97.
Egypt, the plagues of, i. 427-429.
Egyptian and Chaldean chronology, mythical, ii. 171.
Egyptian theology, based on a theory of numbers, i. 109-111; theory of nature, 112.
Egyptians, The Gospel according to the, i. 130.
Elchasai, derives his system from Pythagoras, i. 347; his mode of administering baptism, 348; precepts of, 349; summary of the views of, 389.
Elchassaites, the sect of, opposed by Hippolytus, i. 345; the heresy of the, a derivative one, 350.
Elements, the six, of Empedocles, i. 291.
Eleusinian mysteries, the, i. 147.
Elohim and Edem, of the heresiarch Justinus, i. 186, etc.
Emanation, Simon Magus' system of, i. 201, 202, 209; Valentinus' system of, 225, etc., 234, etc.
Empedocles, his system, i. 36; sketch of his doctrine, 291; the suggester of the Marcionite heresy, 296, 297; followed by Prepon, 298, 299.
Encratites, the doctrines of the, i. 326, 327.
End of the world, the, ii. 99-103.
Engonasis, i. 117.
"Entelecheia," the, of Aristotle, i. 272; adopted by Basilides, 280, 281.
Epicurus, his atomic theory, i. 57; view of providence, ibid.; theory of pleasure, 57, 58.
Epiphanes the heretic, i. 241.
Esau, i. 421, 422.
Esseni, the, the tenets and practices of, i. 352-357; different sects of, 357, 358; their belief of a resurrection, 358, 359; another sect of, 359, 360.
Eucharist, wicked practices of Marcus upon the cup of the, i. 243.
Evil, to be avoided, ii. 235, etc.
Excommunicated persons, advice as to intercourse with, ii. 208; no fellowship to be had with, 249, etc.
Exile, the Babylonian, i. 443, 444, ii. 178.
Eye, and eyes, the, the looks thrown by, i. 431, 432; that mocks, 435.
Ezekiel's temple, the, i. 442.

Fasting, seasons of, ii. 203, etc.; the man who refuses to be reconciled to his neighbour, to be punished by, 272.
Fate, Plato's views of, i. 52; the Stoics' views of, 56.

INDEX OF SUBJECTS.

Father, the, and Christ, distinct, ii. 54, 58.
Fiery god, the, of the Docetæ, i. 313.
Fire, the place it occupies in the system of Simon Magus, i. 198, 199; a primal principle with Simon, 207.
Fire, juggling tricks by means of, practised by the heretics, i. 99.
First-fruits of those who slept, the, ii. 95.
Flaming sword, the, which guarded the tree of life, what, according to Marcus, i. 208.
Flock, the, must not bring a charge against their pastor, ii. 263.
Flood, the story of the, i. 493, 494.
Foal, binding the, to the vine, i. 411.
Forehead, divination by means of the, i. 87.
Fossils, Zenophanes' views of, i. 47.
Friendship and desire, in the system of Empedocles, i. 292.
Fucianus, prefect of Rome, condemns Callistus to the mines of Sardinia, i. 340.

Gabriel, i. 450.
Gemini, the type of those born under, i. 88.
Genealogy of Christ in the holy Gospels, the, ii. 164.
Georæ, the, among the Israelites, ii. 169, 170.
Geryon, i. 127.
Gnosis, i. 127.
Gnostic hymn, a, i. 240.
Gnostics, the Naaseni a sect of, i. 127.
Goat, the, and the ram, of Daniel, i. 449.
Goats, the method of poisoning, practised by the heretics, i. 98.
God, described, ii. 71, etc.; becomes incarnate, 73; the works of, all good, 80.
God, as Father, Word, and Holy Ghost, ii. 60-65.
God, the fiery, of the Docetæ, i. 313.
God, the, of the Jews, according to Saturnilus, i. 290.
God, Plato's idea of, i. 49, 50.
Gospel, The, of the Egyptians, or of Thomas, i. 130, note.
Gospel, the whence and the what of the, according to Basilides, i. 283, 287.

Gospels, the important testimony furnished to, by the Canon of Muratori, ii. 159, etc.; the genealogy of the, 164, etc.
Great Announcement, the, containing the system of Simon Magus, i. 202.
Great Mother, the mysteries of the, of the Phrygian heretics, i. 150.
Greeks, the, a discourse against, ii. 46, etc.

Hades described, ii. 46-48.
Hades, the soul of Christ in, i. 485.
Hebdomad and Ogdoad, the, of the system of Basilides, i. 288.
Hebdomadarii, the, i. 121.
Hebrews, the, ii. 174.
Helen of Troy, Simon Magus' mythical treatment of the story of, i. 210, 211.
Hanotes and Monotes, of the system of Secundus, i. 241, 242.
Heraclitus, the system of, i. 36, 37, 331, 332; his censure of Hesiod, 333; paradoxes of, 333; and Noetus, 334.
Hercules, and the oxen of Geryon, the legend of, i. 184; the twelve labours of, according to Justinus, 190.
Heresies, writers on, i. 30, note.
Heresy, derived from Chaldean astrology, i. 65; alliance between, and the Pythagorean philosophy, 80, 81; the connection of, with magical frauds, 110; compared to the rocks of the Sirens and the stormy ocean, 266, 267.
Heretics, the, i. 26, etc.; opinions of, borrowed from Aratus, 115; confuted by an appeal to a regular succession of witnesses to the truth, 155, 156; pervert the Scriptures, 157-159.
Hermaphrodite man, the, i. 132.
Hermas, The Pastor of, quoted, ii. 162.
Hermogenes, the system of, i. 323, 329.
Herod the Great, the story of his origin and youth, ii. 168, 169; destroys the registers of the Jews, why, 169; the fortunes of, 184, etc.
Hesiod, the cosmogony of, i. 61.
Hexaëmeron, the, of Moses, as expounded by Simon Magus, i. 203; by Hippolytus, 407, etc.

INDEX OF SUBJECTS.

Hind, roe, and stag, the figurative meaning of, i. 432.
Hippo, his duality of principles and psychology, i. 48.
Hippocrates, quoted, i. 133.
History, Hebrew and Greek, taken synchronously, ii. 178.
Holy, the most, to anoint the, i. 452.
Holy Spirit, the, given by the imposition of the bishop's hands, ii. 223.
Honey, the figurative meaning of, i. 431.
Horn, the little, of Daniel, ii. 27.
Horns, the three, rooted up, ii. 31.
Horns, the ten, of the fourth beast, i. 472.
Horoscope, the, i. 66; the futility of, 67; the impossibility of fixing, 68, 69, 71.
Horse-leech, the daughters of the, i. 434.
Hymns composed in honour of Christ by the ancient church, ii. 156.
Hyrcanus and Antigonus, the fortunes of, ii. 184.

Image, the, of Nebuchadnezzar, i. 446, 447, 465-468; the feet and toes of, 483.
Imposition, the, of the bishop's hands, ii. 223.
Incantations, demoniacal, i. 93, etc.
Incarnation, the, of God, without circumscription of His deity, ii. 72, 73, 74, 75, 76; heretical deniers of, 92.
Isaac, Esau, and Rebecca, i. 421, etc.
Isidore, the false decretals of, ii. 144, 145, 203, 217.
Isidorus and Basilides, i. 273.
Isis, the mysteries of, i. 134.
Israel, i. 56.

Jacob, the blessing of, expounded, i. 408-421; the prophecy of, respecting Judah, ii. 8-10; the tent of, preserved at Edessa, 176; displeasure of, with Simeon and Levi, 176.
James the brother of John, ii. 131.
James the son of Alpheus, ii. 131.
Jerusalem, the destruction of, by Titus, i. 489, 490.
Jesus Christ, God and man, i. 425; His ascension, 426; His humiliation, 426, 427; His second coming, 427; baptized by John, ii. 81-85.
Jesus Christ, the legendary account of, by Justinian the heretic, i. 191, 192; Valentinus' view of the existence of, 231; Valentinus' explanation of the birth of, 236.
Jewish chronology, i. 389, etc.
Jewish sects, i. 351-362.
Jewish religion, the, i. 362.
Jews, the, refuted, ii. 43, etc.
Joacim, husband of Susannah, i. 477.
John the apostle, ii. 130; the Gospel of, 160.
John the Baptist, ii. 26; baptizes Jesus, 81, etc.
"Joint fruit of the Pleroma," i. 234, 235.
Jordan, the, i. 138.
Joseph, the blessing pronounced on, i. 416-420.
Judas, called Lebbeus, ii. 131.
Judge, the unjust, ii. 33.
Judgment, the last, ii. 29; described, 122-130.
Juggling tricks of magicians, i. 95-100.
Julius Africanus, a notice of, ii. 163.
Justin Martyr, his statement respecting a statue erected to Simon Magus, i. 214.
Justinus the heresiarch, his system, i. 182; the system of, unfolded in the book of Baruch, 183; the cosmogony of, 184; the triad of, 185; the angelography of, 186, etc.; his idea of paradise and the creation of man, 186, 187; his view of the fall, 189; and of the birth of Jesus, 191; the oath used by the followers of, 192, 193; summary of the views of, 379, 380.

Kardu, Mount, i. 495.
King of the north and of the south, the, i. 458.
Kingdom, the, of Christ, i. 473.
Kingdoms, the four, of Daniel, ii. 105, etc.

Last time, the, ii. 121-125.
Latinus, the name of the beast, ii. 30.
Law, the, i. 431; names of the teachers who handed it down in succession from Moses, 487-489;

curious story of the treatment of, by Armius, 489.
Laymen, the right of, to take part in public speaking, ii. 276, 277.
Leo, type of those born under, i. 89.
Leopard, the, of Daniel's vision, i. 472.
Letters, Marcus' system of, i. 249; symbols of the heavens, 254; the generation of the twenty-four, in the system of Marcus, 255.
Letters, sealed, the illusion of, i. 101.
Leucippus, the atomic theory of, i. 45.
Levi and Simeon, i. 409, 410.
Libra, the type of those born under, i. 90.
Life in common, ii. 218, etc.
Lightning, how caused, according to Anaximenes, i. 40; and Anaxagoras, 42.
Lion, and lion's whelp, Christ predicted under the figure of a, ii. 8, 109.
Lioness, the, of Daniel's vision, ii. 107.
Liver, magical tricks with a, i. 106.
Logos, the doctrine of the, i. 397-400.
Logos, the, fashioned the lyre, according to Aratus, i. 116; and identified by him with the constellation Canis, 118.
Lust, i. 433, 434.
Lyre, invention of the, i. 116; the constellation of the, and Corona, 117.

Magic, the nature and origin of, i. 107, 108.
Magicians, the system of, i. 93; the juggling tricks practised by, 93-108.
Magistrianus, the story of, ii. 97.
Maiden, the, of Corinth, the story of, ii. 95-97.
Man, the creation of, i. 321.
Man, the perfect, according to the Naaseni, i. 142, 146.
Man, his origin according to Saturnilus, i. 289.
Man, the universal, according to Monoimus, i. 317, 318.
Marcia, the concubine of Commodus, obtains the release of Christians from the mines of Sardinia, i. 340, 341.
Marcion, his dualism, i. 290, 291; a disciple of Empedocles, 291; the source of his system, 296, etc.; the theory of, concerning good and bad, 298; rejects the generation of our Saviour, 299; and Cerdo, summary of the opinions of, 383.
Marcites, the, the heretical practices of, in regard to baptism, i. 245.
Marcus the heresiarch, his wicked devices on the Eucharistic cup, i. 243; further acts of jugglery practised by, 244; the system of, explained by Irenæus, 246; the vision enjoyed by, 247; his system of letters, 249; Quaternion of, 250; his interpretation of the alphabet, 251, 252; his system applied to explain our Lord's life and death, 253; letters symbols of the heavens, according to, 225; generation of the twenty-four letters according to, ibid.; why Jesus, he says, is called Alpha, 257; his account of the birth and life of our Lord, 258; his system shown to be essentially that of Pythagoras, 259, etc.; the cosmogony of, 263, etc.; and Colorbasus refuted by Irenæus, 264.
Marriage among blood relations censured, ii. 211, etc., 273.
Mass, the, not to be celebrated by an illiterate presbyter, ii. 274.
Matter, Plato's view of, i. 49.
Matthew the apostle, ii. 131.
Matthias the apostle, ii. 131.
Maximilla and Priscilla, i. 325.
Mediator, the, i. 423.
Melchisedecians, the, i. 304, 386.
Men of good will, ii. 234, 235.
Mercury, position of, among the Naaseni, i. 135.
Metrodorus, i. 46.
Michael, i. 475.
Milky way, the, according to Anaxagoras, i. 42.
Miltiades, the heresy of, ii. 224, 225.
Monad, the Deity asserted by the Egyptians to be a, i. 110; the, in the system of Valentinus, 225; in the system of Monoimus, 318.
Monoimus, the Arabian heretic, the system of, i. 317; man, the universe according to, 317, 318; the monad in the system of, 318; his notion of the Son of man, 319; on the Sabbath, 319, 320; allegorizes the rod of Moses, 320; view of the ten commandments, 320, 321; ex-

INDEX OF SUBJECTS.

plains his system in a letter to Theophrastus, 321, etc.; his system derived from Pythagoras, 320; summary of the opinions of, 382.
Monotes and Henotes, i. 242.
Montanists, the, i. 325, 386, 387.
Montanus, ii. 226; and Maximilla, 228.
Moon, the, illusive appearances of, i. 105, etc.
Moses, i. 486; on Mount Nebo, 456, 457; wrote the *Senna*, 496.
Moses, the rod of, allegorized by Monoimus, i. 320.
Mother, the great, of the Phrygians, i. 150.
Muratori, the fragments of, on the canon, ii. 159-162.
Muses, the nine, i. 61, 62.
Mysteries, the, of the Greeks, i. 27; of Isis, 134; of the Phrygians, 140.

Naas, worshipped by the Naaseni, i. 150; of Justinus, 186, 189, 190, 191.
Naaseni, the, their origin and system, i. 126-128; ascribe their system to Mariamne and James the Lord's brother, 128; the psychology of, 129; the system of, and that of the Assyrians, compared, 131, etc.; derive support for their system from the Egyptian and Phrygian systems and the mysteries of Isis, 135; magnify Homer as their prophet, 138; acknowledge a triad of principles, 139; appeal to the mystery of the Samothracians, 140; their mystical and absurd exposition of Scripture, 142, etc.; their idea of the perfect man, 142, 146; compare the Phrygian system with Scripture, 145; appeal to the Eleusinian and other mysteries, 147; worship the great mother, 150; further exposition of the system of, from one of their hymns, 153, etc.; summary of the principles of, 370.
Name, the, of Christ, its use in the system of Marcus, i. 251.
Natalius the confessor persuaded to become a bishop of heresy, and scourged for it by angels, ii. 156, 157.
Nature, the Egyptian theory of, i. 112.

Nature, the happy, according to the Naaseni, i. 133.
Nebuchadnezzar, the dream of, ii. 464, etc.
Nephthalim, i. 416.
Nestis, i. 291, 292.
Nicolaitans, the, i. 304, 305.
Noah, the names of his sons' wives, i. 491; builds and enters the ark, 491, 492; his coming out of the ark, 495; and the deluge, ii. 173.
Noetus, the heresy of, its source, i. 329; his system an offshoot from the Heraclitic philosophy, 330; a disciple of Heraclitus, 334; his view of the birth and passion of Christ, 335, 336; summary of the opinions of, 387, 388; the heresy of, further described and refuted, ii. 51-70.
Nonentity, a cause, according to Aristotle, i. 269; its adoption as such by Basilides, 274.
Number, the, of the beast, ii. 30.
Numbers, the important place occupied by, in the system of Pythagoras, i. 32, 122, 216; predictions by, 82; quibbles of those skilled in, 86; Egyptian theology based on a theory of, 109-111.

Oannes, i. 129.
Oath, a false, how to be punished, ii. 272.
Oath, the, taken by the followers of Justinus, i. 192, 193.
Oblation of the altar, the, ii. 274.
Ogdoad, the, and hebdomad, according to Basilides, i. 288.
Ogygus, i. 177, 178, 179.
Olympiads, the, of the Greeks, ii. 171.
Ophaz, i. 455.
Ophites, the, 195.
Ordination, the, of presbyters and deacons, ii. 152; of a presbyter not before thirty years of age, 274.
Origen, epistle of Alexander, bishop of Cappadocia, to, ii. 275.
Osiris, i. 134, 135.

Papa, the perfect man of the Phrygians so named, i. 143.
Paradise, Simon Magus' view of, i. 204.
Parmenides, his theory, i. 45.
Partridge, the parable of, in Jeremiah, explained, ii. 32.

INDEX OF SUBJECTS.

Passion, the, of Christ, ii. 187, 188.
Passover, the, and the Supper, ii. 94.
Pastor, the, the flock must not bring a charge against, ii. 263.
Paul, the apostle, ii. 131, 132; the epistles of, 161.
Pentateuch, the, Simon Magus' explanation of the books of, i. 205-207.
Peratæ, the, the system of, its tritheism, 154, 155; and derivation from the system of the astrologers, 156-160; their system explained out of one of their own books, 160-163; their system nominally, but not really, different from that of the astrologers, 163, 164; why they call themselves Peratæ, 164, etc.; their theory of generation, 164-167; their interpretation of the exodus, 165; their view of the serpent, 165, 166; a compendious statement of the doctrines of, 168-170; summary of the opinions of, 371.
Perfect man, the, of the Naaseni, i. 142, 146.
Persecution of the church, ii. 33, 35.
Persia, what occurred in, at the time of the birth of Christ, ii. 195.
Peter, the apostle, ii. 130.
Pharisees, the, i. 359, 360.
Philip, the apostle, ii. 131.
Philosophers, the, summary of the opinions of, i. 367-370.
Philosophy, the Greek, its origin, i. 206.
Philumene, the prophetess of Apelles, i. 306.
Phœnicians, the, their origin, i. 118.
Phrygians, the, the mysteries of, i. 140, etc.; the heresy of, 386; deceived by Montanus, ii. 227.
Pisces, the type of those born under, i. 92.
Plagues, the, of Egypt, i. 427-429.
Plato, and Socrates, i. 48; his three principles, 49; his idea of God and matter, 49, 50; views of demons and the soul, 50; his idea of rewards and punishments, 51; of means and extremes, *ibid.*; of virtue and vice, 52; of fate, 52, 53; of sin, 53; of evil, *ibid.*; Valentinus' system in part derived from, 214.
Pleroma, the, of Justinus, i. 230, 231; "joint fruit" of the, 234, 235.

Pontianus, bishop of Rome, ii. 234.
Predicates, the, of Aristotle, i. 270.
Predictions by calculation, i. 82.
Prepon, a follower of Marcion, i. 298, 299.
Presbyters, the ordination of, ii. 152; not to be ordained before their thirtieth year, 274; illiterate, not to celebrate mass, 274.
Priapus, who, according to Justinus, i. 191.
Priests, may be permitted to minister after a lapse, ii. 214-216; the honour to be bestowed on, 232; the right of, not to be accused or hurt by detraction, 257, etc.; who should not be permitted to accuse, 266.
Priscilla and Maximilla, i. 325.
Proclus, i. 36.
Property, ecclesiastical, by and for whom to be managed, ii. 219.
Prophets, the, ii. 4, 18, 19; their predictions respecting Christ, 98, 99.
Proverbs of Solomon, the, i. 430.
Providence, the Epicurean view of, i. 57.
Psalms, the, Hippolytus' view of, i. 424, 497-504.
Psaltery, the, i. 496.
Ptolemæus the heresiarch, i. 242.
Ptolemy, king of Egypt, i. 458, 459, 460.
Punishments and rewards, ii. 49; Plato on, i. 51.
Pyrrhonean philosophy, the, i. 58.
Pythagoras, the philosophy of, i. 31-35; the place which numbers occupy in his system, 32; held the soul to be immortal, 33; forbade his followers to eat beans, 34; his mode of receiving disciples, 35; taught the transmigration of souls, 36; the heresy of Valentinus derived from, and Plato, 214, etc.; his system of numbers, 216; his duality of substance, and categories, 219; other opinions of, 220; sayings of, 221; the astronomical system of, 223, etc.; Valentinus convicted of plagiary from, 225; the system of Marcion traced to, 259, etc.; Elchasai derived his system from, 347.

INDEX OF SUBJECTS.

Qualities, the, of Aristotle, i. 54.
Quartodecimans, the, i. 324.
Quaternion, the, of Marcus, i. 251.

Rainbow, the, how caused, according to Anaximenes, i. 40.
Ram, the great, of Daniel, i. 449.
Rebecca, i. 421, 422.
Religion, the Jewish, i. 362-364.
Republic, *The*, of Plato, quoted, i. 53.
Resurrection, the, of the saints, ii. 39, 40, 88.
Reuben, i. 488, 489.
Rewards and punishments, ii. 49; Plato on, 51.
Rhea, the Naasene account of, i. 132.
Righteousness, i. 434.
Rivers of Eden, allegorical interpretation of the, i. 151.
Robe, the, woven for Himself by the Word, ii. 67.
Rod of Moses, the, allegorized by Monoimus, i. 320.
Rome, the church of, the duty of following, ii. 249.

Sadducees, the, i. 361.
Saggitarius, the type of those born under, i. 91.
Samothracians, the mysteries of the, i. 140.
Samuel and the witch of Endor, i. 423, 424.
Saturnilus, the system of, i. 289, 290.
"Sayings," the, of Pythagoras, i. 221.
Scorpio, the type of those born under, i. 91.
Sea, the Dead, i. 175.
Seal, the, of Antichrist, ii. 118.
Sealed, i. 433.
Sealed letters, the illusion of, i. 101, etc.
Seasons, the three, of the year prefigured Christ, ii. 90.
Seat, the, of the apostles, the case of an appeal to, by an accused bishop, ii. 267.
Sects, Jewish, i. 351-362.
Secundus, his system of Æons, i. 241.
Self-slaughter of sheep, a trick practised by magicians, i. 97.
Senna, the, written by Moses, i. 496.
Serpent, the, which deceived Eve, ii. 109, 110.

Serpent, the, in the system of the Peratæ, i. 165-167.
Seth, The Paraphrase of, i. 181.
Sethians, the, the system of, i. 170; how they try to support their system—its real source, 176, etc.; their theory of composition and mixture, 179; their doctrines to be learned from the *Paraphrase of Seth*, 181, etc; summary of the principles of, 372, etc., 374.
Seventy disciples, the, ii. 132.
Shadrach, Meshach, and Abednego, i. 469, 470.
Sheep, the, of Christ, i. 428.
Sheep, the self-slaughter of, a trick of magicians, i. 97.
Sidereal influence and names, i. 64, 73, 87, etc.
Sige, of the Valentinians, i. 225.
Simeon and Levi, i. 409, 410.
Simon the zealot, ii. 131.
Simon Magus, i. 96; his interpretations of Scripture and plagiarisms, 198-200; appeals to Scripture, 200; his system explained in the *Great Announcement*, 200, 201; his system of threefold emanation, 201, 202; his double triad of a seventh existence, 202; his explanation of the Mosaic Hexaëmeron, and allegorical representation of paradise, 203-205; his explanation of the Pentateuch, 205-207; fire a primal principle with, 207; his allegorical interpretation of the story of Helen of Troy, 210, 211; the immorality of his followers, 211; his views of Christ, 212; his disciples adopt magical rites, 213; his end, 214; summary of the opinions of, 375.
Simon Magus and Valentinus, i. 123.
Simplicius' commentary on Aristotle's physics, referred to, i. 41.
Sin, Plato's view of, i. 53.
Sirens, the, and Ulysses, i. 266, 267.
Skull, making a, speak, i. 106.
Socrates and Plato, i. 48.
Solomon, the Proverbs of, i. 430.
Song of Songs, the, i. 439, 440.
Song of the three children, the, i. 484.
Sons of God, the, ii. 172.
Sonship, the, of Basilides, i. 277.
Sophia, Valentinus' work so entitled, i. 215.
Soul, the, Plato's view of, i. 50; the Naasene doctrine of, i. 130, 131.

INDEX OF SUBJECTS. 297

Souls, Carpocrates' teaching respecting, i. 300-302.
Stars, the, the influence and configuration of, i. 64; the influence of, in moulding the dispositions of men, 87-92; futility of the theory of the influence of, 93; illusive appearance of, 106.
Stoics, the, and the philosophy of, i. 55, 56.
Stone, the, cut out without hands, ii. 17.
Substance, according to Aristotle, i. 269.
Sun-dial, the, of Ahaz, i. 440, 441.
Susannah, the story of, i. 477-483.
Symphorosa, St., the passion of, and of her seven sons, ii. 191-194.

Tatian, the disciple of Justin Martyr, his views, i. 322, 385.
Taurus, the type of those born under, i. 88.
Temple of Ezekiel, the, i. 442.
Thales of Miletus, his physics, i. 30.
Thallis, or Æthalides, i. 33.
Tharses, i. 456.
Themison, the Montanist, ii. 229.
Theodotus, the heresy of, i. 303, 385.
Theophrastus, letter of Monoimus to, i. 321.
Thomas the apostle, ii. 131.
Thomas, The Gospel according to, as used by the Naaseni, i. 130, 133.
Thratta, i. 31.
"Three things, and four," i. 435, 436, 437.
Thunder, imitation of, by magic, i. 98.
Tongue, the mischiefs of an evil, ii. 269, 270.
Transference of bishops, ii. 240, etc.
Transmigration of souls, taught by Pythagoras, i. 36; by Plato, 51; by the Stoics, 56.
Triad, the, of the Naaseni, i. 139; of the Peratæ, 154, etc.; of the Sethians, 170, etc.; of Justinus, 185, etc.; of Simon Magus, 202.
Trinity, the, ii. 59, 60; the economy of, 60-65.

Ulysses and the Sirens, i. 266, 267.
Unity in Trinity, ii. 60-65.

Valentinus, the heresy of, derived from Pythagoras and Plato, i. 214; convicted of plagiarisms, 224, 239; theory of emanations of, 225, 227, 234; his explanation of the existence of Christ and the Spirit, 229-231; view of the origin of creation, 233; his explanation of the birth of Jesus, 236; further doctrines of, respecting Æons, 237; his vision, 247; summary of opinions of, 376.
Vice and virtue, Plato's view of, i. 52.
Virgo, the type of those born under, i. 90.
Visions, the, of Daniel, i. 445.

Water, the dignity of, ii. 80, 81.
Weeks, the, of Daniel, i. 454; the seventy, ii. 182, 188-190.
Wisdom, i. 430, 431, 438.
Witnesses, the two, ii. 111, 112.
Witnesses, who should be admitted as, ii. 212.
Woman, the, clothed with the sun, ii. 36.
Word, the, His grace, ii. 56; takes flesh, or weaves for Himself a robe, 67; the begetting of, 61; the manifestation of, 62, etc.; described, 65, etc.; becomes incarnate through the medium of a virgin, 68; although God, He refuses not the conditions of a man, 68-70; further described, 72; the first-born, 89; the manifold works of, 90, 91.
Works of God, the, all good, ii. 80.
World, the end of the, ii. 99, etc., 103, etc.
World, the origin of, according to Basilides, i. 275.

Xenophanes, his system, i. 46.

Zabulon, i. 411, 412.
Zarates, i. 34.
Zeno and the Stoic philosophy, i. 55, 56.
Zephyrinus, and Callistus, implicated in Noetianism, i. 329, 330, 336, 337; succeeded in the see of Rome by Callistus, 441, 442; notice of, prefixed to his epistles, ii. 244.
Zoroaster, or Zarates, i. 34.